GOLFER'S Digest

D1556867

DELUXE SEVENTH EDITION

Edited by
EARL PUCKETT, PGA PROFESSIONAL
and
ROBERT CROMIE

DBI BOOKS, INC., NORTHFIELD, ILL.

GOLFER'S DIGEST STAFF

EDITORS

Earl Puckett, PGA Professional
Robert Cromie

ASSOCIATE EDITOR
Charles T. Hartigan

PRODUCTION MANAGER
Pamela J. Johnson

ASSOCIATE PUBLISHER
Sheldon L. Factor

ABOUT THE COVERS

Our front cover shows Jack Nicklaus in a rare display of emotion after sinking an amazing 50-foot putt for a birdie two on the 16th hole at Augusta during the final round of the 1975 Masters Tournament. Jack went on to win his fifth Masters title by one stroke over Tom Weiskopf and Johnny Miller.

The back cover continues the saga of Daniel and Gabriella Klein's progress as junior golfers. Danny (now 7 years old) has been featured on the covers of the 4th, 5th and 6th editions of *Golfer's Digest*. Gabriella (now 4 years old) joined her brother on the cover of the 6th edition. Both are the grandchildren of Milton Klein, founder and President of DBI Books, Inc., publisher of *Golfer's Digest* and a host of other sports and nostalgia books. The children's mother, Hilary Dole Klein is the editor of *Craft Digest,* one of DBI Books' most popular titles.

Material published in this volume has been prepared in cooperation with the editors and publishers of *Golf Digest* Magazine, *Signature* Magazine, *Sport* Magazine, *Chicago Sun Times, Dallas Morning News, New York Herald Tribune, Golfdom, Chicago Tribune, PGA Book of Golf, Fore* Magazine, *Montreal Gazette, Saturday Review of Literature, Esquire* Magazine, *Golf Journal, Baltimore News American, Florida Times-Union, The Jersey Golfer, Newspaper Enterprise Association,* Cardinal Publishing Company, *Los Angeles Times, Florida Golfweek, The Memphis Commercial Appeal, The Quincy Herald,* A. S. Barnes and Co., Inc., *The Columbia Record* and *Sports Illustrated.* Right to reprint any material appearing in this volume without the written permission of the person, publications and/or organizations owning the original copyrights to the individual articles is prohibited. The name Golfer's Digest is used with permission of and by special arrangement with *Golf Digest* Magazine, Norwalk, Conn.

Article starting on page 12 is from *Signature* through the courtesy and with the permission of copyright holder Signature Magazine.

Articles starting on pages 18, 23, 29, 34, 50, 52, 56, 61, 111, 122, 150, 160, 165, 170, 172, 182, 204, 216, 224, 242, and 261 are from *Golf Digest* through the courtesy and with the permission of copyright holder Golf Digest, Inc.

Articles starting on pages 37, 82, 155, and 230 are from *Sport* through the courtesy and with the permission of copyright holder Sport Magazine.

Article starting on page 40 is from *The Chicago Sun Times* through the courtesy and with the permission of copyright holder The Chicago Sun Times.

Articles starting on pages 41 and 159 are from *The Dallas Morning News* through the courtesy and with the permission of copyright holder The Dallas Morning News.

Article starting on page 60 is from *The New York Herald Tribune* through the courtesy and with the permission of copyright holder The New York Herald Tribune.

Article starting on page 66 is from *Golfdom* through the courtesy and with the permission of copyright holder Golfdom.

Article starting on page 70 is from *The Chicago Tribune* through the courtesy and with the permission of copyright holder The Chicago Tribune.

Articles starting on pages 74, 100, 118, and 193 are from *The PGA Book of Golf* through the courtesy and with the permission of copyright holder The PGA Corporation.

Articles starting on pages 89 and 143 are from *Fore* through the courtesy and with the permission of copyright holder Fore Magazine.

Article starting on page 97 is from *The Methods of Golf's Masters: How They Played And What You Can Learn From Them* through the courtesy and with the permission of copyright holders Dick Aultman and Ken Bowden.

Article starting on page 99 is from *Montreal Gazette* through the courtesy and with the permission of copyright holder The Montreal Gazette.

Article starting on page 108 is from *Saturday Review of Literature* through the courtesy and with the permission of copyright holder Saturday Review of Literature.

Articles starting on pages 127 and 175 are from *Esquire* through the courtesy and with the permission of copyright holder Esquire, Inc.

Article starting on page 132 is from *Golf Journal* through the courtesy and with the permission of copyright holder Golf Journal.

Article starting on page 152 is from *Baltimore News American* through the courtesy and with the permission of copyright holder Baltimore News American.

Article starting on page 153 is from *Florida Times-Union* through the courtesy and with the permission of copyright holder Florida Times-Union.

Article starting on page 169 is from *The Jersey Golfer* through the courtesy and with the permission of copyright holder The Jersey Golfer.

Article starting on page 181 is from *Newspaper Enterprise Association* through the courtesy and with the permission of copyright holder Newspaper Enterprise Association.

Article starting on page 186 is from *TPD Annual* through the courtesy and with the permission of copyright holder Cardinal Publishing Company.

Article starting on page 190 is from *The Los Angeles Times* through the courtesy and with the permission of copyright holder The Los Angeles Times.

Article starting on page 201 is from *Florida Golfweek* through the courtesy and with the permission of copyright holder Florida Golfweek.

Article starting on page 202 is from *The Memphis Commercial Appeal* through the courtesy and with the permission of copyright holder The Memphis Commercial Appeal.

Article starting on page 203 is from *The Quincy Herald* through the courtesy and with the permission of copyright holder The Quincy Herald.

Article starting on page 210 is from *St. Andrews, Cradle of Golf* through the courtesy and with the permission of copyright holder A. S. Barnes and Company, Inc.

Article starting on page 228 is from *The Columbia Record* through the courtesy and with the permission of copyright holder The Columbia Record.

Cover photograph by Stephen Green-Armytage for *Sports Illustrated* ® reprinted by permission of Sports Illustrated ® Time, Inc. 1975.

The views and opinions of the authors as expressed herein are not necessarily those of the editors and publisher of Golfer's Digest and no responsibility for such views will be assumed.

Golfer's Digest is a publication of DBI Books, Inc., Northfield, Ill.

ISBN 0-695-80648-3

Library of Congress Catalog Card #66-19804

CONTENTS

DOES THE MAGIC WAND REALLY EXIST?

By ROBERT CROMIE

Zebra putters going through final check before being packed for shipment.

DOES THE magic wand really exist?

Many golfers, from touring pros to high handicap hackers, will tell you that it does. It's called the Zebra Putter.

Gene Littler, the soft-spoken gentleman who has made so remarkable a recovery after major surgery for cancer, was the first ever to use the Zebra in tournament play. He won the 1975 Crosby with it and went on to have the biggest year of his lustrous career: triumphs also in the Memphis, Westchester and Pacific Masters events, and more than $241,000 in prize money.

A woman in Sedona, Ariz., who said she was one of the worst putters in her club, managed to acquire a Zebra (only about 300 are turned out daily in the tiny factory in Carmel Valley Village, Calif., and Zebras are hard to find) and promptly reported that she was taking the club to bed with her and couldn't live without it.

The Zebra's fame is spreading throughout the world. A U.S. Navy commander, stationed in Belgium, saw Arnold Palmer putting with his and wrote—pleadingly—to California. Dave Taylor, inventor of the Zebra, and a soft touch, sent one off to Belgium. This is the response, in part:

"After about 2 hours of practice on the rug in my apartment that first evening I couldn't wait to try it out on our golf course. Several of us went over the next day at lunch time (our course, the Royal Golf Club of Hainut, is only 5 minutes away from work) and I spent 75 minutes on the putting green. Our greens are fairly slow, so I inserted two of the weights in the head and went to work . . . All I can say is that the club is fantastic.

"To date I've played three rounds with the Zebra, and my average number of putts has been 31.7, with the individual putts per round being 34, 28, and 33 respectively. I have yet to have a 3-putt green . . . I might add that I was averaging 35-36 putts per round with my old putter.

"Naturally, I've shown the Zebra to many of my fellow golfers, and a great many have used it on the practice green. Their opinion has been unanimous: 'It's a beautiful club. Where can I get one?' The pro has tried it also, and he said to me: 'Will you get one for me? Money is no problem: 3,000, 4,000, 5,000 francs. I'll pay anything.' Translated, the pro was saying: '$75, $100, $125. It doesn't matter.'

"I also have people stop me at the club as well as come into my office here at work and ask me if I'm the fellow with the new putter. It's gotten so that I am afraid to leave the putter in my golf bag, it's such a celebrity. One of my partners, after my 28-putt round, asked me if the Zebra would give him an autograph . . ."

By this time you must be wondering what distinguishes the Zebra from other mallet putters. The most noticeable thing, visually, is that 11 parallel black lines are set into the top of the gray clubhead. But more of these later. Using it, which the writer has done only twice, there is a feeling that the club almost swings itself. Also, lining up the putt seems a far simpler matter than with other putters. Whether it's the balance—and balls hit off either heel or toe have a habit of running astonishingly straight, the lack of a hosel, the fact that the weight of the head is adjustable after purchase, or simply some unseen wizardry, I couldn't say. Perhaps Dave Taylor's description of how the Zebra was born will give you a clue.

"I've been making putters for Lit for, oh, maybe 15 years, on and off, and about as fast as I'd make 'em he'd discard 'em. And he had his reasons for it. They just didn't seem to fit him. So one day I said: 'I can't afford to keep cutting up putters. I'm buying these things at 20 or 25 dollars apiece and making them over.' And I struck on the idea of putting a ball and socket in it, thereby reducing my own energies and being able to let him adjust it for the lie and loft he wanted. This struck a note with him and he thought it was great.

"Then I had consulted a lot of eye doctors, some of them of some pretty great note, and we determined that the best way to line up a putter was with a series of lines running towards the hole. Parallel lines, not one line, because that was almost too fine an adjustment to have to make. So I proceeded to make up some heads out of aluminum.

"Without telling Gene, I had watched him many times, both as a contestant and when I was playing with him on occasion. He was constantly lining up the putter to the left of the hole. Who am I to tell Gene Littler: 'Hey! You're not doing this right!' He's one of the greatest golfers in the world. But somehow he made adjustments and on occasion he'd win a tournament.

"Well finally—he didn't really agree—but he took a quiescent attitude about the whole thing. This was in about '71 or '72. So when he showed up last year for the Crosby . . . In the meantime I had found out exactly what I wanted. I took the attitude that, look: I can't make a putter to suit every individual professional's desires. It's my opinion that they really don't know this much about what a putter should be like.

"I knew I had to have the lines. I knew I had to have a general look of some gracefulness to the putter. I had to have a low profile or depth of face, because it gives a better feeling as you're looking down on it and allows you to keep the club close to the ground. And I had to have that much distance (indicating the lines) to the mallet.

"So, it's very difficult to take a person who's been using a blade putter with great success and say: 'Here's a mallet putter. I want you to use it.' Strangely, Littler many times used a mallet putter when he was home, but he would say to me: 'I never get out on the tour with it, Dave. I'm not that confident of mallet putters.' There are many good, well-made, beautiful mallet putters on the market.

"So I said Lit—to settle to this—I've got to have it that

Zebra shaft being checked for proper lie.

way. That's the way it's got to be. I don't know whether I can change the whole golfing world or not over to a mallet putter, but I know if I got a putter that's going to cut strokes off their game we're going some place. So to sum it up: We now have this mallet-type putter; has a low profile, and as you look down on it it has, to me at least, a vision of strength but with grace. It's kind of like a 6-foot-2 blonde who's beautiful, but she's got a lot of body at the same time, you know?

"So here we are. I've got that much of it done. Now Littler takes it out and he uses it and comes back and says "'Dave, that's a pretty good putter.' I says, 'I've been telling you that for years.' 'Don't be so smart.' This is his remark, you know. So he goes out on a practice round before the Crosby and he came home. We're sitting in the living-room and he came down and he said—this is typical of Littler—he said: 'Well, I hate to tell you fellows this'—my son and myself were both sitting on the floor—'I'm going to go with that putter tomorrow. I holed some great putts.'

"So he does. He went with the putter. However he still I can see—and he's not very forceful in his objections to you—rather than argue he'd set the putter off to one side and go somewhere else, get something else. I could see he was still wondering about these lines. He says, 'Dave, you're really sure about this?' Now he knows that I have no great technical background. I'm a professional inventor, I'd say. He says I'm a nutty inventor. He's probably right, not me.

So I said 'Gene, I've checked this out with some of the greatest eye-doctors in the country and it's just an irrefutable fact, you see differently every single day, everybody does, after they're 15-16 years old. You can not line up a cross-line as well as you can a series of parallel lines. Now please don't argue with me about it and don't take 'em off. Because if you do, I'm not going to talk to you any more.' He says okay. So, the result is history now.

"He goes out and he just putts the eyes out of everything and he wins the tournament going away. The interesting thing was on Sunday—he had a four-shot lead—I know what he's going to do. He's going to win the tournament, because it's a gusty day, beautiful looking to the public, but a very windy tournament. He's got to play Pebble Beach, and in wind Pebble Beach is an absolute *monster*. And he goes out—some of the better scores were as high as 80 that day—and he goes out and shoots 74, and still walks off with it. Anyway, as he's leaving the house, I say to him: 'Lit, how do those lines look to you today?' Remember now, he's almost set some putting records. At Cyprus he had three birdies in a row from over 25 feet. He said, 'Dave, I have to admit, the more I look at those lines the more they look like the road map to the U.S. mint.'

"Since then he has never taken those lines off the putter. Actually, Arnold Palmer took the lines off the putter, one of the ones that we had equipped him with, and Littler told him: 'Arnold, don't do *that*. That's one of the main things about that putter.' Now he's an advocate of the lines, you see. And so Palmer, being Palmer, one time he painted the whole thing white. Next time he painted the whole thing black. Then I equipped him with a *super*-putter, that he liked, and he went over to Europe and won two tournaments over there, using the Zebra.

"Other fellows would come to Littler and they'd borrow his putter, and Gene keeps calling me up and said: 'Dave, when are you going to get these things on the market? I can't even have time to practice before I tee off in the morning. It's a little embarrassing to me, because I want to putt for 10 minutes before I tee it up. I can't get it out of the other fellow's hands.'

"Well, in the meantime, we've made our arrangements with RAM Golf Corporation and we're doing the best we can. But we do have some factory problems to solve, you know, so that's about the way it got."

The first Zebra putters went on the commercial market in May, 1975, two or three months after Littler's victory at the Crosby with the Zebra prototype.

"As a matter of fact," Taylor says, "we kind of planted the putter on him. We put it in the back seat of my car and I loaned him the car to go to the Crosby. He opened it up and said: 'What's this in here?' I said, 'Oh, that's just a putter I made up.' I didn't push it on him. It was a plant job, that's what it was. You've got to be a con-man with these violin players. They're the greatest guys in the world, but they all know how they want a putter made. And if you could just for a minute have me go over the fund of information that I get from all these *fine* golfers on how a putter should be, you wouldn't believe it!

"If I had listened to Littler I'd have never made the Zebra. As much as I love him, that's the truth. If I had listened to Bob Rosburg, who holds the world's record for the fewest number of putts in a competitive round, I'd still be carving

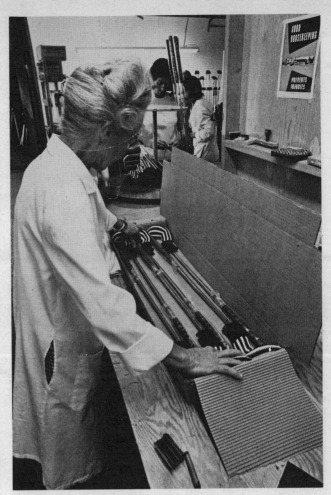

Dave Taylor and son, Dale, trying out finished Zebra for balance.   Mrs. Dave Taylor preparing Zebras for shipment.

out sample putters right now. There are a few of them who are not mechanical, and they say: 'Gee, this is great.' Well now with the success of the putter, last year it won—I say it, the putter in the hands of the fine golfer—won something like $750,000 in the first year, which is a phenomenal success story. And so now, for some reason, and it's pretty obvious, and it sounds a little egotistical on my part, and probably is, they sort of say: 'Well, you're the putter-man, you know. From now on, I'm going to go with you'.''

Taylor remembers one fine player who insisted that two of the lines be removed from the Zebra, because that was the way it should be made. Taylor replied that if the player wanted this done he could pay $40,000 for a special mould and they would put out a putter with the player's name on it. Otherwise, the inventor added, he was removing no lines from *his* putter.

Among other professionals who have used the Zebra with success (although perhaps are not using it now) are Gary Player, Don January, Ray Floyd, John Schlee, Dean Refram and Miller Barber, who dropped into the plant just prior to the Crosby and spent several hours before leaving with two or three different putters made to his needs (upright lie).

The earliest Zebras were adjustable for the relationship between the shaft and head, and then were supposed to be fastened by the owner with a steel pin. Sometimes the head came loose, however, and because of this, and a frown or so

from the United States Golf Association, the Zebra now is fashioned in three styles only, and the one adjustment possible, without violence, are the weights which may be added to the head.

When the first Zebras had been out a while, some of the professional users told Taylor they didn't want to become too fond of the club because of rumors that the U.S.G.A. was considering ruling it illegal in view of the adjustable factor.

"They said it was because the club could be changed from day to day," Taylor explains, "and they were dead right. So we telephoned and said: 'Please don't disqualify our putter by rumor only.' I went to Golf House, and I visited with Mr. P. J. Boatwright, who runs the thing—and make no mistake about it—the U.S.G.A. runs golf, and thank God for 'em because if you didn't have 'em you'd have all kinds of gimmicky things in the *world* out there, everything: hyped-up golf balls, hyped-up *everything*. You'd have club faces that you could make the ball jump back at you 10 feet; you'd have—well, I can imagine you'd have so much gimmickry that the game of golf would not be the same as we know it today if you didn't have the U.S.G.A. A lot of people don't understand this.

"So I met with Mr. Boatwright. I met with Mr. Frank Thomas, the technical director, and they explained their position, most courteous gentlemen, told me: 'Yes, you have

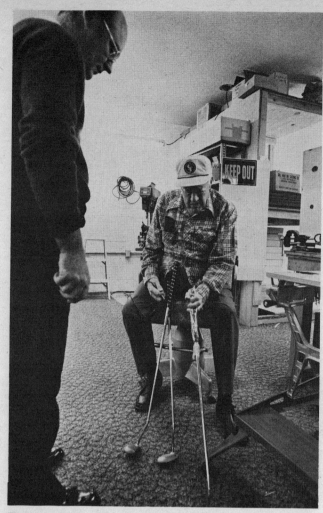

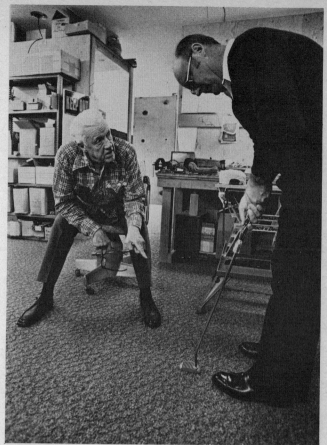

Barber tries out the Zebra.

Taylor and Miller Barber, touring pro, consulting as Barber chooses a group of new putters.

a beautiful club . . .' I said: 'Good, now where do you guys want me to pin it, and how many pins do you want me to put in, and we'll do it. I don't care if it costs us $40.' Because we have a theory here about the Zebra putter. As you know my hobby is old Rolls-Royces, and old fine anythings. I think America is getting away from this fine thing, and my feeling is this—what it costs it costs, but baby we're going to do it right. If you don't want to pay this, you don't need it. I have to say that the price of the putter may go up in time because of the rising cost, but it's going to be the best thing that we, the Taylors, can produce and when it becomes other than that—we'll quit making 'em, if we can't sell 'em!''

Taylor credited Littler's association with RAM for Zebra signing with that corporation as its distributor.

"The president of RAM, Al Hansberger and I shook hands on the deal at Palm Springs and when we did that we sealed it. And, very strangely, 3 days later I got an offer that would make their offer look ridiculous. And I said no, we made a deal with a gentleman and we respect that . . . So I stuck to what I said I would do, and believe me, they stuck to what they said they would do. You can print this if you want to. We agreed on terms on the 'phone. He said, 'Dave, I'm not going to take this to our legal people. What I'm going to do is send you a letter that states all the things you and I talked with on

the 'phone.' Remember, I met this man one time for 15 minutes. He said if you like it sign it and send it back and we will then forward you a purchase order with a check.

"Would you believe, in these times, I got at the end of the week a purchase order and a check for $48,850. I could have cashed that check and told 'em: 'I'm sorry as hell I just plain can't make these putters more than three a day. You're going to have to wait.' There was nothing in that letter that said I got to produce 'em within so many days. Nothing at all. So when you're doing business with a company like that, I have to feel somewhere along the line he looked up somebody who doesn't know me too well who said, yeah that guy's pretty good, do business with him.' Because business is not *done* that way. I don't know of anybody who'll say, 'Yeah, I'll do it,' and send you a check for almost a half a hundred thousand dollars. And he's only seen one club for 15 minutes! So that's the reason we've been working really. Mrs. Taylor and I have come completely out of retirement. I hadn't done anything for 35 years other than just monkey around and do what I want to do."

The Zebra now is made in a small, carpeted factory run by Dale Taylor, the son, who holds a master's degree in business administration from U.C.L.A.; Taylor, and a delightful lady, Marjorie (Mrs. David) Taylor, who cheerfully spends almost every working day packing the newly-minted putters for shipment. There are five or six employees, including a couple of Vietnamese refugees, and the elder Taylor is high in his praise of all of them.

Taylor, born in a Frank Lloyd Wright house at 5858

Woodlawn in Chicago, was one of six brothers. His father died when Dave was less than 18 months old and the family subsequently moved to Winnetka, Illinois, where Dave grew up. He never attended college.

"Hell," he says with a grin, "I couldn't wait to get out of high school, and they couldn't wait to get rid of me."

From the time he was very small he wanted to be an inventor, and early plans were to send him to the Massachusetts Institute of Technology. But an older brother, a patent attorney for whom Dave worked one summer (during which he spent most of his time improving the inventions his brother was trying to obtain patents for), suggested that this would be a waste of time and that young Taylor might as well start right out inventing things.

"You'd probably make a pretty fair engineer," the brother remarked, "but remember that if you're any good as an inventor you can get a better engineer with the snap of your fingers than you could ever become."

By the time he was 27 years old, and after a stint as an advertising executive, Taylor was running a hotel in California and had fallen in love with that state. He never left. Among his patents are ones for a head trainer (to help golfers stop moving their heads too far during the swing); for trimming and cutting asparagus; and for removing the roots and tops of onions.

This last one, created while Dave was the head of research and development for a large concern, was perfected after World War II, during which he was a flying instructor, and he ruefully admits having made a slight miscalculation when he set the terms of payment.

"I blew it," he says. "I could have had 50 percent of their savings on labor costs, or so much per month, and I took that. By their account, after it was all in, it had saved them over $1,056 a day every day, 8 months a year, for the last 12 years. But that's all right."

At the moment the Zebra is his overpowering interest. While he doesn't plan any particular increase in production, at least for now (partly because he fears this might lead to some diminution in quality) Taylor is convinced that the market for the Zebra will keep expanding for years to come. Japan, where Littler is a great favorite, is expected to buy thousands of putters. But don't look for the Zebra imprint in Japan. Because of a name conflict with a Japanese sporting goods firm, the Zebra in Japan will bear the label: "Gene Littler Lineup."

Each Zebra, incidentally, is checked for balance with a spirit level before it leaves the factory, and an excess of glue under the grip or some other almost imperceptible imperfection will cause a club to be tossed aside. There are three standard models available: flat, medium and upright lie, though variations are provided for professionals asking for this or even for the casual buyer who requests his club pro to have the lie adjusted to suit the player's whim.

If room permitted, several thousand words could be added here regarding the Rolls-Royce fever with which Dave Taylor burns and which he has transmitted to his good friend, Gene Littler. Each man has owned a variety of these beauties, (Taylor owns one as this is written and Littler three) and they buy them singly or jointly, work on them together, and sometimes exchange ownership.

The Zebra and its inventor have one thing in common: Class.

A reminder for open orders.

We're Off For Some Golf In

By JOHN R. McDERMOTT, Photographed by RICHARD LITWIN

THE THING THAT got me into the tent was a line in the brochure that Moroccan Consul General Abdeslam Jaidi had sent over from his New York office. The covering letter merely invited me to play in the "IV Trophée Hassan II"—a pro-am golf tournament to us earth people. But on page 8 the lavish brochure stated: "To the first 10 amateur teams His Majesty will award a substantial prize." Visions of a lifetime pass at John Nitti's gas station danced on the ceiling. Or maybe it would be a year's supply of olives. At the very least, a terrific wallet?

I took inventory. I am a 15-handicapper (a pro has to spot me 15 strokes). In a pro-am that is as dangerous as a live grenade with the pin pulled. Furthermore I had never had

the pleasure of playing golf, let alone three-putting, in Africa, but I knew people who got asked out to dinner because they had. Finally, at my club—Winged Foot—a 15 is expected to play like a 12 at most other places.

So much for inventory. My letter of acceptance was grateful, humble and by messenger.

The first thing you have to understand about Moroccans is their basic anxiety to impress without pressing, to be gracious without overkill. The second thing to keep in mind is that you have to reconcile their command of English just as you would your checkbook—send it through two different processes until you get to something that resembles a reasonable bottom line.

Thus at John F. Kennedy Airport that Friday evening we were ushered through the TWA processing as though we were all parents of the bride. When I say all, I mean a full 707 load of amateur and pro golfers—led by Billy Casper, Larry Ziegler and Rod Funseth—from all over the U.S. and Canada. When we found a government security I.D. card on the airport floor and returned it to the Moroccan tourist official whose face it bore, I believe the fellow would have given us his favorite camel if he'd had it with him.

On the plane we discovered that our Moroccan hosts spoke excellent English. It was the punctuation that caused us a few starts—their habit of running some sentences together and stopping in the middle of others. Sample start,

Morocco

from the plane's intercom: "We will begin with drinks after dinner." Pause. My wife and I exchanged uneasy glances. We hadn't eaten dinner. Then the next sentence: "We will be showing for you the movie." It was several minutes before we realized that the steward on the intercom had forgotten to put the period after the word "drinks."

The trip was typical night-trans-Atlantic. Long, mildly euphoric and unremarkable. Except that several of us in the rear kept prowling up the aisle to sneak a look at Loretta Young, who had come aboard without fanfare and was sitting in Row 12. An old friend of Hassan II, she was taking advantage of the event to pay him a visit. By dawn we had been fed, watered, bedded

Par for the tour were such non-golf activities as tribal spectacles and sightseeing. Above left, golf pro Lee Elder joins the floor show after a lunch. Billy Casper, above, preferred serenity at Rabat's Mohammed V Mosque.

Counsul General Abdeslam Jaidi donned his djellabah and chatted with luncheon guests at the Royal G.C.

Aerial act by this dancer was one of several spectacular entertainments staged especially for the tournament.

down and otherwise readied for the great adventure ahead.

First stop was Marrakesh (they rhyme it with quiche). The airport bears a striking resemblance to the one at Augusta, Ga., and since that is the site of the Masters Golf Tournament, I thought that augured well. I had, you see, already prepared a modest acceptance speech for the awards dinner a week hence. We were greeted outside the terminal building by several groups of entertainers—Berbers in white drapery bearing long trumpets, young girls in gypsy prints banging tambourines, old men in flowing tunics, shifting their feet as artfully as Rockettes. It was a marvelous way to start a Saturday morning and it surely beat the television cartoons back home. There isn't much one can say about music that goes back many centuries and which has had minimum exposure back home. I will only observe that I now know where the diesel truck horn was invented.

We were ferried to the Holiday Inn via several large, modern buses which were to hover alongside for the rest of the week. Ditto those entertainers.

Adjustments were many and quick. Hamburgers at the Inn are made from ground lamb. Film is $6 a roll. Seeking bellboy assistance is not a game for shrinking violets. Everyone drinks the delicious mint tea like Little Leaguers into the Kool-Aid. Do not try to buy your wife a bathing cap in the Inn's boutique if, as I do, you speak only English, Japanese and Sign. The nice lady there sells in French and German exclusively, and she concluded my hopeless attempt with what sounded something like, "No, after dinner at the palace." Maybe she was expecting a late shipment.

Dinner that night was at the palace— the Layadi Palace, described as a sort of summer place used by the royal family. It is a masterful mix of three major architectures, each of which stays out of the others' way. The salons are massive, the floors aflame with Morocco's fantastic rugs. And it is very old. It was here that we met His Royal Highness Prince Moulay Abdallah, the king's courtly brother who, among other things, serves as president of the Royal Golf Federation. We made note of still another surprise—the ubiquitous Consul General, Mr. Jaidi, can remember anyone's name after one meeting.

It was here, too—and I tremble as I write this—that we first spied the nefarious Grabaduck. As any international or, for that matter, domestic traveler knows, Grabaduck has defied identification for years. He speaks most languages, is always carefully disguised and you yourself have seen him many times at conventions, resorts, on cruise ships and elsewhere. You probably call him by another name, but we first met him at a luau on an island off New Rochelle, N.Y. A terrifying summer lightning squall had descended on our little rock on Long Island Sound, cutting off escape to the mainland. When it finally moved inland most of us came out from under picnic tables trying to find children, dry towels and dry clothes. I'll never forget him in the middle of that melee. Water streaming down his contorted face, he was barking orders to his poor bedraggled wife: "You go over there and get plates and some of the roast pork! I'll go down to the other end and *grab a duck!*" You know the fellow as well as I do. He gets the first seat on the bus, the first drink at the crowded bar, the table nearest the dance floor and woe betide the man or woman who tries to beat him to the trough. It is said that in 1915 Grabaduck's grandpa was the first person to hit the lifeboats when the band struck up *Nearer My God To Thee*. There he was, in the Layadi buffet line, screaming at an embarrassed chef for more pastry while the dumbstruck guests behind him waited

Tent camp lunch was set up near golf club grounds in Marrakesh, first stop on the tournament-tour program.

for their first course. As we were to discover, his presence in Morocco was to have a serious effect on the outcome of the tournament.

The evening was saved by the dinner itself—a veritable pageant of Moroccan dishes available in most of the country's major cities. The feast was incredible: whole lambs and chickens roasted in a litany of spices and herbs, couscous—the national farina—an armada of fruits, cheeses and pastries, all awash in a fine indigenous wine called Boulaouane. It didn't take anyone very long to get with the local custom of serving and devouring the victuals with one's fingers. I have always believed that we all have that within us. Our eight Arabian Nights had begun in earnest.

Marrakesh is Morocco's sunburnt city, a fascinating maze of russet walls and streets set against the Atlas Mountains. A tour of the town is simple and easily organized. Although we were allowed only a morning and a late afternoon, it was compressed time, well spent. The Saadian Tombs near the markets—where the remains of kings are separated from their concubines—are themselves works of art and set the proper note of reverence for the city's antiquity (1062 A.D.). Many simpler years ago the natives swapped olive oil

for Italy's Carrara marble and the tombs are admissible evidence of who got the better of that deal. There is livelier action in the late afternoon in the Djemaa-el-Fna, a huge open market where farmers come to sell produce and be entertained by story-tellers, snake charmers, acrobats and fellow farmers. On advice of counsel we brought small coins—because it is a felony not to tip the entertainers, whether they entertain you or not. (Memo to Monsignor Skelly: Remind me to tell you how we can make our second collection more effective.)

After the third collection—this one from the carriage driver who took us back to the Inn—we joined two other couples from New York for drinks at La Mamounia, a splendid continental hotel just inside the city's walls. One of its claims to celebrity is the fact that Winston Churchill slept there—and we could see why. Very proper, fittingly ornate and, we decided, not where we wanted to have dinner. I lobbied against the dining room when I spotted Grabaduck therein. Instead we cabbed to La Petite Auberge and had a marvelous meal, sidewalk cafe style. Tip to travelers: Do not leave Marrakesh until you have had a tureen of their onion soup.

Next stop, Rabat, via the king's un-

marked train which takes about four hours to make the 199-mile journey northeastward. By avoiding the lead car we also avoided Grabaduck. Our foresight paid off in coin of another realm: Billy Casper, an old Morocco hand, decided on our car. He tells wonderful stories of golf with the young king, the most memorable of which relates to the extended religious observance—called Ramadan and akin to our Lent—during which Moroccans are not permitted to gad about during the daylight hours. For this reason His Majesty maintains nine holes behind the palace walls under floodlights. "It's different and it's fun," says Casper. "You have a bite to eat and then you tee off at 8 p.m. and play nine."

Rabat is a fairly new imperial city on the Atlantic but old as the Romans who left their mark on the place. Roman columns still line the huge courtyard next to the magnificent Mohammed V mosque. Their forum, most of it uncovered, stands in a section called Chella. It is an impressive city for it combines the flavor of antiquity, a modern ambiance and a very special style, laid on it by the current dynasty.

Visitors—at least it was our experience—are not treated, they are courted. And I am talking about the time we were able to spend away from all the king's men. Even Claude Harmon, our pro at Winged Foot and, as the king's premier golf instructor, the oldest veteran of this tour, is always newly amazed when he comes to Rabat. As a world traveler he also has a discerning eye for the distinguished. For example it is his secret desire to transplant a restaurant called La Mamma Pizzeria back to Westchester County. "If I could get two or three of them going back in the States," says Claude, "I'd be as rich as Hassan." Small wonder. As you wait at the tiny bar for one of the establishment's 35 seats, they serve you complimentary slices of pizza fresh from the woodfired stone oven at the far end of the room. Just something to tide you over. The minestrone is a complete meal if you've got a touch of the vapors some evening. The cruisine is mixed and delicious.

The Rabat Hilton food clearly comes from some mythical cornucopia. Le Relais du Pere Louis should do a cookbook. There are others, all over town,

Former pro at Dar es Salaam, Butch Harmon, brought the advantage of "local knowledge" to the tournament.

Architect Robert Trent Jones followed play in his golf cart, looking like the cat that swallowed the canary.

Roman ruins were kept intact when Dar es Salaam golf course was laid out 5 years ago. Columns line 12th hole.

but, as luck would have it we were consigned, most evenings, to our golf hosts. That wasn't all bad. The feast at Tour Hassan, Rabat's answer to Marrakesh's Mamounia, was extraordinary. The local belly dancer took a backseat during dinner to a young lady from the U.S. State Department who had conned one of the Scottish golfers onto the stage in his dress kilt. If someone could get that act back to Westchester County, he'd be as rich as Hassan *and* Claude Harmon.

About the golf I shall be mercifully brief. Our tounament was played over the 45-hole Dar es Salaam golf club course, where, incidentally, you can play for greens and caddy fees. First, you should understand that the course was designed by golf's most renowned architect, Robert Trent Jones. There is a curse many golf pros visit upon Mr. Jones. It is that he should be made to play all the golf courses he has designed until he makes a par. According to the warlocks who invoke this malediction, Mr. Jones would still be playing the first hole he ever built. Second, it is important to understand

A kiss is just a kiss goes the Casablanca-inspired song, so Lee Elder bussed Brian Barnes at awards dinner.

the nature of a pro-am golf event. It is a contest among teams of four golfers. Each team consists of one gorilla and three chimpanzees. The team objective is to win some bananas for the big guy. If you're ever in the gallery don't spend a lot of time on the chimps.

Third, I'm sure you have heard that the golf handicap system—the game's great equalizer—is very much like what a cracker-barrel Indianapolis judge once told me about our American system of jurisprudence: "It's the best system anyone has ever devised but it surely ain't perfect." Accordingly, one team finished the first round 10 under par even though their pro shot a dismal 82. One four-handicapper opened with a magnificent 91, and he lives in Morocco so it couldn't have been the water.

I was lucky. My teammates and I couldn't get it together well enough to win any silverware but I did get to play with "Butch" Harmon, Claude's son, who had been the pro at Dar es Salaam for a couple of years. Butch had the "local knowledge" and it is a rule of mine that if you can't win you should at least try to learn. Eighteen holes with Butch was a side tour of its own. On the second day our amateur team fell to the lot of one Clive Clark, a delightful young pro from Sunningdale in Eng-

land who was having putter troubles. It was clear from our play that he must have drawn the short straw. It was so bad that I thought one of my teammates—in accordance with the rules—was keeping Clive's score and the fellow thought I was. There was embarrassed reconstruction on the 18th green and I can assure you that we did not call a press conference.

So much for the am part; the pros, when they finally got shed of us on the third and fourth days, didn't exactly "tear it up" as they say. Larry Ziegler won it with a four-round total of seven under par and he had to play like Mandrake to do it. Casper was in contention until the 70th hole—the reasonable par-4 16th to an elevated green. In the foursome ahead Ziegler had just chipped in from the apron for a miraculous birdie. The gallery rushed to the 17th to follow Ziegler while Casper waited in the 16th fairway to hit his second shot. Grabaduck, his movie camera whirring, decided to follow Ziegler, and of course the shortest route to the best vantage point was through a sand bunker guarding the green. I couldn't believe my eyes. Neither could the startled officials and it was a full five minutes before they could find someone with a rake to clear that bunker on 16. Meanwhile Casper

stood impatiently in the fairway. When he did hit his second it went right into the damaged bunker. Anyone who plays golf or who watches it on television knows what happened to Capser's concentration. I have never seen him outraged but I've also never seen him do what he did next. He walked into the bunker and without pausing flailed at the ball. It came out but barely. It took him two putts to hole out for a bogey and he was clearly out of contention. Grabaduck, may the fleas of 1,000 camels infest the place where you lay your head tonight.

And so, eight Arabian days and nights after our touchdown in Morocco, our 707 headed westward with its original cargo and some heady excess—Moroccan rugs, silver tea services, copperware, tinware, jewelry, caftans and just about one of everything else you would expect to find in one of Morocco's souks, their marketplace streets—each passenger sublimely confident that his or her purchase represented the lowest price and the finest bargain that canny American haggling and money could buy. I counted myself among them. But in retrospect, I think our Moroccan hosts, smiling and deferential, had the last word on that subject. The movie they put aboard the flight was *The Sting*.

How to find your Effective Swish Speed

By **DICK AULTMAN**

IF YOU COULD start golf all over again and a magic genie granted you one wish, which of the following would you choose?

First choice: every drive you make will travel exactly 200 yards on the line of your choice. No more second shots from rough, sand, tree trunks or rocky terrain. No more penalties for driving into water or out-of-bounds. You may never lose another ball off the tee.

Second choice: you can drive the ball as far as any living golfer—Nicklaus, Weiskopf, Dent—but with no special assurance of accuracy. You'll probably outdrive every player at your club. You'll reach many par-five holes in two shots, a few par-fours in one. Some courses will play like pitch-'n-putt. But you'll occasionally push or pull-hook into never-never land. Tight fairways will produce that nervous gnawing in the tummy.

Despite the drawbacks, most readers likely would opt for the second choice—distance over accuracy. In fact, most players do, even if not consciously.

Obviously you do not have a choice between 300-yard drives and letter-perfect accuracy. The genie doesn't exist.

On the other hand, distance and accuracy are not incompatible. You need not sacrifice one to obtain the other. In most instances the same fundamentals that add length also increase accuracy.

Simply stated, a golf ball goes farthest when struck squarely with a clubhead moving at maximum speed. The same factors that produce top clubhead speed during impact also deliver the clubhead squarely to the ball.

To make sure you are striking the ball as far and as accurately as you should with the swing you now have it is important that you find your Effective Swish Speed.

ESS is the maximum speed at which you can swing your left

The choice need not lie between hitting your drives straight and short or smashing a long ball into the rough. By experimenting on the practice range to find your maximum controllable arm speed, you can have both distance and accuracy.

**Speed up or slow down
in 10 percent increments
to find your best arm speed.**

To find the speed your arms swing most effectively, take some
normal swings with your driving club and examine the results. If
your shots are flying wildly or you are not making solid contact,
reduce your arm speed by 10 percent. Keep reducing your arm
speed by 10 percent until you are striking your shots solidly and
straight. However, if your normal swing produces acceptable
shots, increase your arm speed 10 percent at a time until you
begin to lose control. At that point, throttle back slightly. You'll
probably find you are still hitting the ball as straight as ever—
and farther than you used to.

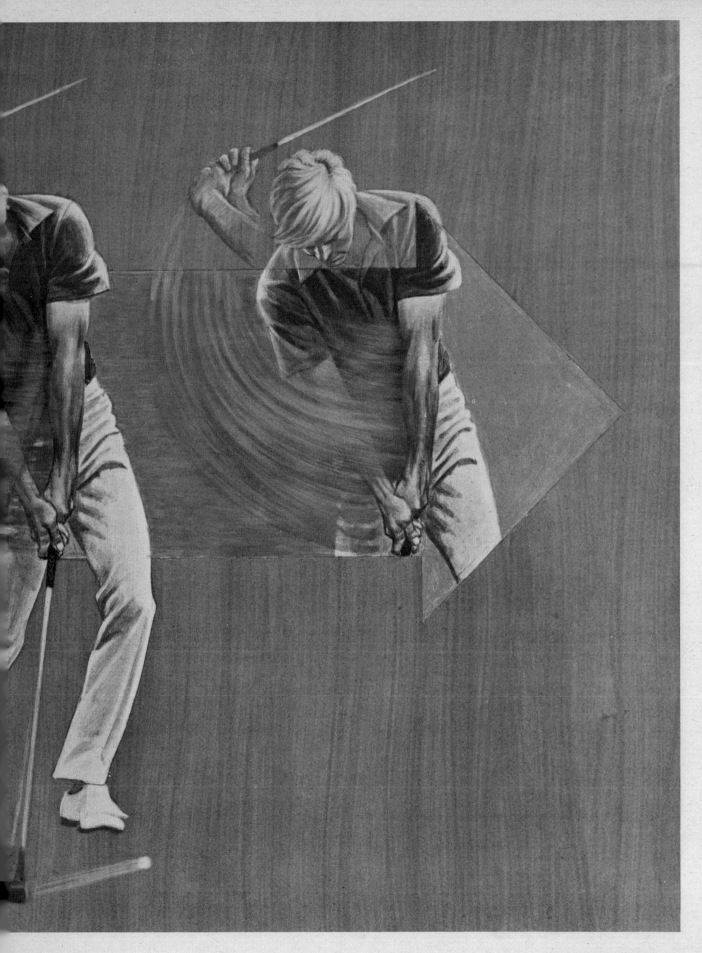

forearm forward *through* the impact area and beyond, yet still make fairly solid contact with the ball consistently (even the best players mis-hit most of their shots slightly). Many players do not achieve their maximum distance simply because they are either too lazy or uncertain to swish their arms forward at their top effective speed. Others try to swing too hard and actually sacrifice both swish speed and solid contact.

Try this experiment to find your ESS. After you are fully warmed up, take your driving club and hit a dozen shots at your normal swing pace or tempo. Analyze these shots and decide whether you are satisfied that you are making consistently solid contact.

If you are not satisfied, hit another dozen shots swinging your left forearm forward with about 10 per cent less swish speed. Again analyze how solidly you struck the balls. Continue this process, using 10 per cent less swish speed each time, until you are satisfied with your ability to strike your shots squarely. At this point you will have reached your ESS.

However, if you are satisfied with the first batch of shots you hit at your normal swing pace, try another batch but swing your left forearm through impact about 10 per cent faster. If you fail to strike these shots as solidly as you think you should, drop back to your normal swing pace. This, for the time being, will be your ESS.

If you find you can handle the faster swish speed, go on to another batch and again increase your swish speed 10 per cent.

Continue this process until you discover your maximum ESS. Once you find it, apply it on all full shots with every club.

"Think target" to swish forward

Golfers often become so absorbed with specific swing movements and positions that they unconsciously reduce their Effective Swish Speed, especially in restructuring their swings.

A good way to counteract this problem—and increase your length and accuracy—is to consciously "think target." Before every shot, first sight the spot where you want to finish. Try to visualize the ball flying and rolling to that spot. Then merely swing your left forearm through impact in the direction of your target at your maximum ESS.

Thinking target reinforces the idea in your subconscious that the object of any golf shot is to drive the ball forward, a simple concept often overlooked in striving for more length. When seeking added distance, the normal tendency is to make a faster backswing. This is a sure way to lose length. The faster you swish going back, the more difficult it becomes to generate maximum swish going forward. Thinking target will automatically make you swish back slower and forward faster.

Decrease tension to increase swish

Freedom of movement—as opposed to sheer muscle power—is vital in adding distance and accuracy through ESS. Tension restricts movement. Here are two ways to decrease tension and increase swish:

One, hold the club lightly in your hands at address and do not sole the clubhead on the turf. The minimal grip pressure required to support the club lightly on top of the grass is all the holding power you need. Any additional grip pressure at address, or any sudden grabbing of the club during your swing, causes undue wrist and arm tension that curtails freedom of movement.

The concept of holding the club lightly atop the grass is a key feature of Eddie Merrins' book *Swing the Handle—Not the Clubhead* and an increasingly popular technique among touring professionals. It not only produces proper grip pressure but also sets the stage for a smooth, free, rhythmical swinging of the arms. The technique is fairly simple to master—a single practice session should suffice—and worth the effort if for no other reason than it eliminates stubbing the clubhead in the grass during the takeaway.

A second way to reduce muscle tension is to shorten or even eliminate the time you are stationary over the ball before swinging. Perhaps 90 per cent of all golfers would automatically add appreciable yardage to their tee shots if they could assimilate Julius Boros' pre-swing drill of simply aiming the clubface, stepping into position, waggling and moving into the backswing.

Ideally, your pre-swing procedure, from aim to takeaway, should require no more than 4 to 5 seconds. In fact, most golfers take less time than this in preparing to make a practice swing which inevitably is vastly better than the actual stroke. It is almost axiomatic that the more time you spend immobile over the ball, the less swish you finally will generate through the impact area.

Condition yourself to plan your shot before setting up. Once you are over the ball, keep in motion. Start your swing back smoothly and swish your arms forward at the speed you have found to be most effective.

This will greatly increase your chances for longer as well as straighter shots—something no genie will be able to do for you.

"Don't think of it as just another putt, think of it as the putt which will determine if I am the company champion—Or if you are the champion of the company where you used to work."

IT'S TIME TO GET TOUGH WITH SLOW PLAY

IN 1965, *Golf Digest* became the first magazine to appear with a cover story advocating that play on the nation's golf courses be speeded up. A couple of other magazines followed with similar efforts. In 1968 the National Golf Foundation launched its "Speedy" campaign to combat slow play.

Unfortunately, there has been no marked effect on the game. The 3-hour round of 25 years ago is gone. Now, 4½ hours is considered speedy, five or longer probably is the average and we are headed toward six.

It's time to get tough in the fight against slow play.

It is difficult to measure the effect of slow play in terms of the game's relative popularity and on the rate of attrition of players. The shocking fact that there is attrition is frequently summed up in the expression, "I'm switching to tennis."

The National Golf Foundation claims the number of golfers in the country is 13,550,000, up five per cent from 1972 and up 13.4 per cent from 1970. There is no concrete statistical evidence to back this up, however.

On the other hand, a 1973 survey by the A. C. Nielsen Co. shows that the number of tennis players has grown to 20,377,000, double the 10,650,000 that Nielsen says were playing in 1970.

The most serious effect of slow play on the golf course is the anguish suffered by those who still play and love the game. And their plight will not get better unless conditions change.

Joe Jemsek, who owns public-fee courses in the Chicago area, cites figures to show he is moving an average of 100 fewer players a day than he was 40 years ago. This is a common problem, and it means lost revenue.

Given this discouraging outlook, it is easy for potential golf course investors to opt for businesses other than golf. That means even more overcrowding until the growth in numbers of players ceases altogether. When that happens, the sport begins to die.

The disease can—and must—be checked. Play can be speeded.

Last July, 60-year-old Matthew Alcorn of Vernoa, Pa., walked three golf courses—including fabled Oakmont—following an average golfer's route of play from tee through green and on to the next tee. The average walking time was one hour and 27 minutes. Since the act of addressing and striking a ball can be done quite deliberately in 15 or 20 seconds, that leaves a lot of dallying time in a five-hour round.

Joe Dey, a long-time executive director of the U.S. Golf Ass'n and for five years commissioner of the PGA Tournament Players Division until his recent retirement, feels that two persons should play a round of golf in 2½ hours or less. Three people should play in three hours or less and four people in 3½ hours or less, he believes.

Dey says, "There's only one thing effective against slow play—a two-shot penalty." He points out that 12 such penalties were meted out on the professional tour in 1973, with the result that the traditionally dilatory pros have cut their average playing time below 4½ hours and are heading toward four.

The two-stroke penalty obviously applies only to the tour. What can be done to make the amateur play faster?

After an 18-month nationwide study in which every known method for speeding play has been evaluated, GOLFER'S DIGEST is presenting six major proposals which could eliminate the problem. Three involve changes in the Rules of Golf. The other three are systems or procedures which can be instituted at clubs and other courses.

These remedies can work. The responsibility lies with you and your fellow players. Demand that your golf course follow these rules. If you belong to a USGA member club, ask the club to push for the rules change with the USGA.

We also are presenting lists of other specific speed-up actions you can incorporate into your club rules and into your personal habits of play. We are giving examples of actions clubs and organizations have taken successfully to combat slow play. And we are detailing one man's battle against slow play on public courses and against equally slow city hall fathers.

1. Enforce this new accountability system.

The low-handicap player in a group keeps his players moving. If the group ahead allows a hole to open up in front of it, the low handicapper warns the low handicapper in that group to close the gap by speeding up or allowing the trailing group to go through. Failure to cooperate is reported to the golf committee by filling out a brief form on the reverse side of the card.

There must be a pre-determined enforcement system with appropriate penalties to be meted out by the golf committee or other governing body. Provisions also must be made to insure that the first group on the course plays quickly. Urge your club or golf association to give it a try.

2. Install slow-play checkpoint signs.

Sign No. 1, setting a 2-hour limit per nine, should be placed on the first tee as a reminder to players to look at their watches and play briskly. Sign No. 2, establishing an 80-minute "par" for the first six holes, goes on the seventh tee. Sign No. 3 should be placed just off the ninth green, clearly visible. Sign No. 4, allowing 80 minutes for the first six holes of the back nine, goes on the 16th tee.

These signs are available at a cost of about $4 each from Standard Manufacturing Co., 220 E. Fourth St., Cedar Falls, Iowa 50613, or from any of Standard's many dealers. Make an effort to see that they are put up on your course.

3. Plant 150-yard markers

By knowing how far he is from the green, a player should not have to walk ahead of his ball. He will be able to make his club selection much more quickly. These indicators—widely but by no means universally used already—would be particularly helpful on resort courses, where most of the traffic is unfamiliar with the layout.

There is nothing in the rules that prohibits these markers, even for tournament play. The USGA normally does not use them in its tournament competition, but it does not force a club to uproot trees or bushes that may be serving as yardage markers. If you use shrubbery, be sure it is clearly defined.

Encourage your club or course to provide 150-yard markers.

SIX HARD-NOSED SOLUTIONS

TO THE SLOW-PLAY PROBLEM

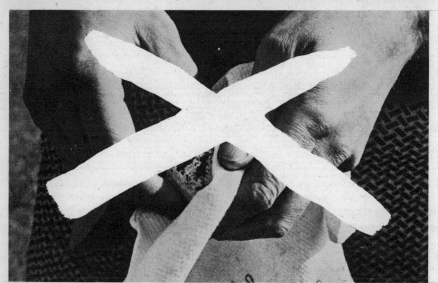

4. Bring back continuous putting.

Marking, cleaning and replacing balls on the green is a proven time-waster. In 1965, the USGA invoked continuous putting and one cleaning on a local-option basis. It never got a fair chance, was soon 'dropped by most clubs and was taken off the books after four years. Wasted time determining if a player was going to step in another player's line and violation of the tradition of the farthest ball being played first are cited by the USGA as reasons.

There are times when tradition must give way to expediency, however. That same player's line probably has been stepped in by 200 players in recent hours. And the strategy advantages or disadvantages inherent in the farthest ball playing first might not be worth all the time spent in re-marking.

5. Allow a putting ball.

Two of the game's greatest players— Sam Snead and Jack Nicklaus—have advocated that a new, clean ball be substituted as a putting ball on each hole. The elimination of cleaning and wiping dirt off the ball, or tossing it to a caddie to do, would speed things up and not change the character of the game.

The USGA has thoroughly discussed the idea, carrying it into talks with the Royal and Ancient Golf Society of Great Britain, the co-rulesmaking body. The R&A objects on the grounds its players might play the smaller, hotter ball to the green, then substitute the 1.68 American ball that is easier to putt. The USGA should know your views and those of your club.

6. Put in the lateral boundary rule.

This would give the player who has hit out-of-bounds the option of dropping a ball within two club lengths of the boundary at the point the ball went out-of-bounds, and incurring just a one-stroke penalty, with no loss of distance. Players always should be encouraged to hit a provisional ball when it appears a shot might be out-of-bounds or lost. But too many don't, and the option of dropping a ball would save a lot of time-wasting treks.

Of course, the stroke-and-distance option would remain in effect.

Again, write the USGA if you favor this proposed change, at Golf House, Far Hills, N.J. 07931.

OTHER WAYS TO SPEED UP PLAY

What an individual can do

• Concentrate and plan ahead . . . be thinking about your next shot, about where to place your bag or handcart or where to park your golf car; save your funny stories for the bar.

• Be prepared to play when it's your turn . . . select your club, line up your shot or study your putt, make your practice swings while others are playing. When it's your turn, address your ball and hit it.

• Walk briskly.

• Carry a spare ball.

• Take no mulligans or practice shots.

• Don't stop with playing partners while they hit . . . go to your own ball.

• Don't walk beyond your ball more than a few paces.

• Watch ball into rough and mark it; hit a provisional.

• Be realistic when waiting to hit to a green or off the tee . . . usually the waiters can't get there with a cannon.

• Learn how far you can hit the ball.

• When out of the hole and heading for triple-bogey, pick up.

• Mark your scores as you walk to the next tee.

• Learn the rules.

What groups can do

• Forget honors . . . first man off green and on the tee, hit it; play when ready in fairway, even simultaneously, so long as you don't interfere with other players.

• Putt when ready . . . don't wait for the outside player if he's not ready.

• Shorter hitters play first as soon as group ahead is out of range.

• If group behind is pressing you, wave it through . . . then speed up.

• Only one man look for his ball in rough and only for two minutes.

• Wave up following group on par-3s, particularly longer ones.

• Make your match and lay your bets before you get to first tee.

What clubs and courses can do

• Insist that new players/members have a certain level of proficiency and knowledge of rules and etiquette.

• Ban winter rules.

• Train caddies properly.

• Allow golf cars on the fairway.

• Be realistic about starting times to avoid over-crowding.

• Start from both No. 1 and No. 10 tees.

• Be sure starter admonishes each group to play briskly.

• Use rangers to push slow players.

• Run a fun tournament to expose golfers to fast play.

• Create a "slow player of the week" award and post the winners.

For faster play in golf cars

• If two are riding, player first to hit should make his logical club selection, then take two more clubs—one longer and one shorter. While he's preparing to play the other rides to his ball. Don't wait for each other.

• Park car in direct line from green to next tee.

• At green, driver should bring other player's putter if he doesn't already have it (which he should).

THEY PROVED

Many clubs, public course officials and golf associations have been battling slow play for many years. In many cases, as the following examples illustrate, the fight has been successful.

Go-Golf in Los Angeles

Ray Goates, manager of the 13 courses operated by the Los Angeles Department of Recreation and Parks, has spearheaded what is probably the country's oldest and most extensive anti-slow play campaign. Since 1966, over some of the country's most crowded courses, the program has reduced the average course round from 4:45 to 4:30.

From time studies by unobserved timers who clocked hundreds of typical foursomes, Goates has concluded that 18 holes can easily be completed in four hours—7-8 minutes for a par-3 hole, 12-13 minutes for a par-4 and 15 minutes for a par-5.

Goates has staged "Go-Golf" demonstrations in which participants are promised a free round of golf if they can finish in less then four hours. In each of two years, more than 4,000 golfers have completed 18 holes in an average time of 3:27 one year and 3:12 the next . . . no one took more than four hours. Not only that, their average scores improved.

Given the opportunity, some incentive and a little know-how, Goates concludes, golfers can play regulation courses in less then four hours without really hurrying the game.

In Rochester, 72 holes in a day

Also disturbed by slow play at the Country Club of Rochester (N.Y.), 16 self-described "middle-aged weekend golfers" have for the last five years conducted a 72-hole Classic Marathon Tournament . . . in one day.

They play in golf carts and abide by "Rules of Accelerated Play"—hit when ready, disregarding honors; no practice swings; pick up once you've reached

GOLF DOESN'T HAVE TO BE SLOW

triple-bogey; search one minute for lost balls, replace in probable lost position with one-stroke penalty; don't remove the flag unless ball is within 10 feet; give any putt within the leather.

The results—an average time per round per foursome of 2:45. More important, over the last three years, there has been only 1/30th of a stroke per round in difference between normal play and the accelerated pace.

Says Alex Hargrave, a tournament regular, "We wish to bring home to our fellow amateurs how much more enjoyable the weekend game would be . . . at no loss of results. Over the years there have grown some ideas of so-called etiquette which bear no relation to the skill of the game, winning the match or politeness. The real politeness is to those behind you on the course."

Crackdown in private clubs

In an attempt to bring the average time per round down to four hours, monitors at The Summerlea G. & C.C. in Montreal, Canada, record the elapsed time between the 1st, 9th and 18th holes. Any player exceeding the time limit is warned the first time and loses prime time playing privileges for the second offense . . . this includes forfeiture of weekend morning starting times.

Ron Reitz, head professional at North Ridge C.C. in Raleigh, N.C., requires his 700 members to view "Courtesy on the Course," a 17½-minute film distributed by the National Golf Foundation that includes about six minutes of anti-slow play suggestions. He shows the films on four evenings during the winter and early spring, following up with a question-and-answer session. Members must sign an attendance sheet at the door and those who haven't viewed the film simply are not allowed on the course. Some members complained at first, Reitz reports, but now everyone accepts it.

Noting that as traffic gets heavier on the course, the distance between foursomes decreases and an automatic

slowdown occurs, the Mount Kisco (N.Y.) C.C. solved its slow play problem by lengthening starting intervals from eight minutes to nine.

This eliminated the "freeway phenomenon" and reduced average loop time from 4:20 to 4:11. Under the new system, players also are more willing to let faster groups play through, since there is more room in front of them and their slow play is more apparent.

Joe Black, professional at Brookhaven C.C. in Dallas, reports his club has a "playing time par" which is printed on the scorecard. After every three holes, there is a sign reminding players what the par time should be and asking them if they are under par. Double tee starting, rules clinics that stress faster play and marshalling by Men's Golf Association officials during tournaments also have helped speed up play, Black says.

Sokits zip in Britain

There is a group of some 50 golfers around London, England, called the Sokits who pride themselves on playing two rounds of golf in six hours . . . including an hour for lunch. This is made possible by three special rules, to wit:

1. Only the player who hit the ball is allowed to search for it in the rough. If he can't find it within two minutes, he drops another in the general vicinity, takes a stroke penalty and plays on.

2. The first player in each foursome who is ready to hit does so regardless of the honor . . . this applies from tee to green.

3. No one is allowed to examine the line of a putt except from behind the ball.

Sub-four in Arizona

John Riggle, president of the Arizona State Golf Ass'n, reports in a survey of 10 state clubs that rounds under four hours are not unusual, even during busy winter months. Some practices that make this possible:

Tucson's Skyline C.C. posts signs on the 6th, 12th and 15th holes reminding

players how long it should take to reach that point. Slow players are refused good starting times in the future . . . golfers who break after nine holes at Skyline lose their places, as do those at Scottsdale's Camelback C.C., which also discourages mulligans and doesn't allow singles or twosomes . . . Tucson National allows golf cars on the fairways . . . Arizona C.C. allows gimmies within 14 inches and circles each cup for reference . . . the club also disregards honors on busy days, except in match play . . . Paradise Valley C.C. in Phoenix tees off on both nines, closing the tees for two hours for cross-overs. A four-hour round at Paradise Valley is considered slow.

The penalty works in tournaments

Denny Spencer, vice president of the Toledo District Golf Ass'n, reports that on the first day of a recent Toledo Amateur Golf Chompiomship the average round took well more than six hours, some more than seven. The next day— after several warnings, two-stroke penalties and the posting of a large sign at the starter's table that slow play would not be tolerated, the average round was cut to less than five hours. On the third day, the low 60 and ties played the final 36 holes in slightly more than seven hours.

"It proved to us that strong enforcement is one of the major keys to handling the problem of slow play in tournaments," Spencer declares.

Bob Hanna, executive director of the Northern California Golf Ass'n, proved the same thing to himself in an area collegiate tournament.

"College kids can be the slowest players in the world, and it was just getting ridiculous," Hanna relates. "We simply posted a notice on the scoreboard that said, 'If any group takes more than 2:10 to play the first nine, each player will add two strokes to his total.' After that, no one took that long to play."

The Cleveland District Golf Ass'n requires its tournament players to complete their rounds in 4½ hours, or 1½ hours for each six-hole segment. If a group is behind after six, it must catch up or incur a two-stroke penalty. After 12, the creepers are asked to leave the course. The 4½-hour limit has been met so far, says CDGA executive secretary Henry Meiers.

The Michigan PGA section levies a two-stroke penalty against players who fall more than a hole behind the foursome in front. The result: foursomes in most Michigan events finish in about four hours.

The Western Washington Branch of the Pacific Northwest PGA Section also levies two-stroke penalties against groups holding up players behind them. The penalties are levied on the basis of formal complaints from competitors, and the system works.

A lot of systems will work, if all of us are aware and willing to help.

Architects incorporate fast-play design

The American Society of Golf Course Architects also is entering the battle against slow play, building design elements intended to hasten play into most new courses.

Former society president Frank Duane of Port Washington, N.Y., suggests that blind shots should be entirely eliminated, leaving the target areas and greens clearly visible at all times. This overcomes the problem of the golfer hitting the ball out of sight and spending 10 minutes looking for it.

An examination of new courses uncovers other subtleties of design which not only speed up play but provide greater enjoyment of the game.

Many golf course architects are giving golfers a chance to warm up a bit before throwing the more difficult holes at them.

These same golf course architects, and others, also agree on another important point—the de-emphasis of water hazards, sand traps, deep rough, and other areas where a ball can easily become lost.

Geoffrey Cornish, Amherst, Mass., says golfers should not be forced to attempt shots—long carries over water, for example—that can't be made with any degree of consistency.

Hitting balls into water hazards, ASGCA architects point out, lends no enjoyment to the game and is not only time consuming but very expensive.

How One Man Fought City Hall and Won

By MARTIN KETELS

You're like me. You play a public course, and you've just complained about your latest Six-Hour Round of Golf.

You grumble your way out the clubhouse, throw your clubs into the trunk, and squeal out of the parking lot. But you'll be back. Before next weekend you'll be on the phone with your partners lining up Saturday's rematch. After all, you can't fight City Hall, can you?

You can. I had the time. Winter was approaching. Before long I wouldn't be able to release my anger by swatting the ball. So I decided to take a shot at City Hall. In my case it actually was County Hall—Westchester County, New York, which operates five public courses.

First I wrote to Joseph Emma, manager of Saxon Woods, the Westchester course I usually played. I argued that slow play limited his weekend greens fees and cut down on potential sales at his golf shop and those of fellow professionals and managers. If he were concerned about the losses, then he'd better work to limit play to 4½ hours—by no means a fast round.

It might only require the placement at the sixth and 12th greens of rangers with the names of players signed up for the day's starting times. The ranger at the sixth green, for example, would know that the foursome which teed off at 10 o'clock could complete the first third of its round by 11:30. If the foursome had been lagging behind, the ranger would instruct the players to speed up their game. If they didn't catch up by the end of the 12th hole (at 1 p.m.), the ranger would order them off the course. If, however, they did speed up according to schedule, they would finish their round at approximately 2:30.

Such a quick finish would be about 1½ hours sooner than my last Six-Hour Ordeal. So I figured the difference represented 15 foursomes—60 greens fees, or $210 at that time.

If that weren't enough of an incentive to speed up play, I thought as I sent off my letter, then Joseph Emma just didn't know his job.

He didn't. Neither did his immediate superior, the superintendent of Westchester's five courses, William Dee.

For example, when asked when play in the morning actually started to b they said it was after the steady

were already out on the course, by 9:30, and the "husband and wife deals" teed up. Asked how many "deals" there were, they said that an accurate count could not be furnished. They then spoke of other nuisances, including people who lack etiquette. They were asked if the "deals" and the violators of etiquette are relatively few and identifiable? Can't really tell, they said.

I finally concluded that if I hoped to get anywhere with Dee and Emma I'd have to have more ammunition. I spent most of the winter researching the slow-play problem and learning what some other areas had done to combat the problem.

Next, I decided to incorporate some of the plans into a questionnaire which I proposed be sent to all Westchester County recreation card holders to be returned by the golfers. The results would give Commissioner Charles Pound a public mandate to make administrative changes in order to speed up play.

Dee promised to submit the draft to the commissioner. He never did, I found out later, but claimed that the commissioner thought that mailing the questionnaire and processing the replies would be too costly.

My next move was to suggest that five persons, including myself, interview golfers as they holed out on No. 18 at each of the five courses on a designated Saturday. Dee didn't commit himself at first but later advised us not to go ahead with our plan.

I finally decided to appeal directly to the commissioner for authorization. On May 6, 1972, I submitted a copy of the questionnaire. After repeated attempts to call on the commissioner, I finally met with him on October 6, 1972. Pound, who is no longer in that job, agreed to propose the survey idea at a golf operations meeting the next week. Here's what was resolved:

The department would prepare and post literature regarding slow play. Golf course managers would more thoroughly instruct their rangers on the procedures for speeding up play. And for test purposes at one of the five courses, the commissioner would survey golfer reaction to a list of suggested changes.

Results haven't come easily or dramatically. Play is still intolerably slow at Westchester's five courses. But if you'll consider that some movement has been made by one individual, think of how successful you and your partners might be if you resolve to do something about the problem at your course.

You *can* fight City Hall. But not in a day.

Martin Ketels is a publisher's representative for The New Yorker Magazine and a free-lance writer. Now a resident of San Francisco, he lived in Yonkers, N.Y., when he conducted the crusade described in this article.

WHAT MAKES A GOLFER UNIQUE IN PRO SPORTS? THE ONLY-NESS

By NICK SEITZ

Hale Irwin

HALE IRWIN responded to my leading question like a true champion. He coined a catchy word.

What, I wanted to know, sets a professional golfer apart from athletes in other major professional sports? What makes him unique?

The serious-visaged, bespectacled Irwin is as thoughtful as he looks. He briefly contemplated his navel in the locker room this day and then answered, "The 'only-ness'."

I found it a marvelous reply. Golf often has been called a lonely game, but to speak of a player's only-ness is to add needed dimension. It is a word that comes from the stomach, the heart and the head, speaking to us meaningfully on several levels.

"You're all by yourself out there in the center of the fairway with only a small ball and your psyche," Irwin went on. "It's a long way to the hole. There are no lines regulating play. You can rely on your caddie, but only one person can hit the shot—you."

The only-ness of the game. Irwin contrasts it with football, America's most popular spectator sport, which he played well enough as a defensive back at the University of Colorado to make all-conference in the rugged Big Eight.

"In a team sport like football there's always something to stimulate you. I wasn't very big, and I felt that every play was for my life. In golf you don't get stimulated by a whack in the kisser. Your stimulation has to come from little things . . . a good bounce, a good lie at a crucial time. Then you tell yourself maybe your luck isn't all bad after all."

The only-ness. Once stimulated, the professional golfer knows he must keep his emotions under tight rein. His sport provides no real emotional outlet.

Tom Weiskopf, by nature tempermental, has trouble selecting the correct club under pressure. "That adrenalin gets to flowing and I'll hit the ball 15 to 25 yards farther than normal," he says. "I've hit a 9-iron 175 yards coming down the stretch when distance is the last thing I want. In other sports you want to be fired up, but in golf you have to be in control of your emotions all the time. You have to discipline your imagination."

Says Irwin, "On the tour you almost never hit a full shot. Every swing demands a different degree of control. It's

very wearing emotionally. I'm most relaxed late in a round, when I'm tired."

George Plimpton, the best-selling author and sporting dilettante, observes that in other sports tension is released once the game starts. But in golf the tension steadily builds throughout the round.

Bad shots are inevitable over a period of 18 pressurized holes, and there is nowhere for the golfer's frustration to go. In tennis a disgruntled player can bash a ball over the farthest fence or berate the nearest linesman. In golf a disgruntled player can only swallow his anger and try to compose himself for his next shot.

It never ceases to amaze me that volatile men like Tom Weiskopf and Dave Hill can win on the tour. The effort it must take for them to subdue their explosive impulses and play this most disciplined of games so well has to be monumental, particularly since they are such perfectionists. Some golfers want to win major tournaments, some want to become millionaires, some want mainly the glory and the beautiful women that go with it. As for Weiskopf and Hill, I am sure thay would trade their kingdoms for a dozen perfectly struck shots.

(What appears to the gallery to be a sensational shot may be largely unsatisfactory to the man who struck it. He alone knows what he intended for the shot and how close he came to bringing it off. A good result does not necessarily signify success in his own mind, where the real game is waged.)

The pace of golf does nothing to ease this kind of psychological pressure on the players. A round usually lasts at least 4½ hours and demands, if not sustained concentration, a greater attention span than other sports. Golf often is played too slowly, but on the other hand it is an activity that cannot be rushed and played well. As Jack Nicklaus puts it, there is no way he can play a shot until he knows he's mentally ready to play it.

The only-ness. In a different way, the only-ness decided Nicklaus in favor of golf over football, basketball and baseball, at which he also excelled as a youngster. He liked being able to play golf by himself in the summertime instead of having to round up enough players for a team game.

Jerry Heard is another pro golfer who was a good all-around athlete. At 6 feet and 195 solid pounds, he would look at home roaming center field for the Oakland A's or bringing the ball up court for the Boston Celtics. Heard typifies the athletic young breed newly attracted to the riches of pro golf.

To him, the game's strongest lure is its ongoing challenge. "Unlike other sports, golf always offers you the chance to improve yourself on your own," he says. "It's exciting to improve."

The only-ness. Not only is golf a game of individual skill, it is based on individual integrity. For all the mass commercialism pervading sports today, including golf, golf remains essentially a gentlemanly activity with a bedrock honor system.

The professional golfer calls penalties on himself. If his ball moves in the rough after he has addressed it, he is expected to assess himself an extra stroke even if no one else saw the ball move. It happens almost every week on the tour. It would be naive to assume that no golfer ever takes advantage of the code, but instances of fudging are so rare, they serve mainly as exceptions to point up the rule.

To Deane Beman, himself a good

Arnold Palmer

tour player until he moved upstairs into the commissioner's job, the honor system is golf's special quality. "Golf stands for what all sports are supposed to stand for," he says. "In the quest for winning and making a lot of money, athletes in other sports learn to cut corners. It becomes part of the game. If you're a cornerback in football and a wide receiver gets behind you and catches a pass for a touchdown, the next time he comes off the line of scrimmage you grab his shirt to slow him down. In golf a player doesn't want to win unless he can win fairly."

Beman makes another point about his game. "There are no specialists on the tour, no designated hitters. You have to be able to do it all, from driving to putting. If you have a weakness, you must correct it in a hurry or you don't last."

That's a commanding insight from the smallish Beman, who as a player lacked power but was known among his peers as the best on the tour with all 14 clubs in his bag. The 15th club in his bag was determination.

The only-ness. Not counting himself, the tour player's primary opponent is the course. In no other game, avers Jack Nicklaus, is it so distinctly one man against the elements.

On every shot, the golfer must consider the lie of the ball, the air density and wind, and the condition of the ground where the shot will land. No two shots are the same, which imbues golf with boundless variety—and also makes it unconquerable for even the greatest players.

Its diversity of venues gives golf an aesthetic advantage over other sports. A tennis court is a tennis court is a tennis court, whether in Vancouver or Venezuela. A football field looks the same in Washington D.C., as it does in Tacoma, Wash.—and is probably laid out on an artificial surface at that.

A golf course, by contrast, is a particular, fetching slice of nature, enhanced (hopefully) by the fine hand of man. If Thoreau were alive and well, I have to believe golf would be his favorite professional sport.

The only-ness. Because each player is competing mostly against the course and against himself, golfers are willing to share their expertise to an extent I have witnessed in no other sport. Visit the practice range at any tournament and you repeatedly will find one player sincerely trying to help sort out the gremlins in the swing of another.

Can you imagine Jimmy Connors offering well-intentioned advice to John Newcombe before they meet in the finals of a major tennis tournament? Hardly. And yet at the Masters Tournament last spring Jack Nicklaus was giving intense counsel to Tom Weiskopf shortly before the tournament started. Weiskopf finished second in the Masters to Nicklaus, by the scant margin of one stroke.

The only-ness. A tournament golfer becomes virtually obsessed by the game, so complex are its demands on him.

"A golfer can't be a man of the world," says Steve Reid, a former tour player who now is pro golf's liaison with the television networks. "The game requires total application. A golfer goes to dinner with other golfers, and the dinner conversation is all about golf. One guy is going through his round shot by shot, and the other five guys are wishing he'd hurry and finish—so they can go through their rounds."

When Reid was traveling the tour and rooming with Frank Beard, it finally reached the point where he and Beard struck a pact agreeing never to discuss their rounds in detail. "What'd you shoot?" one would ask. "A 71," the other would reply and that would be that.

"Charlie Coody is unbelievable," says Beard. "He'll give you his entire round right down to the number of tees he broke. When I see him I say, 'I hope you shot 64, Charlie, so it'll take you only an hour to tell me about it.' "

The only-ness. The typical pro golfer is a staunch conservative. A casual

sampling after the last presidential election turned up one player who voted for George McGovern—young Tom Watson.

"Actually, most of us don't follow politics closely, but if we did we'd probably be somewhere to the right of Barry Goldwater," says the vociferous Dave Hill. "Don't let the bright clothes fool you. We're conservatives about almost everything because we've worked hard for a lot of years at this damned game—hit thousands and thousands of practice balls—and we've learned that you get back from it what you put into it. There are no shortcuts in golf. We have a definite sense of value."

Adds Arnold Palmer, whose future conceivably could include politics, "I keep hearing that golf isn't exciting enough for today's young people, that it isn't violent enough or doesn't relate to the society they're growing up in. That's nonsense. Golf is relevant today. It's a totally individual sport. A golfer pays his own way, pays to enter a tournament. Americans like to look on themselves as strong individuals. You can question the social significance of any sport. I think we professionals give a good many people considerable pleasure, and that's important to me."

Arnold also might have noted that golf is sufficiently violent when played with the robust aggressiveness that characterizes his game. If you've ever seen a stop-action photograph of Palmer at impact on a tee shot, you have seen enough violence to get you through the day.

The only-ness. The professional golfer goes to work knowing he cannot kid himself about what he accomplishes. He will come home—or back to his motel—with a firm measure of his day's labor: his score. All the excuses in the world (and golfers have been known to contrive some highly imaginative ones) won't change it a fraction of a stroke.

If he fails, the golfer has to confront his failure, accept it and overcome it. There's no one else to blame.

What sets a golfer apart from other pro athletes? The answer isn't simple; it has as many varied facets as the game itself. But for a two-word summation it's hard to improve on Hale Irwin's. *The only-ness.*

The above article also appears in the new book "Tournament Players Annual."

Charles Coody

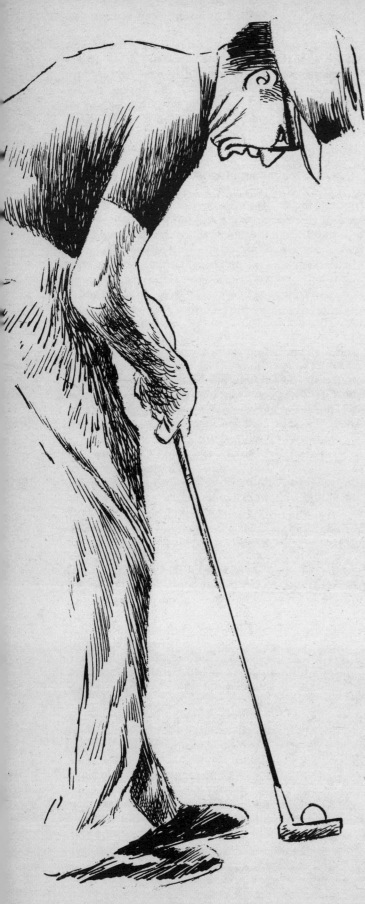

PLUNK. PLUNK. PLUNK. Golf's Greatest Putting String

By CHARLES CHAMBERLAIN
(Associated Press Sportswriter)

RECORDS are made to be broken. Putts are made to be missed.

More is written, and remembered, about missed putts than those wonderful ones that went in. Who will ever forget Sam Snead's missed short ones costing him the U.S. Open? Golf lore is full of missed putts. How many of those made can you recall?

Who can deny that the greatest putting string belongs to Jerry Barber?

On the 70th, 71st and 72nd holes of the National PGA Tournament over Olympia Fields North Course in 1961, little, bespectacled Jerry Barber stroked in putts of 25, 40 and 60 feet for a birdie, par, birdie. The wizardry enabled Barber to make up four strokes on the final three holes on Don January, playing with him, and forced the two into an 18-hole playoff the next day for the championship.

The Monday playoff was a classic, if not anticlimatic, with Jerry winning with a three-under-par 67 to January's 68. Jerry twice rallied from deficits of two strokes and they went to the 18th all even. Both hooked their drives into fairway traps. Barber sent a 4-iron whistling to the green, 18 feet from the cup. January went from one trap into another and came out 15 feet from the hole. He missed the putt to take a five and Barber two-putted for a regulation four and the championship, worth $11,000 in cash, but an immeasurable amount in prestige.

Barber never three-putted through the 90 holes of the tournament. And if that weren't enough to earn him Putter Of The Year honors, his fantastic string of three long ones to lock a playoff certainly did.

Playing conditions added to the dramatic finish. When

Barber rolled in his 60-footer on the last green it was 8:22 PM. With darkness closing in, there was a haze generated by the 90-degree heat and humidity that engulfed the players from the start of the tournament.

Jerry made his 60-footer in the gloamin' and by all standards it should become as famous as Gabby Hartnett's homer in the gloamin' in 1938 at Wrigley Field that gave the Chicago Cubs a ninth-inning victory over Pittsburgh and set them up for the National League pennant.

The late PGA finish on that sweltering July Sunday in 1961 came because rain had washed out the second round Friday. It was played Saturday, and 36 holes were crammed into Sunday after a rain-delayed start, Barber going into them with 136, two strokes ahead of January and Doug Sanders who shared second with 138.

There were several off-beat angles to Barber's triumph. The 5-foot-5-inch veteran tour campaigner became the smallest player in history to win the championship of the Professional Golfers Association and at 45 the oldest.

It also was a homecoming of sorts to the cap-wearing father of five children. He grew up on the farm lands and caddy yards of downstate Woodson and a lot of friends were in the gallery supporting the diminutive Illinois-bred pro from Los Angeles.

There were many dramatics on that final Sunday round by Barber leading up to the climax of his long putts on the last three holes.

Here is a partial account by the late Charles Bartlett, golf writer for *The Chicago Tribune*:

"Pars on tournament scoreboards often conceal the key strokes of a championship, and hidden in the Barber report (on that last round Sunday) was a routine-looking four at Olympia Fields' No. 3 hole, one of the true championship holes of American golf. There won't be many more fours made this season like the one little Jerry wrested from this tiger. Here's how he did it:

"Barber drove into a grove of trees at the left of the fairway. The ball landed near a tree root. He moved it by reversing a No. 10 iron, but the ball only went 10 yards into the fairway. His No. 4 wood third shot was still far shy of the target, halting 50 yards short and behind a sand trap. He took a pitching wedge and hit it toward the elevated putting surface. The ball landed about 4 feet short of the pin, then rolled into the cup."

Barber's birdie putts of 8 feet at No. 7 and 18 feet at No. 9 left him still two strokes behind January for the run to home, the same as at the luncheon break. Jerry hit behind his tee shot on No. 10, heeling the ball into a creek 90 yards away, and took a double bogey six, salvaging it with an 18-foot putt. He was four down again.

He got a shot back when January bogied the long 13th, but lost another stroke and reached the 16th (70th) tee four strokes in arrears.

Barber's 25-foot birdie putt allowed him to pick up two strokes on the 16th as his lanky Texas opponent bunkered his drive and took a bogey five.

On the 17th (71st), Jerry again hit behind the ball and took a 4-wood and a 10-iron to reach the green, 40 feet from the hole. He dropped the putt and remained two strokes behind.

On the 72nd, January drove into a fairway trap. He was 12 feet from the hole after a 6-iron and a 9-iron, but he couldn't sink the putt.

Barber's drive and a 3-iron placed him on the green, 60 feet from the cup. He looked it over, stooped and squinted in the twilight and ran it in—for a birdie three to January's five, tying them at 277.

In a recent interview, Barber, now a grandfather and head pro at the Griffith Park municipal links in Los Angeles, said he still is asked frequently about the putting streak.

"Although I was behind by four strokes on the 16th tee, I had all the confidence in the world I could make it up," he recalled. "After what happened on the third hole, I told myself then from now on I won't lose. I kept going back to that hole and telling myself, 'If you can get a break like that when you're three shots down at the time, you've got a chance to catch him yet.'

"On those last three holes, the line to the cups looked like freeways to me," Barber continued. "It was that wide. On the 16th, the line slid off to the right. I played the break. The ball rolled 25 feet into the right-hand corner of the cup.

"On the 17th, there was a 2-foot break to the right. The ball hit the middle of the hole like it had eyes—from 40 feet away.

"When we reached the last green, there was still enough daylight to see the hole from 60 feet away if you looked real hard. I have to wear glasses but I have 20-20 vision with them. I had to putt up a slope to the right, then out onto a flat, and then a break of 4 feet to the right. The ball rolled squarely into the center of the cup."

Jerry said someone took a picture of his ball suspended in the center of the cup and sent it to him.

"The light wasn't very good and I don't know how he got such a shot," he said.

Barber always was regarded as one of the game's finest putters.

"I used to practice for hours in my earlier days on greens that were near street lights," he said. "I would be putting late into the nights. The secret of good putting is to hold the club firmly and practice mainly on long putts, 50 to 80 feet. This will develop the stroke so it becomes so automatic you can concentrate on the line and distance. And this is what you need to sink the shorter ones. Only a fraction of golfers today practice long putts, and that is a mistake."

Jerry's greens' pistol is a putter he now has had for 28 years and is still in his bag.

"I had been using it for 13 years when I won the PGA in 1961," he recalled. "I wouldn't have taken $5,000 for it on the tour and now its memories make it invaluable to me. I got it from Dale Andreason in Chicago. It's a heavy one with a brass head and a stiff steel shaft taken from a 9-iron once owned by Bobby Locke. Andreason was a big fellow, standing about 6-foot-2. I cut the putter down about 4 inches. It weighs 18 ounces and was balanced out for me by Tom Brandon, the peer in balancing and adding sophistication to golf clubs."

Six Ways the Rules Can Save You Strokes

By P.J. BOATWRIGHT
(Executive Director, United States Golf Ass'n.)

THE AVERAGE golfer knows the rules give him a free drop from ground under repair, casual water or an immovable artificial object. And he knows he may remove a loose natural object (loose impediment) except in a hazard, repair ball marks on his line of putt and clean his ball on the green. However, aside from these benefits and perhaps a few others, the average golfer considers the Rules of Golf to be purely a list of "do-nots" or prohibitions and penalties. Not so. Of course, the rules do prohibit many things in upholding the principles that one plays the ball as it lies and the course as he finds it. But if one knows the rules well, he often can put them to use for his benefit.

Following are some examples:

1 There are several options on lateral water hazards

Ed slices his ball into an unplayable lie in a lateral water hazard. If he drops the ball within two club-lengths of the spot where the ball last crossed the margin of the hazard, which he may do, a large tree will be between his ball and the green. Does Ed have to drop the ball behind the tree or take a stroke-and-distance penalty?

No, alternatively he may drop the ball (1) within two club-lengths of the margin on the opposite side of the lateral water hazard or (2) any distance behind the hazard, keeping the spot where the ball last crossed the hazard margin between himself and the hole. Under the first alternative option, Ed might be able to drop the ball at a point where the tree would be to the side of his line and have a clear shot to the green. Under the second, he might be able to drop the ball at a point where he could play over the tree, especially if the shot to the green was a

relatively short one.

The point is that there are four alternative procedures under the lateral water hazard rule. Most players do not realize they have so many choices.

2 You can make sure ball in rough is yours

Tom plays from heavy rough and knocks his ball into the fairway. On reaching the ball for the next shot, he discovers that he played the wrong ball. Dick, his opponent, claims the hole. Tom protests. He says: "It's not fair. I couldn't see the markings on the ball because of the high grass." Tom should have known that under the rules he had the right to lift the ball from the high grass in the presence of Dick to see if the ball was his ball.

3 If you drop in wrong place, do it again right

Jim hooks his ball into the woods. He declares it unplayable and drops it 25 yards away in the fairway on the line of flight of the previous shot. Bob, his opponent, claims the hole, saying that dropping on the line of flight of the last shot is not allowable. Bob is correct that the unplayable-lie rule (or any other rule for that matter) does not allow dropping on the line of flight. However, if Jim knew the rules, he would know that he could lift the ball dropped in the wrong place and drop it in a right place *without penalty*.

4 If wind is high and green slick don't ground putter

Al and Bill are playing a match on a very windy day. The greens are extremely slick and fast. Al prepares to putt. He takes his stance and grounds his club. At that point, a gust of wind causes his ball to move. Al incurred a one-stroke penalty because, under the rules, a player is deemed to have caused his ball to move if it moves for any reason after it has been addressed.

However, Al could have avoided the penalty if he had not grounded his club, because a ball has not been addressed (except in a hazard) until the player has taken his stance and grounded his club. On many occasions, experienced players playing in windy conditions on extremely fast greens have been known to refrain from grounding their putters before playing strokes on the greens to avoid penalty, if the wind moves the ball before it is struck.

In the 1965 U.S. Open, a player, on the green with his tee shot on a par-three hole, hit his putt too hard and the ball rolled off the green into a pond on the side of the green. The player dropped a ball in high grass on the far side of the pond under the option of the water-hazard rule allowing a player to drop under penalty of one stroke, keeping the spot where the ball last crossed the hazard margin between himself and the hole. From there, he proceeded to dump a couple more shots into the water and ran up a horrendous score on the hole, even though his ball had been on the green in one stroke!

The player could, of course, have dropped another ball under penalty of one stroke at the spot from which he hit the putt which went into the water hazard, under the stroke-and-distance option of the water-hazard rule. Although the stroke-and-distance option of the water-hazard rule is seldom used—as it is generally more punitive than the option allowing a ball to be dropped behind the hazard—sometimes it can be advantageous.

5 Play alternate ball from rut, then ask for ruling

In a stroke-play event, Jack finds his ball in a deep rut made by a maintenance vehicle. The area had not been marked as ground under repair. Must Jack play from the rut or declare the ball unplayable and take a penalty?

Jack could play the ball from the rut (or proceed with it under the unplayable-ball rule) and also play an alternate ball under the ground-under-repair rule, advising his opponents of his plans and telling them that he wishes to score with the alternate ball.

As for an eventual ruling, Jack could ask the club professional for a decision at the finish of the round. At most clubs the pro is empowered by the general golf committee to make rules decisions for casual play. In this instance, if the pro decides the rut where Jack's ball landed should have been marked as ground under repair, then Jack would be allowed to score with his alternate ball.

6 Free-drop rule can give you a better lie

Joe's ball comes to rest against a small mound of dirt created by a gopher. The mound and the ball are a couple of feet in the rough. Ed, Joe's opponent, tells Joe that he is entitled to drop away from the mound but he must drop in the rough. Joe complies. Of course, Ed was wrong. Joe could have dropped his ball in the fairway.

The rule governing such a situation says that Joe may drop within two club-lengths of the gopher hole and it does not provide that, since the ball was in the rough, it must be dropped in the rough. The rules do not distinguish between rough and fairway. Both are covered by the term "through the green."

When dropping a ball under the rules, the player can get a lie worse than his original lie or he can get a better lie. It is not feasible to eliminate this element of luck in the rules. Since a player may get a bad break when dropping a ball, he is entitled to any good break that may present itself.

There are many other positive elements in the rules. Briefly, some are: (a) the right to replace a club broken in the normal course of play; if the club is broken deliberately, it may not be replaced; (b) the right to bend fixed or growing things in the act of fairly taking the stance; (c) the requirement to re-drop if a dropped ball rolls into a hazard or out of bounds; (d) the right to clean a ball when obtaining relief without penalty from obstructions, casual water and ground under repair; (e) exemption from penalty for moving an opponent's ball if it was moved in the act of searching for it; (f) the right to replace a ball if it is so damaged during play of a hole that it is unfit for play; (g) the right to have the flagstick held up during a stroke if, in its position in the hole, it is not visible to the player; and (h) the committee's right to waive or modify a disqualification penalty if the facts warrant.

The rules can help you as well as penalize you. It pays to know them.

HUBERT GREEN WANTS TO BE FAMOUS

BY AL BARKOW

MOST professional athletes will tell you that, as long as they are making a good buck at their game, they couldn't care less if their names are not household words and their faces are not immediately recognized. Most of them will tell you that fame is for film stars. Actually, most of them believe that anonymity is for accountants.

Hubert Green, the pro golfer, is refreshingly honest. "I want the celebrity that comes with shooting low numbers on the golf course," he says. And, in his case, the numbers are there. On the U.S. pro golf tour in 1974, Hubert Green had a stroke average of just over 70, won four tournaments (only Johnny Miller won more) and collected prize money in excess of $200,000 (only Miller and Jack Nicklaus won more). Yet Green has achieved little more celebrity than if he were selling shoes out of a storefront.

The catalyzing elements of popularity are variable, of course, and as inconstant as Bulgarian wine. But, usually, an athlete helps attract attention to himself if something in his manner, his carriage, "says" he is approachable. Hubert Green is approachable. He has a pleasing smile and will talk with anyone anytime. Further, he is tall and slender, dresses well, and has even worked up a few gimmicks in an attempt for recognition. And still, he has not received it.

First, there is the problem of his name. Two years before Hubert Green joined the tour fulltime, a young pro named Bert Greene finished third in the 1969 PGA Championship and made a good run to finish second in the Westchester Classic, a big-money event played just outside New York City, the publicity capital of the world. In 1971, Hubert Green won the Houston Champions tournament, finished second at New Orleans, played well elsewhere

and, with more than $70,000 in total prize money, was selected as Rookie of the Year. It was a good show—far better than Bert's—and Hubert has improved on it every year. But Bert Greene, who arrived first, and whose game has declined, had already cornered a share of the public mind.

During the 1974 Jacksonville Open, which he won, Hubert saw a picture of himself on the front page of a newspaper. The caption read . . . Bert Greene. At the British Open, Hubert was asked to autograph a picture in an expensively-bound program. The face on the glossy page was Bert's, and he wasn't even entered. Green and Greene do not look alike facially—Bert has a small, roundish face set in a grim pout much of the time; Hubert's is long and angular with the protruding browbone of a boxer and eyes buried in exceptionally deep sockets. But they are about the same age and height, have the same slim build and the same Southeastern roots, and swing at a golf ball with similarly quick, upright action. Which does not help explain why, when Hubert Green shot a 69 in the Milwaukee Classic, the news went across the Associated Press wires that one Hubert *Mizell* had done so. Hubert Mizell is a golf *writer,* formerly with the AP.

Like most of his contemporaries, Hubert Green is aware of the benefits that can accrue to an athlete through the media; at the school where golf pros earn their tournament-player credentials, in fact, television executives lecture on which clothing colors show up best on screen. Hubert, therefore, is not benign about typographical mistreatment and is even more sensitive to television slights. Sounding like a Nielsen rating agent, he can recount how his victory in the nationally televised Bob Hope Classic got him more exposure than he'd ever had, "especially in New York," he says, "where a big snow storm kept a lot of people in front of their sets." But, he is sad to report, he was upstaged even then. In presenting the winner's check, Bob Hope ignored Hubert, and did a gag routine with George Burns and Phil Harris.

If you want something badly enough, though, you keep trying, and so Green has been working up "publicity gimmicks."

For seven straight weeks in 1974, not a day went by that Hubert Green did not coordinate his clothes with his name. "I wore green shoes, socks, pants, shirts. I wore green *underwear.* I thought maybe that would help the identification thing, and also maybe a clothing contract would come out of it." What happened? "Nothing, and I haven't worn green since. Got sick of it."

At the 1974 British Open, Hubert wore a multi-colored woolen cap with a thick tassel on top. A lot of people commented on the headpiece, but Hubert's letter to the capmaker, inquiring about an endorsement, went unanswered—and a British golf writer commented, "He got good press wearing those colorful hats, chatting it up with the gallery, and shooting low scores with a bad swing. He does seem a bit dense, though."

A bit dense? That's another Hubert Green gimmick—making himself sound kind of dumb, innocent, naive—the po l'il ole country boy out with the city slickers. This attempt at color often takes the form of self-deprecation. Asked to explain his unstylish, but effective, putting stroke—a wristy quick break of the left hand, an abrupt punch of the ball with the right—Hubert will say, "I've got to make it as simple as I can, 'cause I ain't got but two brain cells workin'." And when asked what he might have done had he not gone into golf: "Well, I couldna gone into medicine 'cause ah couldn' pass hahs-

kool chemistry." Real country, ole Hubert, except. . . .

Hubert Green's sister Carolyn has a Ph.D. in American history and teaches at Samford University in Birmingham, Ala., the Greens' hometown. His sister Melinda was trained as a medical technologist, his brother is a graduate of the University of Alabama, his father is a surgeon and his mother is an educated, sophisticated woman with a long-running interest in music and art, who always had books on those subjects lying about the home. Hubert himself was schooled at Florida State University and, according to Carolyn, was always the smartest one in the family. "Hubert learned to spell and do mathematics faster than any of us," she says.

Hubert's brother Maurice, two years older than he, was a husky handsome high-school football star. Hubert, on the other hand, was a gawky, tall, skinny kid without the natural athletic gifts of Maurice or, for that matter, their father, who played semi-pro baseball as a young man. "Hubert had to work very hard for everything he got," says his mother. "His older brother was more popular, too. Maurice would just walk down a road and everyone would follow him." Including Hubert, tagging along behind.

"It was no contest between Maurice and me," says Hubert. Then he relates, with pride, how Maurice became a career Marine officer and, in Vietnam,

earned a Navy Cross, two Purple Hearts, two Bronze and two Silver Stars. Hubert goes on to tell how Maurice wiped out a pack of Vietcong who raided an encampment, how Maurice became a general's aide-de-camp, then officer in charge of security at Camp David and officer in charge of the color guard at the Nixon White House. It is reasonable to suspect that Hubert Green, in craving recognition, may still be trying to catch up to his big brother.

Because he seeks publicity so openly, and chatters constantly, Green is not overly popular among some of his fellow pros. Newcomers to a big-league sport are supposed to do more listening than talking, or at least very little talking. Hubert Green, however, seems compelled not only to talk, but to talk fast, the words streaking out one atop the other. "Hubert is spacey, a guy you don't seek out," remarks one pro. Another, John Schlee, has complained that "Hubie babbles on about nothing; I don't much enjoy playing with him."

Most of Hubert's patter is harmless, but sometimes he stirs up serious problems. Once, after he had three-putted a green, he blamed it on a distraction, accusing a veteran pro of clearing his throat loudly. Said the veteran later: "They say Hubert was always a cocky, rich country-club kid. I don't know about that, but he came out here and right off began butting in on rule calls that were none of his business."

Hubert butted in most notably at the last Memphis Open, when he was dueling Gary Player for the title. Paired with Player for the last round, Green was only a shot behind him going to the 70th hole. There, Player hit a ball into a hilly area chalked off as "ground under repair." Player was allowed a free drop and, when he took it, the ball rolled back inside the chalk lines. The second drop did the same and Player was then allowed to place the ball by hand. Hubert contended that Player did not place the ball—as the rule demands—exactly where the second dropped ball had landed before rolling inside the lines. Overruled by the PGA official in attendance, Green then huffed up the fairway to find another official for a second opinion and, ultimately, not only lost his claim but was fined $500. And Player won the tournament, with Green finishing in a tie for second.

"He was always a spontaneous, quick-tempered boy, and was brought up to obey the rules," says Hubert's mother. "About the Memphis incident, I told him, though, that in some cases when seeking the truth he must act more diplomatically." Hubert has come to agree that he was out of line in Memphis, and has since tried to become more tactful in many ways. He has even told Jack Nicklaus: "I was trying so hard to be one of the boys that I just talked too much."

Yet Green is not about to turn totally humble. When someone mentioned recently that he had been paired a lot with Nicklaus in 1974, Green quickly retaliated, "No, Jack's been paired a lot with me."

Obviously, Hubert Green enjoys the challenge of trying to promote himself. The card game he plays is bridge, which tests the nimbleness of a mind, and—his wife Judi reports—he went to the movies only three times in a period of one year, and two of those times saw *The Sting*. To see that story of a confidence game a second time, knowing the surprise of the ending, a man must enjoy—even be a student of—the techniques of con jobs.

The legitimate way to earn top billing in golf is, of course, to win a major championship. No one laughed that hard at Lee Trevino's jokes until he won a big one and, as Hubert himself has said, "Guys who play without a gallery get no laughs from the trees." The time may be here for Hubert to win his big one; four years on the tour is the traditional seasoning time and, in his span, Hubert has had more than the usual success. Jack Nicklaus, for one, has told Hubert he has proven he can play well and now must prove he can play great golf. The comment is akin to a company president telling a clerk that he has an eye on him for better things. And in this case, the clerk has *his* eye on the vault.

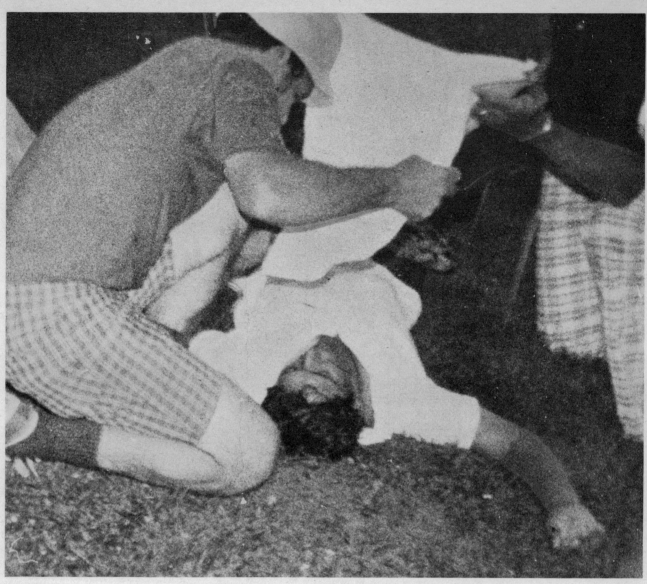

Lee Trevino lies near 13th hole of the 1975 Western Open at Butler National Golf Club in Oak Brook, Illinois after being struck by lightning. He was treated for shoulder burns.

If Lightning Comes—Go!

By LEN ZIEHM
(Chicago Sun-Times)

IT WAS frightening—even terrifying.

The 72nd annual Western Open golf championship started, as usual, as one of the most prestigious events on the Professional Golfers' Association 1975 tour. Before it was over two popular—and prominent—members of the tour, Lee Trevino and Bobby Nichols, were in a hospital and lucky to be alive.

A lightning attack forced both players out of the tournament, briefly hospitalized Trevino's playing partner Jerry Heard and scared the rest of the players, caddies, officials and 16,000 fans in attendance. The same storm severely injured a 16-year old boy in a less publicized but perhaps more serious

(Continued on page 42)

Bobby Nichols holds head in hand after being struck by lightning on the fourth hole at the Western Open. He was treated for head burns.

Each Sweep Meant
I Had Lived a Little Longer

By SAM BLAIR
(Dallas Morning News)

THE FIRST night at the hospital after he was struck by lightning is one Lee Trevino will never forget.

"I was in the intensive care unit and I couldn't sleep," he said. "It's dark in there but I wasn't about to go to sleep. They gave me two sleeping pills but I never shut my eyes. I was afraid I wasn't going to wake up."

That afternoon, while stretched out on the 13th green "like a vibrator" at the Western Open, Trevino had fought desperately to remain conscious and keep breathing. Although the doctors had been reassuring about his condition, he wasn't about to ease up in the hospital.

(Continued on page 42)

If Lightning Comes

(Continued from page 40)

incident at a nearby public course.

The near-tragic episode dramatized one of golf's most dangerous—though all too frequently ignored—enemies. According to the Lightning Protection Institute in Madison, Wis., a typical thunderstorm day will result in the death of seven persons and injuries to 20 others. Another 250 deaths will be caused by lightning-caused fires, and these will lead to another 1,500 injuries.

The Institute declares that lightning causes more deaths and injuries annually than tornadoes, hurricanes and floods, and warns that golf courses are among the worst places to be when lightning storms develop. It's vital that golfers learn from that Western Open incident and know what to do when a lightning storm comes while they are on the course.

Here's what happened on that strange day in the Western Open, and it could just as easily happen to a weekend player as a big name star:

At 4:04 p.m. there was no sign of impending trouble. There was no rain, no hint of it in the clouds. But tournament officials were advised of the approaching danger. They sounded a siren to halt play.

Moments later the storm hit with tremendous fury.

The siren sent Trevino and Heard to the shelter of an umbrella. Instead of joining their group at a somewhat distant refreshment stand, they sat on the grass at the foot of a pond, Heard bracing an umbrella between his legs. They leaned against their golf bags, making themselves an easy target for the lightning. And both were hit at the same time.

Trevino thought his shoulder had been broken; in reality he was burned by the lightning, his shoulder showing both entrance and exit marks and muscle rigidity developed in his upper back. Heard was burned in the groin.

Trevino's legs went stiff, and then hit the ground. He couldn't remember anything else, though a day later the usually jovial Super Mex solemnly admitted, "I thought I would die."

Nichols was playing an another group, and a second lightning bolt knocked both him and his caddie to the ground. Nichols reported to the hospital with a headache and a friend claimed Bobby's breath smelled like "burned wire." But most of the damage was to his nerves. Locker room banter from other players—designed to help Nichols regain his composure—was totally unsuccessful.

"Whatever happens from here on out, I'm ahead of the game," he muttered before heading to the hospital. Nichols left town for home the next day.

"The fact that all four of them were struck and are still living is quite phenomenal," offered their attending physician, Dr. Paul G. Fredrickson. "They're all fortunate to still be here."

Elsewhere on the course spectators reported the hair on their arms stood up straight. Crossing attendants holding onto the metal guard posts received shocks.

Tony Jacklin, Nichols' playing partner, felt "a tingling in my arm" just as he hit an iron shot, and the club flew out of his hands. "It was very, very scary," he said, "like being in a car

(Continued on next page)

Each Sweep Meant

(Continued from page 41)

"The only thing I could see in intensive care was a clock with a sweep-second hand," he recalled. "All night I lay there, watching the hand go around the clock. Each sweep meant I had lived a little longer. I'll tell you I loved every minute of it."

Trevino remained in the hospital at Hinsdale, Ill., another day and night, then flew home to El Paso for a few days of recuperation and further physical examinations. When he passed through Dallas en route to the British Open, he still laughed like the old Super Mex but he wasn't kidding when he talked about his close brush with death on a golf course and how the experience might affect him in the future.

"Psychologically, I don't know how I'll be when I get out there to play again," he noted. "But I know this: if I go out and the lightning starts I'll quit immediately. I don't care if I'm leading the tournament by 10 strokes. If I get disqualified I'll get disqualified, but I'll know I'll be around to play another day."

Trevino took the main force of the lightning which reached down from a low-hanging electrical storm and struck the Butler National Golf Club outside Chicago, June 27, 1975. But Jerry Heard, his playing partner, also was hit as was Bobby Nichols elsewhere on the course. Both joined him in the hospital for check-ups but all three were released over the weekend, realizing they were far more fortunate than were most lightning victims.

Trevino had small marks on his left shoulder which resembled tiny spiders. These were exit marks from the burn. The doctors said they normally saw such marks in the morgue.

Trevino recalled that when the rain began to fall and the storm moved over the course he and Heard thought it was like the other storms which appeared occasionally in the neighborhood since the start of the U.S. Open the week before. They thought it would pass over in 10 minutes and saw no point in going all the way back in to the clubhouse.

"We got up on the green, which is beside a lake, and took off our spikes," he said. "Then we opened our umbrellas and set them up. I stretched out under mine, leaned against my bag and sent my caddie to get some hot dogs and drinks. We figured we'd just relax and have ourselves a picnic."

Seconds later the lightning hit the lake, skipped across the green, shot through the metal shafts in Trevino's bag and into the left side of his body. Heard, who was holding his umbrella between his legs, suffered a lesser burn near his groin.

"Next thing I knew we were stretched out like a couple of vibrators," Trevino said. "They say your whole life flashes before you at a time like that and it does. There are two things I'll always remember. First I thought about my wife and kids. What would happen to them? The other thing was a terrible thought that I was going to die.

"The pain in my left arm and shoulder was killing me, but I kept fighting it. I was lucky I didn't lose consciousness. My breathing was rough but I kept breathing. I was scared and hurt, but I knew I had to hang in there."

By the time the golfers reached the hospital the grim part was over and they could grin again. Heard had started the

(Continued on next page)

If Lightning Comes

(Continued from preceding page)

going at a high speed when something unexpected happens."

The lightning also knocked a club from the hands of Jim Ahern and felled Jim Colbert. Rumors spread rapidly among the spectators as other players immediately fell to the ground—for safety—as the lightning hit. Fans, the uniformed ones, thought the falls were from injury and not a means of avoiding it.

In less than 3 hours the frightening part was over—but it shouldn't be forgotten.

The tour players—though even they don't always follow the proper protective procedures when lightning storms develop—have the right to invoke a "lightning rule" if they feel endangered by an approaching storm.

Oddly, the rule was invoked by Tom Watson just a week before in the U.S. Open at Medinah Country Club—just 15 miles away from the Western's home base at Butler National Golf Club.

Watson, then leading the tournament, went to the safety of the clubhouse after counting out the time between a thunder bolt and flash of lightning at Medinah's No. 1 tee. Tournament officials immediately questioned his decision—something they've tended to do at the major events in an effort to keep playing moving.

"If I'd been Watson, I would have decked the official," said outspoken tour player Dave Hill. "These guys getting burned from lightning should make it evident that the officials should get us off the courses faster during storms.

"Some players, though, are basically afraid of officials. They say play or they'll disqualify you. What can you do?"

Watson was vindicated. As soon as the officials went out of the clubhouse to inspect the weather situation a storm struck with a vengeance. So the establishment urge to keep play moving in threatening weather likely will be curbed now.

As far as the pleasure golfer is concerned, the U.S. Golf Association carries some common sense guidelines in its Rules of Golf:

"If golf clubs could be impressed with the necessity of calling off matches before a storm is near enough to be hazardous, the cases of multiple injury and death could be eliminated.

"Raising golf clubs or umbrellas above the head adds to the element of personal hazard during electrical storms.

"Metal spikes on shoes do little to increase the hazard."

When lightning strikes, a golfer should immediately look for shelter, preferably in large metal-frame buildings, automobiles or trailers with metal bodies.

If none of these are available, search for dense woods—avoid isolated trees because lightning tends to strike the nearest prominent object that offers a path to the ground. Stay clear of hilltops or other high areas.

If you're riding a golf cart, get out of it. Avoid wide open spaces, lakes and ponds, wire fences and overhead wires. If there's no shelter, do as most of the touring pros did at the Western—lie flat on the ground.

"Usually you laugh when the rain and lightning come," said Arnold Palmer, looking back on the Western Open experience. "That time you didn't laugh."

Each Sweep Meant

(Continued from preceding page)

second round that day two under par for the tournament, Trevino two over. But Lee's fine shot to that 13th green had left him only a 2-foot putt to pull back to one over for the day. Meanwhile, Jerry was six over for the day.

"Hey, Mex," said Heard from an adjoining bed in the intensive care unit, "I'm back to four up again!"

"It's a shame," Trevino told him. "I was about to sink that little putt and go back to two over for the tournament. Now they'll probably slap a 2-stroke penalty on me for slow play!"

When he returned to El Paso Trevino underwent three more physical exams, complete with electrocardiograms, and also took a stress test to be certain there was no damage to his heart. After the stress test the doctor told him he had "a heart as strong as a bull's." Thus encouraged, Super Mex packed up and headed for the British Open.

"For a few days my legs were so sore I felt like I had just gone water skiing after a 5-year layoff," he said, "but I'm feeling better now. I've been hitting practice balls, but I didn't do any jogging so I'm 4, 5 pounds heavier than usual.

"I did some reading up on lightning while I was home, and I learned I did everything wrong when that storm came up.

"One, I was near the water. Two, I was on the highest point in the area. And, three, I was leaning on my golf clubs.

"But I did do one thing right," said Trevino, appreciatively, "I kept breathing."

Bobby Nichols and Peter Mortimer, 14, of Hinsdale, Ill., appear a bit dazed after being struck by lightning. Mortimer was holding score stand and standing next to Nichols when hit.

It's Not the Clubs, It's How You Use Them

By HERB GRAFFIS

GOLF CLUBS are like women. Anybody who says he knows all about how to handle them is nutty or soon will be.

The United States Golf Association and the Royal and Ancient Golf Club of St. Andrews long have been afraid that golf clubs might become so good that they would take a lot of fun out of the game in seeing the opponent screw up shots. Often this seems to me to be a sad waste of time by good men. I have been brought up to be respectful and compassionate toward golf clubs and golf association officials. So I began writing about the game and business of golf, when the venerable Joe Davis, golf editor of the *Chicago Tribune* told me the parable of The Stranger in the Clubhouse.

The tale was about a stranger who rushed into the lobby of a golf clubhouse. There was a mournful man standing alone in the lobby. The visitor clenched desperately at the front of his pants and frantically asked the downcast party: "Where is it? Where is it?? I GOTTA GO!!!"

The gloomy man shook his head as one who knows misery. He replied:

"Do it on me. I am Chairman of the House Committee. Everybody does it on me."

That's why I never question golf association or club officials. I know that when there is an assessment at the club or when a golf association does something I don't like, they are only doing it to get even for being elected or appointed.

My saintly attitude is not popular with many of my companions—over the years they have criticized and rebuked me for not abusing the Greens Committee which at every club sins against God and man by spending money on making the course tougher. I must admit that the reason for making a golf course more difficult, 100 cases out of 99, is to get it ready for a Big Tournament. In the tournament there will be several overpaid and under-mannered low and loud males who will complain about the course on which they are allowed to play.

I certainly do not want to revolt against the USGA and the R&A for any of the Rules of Golf. The rules are necessary otherwise we would make up rules as we go along and the rules the other fellows make do not give me a break. So I make up ones that do. Every year I give my playmates Rules of Golf books. The rule books might as well be printed in Coptic. The only rule I think most of the friendly drinking golfers with whom I engage in the game of a lifetime observe is the rule which says, "Thou shalt not tee up in the rough whilst thy opponent is observing."

The 14-club rule is one my kind of golfers, the unsung multitude, can understand. The older ones can remember when many of the pros and the younger talented amateurs had their caddies humped under bales of clubs. The illegal nature of some clubs our people don't understand. What could be illegal about a club that makes a better shot? Does that minimize the demand for skill? Not as long as golf is played by human beings. The worry of the USGA and the R&A is upside down. It expresses a fear that golfers might play too many wonderfully good shots. The nature of golf is that the score depends just as much on the good strokes we make as the bad shots we don't make. The score of the fellow who takes 80 or more is that way not because he didn't make some fine shots but because he made too many bad ones.

Very few golfers, except the very rich, very old and practically hopeless ones, wouldn't buy a new set of clubs if they could afford them. That was true when you could get a very good bench-made hickory-shafted iron fitted to you for $5. The biggest buyer of clubs for his own use I ever knew was a prominent oil man. I knew him first when he was working in a refinery in Tulsa. He wasn't over-burdened with clubs then.

He was very bright, very canny, very lucky and a man you could trust. So when he got rich the angels sang. So did pro golfers. Almost every time he went to another course he bought a new set of clubs and a bag. He left the new outfit with his host or some other buddy. He carried a fistful of bills with him.

Like many fellows who had been poor he never wanted to be caught broke again. I could understand that. When he died in a plane crash with choking thousands in bills in a pocket there was gossip about some situation involving politics and the IRS.

I couldn't go for the scandalous rumor. Neither could the pros who sold him cargoes of clubs. I knew he was a

great fellow who just didn't have the kind of money I did. One time in the airport at Atlanta this friend who was said to never carry less than $20,000 in cash with him borrowed a dime from me. He had to use a pay toilet.

Next to this lamented golfer one who most liked clubs was the once famous playing professional, Leo Diegel. Diegel had Toney Penna make four drivers for him when Penna was with Tommy Armour as a clubmaker and assistant at Congressional Country Club, Washington. One driver was almost flat-faced to use against the wind. Another had a loft to make use of the wind. The other two had a hook and a slice built in.

Penna has seen clubs he designed come back into high favor and sell for mountainous prices. The Tommy Armour iron which Toney designed and MacGregor introduced in 1937 is eagerly sought by pro stars today. Penna says the head is simply a sound design that appeals to the expert because Armour could "think with his fingers." Even with the steel shafts of the earlier models there is a feel that delights the man who knows the sensation of a perfectly hit shot. That wonderful and indefinable sensation of touch fundamentally determines the utility of golf clubs. That's what makes it impossible for any of golf's ruling bodies to determine what club is going to be so happily responsive to a player's feeling that it will do his bidding perfectly, thus altering the nature of the game.

Hundreds and hundreds of clubs have

been declared illegal by the USGA and the R&A but there isn't any evidence that a solitary one of these unlawful devices could have been instrumental in winning any competitions.

An interesting and amusing question in golf is how did golf clubs improve despite the fear of the R&A and the USGA that some diabolical genius might alter the nature of the game by inventing a club so good we'd all be making fine shots?

Putters provide an entertaining area of research for the golfer ambitious to buy a good game. A lot of us who have been around in golf know Curtis Person of Memphis who has won a goodly number of senior championships. He has at least 100 putters in his home. He has collected them while searching for one so deadly accurate it will frighten his opponents, the USGA and the R&A. He continues to buy putters.

The late William Langford, a golf architect, only had one putter the 60-some years he played golf. Langford had polio as a boy and his mother, a nurse, had him play golf as therapy. She gave him a putter she had used. It helped him have the unusual experience of being one who played on both the Princeton and Yale golf teams. After 50 years playing he continued to take putting prizes in the Illinois Seniors and at Palm Beach tournaments.

Putters are fickle. Tommy Armour got disgusted with the putter that had been true to him on Carnoustie's greens and he gave it away. Almost 2 years later the putter appeared in the locker next to Armour's at Florida's Boca Raton Club.

Willie Park, Jr., who won the British Open in 1887 and 1889 and was architect of numerous golf courses in the United States, was reputed to be the deadliest putter golf had ever seen. He is said to have practiced 6 hours a day many days. He was winner of most of the big stake matches he played. To be a consistently superior putter on the greens of his day must have required a talent we haven't got any more. There isn't any special design of putter named after Willie, Jr. He used a rather short-shafted putting cleek that had a trifle more loft than putters usually have. The late John Reuter, Jr., inventor of the Bull's Eye putter was experimenting with a slight loft of a putter face and found the results intriguing. John, who had created the biggest selling putter golf has known, died before he was satisfied he'd found the putting "secret" of Park, Junior. The search for the perfect woods and irons was slowed down when the USGA and the R&A put the 14-club limitation into effect in January, 1938. The number of clubs carried by golfers who were hoping to have a club so reliably good it was illegal had reached the ridiculous point.

In 1908 Fred McLeod had won the United States National Open with six clubs; a driver, a brassie, a putter and three irons. Chick Evans won the National Open and the National Amateur in 1916 with seven clubs. Evans won the Open at Minikahda, Minneapolis, with a new record of 286. This figure stood in the Open for 20 years although contestants carrying as many as 26 clubs in a bag were operating. These fellows had skill too. They included

such heavily equipped stars as Harry Cooper and Leo Diegel.

Lawson Little was another whose caddie transported a bag about the diameter of a power plant smokestack. Little said he used only a few clubs from the stock and most of them were weapons to be used "in case." He recalled that after he'd won all the United States and British National Amateur championships in 1934 and 1936 he was playing in a "Welcome Home" exhibition in California. He had a gallery larger than some he had during his amateur championship matches. He came near the finish and looking into his bag saw a club a friend had given him as the one "positively anti-shank club ever invented."

Little had forgotten there was such a diabolical thing as a shank, so he pulled that bright new club out of the quiver, took a graceful practice swing, then shanked his approach to the home green through the biggest plate glass window west of the Rocky Mountains. Little said he could not explain why he did not wind up throwing the club in after the ball.

That was one club Little didn't have to worry about eliminating when the 14-club limitation came into effect. There were many other club selection problems for the pros then; many of the club choices being in the class of the answer to that old riddle, "If you could save one drowning person would you save your mother, wife or daughter?"

The selection hasn't been answered yet by many professionals, and they have been itching to get the USGA to authorize 16 clubs.

Now even the 12-handicap-and-up ladies and gentlemen are uncertain about what 14 clubs they should carry. It's a question that easily could be either a merchandising opportunity or a horrible manufacturing and inventory program for the club manufacturers and other dealers.

Imagine how embarrassing it must have been to the Royal and Ancient after ruling the center-shafted mallet putter used by Walter Travis in winning the 1904 British Amateur championship an illegal implement to learn that Travis discarded the putter shortly after winning that competition. He said it was a poor club and he just happened to get it when he was putting so well he could have holed putts with a shovel.

In 1921 Jock Hutchison won the

British Open at St. Andrews. Hutchison was born at St. Andrews but in that championship was registered from Glen View, Illinois, where he was professional. By that time Hutchison was an American citizen. Hutchison won that British Open after he and the British amateur, Roger Wethered had tied because Wethered carelessly had kicked his ball. Hutchison was a deft manipulator of irons. He made his mashie and shorter irons backspin the ball like a yo-yo.

The British suspected that Hutchison's magic was dirty work by mechanics and the R&A got incensed about the possibility of sharply filing the ribbing of irons so the rib edges could cut into the ball and backspin it. The USGA, to be very buddy-buddy with the R&A, also got exercised about the sharp edging of irons fearing that the clubmakers and cute pros and amateurs might, like the heathen Chinese, go in for ways that were dark, devious and gain a backspin on a green harder than Highway Number One. Even now in the Rules of Golf books there are diagrams and specifications so tricky the Russian CIA and FBI would give a pretty ruble to get these secrets of the game.

Don't snitch to the Kremlin, but not long ago there were tests made with smooth-faced irons at Winged Foot. Pros who were handy in manipulating the club faces conducted the tests and had no difficulty in getting the leading edge of irons under balls with a spin that controlled the performance of a ball after it hit the ground.

You are bound to be astonished by seeing antique clubs at the USGA Museum in Far Hills, New Jersey, the World Golf Hall of Fame at Pinehurst and other exhibits in Britain and the United States. These clubs indicate there are no revolutionary ideas in golf club construction. Some ingenious fellow gets an idea to use an old hunch in a new way and away he goes.

The resourcefulness of golf inventors is unlimited. There are more than 200 patents on golf tees alone. The basic factor in the patent of Dr. Lowell, the New Jersey dentist who invented the wooden peg tee, was a convex top to hold the ball. Not many fellows have had as much fun or made as much money in golf as the patent lawyers did in finding that the convex top patent detail didn't stand up.

The 14-club limitation came in because the tournament specialists were, like the USGA and the R&A, mislead into believing that something mechanical could do wonders in getting a golf ball from the tee into the hole. They devised every means imagination could suggest to knock the ball straight and the desired distance. It is amazing to see how many modern designs were hinted at in clubs of a century or longer past when playing conditions were considerably different in Scotland than they are in the United States and elsewhere today. The sandy soil, the seaside patches of grass, the shrubs, roads where the gutta-percha ball had to be played required help from the clubmakers. Lifting the ball and improving its lie was a mortal sin in the Old Country then. As a pioneer Scotch-American pro remarked. "Golf is a different game over here than it was in Scotland. In Scotland you hit the ball around the course; over here you cart it around."

There are numerous prototypes of the flanged-sole irons that you may see among the museum irons and these exhibits will remind you that the idea of the wedge isn't as modern as we might think.

Yet, some of the British-born American professionals maintained that when the sand wedge came into popular use in the United States it took out of the game one of the most exacting and masterly shots. The veteran Scots were able to manipulate the niblicks with finger and wrist operations that could pick a pebble out of a bunker. That fine art was perfected where sand traps might be almost the size of a room and the idea of a player smoothing out his footprints still had some years to go before the older Scots accepted this refinement as part of the game.

The sand wedge in its American form first came into the game in 1930. Bob Jones had one in his bag, but in making his Grand Slam that year used the club only once and then with no remarkable result. The word got around that Jones had a cute club that hacked the ball out of a bunker close to the cup, simply by waving the club and wishing. This enchanting fiction got across so well that when Jones was completing his Grand Slam at Merion near Philadelphia, George Sayers, the pro at that club, sold almost a thousand sand wedges out of his shop during the Jones finale. The wedge the spectators bought from Sayers wasn't the same as the Jones tool. It was a club that a Texas engineer and golf nut named Smith brought to the attention of Horton Smith. The club had a convex and concave head, something like a tablespoon. It certainly worked for Horton and he had the Walter Hagen Golf Company, by whom he was paid, add it to the line.

The wedge didn't stay long because the USGA ruled it illegal, saying that the club hit the ball twice as it was exploding the ball out of the sand. A few manufacturers, several of the pro tournament stars of the early '30s, and a flock of the bench clubmakers whose art was fading with the arrival of the steel shaft saw that the sand wedge was sure to be one of the essentials of a set of clubs.

Gene Sarazen got the idea the instant he saw the earliest American wedges, and he improved on the design by having the sole a bit fatter and slightly curved so slashing the leading edge of the club into the sand would slide the club under the ball and up. Milton Reach, the club design genius of the Spalding Holy Family, got the hunch that Sarazen had but he didn't put the weight in the sole that Sarazen (a Wilson staff member whose authority was very high) got the Wilson people to use. It was Milton Reach, though, who named his club the Sand Wedge but, before the name could be legally protected, every golfer was talking about "wedge" as if it were breakfast, lunch or dinner, and it was too late to get a copyright on the name.

Sarazen had a bit more metal put on the sole of the club and rounded the bottom so it would come out of the sand naturally. His club was a deadly weapon, but others on the Wilson staff came along with other suggestions and they all, plus the inspired journeymen of other manufacturers, added little points here and there so the sand wedges and pitching wedges became the most fool-proof clubs. But, as long as golf was played by humans, shots could be missed by humans.

Shortly after Sarazen and Horton Smith began exhibiting their wizardry with the wedge, there was a kid from a small town club in northern Wisconsin who played wedge shots out of sand so consistently good you wouldn't believe his performance. He was Johnny Revolta. He was pro at a 9-hole club where there wasn't much play so he had to stay around the little clubhouse and pro shop and while away the hours

"They usually use a number five iron from here . . . !"

by practicing. He surpassed Sarazen as a wedge player out of bunkers around the green. He had a peculiar way of putting that had his right foot across the extended line of the putt. He was somewhat of a mechanic and his wedge, when he got through welding little chunks of metal to it, was an ugly thing but an electric chair is no Chippendale job either; the Revolta wedge and the barbecue chair both could kill you.

The ancient hack who makes these observations was ghosting the immortal prose of Tommy Armour during the PGA championship of 1935 at Twin Hills in Oklahoma City where Revolta defeated Armour 5 and 4 to win the championship. After the first 18, I consulted my control as we were thoughtfully drinking our lunch and asked how he could explain to the nervously awaiting world how Revolta was beating him. The Silver Scot looked into space and the bartender's eyes and said, "He has a secret weapon. I get one down the middle. He drives into the trees and hits so much timber I think he is bowling. I knock my ball onto the green. Then Johnny comes out of the woods like Lewis and Clark and gets into a bunker. I wait around at ease until Revolta comes out of the sand hole, then I have a hell of a putt to half the hole. What can you write that makes me look good from that?"

Armour hated wedge shots. Charles Koscis, who was an amateur and could use a sand wedge like a Gillette razor, beat Tommy in the Michigan Open one time and the Great Armour felt that scar in his heart and maintained that the wedge ruined the delicacy of golf.

Yet when Armour left Medina Country Club in suburban Chicago to become professional at the course owned by a friend in Connecticut, he saw an amateur who was better out of the sand than Sarazen, Revolta and Smith. This young man, a bookkeeper, who was employed only weekends, Armour said was phenomenal from the bunkers.

The pleasant fellow was Julius Boros. Later when reporters asked Armour how he had helped Boros to become a champion, Tommy replied, "I only suggested a bolder tactical plan for his game. He was so good getting out of bunkers he could dare to play boldly for the flag." Boros won his two National Opens—in 1952 at Northwood at Dallas and in 1963 at the Country Club of Brookline—by using wedges as precision tools. From the sand or the rough, he pitched so many times to a one-putt reach of the hole he killed the hopes of his opponents.

Gary Player and Lee Trevino are regarded as the premier artists in sand wedge use during the past 4 years of the tournament programs. Their sand wedges and the accompanying one-putt greens have erased most of their mistakes.

As wonder-working as the wedge has been none of the professionals generally considered the best technicians in scoring have been rated as magicians with the wedge. Hogan, Nelson, Snead, Palmer and Nicklaus are just a little better than the average expert with the wedge but certainly not super-stars. Talk of tournament contestants who know something about games other than their own and the notes of golf writers point to the guess that if Jack Nicklaus could use a wedge like Lee Trevino, Nicklaus would be known as definitely the greatest golfer the game has known and Trevino would be merely merry Super-Mex of the tournament ensemble.

There have been hundreds of variations of the elemental sand wedge made with not much departure from a 58-degree loft, a 64-degree lie, and a 35-inch length. The overall weight is about 17 ounces but will vary from about the usual pitching wedge weight of a bit more than 16½ ounces to 19 ounces when players add metal to the sole.

There seems to be a temptation never to leave well enough alone in a wedge. Wilson made a sand wedge some years ago that Sarazen, Revolta and Boros worked on with Mike Berend and Joe Wolfe of the Wilson club production staff. The club still is considered by noted players as the ideal sand club. But, as is usually the case, the design and construction was changed a trifle to get a new model for a new year. Different shafts and grips were used. But year-after-year players kept going back to the original model as the masterpiece. The old wedge still is a prize in the expert's bag. The club has a history similar to a set of Tommy Armour irons that MacGregor made one year. Many of the expert players have paid premium prices for those clubs as the perfect tools.

Those irons sold very well. The better golfers were enthusiastic about them, but the clubs weren't anywhere near as miraculous for the average golfer. The average golfer has difficulty getting the ball into the air, hence an application of the wedge idea of a wider and heavier sole that gets weight low and the leading edge of the iron well under the ball helps the player get the ball airborne. Investment casting of iron heads produced precision heads with weight transferred from directly back of the ball to back and under the ball. It produces the desired weight distribution vertically that was achieved horizontally when Willie Ogg introduced his iron design that widened the toe of the iron in offsetting the weight of the hosel. The idea of the veteran Scotch-American clubmaker and teacher became standard in extending the hitting area horizontally.

The wedge notion of getting more weight in the sole of an iron was applied to a set of irons designed by the same Texan named Smith who invented the sand wedge that Horton Smith got the Hagen company to make. The irons were made by the Burke Golf Company of Newark, Ohio. The clubs had a flange that made them wider soled than the usual irons of that period—the early '30s. Burke didn't have good nationwide distribution through pro shops and strong pro pushing was needed to market these unorthodox implements. Nevertheless, the daring buyers who liked the feel of these clubs and didn't mind the unconventional looks found the Smithirons remarkably helpful. The Smithirons didn't last long because of marketing weakness rather than due to any defect in performance. There is a head resembling the Smithiron type used in a versatile club called the Scrambler. It has about a 4-iron loft and a shaft the length of a 7-iron shaft (36 inches). The Scrambler was designed by Ed Rankin, a golf marketing expert who was with the Wilson, Hagen, Hogan and PGA companies. Rankin has been what politicians might describe as a "golfer of the people." He decided most golfers needed the help of a club that would perform in other troublesome spots as the sand wedge did in sand. He finally managed to get the PGA-Victor company to produce the club that many of golf's common people welcome as extraordinarily effective those many times when the players don't know what club to use.

Your Handicap Is Your Head

by BEN J. CHLEVIN

. . . **SO SAYS** Sim Bows who claims, from his 61 years of observing the golf scene as a scratch amateur and former club champion, golf researcher and designated Golf Historian of the Chicago District Golf Association, that many golfers turn off their minds and resort to parrot-like imitations of the "greats" in "developing" their golf swings.

"Take the head position at address, for example," Sim says. "When Palmer was king of the hill, many potentially fine golfers as well as duffers slavishly sought to imitate the picture of Palmer addressing the ball with his head tilted to the left. The 'right-eyed' swingers did all right, but the 'left-eyed' golfer was in trouble—and wondering why.

"Later, when Nicklaus began to dominate the newspaper and magazine pages, showing him addressing the ball with *his* head tilted to the *right,* the left-eyed swingers came into their own and the right-eyed guys trying the Nicklaus address position were thrown into confusion."

Sim says the 'dominant' or 'master eye' concept has been around for a long time. All you have to do to determine whether you are 'right-eyed' or 'left-eyed' is simply to hold a pencil at arm's length in line with a distant object. If the pencil appears to jump to one side when you close your right eye but remains still when you close the left—you are right-eyed.

On the other hand if the pencil appears to jump to one side when the left eye is closed, then your left eye is your master eye.

"That's why," Bows says, "the right-eyed golfers imitating the right-eyed Palmer at address were on the right track while the left-eyed golfers developed problems. And they switched places when they later swung over to mimic the left-eyed Nicklaus!"

Bows claims that when a right-eyed golfer tilts his head to the right at address he is moving his dominant eye out of effective position to pinpoint the impact target, the ball. His 'aim' is thus displaced to almost the same degree as if he *closed* his right eye at address; in effect, moving the point of club-ball impact one to three inches *behind* the ball.

According to Bows, "A right-eyed golfer—unless he consciously adjusts his swing to counteract the tendency—will tend to hit *behind* the ball. A left-eyed golfer, mimicking Palmer's head position, will invariably top the ball.

"Golfers who resort to imitation in favor of cogitation should at least pick a model to imitate who has the same or similar physical characteristics—a right-eyed golfer trying to imitate Nicklaus is almost as bad as a right-handed player playing left-handed to score like lefty star Bob Charles!"

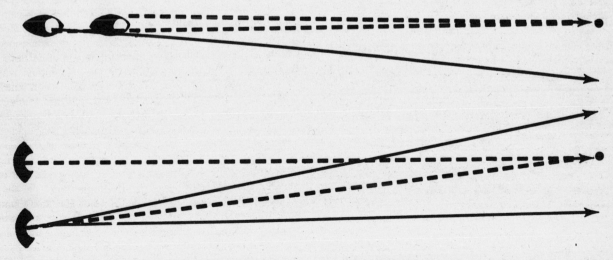

In each of these illustrations, correct vision is pictured by the broken lines, in which the line of sight from each eye converges on one spot. Persons who lack vertical coordination see objects on different levels (top-black line). Those with poor lateral coordination see objects in different vertical planes (below-black lines). Vision training and/or eye glasses can correct these faults.

The Greatest Feat in the History of Golf

By K. JASON SITEWELL

THE BEGINNING of April marked the 76th anniversary of what is probably the most spectacular feat in the history of golf. The records are uncertain whether it was March 31, 1900, or the next day (the only living witness of the event claims it was the latter).

It happened at the Imperial Golf Club in Melbourne, Australia. The principal characters were A. F. Daye, the leading British professional of his time, and Langley Corrigan, the local golf champion and winner of the Australian Open in 1899.

Both men were touring Australia in a head-to-head series. The match at Melbourne brought out a record crowd. Three matches had been played prior to Melbourne, Corrigan winning two of them. The people of the area were ablaze with excitement over the prospect that the local favorite would triumph over the vaunted Britisher.

The Melbourne course was a good test. Par, 73. Length, 7,900 yards. The toughest hole was the par-three No. 17, reminiscent of the famous over-the-water 16th at Cypress Point in California where many pros accept bogeys with equanimity if not a spirit of

thanksgiving. When players approach the 17th at Melbourne, they are close to a precipice; the drop to the floor of the canyon is about 1,200 feet. The green is 215 yards away. Usually, a strong wind whips in from the sea. Some of the longest hitters in golf have challenged the hole with a driver and fallen far short.

On this particular day, Al Daye was one-up coming to the 17th. Corrigan was the first to hit. (In those days, the player who was behind in the match always hit first.) Playing it safe, Corrigan hit a 3-iron into the wind to the dog-leg fairway on the short side of the gap about 170 yards away. He seemed certain to get no better than a bogey.

Daye saw a chance to wrap up the match right then. He was a long-ball hitter, outdriving Corrigan by 20 yards or more on most of the tee shots. He took out his 3-wood and challenged the canyon. The ball started out like a cannon shot; it appeared certain it would carry the green. When the ball reached its peak about 170 yards out, however, it hit gale-like reverse winds and fell about 10 yards short, plopping down to the canyon floor. Knowing he had lost

the hole anyway and being stubborn, Daye took out his driver and belted a prodigious second shot that on an ordinary day would have carried at least 280 yards. The winds were now full force in the faces of the players and the ball fell short again—this time by only 6 or 7 feet. Daye decided on a third try—teed up, fired, and missed.

Now the gale hit in full fury. Daye's caddie, an Australian aborigine of 61 years who couldn't have weighed more than 105 pounds, did something most unusual. He asked for permission to hit a ball over the ravine. Daye promptly put down a ball and offered his No. 1 wood, which the caddie spurned. All this time he had been carrying what appeared to be a walking stick. He turned it around and took a swipe at the ball which he had teed up very low. The swing was entirely original. The aborigine stood about 10 feet to the rear of the ball and then appeared to run at it lashing at it with terrific velocity. It was a low wind-cheating shot and easily made the green despite the long yardage.

Everyone was thunderstruck. When Daye recovered, he teed up a ball and invited the old man to hit again. Once again, the caddie ran at the ball like a javelin thrower, flinging himself at it, then springing into the air at the second of impact. This time, the ball was lost in the deepening fog and rain. No one knew whether it made the green.

The entire party started out for the other side, walking around the semi-horseshoe of the landscape to the green. When they got to the green, no ball was to be seen. The area around the green was flat and open; no ball there either.

Then, suddenly, Corrigan began shouting incoherently. He was holding the pin and jumping up and down. Daye rushed up to Corrigan and demanded to know what the shouting was about. Still yelling, Corrigan jabbed at the hole with the pin. Daye looked down. Two balls were in the cup. Daye bent down for the balls, then looked up and smiled to the crowd. These were the two balls he had given the old man. Two successive holes-in-one by the same player on the same hole! Nothing like it had ever happened before (or has happened since). What made it all the more incredible was that it was done with a stick hardly the size of a walking cane. It later developed that the aborigine, whose name was Vrootengrud, had never played with regular clubs. He had used his cane for everything except putting.

As the result of Vrootengrud's double hole-in-one, hundreds of golfers would pilgrimage early in April each year to the site of the 17th tee. They would congregate close to the precipice, and hold a sort of Quaker meeting, one of their number painstakingly recounting the episode. Inevitably, over the years, the story was embellished. One version described Vrootengrud as being 10 or 15 years older than listed. In another version, his son was the caddie and the old man was trailing along with the crowd, hobbling along on a cane, then stepping forward after Daye gave up, turning his cane around and bashing two balls across the long ravine into the teeth of the gale. According to this version, Vrootengrud announced his feat in advance, much in the manner of Babe Ruth pointing to the bleachers just before swatting a home run against Chicago in 1932.

But these versions are plainly apocryphal. The true story is good enough just as it is and requires no embroidery.

The annual pilgrimages ceased with World War I in 1914. By that time the memory of the Vrootengrud feat had begun to recede. But a marble stone was erected at the site of the 17th tee memorializing the event. And the *Australian Sportsman,* which comes out the first of each month, publishes a short annual reminder of the event in its April issue. Last year, for example, the magazine ran a box in its editorial page which I reproduce herewith:

Vrootengrud Recalled

Seventy-five years ago on this date, the most spectacular feat in the history of golf, two successive holes-in-one, was performed by a caddie, Vrootengrud, believed to be 61 years old at the time. We honor his memory for the glory he has eternally brought to Melbourne.

The Vrootengrud legend is only slightly tarnished by something that came to light in 1905. Everyone had assumed at first that Vrootengrud had performed his feat with an ordinary walking cane, hitting the ball with the handle. Actually, he had used an authentic golf club of the variety in use during the early years of golf in Scotland; that is, a straight branch with a crooked neck. Vrootengrud had fashioned the club when he began to caddie as a youth of 13 and played with it regularly. After he turned 50 he became slightly arthritic and used the club as a cane.

It is not precisely accurate, therefore, to say that he hit his successive holes-in-one with a walking stick. Just the same, the truth detracts very little from the achievement. Even if he had made his successive holes-in-one with a modern graphite club, it still would have to be regarded as probably the most amazing achievement in the history of any sport.

About Vrootengrud himself: his glory, in a sense, turned out to be his undoing. Many players wanted to be able to boast they had been caddied by an old man who had performed a golfing miracle. Despite his worsening arthritis, Vrootengrud tried to accommodate everyone who asked for him—not charging anything extra even though he could easily have cashed in on his fame. His infirmity increased with the years, but he persisted nevertheless.

As might be expected, every time the players for whom he was caddieing came to the 17th hole, Vrootengrud was asked to reproduce his feat. The old man was smart enough to beg off. He kept at his job until four days before his death at the age of 77. The obituary in the "A.S." gave the date of death as August 9, 1916.

To the end, Vrootengrud's only goal in life was to be a good caddie. That he achieved his purpose there can be no doubt.

K. Jason Sitewell is a name sometimes assumed by Norman Cousins, editor of the *Saturday Review.* A few years ago Sitewell threw the golfing world into an uproar with a spoof about the congressman who wanted to abolish all golf courses (see that article elsewhere in this volume). When our editors read Sitewell's latest offering some seemed to feel a slight tug on the leg.

National Open Long Driving Championship Recalls Big Hitters of the Past

By DWAYNE NETLAND

THEY USED to hold one nearly every week on the tour, in the days before the Wednesday pro-ams became fashionable—and lucrative. The long-drive contest. It was the symbol of another time, a hairy-chested era when the man who could hit it the farthest earned the prestige among his colleagues that is accorded today to the leading money-winner.

That tradition was revived in the first National Open Long Driving Championship June 24, 1975 at the Butler National Golf Club near Chicago, during the week of the Western Open. The $50,000 event, with a payoff of $12,000 to the winner if he is a professional, was produced by the Tournament Players Division of the PGA and *Golf Digest* Magazine.

The 18 finalists at Butler included the six longest hitters in the tour contest held the previous August in Atlanta and the 12 survivors of four regional competitions.

The old driving contests weren't quite that formal. It didn't seem to make much difference where they teed it up—any hole that was straight enough for 350 yards, the practice range, Philadelphia's Municipal Stadium, a mountainside near Tucson or the Los Angeles Coliseum. The winner's payoff was between $100 and $200, pocket change by today's tour

Jimmy Thomson (opposite page), first of the long-driving kings, eventually was succeeded by Chick Harbert (above).

standards, but enough then to motivate all the big hitters.

The names are still familiar, evoking a nostalgic touch of yesterday. There was Scottish-born Jimmy Thomson, a stocky powerfully built man who was the longest driver in golf for over 20 years until Melvin (Chick) Harbert broke in during the late 1940s. Then Mike Souchak and George Bayer came along to dominate the long-hitting contests of the 1950s.

The arrival of the big-money tournaments on the tour in the 1960s coincided with the growing popularity of the Wednesday programs. The long-drive contests quietly phased out, like butch haircuts and the twist.

Golf's old-timers, in particular, are delighted by the revival. Among them is Fred Corcoran, who promoted many a long-drive event during his decade as tour manager of the PGA from 1937-1947.

"We had some dandies," Corcoran recalls. "One year we had the boys hitting off rubber mats laid on the concourse at one end of the Los Angeles Coliseum. The object was to drive the ball out of the stadium. Nobody could, not even Jimmy Thomson, and he hit several balls over 300 yards."

Ben Hogan participated in that contest. "I was sure several of the guys could hit it out of the stadium," Hogan says. "I remember watching Jimmy Thomson unloading his Sunday best and landing the ball about 25 rows up. If Jimmy couldn't knock it out in his prime, it couldn't be done by anyone."

Thomson's distance during the 1930s and 1940s was legendary. He frequently drove the ball over 300 yards with a sweeping shoulder turn and strong hand action that produced a low, screaming shot. In 1937, from an elevated tee at the Lookout Point Golf Club near Niagara Falls, Thomson hit a drive measured at 386 yards.

Now 68 and confined to a nursing home in North Miami Beach, Fla., Thomson remembers that shot. "I had a gentle wind at my back," he says. "I caught it just right. I loved those driving contests, and usually I could take on anybody. There was one I didn't win, though."

Thomson was referring to a contest staged by Corcoran in 1947 on the eve of the Tucson Open at El Rio Golf Club. The El Rio pro at the time was Leo Diegel, a two-time PGA champ-

ion. Diegel, by then a chronic hooker, wanted desperately to hit the longest drive.

The players teed off from a plateau up in the mountains. Diegel hooked a shot that bounded down off the rocks. Corcoran recalls that he thought it would never stop rolling. "We measured it out at 455 yards," Corcoran says, "and promptly proclaimed Leo the winner."

On another occasion, Corcoran arranged a driving exhibition involving Thomson and baseball sluggers Joe Cronin and Jimmy Foxx at Sarasota, Fla., where the Boston Red Sox trained in the spring. Thomson was given one ball to hit, Cronin and Foxx three each. In order to count, the shots had to stay in the fairway. The ballplayers sprayed their drives into the rough, and Thomson hit a big one down the middle to win.

Corcoran occasionally matched the tour's bombers against Babe Ruth. "Ruth hit the baseball a mile," Corcoran says, "but he had a short backswing in golf that cut down his distance."

The tour had a new long-drive champion in the years immediately following World War II. Chick Harbert, a swashbuckling extrovert, talked a good game and backed it up on the course. Harbert won nine tour tournaments and the PGA Championship with a superb all-around game, but the big drive was his forte.

In 13 years on the tour, Chick won over 40 driving contests, including several at the Masters and the PGA. One day, from an elevated tee at the Havana Country Club on a tour stop, Harbert pounded a drive that measured 358 yards. It won the contest by 56 yards.

"Nobody could beat me hitting downwind," Harbert claims today. "I hit the ball on the upswing, with a high trajectory. Sam Snead was the best driver against the wind. He hit the ball squarely every time, and kept it down."

Snead, for many years, was the best driver on the tour—period. But Harbert often beat him in the long-drive competitions. "The reason," Chick explains, "was that Sam was so straight he could afford to let it all out on every drive during the tournaments. I could never do that, but I had a little reserve to call on whenever I wanted some extra distance. But Sam was always one of the feature attractions at any driving event. Nobody ever hit the ball so pure."

One contest that Snead did win took place at the 1937 PGA Championship at the Pittsburgh Field Club, in his first year on the tour. Sam hit it 330 yards.

Another big hitter of that time was Lawson Little. Like Snead and Thomson, Little was of only average height, and that fact prompts an interesting observation by Harbert.

"The tall, rangy men of my day were not the longest hitters," he says. "They were the best putters. Horton Smith and Doc Middlecoff are two who come to mind. The big drivers were the stocky men, with the muscles and the full shoulder turn."

Mike Souchak certainly fit that description. He broke in near the end of Harbert's career, just as Harbert had when Thomson was winding down. Chick knew it was time to abdicate when Souchak outdrove him in a contest preceding the Crosby in 1952.

"I hit one flush that day," Harbert recalls, "and Mike put it past me. That planted the first seed of doubt in my mind. From that moment on, Mike was the longest until George Bayer arrived.

Souchak, who had been a football end at Duke University, radiated strength and power. He packed 220 pounds into his 5-11 frame, and he put everything into his swing. Mike won the 1959 PGA Championship driving contest, at the Minneapolis Golf Club, with a belt of 318 yards. He was, moreover, a talented player with a particularly fine record in major tournament and Ryder Cup competition.

Now the head professional at Innisbrook Golf and Country Club in Tarpon Springs, Fla., Souchak looks back fondly on the driving contests. "They were fun," he says. "I used to hit it pretty far, but one day I saw Bayer unload a few and I knew it was time for me to start concentrating on just playing golf."

Bayer, at 6-5 and 255 pounds, was the first exceptionally big man to consistently hit the ball a long way. In 1955, his first year on tour, he won 12 of 13 driving contests. "I drove it out of the fairway on the other one," Bayer says. "Paul Harney won it."

Harbert, who always had a keen eye for any driving competition, remembers the first time he saw Bayer swing. "What an arc!" Chick says. "George

The list of longest hitters includes Mike Souchak (above), George Bayer (opposite) and Jim Dent (below).

was prodigious. He just pulverized the ball."

Bayer once drove the 426-yard seventh hole at El Rio during the Tucson Open. It was only four yards short of the longest recorded drive in tournament competition, hit by Craig Wood on the fifth hole at St. Andrews during the 1933 British Open.

On a 589-yard hole in Australia, Bayer hit his drive so far he had only a 50-yard pitch shot for his second. "I better explain that one," says Bayer, now the Detroit Golf Club pro. "I had the advantage of a tailwind, hard ground and the small British ball. But I did hit it pretty good."

Bayer won two driving contests at the PGA Championship, and two more at the Masters. The long-drive event at Augusta was supplanted by the par-three tournament, and in 1963 George Bayer finessed the ball around the little par-27 course for a winning score of 23. The big fellow had a nice touch around the greens as well.

"I was proud of being a big hitter," Bayer says. "It got me a lot of exhibitions in my 10 years on tour. I've lost a little distance now, but I drove a 376-yard hole last winter in Florida. Unfortunately that doesn't happen very often anymore."

Bayer, 50, is interested in the National Open Long Driving Championship, and is naturally curious to see what Jim Dent can do. "I'm afraid he's got too much youth for me to handle," Bayer admits. "But it would be fun to find out.

"Dent has the same reputation I had. He's earned it. I'm not going to live in the past. I remember guys from my day saying they used to do this and used to do that. A man's records ought to speak for themselves."

Bayer and Dent. It would be an intriguing matchup, with the generation gap between them providing additional flavor. Dent won the tour contest in 1974 in Atlanta with a smash of 324 yards, 18 inches.

One of the CBS television commentators at that event was Ken Venturi, whose tour success was built far more on iron play than long driving. Observing Dent, Venturi sidled over to Deane Berman, the TPD commissioner who was even a shorter hitter than Venturi.

"We could put our drives end to end," Venturi said in jest, "and we still couldn't match Dent."

The Jock-Mystic Approach to Better Golf

By LARRY SHEEHAN

THE LATEST from California is psycho-energetics—a way to play golf in a better frame of mind and maybe even with fewer strokes. The offbeat, non-technical approach is being explored at Esalen Institute, a 100-acre psychological and spiritual laboratory along the ocean in Big Sur. Esalen holds some 500 workshops a year on everything from body-flying to learning to fight with your spouse more constructively. Now it has started research in athletics and has run golf, tennis and skiing workshops.

"We are still in an early stage as far as sports go," says Michael Murphy, the 43-year-old co-founder of Esalen. A sports buff and 4- to 7-handicapper himself, he is best known to golfers as the author of *Golf in the Kingdom*, the fantastical novel set in Scotland which appeared in 1971.

Murphy points out that improvement in the conventional sense of the word has not been a goal of the few golf workshops that have been held so far. "We are not offering to reduce someone's handicap three strokes in two weeks," he says. "All we're trying to do is build more awareness and more enjoyment of the game for the long run."

The workshops are a combination of talks on the theories of Eastern philosophies and martial arts and teaching players to more effectively draw on their energy fields. Despite the de-emphasis on improvement, there have been success stories. One man claimed he shot the best game of his life shortly after attending a workshop. Another broke 80 for the first time and also reported greater emotional resistance to pressure at the office. Another participant said he learned to settle his weight around his stomach rather than in his shoulders during his swing, with a smoother, more rounded swing the result.

There have been flops, too. During one weekend two building contractors from San Francisco dropped out after they were told to lie down on the floor so they could experience nothingness and be in the here and now. The builders didn't think that was too swift.

"Many people react to metaphysics as a lot of baloney," says Buddie Johnson, a National Golf Foundation consultant who helped Murphy set up the first golf workshop over a year ago. "But this approach can help people relax and perform better and more enjoyably, not only in golf but in their careers and family lives."

Johnson, who has had experience as a Methodist minister in group psychological work, sees two main problems in the American way of golf.

"First, we are often 'over-techniqued,'" he maintains. "We're aware of so many specifics in the golf swing that we tend to tighten up and get nervous before hitting the ball. The details wreck our swing. Second, we have a tendency in our culture to meet one crisis with another crisis, to meet force with force. If our boss, or wife, gets mad at us, we get mad back. Same thing happens on the golf course. We treat the tee shot on a long hole, say, or any trouble shot, as a crisis. And generally, we try to force our way out of the crisis by trying to kill the ball, which also destroys our swing."

The workshops have two main thrusts. The first is to help the player understand how his subconscious may be affecting his performance and enjoyment. The golfer who hurries shots when playing with better golfers, for example, could start to lick the problem by realizing that he does so because he doesn't feel worthy enough to take the time. Being able to understand the reasons behind your actions on the course is the "psycho-dynamic" level and the foundation of a rewarding game. When great players go into a slump, it is usually because they have failed to discipline this mental aspect of the game.

The "psycho-energetic" of "energy dimensions" stage involves making the player visualize and execute a fluid swing. Exercises and practice are used to encourage each player to call upon the stream of energy flowing within and around each person. Players are taught to "center" their energy, which means releasing tension, which surfaces in such things as clenched fists and knotted shoulder muscles. Another technique used to promote a strong, fluid swing is visualizing a perfect swing, which Murphy claims becomes an irresistible path and seems to create the energy to make the image a reality.

The golf workshops have been held irregularly but basically have run along the lines of the first. That took place on two weekends a month apart. A group of diverse golfers, including a psychiatrist frustrated with the game, first met on a Friday evening to perform exercises in "energy dimensions." These were led by an expert in the Japanese self-defense form known as *aikido*.

The next day was spent on the driving range trying to put the concepts into

Mike Murphy

practice under the tutelage of Murphy, Johnson and the *aikido* expert, a 37-year-old San Franciscan named Bob Nadeau. A month later, the same group met to report on their various experiences playing on their home courses. They performed more exercises, worked on the driving range and finally played half a round of golf.

"That first time out on the course together was strange," Johnson recalls. "All of them kept closing their eyes for a while before each shot, to get into the right frame of mind. We didn't slow anybody else up, because it was late in the day and there were no groups behind us. But it was a most deliberate nine holes."

A practical aim of the workshops is to talk the golfer out of having conscious perceptions of what he is doing with a golf club.

"Most golfers are head-trippers," observes Nadeau, who had never worked with this breed of sportsman before the Esalen program. "They appear to be businesslike and intelligent and quick on the draw. But if you tell them to do something, they have a tendency to start *thinking* about it rather than *feeling* it."

In the workshops, Nadeau tries to get the golfers feeling "centered" rather than thinking "technique," and to help them relax under pressure. He leads them through a series of exercises, some as simple as sitting down and standing up again, others related to the *aikido* discipline, until everyone seems to be moving in a reasonably natural flow. Out on the practice range, however, the golfers tend to revert to their original aggressive state.

"As soon as a ball is put in front of

them, challenging them to action, people suddenly jump out of their 'center' again," Nadeau observes. "So then our job is to go up and down kind of nagging them back into repose. We aren't teaching them to learn something so much as to *unlearn* whatever is interfering with their natural performance."

Exercises also are used on the practice range to show how people misapply their energies. For instance: a golfer might walk along while another person, walking backwards at his side, presses across the golfer's chest with his arm. It is found that most people respond to this force by hunching up and pushing forward with the right shoulder. Those who respond by pushing their stomachs out tend to have freer, more effective golf swings. The others tend to hit from the top, which indicates a need to get the bulk of their strength and nervous tension out of the right side and back down in the center of the pelvic region where it belongs. During workshops, meditation and massage techniques are used to help persons with lopsided distribution of power get back on center.

"Some time is spent on simple fault correction," reports Johnson. "But the main emphasis is on feeling the swing, and on using sources of energy most effectively."

Mike Murphy, a native Californian who studied philosophy at Stanford University and in India before starting Esalen 12 years ago, is a cheerful, articulate jock-mystic who can make all the metaphysical aspects of golf sound perfectly clear and logical—or at least pleasantly obscure. So I was glad for the chance to talk to him when he came east recently to meet with publishers and look after various matters relating to Esalen. He had just resigned as president of the Institute in order to write and to deepen his research into the psychological and spiritual "glimmerings" in the world of sport.

He had a datebook to keep him organized for his few days in Manhattan, but otherwise he did not look all that businesslike in faded corduroy slacks and white net sweater. His face was tanned, unlined, with bright brown eyes and a frequent disarming grin. Under the desk in his hotel room were blue jogging shoes, which he had worn to knock off 6 miles in New York's Central Park that morning.

Since the Esalen workshops are the result of Murphy's abiding interest in golf, I asked him to give me his background in the game and his feelings about it. He lay on the bed or sat crosslegged on the bed, or stood up and went through the motions of his swing, or putting stroke, while he told me.

"I played golf a lot when I was younger but I stopped playing except irregularly for about 15 years. I didn't get into it again until I started writing the novel. Then the game became wildly alive for me. I began to have unusual experiences on the golf course. For instance, during one period I had a terrible time getting lined up on shots, even putts—the golf course looked like a cubistic painting through my eyes. It reflected the chaos in my personal life at the time. When I solved my personal problems, the problems on the course cleared up, too. That's an example of why I say that golf mirrors our basic conflicts.

"I hate cheap psychologizing, but the golf course can be a marvelous theater for the psyche. It's easy to read things like aggression, or greed, into the way some people play. Of course a certain amount of our playing style has to do with how we're wired up physiologically. Some of us have to learn to live with a slice, probably. But the reason most people have problems on the golf course is that they're carrying around a lot of unfinished business in their lives. If they can clear that up, there'll be fewer things to interfere with their game, or their pleasure, on the course.

"My own game is kind of boring. I never drive out of bounds, or very far. My golfing friends blame my poor distance on lack of enough leg action, but I believe it's because my wrists aren't that strong. Anyway I invariably shoot between 75 and 82. I love to drive. I can play a 2- or 3-iron very well, and my sand game is weak because I never hit into bunkers so I don't get the practice. A round of golf in America often is a gigantic social event. That's why I like to play on rainy days sometimes, when no one else comes out, and you can feel the great, wild, introverted drift of the game.

"On the other hand, I also like the humor and needling that goes on when you're playing in a good foursome. It's one of the best parts of the game. It provides a testing quality that exists in mystic religions, too: you have to learn to laugh at yourself, to relinquish your ego, in order to keep needling from ruining your game. In a way needling is mean, but at a deeper level it can be very liberating."

Murphy also admitted that he has been a passionate follower of the pro tour since his high school days. He's been to almost every Crosby Clambake since 1948. It was at the 1950 Crosby that he first watched Ben Hogan play. Hogan he rates No. 2, behind his fictional creation, Shivas Irons, on his All-Time True Gravity Team ("true gravity" is a higher form of "centering").

Murphy believes that the careers of Hogan and Jack Nicklaus in particular, as well as such extraordinary winning streaks on tour as those of Johnny Miller, Tom Weiskopf and Lee Trevino in the past three years, are the result of the players having achieved an edge in the psychic or what he calls the "psycho-energetic" dimension of the sport. To a limited extent, ordinary golfers can experience this dimension, too, Murphy contends—but not necessarily in fewer strokes.

"The trouble with the purely rational, technique-oriented approach," he says, "is that it has made people focus compulsively and exclusively on score and performance, and they have often lost the whole deeper joy of the game."

Some California club professionals have shown interest in hearing about Esalen's more spiritual approach to learning and playing golf, and at one point there was a move afoot to acquaint the PGA with its program. In any case, Esalen is not opposed to conventional golf instruction. It is simply espousing a complementing approach which seeks to heighten the experience of playing the game. Indeed, it views the club pro as potentially a kind of guru, a teacher of the spirit as well as the body, working on your personality problem and putting problem simultaneously.

There is no mysterious ingredient, or secret, offered by Esalen which an enterprising, sensitive fellow can't get on his own. Golfers who believe they aren't enjoying the sport fully, or who suspect they would play much better if they weren't so tense and jumpy out on the course, certainly should consider finding out for themselves what Oriental philosophies may have to offer.

That can be accomplished by dipping into texts such as the much-recommended *Zen in the Art of Archery* by Eugen Herrigel, or even enrolling in a yoga class at the local Y or health club. Of course, applying your newly found precepts of consciouness and energy to the game of golf may not be easy, but then neither is setting your club early on the backswing, or leading with your hands on the downswing, or any of the other myriad dictums of instructional technique.

If Michael Murphy is correct, the approach offers at least a more highly evolved form of beating your brains out on the golf course.

"Doctor Hampter has taken time from his very busy schedule in order to be with us today."

You May Remember This— It Happened 30-plus Years Ago

By Red Smith

AUGUSTA, GA.—The tall man with the look of one who has known great sorrow sat in the Augusta National Golf Club unmoving, expressionless, not drinking or eating or saying much. Just sitting there like a ball player in a hotel lobby.

"Get a load of Laughing Boy Keiser," somebody said. "And hey, look who's talking to him. That a picture, eh?"

It was Craig Wood talking to him, and it was indeed a picture. For here was Herman Keiser, who looks like a Missouri mortician, sweating out the time between his finish in the Masters championship and the moment when they'd say his score was good enough to win. And there, talking quietly, was the guy who had done the same thing in the same place 11 years earlier.

Eleven years earlier Wood sat in this club with a score of 282 on the board—exactly the score Keiser had tonight—and the mob was thumping his back and buying wine and shouting: "Boy, oh boy! What a wedding anniversary for you, Craig old pal!" And then just when the committee was ready to draw him a check for first prize, Gene Sarazen shot a double-eagle two on the 15th hole and came home tied for first and the next day Gene won in a playoff.

Maybe they both remembered that as they talked, although Keiser hadn't been around in those days. At any rate, they could hear the gallery cheering for Ben Hogan as he came ripping home with his sights on that first prize of $2500. Every cheer meant Hogan was one stroke closer.

When Ben was on the 17th green Keiser heard that Hogan was three under par, which meant they were tied. As he sat there in the club, he was told Hogan needed a par four to preserve the tie.

"I hope," he said, "Ben shoots either a three or a five."

He is a curious guy, this newest and most obscure winner of the Masters. Ten thousand people paid $5 apiece today expecting to see him chewed up like a sad-faced Christian flung among lions. They went clamoring and skidding up slippery slopes and trooping through sand traps and stomping across greens and every now and then they caught up with the parade and, standing tiptoe, saw Keiser's white sun visor as he straightened after hitting a ball.

But they didn't see him blow up. They caught, for their five-spot, occasional glimpses of a guy who approached and shot with sad detachment, like an undertaker approaching a job he didn't particularly fancy. He is the walkingest and waitingest and studyingest guy that ever won a major competition.

He hits a shot and then he ambles down and stares with distaste at his lie and then he walks over some nearby hill and stands gazing unhappily at the flag. He comes back, glares at the ball again, lifts a club from his bag and takes a few practice swings. At last he stands over the ball and shifts his feet and waggles his hips and brandishes his club threateningly, and at long last he hits his shot.

When he gets on the green he slows up. He walks from the ball to the pin. Then he walks from the pin to the ball. Then he gets behind the ball and squats and studies the line. Then he takes his putter from the bag and aims it like a rifle across the ball. Then he swings it crosswise, tilts it this way, tilts it that way and sights across it like a painter stepping back and measuring his canvas across his brush. Then he creaks up and pokes the bloody thing into the cup.

He never varied this routine today. He never showed a real trace of nervousness. He hit his shots firmly and patted his

putts deliberately. Even on the 18th green he gave no sign that he heard the applause that greeted him after coming out of the rough. He walked up and took his time and then swung his putter, aiming for the cup 20 feet away.

He gave the ball a bit of body English as it rolled, swinging his hips and taking two or three prowling steps to his right. The ball rolled past the cup. He tried again, deliberately, and when he missed again his tall, lank figure sagged. That meant three putts on the 18th and that could mean the tournament. Even as he tapped the ball in, a cheer rattled across the hills from Hogan's gallery.

Keiser went into the clubhouse and waited. The whole gallery flocked back up the course to meet Hogan. Ben was playing along about as usual, his face impassive, a cigarette always between his lips. He came to the 18th green needing a par to tie, a birdie to win.

He putted downhill and missed. He putted uphill and missed. He straightened, shuddered a little and looked down at the grass. Then he stepped over and pushed the ball in, and then they gave the prize to Keiser. Even then Herman's face was mournful.

AIM CORRECTLY, NOT RIGHT

By BRAD WILSON

Brad Wilson is a 37-year-old associate professional at the Mesa Verde C.C. in Costa Mesa, Calif. Considered one of the west coast's outstanding teachers, Wilson has worked with Gene Littler, Phil Rodgers, Cesar Sanudo and others on the professional tour. He has been an instructor in two PGA business schools and at a National Golf Foundation seminar for teachers.

ONE OF THE most common faults in golf is aiming too far to the right of the target. It's the cause of many errors committed during the swing itself and it can seriously undermine your chances of developing a sound, repeating action.

Ever wonder why your practice swing feels so good and your real swing so bad? Usually it's because in your practice swing you are not committed to hitting the ball toward a specific target. Your subconscious doesn't need to compensate for any faulty aiming and mis-alignment. Therefore, it allows you to swing in the same direction you are aligned. All goes smoothly.

But when you aim off target, your subconscious mind realizes your true objective and literally *insists* that you swing the clubhead in that direction.

So you will tend to start your downswing with your upper body pulling or shoving your clubface to the left, in an attempt to square it to the target by impact. With your shoul-

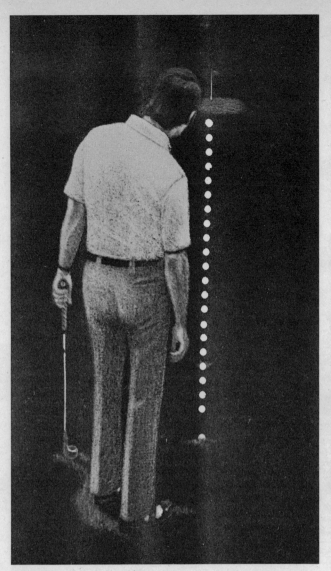

1. Stand behind the ball and sight from the ball to your target.

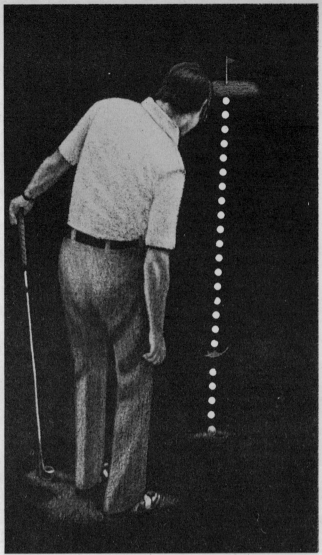

2. Pick an intermediate spot—a leaf or divot or other distinctive mark—a few feet in front of the ball on the target line.

ders so active, your hips and legs must remain relatively inactive, blocking the way for you to swing your arms freely and aggressively toward the target and making it impossible to achieve maximum clubhead speed.

Since the overactive shoulders pull the clubhead across the ball from outside the target line, the ball normally will start out to the left of target. Depending on how your hands react in aligning the clubface, you can pull, duck-hook, or pull-slice the ball. Topped shots, sclaffed or "fat" shots and shanks often result.

Not until you get your conscious and subconscious minds in agreement on direction will you start correcting these swing errors. I'm not claiming that proper aiming and alignment is a cure-all, but it will help create harmony between your conscious and subconscious, therefore encouraging you to swing the club freely in the direction in which you are actually aiming. The grooved compensations that have developed from aiming too far right can be changed only through practice.

A word of definition here. When I speak of aiming I'm talking about the clubface. When I speak of aligning I'm referring to the body—the shoulders, hips and feet. Usually, though not always, faulty aim and bad alignment go together.

Why do most golfers aim and align too far to the right? One reason involves optics. Often the golfer "sees" the clubface aimed toward the target when actually it is not. A clubface aimed square to the target may looked closed to you until you learn that this is how it really should look.

Another common reason is that you don't know what proper alignment really is. Often you indirectly have been advised to aim to the right. This happens when you are instructed to align your feet, hips, and hands or shoulders *to the target*. Only after you have done this do you position the clubface behind the ball. Naturally, you place the clubface square to your stance and body alignment. Also quite naturally, this aims the clubface to the right of the target.

Once you fall into this pattern and begin producing shots that start out to the left, the normal tendency will be to aim

 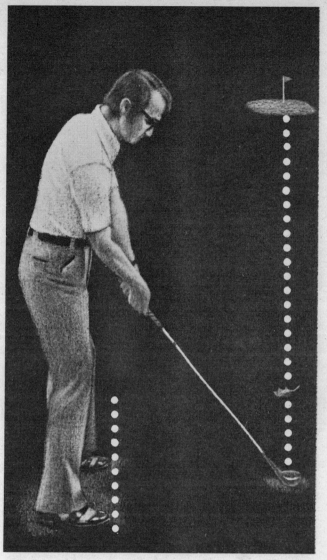

3. Aim your clubface at that intermediate spot and align your body square with the clubface.

4. Once your clubface is aimed at the spot and your feet and body are properly aligned with the clubface, once again glance at the target to visualize sending the ball flying to it.

even farther right to compensate. This merely compounds the problem.

The solution is to reverse the procedure. Instead of aligning the clubface square to your feet and body, first set the clubface behind the ball and aim it toward the target. Then align your body square to the clubface.

You will feel you're standing open. Now if you place a club on the ground in front of your toes to check your alignment, you'll find it points straight to a spot to the left of your target. But remember, your clubface is aimed directly at the target.

There is one warning I must make and it gets back to that business of optics. Aiming the clubface first will go for naught if your eyes give you a distorted line to the target. You may think it's aimed there when it's not. Let me give you a system to eliminate this chance for error.

The only "foolproof" way I know to line up properly is to *spot aim.* Bowlers do it all the time. Facing down the alley, they look at the arrows just a few feet out in front of the foul

line instead of at the pins at the end of the alley. The same theory holds true for golf. It is not a new concept. Many good players spot aim, the most notable being a fellow named Jack Nicklaus, who considers it an integral part of his alignment procedure.

To properly spot aim, stand a few feet behind your ball so that it is directly between you and your target. Draw an imaginary straight line through your ball to the target. Select a spot or blemish such as an old divot mark, broken tee or clump of grass on that line a few feet in front of your ball. Then draw *boldly in your mind's eye* a short line from the mark you've selected back to your ball.

Next, place your clubhead behind the ball so that it looks directly down that line to the spot you've chosen.

Finally, merely position your feet and body square to the clubface. Thus, you will be aligned parallel to the target line and in position to swing the clubhead squarely into the back of the ball. Your *conscious* and *subconscious* now will be working in concert to help you do just that.

The Calm Golfer Is the One Who Collects

By CHUCK FRANK

FORGET ALL those golf gadgets, gimmicks, and gizmos geared for us incurable addicts—or at least hold them in abeyance until you get your mind right. It turns out that honing your golf game '70s-style isn't exclusively a matter of sinew and sweat after all.

The often frustrating process of learning and perfecting your on-course routine has developed a distinctly mystical ring these days. And according to advocates of two influential and pioneer movements of the cerebral-fitness approach to athletics, their updated forms of swivel-chair calisthenics for the mind, soul, and body can indeed do anything from putting points on your batting average to taking strokes off your golf score.

Call it the knack of knowing your own noggin.

Among the most widely-acclaimed methods for achieving tranquility (and possibly lowering your handicap) are Transcendental Meditation and the Inner Game approach. In some important and potentially beneficial ways, the two systems complement each other.

The first proposes to help the athlete take his nervous system down a peg or two, thereby effecting heightened levels of perception, endurance, and concentration; the latter, while offering a first-tee calmative of its own, tries to help the athlete learn by forgetting, achieve by not trying too hard, gain control by letting go—and perhaps most importantly, to lose that blasted ego that has a nasty habit of tripping him up every time Bill, Harry, and both their wives are watching.

In their own rights, both approaches can prove powerful aids to better learning and performance. But employed together . . . well, it might just take a shower of kryptonite to keep you down.

The TM system, which consists of 20-minute meditative sessions with the mind dwelling on a meaningless mantra (Sanskrit word) each morning and afternoon, is on the world-wide marketplace with 1,200 centers and 8,000 teachers in 89 countries. The latest pitch for this twice-daily pause that refreshes is slanted toward athletes, and the campaign is as convincing as an old Arnold Palmer charge.

Athletes in every sport, from football's Joe Namath, to baseball's Willie Stargell, to tennis' Arthur Ashe, and right on through to golf's Gary Player, are practicing this condensed form of Eastern meditation which has been mashed down and molded to suit the palate and pace of the Western world. It's no wonder that *TM—Discovering Inner Energy and Overcoming Stress* (Bloomfield, Cain, and Jaffe) is a current Sports Illustrated Book Club selection.

Scientific studies, conducted at universities and hospitals including Harvard, UCLA, and Boston General, indicate that meditators achieve a restfullness twice as deep as deepest sleep while meditating, and benefit from effects ranging from lower blood pressure to denser alpha waves in the brain. As a result, TM's own testing concludes, meditators react quicker, endure longer, run faster, and—the golfer's byword—concentrate better and with crystal clarity.

"A very important factor is that TM improves reaction times and helps perceptual motor performance (eye-hand coordination)," said Steve Schulte, a Chicago-area teacher of TM and a former Southeastern Missouri State University basketball player. "Those are things that can be a big plus for athletes in any sport."

This seeming panacea is available to anyone—but only for a fat price and a substantial commitment of time. The TM method is taught only at authorized centers, involves a 7-step, week-long training process, and costs $125.

The Inner Game technique of improved performance, on the other hand, is yours for $6.95 and a short perusal. It is described in Tim Gallwey's bestseller *The Inner Game of Tennis* (Random House, 141 pages), but its implications extend far beyond the claylike Har-Tru courts of Forest Hills—possibly all the way to the undulating greens of Augusta. "It's an approach to learning and an approach to doing, and therefore it applies to any kind of learning, period," said Gallwey, when specifically asked of the Inner Game's application to golf.

Gallwey proposes to build and strengthen your golf game by tearing down your ego, and thereby letting your natural instincts control your nervous system without psychological interference. His principles are a blend of Eastern philosophy and modern psychology aimed at quelling the high-pitched ego-nervous system struggle, while at the same time increasing your awareness of what is happening around you. The Inner Game is a technique of calming the nerves, banishing the mental obstacles and ingrained performance demands we all suffer under, and *letting* things happen—as opposed to *making* them happen.

"As far as the pure Inner Game goes, it requires almost no instruction whatsoever," said Gallwey, and then he made a case in point. "Normally, if you want to instruct a student in golf, you tell him how to stand, how to hold the club, how to take it back, how not to bend his elbow, how to cock his wrists and how to come through. Basically, you would give him a lot of instructions on how it should be done."

Not so with Gallwey's approach.

"The Inner Game principle is that learning takes place fastest and most effectively not by pressuring the student with what should be done, but by increasing his awareness of what is happening," he said. "Most students react to instruction ambivalently, with part of them willing to do it and part resisting being told what to do."

So the teacher of the Inner Game concept does not instruct—he questions and points things out. He would ask, in Gallwey's words, "Where is it (the club) exactly, when, and what are the results? As the player sees more accurately the results of his actions, those elements of behavior which produce the more desired effect will be reinforced. But if a player has to think about six things to do at once, he'll definitely foul it up."

The beginning student would take a swipe at a dozen balls. If a single one got airborne, the teacher would force the student to become aware of what he did on that particular shot.

"What the Inner Game is about also," said Gallwey, "is who is in control of the human body, the ego or the second self (the nervous system). The objective is to quiet the mind enough to get back in touch with our own innate intelligence. You have to let go of control to gain control—you can't steer from both centers of the mind at the same time.

"There's a point that people gloss over, and that is that there's a natural learning process that takes place and we really do interfere with it when a person is no longer a child. When the ego mind develops, it severly interferes with our capacity to learn. I'm interested in doing whatever I can to minimize the blockages in the mind."

Does this mean that, given a proper mental framework, we can all learn to hit the ball like a Jack Nicklaus or a Johnny Miller? Hardly. "I definitely feel," Gallwey hastened to emphasize, "that a person's effectiveness is dependent on the endowments of his or her body."

Another key for the serious student of the Inner Game is to shut out useless data (i.e. the situation one shot ago) along with the excess psychological baggage. "In very simple terms, what's useless is thinking so much about things and about how to change them, as opposed to directing one's experience to what is happening," Gallwey said. "The human mind has a lot of bad habits, and it's amazing how much faster learning goes and how much better performance gets when you turn that part of the mind off."

Where exactly does TM fit into this blissful learning and improvement policy? "TM can bring the mind to a relative state of calmness," observed Gallwey, "but even if you perceive more clearly and still think that your self worth rides on how well you play—which is what most athletes are deceived into thinking—then you're caught in a trap and you're not going to be calm when the competition begins."

In one sense, TM teaches how to calm the body, and the Inner Game teaches how to keep it that way on the course or court. "What I consider the limitation of the TM approach is that the last time an athlete has meditated is that morning," said Gallwey, "and while he may have it calm going into a contest, something like a desire, fear, or anxiety not to blow it can destroy that calm. This is what the Inner Game is for. It's something to focus the mind on and calm you when you need it.

"My Inner Game and TM are alike in that they're both first steps for Western people, and they both come on as something that can help you in your life. The real purpose is to see that if this kind of thing works with tennis, then maybe it'll work with golf and then maybe with life. Then the person says, 'ah yes, the mind is where it's at. I just change the mind and everything changes.' That's better than trying to change everything out there—and that's the Inner Game."

Five dollar Nassau, anyone?

HOGAN ON BUSINESS

By NICK ROMANO
(Associate Editor, *Golfdom*)

TODAY, Ben Hogan is a businessman—an asset to the golf industry.

Among the game's all-time greats, he recently spent a morning in his Fort Worth, Texas, office talking about the business of running his own golf equipment company.

"Golf is a great business," he said. "But there is a lot more to do yet. More people are playing now than ever. People play for health and enjoyment. Some are competitive, some aren't. People keep striving for improvement."

The same can be said for Hogan. Since retirement from full-time tour golf in 1960, he has channeled his efforts into the business side of golf and is involved in several facets of the industry.

At 62, Hogan's interest as head of the AMF/Ben Hogan Company is providing new innovations in club design. He has developed 21 models since the firm began business in 1953.

Hogan is as much a reflection of Fort Worth, as it is of him. Just miles away from Dallas, Fort Worth is a modest, mild-mannered city of some 394,000, that seems to enjoy being set apart from the hustle of the Big D, to the east.

Beyond the downtown area, the Hogan Company is situated over 10 acres of one of the city's industrial parks. Squeezed in between two older buildings, lies the main office of the plant and Hogan, himself.

"We're a long way from perfection in this business. Equipment is improving every day, through advancing manufacturing techniques. We're putting out better merchandise, because of this," Hogan added.

It's ironic, but after you talk to Hogan for a time, you realize with so many people wanting to know what he thinks, Ben Hogan doesn't consider his opinions all that important to the industry. He is thoughtful in his answers, but modest and humble in his approach—unawed by his own reputation.

Hogan explains that the process of club design is long and involved. If something doesn't feel right to him, it never reaches the market. "I guess, if I ever had a goal to strive for in this business, it's that I could really contribute something to the game," he said.

There are still stories at the plant about how Hogan once threw out $150,000 worth of clubs because he didn't feel the quality was right. He is firm in the belief that nothing carries his name he is not proud to have it on.

From time to time, he gets letters from customers concerning his products and tries to scrutinize suggestions, both praise or complaints, which there are usually few.

"I think we have a quality line and that helps us sell. Along with that, we have a dedicated sales force, but like any business, there are peaks and valleys," Hogan remarked.

Ben Hogan believes in the club pro concept. "I don't think I have the expertise to advise pros on how to run their business," he says, "but, I remember when I was a club pro, I tried to operate a good business. One of the most important things a pro has to do is to evaluate his membership. You have to tailor your operation to fit them."

If there is a sure road to success for a pro, Hogan believes it is in always selling quality merchandise. "It isn't worth it to sell less expensive merchandise. Further, lesser merchandise nets smaller profits," he said.

Asked about the current number of legal battles to strip the exclusivity away from pros selling pro-line clubs, Hogan immediately backed his company's policy. "We won the suit in New Orleans. We dropped out of that case, because there was no case against us."

On the future of the pro-only policy being changed by a legal decision,

Hogan is clear. "If they pass a law saying we have to sell our clubs to people other than the pros, I guess we'll have to do it. Until then, I'll just wait and do what we've always done."

If litigation ultimately involves the pro shops, Hogan thinks it will adversely affect the game. "Taking pro-only clubs away from pro shops will damage the competition of the market and hinder golf."

Commenting on the tight money situation facing many pros right now, Hogan explains that this situation isn't a new one. "Those problems have been going on for as long as I can remember. I suppose there will always be some pros that are in trouble. It happens in every business. Today, pros are getting much better at paying their bills on time."

Intelligent solutions are the answers Hogan offers today's pro in keeping out of the red.

"A lot of businesses are underfinanced. A lot of small businesses are in trouble. A lot of pros are in trouble. The remedy is to carry less inventory. Buy things that move. There's enough business history to back that up," he points out.

While still a touring pro, Hogan realized that he would one day turn to the business side of the game. "I knew that I'd get old someday. This business looked good, because it seemed that I knew something about it."

Since becoming involved with his equipment company, Hogan has been an active overseer. He is no figurehead. When AMF purchased the Hogan Company in 1960, part of the agreement was that the name of the company and its principal namesake would continue.

If any group is happy about the arrangement, it is his employees. Touring the plant with a company public relations man, one sees dedication in the work. Hogan himself, has trained a lot of people that now work on his assembly line.

Quality of the finished product is the prime goal at the Hogan plant. Numerous inspections are made before anything leaves for the marketplace. This may slow production, but assures a demand for the Hogan lines. AMF's annual corporate report for 1974, showed that the Hogan Company celebrated its best year ever.

Hogan's business interests in golf extend beyond equipment. He is involved in course architecture and construction.

He is currently involved in a course being constructed near the Dallas-Fort Worth Regional Airport. Called the Trophy Club, the project's chief designer is architect Joe Lee, but Hogan himself will have a lot of input in the complete result.

"I always wanted to find a good piece of land and build a course that should be played. People should enjoy playing it. There will be no blind shots on this course. When you design a course, it should be built to allow for the greatest enjoyment. You build with that thought in mind. Each hole should be different and need to be negotiated differently."

"Courses should be built for enjoyment. Anybody can make a course impossible to play. A course should be constructed with framed fairways, bunkers and ample-sized greens. There has to be character in each hole," Hogan said.

There will be 36 holes full of character at the Trophy Club and Hogan feels that's the only way to build a course. "There has to be that many, at least, because a course with only 18 holes more easily lends itself to slow play," he said. "I realize there is a slow play problem right now. I don't have solutions for it, although, a lot of the problems may be a matter of management."

He described how two Texas pros are now handling over 600 people a day on weekends on a 36-hole course. He was sure slow play can be dealt with. "There are people in this world that don't mind waiting. Take Japan for instance, there are people there waiting two months just to get a tee time. If you miss, you wait two more months. Japanese people play golf as a status symbol."

Realizing there is a maintenance side to the course, too, Hogan wonders out loud about the escalating costs of country clubs. "As expenditures go up, the dues at courses go up. A lot of clubs are having a tough time right now. Even though it might cost more to play, I don't think the game will suffer. People will continue to have recreation. Golf, skiing and tennis are continuing to expand," Hogan said.

Ben Hogan as a player influenced two generations with the game of golf, and helped it to build a prominent niche in the life of America. As a member of the golf industry, he continues a pattern of influence which is helping make the business of golf a major one, important to the economy.

"This is going to be a tough shot!"

Spain, Australia, Athens— Where Do *You* Want To Tee Off?

By CAROL McCUE
(Executive Director, C.D.G.A.)

IN RECENT YEARS, golfers have been turning with the joy of a holed 6-footer to their local golf associations for new fairways to follow, new bunkers to cross, and new greens to fathom.

Since 1968 when the Chicago District Golf Association launched an air-lift to the Costa del Sol, golfers have discovered the easy way to combine new golf areas with foreign travel and a brush with history. And in almost every instance — like the ubiquitous Kilroy — Robert Trent Jones was there. His magnificent courses pop up everywhere.

During the fall and winter of 1968/69, the CDGA sent 3200 members to Marbella, Spain, the golfers new Valhalla. As with many new projects, too many promises were made to be kept and the hotel and airline promoters who promised airfare, bed, board and green fees at five golf clubs for 8 days for $350 had somehow neglected to spread the glad tidings to four of the golf clubs involved. This was overcome in a day or two, however, which in itself was record time in Spain, and the golfers happily toured the 50 miles of sunny green coast leaving divots and dollars wherever they went and raising the standard of living in an area that hasn't been the same since. Golf clubs started one-room schools for caddies, and caddies took home in 1 week more than their fathers earned in 6 months. Waiters finally earned a living and the youngsters who delivered *hielo* (ice) jingled all the way home.

The golf courses were magnificent. The golfers' welcome was warm and when not on the links, they strolled the villages, patronized the cafes and shopped. Oh, how they shopped! The charters returned to Chicago 2000 pounds heavier than they went over and that wasn't all *paella!* The first charter, in September of '68, was diverted on return to Reykjavik for fuel because of hurricanes in the North Atlantic. The airport souvenir shop was stripped bare by nervous golfers who thought they had already blown the shopping wad in Spain only to find more watches and rugs in Iceland. Being the first such group ever dropped on this unsuspecting, remote airport, the exhausted shop keepers stared in amazement as crazy Americans crammed more merchandise into their already loaded jet.

The following year sponsorship of the golf charters was switched to the Chicago District Golf Charities, a smaller affinity group dedicated to providing golf facilities at veterans hospitals, and contracts were negotiated with Pan American and Hilton International— not as exciting as the Spanish adventure but 100 percent more reliable. Since then CDGC has flown 13 charters to Athens, six to San Juan, five to Paris and Cannes, and one each to Australia and the South Pacific, Lisbon, Rome, Florence, Vienna, Bermuda, Caracas, Copenhagen, Rabat and Tokyo and through those years remarkable vignettes are nailed in the memory, as un-

forgetable as three birdies in a row:

● The man of the cloth teaching a bartender in Marbella to use only English gin and 3 drops of vermouth in a martini. We understand this elixir now has spread all over southern Spain, but in 1968 the dry martini was unheard of.

● The woman who broke her leg when she fell off a donkey sightseeing near Athens and the next day was climbing the Acropolis in a cast.

● The lady who couldn't be convinced she was getting the right amount of currency exchanged because she was swapping U.S. dollars for New Zealand dollars and wasn't getting an equal amount.

● The fuel stops in Shannon, where the shops weren't quite wiped out, but the golfers certainly helped build the new, expanded Irish shipping center.

● The couple in Copenhagen who discovered they could get a 2¢ refund on soft drink bottles at a little shop around the corner and hauled two shopping bags back for refunds on the day of departure.

● And romance—one couple met in Copenhagen and married in Chicago, one couple married in Greece, and the loveliest of all, the couple who renewed their vows in Australia 25 years after the date of their marriage. He had been a doctor and she a nurse during World War II, and 25 years later they returned via CDGC charter with their original witnesses to the same small church where the priest who had married them said the anniversary mass.

Among the other associations sponsoring golf junkets are Wisconsin, Arizona, Pacific Northwest, Northern California, Carolinas, Cleveland and two that will start in '76, Kentucky and Massachusetts. Most golf charters are 8 or 9 days, though of necessity a few, such as the South Pacific or Tokyo, must run longer.

New government charter regulations will make it even easier for golfers to join groups to play on faraway greens which 'til now they've only dreamed about. Affinity charters are being phased out by the government and travel industry. In fact, the cost of these charters is no longer competitive with the new OTC charters (One Stop Inclusive Tour Charter), a change which will open wider vistas and give more choice to those merry souls who have clubs, will travel.

CROMIE'S CORNER

Golfer's Digest Co-Editor, noted TV personality and newspaper columnist Bob Cromie looks at various aspects of his favorite game.

Golf Can be Annoying But You Like It

GOLF season is here once more, or at least no further than a good brassey shot away, and we might as well set down right now a number of the annoying things that will befall us on the links during the next few months.

This will do no good, of course, except that it will enable us to cry an anguished I-told-you-so or two, which is somewhat soothing in an obscure sort of way. Now:

A redheaded guy we play with will show up late. This will enable one of those odd-ball foursomes—which always lurk in the bushes off the first tee for just such an opportunity—to get out 10 seconds ahead of us. This is sure to include:

1. Four women with golfing handicaps of 27 and other handicaps which the shorts they wear do nothing to conceal. Each will teach the other, a classic case of the blind leading the blind from trap to trap. Or:

2. Four giggling girls who spend half their time missing the ball completely or moving it a maximum of 5 feet and the other half peering about to see if anyone is watching them. Or:

3. Four men, obviously more concerned with some business deal than golf, who chat on each tee, chat between each shot, chat on each green and always seem surprised when anyone expresses a desire to shoot thru. Or:

4. Four playboy types, with a dime riding on each hole and a wide acquaintanceship. They haggle over the rules—or their own version of the rules—insist on paying off on each green, and keep the rest of the course (they know everyone on it but us) appraised of their winnings or losings by shouting at the top of their lungs.

There are variations on this foursome, but you get the idea. And besides, this is nothing. After all, it's quite possible to get thru a group as early as the 16th or 17th hole, especially if you're lucky enough to have one of them fall into a fast moving stream and get carried away, or hit himself in the head with his own backswing.

Sometimes we wind up behind some human measuring worm. (This happens even on the rare occasions when our redheaded friend is on time.) He is forever pacing off distances: From tee to drive ("Hey, fellows, it's 175 yards if it's an inch."); from drive to green ("Don't know whether to use my wedge or a three-quarter 9-iron."), or from putt to cup ("You lucky stiff, that putt was 34 feet 6 inches!").

The only answer to this is to stretch out on the fairway for a snooze while he measures away, a device which gives the course a cluttered appearance reminiscent of some plague stricken countryside, especially as those behind begin to pile up about the 13th hole. Other grievances certain to arrive:

We will be driven into while putting, waiting to make our second shot or leaving the green. The excuse will not vary: "Didn't expect to carry so far, old man," the offender will say. "My, that's a nasty cut you put in my ball. What *do* you carry in that hip pocket of yours?"

Our opponent, at least five times during the year, will hit a cinch out-of-bounds shot which will catch a tree, fence post or some idiot bird and come back into play. This will *never* happen to us.

Someone will find our ball in the middle of our own fairway and hit it, under the impression it's the one he just sliced from two fairways over. Ours will be new. His, which we will find after he has disappeared behind some distant hill, *could* be one lost by Harry Vardon during his match with Francis Ouimet in 1913.

Taft Beat Ike to Fame in Presidential Golf Race

GOLFERS EVERYWHERE today are delighted that some of our chief executives' interest in the game lends dignity and prestige to their own enthrallment. But President Eisenhower was not the first, which may surprise you.

President William Howard Taft, so far as we know, was the earliest President to play the Royal and Ancient game, and if you believe Walter J. Travis, winner of the national amateur in 1900, 1901, and 1903, William Howard was a pretty fair swinger.

Travis, in an article in the *Century* magazine for September, 1910, "Golfing with President Taft," credits President Taft with having done much to popularize golf in the United States:

"A dozen years ago (says Travis) the game was confined to a few of the larger centers. Now nearly every small town has a golf club. A decade hence, at the present rate of progression, it will be played everywhere. Not a little of this undoubtedly is due to President Taft's example. Many men who otherwise might not have been led to take up the game have done so since Mr. Taft became Chief Executive, a little over a year ago.

"Brushing aside the undisguised lack of sympathy, and ignoring the ridicule which surely would have been their portion a couple of years ago, they have consoled themselves with the reflection that what is good enough for the President is good enough for them."

Travis says that a year previously Taft himself had described his golf as of a quality deserving the description "bumblepuppy." But, adds Travis, "he was altogether too modest. I personally know scores and scores of golfers who would almost be tempted to sell their immortal souls could they but put up such a game as he does.

"A player for 15 years, the President is not a novice. No man can serve an apprenticeship of that length of time, and have so keen a love for the game as Mr. Taft has without being able to play well. And the President does play a good game—a very good one considering, if I may be allowed to say so, the handicap of avoirdupois."

After describing Taft's stance and address (closed stance, feet nearer together than usual, and a habit of addressing the ball without any waggles, for "much longer even than with the ordinarily slow player"), Travis tells of a round played at Chevy Chase Country Club, just outside Washington with the then President, a course, Travis says, which Taft normally shot in the 90s.

Taft's clubs were fairly long and heavy . . . "driver and brassey about 47 inches . . . and weighed about 14 ounces. His putter would not allow him to compete in any of the British championships. It is of the center shafted type that has been barred at St. Andrews."*

During this Taft-Travis round—in which the two played their best ball against that of Capt. Archie W. Butt, military aide to Taft, and a brigadier general—the President started with a par 3 on the 292 yard first hole (dropping a "downhill putt of 8 yards").

Taft then remarked that "he could not keep up that pace" and promptly topped his tee shot on the second. He got a par 4 at the third (344 yards) and Travis grows vague about the next four holes. But of the eighth, he says:

"It was on this hole that the President displayed the one and only outward sign of irritation during the match . . . he had an easy putt which he failed to make. And he missed the next, a little bit of a thing! Scores, hundreds, nay, thousands of men have been known under like circumstances, to say and do things which could not be repeated here. With an air of mild disgust the President contented himself, however, with a mere, 'O, pshaw!' "

The Travis-Taft combine finally won, 6 and 4 (with a best-ball of 69 after the remaining four holes were completed) and Taft persuaded Travis to remain over for another round the next day.

"Despite the fact that it rained, and rained hard, Mr. Taft was duly on hand, and the entire match was played—the full round—in an ever increasing downpour."

As you can see, the man was a golfer.

---

*Barred after Travis himself had used a similar putter while winning the British amateur title in 1904.

A Golfer Can Dream, Doctor Game Indoors

IF YOU'RE lucky enough to be a golf enthusiast living where it's summer the year around, read no further. You're just plain lucky and we envy you. Maybe even hate you a little.

But if you live in a northern clime, where the snow flies, the wind whistles, the greens become like rocks and the flags freeze into the cups (assuming the course itself isn't locked up until April) then listen. Here is some good advice:

Don't quit the game until spring. Even if you don't care to face a wintry breeze with the mercury somewhere in the 30s—and some members of the clan play when it's 20 or below—then hunt up an indoor range. Take lessons from a competent pro, or at least keep limber by driving balls into a net.

Or if you're too indolent to do that, then practice in your living room or your basement. If the basement is large enough, and the ceiling permits, set up a small range of your own, complete with driving mat and canvas. Small mats, incidentally, which can be used either for wood or iron shots, are now on the market.

If none of these things appeals to you or if you're strictly an armchair athlete once the warmth disappears from the air, then at least do this: Get some golf books, or subscribe to one or more of the fine golfing magazines available. Read a little, either instructional or simply time passing stuff dealing with the royal and ancient game, then sit and reflect.

(Continued next page)

(A Golfer . . . continued)

It's easy enough to create a mind's picture of how you should swing. And it's also possible, believe it or not, to improve your game by telling yourself, even as you nod and smile while listening to some non-golfing idiot at a cocktail party, how your swing should be made. Remind yourself to grip the club properly, not to swing too hard, and to try to capture the timing which distinguishes a good game from a bad.

As has been said, the best way to improve a bad game over the winter, or to keep the edge on a good one, is to seek out some member of the Professional Golfers' Association, who has a wintertime school, and enlist for a course of lessons.

But if that's too much trouble set up your own school, either on an active or passive pattern, and get the jump on the rest of your foursome when you and the first robin return to the links together.

P.S.—And do it NOW!

Tee Time Lesson: Courtesy Big Factor In Golf Behavior

IN 10 YEARS of running the Sportsman's Golf Course near Wheeling, Ill., built by his father, George, more than 45 years ago, Dick Chamberlain developed a few ideas on links' behavior. His first rule was a simple one:

"Even if you've never before held a club in your hands," he says, "remember to observe the rules of common courtesy. Then you can't go too far wrong.

"To carry this a little further: Let's suppose you've lost a ball and the players behind ask permission to go thru. That's no reason to start wrestling—which happens! Not knowing the rules is no excuse for being rude. And if you lose a ball and do know the rules, simply wave the people behind on as you continue to look for it.

"When you're teeing off, if there's someone else waiting to follow, don't take an excess of practice swings. And once on the fairway, if you're slower than the people behind, a circumstance you can determine by whether or not there's an opening ahead of you, ask them to go thru.

"On the other hand, if the course is moving slowly and there are no open holes ahead, it's not your privilege to go thru the group ahead of you even if you happen to be faster than they are."

Many players, Chamberlain adds, waste too much time on the greens after they've finished putting.

"When you drop your putts," Chamberlain says, "get off the green. And if you're playing a short hole with people on the tee behind you, wave them to hit their tee shots before you start putting out.

"Remember that golf is an 18-hole game, too. If you stop for refreshments at the end of nine, don't come out of the clubhouse and expect to go right off on the 10th hole ahead of others coming from the ninth green. They have the right of way."

Chamberlain feels that too many golfers, both veterans and tyros, forget that golf is a game of relaxation and sportsmanship.

"Never take a chance on driving a ball into anyone," he warns, "either on a blind shot over a hill or because you're trying to hurry them up. It isn't worth the risk of doing serious damage to someone. Occasionally players are hurt by accident and no one is to blame. But to hurt someone because you lose your temper is unforgivable. Shouting the word "fore" isn't the equivalent to taking out a hunting license. It doesn't make it open season on the rest of the players."

Chamberlain, as the master of a 36-hole layout, had plenty of chance to watch both men and women golfers. And he scoffs at the average masculine belief that women are slower than men.

"The average male score is pretty high," he reports, "about 110. So this business about women holding them up is something left over from the old double-standard days. In most cases it turns out the women are being held up by someone ahead of them and can't go any faster."

Chamberlain, a fair-to-middling golfer himself, also suggests that more respect be paid to sandtraps, greens, and the fairway.

"Don't walk thru traps needlessly, and if you won't smooth them out at least take the shortest way to and from your ball. Don't run your carts on the apron of the green, thus wearing it out, and when you leave your cart to begin putting, place it so it's in line with the next tee.

"And on the greens themselves, be careful of scuffing the turf with your spikes. Be careful of dropping the flag or a club so it digs into the putting surface, and on extremely wet days, be careful of walking carelessly and leaving permanent marks. Also when playing to a soft green, be sure to repair the mark left when the ball hits and bites."

This concludes this lesson, except for a brief tip on what to do when you hit a ball out of bounds into someone's newly plowed or planted field or rose garden. The tip: Let the ball go. The error was yours. Don't add discourtesy to a bad shot.

Shoe Man Sizes Up Sports Stars

AL ROBBINS, a native of Manchester, England, who now calls Chicago his home, has been in the shoe business more than a quarter of a century. During that time he's developed a strange compulsion. You mention a famous sports figure (or theatrical or business figure) and—assuming Al ever fitted them with brogans—he automatically states their shoe size.

"Bing Crosby," you say.

"Eight and a half," returns Robbins.

"Patty Berg?"

"Six-B."

"Sam Snead?"

"Nine-C."

"Eddie Arcaro?"

"Five and a half."

"Walter Hagen?"

"Nine."

"Charley Penna?"

"Ten-D."

"Babe Zaharias?"

"Seven and a half-B."

"So-and-so?"

"Leave her out," says Al.

Robbins, whose downtown store resembles a misplaced pro shop, what with a rack of putters, golfing photos on the wall, a bunch of irons in one corner, including some of Ben Hogan's new models, and a putting machine, is himself a hopeless golfing addict who—when he plays regularly—is in the 70s.

Al believes that a golfer's shoes should be fitted to his needs just as his clubs are, or should be chosen for his physique. He thinks it foolish, for example, for an older man, used to light shoes, to climb into a pair of heavy golf shoes and wear himself out just lifting his feet. Al points out that it's possible to remove as much as half a pound from a pair of golf shoes by such devices as hollowing out the heels and using plastic instead of steel spikes.

He feels, also, that most people, both golfers and non-golfers, wear shoes that are too small.

"People should beware of the false comfort of shoes that don't fit," says Robbins sadly. "When a customer comes in and says he should wear an eight and I know he should wear a nine, I have to tell him he doesn't know what he's talking about—in a nice way, of course."

Never have golf shoes fitted when you're wearing heavy socks, because the action of hitting the ball tends to make the shoe stretch in width. And never put shoetrees in a wet pair of shoes, unless you want to stretch them as much as a full size larger. Robbins suggests stuffing a towel or some absorbent paper into each shoe instead.

He also advises using Castile soap for adding to the life of the leather, and avoiding over-polishing, which clogs up the pores of the leather and prevents its breathing. It also is wise to give your shoes a day of rest for each day of use, if you wish maximum service.

Robbins, no stuffy conformist, is delighted with customers who want such exotic (and repellent) items as plaid footgear, or shoes made of unborn calf ($50 a pair), alligator hide, ostrich, ring lizard, python or waterproof seal-skin. He also views with equanimity such shoe colors as blue, yellow, or burgundy, and if you want a flannel inlay to match your socks, just say the word.

Never Laugh At California Greens

THEY USED TO tell us about the golf courses in California, where the greens seemed to tilt one way and the ball rolled the other. And we would laugh and say: "Yeah! Yeah!"

Now we're a believer.

It was our fortune recently to play the Annandale Golf Club at Pasadena with a gentleman named Lathrop Leishman, a descendant of the Clan MacGregor and possessor of that most annoying (to the opponents) of all golfing habits. No hook, no slice, just straight down the middle.

When we reached the first green, we refused to believe the counsel offered either by Leishman or our caddie, Percy, who—we were told—shoots Annandale in the low 70s. Anyone could see that the break was exactly opposite to what my host and Percy advised.

So we putted against their advice and missed the hole about as far as we've ever missed a putt of that length.

One lesson was enough. From then on we listened to the experts and even managed to sink a couple of long and impossible putts, which defied all the laws of gravity to fight their way into the hole. When we expressed disbelief at what we saw, Leishman explained:

"Everything breaks toward the highway," he said, "and away from the mountains."

When someone tells you about those California greens, fellow hackers, believe him. He tells you true.

Annandale winds up and down fairways which would be ideal for cowboy and Indian chases, since there are brush and tree covered hills on each side and the fairways themselves are narrow. Percy told us of one tormented soul who a few seasons ago drove a couple of brand new balls far off the course and into the hilly wilds.

He started off the tee, after finally landing a timid poke on the fairway, and the caddie followed hard in his wake.

"Aren't you going up after those first two?" the startled player asked.

"Snakes up there," said the caddie, continuing to plod ahead.

"You're a helluva caddie," the golfer cried in exasperation.

"You're a helluva golfer," was the placid answer, "to hit the ball up there."

Fellow never did find them, either.

(Reprinted by permission of *The Chicago Tribune*.)

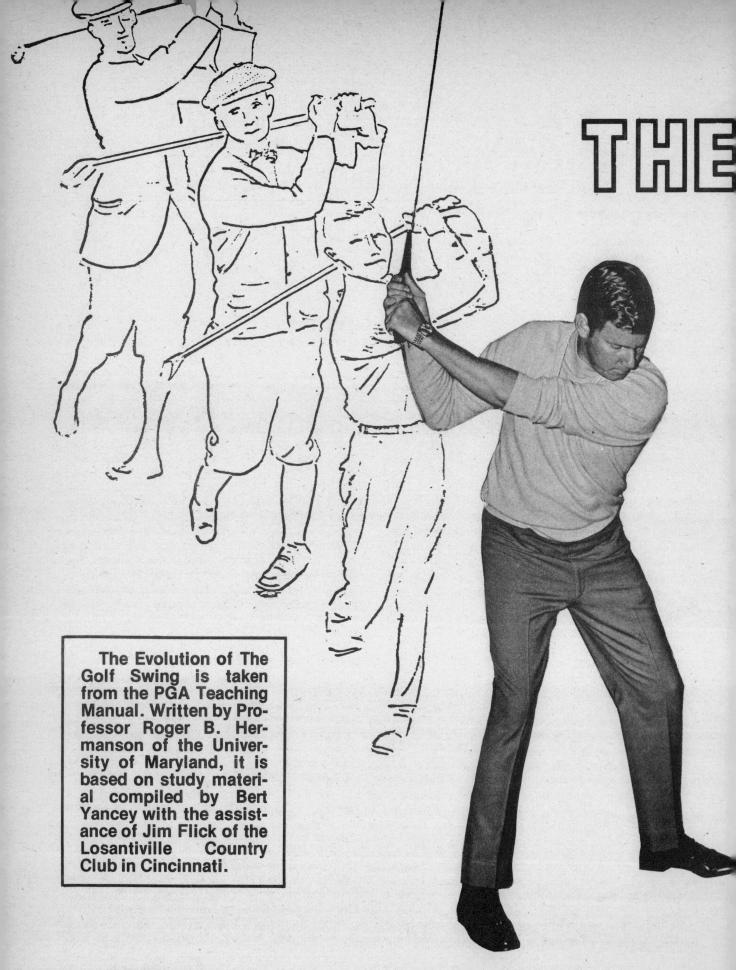

THE

The Evolution of The Golf Swing is taken from the PGA Teaching Manual. Written by Professor Roger B. Hermanson of the University of Maryland, it is based on study material compiled by Bert Yancey with the assistance of Jim Flick of the Losantiville Country Club in Cincinnati.

EVOLUTION Of the GOLF SWING

By Roger B. Hermanson

FROM THE beginning of time man has sought to improve ways of performing certain tasks. Our purpose is to trace the evolution of the golf swing from its beginning, around the middle 1800's, to the present time.

The golf swing did not evolve in a vacuum. Among the important influences were type of clothing worn (a function of both style and weather conditions), type of equipment in use, the playing characteristics of the courses, and the level of communications and exchange of knowledge. In the early days of golf in Scotland the golfer was well bundled against the cold Scottish winds, and he was using clubs with wooden shafts each having different playing characteristics and a very "dead" ball by today's standards. Prior to the first British Open in 1860, golfers had very little intercity or club competition so they could not observe, evaluate, or compare swings of successful players. Therefore, many players developed the style used by the professional and most successful players at their geographical location— so much so that players could be identified by their motion as follows:

St. Andrews—long and flowing motion

Hoylake—open stance, ball played off right leg.

Laidlays—ball played off left leg

No particular orthodox swing had been developed and communicated to others outside a small region.

In contrast, today in the United States, the modern-day golfer is dressed in light clothes that allow maximum freedom of movement, he plays with metal-shafted clubs having a uniformity of playing characteristics and a "live" golf ball, and he has witnessed the swing techniques of the greatest players of the game in person, on television, and in various books of instruction. It would be a wonder, indeed, if the techniques of the golf swing had not changed since the early days of golf.

Golfers throughout the history of the game have sought to improve their standard of play. They watch the great players of their era, read their books, and seek the help of their local professional. They are members of a group who have found frustration, enjoyment, and challenge in the pursuit of the game. How is it, they say, that great players can make such a difficult task look so easy? The simple and fluid motion they so admire is a result of two major factors:

● Years of practice and dedication as illustrated by the touring professional you see on the practice tee.
● The evolutionary process, which throughout time has eliminated unsuccessful methods and preserved those methods which have proven to be successful.

We will now trace the evolutionary process of the development of the modern fundamentals of golf. In the early days of golf when men played golf on difficult courses with golf equipment that was quite different from that used today, the swing techniques were very complicated and very different. Players wore bulky, restrictive jackets that would not allow a free turn of the upper body if the left arm stayed straight. Also, players generally used a flat arc so as to keep the ball low under the wind and have it run on hard ground up to the greens that were bunkered on their sides and would not hold. Clubs had whippy and long shafts and were set flat, all of which encouraged the use of flat wristy motions. These characteristics would be general of most swings prior to the 1890's, although there were many individual differences caused primarily by the lack of communications and the resulting lack of exchange of knowledge.

At this point, Horace Hutchison, highly regarded authority and swing analyst of that era, described the "ideal orthodoxy" of that period. The swing described by Horace Hutchison was as follows:

Grip—Palm grip with thumbs off shaft.

Set Up—Ball in center of stance, left arm bent, both feet turned out so both legs could move considerably.

Take Away—Flat arc, wristy motion to inside, too long (past horizontal).

Top of Backswing—All weight wholly on right leg, (sway), on left toe (heel way up), right elbow flying to position above right wrist, big body turn (hips

HARRY VARDON was the father of the modern style; characteristics included a straight left arm, deep wrist cock instead of flippy wrists, slightly open stance, both hands firm on the club, smooth tempo but with slashing hands from upright plane and shorter arc.

BOBBY JONES was king of the 1920's and was influenced by Vardon but developed his own style based on a more sophisticated body turn, source of power came from long arc and perfect timing; raised up on both toes at impact and hit against a very rigid left side.

and shoulders in unison), club very loose in both hands.

Forward Swing—Little mention is made of this but it was obviously a wristy slashing with the arms to a finish that is flat and upper body forward on left leg, with head moving forward to over the top position.

The Classical Swing

HARRY VARDON

The great Harry Vardon virtually dominated golf in the 1910-1920 era. Vardon is sometimes considered the "father of modern golf" and used a style very common in his day. He illustrates the ancient slashing style of play where the hands and arms dominate the swing. His source of power was his long arms and powerful wrists, and he

depended on perfect timing for long drives of over 200 yards. While Harry Vardon is most famous for his Vardon overlapping grip, he did make other notable contributions to the evolution of the golf swing. His swing characteristics included:

● Both hands firm on club.

● Left arm straight.

● Deep wrist cock instead of loose hands at top.

● Slightly open stance.

● Ball more forward.

● Body rotation—weight staying slightly more centered (straight right knee at top to straight leg at impact)—some body coil.

● Shortened and lightened clubs to get a more upright plane and shorter arc.

● Smooth tempo—but slashing hands resulted in quick turn immediately after impact.

Vardon dominated the game during his era because his style was so well suited to getting the most out of the equipment he used. Professionals of today would not dare imitate his style because of the changes in equipment, clothing, and so on.

Other players around this time made other contributions. Ted Ray popularized the idea of a short backswing with little wrist cock but used a large body sway during the swing.

James Braid used resistance of the legs on the backswing and thus reduced body sway and also used a shorter arc. He was probably the first man to have

BRYON NELSON was the first to dominate the game in the steel shaft era; featured a more upright swing with greater use of the legs on the forward swing; club stayed on the flight path longer after impact; some lateral body motion on backswing.

BEN HOGAN dominated the game in the 1950's and popularized the idea of body tension or torque based on restricted turn of the lower body; introduced the shorter swing with less clubface rotation on the backswing; wonderful use of leg muscles and body dynamics.

the feeling of upper body tension but released it too quickly on the down-swing.

Walter Simpson was one of the first players to keep the right elbow down at the top of the backswing and to not rotate the club on the backswing.

Jim Barnes was the first person to advocate forgetting about the flight path and enter the hitting area with wrists cocked and then release from the inside. He said the proper way to strike a golf ball was to drive the hands down and hit from the inside-out.

BOBBY JONES

The 1920-1930 era clearly belongs to the great Bobby Jones. The influence of Vardon can be seen in Jones' long fluid style, but Jones developed a much more sophisticated body movement. This can be seen in the rotation of his

hips and the alternating rigid movements of the right and left legs. The true source of power in Jones' swing came from the long arc and perfect timing of hands and arms as the body rotated into position for impact. He raised up on both toes and the left side was very rigid at impact. Like Vardon, Jones' swing was perfect for the wooden-shafted clubs he was using. The wooden-shafted clubs had two clearly identifiable characteristics:

● Because each club was handmade each one had a different flex pattern, thus resulting in different playing characteristics. The 5-iron might be much whippier than the 6-iron, and so on.

● The wooden shaft had a great amount of torque (or twisting) during the swing

as compared with the modern steel shaft.

Bobby Jones developed a unique ability to swing the club in such a way that the flex and torque characteristics were minimized. He did this by "throwing" the club with the right side much as Vardon had done so as to allow the clubhead to catch up with the shaft long before impact. To repeat, this action minimized shaft deflection thereby minimizing inconsistency, and also harmonized the amount of torque (or twisting) in each club.

One important difference between what Jones did and what Vardon and others before him did was in the plane of his swing. Jones' swing plane was much more upright, thus much more in the direction of the flight of the ball. This enabled him to "release" the club down the intended flight path at a later moment than did Vardon. Vardon, because he initiated the downswing from a flatter plane had to release quite early in an attempt to get the club on the intended flight path. Jones' release enabled him to maintain body tension to a later moment in his swing. This resulted in high clubhead speed with minimum deflection and torque.

The extent to which Jones had mastered the technique of minimizing shaft deflection and torque is illustrated by a true story he related in an article he wrote. A lady approached the practice tee where Jones was hitting shots in Atlanta, Georgia. She had a club which was shafted with a bull whip and asked Jones to swing it. Bobby obliged, and he said the ball went as far and as straight as any ball he had ever hit. He didn't try to explain how this was possible except to speculate that it must have been due to centrifugal force. It did convince him that he would never discard one of his old clubs merely because the shaft had gone weak. This example would seem to prove that the great success of Bobby Jones can be attributed primarily to his ability to swing a club of any flexibility with good timing. He did this by perfectly applying the right-sided, classical style. He also had an uncanny ability to "feel" the club and thus select a fine set of clubs. For instance, it was not uncommon for Bobby Jones to take 20 different 4-woods to the practice tee to find the one with the perfect feel.

It is interesting to note that although he used a right-sided motion on the downswing he did mention using all left side getting the club back on the backswing.

Jones' major contributions to the evolution of the modern swing were:

● Increased resistance of legs on backswing.

● Less looseness in body movements than Vardon.

● Ball is played more forward in the stance.

● The club is placed on the intended flight path earlier in the downswing.

● More upright swing (in closer to ball).

● Left-side control on the backswing.

● Stayed centered on the ball during backswing rather than shifting weight way to right side.

The Steel Shaft

In the final days of Jones' career, a great change took place in the manufacture of golf clubs. The "steely" feeling that was so widely sought in the wooden shaft induced the production of clubs that actually had steel shafts. With this change in equipment the golfer of the 1930's no longer had to worry about inconsistency of shot making caused by the varying deflections and torque that was so prevalent with handmade wooden-shafted clubs. Now, suddenly, Bobby Jones' ability to achieve consistency in shot making would be achieved to an increased degree by other players using steel-shafted clubs. The severe torque which was so characteristic of wooden-shafted clubs was no longer a problem with the steel-shafted clubs. Although there was still some deflection with the steel-shafted clubs it became an advantage rather than a disadvantage. Deflection without torque enabled the player to combine distance and accuracy. A whole new group of young players was finding a simpler and more powerful way to swing a club.

It took some time for the players to realize the changes in the golf swing that would maximize the benefits of using steel-shafted clubs. Also, Jones was so successful with his method that many great players and teachers tried to use his techniques even though they were more perfectly suited to wooden-shafted clubs. We believe that many of these players had not yet realized that there was a more efficient and simpler way to play effectively with steel-shafted clubs than the old classical style of throwing with the right side with a great body rotation or pivot. It is to their great credit that several of them achieved "star" status in spite of using the classical method with steel-shafted clubs.

The Modern Swing

BYRON NELSON

Byron Nelson was the first player to dominate the game in the steel-shafted era. He was the controlling figure in the late 1930's to late 1940's. He was the first of what we call the modern swingers; those who moved away from the classical method and began using important parts of the swing being used by touring professionals in the 1970's. Nelson used a lateral body shift rather than a rotational movement to obtain maximum accuracy and distance. This could be seen in his flexed right leg, in the backswing, and more specifically in his flexed left leg through impact. This was an entirely new style, and for the first time we see the body moving "in front" of the club. The result was a more upright plane in the backswing because of the lack of hip turn, a more compact backswing, and the club staying on the intended flight path longer after impact.

The specific contributions of Nelson were:

● Increased use of legs on the forward swing.

● More upright swing and a straighter back at position of address.

● Club stayed on the intended flight path longer after impact.

● Less flex and looseness in the left hand at the top of the backswing, thus stressing left-side control.

● Upper body remained back behind left hip at follow through with the left knee flexed at impact and well into the follow through.

● There was some lateral body motion on the backswing to eliminate body rotation of Jones—this produced the beginning of the coil and resistance concepts emphasized by Ben Hogan.

BEN HOGAN

The next great player to dominate golf was Ben Hogan in the 1950's. Ben Hogan popularized the idea of body tension or torque which develops as a result of restricting the lower body turn and maintaining the upper body turn or shoulder turn. In the old classical style, body tension was thought to be destructive, and the complete rotation of shoulders and hips indicated by the raised left heel prevented this tension from developing. However, Hogan says this torque can make the body work like a powerful spring and can be a source of great power.

Hogan also stated that the left wrist should bow out (or supinate) at impact rather than rotate or pronate as it did in the old classical style. This allowed a final surge of power to be released at the last possible moment from in front of the ball, in a pulling motion, and further extended the time that the club remained on the intended line of flight. While Nelson's lateral motion allowed the club to remain on the intended line of flight after impact, Hogan's supination caused the club to arrive on the intended line of flight sooner before impact while still retaining the power for impact.

Hogan's contributions include:

● Shorter swing.

● Left hand moved to a weaker position (especially later in his career).

● Less clubface rotation on the backswing.

● Wonderful use of legs resisting, with great body coil (upper against lower).

● Shaft now being swung dynamically as legs lead forward swing.

● Better explanation of plane—the shaft was worked "up," not "around" at ¾ mark.

● Supination of left wrist at impact.

● Hands less active and use of body and legs gaining importance as evolution begins to unfold even further.

The lower body movement of both Nelson and Hogan necessitated playing the ball more forward in the stance.

As with an evolutionary process you would expect some overlap of the classical and modern swings for some time. We believe that we must mention the great Sam Snead at this point. In our opinion, he is the last great player to use basically the classical style. Although Snead uses some of the modern trends in his swing, the grace and beauty of his fluid motion can best be described as classical because of the great body rotation and the firm, rather than flexible, left side at impact, giving him a rotational, rather than lateral, move at impact.

As the simpler, modern style became more popular, more and more fine players became prominent. It seemed that no longer could one man dominate

the game because the increased communications and improved teaching techniques began to mold all players into this one basic style. Demaret, Burke, Middlecoff, Boros, Bolt, Venturi and many others began to show that the modern swing is best.

ARNOLD PALMER

Then, suddenly, there emerged out of the pack of these fine players one who more than anyone since Hogan began to dominate the game. Could it be that Arnold Palmer had developed a new addition to the modern swing which made him more efficient? One can often be mistaken when making a historical study in the same period that history is being made, but we believe Palmer contributed something very important to the modern swing.

Many players using the modern style of lower body restriction and lateral movement forward to pull the club did so with quite a weak position of the left hand at the top of the swing. This was necessary because of a very strong left hand position in gripping the club at address, which resulted in quite a bit of pronation on the backswing. This could be seen quite clearly in Ben Hogan's swing and especially so early in his career. He found it necessary to adjust the wrist position during the backswing so that it would be in a supinated position before impact. We believe that Hogan weakened his left hand grip at address later in his career.

Palmer's most important contribution was that he greatly simplified the modern swing by setting the left hand in a very "weak" position at address with the back of his hand more directly facing the target, and he set the left hand in a very square or almost bowed out or supinated position at the top of his swing. This action eliminated the necessity for recovery to a supinated or bowed out position before impact. It also served to prevent a whiplash type of result which comes on the downswing when the wrists are pronated on the backswing. The supinated wrists at the top of the swing could also be seen in the swing of Tony Lema, and can be seen in those of Billy Casper and Jack Nicklaus. Gary Player still prefers the pronating position used by Hogan and has had great success with his method. Other than this difference he used the "modern" swing techniques.

ARNOLD PALMER set left hand in a weak position at address with the back of the hand more directly facing the target and set it in a very square position (or supinated) at the top of his swing, eliminating the necessity for recovery to a supinated position before impact.

(Continued on next page)

But we believe the Palmer supinated position at the top to be superior.

It would be a mistake to infer that Arnold Palmer's great success was only the result of a superior playing technique. Mention must be made of his great desire, attitude, and strong mental qualities that are exemplified by the tug on the pants and his "let's charge" philosophy. Besides the competitiveness and mental tenacity of Palmer, he did contribute these physical aspects to the modern swing:

● Left hand in a "weaker" position at address with line formed by thumb and rest of hand pointing approximately toward the chin instead of toward the right shoulder.

● Acceptance of more square position of club as it moves away from the ball on the backswing.

● Supinated left wrist at the top of the backswing. This also meant the clubface was more "closed" at the top.

● Stressed more left-hand control at impact and clubface square to intended line of flight longer.

● Reestablished big shoulder tilt and turn.

Palmer has become a straighter and better driver later in his career as he has reduced his hip turn on the backswing and the legs resisted more on the take away. His take away now promotes better leg muscle activation.

JACK NICKLAUS

The next prominent figure in golf was Jack Nicklaus. In view of the increasing numbers of Tour players, beginning to use the modern, super method, there may never be another golfer who will completely dominate the game for any extended period of time.

Jack Nicklaus' swing seems to incorporate the best in all the modern swings which preceded it. He has the swing plane of Byron Nelson, the leg action of Ben Hogan, and the left-hand position and ball control of Palmer. These characteristics exist in his swing for all to observe, copy, and develop. In our opinion, Nicklaus is the perfect illustration of the complete evolution up to this point in time.

JACK NICKLAUS seems to incorporate all the best features of the earlier style pioneers—Nelson s swing plane, Hogan's leg action and left hand position and ball control of Palmer—and is considered the perfect illustration of the complete evolution up to date.

What Decides Tourney Importance? Money? Tradition? The Field?

By LINCOLN A. WARDEN
(Former *New York Times* Golf Editor)

STATISTICS can reveal both the pleasant and the unpleasant facts of life. We learn with sadness of a friend listed among the weekend total of auto accident casualties. But we smile when a neighbor brings good news that a baby boy arrived weighing 7 pounds, 3 ounces.

Long ago a high school "math" teacher advised his class that the study of statistics could be worthwhile. He suggested that "figures don't lie but sometimes liars figure." At the time our classmates, who included Lou Gehrig, thought the "prof" was either exaggerating or being silly. Yet strangely enough the best known statistic that emanated from that class was one pertaining to Gehrig, who later played 2,130 consecutive games at first base for the New York Yankees, an incredible record.

Golf, of course, has already accumulated an imposing mass of statistics for the record books. This was further substantiated at the beginning of 1976 by the report from the energetic staff of the Tournament Players Division.

In 1976 the prize money total on the tour of $9,073,450, spread over some 44 events, establishes another statistic. A new high of this proportion seemed only visionary a decade ago.

Although there were indications when the $500,000 World Open was first scheduled that a skyrocketing money race might get under way among sponsors, it never materialized. When some of the top name pros failed to enter for the World Open with its $100,000 first prize, it proved that money may be important but it is not necessarily the conclusive lure, should the pros as free agents, decide they don't want to play.

Despite the lack of a gargantuan purse, the World Open is still on the schedule. So are some hefty $300,000 tourneys and an overall attractive 1976 menu with 29 offerings of $200,000 in prize money or more to shoot at.

If the trend has been against gigantic purses, there has been a tendency to add more championships. The U.S. Open, the Masters and the P.G.A., with their prestige, once appeared to monopolize the big league. Now the titled group is expanding, nudging the old stalwarts for room. Commissioner Deane Beman says he believes the new World Series with its international format, will become "*The* Championship." That almost sounds like heresy to the historians. But what will the reaction be of the players and public? The statisticians will be standing by to see.

Another event seeking a prominent spot in the sunshine is the tournament players own championship. Since all top stars are required to compete, it is another title the pros want to win. It is easy to conclude that an ambitious campaigner will be able to find more money and more laurels at home than by testing his skill abroad.

If Beman's prediction comes true, what will it mean to the statistics that establish the Big Four as the traditional gems to win? Will we have to scuttle the time-honored combination of the U.S. and British Opens, the Masters and the P.G.A. for another? With the World Series, will these automatically form a Big Five? Or will one diminish in prestige and drop into the rough, leaving a new style Big Four? Then what about the rating of the T.P.D. championship or the World Open tourney? Are these destined to bring greater glory to their winners?

While the statisticians go to work, they will also have to watch Jack Nicklaus. His influence and impact on golf still are immeasurable. Each time he wins a tournament he adds to its prestige, besides his own. Walter Hagen once dominated the P.G.A. championship by his consistent match play victories. But Big Jack is in his own class and as yet the statisticians haven't been able to keep full stride with him.

Of course, he led the money winners with $298,149 in 1975. But how did he do it? He played only 64 rounds, while most of those who finally joined the low 60 exempt group with him had to play 90 to 100 rounds to make the grade. It meant his rivals sometimes had to finish in the money in four or five more tournaments than he did to qualify automatically for the 1976 tour.

Jack has an advantage with more prestigious tourneys on the schedule. He might now pick up four or five or even six titles. Should he eliminate the British Open and stay at home for the top American events, he would add to the importance of the ones in which he competed. It's easy enough to say "figures don't lie" but neither does Jack's game nor the kind of statistics he will bring to his record this year.

Lee Elder's Masters Journal

WITH PHIL MUSICK

THE FIRST week of April, 1975, was an historic one in sports. Eight teams stayed alive in the NBA playoffs, and for the first time in recent years, none was the Knicks, Lakers or Bucks. Eight teams stayed alive in the NHL playoffs, and for the first time ever, one was the Islanders. Frank Robinson, in his first season as baseball's first player-manager in 15 years and first black manager ever, hit a home run in his first time at bat.

And, perhaps most significantly, down in Augusta, Georgia, a 40-year-old man named Lee Elder became the first black golfer to play in the Masters tournament. He broke the final obvious racial barrier in American sports.

The 1975 Masters was one of the most dramatic ever, and Elder's participation was partly obscured by the finishing drama. But only partly. The people who shared Lee Elder's life in Augusta in the first week of April, 1975, called him by a special name: They called him "History." Here is Lee Elder's diary of his historic week.

Monday

"Georgia, Georgia . . . Georgia on my mind."

I heard that tune on the radio driving to Augusta from Greensboro today. I've had Georgia on my mind for 51 weeks now, since I won the Pensacola Open and qualified for the Masters. Driving here I remembered my first visit to this state some 15 years ago.

My wife, Rose, and I were traveling to a United Golf Association tournament. The "chittlin' circuit," we called it. All black golfers.

Late one night we stopped for gas and I asked the station attendant where the restroom was. The gentleman stuck a shotgun in my face.

"Ain't got no restroom," he said.

My wife Rose said, "That's impossible." She wanted to argue.

But the shotgun barrel looked bigger than a sewer lid and when he yelled, "Git you niggers," I picked Rose up and stuffed her in the car and pulled out of there. It was the only time in our marriage that I was rough with her.

Niggers. Now the niggers were invited to spend a week at the exclusive Augusta National Golf Club. Fifteen years ago the Professional Golfers' Association bylaws read ". . . for members of the caucasian race." Gradually that had changed—and now the Masters.

I couldn't wait to get here. Since I qualified, the world has turned upside down. Suddenly I became a celebrity. Country clubs where they still call the black caddies "boy" wanted Lee Elder, Mr. Lee Elder, for exhibitions. Companies that wouldn't let me get past secretaries when I was searching for sponsors now wanted me for endorsements. And people everywhere wanted me for speaking engagements. I felt obligated to go everywhere. I was making history in the eyes of many blacks. I had a responsibility. But I became so involved with my responsibilities, that golf became something I did in my spare time.

I appeared on the Sammy Davis Show. I got a good connection with the

Little David Golf Tool company. There were also other endorsements. But when you endorse golf products, you don't just sign your name and cash the check. You talk to sales managers. You play a round with the vice president in charge of marketing. You have dinner with the president. You shake a lot of hands. When you're shaking hands or correcting some sales manager's slice, you're not out there with a new set of irons trying to figure why the hell you can't get any height on the three-iron.

Then I was knee-deep into my own tournament. It's not some ego-massage for me. I have a scholarship fund and it costs us $5,000 a year to sponsor a kid in college. To make the tournament pay off, you have to bring in celebrities. You don't just call up Flip Wilson and say, "Hey, baby, come in, we need you." A man like that has commitments. We had to work on that. This year we had a guy named Gerald Ford in the tournament. Nobody can call the White House and say, "Send the President over Saturday at 12:20. Every-

thing—the endorsements, the exhibitions, the speaking engagements, my tournament—took time. I knew I was gambling on my game staying sharp. But after Pensacola, I decided to take that gamble.

Funny thing is, if it hadn't been for Rose, I wouldn't have even gone to Pensacola. A few days before I was to leave I went to the track. The ponies got me. Cleaned me out. I lost every dollar I had in my pocket. I called Rose and told her to call the Pensacola people and tell them Lee Elder died on the backstretch.

"Honey," she argued, "you better go down there. You're playing good. You might win." I hadn't won anything in 7 years. She talked me into going. Rose the Prophet, we call her now.

I beat Peter Oosterhuis in a playoff and Cliff Roberts—he's the Masters committee chairman—got a monkey off his back. For years reporters had been asking why the only blacks at Augusta National were in the kitchen or at the ball-washers.

When a writer called to ask him if he knew who was coming to Augusta National, Mr. Roberts said he thought I'd be a credit to the tournament. Like Joe Louis was to his race, I guess. "We're pleased Lee Elder is the first representative of his race to qualify because he's been a fine player for a number of years," Mr. Roberts said. "He's quite likely to make a fine showing."

He hasn't seen me play lately. Realistically, I can't hope to win here. No rookie ever has. Lord, I'd love to though. I'd love to slide into that green jacket and wear it to dinner in the Grill Room. Order ham hocks and black-eyed peas.

But winning's not the goal. First, there's too much pressure. I'm not nervous—the people around me are—but I feel the intensity. I can measure it in demands on my time. I've been interviewed by every publication from *Golf World* to the Congressional Record.

Then there's the course. Sort of a leafy Godzilla. Like no other tournament in the world. A different league. I want to finish in the top 24 and come here again without being looked at like a tarantula on a slice of angel-food cake. I want to be a golfer, not a symbol, not a cause, not an integrator.

I don't want this to be a one-time thing. I don't want people to remember me as, "Lee Elder? Oh, yeah, the black guy that played in the Masters one time."

I've wanted this for a long time. All those years on the UGA tour. The hustling. A long time. But I wanted to qualify, to belong here—and I made it.

The course is lush. It looks like they chipped off a corner of Bora-Bora. Azaleas and wisteria everywhere; Georgia pines sticking their fingers up into the sky. Everything is tasteful. I get the chills looking at it. I think about the courses I had to play when I was younger—bare tees and burnt fairways and sand greens. And now here I am, little old Lee Elder off the scrub courses of Dallas, walking Augusta National. When I think about that, I can't even swallow.

There's a dignity here you don't often see. The place keeps a low profile. The Augusta National listing in the phone book isn't even in bold-face type. Old South cool.

I slipped out onto the back nine about 4:30. Nobody tried to lynch me. I'd wondered about how the gallery would react. But the people treated me like the other golfers and I must have signed a couple of hundred autographs. One lady said, "Mr. Elder, we're delighted to have you here. I hope you win."

Me, too, Ms. Dixie Belle. Keep the faith.

Once I hit a duck-hook out of the fairway and four people applauded. These people seem genuine. Oh, there are a few rednecks. I got a look or two. *What you doin' here, boy?* But nothing like the back nine at Greensboro. George Foreman wouldn't be safe there. Fans sit and drink beer in the hot sun all day. When they see a black golfer, it gets a little ugly.

Several reporters wanted to talk as I walked the course, but I stalled them. Tomorrow I'm holding a press conference. Later somebody said, "History came to Augusta today, but History wasn't talking."

I ate dinner late—at a restaurant called The Green Jacket.

Tuesday

I wore green to the course this morning. Hubie Green and I wear it all the time, feeling green draws green. Or at least hoping green draws green. I'll wear it again Sunday. It'll go nice with the coat.

It rained some this morning—fine old Masters tradition, I understand. The greens were slower than they'd been yesterday. I was paired with John Mahaffey and Lu Liang-Huan.

The round went pretty well for a guy who hasn't had much time for golf lately. I had a couple of birdies early and that's always a nice way to start.

I spent the round today getting a feel for the course. There's no time to learn it properly. What I have to do is get an instinct for it. The course isn't that long, but it's subtle. They call 11, 12, and 13 Amen Corner. On TV it doesn't look so difficult. But that's on TV. You could easily put three or four shots in the water on 11 and 12.

If you don't putt well on the entire course, you need a calculator to keep score. The greens are that treacherous. A lot of putts break twice.

Tom Weiskopf was telling me they put the pins in places you'd never expect them. He says there are several holes you can par the first three days, then on Sunday be praying for a double bogey if your approach shot ends up in the wrong place. His caddy told me, "Defense. You always have to be on defense in the Masters."

One thing you need is a high ball, which is what a lot of guys have when they come off the course. Seriously, you have to hit it high to hold these greens. Great. I've always been a low-iron player. I got some new irons, and bent them to get more height.

That's the only change I've made. Everyone says you can't play here without a hook, but I'm going to try. I have a tendency to duck hook, so I'll play my usual fade and pray a lot.

Without being familiar with the course, I scored well today. Even three-putting 18, I had a one-under 71. I'd settle for that on Thursday. But I can play well here. I know it. The course is just not that tough unless they get tricky with the pin placements.

After finishing my round, I went into the press building for the press confer-

ence. Rose had scheduled it for 3 o'clock and the building was full. No new questions though.

Someone asked me who I was playing for and I told him, "Rose and Lee Elder . . . and a few creditors." I don't think blacks are looking at me as some kind of saint. I know there's a statue downtown here inscribed, "No nation ever rose so white and so proud." But I'm just a golfer who happens to be black and qualified like everyone else. My attitude doesn't seem to bother too many local people except James Brown, the singer. He owns a radio station here. He went on the air and said I'm all wrong, that I'm playing for all blacks. I wonder if he sings for all blacks.

I wasn't Flip Wilson, but the interview came off OK. I'd have stayed four hours if they'd wanted me to. But now I've got to quit talking and get back to playing, the way I *can* play. I wish another black guy had qualified. Maybe they'd be after him then.

I need time. The year's rushed by too quickly. My mind's tired. Too many decisions. Too many questions. Too many emotions. Tears at Pensacola when I won. Pride at being the first black man here. Anxiety about the galleries.

Rose is holding up fine. I was concerned about that. I wondered if she'd be lonely. If I would be. But the house we rented is full of friends. A smiling face can sometimes help you forget a missed 4-footer. If I want to play blackjack, my attorney, Reuben Payne, is ready. And if I want a little sweet potato cobbler, it's right there.

An insurance company here in Augusta held a reception for me tonight at a downtown hotel. Almost a thousand people there. I was tired, but I enjoyed it. Made a little speech. Smiled some more. Fellow offered to do our cleaning free here. Won't he be surprised when he gets a basketful tomorrow?

Wednesday

An Oldsmobile dealer I do some work for in Washington had some "Good Luck, Lee" buttons and bumper stickers sent down. I was holding a button and someone reached out to shake hands. The pin almost went through the middle finger of my right hand. An hour later, my finger

was sore and stiff. Wonder if that's a bad omen.

I was tired this morning, so Rose and I sat around drinking coffee. I didn't go to the course until noon. Did some putting and took my 7-iron out to the practice tee instead of wrapping it around a Georgia pine, which I considered briefly. My caddy, Henry Brown, was a big hit at the putting green. He's a one-handicapper, but plays at scratch in interviews. Reporters been talking to him all over the course. Maybe we ought to switch around and I'll carry the bag. When this gets to crunch tomorrow, I'm going to need him. He's Mr. Roberts' caddy.

Today it was mostly for laughs in the Masters Par-Three tournament. I shot a two-under 25 playing with Gene Sarazen and a buddy of mine, Jim Colbert.

I went back to the practice tee afterwards and worked some on my 7-iron. I'm a good iron player. Today I had problems with the seven. I *never* have problems with the seven. But I've played too little golf recently. Think I straightened it out. The three's the one I can't hit now.

I *knew* this week was going to be OK when the cook at the house we rented served us a great dinner—sweet potato cobbler, collards, corn bread and ham. Bet no Masters rookie ever had soul food for dinner.

Then we went off to church, to the Greater Mt. Canaan Baptist Church. The preacher was inspired. "It's been a long time coming, Lord," he prayed. "A *long* time. Now this man, Lee Elder, is here to play in the Masters. Tomorrow, a black man will walk on that country club course . . . right here in Augusta. Lord Jesus, be in his arms and his hands and in his feet and in his heart. Lord, give that little white ball eyes so that it might see its way."

Amen.

Thursday

The big day. Teed it up at 11:50. Me and The Machine—Gene Littler. Glad to be paired with him. He doesn't say much, but when he opens his mouth, it's worth hearing.

I hope the last shot I hit on this course is as good as the first one. I held my breath and let out the shaft on No. 1. The ball landed about 260 yards away, right down the middle of the fairway.

I looked around to see how Flip Wilson had liked it but he wasn't in the gallery. He'd told Rose he was going to show up on the first tee today dressed as Geraldine. Roberts would've loved that. Making a mockery of the grand old game.

Anyway, Flip was a no-show, but Jim Brown and Leroy Kelly were there. For a while, I thought old History was going to put on a show. Nerves and all. I wasn't putting well, but the last two days I'd hit the ball pretty fair. Now I'd find out how much the year since Pensacola had hurt my game.

Would four speeches a week take 15 yards off my drives? Would I slice an iron shot for every five cocktail parties where I'd listened to some sales manager's wife talk about *her* slice? Would I jab too many short putts because golf's in your head as much as your hands and my head hadn't been in the right place for too long?

The smoker I'd hit on No. 1 set me up for an 8-foot putt for a birdie, but I rimmed it. Next hole, I stayed hot. Ran a wedge across the fringe and holed out a 15-footer for a birdie. One more and maybe I'd make the leader board.

There was a burst of thunder after my bird on two. Someone told my lawyer, "that's Bobby Jones up there kicking the tee markers."

Some guy talking to Reuben said, "Elder birdies three, there'll be lightning all over the course." No danger. My putting went sour. I blew short putts for bogeys on No. 4 and No. 8. Littler kept talking to me about the course. Little things. Take your time. Think it out. Watch your tee shot here, your approach there. He was a help. Wish he could've putted for me, though.

I scrambled pretty good, making the turn just one-over. Maybe I could slide through. I was hitting it good off the tee and my irons were holding up. A birdie here and there, I'd get done what I'd planned. Play par golf. Hang in the first two days, then try to make a move.

I played Amen Corner in par, and on the 15th hole, I had a chance to get even. It's the hole everybody remembers because Gene Sarazen made his famous double-eagle there in 1935. I'll remember it as the hole where Lee Elder made a decision that was for the birds 40 years later.

It's a par-five, 520-yard, straight-

shot birdie hole. In five swings, you ought to par anything man-made. But on this par-five, you have to think before you hit. Should you drive the water hazard on your second shot or lay up in front? I decided to lay up.

I'd made a mistake. A two-shot mistake. I could've hit the green in two and been in position for a birdie. I know it. Only I looked at the water too hard.

I layed up nicely and had a sand wedge to the green, but I missed it and ended halfway up the bank between the water and the green. Lovely. Another wedge . . . 8 feet short of the pin. I missed the putt. Bogey.

They say you can play from tee to green on memory but that you've got to concentrate to putt. I didn't concentrate on 16. Two-over.

I went the Sahara route on 18. Into one trap, out of it, into another. I'm going to have to talk to Henry. That was the umpteenth time today I was underclubbed. But the old putter steadied up on 18. I snaked in a tricky little putt and it was done. A two-over 74. Not good, but not bad for a rookie with historical overtones.

In the press building, I told the writers I hadn't been nervous. And after the first hole, I hadn't. Nerves didn't shoot that 74. Mistakes did. I should've gone for it on 15. But I'd been underclubbed all day and that water hazard had looked like the Indian Ocean.

I tried to attack the course. It fought back, and when you bogey par-fives instead of birdieing them, some of the fight goes out of you. Tomorrow I'll be more aggressive. Knock a stroke off that 74 tomorrow and Old History will make the cut. I didn't come down here to miss the cut. Maybe not to win. That's dreaming. But not to miss the cut.

Friday

As I was saying, you have to putt well here. I didn't again today. And I was still underclubbed. I should've fired Henry after yesterday. Henry's a one-handicap golfer, but a bigger handicap as a caddy. I hate knocking caddies, being that I've only carried 10,000 or so bags myself over the years. For Henry Brown, I'm going to make an exception.

Henry didn't knock me out of the Masters. He nudged me out. You have to have correct distances on a golf

Lee Elder and his wife Rose

course, especially on one you don't know. A golfer expects to be able to ask a caddy for the distance to the pin from anywhere on the course and get it. Otherwise, you take a risk of injuring the spectators. Or worse, underclubbing.

All day I'd ask Henry, "How far from here?" He'd miss it by 10 or 15 yards. That made for some long putts. I wanted to fire him and I got talked out of it. My mistake.

On No. 1, I drove into the left rough. The ball snuggled up to a pine tree and I couldn't reach it right-handed. I turned a four-iron around and hit it left-handed with the back of the blade. Neat, huh? Bogey. On the next hole, my putter bit me some more. Bogey. On seven, I buried a shot in a bunker. A bogey . . . for Henry. I was underclubbed. On nine, I faded my approach into the gallery. Bogey.

It was all over for Old History before the turn. The back side was better, but I was in at 78, for 152. I'd missed the cut by a mile.

Back to the press building. Smile still in place. Told them they wouldn't have Lee Elder to kick around any more. Got almost as big a laugh as my game did.

One of the writers said, "You don't seem disappointed about your play." I told him, "I've played that way before." I wonder what he thought I was going to do. Cry? Come down here and keep my cool for a week, then blow it on the way to the parking lot?

Sure I'm disappointed. I wanted to take the Masters by the neck and strangle it. Not for some cause. Not for money. Just to do it because playing golf is what I do best.

But it didn't happen. I feel bad. A lot of blacks were pulling for me. Lots of whites, too. But History missed the cut.

Sunday

Washington, you never looked so good. Didn't do much today except refill the Kleenex box. Rose and I had a long talk. Seemed like we hadn't been alone in years.

The Masters was a letdown for both of us. We'd looked forward to going there for so long. Then I played so poorly. Rose and I are a team. She runs the business end. I should run the golf end so well.

We went over the whole year and asked each other a thousand questions. Should we have gone to Augusta earlier? Yes. Spent more than a week getting used to the course? Definitely. Maybe longer. Should we have checked out the caddy situation further? I blew that one.

What could we have done that would've sharpened my game? More practice. Maybe hold the press conference at Greensboro. Did we handle the whole year wrong? I don't think so.

In the afternoon I watched the final round on television. It was a fantastic finish. Greatest thing I ever saw in sports. Nicklaus, Miller and Weiskopf coming to the wire.

Wish I was there. Next year.

Best of Chick's Records Has Meant College for Thousands

GOLF, ILLINOIS—Five thousand dollars . . . what to do with it?

You say it's an easy problem. Well, Charles Evans, Jr., famed in the golfing world as Chick Evans, faced just such a problem 59 years ago.

The answer wasn't easy. But Chick's answer proved to be a wonderful break for the youth of America.

It resulted in the Evans Scholars Foundation. This organization, nationally hailed as "Golf's Favorite Charity," has made possible a four-year college education for more than 4,000 boys.

Let's go back to that $5,000. Chick Evans received it in a way familiar to those who have seen modern-day stars like Arnold Palmer and Jack Nicklaus realize a tremendous income from royalties and endorsements.

Over a span of several years, Evans was ranked by many as the world's finest golfer. Chick became the first player to win all four major titles of his era. These were the USGA Open, the Western Open, the USGA Amateur and the Western Amateur. He also was the first to win the USGA Open and the USGA Amateur in the same year.

For a golfer of that stature, the $5,000 came to Chick Evans in a routine manner. He made a series of phonograph records

giving golf instruction, and the money represented his royalties.

Why the problem with the $5,000?

One reason: To accept this money for himself would mean giving up his amateur status. That was not in Chick's plans then. Nor is it today. He remains the dean of America's amateur golfers.

"I guess the question first came up back in 1916," Chick relates. "Within minutes after I won the National Open, I had several very lucrative offers to turn professional. My mother and I talked it over, and we decided that I would remain an amateur—forever."

As a result, Chick never held the $5,000. It went to a bank, was placed in escrow, and was joined by additional money which materialized in similar fashion.

What to do with this money?

Chick gives all the credit to his mother for the solution:

Since the money came from golf, she insisted that it go back to golf. She believed that it could be used to help caddies, by sending some outstanding boys to college.

"It was all her dream, her idea," Chick relates.

The dream turned into a reality in 1930. Chick was close to the men of the Western Golf Association (he won WGA's Western eight times between 1909 and 1923). He asked WGA to take the money, set up a caddie-scholarship program and administer it.

That was the original concept. It still is in effect today.

Evans Scholarships are awarded to those who have outstanding caddie records, who have shown college ability by ranking in the upper 25 per cent of their class and who cannot afford college otherwise.

The first two Evans Scholars were appointed in 1930; in 1975 the 4,000th Evans Scholar was selected. There are 867 Evans Scholars currently enrolled at 27 universities across the nation. Approximately 230 new Scholars are appointed every year.

An Evans Scholarship is a grant, not a loan. It covers full tuition and housing and is renewable for four years. The average value of each grant is about $4,500. To insure the caddie scholars of a well-rounded education with all the advantages of fraternal living, the Evans Scholars Foundation has purchased its own Chapter Houses at 14 midwestern universities. These Chapters, which range in size from 93 to 32 Scholars, are at Northwestern, Marquette, Wisconsin, Minnesota, Illinois, Michigan, Michigan State, Ohio State, Purdue, Miami of Ohio, Colorado, Missouri, Kansas and Indiana.

This unique program, blending sports and education, is supported by the contributions of individual golfers—more than 87,000 contributors in 1975 alone. It offers all golfers an opportunity to give back to "the game of a lifetime."

Chick's dream spread throughout the country. A total of 28 golf associations now sponsor caddie-scholarship programs. Fifteen of these are grouped under the WGA banner in the Evans Scholars Foundation.

All this has given a unique twist to Chick Evans' own place in golf history. He compiled one of the great playing records, still is a durable competitor today at 85 and has been given every honor, every possible recognition which the game offers.

Yet, Chick Evans is destined to be remembered equally well by golf historians as the father of caddie scholarships.

Are Forgings Being Cast Out?

Text and photos by Will Hertzberg

EVER SINCE the California aerospace slump of 1970-71, and the ensuing glut of available investment casting houses, there has been a battle raging between iron manufacturers for control, or at least their healthy chunk of the potential club sales represented by over 11 million golfers in the United States alone.

The competitors are broken into two distinct groups—the forgers and the casters (further elaborated upon in the accompanying sidebar). Forging has been the traditional method of iron manufacturing since the period of King James I almost 400 years ago. Annual production of forged heads outnumbers cast heads 15 million to 6 million, with the majority of cast heads in top quality lines. Iron casting via the ancient "lost wax" technique, which has been highly sophisticated in recent years from the crude samples produced by early Egyptians and even primitive tribes in Africa today, started in the early 1950s. Pioneers such as Bob McClelland laid the groundwork for what would eventually become an explosion in the 1970s. Prior to the late 1960s and early 1970s, the investment casting process had been used almost exclusively in the production of aerospace parts, jewelry and bridgework.

As the advanced investment casting technology utilized in the production of aerospace parts began rubbing off on the iron manufacturers, a whole new field opened up for the budding entrepreneur. For once the little guy got a break. No longer was it necessary to invest millions of dollars in machinery, toolings and a plant, nor was a lengthy production run of every design necessary to amortize the costs, as it was in forging. For as little as $25,000 to $50,000 an individual could now be in the manufacturing business; working out of his basement or two-car garage. That may sound like an exaggeration, but remember, today's multi-million dollar companies such as Lynx, Ping and Confidence, were yesterday's struggling enterprises.

The tremendous fanaticism over golf in Japan was also instrumental in spurring investment cast iron production in the United States, particularly in Southern California. In fact, by 1973, approximately 30% of all investment cast irons manufactured in the United States were being shipped to Japan.

This lure of additional foreign sales turned mild-mannered businessmen into overnight fanatics. Golf companies began springing up faster than toadstools in wet moss, with each firm boasting the latest in revolutionary investment cast design. In 1971, there were 30 different companies selling one or more lines of investment cast irons; now there are 90!

However, during the last 18 months, the Japanese market has dwindled to accepting only approximately 5% of the total U.S. production, retailers have found themselves overstocked with high inventories and many manufacturing plants are working at only 50% of their production capability. With the added burden of an unstable economic future and spiraling inflation, many of the smaller companies who got into the picture on the crest of the tidal wave, are now slowly suffocating in the residual foam. A thinning out of companies appears inevitable, with only the strongest likely to survive in competition with the forgers.

As it has been from the beginning, most of the competition for sales between the forgers and casters has been in the top quality of "pro-line" models. The cost of raw castings versus raw forgings ($2.75 to $3.10 vs. 50¢) makes the top quality cast iron too expensive to be accepted as a store line product, distributed through department and discount stores. Finished investment cast irons usually retail for about 15-20% more than comparable quality forged irons. The difference in price is mainly attributed to the greater amount of hand labor involved in the production of an investment cast head over a forged one. Shafts and grips vary little in cost from manufacturer to manufacturer.

Other than the obvious difference in cost, the major factor that the consumer must take into consideration is the relative quality of the finished product. And here is where the forgers and casters are sharply divided. The forgers feel they've been maligned, and unfairly trampled upon during the casting explosion of the 1970s, while the casters contend that there are few advantages in a forging over a casting—other than the cost factor.

To get a better picture of the forging

versus casting controversy, and to obtain comments on the state of iron production in the United States, we talked with industry influentials including: Carl Ross, founder of Lynx Precision Golf Company; Bob Mader, founder of Confidence Golf Company, Bob McClelland, general manager of Fansteel; Phil Skovronski, the most prolific designer of top quality investment cast irons in the world; and Ed Holmwood, a 15-year-veteran with Cornell Forge Company, one of the two major producers of forged irons in the United States.

The following are discussions I had during a three month span.

W.H.: What are the major advantages in a cast iron over a forged one?

ROSS: In my opinion, castings represent a much better product because of the closer tolerances that the casting system allows. With a cast club you can cast a hosel hole into the club and the wall thickness of the hole remains the same all around the hosel, resulting in a perfect hole every time. When you drill a hosel, which you have to do on a forged head, out of 10 heads you'll get four good ones, four fair ones, and two bad ones. You're going to get 20% bad heads every time you drill hosel holes. Then they put those heads right into the top line clubs; I would never do that. You can get a cast head to weigh within two grams of what you want it to weigh; with a forged head, you can only get it about as close as ½-ounce (14 grams).

McCLELLAND: Advantages of a forging over a casting other than price? I say absolutely nothing!

SKOVRONSKI: Everything about a casting is better and more advantageous to the manufacturer except for one thing: cost. You get more consistently accurate specifications.

MADER: The main point of an investment casting over a forging is the consistency between one iron and another, because if you make masters up and do them right, you can get every one of them exact in every detail.

HOLMWOOD: McClelland has done a great job of promoting his product for nothing through articles (and if I had been that clever I would be patting myself on the back), so I'm not stabbing him. But the advantages that are talked about in the articles are not advantages to the consumer; they're advantageous to the manufacturer.

(Continued on page 93)

INVESTMENT CASTING

The laborious art of investment casting an iron head begins with an original idea or design, which has usually been drawn and then sculptured in clay or wood. From this original, a bronze or aluminum master is machined to exacting specifications. What results is a metal replica of the designer's original conception. From the metal masters, a skilled craftsman, such as Bob Mader or Phil Skovronski, will produce epoxy or aluminum molds, identical in every way to the metal masters. For creating a set of 11 metal masters and molds (which are manufactured in two pieces, split down the center), designers such as Skovronski usually charge anywhere from $12,000 to $20,000. Once the molds have been manufactured, they are sent to a casting house, such as Bob McClelland's Fansteel operation, where the processes continue. Wax, heated to 130-135 degrees Fahrenheit, is injected into the mold through a small hole in the bottom. This wax fills the hollow area inside the mold, which was designed after the original metal master of the iron head. After the wax has cooled (about one minute), the mold is opened and the wax iron head replicas are removed and inspected for blemishes. This wax replica is exact in every detail to what the finished product will be, including loft, lie, static weight, and scoring. The wax replicas are usually grouped together in what is referred to as a "case, cluster or tree,"—five to seven replicas attached to each other for the purpose of convenience throughout the rest of the process. The cluster is next dipped in a ceramic slurry (about the consistency of pea soup) and then sprinkled with refractory sand to cover all areas that have previously been wetted in the slurry. The cluster is then allowed to dry overnight. This process is repeated for seven days until a ceramic-like shell about 3/16-inch thick is built up around the cluster. Once the clusters have gone through their dipping and drying routine, they are placed in an auto-clave (a device which resembles a cross between a laundromat dryer and a pressure cooker), where under heat, steam and pressure, 98% of the wax replica is melted away and runs out the pouring sprue (a hole in the hosel area). After the melting occurs, all that remains is a cavity encapsulated in the ceramic shell. The hollow ceramic clusters are next cured in massive ovens and immediately filled with molten stainless steel. After cooling, the ceramic is simply knocked off with a hammer. What results is an investment cast iron head, perfect in every detail to the original metal master. After the heads are cut apart from the cluster, they are sand blasted, heat treated, sand blasted again, categorized, inspected, then ground and polished if the client so desires.

FORGING

As with investment casting, the forging process begins with a metal master which is delivered to the forging house. From the original master, a series of dies are fashioned to correspond with the club's configuration. The head itself (made from 10-30 carbon steel) begins as a round bar of metal about one inch in diameter and six inches long. This bar is heated electrically to 2,235 degrees Fahrenheit, before being placed between the dies. With the aid of a 2,000-pound ram, the steel is sequenced through four cutting and shaping operations, one a little more precise than the last, leading up to the final blows which are done in the finishing impressions. It is usually the responsibility of the individual manufacturer to drill, polish, chrome plate and score the head after it leaves the forging facility. Traditionallyn the forging house supplies only the raw heads which have been trimmed of excess flash, inspected and placed into general weight categories (plus or minus 1/16-ounce).

The Investment Casting Process

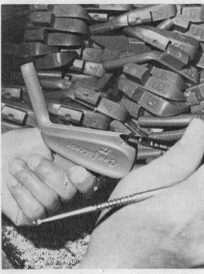

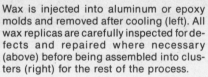

Wax is injected into aluminum or epoxy molds and removed after cooling (left). All wax replicas are carefully inspected for defects and repaired where necessary (above) before being assembled into clusters (right) for the rest of the process.

Wax clusters are dipped in silica slurry, and covered with a special sand.

Under heat and pressure, wax inside clusters is melted away in an auto-clave.

Ceramic clusters are cured in massive ovens before being filled with steel.

Raw stainless steel castings after ceramic is knocked off clusters.

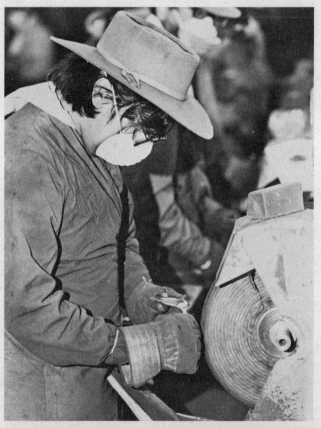

After stainless steel cools and ceramic is removed, clubs are cut off cluster.

Skilled hands grind and polish each stainless steel iron head to perfection.

Now what difference does it make to me as a consumer *when* the club gets scored? The fact that there is a tight weight tolerance on the castings . . . what does that matter to me as a consumer? I can get that same precise weight, if not closer, by buying a good line of forgings, because they've been ground to a precise weight, and they're weighed two or three times in the manufacturing cycle. I have no fault with castings. I just happen to think that if you're going to pay $35 for something, then somebody, somewhere, in the manufacturing process should assure me that I'm hitting the ball with a flat face. Investment cast faces are not terribly flat, and if you don't believe me, take a straight edge and go out to one of the pro shops in your area and put it across the face, and if I'm wrong, I'll buy you a dinner.

W.H.: A recent survey of touring pros shows that over 90% are still using forged clubs. If the cast clubs are indeed better in most respects, or at least more consistent, why haven't the pros taken up the banner for castings?

ROSS: The guys on the tour can hit anything. The forgings they use are not the forgings the consumer can buy in the golf shop . . . and that's what Cornell won't tell you. However, the cast club that the pros use is the same cast club that any man can buy in the golf shop. But the pro using forged clubs is getting a *hand-made* set, which costs the manufacturer $300 to $400 to make.

McCLELLAND: It's the old witches tale that says that the forged iron is a little softer and the ball comes off a little differently. The younger player who is not involved with the old ways of thinking knows no difference.

MADER: Well, you look at the guys on the tour, the guys who put the tee down for money, and most of them are using forged irons. They say it's a softer feel. Whether it is or not, who knows? They hit 10 buckets of balls a day, and I hit 10 buckets a year. I can't feel the difference when I hit a forging, but they might be able to tell the difference. The average golfer doesn't have to worry about that. He only has to worry about having an iron that's well-designed, well-engineered, and that *he* gets better performance out of.

W.H.: How much consumer buying is based on cosmetics and/or prestige in the golf club industry?

HOLMWOOD: The real appeal for the casting is that snob appeal. I went to the PGA merchandise show and was quite amazed at the techniques the manufacturers were using to attract attention to the pro. They were selling back design. Which is fine, and all well and good if you are going to make it a fixture in your office. I think the other side, the face side is what is more important to the golfer.

MADER: There's a lot to the psychological, and there is a lot of prestige too. When a guy drives up to the country club with Lynx or Ping or Confidence in his bag, everybody knows that he takes the game seriously. He put out a couple of bucks; he didn't walk up with a Pennys' or a Sears' brand. They know that he got the best shaft, the best grip, and the most expensive head that can be made. There's a little bit of care that goes into making the set up. If he orders a D-2, he gets a D-2. You know, there's a lot to be said about that.

McCLELLAND: I have manufactured about 120 parts in every lunar module that went to the moon. It's ironic, but what's on the moon has less cosmetic qualities than the golf club. One pit on a golf club negates it as a saleable item. It's far more critical in its cosmetic values than anything I've ever made in my life. There's seven grams difference between one club and another; two grams is a swingweight.

W.H.: How do you feel about the current state of advertising in the golf industry? Are false claims being made by golf club manufacturers, and if so where does that leave the consumer?

SKOVRONSKI: The public just buys what it says on the advertising. If it says it'll go farther, they buy it.

ROSS: The consumer does have a problem. It's confusing as hell, and I'm the first one to admit that. We call our advertising 'dumb, honest advertising.' You'll never see us saying in our ad that 'Our club will hit it farther.' We don't talk like that. That's B.S. I don't believe in lying. We just try to tell the consumer that we have a super fine product. I don't believe in all that noise that some of the companies are making—'Our golf club will do this', and 'our golf club is shank proof.' It's all crap. It eventually catches up with you. I just don't believe in that. I'm not a promoter; I'm a merchandiser. The consumer is getting smarter and the

people who are using all these fancy words with their advertising are going to get clobbered.

McCLELLAND: There ought to be a Ralph Nader of the golf business to stop this B.S. Ninety-nine percent of what you read advertised about golf clubs is a little bit of B.S. It's absolutely terrible what some of these companies come out with for claims. It's totally untrue. Total lies. I think the public likes to be fooled.

W.H.: With so many brands of clubs currently on the market, how does the poor consumer know what to look for?

HOLMWOOD: The consumer isn't going to be able to tell the difference between a casting and a forging with the untrained eye. Forging represents value in terms of workmanship and quality of all the particular parts. Obviously the shaft that goes into a casting and the shaft that goes into a forging are identical quality. The grip can be identical quality. What we are talking about is the difference in the head, what it weighs, how accurate it is in terms of lie and loft. It's pretty tough for the consumer without any knowledge to tell the difference. What he ought to demand is that there's an orderly sequence in the weight of golf clubs from the 2-iron to the wedge, that they swingweight the same, that they have flat faces, and basically after that it is the eye appeal that is the most important thing. The problem is what is grabbing the grip, not what's below the grip. You can swingweight a telephone pole to D-1, but can you swing it?

McCLELLAND: "I'm sure that there's not just one good golf club, but that there are probably 10 good golf clubs. People buy golf clubs because they have an extra dollar or they think it will help their golf game. Golf is a disease, it's a way of life. It's an impulse buy. Theoretically, if you buy a set of golf clubs, you should be able to play them the rest of your life. But people don't think that way.

W.H.: What can we look for in the years to come as far as investment casting versus forging and the designs that emerge from both processes?

SKOVRONSKI: There isn't anything different today that can be done to the back of a golf club that will have any effect on its performance. It's all gingerbread.

McCLELLAND: Normally investment

cast irons aren't something you change year to year like forgings used to be. After you get to a certain point in a golf club, there really isn't much more you can do to the design of that club as far as its hitability, unless you become ridiculous. The exception to the case is the Slinger. In the future you'll see a more rounded sole to prevent heel catching and thus hooking. More people are moving toward shaft in hosel designs because of scares of breakage from poor heat treating.

HOLMWOOD: I'm glad castings came along. We've been stuck in that low price category for a long time. The advent of the investment cast head at $2.75 to $4 all of a sudden has opened up a whole new gap between 50¢ and $4. We can now start doing things differently than we ever could before because now the market *demands* a better product and will take the increased cost. So now we are in the process of spending $500,000 for new equipment. We are going to be able to do the back design that the casting people are doing now and we will have more precise weight control than they have now. There will be less work done by our customers. There is a market for a more precise forging for significantly less than a casting. But I don't think we'll ever cause castings to go out of business because I think there is definitely a market for them. I think they overkilled and there are going to be some adjustments, and forgings are going to come back and take a bigger share of the market. But we will never wipe out castings, even with the new process.

ROSS: If I see the pendulum swinging back to forgings, I'll get in 'em. If I see it swinging, I'm not going to let my company sink.

MADER: Who knows? Right now, my personal feelings are that it will settle on the lines we've got now. I think if there are going to be any major improvements, they will probably be in the alloys used, not so much in the designs. I would say down the road, there might even be a combination of metals and plastics . . . different types of metals. This would be my trend of thinking rather than radical designs. There's only so radical you can get. I'd say that Flood (Jim Flood, president of Lil' David Gawfe Co., which currently sells its revolutionarily-designed

Slingers) is as radical as you can get.

Regardless of what the future may hold, one thing is certain, and that is that both forgers and casters have come a long way from their primitive beginnings. Along the road numerous technological improvements coupled with increasing consumer demands have brought both processes to their peaks. Many problems such as cavitation (uneven surfaces) in investment casting, and out-of-center-hosel holes on forged irons, have been almost completely eliminated on top quality clubs. Both forgers and casters are gearing up for stiffer competition in the marketplace ahead.

As a consumer, you should weigh the advantages and disadvantages of both forged and cast irons before making your final decision. Don't go shopping for clubs blindly. Talk to your friends about their choice of clubs and why they made such a decision. Discuss the matter with your club pro. And most importantly, hit a few balls with each of the clubs you are contemplating buying. A pro can guide you toward the club with the right mechanical specifications (length, shaft flex, swingweight etc.), but only you can determine such subjectives as "feel" and "cosmetic appeal."

If price is no object, you will probably find yourself torn between the dozens of investment cast irons on the market. Conversely, if you feel your game isn't worth an extra $50-$75, you will still have a huge array of forged irons awaiting your judgment. Whichever route you choose to take, travel it carefully. Dangers lurk around every corner for the naive or uninformed buyer. Analyze advertising for what it is—an attempt to inform and convince you that a particular product is better than its competitors. Watch for exaggerated claims aimed at luring your hard earned dollars into the corporate coffers. This is not to say that golf club advertising is dishonest, but rather a gentle reminder to all consumers to think for themselves, to question exaggerated claims, to test a product before buying it, whether it be a set of $250 irons or a new lawn mower. You will never be sorry for being overly cautious when you are dealing with two of the things most dear to every golfer's heart—his handicap and his bank account.

Introdu

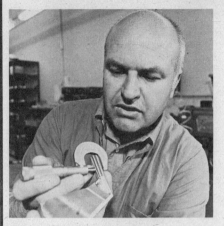

Phil Skovronski

With over 30 different irons to his credit, including clubs for PGA, Pro-Dyn, Royal, H&B, Keller, Dunlop, Slazenger and Lynx, Phil Skovronski has firmly established himself as the most prolific investment cast iron designer in the world. And Skovronski's outstanding reputation has not been built on mere numbers, but on his consistently high quality products, which he manufacturers with the aid of $250,000 worth of the finest

Bob Mader

"I've always been an idea man," said Bob Mader founder of Confidence Golf, and the man mainly responsible for promoting the feasibility of investment cast irons in the early 1960s.

Before founding Confidence, the 51-year-old inventor, designer and manufacturer was a chief engineer in the Merchant Marine. In 1957, after his stint at sea, Mader decided he would try to make it as a freelance inventor. After three major enterprises, and a moderate degree of success, he was approached by a gentleman (involved with one of his projects) who instigated Mader's initial involvement with golf club manufacturing.

"The gentleman said: 'Bob, with your design ideas, you ought to get into golf. It's the fastest growing industry in the world.' This was back in 1961. So I said, 'O.K., I'm in golf.' Whether I design a chair, a dress or whatever, it's just a series of lines that go together. Other than joking around as a kid in high school, I didn't know one end of a golf club from another; I didn't know a club from a hockey stick."

It was through this same gentleman that Mader met Bob McClelland, and the chemistry between the two individuals began to work. "He kind of liked me, and I admired him for what he accomplished in the casting business," recalled Mader. "The investment casting process just fascinated me be-

Swiss and German machinery, in his Oxnard, California facility.

Skovronski, 42, began his involvement with golf at the tender age of seven when he was a ball boy in Wisconsin. When he was only 12, he made his first set of forged irons—from scratch. "I've always been involved in making clubs, but I never had any aspirations of what today has brought about," said Skovronski, who at one time was a teaching assistant at Cincinnati Country Club and who now plays to a 7 handicap.

After a stint in the service, Skovronski began making putter heads in 1958, and was selling for Matzie. During this time he was gradually adding to his growing collection of machinery. Skovronski met Bob McClelland in 1959 when Phil moved to California, and the two have been more or less teamed together in the investment casting business since—Skovronski doing the designing, while McClelland handled production of the iron heads at his Santa Monica plant. During the late '50s and early '60s, Skovronski and McClelland made putters, wedges and chippers, but weren't very successful with irons.

"We were doing anything just to get by," recalled Skovronski when questioned about the lean years. "We were giving tooling away just to see if we could get our foot in the door. I remember when we were selling putters and reached 150 per month. We were *really* living. In 1961, when we rented a building in Santa Monica for $150 a month, we didn't know if we were biting off too big a chunk."

With encouragement from the PGA people, Skovronski's investment cast clubs got a much needed boost and paved the way for what was to follow.

In 1965, Skovronski made his first set of investment cast irons (masters and patterns) and sold them to a company in Japan. "I originally made them for the Palmer Company, but they weren't interested. I was broke so I sold them to a tool company for $5,000."

By the time John Riley approached Skovronski to make the tooling and patterns for what would be the Lynx irons, Phil was already on his own. Besides the Lynx iron, Skovronski also made the first set of Pings, and is currently working on his own line called Pro-file.

Despite his fine reputation and monetary success, Skovronski remains modest and praises the entire "team effort" within his 11-man production unit. "I don't have anybody working here who doesn't believe he's going to be here for life," noted Skovronski, who still puts in his share of 16-hour days in a tireless effort to seek perfection in his work. He gives a lot of the credit for his success to his wife, for her fine business sense and money management within the company.

McClelland recalled the day in 1959 when Skovronski approached him and asked if "there was anything he could do to help out": "Phil didn't know a lathe from a mill when he first started out, but he's *very* talented."

Skovronski returned the compliment: "If not for Bob McClelland, I'd be back looping (caddying) at Riviera or something. Because regardless of what anyone says, he is the one that is responsible for things being what they are today in this golf business. Bob is the best there is; there's no middle ground. You go from mediocrity to the pinnacle. No one can approach what he can do with surfaces, soundness and casting holes. He's really the oracle of this thing. He has no peers, and there is no one on the horizon."

And what is Skovronski's goal in producing irons?

"We're trying to do what the Mercedes Benz (he owns two) people try to do, and that's to make something as well as we can, and to make certain it is pure within."

---

cause I thought there were no limitations to what you can do with the thing."

As the relationship between Mader and McClelland developed, Mader was given the run of McClelland's shop, including the use of any equipment. "I could walk in there and use any equipment that he had, and shoot waxes, and try this and that," said Mader. "Without his cooperation, I don't know what would have happened. He helped both Phil (Skovronski) and me out tremendously. As a result, he benefited by this too."

At this time, the two were doing aerospace work just for eating money, and investment cast golf clubs were still in the experimental stages. In 1962-63, McClelland was doing some casting work (putters) for his own use and to give away to his accounts in the aerospace industry.

As the demand for clubs increased, and Mader was able to develop epoxy molds to increase the production rate, the two began receiving more recognition, and as a result, requests for wedges and standard irons.

By 1964-65, Mader and McClelland had ironed out most of the major problems they faced in constructing the molds and injecting them with wax. About the same time they started doing cast work for the Arnold Palmer Company, Mader developed a line of product putters (remember the pickle and hot dog heads?). While busy promoting these novelty items, Mader began receiving orders for conventional clubs. As a result, he developed the Confidence line to satisfy the customers he had originally met through the product putter field. Mader recalls well his initial attempts to sell his original investment cast irons.

"I would walk into a pro shop and say, 'I'm Bob Mader and I made a set of golf clubs I call Confidence, and they sell for $25 a club. The pro would laugh me right out of the shop because the top line of Wilson, Macgregor and Spaulding was $18 . . . and they were well-known, well-advertised clubs.

"I explained the process, the accuracy and consistency and everything else that goes along, but at this time I was talking to the wall because they didn't understand what I was trying to accomplish. This was around 1965-66."

Mader continued to promote his clubs through contacts in the product putter field and with guys he met on the course during a casual round of golf. Little by little, through word of mouth and golf magazines, the club gained recognition. Ping came out a year later, giving credence to the "new" process. But it wasn't until Lynx came out that the whole thing really took off, and the public was made aware of the investment cast iron. All this time, Mader had been working out of his garage, due to lack of finances for a larger facility, and had specialized in selling to the better golfers.

A fortunate meeting with Jerry Heard, who fell in love with the clubs, helped Mader gain recognition among touring pros. In fact, within a year, 35 tour members

had purchased clubs from Mader (he didn't give any away), and at one time there were as many as seven of the top 10 golfers in several tournaments using Confidence clubs.

Since those bygone days of frustration and struggling, when no one would give Mader the time of day, much less an order for any of his "over-priced" clubs, Confidence has gone on to become the third largest independent manufacturer of investment cast irons in the world (behind Lynx and Ping).

(Continued on next page)

Introducing the Cast of the Industry

Bob McClelland

"I guess you might say I'm the father of the investment cast iron," said 60-year-old Bob McClelland, general manager of Fansteel (formerly Advanced Casting), the world's largest manufacturer of investment cast irons.

McClelland started Advanced Casting in the late 1950s when he was dabbling with the possibilities of producing investment cast irons. Prior to that, his realm of expertise had been in the aerospace field. As his reputation and production volume increased during the 1960s, Fansteel became interested in his operation and finally negotiated the purchase of Advanced Casting in 1967 for several million dollars. However, McClelland remains at the helm, supervising all facets of design and production, which is currently running 5,000 heads a day. Combined with Fansteel's plant in Newberry Park, the two facilities are capable of turning out as many as 28,000 to 30,000 heads a day if the demand exists.

Besides manufacturing, McClelland also handles assembly and polishing work for customers who don't have their own areas for these services. Fansteel (Santa Monica) currently employs 130 workers, with 30,000 of its 35,000 square feet devoted to manufacturing. The remainder is assembly area.

Like Skovronski, McClelland grew up in the Midwest, and began caddying at age eight. Although he had been doing minimal

amounts of investment casting of irons for 25 years, it was more experimenting with his favorite hobby, than trying to revolutionize the world of golf club manufacturing.

"It wasn't until about four years ago that we really started to rip this thing out and to cause a lot of competition," noted McClelland. "But I still say we're the best because we're the originators of it."

McClelland first started with Bob Mader's Confidence line in 1970-71, but has since exploded to the point where he now does work for every major golf club manufacturer in the world except Hogan. "I feel I've

reached the pinnacle of this business; I don't think anyone else can truthfully say that," said McClelland proudly. "I find that I'm still learning, but from a competitive standpoint, I feel I have a lock on it."

Despite his millionaire status, McClelland continues to work 7 days a week doing design work and overseeing the operations at Fansteel. "I'm continually developing new techniques," said McClelland, "My whole life is golf. I never had the talent to play as well as I knew the game. I guess I could have been a good 2 or 3 handicap, but not good enough for the big time."

Like Skovronski, McClelland prefers working with a team of employees, rather than a chief with many grovelling Indians going through the motions of their jobs without question or comment.

"We have no politics within the plant. If people working here have something to say, they say it," noted McClelland. "It's sort of like a family-run operation. It's not what the Harvard Business School would advocate, but I'll take my bottom line over theirs. You must be surrounded by the finest people in the world. Anything coming out of this shop is as close to perfection as we can possibly make it. There are only four or five major houses in the United States today making investment cast irons, but I look at them and they're not my standards, my quality."

When you're already at the top, how does a person like McClelland keep his enthusiasm and drive?

"I'll tell you . . . It's a romantic business. At least I guess it's still romantic to me. Every day you knock out a case, it's like opening a present at Christmas. You have to have the desire. Your total devotion has to be the golf club."

Carl Ross

As head of Lynx Precision Golf Equipment, the world's largest independent manufacturer of investment cast irons, Carl Ross holds an enviable position. His company produces approximately 8,000 sets of irons, and 5,000 sets of woods per month, with total sales around $15 million for 1975.

But as the 39-year-old bachelor, who plays to an 8 handicap at Lakeside Golf Club, will tell you, the success did not come without adversities. In fact, in November, 1971, after only nine months in business, his entire Salinas, California factory burned to the ground, dampening the optimism that resulted from Lynx's initial consumer acceptance (they started making 20 sets a week, but had escalated that figure to 100 within the first six months).

After meeting with his 14 original investors, including Glen Campbell and other noted entertainment figures, the decision was made to come back stronger than ever with a new factory in Paramount, California. Within four weeks after the fire, Lynx was once again shipping clubs.

Despite skepticism in many circles about the playability of investment cast irons, Lynx sales boomed. And when the Japanese golf craze hit in 1973, Lynx continued to

step up production to meet the ever-increasing demand for their clubs. The rest is history. Today Lynx outsells Ping, its nearest independent competitor 3 to 1, and Confidence 5 to 1.

Ross first entered the golf arena as Arnold Palmer's pro shop manager at the Miami

Country Club in 1961, and later joined the sales force of the Arnold Palmer Golf Company.

"I didn't have the natural ability to play in professional sports, so Arnold was nice enough to hire me," recalls Ross, who grew up in Plamer's home town of Latrobe, Pennsylvania, and sold clothes to him when Ross still worked as a clerk in the local clothing store. "That's how I got to know him pretty well."

Ross, who worked for the Palmer Company until 1970, when he decided to form his own company, says that a great deal of his technical knowledge was absorbed via association with industry influentials such as Phil Skovronski, Bob Mader and Bob McClelland.

Already a self-made multi-millionaire (he never went to college), Ross continues to strive for higher peaks, and spends about six months a year in foreign countries promoting the Lynx line. His down-home honesty makes him easy to talk with, but don't let his nature fool you. He is still a shrewd businessman, who wants to do well in a field he happens to enjoy tremendously.

"Right now I just want to run my 'little' company, and give something back to golf," says Ross. "I don't need the money anymore. I'm going to be in the golf business for the rest of my life. I don't want to do anything else."

Vardon Left Us Much More Than a Grip

By KEN BOWDEN

PROMINENTLY displayed in the foyer of the South Herts Golf Club, north of London, is a commanding bronze sculpture of a golfer's hands gripping a club. Because this was the course where Harry Vardon ended his days—he is buried a few paces away in the Totteridge parish churchyard—every visitor knows or quickly guesses whose hands they are. But take those hands of golf's first true superstar out of their commemorative setting, and not one golfer in 10,000 would be able to identify their owner.

The sheer size and muscular power of the hands would surely prompt a strong vote for Arnold Palmer. To the more intense student of technical nitty-gritty, the fairly "strong" placement of the left hand might suggest Billy Casper or Lee Trevino. Perhaps the purposeful "short-thumbed" snugness of the over-all grip would even bring Jack Nicklaus to mind. But it would be a guessing game at best because the fact is that this grip, for all practical purposes, is the grip of just about 99 per cent of today's top professional and amateur golfers the world over.

It won't, of course, be news to anyone who can break 90 that Harry Vardon popularized the principle of "wedding" (to use his word) the hands together by wrapping the little finger of the bottom hand around the forefinger of the top hand. What may be news is

Excerpted from the book, *The Methods of Golf's Masters: How They Played and What You Can Learn from Them*, by Dick Aultman and Ken Bowden. Published by Coward, McCann and Geoghegan, Inc. Copyright © 1975 by Dick Aultman and Ken Bowden.

that he didn't actually invent this overlapping technique: his fellow member of the "Great Triumvirate," J. H. Taylor, developed it simultaneously but independently, and a fine Scottish amateur, John E. Laidlay, had used it in winning the British Amateur championship in 1889, the year before Vardon played his first round of tournament golf. What may be even bigger news to the modern golfer is the exceptional degree of influence that Vardon had on the golf swing as a whole, far beyond his popularization of a grip style.

Harry Vardon's achievements were awesome—every bit as overwhelming in his own time as Nicklaus' are today. But looking back now, what impresses most about him is not so much his inevitably mist-shrouded victories as the method through which he achieved them. The deeper one gets into his technique, the more dramatically apparent it becomes that he was the greatest technical innovator in the history of golf.

The swing style of his predecessors is so foreign to the form we know today as to be almost unrecognizable. But when one watches Vardon on film, one sees, in essence, the swings of Gene Sarazen, Walter Hagen, and Bobby Jones—even the timeless Sam Snead. In basic principles at least, here is the swing with which countless good senior golfers—and others who cannot physically or temperamentally accommodate the stressful body-controlled actions of the game's young lions—still continue to win golfing prizes and pleasure. Here, in short, is the master mold; the mold from which Byron Nelson built in initiating the method now so successfully refined on the U.S. professional tour; but a mold which remains, almost in its

original form, a wonderfully valid swing pattern for the purely recreational golfer.

Harry Vardon was born the son of an artisan in 1870 in Grouville, Jersey, one of the Channel Islands between England and France. Almost from the time he could walk, he would occasionally swing a homemade club in rudimentary backyard golf games with his five brothers and two sisters, but he had slight interest in the sport. When he began work at 12, in domestic service, cricket and soccer consumed most of his sparse leisure time, and the rest was spent supplementing family income by such means as collecting and selling sea shells.

Golf was no more than a casual pastime for him during adolescence. He never had a lesson, never formally studied technique, never consciously copied anyone's swing. His clubs were a ragbag of discards and homemades, and he ferreted his gutta-percha balls out of Royal Jersey's wiry sea grasses.

By the time he was 20, Vardon had, by his own estimate, played no more than 20 full rounds of golf, and the closest he had come to practicing shots had been hitting balls around a cultivated field to scare away crows. Then, while still in his 20th year, he entered a tournament at the local workingmen's club and won. Simultaneously, news arrived that his brother Tom had won a professional tournament in Scotland and with it a prize of £20. Said Vardon later: "This seemed an enormous amount to me and I pondered long and intently over it. I knew that, little as I had played, I was as good as Tom. If he could win that vast fortune, why shouldn't I?"

So began a career that was not only to

immortalize the name Vardon but was to massively and permanently alter the character of the golf swing.

Prior to Vardon's appearance on the professional tournament scene, such as it was in the mid-1890s, golf was played at every level with what had become known as the "St. Andrews Swing." As today, there were individual variations on its basic theme, but fundamentally the St. Andrews Swing consisted of a long, flat, slashing action deriving from an ultraloose grip, a huge swaying body turn away from and through the ball, and an uninhibited slinging of the clubhead through the ball with the hands, wrists, and shoulders.

Vardon changed all that. His first three British Open wins in 1896, 1898, and 1899 severely dented confidence in the old Scottish style, even though many leading Scots vigorously defended their invention often to the point of bad-mouthing the "English" method that was beating them so soundly. By the time Vardon won his record sixth and last British Open in 1914, the St. Andrews Swing—at least in its most extreme form—had disappeared.

His greatest victories were won with the guttie ball, which he always preferred to the rubber version because of the thoughtfulness and precision it demanded in conceiving and executing every shot. From tee to green he was in his day totally without peer. He flew the unresponsive guttie appreciably higher than his rivals, thus gaining the twin advantages of long carry and soft landing that have so aided Nicklaus. He drove straight and, when necessary, extremely far.

No one before—and probably no one since—played more majestically with the brassey: Vardon himself said that, on form, he could expect to hit the ball consistently within 15 feet of the pin with this equivalent of the modern 2-wood. With the shorter clubs he grew, if anything, even more adept. "No one ever played irons more prettily," eulogized Bernard Darwin, Vardon's equivalent among writers of the game. "He merely shaved the turf and did not take cruel divots out of it." He was an expert manufacturer of special shots with every club in the bag.

It was only when Vardon reached the green that he sank to the level of his contemporaries. "A grand player up to the green, and a very bad one when he got there," was how Darwin—never a

man to mince words—put it. "But then," he added, "Vardon gave himself less putting to do than any other man."

The overlapping grip, although Vardon's most famous legacy to golf, was actually one of his least drastic departures from the St. Andrews Swing, which featured a mechanically passable if somewhat loose and sloppy 10-fingered hold on the club. Vardon was an average-size man—5'9½" and 165 pounds in middle life—but he had unusually large hands and long fingers. Almost certainly, wrapping the little finger of his right hand around the forefinger of his left was originally simply a way of compacting his hold on the club. It took him no time at all, however, to discover the real value of this type of grip, which is the "wedding" of the hands into a single unit, and he strongly advocated it for this purpose for all players.

The modern golf teacher would find little fault in Vardon's grip and a lot to praise. The club passed from the inner knuckle joint of the first finger of his left hand across the base of the second and little fingers, which placed it a little more in the fingers than is currently fashionable. But this was essential to the light grip pressure and fluid motion of Vardon's swing, as it is to many good modern "hands" players. In most other respects Vardon's grip could have come right out of the 1970s. His left thumb sat just to the right of the center of the shaft and was snugly covered by the right palm when this hand was added. The club lay at the roots of the fingers of the right hand, and the right thumb rode just to the left of top-center on the shaft. The V's formed by the thumb and forefinger of both hands matched exactly, both pointing somewhere between his right ear and shoulder.

About grip pressure he expressed himself with a bit more flourish than might your 20th century teaching pro, but the message was the same:"In the ordinary way of things, the tight grip creates a tautening of the muscles in the body and when the player is in this condition the chances of executing a perfect stroke are remote. The golfer's muscles should be at once healthy and supple—like a boxer's. When they are encouraged to develop hardness and size—like a weightlifter's—they retard the ease and quickness of hitting, which count so much at the instant of impact." Vardon did vary from modern theory, however,

when he added that "it is quite sufficient to grip a little tighter with the thumbs and forefingers. They will prove sufficient to keep the clubhead in position. The other fingers may be left to look after themselves in the matter of the strength they apply."

Modern grip principles call for maximum pressure in the last two fingers of the bottom hand. But this is much more a matter of feel than mechanics. From photographs of grips only, few average golfers today would be able to distinguish Vardon from 70 per cent of the present-day tour players.

The modern golfer is frequently advised to face the back of the left hand and the palm of the right to the target at address. This point was also stressed by Vardon: "The left-hand knuckles should face down the line of play and the right-hand knuckles the other way," he instructed many times in his books and magazine articles. Then there is the question of which hand should grasp the club most firmly. Modern teaching favors either equal grip pressure or a slightly softer hold with the bottom hand. Said Vardon: "I grip equally firmly with both hands at the start, but the pressure of the right hand decreases during the backswing." And finally the matter of which is the master hand and arm. Although the very latest theories lean strongly toward "left-sidedness," a consensus of international teaching opinion would probably favor a balanced effort. Wrote Vardon: "I don't believe in a master hand or arm. All should work as a unit, and I believe the overlapping grip best achieves this."

Harry Vardon played all his competitive golf in knickers, fancy-topped stockings, a hard collar and tie, and a tightly buttoned jacket ("A cardigan or jumper permits too great a freedom in the shoulders," he said). Re-dress him in a sport shirt and double-knits and he would still look incongruous on today's pro tour because, champion innovator that he was, certain elements of his swing definitely conflict with modern theory.

His manner of starting the club back, for example (although also employed by Jones and Hagen), would create horror at any present-day PGA teaching seminar. Vardon's first move was a pronounced drag backward and inward of the hands, with the clubhead trailing the hands almost until they reached hip height, at which point a free wrist cock from a cupped left wrist position set the hands very much "under" the shaft and established a wide-open clubface. That is certainly about as far as you can get from the "one-piece" policy of the 1960s and light years away from the "square-to-square" and "set-the-angle-early" edicts of the 1970s!

Conceivably, Vardon's famous bent left arm would be less sinful in principle today than his takeaway, in that a number of top golfers currently play with discernible "give" at the elbow (including Europe's top teacher and former tournament star, John Jacobs). But Vardon's elbow didn't just "give"; it categorically *bent*—during his early years almost at right angles! When teaching, he did not insist on so great a kink, but he strongly advocated relaxation in the elbows to prevent tension and to produce smoothness and rhythm, arguing that centrifugal force would automatically straighten the leading arm at the appropriate moment in the downswing. "I am constantly having to cure patients ruined by the stiff left arm," he wrote in an American golf magazine, and he stressed the bent arm frequently and persuasively in his books.

Vardon's swing contained other departures from what is presently regarded as good form; for example, he allowed his hips to turn freely in the backswing; his right elbow to rise high and away from his body (into almost the same position as Nicklaus!); his left heel to swing high at the completion of a full backswing (again like Nicklaus), and he "crossed the line" at the top—pointed the club right of target.

Whatever Vardon's variations from modern standards, they are vastly outweighed by his similarities.

Good action photography of Vardon is scarce today, but what is available of his mature swing depicts a number of strikingly modern features—all of them seminal departures from the St. Andrews Swing.

Vardon's "centeredness" throughout the swing is one such. A 1927 commentator graphically described it thus: "Imagine that, as he addresses the ball, a pole is passed downward through the center of his head and body, and into the ground: then his swing is a rotating movement performed by the shoulders and hips, around the pole, while the arms are being lifted up and the left knee is bending inwards." The writer goes on to quote Vardon as saying that his abil-

ity to maintain a fixed axis was perhaps the major factor in his accuracy and control—why he "would not be off the fairway six times in six rounds."

Another remarkably modern feature of Vardon was his address posture: knees slightly flexed; upper body angled forward from the waist; back straight; arms hanging easily and freely; head high; hands slightly below a straight line from the club-head to the left shoulder.

Leg action, the core of the modern golf swing, was little discussed as such by Vardon in his writings, but he did recognize it obliquely, and he certainly employed it, albeit unconsciously, as an effect rather than a cause. His lower-body movement was a natural, unconscious, *reflex* reaction to the winding of his upper body in the backswing (as it is with every golfer who makes a full body turn and free arm swing). Thus, because his legs operated so instinctively and automatically once he'd got to the top of the swing, Vardon never had occasion to think about them consciously—or, if he did, he could quickly put the matter out of mind as being a natural reflex movement not needing or warranting conscious direction.

It would seem that Vardon was definitely way ahead of most of the moderns in at least one respect, that being his swing's appearance of grace, ease, and economy of effort. Today only a handful of tour players, such as Sam Snead and Gene Littler, would seem to come close to matching what Bernard Darwin called the "beautiful free movement of one having a natural gift for opening his shoulders and hitting clean. Time after time Vardon would come right through, drawn to his full height, the club round over his left shoulder, the hands well up, the left elbow tolerably high. It was the ideal copybook follow-through, and he did it every time with an almost monotonous perfection."

An even better word picture of Vardon's over-all motion comes from Walter Cavanaugh, writing in *The American Golfer* in 1924: "The outstanding impression of watching Vardon play is that of utter ease and lack of physical effort. His hands, arms, body and legs appear to work as a well-oiled machine, and there is always present that element denoting complete coordination, ordinarily referred to in golf matters as rhythm."

How many of today's stars, one wonders, will evoke such prose?

Golf Traditionalist Cotton Right-Hand Power Booster

By MARV MOSS
(Montreal Gazette)

IN RETURN for an allowance of peppermints, a donkey named Pacifico lugs Henry Cotton's clubs around the golf courses of Southern Portugal with an impeccable manner while the master cracks out balls with a swing dominated by the right hand.

The animal may be a complete ass in matters like reading the greens but few caddies today work as inexpensively.

In a school remarkable for the diversity of its theory Cotton has meanwhile become the foremost exponent of the passive left hand.

"If it's educated, you can't use too much righthand in the golf swing," says the three-time British Open champion, now 68 and still ensconced as resident professional at posh Penina although he admits that at one time he feared his outspoken comments on socialism might antagonize the revolutionary regime and lead to his expulsion.

To develop the groove, Cotton's proteges whack an automobile tire with the driver, gripping the club solely with the right hand, the reverse if the student is lefthanded.

Neither the drill nor his premises have achieved widespread acceptance among his peers.

"But think about it," he says. "If you were asked to strike an object as forcefully as you could with a mallet, or perform a subtler task like return a table tennis ball with a bat, in both instances you would use the hand that is the essence of power and sensitivity. Why suppress the instinct for golf?"

SEVEN KEYS TO A SOUND GOLF *Swing*

Standing up to the shot.

Roland Stafford, Longue Vue Club, Verona, Pennsylvania. Tri-State Section Champion.

A good golf shot begins with a good set-up. First, place the club-head to the ball so it is square to the line of flight. Now take your stance so you are comfortably positioned with your knees slightly flexed. The left arm serves as an extension of the club shaft in a straight line to the left shoulder. When the right hand is added to complete the grip the hands will be directly over the ball in the same position as at the moment of impact. The vees formed at the base of the thumbs will point directly at the right eye. The right shoulder is necessarily slightly lower than the left shoulder because the right hand is lower on the shaft and the right knee is cocked in toward the ball. Now you're ready to swing . . .

Starting the backswing.

John Frillman, Happy Hollow Club, Omaha, Nebraska. Nebraska Section Champion.

Think of the backswing as the winding of a spring which must be wound carefully. The clubhead moves s-l-o-w-l-y away from the ball on a low flat plane. Think of it as being thrust back by a nearly rigid left arm and firm wrist—not as being drawn back by the right hand. Actually, the right hand just goes along for the ride. The clubhead moves back on a straight line for several inches before starting to rise in a wide arc with the extended left arm serving as a radius. There is no rolling of the wrists. The right upper arm remains folded against the body until it is drawn away to accommodate the sweeping radius of the arc as it approaches the top of the backswing.

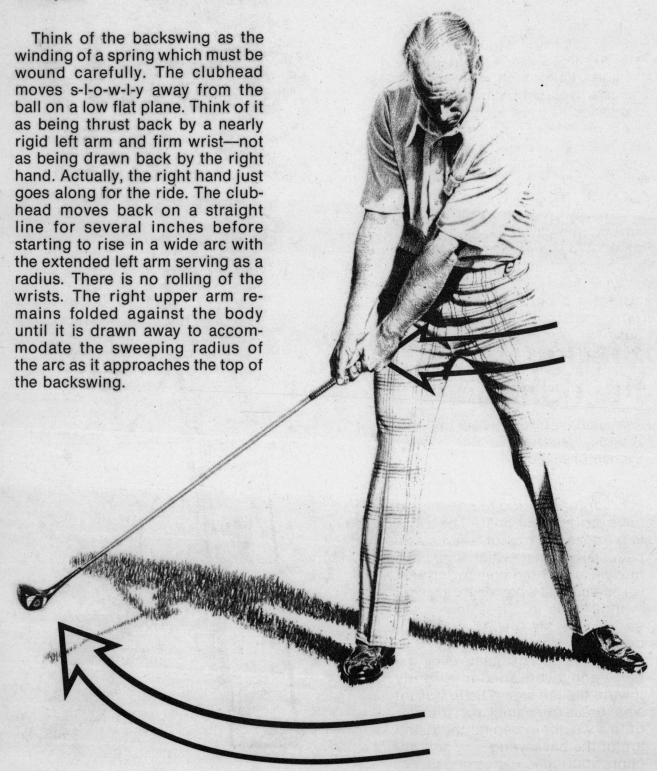

Bracing the right side.

Ken Lindsay, Colonial Country Club, Jackson, Mississippi. Gulf States Section Champion.

In order for a spring to coil it must have an anchor post. The right leg, from knee to foot, serves as a pedestal against which the body muscles build the coil spring that will unleash its power in the golf swing. While all these forces are gathering at the top of the backswing, the body weight must remain even distributed over the ball—and even shaded slightly toward the left side. The firm right side brace prevents any transfer of this weight in behind the rising arc of the backswing . . . and anchors your head over the ball.

Making the full shoulder turn.

Al Chandler, Columbia Country Club, Columbia, Missouri. Eastern Missouri Section Champion.

A common fault of the high handicapper, and especially to the lady and senior golfer, is failure to complete the body wind-up. Basically, it's a lazy fault. Bring the left shoulder under and all the way around until it's under your chin. Don't leave anything behind! Think of it like this: If the wide arc is the vehicle and velocity is the fuel; thus, the shoulder turn is the ignition of a good golf shot. The full turn is the source of tension between the upper body and the resisting lower body which creates the spring action. Further, combined with a firm left hand grip and arm, the shoulder turn helps to insure a one-piece takeaway and avoids the tendency to pick up the club.

Moving into the ball.

Gordon Leishman, Idle Hour Country Club, Lexington, Kentucky, Kentucky Section Champion.

The golf swing really starts from the top. All the rest is prologue. When you've got that club at the top of the backswing the spring is all coiled and the trigger is cocked. The uncoiling of the body begins with an initial push off the right foot. And this is accompanied simultaneously by a sliding swivel turn of the hips and a lateral forward move of the flexed knees. This has the effect of clearing the left side and opening the path for the clubhead to move through the ball.

The moment of truth.

Bobby Brue, Ozaukee Country Club, Mequon, Wisconsin. Wisconsin Section Champion.

There is a popular misconception that the golf swing follows an inside-out track. This isn't the case at all. The golf swing actually is an inside-to-inside swing. The clubhead comes down along an inside-out track, but at the moment of impact it begins moving back along an outside-in path. In essence it's an inside-to-inside plane with the clubhead continuing along the line of flight for a few inches before beginning to rise along an inside plane after striking the ball. As a reminder, I often place a favorite club on the ground and tee up the ball just inside the club which is aligned toward the target. You can bet I'm going to take pains not to hit that club. I don't recommend this for you, but you might try using a stick or block of wood.

No unfinished symphonies, please!

Sam Harvey, Pinecrest Golf Course, Fairfax, Virginia. Middle Atlantic Section Champion.

Most high handicappers hit at the ball, instead of hitting through it. The result is a collapsing left arm and left side with disastrous consequences, ranging from a 40% loss of power to fly-away pulled shots with long and medium irons. Picture in your mind a weight tied to the club-head which must be swung through the strike zone and well beyond. Collapsing left side also results in the familiar "Fire and fall back" posture with the weight recoiling to the right, pulling the left foot off the ground. Let that imaginary weight at the end of the clubhead pull your right through the shot, carrying your weight over to the left side and drawing your head up as the arms complete the sweeping arc to a high, full finish.

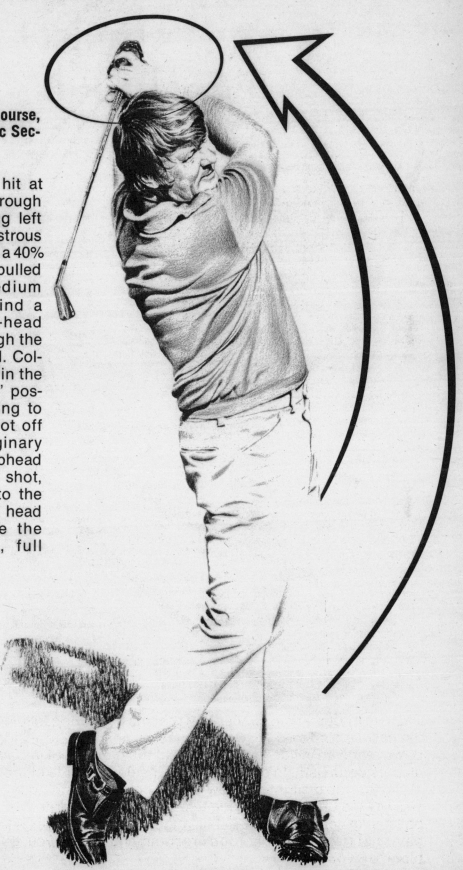

The Abolition (Almost) Of Golf

By NORMAN COUSINS
(Editor, *Saturday Review*)

THE *Saturday Review* has a tradition for spoofing on April Fool's Day. Perhaps the most successful spoof took the form of the following letter, published in the first April 1971 issue of the *Saturday Review*.

A Call to Defeat HR 6142

I come before you with a cause that I trust you will not regard as too inconsequential to warrant the kind of personal eloquence that has been so characteristic of your editorial page. I refer to the need to defeat Congressional Resolution 6142, introduced by Representative A. F. Day and co-sponsored by some 40 members of the House. This bill, which for some inexplicable reason has received virtually no attention, would abolish all privately owned parks of more than 150 acres that are used by fewer than 150 persons per day, averaged over a week.

The bill sounds democratic enough until one recognizes its principal effect would be to eliminate the nation's golf courses. This is not the stated purpose, of course, but it would certainly be the principal effect.

The minimal amount of land required even for a private nine-hole course is 75 acres. By definition, therefore, all private golf facilities would be closed.

What about public golf courses? The average public golf course, running between 175 and 250 acres, is played on by fewer than 150 persons a day, averaged over the week. This average is made up of about 400 playing on Saturdays and Sundays and 60 playing on weekdays. Congressman Day very cleverly specified "fewer than 150 persons per day, *averaged* over the week." There is not a public golf course in the country that would not be shut down under this definition.

I believe that I can prove that Congressman Day is deliberately seeking to destroy golf. Permit me to speak personally. I have known A. F. Day since childhood. We went to the same public elementary school in Brentwood. In our eighth-grade English class, we had to write a 500-word essay on the subject: "What is the first thing you would do if you were President?" Day's little composition, which was not a joke, said the first thing he would do as President would be to abolish golf. He wrote that it was worse than alcohol as a disruptive influence within the family.

What Day's classmates didn't realize at the time was that he was writing out of his own tragic family experience. His grandfather perished in a sand trap on the fifth hole of the public course at Hillsborough, California, the victim of a heart attack caused by massive exasperation and exhaustion. Day's father was fired from at least three jobs because he persisted in goofing off for golf. He would take the family's grocery money to buy expensive golf equipment. The family never saw Mr. Day on weekends. He would leave the house before 4 A.M. in order to wait on line for a starting time. He played miserably. He anguished over every slice and hook. He would have golf nightmares in which he would six-putt greens. His blood pressure was amost as high as his score.

Inevitably, Mr. Day developed a serious case of hypertension and ulcers. One day, playing at San Jose, not far from the site of the grandfather's tragedy, Day expired from a coronary undoubtedly caused by his uncontrollable frenzy after hitting 19 successive balls into the pond in front of a par-three green. Little wonder that the son should have developed such a fierce antipathy to the game.

When we were seniors together at UCLA, A. F. Day wrote a term paper for our economics course that clearly reflected his embittered feelings about the sport. His paper differed from the one he wrote in the eighth grade only in its additional sophistication. He used ostensibly detailed research to disguise his psychotic hostility. His paper revealed that in just one year 18,000 men died on golf courses from heart attacks; 72,000 men developed ulcers or gastritis from acute anguish over their inability to hit the ball properly; 930 men were killed and 8,600 were injured in overturned golf carts. His paper further disclosed that golf was the prinicpal cause each year of more than 60,000 broken homes; that it was by far the greatest single cause of alcoholism and acute melancholy in the United States; that it kept 3,642,000 acres—twice as much acreage as that devoted to the national forests—out of productive cultivation or from other important social uses, of which low-cost housing was the most conspicuous.

When Day was elected to Congress 3 years ago, I naturally wondered how his malicious obsession would manifest itself. Now I know. But what about the 43 Congressmen who have announced their support for Day's bill? Do *they* know? Day's bill is all dressed up in the ecological and conservationist fashion of the day. It is made to appear that the bill will protect what are cleverly described as private parks, insuring their use for the public good. For those Congressmen whose constituencies consist largely of the poorly housed or impoverished, the bill holds out the prospect of low-cost housing in verdant settings.

A. F. Day is not the first man elected to public office in our history who has been motivated and energized by a secret or absurd purpose. It is a terrible error to underestimate him. I regret deeply having to make all this known, but history has often been twisted all out of shape because not enough people took seriously a few men who acted out of their obsessions or deep-seated aversions.

I urge *SR*'s editors to oppose HR 6142; I urge all your readers, especially those who regard golf not as a vicious and extravagant diversion but as a prime manifestation of the American way of life, to write to their Congressman making known the real facts about Congressman Day's bill. Everyone who knows what weekends are for has the obligation now to act.

K. Jason Sitewell
Burlingame, Calif.

The letter was followed by an Editor's note saying that Congressman Day's reply would appear the following week. But even before that issue came out, K. Jason Sitewell's letter made an impact on the sports world that was certainly as unprecedented as it was unexpected. *Golf World* magazine reported Sitewell's letter on its editorial page under the banner headline: "A Frightening Bill." The editor appended his own comment: "This somewhat innocent appearing bill is the most ominous threat to golf that has come along."

Then the floodgates opened, with sports editors throughout the country becoming engulfed in the episode. One syndicated columnist wrote cautiously:

I'm not trying to be an alarmist, but there is a bill before Congress that would, if passed in its present form, destroy the game of golf. It might be prudent for all golfers to drop a line to their Congressmen concerning this matter.

Letters poured in on Congress. The *Saturday Review* began to feel the reverberations. One congressman wrote in to express "unequivical opposition to HR 6142." In a flourish of political style he added:

And I want to make it perfectly clear that I do not play golf, nor do I have any vested interest in private golf clubs.

Gerald Ford, at that time Representative from Michigan, wasn't altogether stymied, as is clear from his letter to *SR*:

I am wondering whether this was meant to be a hoax and whether Congressman A. F. Day referred to "April Fool's Day." If this was the intention, it has amazed the readers of your magazine whose reputation is based on something much more solid. I would very much appreciate an explanation that I can pass on to the folks in Michigan, who took these letters very seriously.

The repercussions extended beyond Congress. I received one call from a swank country club near Chicago that had called a special meeting of its board of governors to plan special strategy to defeat the bill.

A letter on official golf-club stationery sounded a cry of distress.

Imagine my embarrassment when members keep calling me at home or stopping me in the club rooms to ask "What is your relationship to A. F. Day?"

It was signed, R. D. Day, Jr. President, Merion Golf Club.

Most of the letters we received had one especially notable—perhaps especially distressing—thing in common. There wasn't a journalist, golfer, golf organization, or politician—except for Gerald Ford—who expressed any skepticism, much less concern, for A. F. Day's statistics specifying nearly 19,000 deaths and more than 80,000 injuries and diseases caused by the game of golf.

Amidst all this flurry came the publication, in the April 10 issue of *Saturday Review*, of the distinguished Congressman Day's response:

Congressman Day Defends Himself

K. Jason Sitewell makes it appear that the bill I introduced in the House of Representatives has a secret and pernicious purpose. He says I am dominated by a "malicious obsession" to destroy golf.

The 43 members of the House who are co-sponsoring my bill will bear witness to the fact that I have never made any secret of my opposition to privileged use of parks, public or private. I believe it is undemocratic and indeed arrogant for large tracts of land to be pre-empted by small numbers of people for any purpose, be it golf or any other so-called sport. I have no objection to public golf courses so long as they are used by enough people to justify the public taxes that support them.

I trust this sets the record straight so far as my purposes and objectives are concerned. Now let me raise some questions about K. Jason Sitewell and the *Saturday Review*.

Mr. Sitewell says he has known me since early childhood. That is correct. Obviously, therefore, my own knowledge of him is of equal duration. Would it surprise the readers of *SR* to learn that Mr. Sitewell is one of the largest investors in sporting goods equipment in the country?

Now for *SR*: The letters page is usually reserved for comment on material that has previously appeared in the magazine. The Sitewell letter was totally unrelated to any earlier article in *SR*. Yet the editor gave it a full page. Why? I point a finger at the editor himself.

The public image of N. C. is of a man dedicated to literature, philosophy, and important public causes. He has been known as a confidant of such men as Schweitzer, Nehru, President John F. Kennedy, and Pope John XXIII. This is not the real N. C. The real N. C. became revealed to me the other night when I listened to Arnold Palmer on the *Tonight Show*. Palmer spoke of playing golf with his "good friend Norman Cousins," and of dedicating his latest golf book to him. Good Lord! The next thing we know, Spiro Agnew will be writing editorials for the *Saturday Review*! Sic transit gloria mundi.

A. F. Day
House Office Building
Washington, D.C.

This produced a hot response. Larry Dennis, a columnist for Chicago's suburban papers, wrote:

Congressman Day's obfuscatory thinking confuses commonweal, if indeed that is his noble purpose, with eradication of private enterprise and ownership. Laying aside for a moment the recreational and ecological repercussions from closing any golf course, and they are frightening, it is enough to point out to Mr. Day that a private golf course is not a park. It is a club, equivalent to a man's home. If you are fortunate enough to own an estate of more than 50 acres, I imagine Congressman Day would well like to abolish that, too.

A *Saturday Review* reader rushed to my defense:

The Honorable Mr. Day concludes his letter with the shattering revelation that N. C. *plays golf*! (The implication is inescapable that any magazine whose editor suffers from such moral degradation is automatically suspect.) To this, may I offer two words: Dwight Eisenhower.

But the real issue raised by the introduction of this bill is more serious: It is unspeakably frightening that a man who is as sick as Congressman Day is should be elected to any public office. It can only be hoped that any further bills he sponsors will be reviewed with extreme caution by our nation's legislators.

One subscriber wrote to me:

It is certain that HR 6142 will be defeated. (Just to be safe, I have written the Representatives from my district.)

Some of *SR*'s readers displayed both compassion and imagination. Consider this letter, which appeared under the fanciful name "Andrew Long Woods, Professor, Department of Suburban Planning, UCLA":

Congressman Day's bill, while evidently not perfect, has considerable merit. Perhaps it will force the American golfing community to adopt some of the practices of the East—the Japanese practice, for instance, of placing picnic tables and cooking areas in the fairways, thus opening these lovely stretches of green to the general public. With picnickers, the golfers and the non-golfing public will feel a closer kinship. They will be kept on their toes, and the nation's golf links may at last help forge the social links our society so desperately needs.

Long Woods's letter drew a response of its own:

I myself cannot visualize the game of golf being played on a course covered with beer cans, pop bottles, half-eaten hot dogs, watermelon rinds, newspapers, sun-tan lotion tubes and all other excreta that picnickers, nature lovers and bathers produce. Perhaps the Japanese are neater than we are; in any event, if this is the best we can think of to re-establish those "social links," I think I may take up some other sport—like jalopy racing.

Wrote the distressed Dean of UCLA:

There is no Department of Suburban Planning at UCLA and Mr. Woods is not listed in the UCLA Directory as being in anyway associated with the University. I would think that even a superficial check would have revealed that some sort of problem was involved here.

More and more people were beginning to catch on, however. Finally, the *Wall Street Journal* ran a delightful front page story exposing the spoof. Entitled "Holy Niblick! Have You Golfers Heard About Rep. Day's Bill?" it disclosed the fact that HR 6142 was actually a bill to limit the liability of national banks for certain taxes.

The UPI picked up the story. So did newspapers and magazines across the country. A good many people got a few chuckles from the hoax—but many of those who had been taken in thought that my sense of humor lacked both humor—and sense.

Wrote the editor of *Golf World*:

The editor apologizes to the golfers of the world for accepting the integrity of the magazine, *Saturday Review*, as gospel, and reprinting from its April 3 issue a lengthy letter which would have upset the entire structure of golf. The initials and name of the congressman fit Cousins's somewhat cruel, distorted idea of a joke.

One of the "taken" columnists wrote:

At this point, *Mad Magazine* stands head and shoulders over this supposed literate publication. We congratulate Cousins for writing such a convincing piece, but question his judgment. At the same time, we're on the first tee, questioning our own.

The PGA was smoldering:

Your shocking, unprecedented article of April 3 has left the PGA golfing family aghast. You caused the PGA a tidy sum of money in phone and clerical work to our almost 7,000 members.

Two members of the clergy showed that God's representatives may have irreverant, if mysterious, ways:

As a member of the cloth let me simply say that your crude (and cruel) joke chipped off one more piece of the remaining fabric of trust, morality, and respect for authority left in America. As a result we will have a little less faith in anything that appears in your pages henceforth. May God forgive you and have mercy on your soul.

And a Yale Divinity student wrote:

I have been puzzling as to whether Congressman Day's bill will affect any of the nation's enormous cemeteries and burial parks. Surely many exceed the minimum acreage. As both a golfer and a divinity student, this question is of dual concern to me. I rarely pass a cemetery without remarking to myself what a great pity it is that the stones are not leveled, the ground seeded and sodded, and the lot of them made into golf courses.

One subscriber's letter fairly well represents those of many readers who had been gulled:

Here is my joke to you: I will certainly not have my subscription to *Saturday Review* renewed when it expires. I make a fool of myself often enough on my own and do not need your help.

I wrote apologies to each subscriber who had been offended or angered. I begged my golfing friends, who threatened to have me barred from every course in the nation, to forgive me for my joke. I suffered enough every time I played, I told them, and penance was awaiting me on each tee.

Still, I wasn't entirely humbled. *Saturday Review* to be sure, is a literary magazine, but I've always seen a distinction between a serious publication and a solemn one. I had never seen anything inconsistent in publishing articles about grave world problems while interspersing them with humorous cartoons—or, for that matter, with a practical joke or two. Indeed, I always zealously guarded the job of writing those jokes and picking the cartoons for myself. I relished that part of the job. I still do.

N. C.

A POEM

I think that I shall never see
A shot like one that gave me a 2 on 3

A shot that through the air did fly
Only to hit a branch to die

To drop to the waters edge of cement
And bounce on high, flagstick bent.

To bound up on the green, curl 'round the cup and drop
Never will I hear such a heart-stopping plop.

If only I could make a hole in one
My star would shine as does the sun

To go one better, I'd be the worlds greatest hero
But, alas, I know that only God can make a zero.

Stanley Rosin

New Listing of America's 100 Greatest Courses

Winged Foot Replaces Medinah In Top Ten

A PANEL of leading amateur and professional players helps us pick "America's 100 Greatest Courses." The judgements of the regional selectors are carefully tabulated. A national panel then considers the results and, in collaboration with our editors, makes the final rankings. The primary goal is to recognize the best examples of American golf architecture, while retaining to some degree the basis of tournament toughness.

In the process, the panel has diligently attempted to avoid rating any courses strictly on their tradition as major tournament sites, although in many cases that appeal can hardly be overlooked. There are courses on our list that have never held a tournament of notable consequence, and yet their credentials are so obvious that there is little question of their selection.

Seven courses are making their first appearance in the ratings this year, but the most prominent change from the previous list has the West Course at Winged Foot Golf Club displacing the No. 3 Course at Medinah Country Club in the top 10. Ironically, these courses were the sites of the two recent U.S. Opens. Attention inevitably was focused sharply upon them as a result, although great care was taken to minimize the impact of these Opens as the basis of a change in ranking.

Winged Foot drew heavy support almost in spite of the preparation it was given by the USGA for the 1974 Open. Most of the panel felt strongly that the alterations at Winged Foot actually detracted from its appeal. Two par-5 holes, for example, were changed to par-4s that were just too severe. Players had to hit woods to greens designed to receive mid-irons. The panel rated Winged Foot, instead, on the merits of its original design.

Located amid the lush greenery of Westchester County at Mamaroneck, N.Y., less than an hour's drive from Manhattan, Winged Foot is a classic parkland course. Opened in 1923, it was designed by the distinguished architect A. W. Tillinghast, whose imprimatur appears on many championship courses throughout the country. Among its dominant characteristics are deep bunkers, slick greens and a reputation as a demanding second-shot course.

Frank (Sandy) Tatum of San Francisco, chairman of the USGA's championship committee for the last two Opens, offers some revealing insights on the character of Winged Foot—and Medinah as well.

"The basic appeal of Winged Foot," says Tatum, "is the remarkable balance of its par-4 holes. Its par-3 holes have gotten a lot of recognition—and deservedly so, particularly the 10th—but to me the par-4s make the course. There are short par-4s, such as the sixth and the 11th, that require some real finesse. And there are muscle par-4s such as the first, the fourth, the 17th and the 18th. The latter force the golfer to make some strategic decisions on the tee—whether to gamble with the big drive or play it more conservatively. Either way they absolutely demand that you hit two first-class shots."

Joe Dey, the retired PGA tour commissioner who spent 35 years as executive director of the USGA, points with emphasis to Winged Foot's distinguished record as the venue of major events. It held the U.S. Amateur in 1940, the Walker Cup in 1949 and the Opens of 1929, 1959 and 1974 on the West Course, and the U.S. Women's Opens of 1957 and 1972 on the East Course.

"In each case, the course played severely and yet very fairly," he notes. "The greens have always been one of the

Framed by the lush greenery of the Westchester County parklands in suburban New York City, the 190-yard tenth (above left) has long been considered one of the most appealing holes on the West Course at Winged Foot. The fifth at Butler National (above right) is another 190-yard hole that offers a far different type of problem.

strengths at Winged Foot. When the pins are placed strategically, they demand the maximum of skill and concentration.''

Hall of Fame inductee Fred Corcoran, who lives near the 15th green at Winged Foot, has been a member at the club for years and been connected with it in some capacity ever since he served as a scoreboard boy at the 1929 Open. ''You've got to bring your putter with you at Winged Foot,'' says Corcoran. ''And the fellow who gets it up and down in two from those bunkers has to be playing with a prayer book in his pocket.''

Another incisive assessment of Winged Foot comes from its longtime pro, Claude Harmon. ''There's nothing unfair about the course,'' Harmon says. ''There are no blind holes or blind shots. Everything's right out in front of you where you can see it.''

There are some who claim that Medinah lacks that characteristic, that it contains too many blind holes. If our panel found anything wanting in Medinah, however, it lay in a certain monotony of design. Maybe there was another, more subtle factor. In the minds of many people, including several USGA officials, the 1975 Open at Medinah was a ''downer.'' It lacked charisma and excitement, it was harrassed by inclement weather, and it had the specter of so many contenders, including Jack Nicklaus, backing off at the end.

It was unfortunate, since the course itself proved fair and eminently testing.

There was widespread agreement among the panel that Medinah is even tougher than Winged Foot. Tatum, who admires Medinah as much as he does Winged Foot, believes Medinah may be too severe in some areas, notably the 13th. A man who belongs to both clubs rates Medinah ''at least three strokes tougher.''

At any rate, the switch in the rankings was not so much a demotion for Medinah as it was simply that something had to give in the top 10 to accommodate the overwhelming support for Winged Foot.

It is also true that our ratings panel has shown its willingness to delve more deeply than ever into the qualifications needed for high ranking. Another top-10 course, Pinehurst No. 2, was nearly demoted owing to a combination of spotty conditioning and slight architectural changes in the last two years. The famous old Donald Ross masterpiece, which the likes of Nicklaus and Ben Hogan rate high, is a symphony of design. Then some of the subtleties were removed. Mounds were shaved, the natural love grass and piney rough replaced by Bermuda rough, scrub cleared in strategic areas. Among those expressing their dismay were Sam Snead, who has long considered Pinehurst No. 2 the best course in America, and amateur Bill Campbell, whose

adulation of the course has been equally ardent.

The panel holds the course in such high esteem it was reluctant to drop Pinehurst from the top 10, but indicated that if the course is not restored to its original state and the condition improved, there would be no such reluctance when the list is next revised.

Heading the group of seven courses named to the list for the first time are Butler National G. C. at Oak Brook, Ill., and Muirfield Village G. C. at Columbus, Ohio, so highly regarded they were placed in the fifth 10. Although they are barely three years old, to be ranked that high so soon marks them as impressive courses.

Butler National, designed by George Fazio, is the new permanent site of the Western Open. Muirfield Village began as a collaboration of Desmond Muirhead and Jack Nicklaus. When their partnership in course architecture dissolved, Nicklaus assumed full command and it is certainly the course on which he has lavished his most careful attention. He plans a prestige tournament there each spring, modeled somewhat after the Masters. Although both new courses will need maturing to be fully evaluated, they are intrinsically sound, and potential candidates for higher ranking.

The normal gestation period for a golf course is from six to eight years. Turf must have time to settle and drainage a chance to find its new course, rough spots must be worked over, plantings must mature, a bunker must be replaced here or a tree removed there. This period of settling in and maturing can take even longer in northern climates. Only one course built since 1960 appears in the top 20, and that is Pine Tree in Florida, perhaps the greatest of Dick Wilson's many fine courses.

Wilson has 10 courses on the list of 100, an excellent showing, but nowhere near the leader—Robert Trent Jones. Jones has either designed, co-designed or redesigned 17 courses of the top 100, including one in the top 10 (Oakland Hills) and one in the second 10 (Firestone). The late Donald Ross, who designed almost as many courses (600) in 50 years as Jones has done in 40, has 14 courses on the list, including two in the top 10 (Pinehurst and Seminole). A. W. Tillinghast has six courses on the list, and William Flynn, George Fazio and Englishman H. S. Colt each had a hand in five.

Fazio, the architect of Butler National, designed another newcomer to the list, the new course which bears his name at Palmetto Dunes resort on Hilton Head Island, S.C. Two other courses that make an appearance for the first time are the work of Texan Joe Finger. They are Cedar Ridge in Tulsa, Okla., and Colonial Country Club's South Course in Memphis. Other newcomers to the list are Arcadian Shores, Myrtle Beach, S.C., the work of Rees Jones, one of Trent

(Continued on page 117)

AMERICA'S 100

As Ranked

FIRST TEN (In alphabetical order)	YARDS	PAR	YEAR	SECOND TEN (In alphabetical order)	YARDS	PAR	YEAR
Augusta National G.C. Augusta, Ga.—Alister Mackenzie	6,980	72	1932	**Baltusrol G.C. (Lower)** Springfield, N.J.—A. W. Tillinghast	7,069	72	1922
Merion G.C. (East) Ardmore, Pa.—Hugh Wilson	6,498	70	1912	**Colonial C.C.** Fort Worth, Tex.—Perry Maxwell	7,142	70	1935
Oakland Hills C.C. (South) Birmingham, Mich.—D. Ross/R. T. Jones	7,088	72	1918	**Cypress Point Club** Pebble Beach, Calif.—Alister Mackenzie	6,464	72	1928
Oakmont C.C. Oakmont, Pa.—William and Henry Fownes	6,938	72	1903	**Firestone C.C. (South)** Akron, Ohio—Bert Way/R. T. Jones	7,180	70	1929
Olympic Club (Lake) San Francisco—Sam Whiting	6,669	71	1924	**Los Angeles C.C. (North)** Los Angeles—George Thomas	6,813	71	1911
Pebble Beach Golf Links Pebble Beach, Calif.—J. Neville/D. Grant	6,815	72	1919	**Medinah C.C. (#3)** Medinah, Ill.—Tom Bendelow	7,102	71	1930
Pine Valley G.C. Clementon, N.J.—G. Crump/H. S. Colt	6,765	70	1922	**Pine Tree G.C.** Delray Beach, Fla.—Dick Wilson	7,197	72	1962
Pinehurst C.C. (#2) Pinehurst, N.C.—Donald Ross	7,051	72	1925	**Riviera C.C.** Pacific Palisades, Calif.—George Thomas/Billy Bell	7,022	72	1926
Seminole G.C. North Palm Beach, Fla.—Donald Ross	6,898	72	1929	**Shinnecock Hills G.C.** Southampton, N.Y.—William Flynn	6,697	70	1931
Winged Foot (West) Mamaroneck, N.Y.—A.W.Tillinghast	6,956	72	1923	**Southern Hills C.C.** Tulsa, Okla.—Perry Maxwell	7,037	71	1935

	YARDS	PAR	YEAR		YARDS	PAR	YEAR
Arcadian Shores G.C. Myrtle Beach, S.C.—Rees Jones	6,960	72	1974	**Coldstream C.C.** Concinnati—Dick Wilson	7,170	71	1960
Aronimink G.C. Newton Square, Pa.—Donald Ross	6,958	70	1928	**Colonial C.C. (South)** Memphis—Joe Finger	7,193	72	1972
Atlanta C.C. Atlanta—J. Finger/W. Byrd	7,053	72	1965	**The Country Club** Brookline, Mass.—F. Hood/L. Curtis/W. Flynn	6,464	72	1927
Baltimore C.C. (Five Farms) Baltimore—A.W. Tillinghast	6,833	70	1921	**C.C. of Birmingham (West)** Birmingham, Ala.—D. Ross/R. T. Jones	7,000	71	1959
Bethpage G.C. (Black) Farmingdale, N.Y.—A. W. Tillinghast	6,873	71	1936	**C.C. of Detroit** Grosse Pointe Farms, Mich.—H. S. Colt	6,875	72	1914
Boyne Highlands G.C. Harbor Springs, Mich.—Robert Trent Jones	7,131	72	1968	**C.C. of New Seabury (Blue)** Mashpee, Mass.—William Mitchell	7,175	72	1964
Cedar Ridge C.C. Tulsa, Oakla.—Joe Finger	7,112	71	1971	**Crooked Stick G.C.** Indianapolis—Pete Dye	7,086	72	1964
Champions G.C. (Jackrabbit) Houston—George Fazio	7,121	72	1964	**Desert Forest C.C.** Carefree, Ariz.—Red Lawrance	6,831	72	1962
Cherry Hills C.C. Denver—William Flynn	6,955	71	1922	**Disney World G.C. (Palms)** Lake Bunea Vista, Fla.—Joe Lee	6,951	72	1971
Chicago G.C. Wheaton, Ill.—Charles B. Macdonald	6,553	70	1892	**Goodyear G. & C.C. (Gold)** Phoenix—Robert Trent Jones	7,220	72	1965

GREATEST GOLF COURSES
by Golf Digest Magazine

THIRD TEN
(In alphabetical order)

	YARDS	PAR	YEAR
Cascades G.C. (Upper)	6,895	71	1923
Hot Springs, Va.—William Flynn			
Champions G.C. (Cypress Creek) Houston—Ralph Plummer	7,166	71	1959
C.C. of North Carolina	6,973	72	1963
Pinehurst, N.C.—E. Maples/W. Byrd			
The Golf Club	7,237	72	1967
New Albany, Ohio—Pete Dye			
Harbour Town Links	6,655	71	1969
Hilton Head, S.C.—Pete Dye			
J D M C.C. (East) (formerly PGA National) Palm Beach Gardens, Fla.—Dick Wilson	7,096	72	1962
Juipter Hills Club	7,248	72	1970
Tequesta, Fla.—George Fazio			
Oak Hill C.C. (East)	6,962	71	1926
Rochester, N.Y.—Donald Ross			
Point O'Woods G. & C.C.	6,906	71	1958
Benton Harbor, Mich.—Robert Trent Jones			
Quaker Ridge G.C.	6,745	70	1916
Scarsdale, N.Y.—A. W. Tillinghast			

FOURTH TEN
(In alphabetical order)

	YARDS	PAR	YEAR
Bellerive C.C.	7,310	71	1960
Creve Coeur, Mo.—Robert Trent Jones			
Concord G.C.	7,205	72	1963
Kiamesha Lake, N.Y.—Joe Finger			
Congressional C.C.	7,154	72	1924
Bethesda, Md.—D. Emmett/R. T. Jones			
Doral C.C. (Blue)	7,028	72	1962
Miami, Fla.—Dick Wilson			
Laurel Valley G.C.	7,045	71	1960
Ligonier, Pa.—Dick Wilson			
Peachtree G.C.	7,219	72	1948
Atlanta—Robert Trent Jones			
Prairie Dunes G.C.	6,522	70	1937
Hutchinson, Kan.—Perry Maxwell			
Saucon Valley C.C. (Grace)	7,044	72	1957
Bethlehem, Pa.—David Gordon			
Scioto C.C.	6,822	71	1912
Columbus, Ohio—Donald Ross/Dick Wilson			
Spyglass Hill G.C.	6,810	72	1966
Pebble Beach, Calif.—Robert Trent Jones			

FIFTH TEN
(In alphabetical order)

	YARDS	PAR	YEAR
Bay Hill Club	7,015	72	1961
Orlando, Fla.—Dick Wilson			
Bob O'Link G.C.	6,731	72	1916
Highland, Park, Ill.—D. Ross/Colt, Allison			
Butler National G.C.	7,002	71	1974
Oak Brook, Ill.—George Fazio			
Canterbury G.C.	6,877	72	1922
Cleveland—Herbert Strong			
Cog Hill G.C. (#4)	7,224	72	1964
Lemont, Ill.—Dick Wilson/Joe Lee			
Dunes G. & B.C.	7,008	72	1949
Myrtle Beach, S.C.—Robert Trent Jones			
Innisbrook G. & C.C. (Island)	6,965	72	1970
Tarpon Springs, Fla.—Lawrence Packard			
Lancaster C.C.	6,672	70	1920
Lancaster, Pa.—William Flyn			
Meadow Brook Club	7,101	72	1948
Westbury, N.Y.—Dick Wilson			
Muirfied Village G.C.	6,983	72	1974
Columbus, Ohio—J. Nicklaus/D. Muirhead			

SECOND FIFTY
(In alphabetical order)

	YARDS	PAR	YEAR
Grandfather G.C.	7,220	72	1968
Linville, N.C.—Ellis Maples			
Greenville C.C. (Chanticleer)	6,815	72	1971
Greenville, S.C.—Rees Jones			
Hazeltine National G.C.	7,134	72	1961
Chaska, Minn.—Robert Trent Jones			
Hershey C.C. (West)	6,928	73	1930
Hershey, Pa.—Maurice McCarthy			
Interlachen C.C.	6,726	73	1919
Edina, Minn.—Donald Ross			
Inverness Club	6,815	71	1903
Toledo, Ohio—Donald Ross			
Kittansett Club	6,545	71	1922
Marion, Mass.—Fred Hood			
La Costa C.C.	7,013	72	1964
Carlsbad, Calif.—Dick Wilson			
Maidstone G.C.	6,510	72	1891
East Hampton, N.Y.—Willie and John Park			
Manua Kea G.C.	7,200	72	1965
Kamuela, Hawaii—Robert Trent Jones			
Moselem Springs C.C.	7,003	70	1965
Fleetwood, Pa.—George Fazio			
National Cash Register G.C. (South) Dayton, Ohio—Dick Wilson	6,910	71	1953
North Shore C.C.	7,009	72	1924
Glenview, Ill.—Colt, Mackenzie, Allison			
Old Warson C.C.	7,272	71	1955
Ladue, Mo.—Robert Trent Jones			
Olympia Fields C.C. (North)	6,750	71	1922
Olympia Fields, Ill.—Willie Park			
Palmetto Dunes (Fazio Cse.)	6,855	70	1974
Hilton Head, S.C.—George Fazio			
Pauma Valley C.C.	7,003	71	1960
Pauma Valley, Calif.—Robert Trent Jones			
Plainfield C.C.	6,817	72	1920
Plainfield, N.J.—Donald Ross			
Preston Trail G.C.	7,113	71	1965
Dallas—Ralph Plummer			
Princeville G.C.	6,948	72	1972
Kauai, Hawaii—Robert Trent Jones Jr.			
Salem C.C.	6,796	72	1926
Peabody, Mass.—Donald Ross			
San Francisco G.C.	6,794	71	1915
San Francisco—A. W. Tillinghast			
Sea Island G.C.	6,692	72	1929
St. Simons Island, Ga.—Colt, Allison/D. Wilson			
Stanford University G.C.	6,782	71	1930
Stanford, Calif.—Billy Bell			
Stanwich C.C.	7,179	72	1966
Greenwich, Conn.—David Gordon			
Univ. of New Mexico G.C.	7,246	72	1966
Albuquerque, N.M.—Red Lawrence			
Wannamoisett C.C.	6,583	69	1898
Rumford, R.I.—Donald Ross			
Wilmington C.C. (South)	6,912	71	1960
Wilmington, Del.—Robert Trent Jones			
Winchester C.C.	6,659	71	1902
Winchester, Mass.—Donald Ross			
Yale University G.C.	6,628	70	1926
New Haven, Conn.—Charles B. Macdonald			

From the tee it looks reasonably wide open, but the 375-yard fifth hole at Cypress Point (above) annually poses a world of trouble for participants in Bing Crosby's National Pro-Am. The target area narrows perceptibly into the green, which is well bunkered. One of the showcase holes at Jack Nicklaus' new Muirfield Village Golf Club is the 482-yard 15th (below), an undulating par-5 cut through the woods.

Jones' two architect sons, and a real old-timer, Wannamoisett C.C., Rumford, R.I., a little gem that dates back to 1898 and is the perennial site of the Northeast Amateur.

For the statistically minded, the average course from the list of 100 measures 6,900 yards, plays to a par of 71 and is 30 years old.

In evaluating courses, the panel follows several general guidelines that determine a great course. They are, breaking them down into two primary sections:

1—Qualities of Play

The course should require that you play most shots with a maximum of skill. It should fairly test the skills of the scratch player from the tournament tees, requiring that he play all types of shots and most of the clubs in the bag. It should reward well-played shots. And it should require the golfer to blend harmoniously the use of power and finesse.

2—Aesthetic and Emotional Factors

Each hole should be memorable. The visual lines and playing characteristics should be clear, all problems in full view from the tee so you can make decisions as to how to play each shot. The over-all design of the course should offer a balance in the arrangement of each nine holes so there is a variation in the length of par-3s, par-4s and par-5s, with different types and degrees of problems involved in each. There should be a feeling of enticement, of challenge, and a sense of satisfaction in the well-played round.

In summary, the condition of the course—including turf, sand, putting surfaces, drainage, plantings—should pre-

serve, even enhance these qualities. Condition varies with climate, season and location, but it is a truism that any golf course, regardless of the quality of its design, will seek the level of its maintenance.

There are, to be sure, exceptions to all rules. Nobody has yet built the golf course that perfectly combines all the virtuous traits. There are knowledgeable people who insist that Merion is too tricky, Pebble Beach has too many average holes, Augusta National is too wide open, Harbour Town is too narrow, Seminole depends too much on the wind, Jupiter Hills is too long, Cypress Point is too short, Oakmont is too ugly, Olympic's finishing hole is too weak, Pinehurst is too plain, and so on. Whether these flaws are real or imagined, each of these courses exhibits enough elements of greatness to earn lasting recognition.

Perhaps no other course exemplifies the philosophy expressed above better than Cypress Point, that remarkable jewel perched on the Monterey Peninsula. Without doubt, many golfers could name 40 courses that are tougher or more testing than Cypress Point, a fact reflected by its ranking in the fifth 10 of the 1973 listing. But can there be more than a handful of courses that are greater? Not in the opinion of the panel, which voted it into the second 10 on the 1975 list. Stong objections came from panelists Jimmy Demaret, Bill Hyndman III and Sam Snead. It is not surprising that good players might find Cypress Point wanting; it has several easy holes and a weak finisher.

It has consecutive par-5s (holes 5 and 6) and consecutive par-3s (holes 15 and 16), and three of its par-4s are less than 340 yards. The reason Cypress is ranked among the greats is that it possesses some truly classic holes and many of the qualities of play and emotional factors which the panelists feel comprise greatness.

Two other courses with similar qualities are Pine Valley and Merion. Like Cypress Point they are short by modern standards, but both are top-10 courses. The past summer, Gene Sarazen, one of our most peripatetic and voluble panelists, went back to play these two courses. He called with his re-evaluation.

"Pine Valley is the greatest course in the world," he declared. "It burns me up that with the billions spent on course construction in the past 50 years, all the architects together haven't been able to build anything that touches it. In replaying Merion, I couldn't help but be struck that the modern architect places too much emphasis on length and not enough on the character of the greens. And when they go to remodel a course the more they lengthen the more they reduce the feel of the hole and ruin the original intent of the designer."

Sarazen neatly puts his finger on some of the beliefs that guide us in selecting America's 100 greatest courses. A course is not great just because it is long, or even because it is relentlessly tough. If there were no Pine Valleys or Merions, no Cypress Points or Harbour Towns, we might be excused for making golf courses that are bigger and duller. But happily they are there, along with Seminole, Pebble Beach, Oakmont, Upper Cascades, Shinnecock Hills and all the other superb courses that so vividly show the results of the course builder's ingenuity, his technical competence, his tenacity and his artistry. Our list of 100 greatest courses is intended above all to recognize the great courses and encourage the development of more like them.

WINNERS WALK
...While the losers

IS IT REALLY true that some golfers carry the label of consistent winners? And that there are those who will always be remembered as nice guys who just couldn't win?

It's often been said that every great champion in golf has had his share of breaks. True. But even the consistent loser will admit to enjoying his share of breaks. Added to that, many golfers have been quoted as saying "The more I play, the luckier I get." However, there is a lot more to winning at golf than luck. Much more. One of your first questions now has to be "Why?" Why the Jack Nicklauses, the Bobby Joneses, the Ben Hogans, the Arnold Palmers, the Lee Trevinos? On the other hand, why are there players who come close—oh, so close—to the threshold of being a champion, then something always seems to happen to keep them in the ranks of the majority—the non-winners.

How many times have you heard "I could have set a course record if that putt hadn't lipped out on number 17" or "I could have broken 100 if only—."

Why does golf attract so many and what are the appeals of the game. It is important to contemplate and understand the psychology of the game itself before understanding the player, winner or loser. First, it's unique that most of the problems surrounding it are mental. Picture yourself on the tee. Is my stance correct? Is my grip right? Keep my head down, take the club straight back, pronate, follow through, etc.

One of the special features of golf is that it doesn't require you to be big physically. A little man in stature can have success. Such players as Chi Chi Rodriguez, Gary Player and Lanny Wadkins are prime examples that you don't have to be 6 feet tall or better and weigh over 190 lbs. The fact that even my weight (150 pounds) is over 3,000 times that of the ball proves physical appearance and strength are of minimal importance in golf.

Another appeal of golf is that a man can blame only himself if a shot goes wrong. And this applies all the way from the tee to the cup. The man is the only one in control of the shot. Still another attraction is that every course is different and each presents some kind of different challenge. You have hilly courses, the long wide open ones, the short ones with seas of traps and enough woods for a hunting preserve, the ones that require what many golfers refer to as "shot-making" and the ones where you can "just crank up and let it fly." Added to that is the fact that every hole on every course is unique in its design. The only consistent thing in the game of golf is the diameter of the cup. This is what presents the great challenge of golf.

The emotional appeal of the "addictiveness" of golf was recently demonstrated by one of the Viet Nam POW's recently released. He stated that he was able to maintain his sanity by replaying in his mind all of the golf courses that he had played in the past and picturing each shot on each hole.

You often hear the more you practice, the better your game will be. But this isn't always true. This goes back to the fact that in golf so much is mental. Many golfers say the more they practice, the "tighter" they get.

Let's examine a term that is used in all sports and is especially important in golf: being "psyched up." One hears players who say "I'm really psyched up and ready for this one." But if you carefully watch the scores of tournaments, the ones who get psyched up generally do not play well. Their approach has turned purely physical.

Being psyched up is fine for football players, basketball players, boxers and track stars. The adrenalin starts flowing, the heart rate increases, the blood pressure increases and the respiratory rate increases, forcing more oxygen into the blood stream. That's fine if you're a football player and you're going to overpower your opponent. In golf, however, it's just the reverse. You've got to be relaxed, in complete control of yourself and your emotions. You can't be psyched up and be relaxed at the same time and in golf it's the one with the relaxed swing who is going to have more success.

Competition is another key word in all sports and again, especially in golf, because it takes on a somewhat different meaning for the golfer. In golf, competition is primarily symbolic. The only time the players are physically close to each other is either on the tee or the green. The player with an aggres-

By Richard C. Proctor, MD
Chairman, Department of Psychiatry
THE BOWMAN GRAY SCHOOL
OF MEDICINE
WAKE FOREST UNIVERSITY

ALONE...

are buying drinks

A Psychological Profile

sive personality has many advantages over the one who does not. Later on, we will examine examples of aggression and why some are afraid to win and why their aggressive tendencies make them afraid to win.

Some athletes are naturally better at team sports. Their efforts fit in with others and individual solo sports have little psychological meaning for them. Successful golfers are also a little paranoid (suspicious) and they compete well only if they maintain some physical separation from their opponents. Otherwise their paranoia tightens up their muscles and they can't swing the club in a relaxed manner. The weekend golfer is able to ventilate his hostility and aggression on the course. He is not the champion for he uses golf to get rid of certain feelings he can't get rid of elsewhere. He may not be able to cuss out his boss but he can cuss out the ball. He may not be able to hit or strike a person but he can picture his face on a ball and knock hell out of it and feel better.

Other key words in this area are "compensation" and "denial." Some golfers compensate for their aggressiveness by being overly friendly. Some compensate by spending hours on the practice tee (ventilating?). Others become withdrawn and quite reserved while still others spend a lot of time around the clubhouse, socializing.

Physically our bodies compensate for certain "weaknesses." The blind develop keener sense of hearing and their tactile sense is more acute. Consider the grammar school bully who is basically a coward and tries to deny his fears by being the big man around the school.

Another area that distinguishes the successful golfer is that he will never play his opponent. It's the course that presents his biggest challenge. The not-so-successful golfer will tend to play his opponent, to drive as far as he does, etc. When he starts doing this (and feeling that he has failed when his drive is 40 yards short), to put it bluntly "it ain't no good."

The explicit goal of all sports is to win and to win within the rules. The rules may vary in many sports, but still the main objective (at a conscious level) is to be a champion—to win.

Now for the big question: *Why are there consistent winners and consistent losers and what is the difference between them?*

The history of all sports is filled with the bad luck athlete who faltered on the threshold of victory. This man is simply a "choker." At the same time, you can take a look at any sport and find the consistent champion, the clutch player who comes through when he seems beaten or when there seems no way for victory. The illustrations are many in all sports. Take for example Bob Cousey, Johnny Unitas, Bobby Hull, Stan Smith or Mark Spitz—true winners who were not afraid to win. Yet every sport is full of what we call the majority—the loser.

Why the difference?

A good competitor uses his opponent

as a temporary enemy. To the golfer, the enemy is, or should be, the course. He may even appear angry at it, ready to take it apart.

Did you ever watch a champion come off the course after a bad round? He isn't very pleasant to be around. He will be angry, appear sullen, mad at himself, never making excuses. When he goes to the first tee to begin play he is not chatty or friendly.

However, watch the chronic loser after a bad round. There will be alibis, excuses. He seeks to be consoled, and after only a few minutes he's in the clubhouse mixing and mingling with the other professionals. He didn't win and unconsciously he is relieved that he didn't win because he has a deep-seated fear of his aggressive impulses.

Where did this fear come from? When children are in their formative years they learn that a display of aggression could have unhappy consequences. For example, if he tears something up in a show of aggression he is chastised or punished or (even more important) is told "Mother doesn't love you when you do that." He quickly learns that being aggressive and *expressing* it may bring harmful results. Yet aggressive and hostile feelings are present in all of us and are not necessarily abnormal. Into this brain goes the question, "Should I or should I not be aggressive?" Instead of expressing aggression he quickly learns to deny it and turns to niceness and politeness.

Fathers, too, play a part in this whole area. A father who pushes his son into sports (sometimes to satisfy his own frustrated ambitions through his son) may contribute to the development of a loser. If the father demands winning, is not satisfied with anything less and yet does not allow the boy to express hostility or anger at this treatment, he may find the son not winning. The not winning may be the only way the son can get back at the old man, the only way he can express his resentment. The boy resents the fact that he can't have a normal childhood, that he is spending a lot of his spare time on the practice tee and not doing other things. Yet he is trying to please his father, is afraid of rejection, afraid that love will be withdrawn. But no matter how hard he tries, he can never please his father. When he becomes an adult (physically) he does fairly well on the Tour but

never is a consistent winner. He comes close but never quite makes it.

All of us are products of many factors: environment, genetics, physical development, basic intelligence, etc. Some of these factors we have little control over but some we can modify. Motivation is important—desire. For even if all factors are ideal, without the motivation we accomplish little. There is little difference between a Cadillac and a VW if you never turn on the motor.

A composite picture of a loser shows a mother who was a good golfer or athlete, a dominant person but in a quiet subtle manner, a father who was passive and showed little interest in golf, and raised in a small conservative community. He was a nice boy, well liked in high school and in college. He had a brilliant amateur career except for one big tournament that he "blew" and later admitted that he was scared at the time. He never made it on the Tour.

A winner comes from a larger family, usually is the oldest, has some athletes in the family (but not generally the father.) The mother is strong and dominant, but aggressive and obvious about it and is personally ambitious. The father is a "weak person" and may have emotional problems himself. The player grew up in a larger community, was always a loner, had few close friends in high school and college. He was suspicious of others and was hard to get close to. He was determined to be successful and cared little, on a conscious level, whether people liked him or not. The successful champion has this aggression and is not afraid of being punished because of it. He has this drive and has no fear of displaying his aggression by winning for he is not afraid of not being loved.

Some athletes can learn to handle this fear of aggression outside the world of sports. If they find out they can be successful in business or in some other venture, then their thoughts can turn to "If I can do it here then I can also do it in golf." This has worked for several.

What do you do when you are a winner—a champion? You are at the very top and the top is a very lonely place. There is no place to go but down.

Everyone thinks that being a champion is a great spot to be in. "Look at

him—powerful, strong, with all the benefits that life can offer, and all the fringe benefits." But a champion is sub-consciously convicted of murder. He has destroyed his opponents and his friends and this is not a very comfortable feeling. Sure, his name is in the headlines and he has all the material "goodies" that go with being a champion but he may not be very comfortable. His aggression drove him to do away with his opponents—all at the not-conscious level, of course.

Another factor a champion has to contend with is that all future opponents are out to get him. They all want to knock him off. Look at UCLA in basketball. How many people want to see the Bruins get beaten? It's just a fact of life that the majority of people will pull for the underdog. If UCLA plays Podunk U on a neutral court, the crowd will pull for P.U. But the consistent winner looks forward to this competition and enjoys defending his championship position.

The consistent loser is not isolated from his peers as is the champion. He is not apart from the crowd, and his security comes from being in the crowd and part of it. One of the biggest comforts of a loser is the pity he receives from losing. He thoroughly enjoys the pat on the back, the "sorry you lost" jazz—"you came so close"—"that was a bad break on the 14th hole"—"that putt should have dropped"—"it was in all the way."

In short, one of the big differences between the consistent loser and the continual champion is being an adult. The comfort, the pity, the condolences mean nothing to a champion; while it's just what the loser needs and thrives on. He is afraid to stand alone as champion and you can always find all the losers together.

The champion can tolerate aloneness. He has learned to live with it and much of this learning came during his childhood. It is very difficult to be a winner and a nice guy at the same time. Look at the consistent winner and you will see that he is not very close to many people and never has been. You can't be a consistent winner and one of the "regular boys."

It takes a very secure person to be different (a winner). Look at children—they get their security out of belonging to the pack and being like others in the pack. "But Mother, all the other kids are doing it''—or, ''But everybody wears their hair like this.'' It takes a tremendous amount of security to stand alone and to be different. What would you do if tomorrow at noon you stood at the busiest corner in your home town and everybody but you was naked? You would either take your clothes off or leave. You couldn't stand everybody looking at you and being that different. The champion is giving up the comforts of childhood to take on the responsibility of an adult. He has emerged out of the crowd into a unique alone position.

Many times you hear, ''If he could ever win. He just needs a win, a victory, and he would be over the hump and on his way to the top.'' To some extent this is true. All of a sudden the loser has won and the unconscious fantasy of how terrible it was going to be when that victory came along is shown not to be true and is a much better feeling than the one experienced when he was afraid to win. He was not punished and did not commit murder. Now he can safely win. But he will not be a consistent winner unless he is completely satisfied that the winning feeling is much better than that of a loser. Now he can live with and accept all the things that were once considered unbearable, that go with being a winner. It will not be true when winning and being alone is a worse feeling than when he was a loser. He will return to his old role and once again seek the pat on the back and the pity from his old friends.

Age also plays a big part in being a winner or loser. The older a golfer gets it's only natural and a fact of life that the nervous system and the muscles become more difficult to control. We can recall the missed putts of the past and automatically tighten up. Timing and coordination become more difficult with age. Wouldn't it be something if we could all be Sam Sneads?

Once again, let's bring in the fact that the mental discipline of golf has to be the opposite of other sports. A golfer has to learn to do the reverse of what he sees all other athletes doing in regard to emotions and nervous systems; yet it is a very difficult thing to deliberately and willfully control. Can you willfully control blushing? No, for the harder you try the more you may blush. Yet blushing is a physical response to a feeling (or an emotion) of embarrassment. Can you deliberately slow down your heart rate after seeing the running back of your alma mater scurry for an 8-yard touchdown? How difficult it is then for a golfer to deliberately make his muscles relax when he wants so hard to win, yet may be afraid to win.

Positive thinking is an overworked phrase. Concentration may express the idea better. The ability to concentrate on the matter at hand—not past events or mistakes—is essential for the winning golfer. When thoughts of missed putts, shanked shots, duck hooks, etc., crowd into consciousness, they are liable to occur again. As in blushing, when one thinks, ''I must not shank,'' the chances of doing it increase. When one thinks ''I must not blush,'' he probably will. By the same token, when one thinks about the duck hook on the previous hole or the last time he played the same hole, it may occur again. The winner is able to blot out the thoughts of past mistakes. But he blots them out by replacing them with something—another thought.

The first commandment of psychiatry is ''Taketh not away unless thou putteth back—otherwise thou leaveth a hole.'' It is more effective to tell yourself ''I *am* going to think about this'' than to say ''I'm not going to think about something.'' If I try not to think of a slice, the thought is placed in the mind for there is the word ''slice.'' I will automatically tighten up and try to guide the ball and end up slicing. Satchel Paige put it another way by saying ''If your stomach disputes you, lie down and pacify it with cool thoughts.'' A winner can concentrate on ''cool thoughts.''

Inexperience can also play a major role in being a winner or loser. There is always a growing-up process we all have to go through in our lives. The younger a golfer can experience being a winner the better off he is likely to be.

Examine players like Jack Nicklaus and Lanny Wadkins. During their amateur careers they dominated the tournaments. They experienced success and had to stand alone at an early age. Then came the professional tour. Instant success for both of them. They had already learned to live with many things a winner has to contend with. With some golfers, it takes much longer to go through this period of adjusting. Some never do. All consciously want to win and have the skills to do so. The talent is there or they wouldn't be on the professional golf tour. Their scores will indicate the kind of golf they are capable of shooting 71-72-66-74—just enough to lose, to receive the pat on the back, condolences—a loser.

No matter what some people say, one fact of life is unassailable: There are many who will never be a winner.

Another fact: There will always be the few who are willing and able to stand alone—the winners.

About The Author
Dr. Richard C. Proctor is the Chairman of the Department of Psychiatry at the Bowman Gray School of Medicine at Wake Forest University. A native of Raleigh, North Carolina, Dick Proctor is a past president of the Southern and Southeastern Psychiatric associations, the North Carolina Neuropsychiatric Association, and past treasurer of the American College of Psychiatrists.

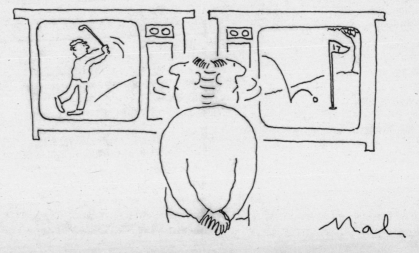

WHAT YOU CAN LEARN FROM THE SWING THAT WON THE WOMEN'S SLAM

By **SANDRA HAYNIE**
1974 U.S. Women's Open
and LPGA Champion

Because most women golfers are relatively slight in weight and stature, they must make maximum use of their physical attributes to hit for suitable distance. I believe my swing is a good one for women and smaller men to copy.

What produces distance, in my opinion, is the combination of a larger shoulder turn and lesser hip turn on the backswing along with definite use of the right side on the downswing. While this may seem violent, it will work if the golfer maintains a steady head, stays in balance and remains in easy control.

The larger shoulder turn serves to coil the body, storing up power to be released on the downswing. Right-handed golfers must use their strength—in the right side—down and through the ball. Any holding back here will diminish clubhead speed and distance.

Let me explain the more important points demonstrated in these photos of my swing with a driver.

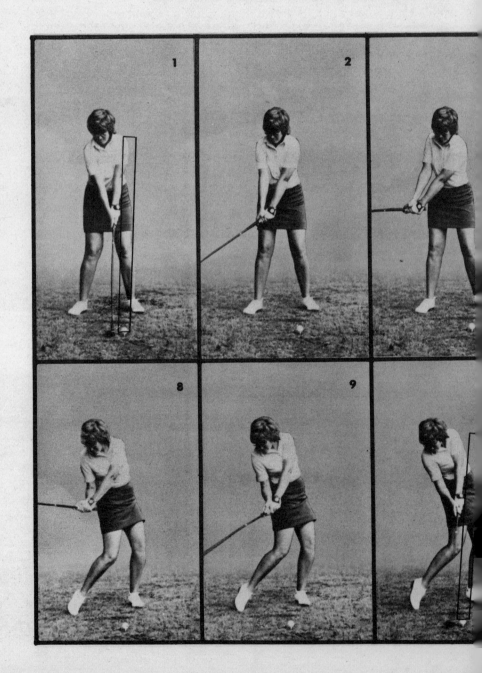

At address (photo 1), the left arm and clubshaft form a straight line. This helps me start the clubhead back with a unified motion (2) without any sudden hand or arm action that would tend to throw me off balance. I can tell you that my muscles are solid but not tense at address. My straight left arm produces good extension halfway back (3). This wide backswing arc is a necessary prelude to a proper body turn.

A point I especially want to make is that while my head stays behind the ball throughout the swing, it does rotate. As I near the top of my backswing (4) my chin is being forced around by my left shoulder. If I tried to keep my head from rotating I could not achieve the big shoulder turn I want.

Perhaps my backswing is a bit long (5), but I'm in control. My right hand is in the "tray" position and my right elbow pointing down, positions which indicate a properly upright swing path.

My left heel is solidly planted as I start my downswing (7). I set my left side quickly here because I want something solid to hit against. That strong move with my right side I mentioned earlier is evident in 7. My head and upper body remain behind the ball (8 and 9), allowing centrifugal force to add speed to the clubhead as it approaches impact. Any upper body movement toward the target would diminish distance.

Note that at the hit (10) my left arm and the clubshaft have duplicated the straight line they formed at address. This indicates I have swung in a consistent pattern which will return the clubhead into the back of the ball and produce a straight shot.

The force of my swing has carried the clubhead out toward the target (11 and 12). My hands are high (13), showing a wide arc, and I'm in complete balance at the finish (14) with my shoulders parallel to the target line—the perfect finish of a big-turn swing.

The Long Road From Longniddry

By FRANK LITTLER

IN 1976 the United States Open, in Atlanta for the first time, will again be handled by Nancy Jupp, tournament manager. Miss Jupp, for whom one year's preparation is the norm, brings to each annual assignment two secretaries (one local), an assortment of files, folders, and official stationery, and her own accumulation of Scottish-American expertise.

This, when pried open, discloses journalism in England and Australia sandwiched between.

She is small and sturdy, moves with a light, springy step, and speaks with a Lowland accent her 19 years in the United States haven't neutralized. She is the only Scotswoman to fill a responsible position in American golf—and with the growing obscurity of old-time immigrant pros, she may be the only Scot of either sex.

Ironically, she made more headlines in 1934 than she is making now.

In that year, as a 13-year old from Longniddry, near Edinburgh, she traveled down to London to compete in the British Girls' championship at Stoke Poges. Almost nobody mentions Stoke Poges without pointing out that it adjoins the country churchyard that inspired Gray's Elegy. The plowman

homeward may have plodded his weary way, but there was no such fatigue in Nancy Jupp's five trips around the course. Wearing a gray kilt and knee-high's she won every match and—6 years younger than the age limit—walked away with the trophy.

How does a schoolgirl title, captured 40 years ago, prepare the holder for mounting US Opens from coast to coast?

The answer is long, tangled, and intercontinental.

Stoke Poges gave her, naturally, a knowledge of spectator behavior (there was a gallery of 5,000 for the final) and an early understanding of the rigors of competition. Her career on the course, however, was short-lived. She was undeniably the youngest winner of a national championship in golf history—and peewee events aside, she still is. But her victory launched such an avalanche of press hyperbole that by the time she dug herself out of it she found that other sports had become more appealing than celebrity golf.

"One reporter," she recalls, "described my attitude as 'blissful indifference,' and it's true that I entered only because my sister Rhoda was playing and I wanted to keep her company. I beat a girl named Joan Montford in the final, 3 and 1, and I didn't have a thought for the future."

At least three futures, if somewhat cryptic ones, opened up for her when her victory hit the headlines. She received that many proposals of marriage—two from correspondents in the former Gold Coast, and one from a man in Aberdeen. The Aberdonian mailed his offer to the principal of her Edinburgh college, who called her in and showed it to her. "How," she asked Nancy, "am I supposed to reply to this?"

And from Canada came an inquiry from a woman anxious to trace a missing Aunt Jemima Jupp—of whom no details were given. This letter was addressed:

Miss Nancy Jupp
British Girls' Golf Champion
c/o King George V
England

Nancy replied politely that she knew of no Jemima in the family.

Meanwhile, a Scottish golf reporter, musing on her triumph and the probable reaction to it of what he called "stockbroking and torso-dropping males," wrote: "Don't trust their praise, Nancy. They hate you. You have shown that golf is a child's game."

Today, in the busy tournament office at Atlanta, she displays a different aphorism. It reads: "Be it ever so humbling, there's no place like a golf course."

Not feeling that way after the paroxysms of the British press, she turned to swimming, hockey, cricket and other sports, and didn't tread the fairways again until she was 25. Her proficiency in games she inherited from her father. He was a civil servant, who had been a county cricketer in England before he took up golf in his forties (and was soon playing to a 4 handicap). Off the playing fields she studied voice with the encouragement of her Scottish mother, who had sung with the D'Oyly Carte Opera Company, and in the early stages of World War II she had worked in an Edinburgh bank. Then she served for 5 years as a flight mechanic in the Women's Royal Air Force. The war over, she moved to London, took an apartment in Chelsea, and went to work in a sporting goods store.

"In London," she says, "I started to think seriously about journalism. So I went to a woman in Kensington who conducted a small class—there were about 12 of us—and she taught shorthand too. In 1948 I got a job with a British golf magazine."

As a child she had watched Walter Hagen win the 1929 British Open at Muirfield—"my father held me up over the heads of the gallery"—and as a golf writer in the late 1940s she was back at nearby Gullane to see Babe Zaharias. "I never saw a woman hit a ball so far, and as for her personality, when the LPGA tells you they need another one like hers they're absolutely right. I did see Joyce Wethered, but that was after her great days, and it's hard to compare golfers of different generations. When you read about what Bobby Jones might have done in a later era, you could speculate the same way about Joyce Wethered. I can only guess at how far her flawless style and her tremendous concentration would have taken her if she'd been using today's equipment."

Anxious to leave Britain in 1955 after two personal misfortunes, Nancy wrote to a relative in Adelaide, Australia, and he passed her letter to the Adelaide Advertiser. The response surprised her. She was commissioned to cover the Australian Open and Amateur—both were played in Queensland that year—so it meant going as far as Brisbane before traveling back to Adelaide. "They seemed to like what I'd written, and I went to work on the paper."

Unfortunately she soon discovered that Australian editors were inclined to put women sports reporters into journalistic purdah. "The men cover male sports, the women cover women's sports, and they even occupy different sections of the paper. You could call it sex discrimination by pages. Things may be different now, but in the 1950s Australia really was a man's country, in all sorts of ways."

So she came to America and joined the staff of the United States Golf Association in New York City.

At that time the USGA was still functioning from a dignified town house on E. 38th Street. She wrote its press releases, edited its Journal (an authoritative publication unavailable on bookstalls), and looked after the museum and library. The library had recently acquired many of the historic volumes amassed by Colonel R. Otto Probst, of South Bend, Indiana, and in sorting and cataloguing them she expanded, through random glances and gleanings, her knowledge of golf in past centuries.

Then the pace quickened. After a spell on Golf, at that time a new magazine edited by Charles Price, she was appointed to a New York office opened by J. Edwin Carter. Carter is a former PGA tournament director—a fast-talking, fast-thinking employer, from whom she learned a great deal about the intricacies of tournament organization and the multitude of decisions a director has to make.

"The men," she explains, "are called tournament directors. I call myself a tournament manager to soften the impact on my committee chairmen!"

In the early 1960s she was assisting Carter in the operation of pro tournaments, but took a leave of absence to write for Shell's Wonderful World of Golf. "I have to be grateful to a game that's given me two world tours. I wrote eight TV shows for Shell—the matches were played from Ireland to the Philippines, and I visited Scotland for the first time since I emigrated."

By 1963 she had branched out on her own. She managed the US Opens of 1964 and 1967, and between times free-lanced through Ed Carter on tour events, one of them the first Hawaiian Open.

Toward the end of the decade another personal problem suddenly left her unanchored. She had vacated her home, was no longer working for anyone, and had to start updating her contacts. Ed Carter came to her rescue by offering her some work on the revived Milwaukee Open and the new Kemper tournament at Pleasant Valley, Mass. By 1969 she was back in business for herself, and she has managed every US Open since 1970.

She establishes her temporary home wherever the championship is, being quite literally a person of no fixed abode. Into it she moves her furniture, linen, books, TV set, and ginger cat. Increasingly alienated from downtown areas, as many of her generation are, she bypasses the great cities as constantly as any touring professional. To meet her in any of them would be like meeting Henry Kissinger in a streetcar. She drives to and from the course in an Oldsmobile Cutlass.

In the apartment there are no indications of her profession, except that a few golf photographs decorate the walls and a selection of golf books can be seen in the bookcase. The rest of her library includes such contrasted authors as James

Michener, Sir Winston Churchill, and Compton Mackenzie, and she has a penchant for cook books and cat books. One of the latter, written by Mackenzie, bears his autograph—he was at one time an Edinburgh neighbor of the Jupps.

In carrying out her strangely unpublicized assignments she contracts not with the USGA but with the host club. "The clubs usually approach me 2 or 3 years ahead of time, and as soon as I'm hired I start feeding them material."

She sees little of the USGA until about a month before the date, when James F. Gaquin, Jr., tournament relations manager, arrives in order to take care of press credentials and set up the course, particularly with respect to ropes, stakes, and scoreboards. However, there is considerable liaison throughout the year.

Except for an occasional contretemps, Nancy Jupp's championships have unfolded smoothly. But at Baltusrol a few years ago she was involved in an auto accident the week before the contest, when she was returning to her Manhattan apartment. The collision occurred in the underpass at the approach to the Holland Tunnel. She suffered a broken knee, bruises, and facial injuries, and was taken to Jersey City Hospital. When asked to whom messages should be sent, she requested that a friend be instructed to go to the apartment and take care of the cat, and that Baltusrol be advised not to expect her the following morning.

Shortly afterward the Baltusrol chairman of the championship, accompanied by his wife, the chairman of the championship's legal committee, and the president of the club, arrived in a fretful party at the hospital and arranged for her to be transferred to another hospital, one much nearer to the course. One more official, however, had still to appear—when she got to the next hospital the chairman of the championship's first aid committee was in the admitting office. He was given one directive: "Get her back on the job!"

No doubt it was good pre-championship practice for all of them.

"But I remember something else about that accident," she says. "Before I got into the car to drive back to town I'd watched Arnold Palmer play a few holes—a little earlier I'd secured some extra hotel reservations for three guests he was bringing. Well, two mornings later I had a get-well letter from him. As soon as he'd heard about the accident he asked for some Baltusrol stationery and sat down and wrote to me."

She has never directed a women's tournament, but she agrees that the LPGA needs more media exposure, and bigger prize money. "And a firm and articulate spokeswoman, who has no fear of getting hurt. It's a pity the sexes are separated. One thing about tennis—when you go to Forest Hills you can hardly watch the men without seeing the women as well. It isn't possible in golf any longer—the one mixed event the pros did have has faded away. Perhaps the girls would prefer bigger purses and more TV coverage to playing with Johnny Miller and Gary Player—but as I say, it's a pity."

Asked whether the doubting looks she occasionally gets from the male committee chairmen derive from the sheer uniqueness of a woman in tournament management, she shakes her head. "No, I think some of them really suspect a woman's ability. I've noticed, though, that the more important the person the less the skepticism, and as soon as they realize I know what I'm talking about they turn right around and are great to work with."

She lifted the ginger cat from the top of her bureau and set him down on the carpet. "These days I'm a loner, and I like it. I run into former boy friends from time to time, and think to myself: 'There goes another of my lucky escapes!' To be frank, I'm delighted now that I didn't marry. I had 200 cards at Christmas, which proves that being alone isn't being lonely. The drawback, of course, is that after you've made a succession of friends in one place you have to pack up and go somewhere else for the next event."

And her game?

"Yes, I still play—but only about two or three times a year. If I had a handicap I suppose it would be about 16."

"He's played this course before."

Shooting with the Stars

by Dave Marr

The former P.G.A. champion clears up some misconceptions
about all those celebrity golf maniacs

SINCE GOLF is my business, I obviously have more than a passing interest in anything that promotes the tour. What's promoting it right through the roof these days is, of course, television, but I doubt very much if televised golf would have achieved the enormous following it has were it not for the number of celebrities both sponsoring tournaments and lending the marquee-value of their names by participating in the pro-am events. While I in no way discount the attraction of such stars as Nicklaus and Palmer, at the same time the prospect of watching yours truly miss the cut is hardly calculated to keep you glued to the set. But pair me with a Glen Campbell or a Bobby Goldsboro and it's a different story.

No sport has attracted such hard-core devotion among the show biz set as trying to break a hundred—well, make it ninety—but at the risk of losing a passel of prominent friends, I'll say right out that the majority of stars you see on television playing in the various tournaments are average, albeit dedicated, golfers playing against a handicap you don't exactly count on the fingers of one or even two hands. I say it right out because of my immense admiration for these celebrities who, for the sake of charity, continually risk making asses out of themselves in front of galleries that number in the thousands on the course and in the hundreds of thousands on television. I may sing *Moon River* in the shower and think I could give Andy Williams a run for his money, but I'm not about to put it

to the test by warbling a fast chorus in my Texas twang over national television and find that huckleberry friend has switched to a raspberry. Not for the worthiest cause in the world. Yet Andy Williams not only sponsors his own charity tournament but gladly participates in many others as well, and Andy is, in fact, an average player who shoots his handicap. Andy's not very big physically, but he makes up for it by working harder at his game than some big guys. He loves the sport, has made a tremendous contribution to it and, heaven knows, is a better golfer than I am a singer. A pro he's not.

By calling Andy an average player, I am not for a minute knocking his game but rather trying to stress what I consider an important point about celebrity participation in tournaments. I often think the galleries and TV public expect too much of the stars playing in pro-am rounds because they have seen them bring down the house with a song, or wipe out a machine-gun nest in the movies, or solve a burglary on TV; the public consequently thinks the stars can do anything. As professional performers, they can; as amateur golfers, they should not be expected to do more than play their game.

I believe there are a number of other misconceptions about what might be called celebrity golf. Fans ask me a lot of questions that are based on false assumptions, and I think it may well be time to separate fact from fiction.

To begin with, the stars you see on television are consider-

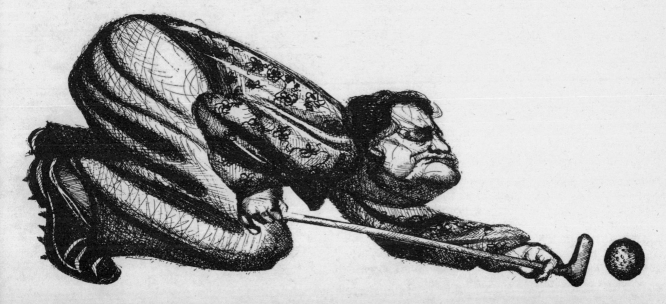

ably more serious players than it would appear from the quips exchanged with the gallery and the needling they give each other. Naturally, a lot of joking goes on while a group is waiting to tee off or walking down the fairway. These are performers, after all, and they know the public expects them to perform. The galleries haven't paid their admission fee to watch a bunch of somber-faced comedians, so the celebrities give them their money's worth and then some; but they never forget that they are in a golf tournament. They are primarily concerned with playing, and playing well. When it's time to address the ball, addressing the gallery stops. I know of only one celebrity who doesn't know where to draw the line. This guy, who for obvious reasons will remain nameless, is onstage all the time and is a real bore to play with because of it. I'm not the only pro who prays not to get paired with him, because this not-so-much-of-a-gentleman will never let the fact that it's your time to play interrupt his endless routine. There is a certain etiquette involved in golf, and if he were doing his nightclub act, you can bet he'd expect me to shut up and let him get on with it. Not that he'll have to worry: I wouldn't go near any nightclub where he's performing. Fortunately, he's the exception; the rest are like Hope and Crosby, who will toss out the perfect quip and then proceed to the serious business of golf.

At the same time the celebrities are performing for the gallery as much as the game permits, there is often another show going on. Many celebrities put on an astounding act of appearing relaxed and nonchalant when they are actually damned nervous. And with good reason. Take a typical celebrity playing in a pro-am. He is no Dean Martin, Jim Garner or Glen Campbell, who are probably the three best amateur players. He knows that the public is probably expecting more than his game is going to deliver. Right there, it's trauma time. But it doesn't stop there. The pressure of playing in a big tournament is tremendous. Here's a guy who is used to playing with friends in a foursome, teeing off with maybe a few club members standing around. Suddenly, he's teeing up in front a sizable gallery. All he can do is try to keep his hand from shaking and thank God he isn't paired with Jack Nicklaus or hasn't Arnie's Army to contend with. And while the gallery is remarkably good about keeping quiet, there's always the chance that, just as the poor guy starts his swing, an earth-shattering cheer will go up for a birdie at an adjoining green, and a beautiful topped ball will dribble down the fairway. Then, as he heads for it, doing his best not to look embarrassed, one of his fans may dash onto the fairway and steal his ball for a souvenir. He may play a new one without penalty, but the penalty to his concentration is something else.

There is another hazard of a more delicate nature our pal may have to cope with. Tournament play is notoriously slow and, for a guy who is used to whipping around his country-club course, the invariable logjam that halts the action can make the rest rooms at the end of the ninth or eighteenth hole seem awfully far away. As one very big Hollywood star learned when he was stuck at the 16th tee at Cypress Point, there's always someone you're playing with who is happy to point out to the gallery that that little nature stroll into the woods isn't prompted by ecological concerns.

With all the pressure the celebrity is under, the pros want to do everything possible to help him. Not only are we altruistic guys, but the better player you're paired with does, the better

you play yourself. But helping a celebrity partner can be a touchy thing. It's very easy to help a partner with something in his game and wind up hurting him instead, which can sort of spoil a nice day, to say nothing of a friendly relationship.

Pairing can make a very real difference. While it is usually done by tournament officials, when a celebrity is invited to a tournament he is often asked with whom he likes to play. Glen Campbell, for instance, prefers to play with Bobby Nichols. They have been friends for a long time and feel comfortable with each other. I can see why Bobby enjoys playing with Glen, because I played with him last year in San Diego and he's a fine golfer and a very nice fellow to go around with. I also have had a terrific time playing a few tournaments with Bobby Goldsboro. He's an avid fan and works very hard at his game. If he'd just spend a little more time playing golf, he would be even better. But when you're busy turning out a million-seller record, you don't have enough time to keep your edge. That's another reason I have so much respect for the celebrities who commit themselves to the tournaments. They may have just come back from making a movie in Spain or a long nightclub tour and will be off their game by a country mile, but they'll play for the sake of the charity and make no excuses for their score.

I am sometimes asked if I've ever been beaten by a

celebrity, which again seems to indicate a certain misconception about how much the public should expect from the famous. No, I have not been beaten by a celebrity amateur, and I'd feel pretty damn incompetent at my business if I were to be beaten by an amateur. I've been on the pro tour since 1957. All I do is play golf. The chances of any amateur beating any pro are pretty slim. An amateur simply can't devote enough time to his game to compete against the pro who does nothing else but work, work, work on his game. I have been beaten by Don Cherry—Don Cherry the pro, that is, not Don Cherry the singer. Since Don has been a regular on the tour and one hell of a golfer for 25 or 30 years, that he sings a little on the side doesn't count. I'll confess I came close to being beaten by Jim Garner when we were playing together in a tournament at Riviera Country Club in California. We were even as we came to the 18th tee, and I was getting a lot of teasing from the gallery. Happily, Jim was considerate enough to bogey the hole for a 71, and I finished the round with a 70, one up on him. One is all it takes.

Another thing people invariably ask me about is the practical jokes and gags they imagine take place in the locker room with all those famous comedians trying to outdo each other. Well, I'm sorry to disappoint you, folks, but the locker room is a pretty businesslike place. Tournaments are extremely complicated affairs. Instead of snappy remarks, you're more apt to hear that world-famous clown asking an official if he's on Team 31A that tees off at twelve-fifteen or Team 31B that tees off at twelve-twenty and what the hell time is it now, for God's sake? The only funny thing I remember happened in the locker room one year at the Crosby when the tournament was snowed out, which is going pretty far even for the Crosby. The morning after the storm, it was still bitter cold, but the tournament was on. Phil Harris had the locker next to mine and, when he opened the locker door, I saw a whole row of little airline-size liquor bottles. I asked, "What are those, Phil?" Phil held up one in each hand and said, "These? Haven't you ever seen hand warmers before?" It was a day I could have used a few shots of hand warmer myself.

Phil Harris is undoubtedly one of the funniest celebrities playing in the pro-ams. He's also a fine golfer, a real competitor, and an excellent putter. One year at the Crosby, Harris sank a pressure putt from 60 feet that won the pro-am for him and his partner, Dutch Harrison. There's always some luck involved in making any distance putt, but you also have to know what you're doing in order to get the ball anywhere near the cup. It is usually true that the better amateur putters are the players who don't hit the ball a long way, so they work harder at the part of the game they can improve. Bob Hope is another very good putter, though not a terribly long hitter. Tom Shaw, who plays a lot with Jackie Gleason, tells me that Gleason is also excellent on the green, which may well come from his pool playing. A lot of times it turns out that a guy who is a good putter has had what could be called a misspent youth.

Ever since color television came along, I've heard a lot of comments along the lines of, "Boy, that was some fire-engine red outfit Dean Martin had on at the Desert Classic." Celebrities do dress a little differently from your average citizen. Most of them live in California, where colors are generally brighter and clothes more flamboyant. I think the three celebrities who are the most, shall we say, noticeable dressers are Dean Martin, Glen Campbell and Bobby Goldsboro. They're almost in the Doug Sanders league. But the rest aren't too far behind, and I'm always kind of amused when someone comments on, say, Peter Falk's snazzy outfit. I mean, if he played in that old Columbo raincoat, he might find it a little hard to swing.

The other day someone wanted to know if I could remember the first celebrity I ever played with in a pro-am event. I sure can. It was Bing Crosby, with whom I was paired in a tournament at the Eldorado Country Club near Palm Springs. It was not, however, the first time I had met Bing. When I worked at Seminole in Florida, Bing was a member, and I knew him casually. But knowing someone casually and playing in a tournament with someone of the stature of Bing Crosby are two very different things. This was well before I'd won the P.G.A. I was just another young pro on the tour, and there I was playing with Bing Crosby, a name that was as much a part of my life as Roosevelt and Pope Pius XII. Believe you me, I was awed by the whole thing and far more nervous than any celebrity playing in his first pro-am today. But Bing made it easy. He is not only an institution, but a good and gracious player, although he hasn't been playing so much in the last few years.

Bing, along with Bob Hope, has done more in the cause of furthering golf than any dozen other people you could name. That's one reason I'm delighted that, when people ask me about what stars have made holes in one during the pro-am play, the only name that comes to mind is Bing Crosby. It may well be that others have, and I certainly wouldn't belittle their achievement, but I doubt if any hole in one can top Crosby's at the 16th at Cypress Point, one of the great golf holes in the world. The green sits out in the ocean, and from the tee you must shoot over an ocean-water hazard to reach it. You're lucky if you manage to knock the ball onto the green, much less into the hole. It was a remarkable feat. In the beginning there was Bing Crosby and Bob Hope. Today, thanks to them, just about every celebrity is addicted to golf and joining in pro-am tournaments. While the stars of the pro tour will always draw dedicated golfers to the gallery, it's the celebrities that draw the general public and make the tournament a success. And do they draw! You don't notice it so much around Los Angeles, but go somewhere like Atlanta or Pensacola, where the public has never seen a celebrity except on television or in a stage show, and the crowds for the Wednesday pro-am are tremendous. These people couldn't care less about golf; they've come to see the stars, and stars they get. Stars like Buddy Hackett, who one year at the Sahara Invitation had a house on the golf course and every morning had a huge gallery. He'd be breaking up while he was drinking his coffee before the tournament even started. Hackett has to be the funniest celebrity player of them all. I start laughing when he shows up.

The gallery will keep moving from one group of stars to another, trying to see them all, from a Hackett to a Jack Lemmon. Lemmon is a golf nut and real sport. I remember at the Crosby a couple of years ago, Jack muffed a little shot and it ran about halfway up a hill and back again. The television cameras had it on tape and played it in slow motion. Then a few minutes later they played it several times so that the ball would go up the hill and down, up the hill and down. Then the TV boys set it to music, and they kept running that shot all through the TV coverage. I felt kind of sorry for Jack because it did make him look pretty silly, but Jack took it in great good humor.

The pros also take a lot of kidding from the celebrities. One of the funniest incidents was when Foster Brooks, who did the drunk act on *The New Bill Cosby Show*, was playing in a group with Jack Nicklaus. This was before he was famous for his drunk bit, and Jack didn't know him. Foster, who in reality doesn't even drink, began putting on his act, and Jack didn't know whether he was kidding or not. Then Foster started getting belligerent, as drunks will, and Jack was getting pretty nervous about what the guy would do next. Finally Foster said, "Nicklaus, you play so slow that when I started out I was clean-shaven." That broke Jack up, and he finally knew it was all a gag.

One person who really tricked me was Bobby Goldsboro. Bobby can make a sound that's exactly like a cricket. At one green, I was studying my shot and kept hearing this cricket I couldn't see. Then, when I got to the next green, damned if the cricket hadn't followed me. The same thing happened at the next hole and I couldn't figure it out and it was driving me crazy. Finally the gallery was laughing so much I caught on.

By the end of the day, the gallery has seen enough stars to last a lifetime. And next week, a whole new gallery in another town will see the stars. And they'll continue to see them as long as God, in His infinite wisdom, keeps turning celebrities into golf maniacs. So please, God, enough of this tennis nonsense.

EDITOR'S NOTE: The following letter, received by Sidney Harmon, one of Hollywood's top producers, proves once more that golf is an international game whose appeal is universal.

To: Mr. Sidney Harmon

Dear Mr. Harmon,

I am hopeful that you remember me. I am Esteban Cardoza. I am still the senior golf teacher at the Real Sociedad Espanola Club de Campo in Madrid, Spain, but I am already 80 years old, but I am still Professor of Zen Philosophy at the University of Madrid.

I shall never forget how we met. It was in the motion picture studio in Madrid while you were making the Battle of the Bulge. You were having lunch with some of the actors on the picture, and I came over to get the autographs of Henry Fonda, Robert Ryan, Telly Savalas, Charles Bronson and Robert Shaw. I wanted the signed photographs for my grand-children and all of those wonderful actors were happy to cooperate. You asked me why I was wearing a baker's apron and I told you that I had been chosen as an extra in the picture just to tell my grand-children that their grandfather was an actor for a day. They never cared about golf or philosophy.

I also told you that I taught golf, not as an instructor, but as a philosopher and I tried to explain in my bad English what I meant by the spirit of Golf—but no one could understand me, even when I spoke in French and German, which some of your actors could understand, but they could not understand, so I determined that I would learn English so that I could write to you and make clear what I mean by the spirit of Golf.

You were the only one who said that you would like to take some lessons on the spirit of golf, since you had never played the game before.

We worked out a wonderful arrangement so that I could tell my grandchildren that I was a regular actor. You would keep me on the picture for the remainder of the production and I would teach you the spirit of golf three times a week at 6 A.M., rain or shine.

I must remind myself that this is my first letter in English. It is really my graduation paper for the American School here in Madrid. My grandchildren also go there every other afternoon and they have checked my spelling but they tell

SPIRIT OF GOLF

me that my grammar is impossible, so that I hope that you will forgive me. I must tell you that my grand-children think that I am a crazy old man because I want to learn English in order to write to you to tell you the philosophical idea behind the spirit of golf. They only want me to get them acting jobs in American movies.

It is no wonder that my children say that I am getting senile. They say I am always getting off the point. They should know the difficulty that I am having with the censors here in Madrid concerning my modern version of Plato's Republic which I finished writing last year and my manuscript is still waiting the proper stamps from the Ministry of Publications.

Beginning with our first lesson on the spirit of Golf, I tried to tell you something of the philosophy of Plato and its relation to golf especially when it came to your attempts to pay me for the lessons. I could never convince you that one cannot be paid for teaching spirit. It cannot be bought and it cannot be sold. It can only be shared.

It did not mean very much to you when I kept repeating in very bad English: "Look ad dee bola," "Bock Sweeng," "Bock Sweeng," "Feenish." I could not tell you at the time about the philosophy of the spirit of golf because I did not know the words for those ideas in English. It is the purpose of this letter, I hope, to make clear these ideas.

All of golf is an enigma and a mystery. I have never understood the mystery of the stars in the sky or the stars in the movies. I accept them.

I have tried to learn why hitting a little white one-and-one-half ounce ball with a club so far away from the hands gives me such a thrill even though I almost miss it over fifty percent of the time. Although I am able to go around the course in 80, which is exactly my age tomorrow. I must confess that there are times when I hit 90 or 94. This is another frustrating mystery that I shall never solve.

It is something like the task that I set for myself when I gave you your first lesson. I said that I would learn to write in English, so that I could explain what I mean when I talk about the poetry of golf. But in a way golf is not like anything else at all. It is possible for me to learn how to write and talk in English very well all the time. It is not possible to play golf well all the time, but one has the opportunity to observe the world with your eyes and your hands and your heart and only when you look out and up at the sky just before you tee off do you realize a little bit how lucky we are to be here at all. We must be aware enough to observe the color of the tee and how far it is teed up over the ground and how nicely the ball sets on the tee and observe the name of the ball and whether the grass is thick or thin under the tee. We are now ready to look out to where we are going to hit the ball. Look at that beautiful cloud or that high maple tree or to the right of that bunker.

Look around you every time that you are ready to make a shot. Of course, there are difficulties, but looking where you are and feeling where you are is where the beauty of the game is. If you look carefully you can see the slight breeze flow down in transparent cascades from the sky and you can feel the warm sound of your club as you swing it past your ear on your backswing.

You are no longer just playing golf. You are entering a new door to the mystery of life which will open your eyes more fully when you see the ball arc over the fairway on a cushion of air and then settle on the grass like a swan, embraced, sometimes, by a few leaves as it comes to a slowing stop.

If you have been able in 18 holes to have hit one magnificient shot, you will have achieved a special kind of inside feeling. Perhaps I can express my thoughts in another way.

Golf is more than hitting well.
It is some kind of Scottish spell.
Once in a while and only once in a while,
You feel that you have hit the ball a mile.
Your face has a glorious golf smile
That is not like any other feeling.
It is more like your soul singing.
It may or may not be amusing
But there is no other game so simple and confusing.
The ball is always there,
But who can tell whether there is where?
That is the confusing, confounding,
frustrating, exhilarating dilemma
and mystery of golf.

And give my very best wishes to all of my philosophic golfers in America.

Fondly,

Esteban Cardoza Jan 25, 1976

STALKING THE ELUSIVE FEATHERIE

By JOSEPH S.F. MURDOCH

THERE IS a peculiar form of madness within the sometimes mad world of golf known as collecting. Collecting, that's right. Some golfers collect books, others save clubs with wood shafts, some specialize in such items as old golf balls, prints and statuary, score-cards, ball markers, bag tags, tournament programs and magazines.

The collecting bug afflicts many golfers. The exact number, of course, will never be known; but there is a group called the Golf Collectors Society and the membership exceeds 150. One of the members is called Doc because that's what he is, and, while there is no such thing as a typical collector, Doc has an overdose of the one quality present in all forms of collectors: tenacity.

The good doctor has a bustling medical practice and takes the month of February off each year for vacation and goes to his seashore home with an accumulation of reading material for relaxation. Doc was browsing through some old golf magazines and spotted a letter to the editor from a woman who wanted to sell a feather ball, one of the true rarities in golf collecting.

Despite the fact that the magazine was six years old, Doc sat down that evening and wrote to the woman, asking about the fate of the elusive

featherie. In time he received a reply and, to his astonishment, the lady had never gotten a nibble on her offer. The ball was still available. After a bit of delicate negotiation, the ball was duly delivered and now occupies a spot of prominence in the Doc's fine collection.

A collector learns, too, that if persistence is rewarding and somewhat time-consuming, seizing a rare opportunity oft-times produces immediate results.

This was demonstrated by another collector we'll call Frank. He spent a happy weekend at Monterey, playing the great golf courses in that beautiful part of California.

One day after his round Frank repaired to a neighborhood bistro for refreshment. While sitting and sipping, he spotted a few old woodshaft clubs nailed to the wall above the bar. A few moments conversation with the barkeep revealed that an absentee owner arranged the display and might be willing to part with them.

Never at a loss for words or a dime, Frank immediately called the owner and, before hanging up, had arranged for the purchase of the clubs behind the bar. After finishing his beer, Frank walked out with them. One of the clubs, after careful cleaning and examination at home, turned out to be an antique wooden-head putter worth many times the price Frank had paid for the entire lot of clubs, the beer and the phone call.

It is suspected that one begins to collect golfiana almost by accident. A

collector can be entirely convinced he is unique in getting hooked. It is usually with some surprise that he later discovers there are others who share the interest; a modest study of golf history should have brought the news to him earlier.

Anyone who has played golf for only a short time realizes the game was by no means the invention of Dwight D. Eisenhower and Arnold D. Palmer. Just who did invent it probably will never be established but it is a matter of record that the game was played, in its present form, as early as the 15th century. Many years passed before it was recorded that men began to collect the implements and equipment of the game.

Perhaps the first such reference to collecting appeared in a footnote to a poem published in 1793 in the third edition of a book whose previous editions (1743 and 1763) were devoid of the revealing footnote.

In the poem, which describes an epic match played on the ancient links of Leith, reference is made to a certain Mr. Falconer. The note refers to the fact that Mr. Falconer had an accumulation of several hundreds of old clubs, a thought which can induce a state of frenzy in the modern-day collector.

Again, in 1866, while golf was still generally confined to the links of Scotland, a small book was published in Ayrshire which carried a number of advertisements on the back cover. One of these indicates that interest in the old and the antique was already fes-

tering. The advertisement follows:

TO GOLFERS
A MUSEUM
Has been opened in the UNION
CLUB HOUSE, St. Andrews
OLD RELICS OF GOLFING
CELEBRITIES
and other objects of interest in
connection with the game.
Contributions to the Collection will be
thankfully received.

A great burst of golf's popularity took place between 1885 and 1895 in England and even beyond to the colonies and America. Rising to the need for news, information and, perhaps more importantly, instruction, the first golf magazines began to appear. Even in some of those early issues, an occasional advertisement would appear offering to buy or sell collection of golfiana. In a September, 1899, issue of (British) *Golf Illustrated,* the following ad gives evidence that collecting was already a serious matter to some.

"Liberal prices given for old feather balls, Philip and other old clubs, prints of Golf subjects, early Gutta Percha balls and for any Golf curiosity whatever. Send price and full description to F. W., South Hill Park."

It should be obvious, then, that the collecting of golfiana is by no means a new hobby. Men have always exhibited an almost animal ferocity in pursuing a hobby, and the golf collector is no exception. As he strives to improve his game, he also demonstrates his tenacity to enlarge and improve his collection.

Equal parts of hard labor, detective work and simple good luck are the ingredients that make up a collection. Frustration must be endured and short of sinking a 18-foot putt on the home hole to win a match, the highest elation is experienced in adding a much-desired item to the collection at the expense of a competitor.

No collector of golfiana ever enjoyed better luck than one Harry B. Wood, a noted English collector in the early part of this century. He owned one of the finest golf libraries in the world, and perhaps the greatest collection of old golf clubs, golf balls and golfing curios.

There is no limit to a collector's desire to save material about his favorite sport, as these photos prove.

At that time, one of the rarest books of all on golf was a poem, entitled "The Goff" in three cantos by Thomas Matheson. There were three editions, the first being published in Edinburgh in 1743. The other two editions, 1763 and 1793, were rather more common, but the first was extremely scarce. Mr. Wood had been looking for years to find a copy.

One day, in a catalog of books for sale in Edinburgh, he noticed a listing for six packages of books on golf. He put in an order and obtained them for 6s, or about $1.50, current U.S. currency. Among them was copy of the first edition of "The Goff" in its original cover. To relate Mr. Wood's find to another field of collecting, it would be like finding a Rembrandt in a pawn shop for $10. That's luck.

Another example of luck was experienced by a present-day collector, an American who lives in England. One morning, annoyed by a persistent drip of a kitchen faucet, our collector called in a plumber. The artisan arrives to fix it and while performing his tasks, pulled a small black object from his pocket.

"Here," he said to the collector, "I found this under the floor of a house I was working in last week. Is it of any interest to you?" To our friend's delight, the object turned out to be a hand-hammered gutta percha golf ball, one of the rarest to find today. It was the kind used from about 1848 to 1852, when the transition was being made from the old feather ball to the molded guttie.

There is the story of a collector who was determined to obtain a copy of a little-known golf book published in Kenya entitled *Golf in East Africa.* This history of golf in that area had been written by a British civil servant and, because it was published in the relative anonymity of that small country, it did not exactly enjoy booming sales.

This story's hero, we'll call him Jim, visited Golf House, headquarters of the USGA, and spotted a copy of this book in the library which revealed on its title page the author's name and the name of the publisher in Nairobi.

Off to far-away Africa went a note of inquiry as to the availability of the book and after a couple of months a reply was received. The publisher had gone out of business and this answer, received from the firm that now occupied the same quarters, announced that a search of old files turned up no information or hint about the aging book.

Somewhat desperate, but still persistant, Jim wrote to the editor of *South African Golf,* the official golf magazine in South Africa, asking for help. Oddly enough, the editor not only helped but he provided Jim with the address of the author, now retired and living in England.

Off went another letter, and, despite the fact the author had since moved to still another address, it was received and acknowledged. In fact, so flattered was the author that he sent Jim his last remaining copy of his book.

Thus, from the United States to Nairobi, Kenya; to Cape Town, South Africa; to a small village in Sussex; letters had traveled almost 25,000 miles just to obtain a small book that now fills a rather narrow niche on the shelves of one collector's library.

If there are stories of success in golf collecting, there are also stories of failure and frustration. The pain that results is somewhat like taking three putts on the 18th hole when getting down in two would have returned a 79. This writer can tell such a tale of woe.

Once upon a time in Philadelphia there was a violin-maker who displayed four charming woodcarvings of golfers in his shop window. Puzzled by the incongruity, we stopped in the shop and learned that the four statues had been sent in error with a shipment of fiddle frames from Italy 'way back in the early Thirties.' Not knowing what to do with the swingers, he had placed them in the corner of the shop window where they remained undisturbed for years.

Pleased with the prospect of adding these beautiful carvings to our modest collection, we began to negotiate a price, but alas, the price quoted was a little more than a modest budget would allow. Buoyed by the thought that they had been there for more than 30 years, we began to save until the required sum could be accumulated. As the weeks went by and the kitty grew, we contented ourselves with visiting our statues every couple of weeks to savor them from the sidewalk.

Finally the day came when the pennies had grown into the necessary dollars and our dream of owning the

This handsome statue is of unknown origin but is believed to be modeled after Joyce Wethered, famous English golfer.

beautiful carvings was about to come true. An impatient morning in the office and then almost a dash down into town at the lunch hour. Flushed with the sense of impending success, we arrived at the shop, glanced in the window and stopped mid-step. Our statues were not there!

Every man experiences black days, like when you shank your approach on the 18th and lose in the final of the Fifth Flight of the Club championship, or the day your wife leaves you in favor of an old friend who plays to a three handicap, or the day you open some wine and taste vinegar. This was our black day. Our statues had been purchased the previous week by an unknown enemy, another collector.

JOE MURDOCH is a member of the Philadelphia, Pa., Cricket Club and a co-founder of the Golf Collectors Society.

ST. JERRY AND THE SHANK

By ROBERT ALLEN

IF THE NATION'S weekend golfers have any say in the matter, it seems at least an even-money bet that Professional Jerry Barber may some day be canonized for his dedicated efforts to wipe out the shank, that most demoralizing of all the game's wide variety of horrible shots.

Barber, a former P.G.A. champion, who now runs the range and pro shop at Griffith Park in Los Angeles, with his son, Tom, developed a new concept in club design a couple of years ago that resulted in a shank-proof set of irons—at least for shots hit in normal fashion from a fairway lie. Barber, a highly articulate and amusing man, also has created a new design in woods that is aimed at improving the accuracy of the run-of-the-mill player and lessening any tendency toward the accidental hook or slice.

The clubs are not *only* for the average player. In fact some highly-skilled swingers are using them with good effect. But they are, as Barber is the first to insist, aimed principally at the golfing multitudes and not his fellow professionals. However, he is dismayed to find resistance to his clubs from many pros who—he feels—should be selling them to make the game less of an ordeal for a host of frustrated addicts or beginners.

"I have seen," Barber says, "where people will come down to our range to sign up with my assistant for a series of lessons. They're housewives, they're office-girls, they're salesmen, they're lawyers, they're judges or whatever. They want to learn to play golf. But they can't learn to play golf as well with the conventional clubs as they can with a golf club that is virtually impossible to shank with. So I watch these people sign up for lessons, then disappear back into the woodwork because they couldn't handle the game.

"I had been a machinist before I went into the army in the Second War, and I began to realize that a club like this could be developed and put into the market. So I started to do some work as far as getting from foundries certain test heads and building them up with weld and machining them."

By moving the hosel out of its previous relationship to the head, after checking with a number of persons to find if this were feasible, Barber determined that he *could* build a club "that would make the game a little bit easier to play.

"Ever since they've developed the game," Barber says, "the shank has been part of it, not that it *needs* to be part of the game but because it has been when a player swings over at the top and out and doesn't quite get the club back on line

with the shot going thru, and hits the ball up on the shaft. That's what a shank is.

"A lot of people don't distinguish between a shank and a toe shot. A lot of people who hit the ball clear out on the toe and hit it at right angles think perhaps they have shanked it. That's the only thing you can do with these clubs that will even *resemble* a shank. Dan Topping in New York probably would have given $10,000 for a set of clubs like this. He used to lose that much in an afternoon because he shanked a shot. And I got a message from a man up near San Jose through my son the other day who said, 'I bless your father for developing these clubs, because I quit the game 8 years ago and now I'm playing again.

"What restricts and inhibits the swing and movement of the average player is that he thinks he might—or occasionally does—shank the ball. This club here is a boon to all of these players, and there are far more of those than there are of the other kind.

"With the average club the hosel goes all the way to the ground, to the base of the sole, and it's round in structure. On this club the hosel stops at the top edge of the clubhead, and in that way when you hit the ball at the lowest end and closest to the shaft, you get a fair shot and sometimes an excellent shot. But you do not get a shank shot. You do not get a *total* shank, even if you hit the ball up on the shaft. It has to be sitting up in the grass, and you have to swing completely under the ball, to get a shank.

"I had a letter from a man in Texas I've known for many years. His name is Frank Jones. He wrote and said this would renew our friendship on a very friendly note. He said, 'I was playing so badly, and shanking the ball so much, that when I walked into the golf shop the other day and saw a set of your irons I grabbed 'em up and took them out to the practice tee, where I hit balls for half an hour or so. Then I went back to the shop and told Clayton Jones, my professional, 'I don't know what they cost but put 'em on my bill. I am now playing at least 10 shots better than I was.'

"John McKay, the football coach at Southern California, I ran into him the other day at Julie's restaurant in Los Angeles, and he said, 'Jerry, I won't go on the golf course without your 8 and 9 and pitching and sand clubs. I just feel so much more comfortable with them.'

"These clubs enable you to take a more natural swing at

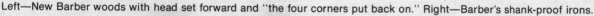

Left—New Barber woods with head set forward and "the four corners put back on." Right—Barber's shank-proof irons.

the ball, which means a better swing. Because the shanker is a guy who's trying to guide the club through the ball, and in so doing he gets so tense where his arm runs into the shoulder socket that he twists, instead of going into a lateral movement by swinging the club up on the backswing and down on the downswing and up in the follow-through. He loses a great deal of power, and that's how there came into being what they call the one-piece take-away, which is death to distance. It just *kills* the distance.

"It allows a person to kind of scoop the club along, because they cannot handle the club, and as a result of that they have no wrist action. If you can imagine Henry Aaron hitting a homerun with no wrist-action in the bat—I don't think he'd hit it much beyond short center field. You've got to have wrist-action in golf whether the players want to admit it or not. And if you want to slow down all of the good players, you'll find at the base of the swing they have fantastic wrist-action. I don't care if there are those who deny this, whether they're Jack Nicklaus or Arnold Palmer or whoever, they have the wrist-action at the bottom of the swing.

"I used to play golf with Byron Nelson. Byron had a unique swing. He had no hand action in the backswing, and as he started down he dropped his wrists in, pulled his hips back, and he went through the ball with tremendous wrist-action. He and Al Geiberger and Lloyd Mangrum belonged in that group. Geiberger does it now. People don't realize this, and very few people are able to discern that Geiberger is cocking his wrists as he moves down into the swing. But the elimination of wrist-action from the game is the elimination of power, as well as quite a bit of direction. But a *tremendous* amount of power.

"Now this club: You don't have to be as accurate swinging our golf club, but you become *more* accurate, because you lose this tension where your arm enters your shoulder. This is all locked up if you're afraid, or if you've been taught to hold the club lightly. If they just thought a little more carefully, people would realize you don't hit the ball at the bottom of a swing, with the clubhead going anywhere from 60 to 100 miles an hour, without having a good strong grip on the club.

"I had a game with Johnny Bench in Palm Springs a couple of years ago and he was the victim of a light grip. I said, 'Johnny, do you have a light grip on the bat when you hit a homerun?' He said, 'well no'. Then, I said, 'don't have a light grip on the golf club when you're trying to hit a 275 yard drive'."

The new Barber woods have the head set forward, as a visual aid to confidence, and "the four corners put back on."

"The thing that I have done," Barber explains, "is to straighten the top line, take off the crown, knock off the end of the club, and knock off the back of the club. The reason I knock off the end and the back of the club is two-fold. One, it gives you a feeling of having a straight-on shot with the club. Sort of a battering-ram thing. Second, that wood had weight. Now that weight can be underneath the sole plate where it can be more beneficial than it is out at the end of the club. And by squaring up the club-face and squaring up the look of the club itself, the player is able to line up his clubface to the intended line of flight.

"I've also decreased the amount of what we call bulge on

By squaring-up the clubhead and stopping the hosel at the top edge of the clubhead, the player is able to line up his clubface to the intended line of flight.

Even when the player hits the ball at the lowest end and closest to the shaft, the chances of an accidental hook or slice are greatly reduced.

the clubface. The ball hit toward the heel actually came out from underneath your left hand because of the tremendous amount of bulge. They figured that the less of the club touching the ball the greater the compression and the less spinning but the ball is on the clubface such a small amount of time—like 1/950th of a second or something like that—that is not really a factor. The fact is that the way the toes were rolled away and the heels were rolled in, if you caught the ball in toward the heel the ball actually went left. The *theory* was if you caught it on the heel the roll there would spin the ball and cause it to fade back in, or if you caught it on the toe it would also spin the ball, but conversely, and cause it to come back in. But I haven't found that to be a factor in playing at all. The fact is I've found it to be a detriment. It actually creates an *increased* slice or hook.

"When I developed this wood club, which I'd had in mind for a long time as I have a lot of things, I got a prototype and played with it. It had no insert in yet, but I called it my 'laughing-club' it was so easy to play. What we're really interested in is to get the club professional to realize that this unit of woods and irons will so definitely help the average player that he'll come off the golf course feeling much less frustrated, much happier, and much more anxious to get back to playing again, and his handicap will be reduced. And believe it or not, he'll be a much more livable person. I have one professional in Alabama who has sold about four sets to the same player. Fact is, he has been called, I think, by the U.S.G.A. because he's over the club limit. He belongs to too many clubs. He's over 14."

Barber also mentioned his new grip, which he believes permits the club to be held more easily because of its composition and conformation. This is optional, since the more conventional grip also is available. And he was asked how he had done during play in a tournament at Phoenix the week before.

"We could have done without *that* question," he said. "I shot two 75s, made one birdie. I'm inundated with development, production, and research. If I were twins I couldn't get all done that I need to do."

Asked if the shank were a problem for professionals, Barber had an apt story:

"I was standing in the middle of the fairway at Phoenix a year ago playing with a fellow who shanked the ball right over my head. And I waited for him and I'm sure he didn't appreciate the remark I made. But as he walked by I said, 'I've got a club that will cure that.' You won't believe this, Bob, I got no response. I got a stare-straight-ahead stone look, and it really called for some kind of remark whatever because neither he, nor I, nor the other members of the group were going to qualify to play out the last 36 holes."

"And you made the remark out of friendship?"

"Total. Total. I was going to help him.

"A former Masters champion told me he had a set of my clubs and that at least half the people playing golf should be playing with them. And a former tour player who now plays with the clubs told my brother, Willie Barber, the National Open Seniors champion, 'I've had a lot of golf clubs in my life and hit lots of them (he's over 65 now) but I never had a set as good as these'."

Barber, born and raised on a farm near Jacksonville, Ill., began playing golf left-handed when he was 6 years old.

"I've always thought if I had just stayed playing lefthanded that I would have made a terrific farmer," he says.

He moved to California in 1942, the same year he became a professional golfer. As you will hear later, he feels that his size has been a handicap to his career as a player.

"Actually, I'm 6 feet 3 and weigh 240," he says, "but the Army got me in at 5-5 and 138. I think when I went into the Army they scared me and I shrank. My best year was 1960, although I won Player of the Year in 1961. But in 1960 I won the Tournament of Champions and set a still-standing record at the Desert Inn in Las Vegas. I won the Yorba Linda tournament to get me in there. In '61 I won the PGA championship. I played in the Masters 12 times and finished as high as fifth twice. One year when Snead and Hogan tied I was three shots behind, and Snead beat me four shots on the 12th hole one round! He made two and I made six. I mentioned this to him one day and Sam said: 'Well, do you think you'd of played that good if you hadn't made that six down there?' Who knows."

Barber has a lot of merry memories:

"I was playing in the PGA championship in St. Paul at the Keller course in 1954. I was playing Freddie Haas, and he had me two down and three to play and I beat him the first extra hole. So as I'm going down to the locker-room I meet Walter Hagen, coming up the steps. Walter stops me and says, "Jerry, you're fouling up my scorecard. When I heard you were two down and three to go I put Haas's name in here, and I had to scratch that out and put your name in. I want you to be careful about that. I said 'Okay, Walter.'

"That afternoon I played Charlie Bassler from Baltimore, and he had me four down and six to play and I beat Charlie on the second extra hole. And who do you think I met going into the locker-room—Walter Hagen. Walter said, 'Jerry, you're not doing what I told you. You're fouling up my scorecard. When I heard you were four down and six to play I put Bassler in there. Now look at my card. I'm keeping it in ink and it's all fouled up with your beating these guys when you're so far behind.'

"But that's how golf is, it's not over until the last putt unless you get beat way out on the course.

"The best player I ever saw? I think the one best player that I have ever seen would have to be Snead. It would be hard to say that Snead was better than Hogan or Hogan was better than Snead. Now they are two different types of players altogether. Snead is a natural player and Hogan is a mechanical player. Hogan had to dig it out with his clubs day after day, week after week, year after year, and Snead fell out of bed with his game.

"But Snead liked golf as well as anybody I've ever known. I've played a tremendous amount of golf with Sam, and I've seen him hit shots that are just almost unreal. For sheer power and rythm and movement I think that Snead probably is the greatest player I've ever seen. Now somewhere in this conversation probably belongs Byron Nelson. Because Byron was a great player. And another player that would make a fantastic foursome if you wanted to tee the four of them off in their heyday would be Dick Metz. Dick Metz was as great a shotmaker as I believe I've ever seen. Dick was a horrendous putter.

Nicklaus?

"Well, Jack is a very dear friend of mine and is reputed to be the greatest player that ever played, but I would have to say that I've played quite a bit with the fellows we've

mentioned and I've seen Jack hit more bad shots in one round than Ben Hogan would hit in 72 holes.

"Jack is a fantastic concentrator, a great putter, and at times a fantastic shotmaker. He has won a lot of tournaments. Jack Nicklaus has probably as great an attitude to golf as anybody I've ever seen. His self-control—if you're holding a conversation with Jack and there are 40 people around you have his undivided attention. He's an incredible individual. But as far as swinging a golf club is concerned he's not even in the same room with guys like Metz and Hogan and Snead and maybe Nelson and two or three others I might mention. Jack doesn't have the rythm and timing that are natural. He's more of the mechanical type, where he had to practice and practice in order to do it.

"I've seen Bobby Jones play. I saw him play one afternoon in Belleaire, Fla., and he had a magnificent, flowing golf swing. As far as I'm concerned Bobby Jones could be in a class all by himself. I never played golf with Bobby Jones, but it would be hard to imagine anybody who could swing the golf club any better than Sam Snead."

What do most people do wrong when they play the game?

"There are three things most people do poorly at golf, because they don't quite understand the game. I said that to a man one day and he said, 'I'm not paying you to be insulting.' I told him, 'I didn't mean to be; if you want to we can stop the lesson now.' He said, 'Oh, no, I was just kidding.' But I knew he wasn't. Most people don't know how to put their hands on the club and the single most important thing is that they don't keep the hands on the club while they're swinging—for the duration of the swing, which takes less than 2 seconds. This is the single biggest problem. The grip is too loose.

"The other two things that are so important—and they're taught this, incidentally—they're taught to stand with their feet the width of their shoulders, and to stand too close to the ball. Nothing could be worse. You put your feet far enough apart to maintain your balance. If I had a pair of shoulders the width of my golf stance, I would be able to take Muhammad Ali on, I think. Because I put my feet out far enough to maintain my balance.

"Most people that play golf stand too close to the ball, not only after they hit it but before they hit it. And because they stand too close to the ball they're apt to make a lateral travel at the top of the backswing which goes out. Then as they come down—they don't know this, but they're too close to the ball and they have to pull the club in, the left shoulder goes out into what we call left field, and this accentuates the already positive slice most people have.

"*Most* people have a poor grip, not secure enough, not firm enough. They stand with their feet too close together, and they stand too close to the ball.

"I never teach a person to squat. A person should take his grip with the club up in the air, and then as he brings the club down to the ground he should bend forward at the waist and set the club on the ground. Then he breaks his right knee in quite a bit more than the left knee, because the right hand goes beneath the left hand so the right shoulder has to be dropped lower and you get this by breaking in your right knee. If you squat, you set up a strain through the center of your back and you build up tension in your shoulders and arms and then you're almost dead before you start . . ."

How could the average player get more distance?

"Most people stand too close to the ball, as I've said, and because they stand too close they have to turn away from the ball as they're hitting it in order not to shank it or hit it so far into the heel that they're going to get nothing out of it. Because of this they have to uncock their wrists way, way early in the downswing, which means they're just flailing at the ball with their arms. All the power is gone before it gets to the ball. Most people would be better off if they stood too far from the ball, with their feet too far apart, with too tight a grip. They'd play a lot better.

"I had a young boy from the University of Southern California golf team out here yesterday for a lesson, and he was standing right on top of the ball. All he has to do is lay off for a few days and he's dead. He can't play a lick. Golf is a sadly misunderstood game and, I think, probably the poorest-taught game of all the games I know. Many of the teachers get what they teach out of books, and the best book has not yet been written.

"The game of golf is between your mind and your fingers. If you take your mind off your hands you're a dead pigeon. As soon as you turn loose of that golf club that shot is gone, lost, destroyed, ruined. The follow-through should be easy, natural, and on the same plane of the swing. If you swing a baseball bat you have a level swing, parallel to the ground. If you took that same swing and bent forward at the waist, now you're going to swing in a tilted plane. So the club coming up high on the follow-through doesn't mean a thing. If you're thinking of coming up high, you may forget to hold onto it. The player's mind must be on holding onto the club and retaining control of the club for the duration of the swing. You can do more with your hands, and thinking about holding onto the club, than you'll ever do thinking about finishing high or getting the club flat or upright or back or whatever."

Graphite shafts?

"I've tried several graphite shafts. I've found one I think is pretty good, but I cannot hit a graphite shaft any farther than I can hit any other shaft. I think the one thing that is good about graphite is for the average person who doesn't have as much physical strength as a lot of the professionals have and a lot of the good amateurs. Just the lightness of it is beneficial. But as far as knocking the ball farther, I can't do it. I've found out I can drive the ball much farther on ice than I can with graphite."

What would you change if given the chance?

"I don't know. I would do it a lot differently if I were a touring golf pro again. I would work much harder practicing than I did—and I practiced very hard. I had a reputation when I went around to the different tournaments, and the kids would see me coming and all go and hide. Because they knew I was going to practice before breakfast and after lunch and after dinner and back in the evening and whatever. I would be a golfer or maybe a musician or something. I like music. I love piano. I have a sister who's a natural pianist. She can hear a song and play it.

"But if I were to be a professional golfer again I think I could have done a lot better. I go out to the tournaments and watch the professionals play and I hear the young fellows teaching each other, and I sometimes feel it's the blind leading the blind. Because it's just a matter of experience and they haven't had enough experience to know what to

look for. They can play well because they're well-coordinated, they're young, and they're strong. But actually, in today's market, I'm too small for the tour, much too small.

"Those guys out there are hitting the ball! When I tee off with a driver and they're laying up on the hole with a one-iron and we're out there the same distance, I know I'm in the wrong league, see? But the name of the game is to get the score.

"But there again—the architects have made the golf courses longer, like that Butler National. I wouldn't go near that place unless I could hit it as far as George Bayer, Jack Nicklaus, Sam Snead or Ben Hogan or some of those guys. That's just an *impossible* golf course.

"You see, they took the quality out of the game in many areas and put quantity in. It's not a matter of being able to *think* your way around a course, it's being able to blast it over the bunkers they build out there to a wide-open fairway, to a golf course where a guy who has a 280- or 290-yard tee shot has so much advantage over you.

"If some of these young fellows who have so much power had the dedication to the game that some of the players had before, there's no way of telling what they could do. But they do not have the dedication. You see 'em out there—to them practice is hitting one or two bags of practice balls and 15 or 20 minutes of putting and a little chipping and that's the end of it. Although they do a lot of putting. They hit a lot of drives and then a lot of putts. They don't hit the ball up on the green like I think they should, and they don't have the quality of the swing that I think they should. They're not nearly as good as they should be from a hundred yards in."

What about today's big purses?

"I was just getting in to the edge of it. The first big purse we had was the Tam O'Shanter purse. I came the year that Ted Kroll won.

"At the end of the 57th hole I was leading the tournament, but Ted went on a birdie binge, where on the last round he birdied 5, 6, 7, parred 8, birdied 9, 10, and 11. He made six birdies in seven holes and he just ran away and hid. We kept walking down the fairway, and I never saw so many people on a golf course. They were 30-deep around the green, at that time they estimated they had 30 or 35,000 people on the golf course. Ted said, 'Don't leave me! Don't leave me! Just walk right next to me.' If you hit a ball off line to the green it had to hit somebody 'cause you couldn't get out of the way.

"Yes, I missed the days of the big purses. The year that I had my best year, in 1960, if I would have had it in the last few years I would have won between 175 and 200 thousand dollars. Because I won $36,000. I won two tournaments. That would have been good for 60 or 70 thousand, but I had a lot of good finishes that year. The fellow who was second at Phoenix the other day won $22,800! We used to tee off in a $10,000 tournament!"

Perhaps a second Barber son should be mentioned here. His name is Roger, he's only 17, and he has a magnificent swing. Maybe he'll get a chance to cut up some of those rich pots his old man missed.

The Jerry Barber clubs are distributed by the Golf International Corp. of Irvine, Cal.

And the next time I shank . . .

Golf Hawaii

Text and Photos by WILL HERTZBERG

Golfers must carry 150 yards of ocean on Mauna Kea's treacherous 225-yard par-three 3rd hole.

WHETHER you're the type of person who enjoys sightseeing and shopping for colorful native clothing or of the walk-on-the-beach-at-sunset-with-a-mai-tai-in-hand persuasion, the outstanding golfing facilities that await you in Hawaii are sure to lure you from your scheduled activities and have you seduced at the turn.

Hawaii is everything you've read about it and then some—beautiful weather, a crystal clear warm ocean, magnificent beaches, fine restaurants and an outstanding array of golf challenges.

Of course, you'll hear skeptics who complain that Hawaii is way too commercial and touristy, that they could have just as easily stayed on the mainland and saved a bundle. While this may be true of the Honolulu/Waikiki area, which looks like Miami Beach West with roaming groups of Hare Krishnas, the outlying area of Oahu and the other populated islands are very sparsely populated. An amazing 80 percent of the state's 850,000 population live in Oahu, justifying the name the old Hawaiians gave it—"The Gathering Place." Honolulu is where the majority of the flights from the mainland land, and nearby Waikiki is the main beach/entertainment/hotel area. And while get-away-from-it-all purists may find the pace a bit hectic and the conditions overcrowded, Waikiki is where the action is. Stage shows, discoteques till dawn, rooftop restaurants, and eligible singles of both sexes make the Waikiki area the place to be for an active nightlife. Days are usually spent soaking in the glorious rays at the beach, catamaran riding, or sightseeing around the rest of the island's 608 square miles, and 112 miles of fantastic coastline.

Oahu

Resort golf on Oahu is centered around Makaha on the leeward side and Kuilima on the windward side. Makaha is located about an hour drive north of the Honolulu/Waikiki area, while Kuilima is about an hour drive through the mountains to the other side of the island.

Makaha Inn and Country Club is the only facility in the islands that offers two full 18-hole layouts—the 7,252-yard par-72 monster West course, and the more reasonable 6,403-yard par-71 East course. With a championship rating of 75, the West course is one of the toughest in Hawaii. It's certainly one of the most memorable, with huge mountains rising from either side of the fairways on the back nine. The East course follows the sloping edge of the lush valley's eastern mountain range and requires accuracy and finesse with both woods and irons rather than crushing drives. The greens are well trapped, and are generally faster than those you may be accustomed to. Guest accommodations are situated in 13 acres of green lawns, flowering shrubs and uncluttered arbors. A total of 196 rooms are available at the inn ranging in price from $36 to $75 double. The sunny accommodations are Polynesian inspired in decor and are set against a setting of tropical, natural foliage, with each room commanding a panoramic view of mountains, valley or ocean. Other amenities at Makaha include two lighted tennis courts, two swimming pools, shuffleboard courts, croquet green, driving range, archery field and trap shooting. Also of note to deep sea fishermen is the fact that the world's largest recorded marlin (1,805 pounds) was caught just off the shores of Makaha.

Located on the North shore of Oahu near the famed surfing areas of Waimea Bay and the Bonzai Pipeline, the Kuilima Resort Hotel and Country Club offers visitors splendor and seclusion.

The Kuilima is the only hotel on Oahu right on the beach with its own 7,061-yard par-72 golf course. Each of the hotel's 500 rooms, cottages and cabanas has a spectacular ocean view, and most have their own private lanai. Rates range from $45 double in the main building to $175 for a three-room suite. Special golf and honeymoon packages are also available. Two swimming pools, four lighted tennis courts and paddle tennis facilities provide ample recreation while not lounging on Kuilima's beautiful sandy cove or playing a round of golf. Although pro Palmer Lawrence does a fine job at his course, the Kuilima area is more noted for its outstanding hotel facility than its golf course, and rightly so. Unpredictable winds on the north shore play havoc with your game, while the lack of rain has left the course dry and brown. The layout itself is relatively flat, with little trouble. Greens are fast (perhaps due to the dryness) and some have considerable undulations. It is a fair tract, but not very stimulating visually.

Maui

With two 18-hole golf courses and a stretch of hotels fronting one of the world's great beaches, the Kaanapali area may prove to be one of your favorite stops on your visit through the Islands. Only a 45-minute drive from the airport, the Kaanapali facilities are impressive, with over 2,000 rooms available along a one-mile strip of sandy beach. Outstanding hotels in the area include: the Kaanapali Beach Hotel, Maui Surf, Maui Eldorado, Royal Lahaina, Hilton Hale Kaanapali Hotel, and the Maui Sheraton. There are also more than 20 tennis courts in the area, and a list of amenities that won't quit. Rates in the area generally begin at $32 double. Centrally located amidst the mini-vacation metropolis, are the two Kaanapali golf courses— The 7,179-yard par-72 Royal Kaanapali, and the smaller par-64 Kaanapali Kai executive course. Played from the back tees, the Royal Kaanapali is strictly for the long knockers. Its varied terrain, beautiful greens and breathtaking ocean views (except for the new hotels under construction) make it an enjoyable test. There are six par 4s over 420 yards and the 645-yard par 5 18th is the most difficult finishing hole in Hawaii. However, the executive

course leaves much to be desired. It is flat, dry and unimaginative, but could serve as a tune-up if the Royal course is too crowded.

Located only about 30 minutes from the airport, the new resort community of Wailea presents one of the finest yet least discovered of all golf resorts in Hawaii. It has not only an outstanding 6,700-yard par-72 golf course with a $1 million clubhouse, but the largest tennis facility in Hawaii with 11 courts and a center-court stadium that seats 1,500. The unique residential resort community embraces five crescent shaped sandy beaches and covers 1,500 acres. All construction and amenities have been carefully master planned to ensure retention of the beautiful scenery and wide-open spaces. The 600-room Maui Intercontinental hotel is scheduled for completion in January 1976, as well as 300 low-rise, two-story condominiums. Wailea is gearing up its efforts to become the top resort on Maui, and optimistically the best in the Islands. They have a fine start, particularly with their tennis facilities and the *finest* maintained course in Hawaii. Wailea has spared no expense in producing lush fairways and perfectly manicured greens. Wailea is a joy to play, despite its 76 bunkers which add an extra challenge to its moderate length. It is a fair course, where *all* par 4s are reachable in two by the average golfer. Beautiful ocean and island panoramas add to the blissful feeling one gets when playing a round at Wailea, known for the finest climate (least rain and wind) in Maui. Another full 18 holes of golf are scheduled for completion by January, 1977.

Kauai

Kauai, "The Garden Isle", boasts two fine golf resorts on opposite sides of the 627-mile square island. With a population of only 31,000, Kauai offers majestic scenery in an uncrowded, relaxed atmosphere where golf is just another digression from the tranquility of Hawaii's oldest island. Only a 10-minute drive from the airport, the Kauai Surf offers one of Hawaii's most complete resorts. Two-hundred acres of green, combined with a half-mile of white, sandy, uncrowded beach, afford the visitor a visual feast as well as a relaxing vacationland. Rooms range from $34 to $44 double. There is the serenity of their Japanese garden com-

Princeville's 180-yard par-three Ocean 3rd is the most scenic hole in the Islands.

bined with the challenge of eight tennis courts and a 6,808-yard par-72 golf course. Water hazards and large fairway bunkers make golf a fine test at the Kauai Surf.

Although not a resort development, the Wailua Golf Course, just a few miles south of the Kauai Surf, offers the finest municipal golf challenge in Hawaii. The 7,028-yard par-72 seaside layout is well maintained and was the site of this year's National Public Links Championship. Play the Kauai Surf in the morning, and Wailua in early evening as the sun sets into the deep blue Pacific.

Lush green mountains, cascading waterfalls and miles of virgin beaches characterize the northern edge of Kauai, home of the beautiful Princeville Makai Golf and Tennis Club. Princeville is only 45 minutes from the airport and just a 4-wood from Hanalei Bay where the movie "South Pacific"

was filmed. Princeville utilizes the natural terrain and ocean panoramas to make the Robert Trent Jones, Jr. course one of the finest in Hawaii. Princeville's 27 holes—a woods nine, a lake nine, and an ocean nine—offer golfers a total of six different 18-hole par-72 playing combinations. Each nine plays over 3,400 yards from the back tees, and about 3,100 from the regular markers. Of the three nines, the 3,460-yard par-36 Ocean nine is by far the most inspired, with varied elevations and fantastic ocean views. This is unquestionably the finest nine consecutive holes of golf in the Islands. If you play the ocean nine first, you may never want to try the rest of the course. It's that intoxicating. And the beautifully manicured greens make putting a joy at Princeville. As an indication of the courses' potential, it moved into *Golf Digest's* Top 100 after only three years of existence. Another complete 18' holes are in the master plan, which would make Princeville the largest golf facility in Hawaii, and certainly one of the most beautiful and secluded. For tennis enthusiasts, Princeville boasts six fast-drying courts. Princeville has some of the finest accommodations of Kauai, including a total of 125 cottages, sealodges and condominiums in both 1- and 2-bedroom models. Rates range from $32 to $78 per day, depending on size and location. The 86 Pali Ke Kua low-rise condominiums, situated above a secluded beach, offer incredible mountain and ocean views and are priced from $46 to $75 per day for 1- and 2-bedrooms, respectively.

Hawaii

When you speak of luxury golf resorts in Hawaii, none can compare with the fabulous Mauna Kea Beach Hotel and golf course. Situated some 25 miles north of the Ke'ahole airport (over an endless expanse of residual lava), Mauna Kea is a jewel at the end of desolation highway. It's like arriving in Palm Springs after baking in your car through miles of lifeless desert. Mauna Kea is an oasis blasted out of lava by Robert Trent Jones some 12 years ago at the request of Laurance S. Rockefeller, chairman of Rockresorts. When construction first started, the project appeared almost impossible. But, little by little, the desolate lava fields were transformed into lush greens and fairways. A magnificent luxury hotel

Golfers are afforded a magnificent ocean panorama playing Wailea's 138-yard 16th.

Looking down on the 18th green of the Mauna Kea course and the ocean front hotel.

was built, and $20 million later, Mauna Kea had established itself as one of the finest resorts in the world. The golf course is listed in *Golf Digest's* Top 50, and is aiming for the top 25. Each hole on the 7,016-yard par-72 layout affords an ocean view. Holes are designed with broad fairways, and well-undulated greens, seven of which are being rebuilt to increase playability. In the past, some visitors have complained that the greens were just too severe and that three- and even four-putts were all too frequent. With the greens leveled, the course should play a couple of strokes easier, which will still make it the toughest in Hawaii. The greens themselves average 6,500-8,000 square feet. Even if you decide to play from the regular tees, you will have to contend with 106 bunkers over 6,593 yards. The course sprawls over 230 acres, giving the golfer a feeling of uncrowdedness not generally associated with resort layouts. Mauna Kea was built on the Jones' philosophy that: "Every hole should be a demanding par and a comfortable bogey." He has succeeded in every way, while providing a dazzling

Seven devouring bunkers guard the 145-yard 7th at Kauai Surf.

visual feast during your round. The Mauna Kea Hotel is the perfect blend of a grandiose Southern Plantation and a tranquil South Pacific retreat. With 310 rooms overlooking the ocean, gardens and distant snow-capped 13,796-foot Mauna Kea, the hotel is not a high rise eyesore, but rather a harmonious addition to a beautiful setting. You may find yourself brushing elbows with international entertainment celebrities, high ranking political figures or million-dollar-a-year athletes. They all come to unwind at Mauna Kea. When you're not out doing battle with the golf course, you can relax on Mauna Kea's fantastic beach or play a game of tennis on one of their nine courts. At $100 to $125 double, you may find Mauna Kea a bit steep for your vacation budget. But remember, that price includes breakfast and dinner, and you haven't dined until doing so at Mauna Kea. If you happen to drop by for a round of golf in the morning, be sure to stay for the buffet lunch served on the open air terrace overlooking the beach and ocean below. For $6.50 you get a feast fit for anybody's king, with a huge variety of salads, entrees and a desert area which resembles the spread at a French bakery. But whether you're taking advantage of one of Mauna Kea's five special five day/four nights plans—family, honeymoon, golfer's, tennis or scuba—or just dropping by for a round of golf and buffet lunch, Mauna Kea is an *absolute must* during your stay in Hawaii.

Just a few miles before reaching Mauna Kea, is the relatively new 31,000-acre Waikoloa development, complete with a 6,833-yard par-72 golf course, tennis courts, swimming pool and complete stable and riding facili-

What To Know Before You Go

TRANSPORTATION

Air: Hawaii is serviced by five carriers out of Los Angeles including Northwest Orient, Pan American, United, Continental and Western. Round-trip fares range from $238.75 (economy weekday flights) to $252.75 for coach weekday flights. First class fare is $408.80 Flying time is approximately 5½ hours. Special golf tour packages are available from all air carriers. Hawaiian Airlines and Aloha Airlines provide intra-island transportation with a common fare of $11 per stopover for passengers from the mainland. Residents of the Islands have to pay $25 to $30 for the same flights. Sea: The Pacific Far East line has two ships, the SS Mariposa and the SS Monterey that cruise to the Islands. Travel time is five days each way, and fares range from $516 per adult (one way) to $1,253 for a suite. Eighteen-day package cruises including four islands range from $1,752 to $4,265. Seaflite: A new hydro-foil boat offers a unique form of intra-island transportation for about $20-$25. Travel time is about 2½ hours, compared to 20-30 minutes by air. Regardless of what form of transportation you decide upon, be sure to check with your travel agent for special package tours and/or charters that you may be able to take advantage of at considerable savings.

CLIMATE

Hawaii's near perfect climate is one of the state's major tourist attractions. Days are usually in the 75-85 degree range, while the nights are a beautiful 70. Temperatures vary little from summer to winter. Rainfall averages 20 to 30 inches per year, but visitors should be warned that it can and does rain without warning almost every day. The refreshing "pineapple mist" as the locals like to call their sudden downpours, may last for only a few minutes, or can turn on and off like a water faucet during your afternoon round of golf.

WHAT TO BRING

Although most golfers visiting Hawaii usually bring their own clubs and balls, it is not an absolute necessity. Most resort courses have rental clubs available for $6 to $8 per round and all have well-stocked pro shops. Clothing should be casual, cool and of the drip-dry variety. Don't make the mistake of packing heavy sweaters or overcoats. Even sports jackets are a rare sight in this relaxed atmosphere, where patrons at fine restaurants wear their Bermuda shorts, Hawaiian shirts and sandals . . . as do the waiters! An umbrella is a must, as is a windbreaker if you're headed to the windward side of any other of the Islands. A beach blanket is a wise addition if you're planning to bronze your body.

YOUR BUDGET

If your wife is the type who loves shopping, you better bring a Brinks truck full of the green folding stuff. Prices on the whole are about 15% higher in Hawaii than on the mainland. Dining and drinking (especially those habit-forming tropical concoctions) can gouge deeply into the family piggy bank. Hotels are fairly priced. Plan to spend a minimum of $32 per night for a double room and $20 per person per day for food. If you plan on renting a car, and I highly recommend it, that will cost you a minimum of $15 per day plus gas. Hawaii's cost of living is approximately the same as New York City's, but we think you'll agree that your visit there will give your lungs a much needed rest, and you'll never have to shovel soot-covered snow from your driveway.

TOURIST ATTRACTIONS

Upon arrival in Hawaii be sure to pick up a copy of *This Week,* a fantastic publication covering all the major sight-seeing attractions, dining and entertainment establishments in the Islands. There are also numerous other publications available at most hotels outlining tours available. Besides golf Hawaii offers excellent diving, fishing, hunting, hiking, sailing, and hang gliding.

FOR FURTHER INFORMATION

Contact your local travel agent or the Hawaii Visitor's Bureau, 3340 Wilshire Blvd., Suite 203, Los Angeles, CA 90010.

Above—Par-five 18th at Waikoloa golf course. Below—A cinder cone looms in background of Seamountain's 147-yard 14th.

ties. The Boise Cascade project is still in its infancy, but big things are planned for the future, including a beach resort with another 18-hole championship golf course and as many as six beachfront hotels to challenge the monopoly currently held by Mauna Kea. The Waikoloa golf course, designed by Robert Trent Jones, Jr., was first opened for play in early 1972. And although it lacks the maturity that will add to its stature, it is still a fine test of golf, with sharp doglegs and strategically placed traps. During our last visit, the course was in excellent condition, enhanced by the dramatics of snow-capped Mauna Kea and Mauna Loa (which just recently erupted after 25 years of relative inactivity). For those wishing to stay at Waikoloa, condominiums are available for rent from $20 per day for a studio, to $31 per day for an upper level 1-bedroom.

Heading south 12 miles from the Ke'ahole airport along the Kona coast, you will encounter the Keauhou-Kona Country Club, complete with a 6,814-yard par-72 course designed by architect Billy Bell. Varied terrain and fine greens, plus the inviting lava fields bordering the fairways make Keauhou-Kona a stiff challenge for the golf vacationer. Two luxury resorts, the 318-room Keauhou Beach Hotel and the 550-room Kona Surf offer excellent accommodations, food and entertainment within a few minutes of the first tee. Rates at the Keauhou range from $31 to $41 per night double, while the Surf commands $37 to $44 double. Both hotels have tennis facilities and swimming pools.

About 60 miles south of the Keauhou (along a narrow, winding two-lane road through mountains and lava flows) lies Seamountain, one of the finest new courses in all the Islands. The 6,492-yard par-72 layout is the first in a series of recreational attractions at Seamountain-Hawaii, a major new Big Island vacation region extending from seaside lagoons to cool green upland forests. Designed by Arthur Jack Snyder, Seamountain is beautifully maintained and offers the golfer a variety of shot-making challenges not generally associated with a course only 1½ years old. Double doglegs, water hazards and 24 traps add interest to the well-planned layout. There are no fairway bunkers, and only two parallel fairways. Seventy four condominiums have just been completed and are available for renting. In addition, a 230-room hotel built over a lagoon at the ocean's edge is scheduled for completion by 1978. Numerous homesites are also available for those interested in living at Seamountain. Tennis and swimming facilities are coming in the near future.

About 30 miles further along Highway 11 toward Hilo (where your plane may have landed in the first place) is Volcano Golf course, a relatively short 6,219-yard par-72 layout owned by the Brewer company, the same firm responsible for the Seamountain development. Unfortunately, Volcano doesn't live up to its billing, and is forced to take the backseat to Seamountain in every way. During a recent visit, the course was in mediocre condition and was suffering from a severe lack of rain (as were many courses in the Islands). However, you may want to stay overnight at the famed Volcano House on the rim of Kilauea Crater. There are 39 rooms ranging in price from $20 to $28 per night double. If you're just passing through on a visit to Kiluaea Crater, be sure to stop for their buffet lunch at the Volcano house, where as many as 1,000 guests are served daily. If you eat there, you'll understand its popularity.

Remember, before you make any decisions as to where you want to spend your golfing vacation in Hawaii, be sure to talk it over with friends who have been there or consult your friendly travel agent, who can guide you in your selection of hotels and courses best suited to your travel objectives. Hawaii is a state of mind that should definitely be visited at least once in a lifetime, but prior planning is a must for maximum enjoyment of your vacation.

Golfers must hit over huge expanse of lava to reach Keauhou Kona's 150-yard 17th.

HOW TO HELP YOUR GAME BY WATCHING TV TOURNAMENTS

WHEN YOU ARE watching a professional golf tournament on television you can learn a lot more than just how the players are scoring. If you'll study what's going on, you can help your own swing and improve your game.

The key is to know what to look for. Mostly you'll just get a general impression of the players' swings as you watch the action, but there will be a bonus "instant lesson" for you with each slow-motion replay.

Some fundamentals you can improve by watching the stars in action on the TV screen are: setup routine, posture, swing tempo, rhythm and balance.

It is a good idea to pick out players with physical characteristics similar to your own and watch them closely. If you're tall and slender, for instance, you might want to choose Al Geiberger or George Archer for a model. If you're short and stocky, pay close attention to the way Gary Player and Lee Trevino swing.

No matter how you're built, you can benefit from watching the smooth swings of Sam Snead, Gene Littler, Bruce Crampton and Julius Boros. If you have a tendency to swing too fast and lash at the ball, notice the way these pros swing with ease.

One reason most touring stars make such good free swings through the ball is their excellent posture as they set up for the shot. Study Tom Weiskopf next time he's playing in your living room. Note how he positions his lower body nearer the hole than he positions his torso. Watch how he bends slightly at the waist, keeping his back straight and allowing his arms to hang freely. As you watch him, try to imitate his setup. You might even want to hang a large mirror close to the TV so you can check your setup against what you see on the screen.

Notice that almost every player has a set routine in preparing to make a shot. Pick out a player whose routine you like and try to copy it.

Steve Reid, the former tour player who is now the TPD's television coordinator, points out that Bert Yancey has a routine that follows the same pattern right down to the second. "Watch him sometime," Reid says. "After he chooses a club he always takes exactly 13 seconds waggling and checking his line until he strikes the ball."

Another part of your game you can help watching TV is footwork and balance. Watch how Johnny Miller pushes off his right foot and finishes on the outside of his left. Dave Marr, the 1965 PGA champion who works with the ABC telecasting crew, says many average golfers lack this good weight shift and could improve their play by trying to imitate Miller's footwork. "Good balance encourages good swing movements," Marr says. He also advises that you "try to hold your finish the way Crampton and Littler do."

Byron Nelson, the former tour great who does some TV commentating for ABC, points out that even though you'll see a lot of different swings, almost all of the good players have one thing in common. "Watch how they swing the club around a steady head," says Nelson. "There is no lifting, just a swing."

You can learn more about putting than other parts of the game, for two reasons: the telecasts show much more action on the greens, and the slower tempo of putting gives you more opportunity to analyze it.

You'll see a greater variety of strokes on the greens than on the tee or in the fairway. Don't let it confuse you. Pick a player whose putting style you prefer and pattern your putting after him. Keep your putter in hand as you watch the telecasts and practice setting up and stroking in synchronization with your model player.

Many golfers could improve their putting by setting up with Jack Nicklaus each time he addresses a putt and copying his tempo in striking the ball.

Note how quickly many of the good players line up their putts—much quicker than many club players think when they go to the course the next day and wander around the greens. The tour players all survey putts carefully, looking over the line from at least two directions, but they do all this relatively quickly.

You can sharpen your course strategy watching TV too. See if any of the holes shown are similar to holes on your course. Watch how the various players attack the hole and perhaps their strategy can help you later. Note how a player trying to protect a lead will play one of the finishing holes safely, while a player trying to make up ground will attack the same hole entirely differently.

You can pick up tips from the telecasts if you watch them with the idea of helping your game rather than just being entertained.

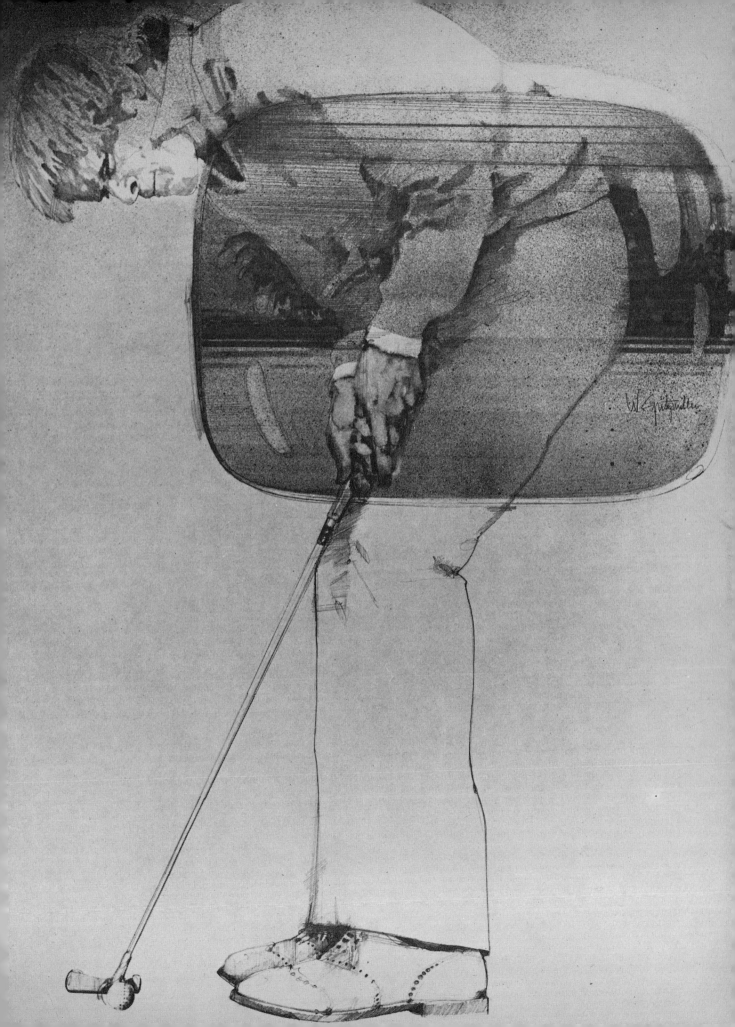

Golf is a Game of Honor

By JOHN F. STEADMAN
(Sports Editor, *Baltimore News-American*)

MEN HAVE been known to cheat on income taxes, to fill out erroneous expense accounts, to pass bad checks and even to wrap their enemies in jackets of concrete.

But don't touch that golf ball.

And, if you're going to pick it up, make sure it's replaced on the exact spot from where it came and you don't improve the lie. Play it where you find it.

Golf is a game of honor.

Men who would stack the deck against their own mother, who would lie to themselves wouldn't do a dishonest thing on a golf course—even if they shot 162 on the front nine.

But golf is this way.

The essence of the sport is trust.

Each player is an official scorekeeper, for putting down his own count and also in paying attention to his opponent.

There are no certified public accountants on the golf course.

This is the foundation, the basis, the bone marrow of golf, the heart, the soul.

If you don't report an accurate figure on a hole, or if you influence the position of the ball in any way, then it must be recorded and the penalty accepted.

Each golfer is his own "private eye," his own judge and jury, his own policeman and his own personal and public conscience.

In some games, it's considered a part of competitive astuteness to find a way to beat the rules or to get-away with an illegal play when an official isn't looking.

Golf, though, is a sport unto itself. It's royal and also ancient.

If permissiveness is permitted or the code violated, then it is no game of equality. And the same regulations must apply to all.

Allow a breakdown in the honor system and there is no accomplishment or respectability left to the laws of golf. This leads to absolute chaos.

There is no flexibility. Penalties are assessed for hitting out-of-bounds, grounding a club in a sandtrap and even if your caddy absent-mindedly touches the green.

No, you can't even breathe against a golf ball.

Anything that happens from the time a player gets in an address position is his responsibility. If you're about to hit and a 90-mile wind turns the ball a revolution before you have even struck it, then there's a penalty.

You can be searching in 10 feet of saw grass and inadvertently step on your ball and, again, there's an infraction.

Lloyd Mangrum, in a playoff with Ben Hogan and George Fazio for the 1950 U.S. Open Championship, staged at the Merion Golf Club, thoughtlessly picked up his ball to blow off an insect at the 16th green and incurred a two-stroke penalty.

The severity of the rules can be difficult. Even an act of God is charged against the golfer if it results in a hurricane or an earthquake lending assistance to improve the lie of a golf ball.

Sometimes, the rules are relaxed for an informal match. But this is agreed upon before the first ball leaves the tee.

In competition, be it amateur or professional, the laws of golf are the same for all—the world over, be it St. Andrews, the shrine, or Possum Hollow, where they have nine holes in a cow pasture.

Like love, golf is a universal language. You don't speak it, you live it.

If one golfer violates a rule his rival is duty-bound to call it and, if a penalty is not voluntarily assessed and accepted by the offending party, then it's up to a tournament official to take testimony, ask opinions of witnesses and make a judgement—that can lead to disqualification or, worse yet, suspension or banishment.

Since the game is played and officially scored by the golfers participating, there is no such thing as a referee or an umpire accompanying each group that tees-off or going along to see that proper jurisdiction prevails.

Men have been known to have their scores questioned. To raise such an issue is to make a player suspect. But this is the character of golf.

It's a simple game, counting up strokes with the fewest number winning, but it also can be complex and frustrating and entwined with deep emotion.

Yet the only precept has to be total honesty. There can be no deviation from a common rule book that has been in vogue for centuries.

Allow golf to be penetrated by those interested in taking a short-cut, either by calculating design or mere happenstance, and this game, by its innate nature, comes crashing down to utter destruction.

It hasn't happened yet. Pray God that it won't.

PLEASE, Mr. Seely

By FRED SEELY
(Executive Sports Editor, *Florida Times-Union*)

FOR MANY years now, you've picked up your copy of GOLFER'S DIGEST and, by careful perusal of its many pages, you've learned how to cure all ills in your swing and become Johnny Miller and Jack Nicklaus put together, only without all that hair.

But you haven't learned the most important thing.

How to cheat.

Ah, you say . . . I don't cheat. Not me!

But remember that day your ball came to rest on a root and you nudged it a few inches away? Or remember that day you moved a branch and your ball moved ever so slightly, and you didn't add a stroke? Do you think Diogenes would come after you with that lamp?

If you're going to cheat, you might as will do it right. And here's how, with the help of some club and touring pros.

Lost Ball

Don't let that bother you, unless you've lost it in a lake and the splash was clearly visible to your playing partners.

You're not a slicker if you go out without a hole in your pocket. It's the best method, and it's almost impossible to catch, unless you manage to drop a ball of another brand or number.

Hole-in-One

Never made an ace? C'mon—it's easy.

"One guy on tour would make a lot of holes-in-one," recalls part-time tourist Chris Blocker. "We finally figured it out. He got to the green first, and that was the key.

"His system was simple, and he usually pulled it in pro-ams when his playing partners weren't too sharp. Say a hole was 150 yards, which would be a 7-iron. Preferably, there would be a swamp behind the hole, although dense brush worked just as well. He would tell everyone he was hitting a 7-iron, then pull out a 5-iron and slam the ball over the green and into the trash.

"Then he would hustle to the green first, palming an identical ball. He'd reach into the cup and seemingly pull out his ball.

"That's how to make a hole-in-one."

Short Putts

There's really no reason for you to have a long putt. Or, for that matter, there's no reason to have a 3-footer. Employ the goal line offense and you're in business.

"I know a guy who's better than Larry Csonka near paydirt," says Bill Maxwell, another frequent tour player. "If a pro football player could gain ground by spotting his ball illegally, this guy should take up that sport."

It's like playing tiddlywinks. The first step is getting to the green first. Second, use a penny to mark your ball—it doesn't shine as much.

And the method: Pretend to spot the coin behind your ball, pick up the ball with your other hand, and flip the coin toward the hole.

"This guy turned more 3-footers into tap-ins than any football player has scored touchdowns, I'll guarantee you that," says Maxwell.

Long putts can be shortened, too. "There are guys who can flip a coin 25 feet without anyone knowing," says Maxwell.

Spike Marks

It's the same idea—get to the green first and examine your putting line. If there are spike marks in your way, flip the coin diagonally—you'll be closer to the hole, and you'll also be away from the humps.

Train Your Caddie

In this era of golf carts, you're usually under surveillance. But, in this era of the motorized vehicle, you have an advantage—who wants to walk?

You, that's who . . . and the American caddie will do almost anything for an extra buck.

"I've seen many a barefooted caddie with big toes who could take a ball out of a buried lie and place it in the prettiest place you ever saw," says John Beckmann, one of a family of golf pros. "And I've seen caddies—and players, too—with holes in their shoes who could drag a ball 30 or 40 yards closer to the green."

Gator Steadman is presently working out of Florida's famed Ponte Verda Club, but used to work the tour regularly.

"I've never done anything on the tour that was illegal," he says, "but in local matches I've done plenty—from dropping balls in better places to stomping opponents' balls in the mud."

Norrie Wright, a young pro who rapidly is gaining attention for his radical teaching methods with young golfers, recalls a college golf match.

"My opponent was deep in the woods," he remembers. "I didn't see how he could get out, but I heard him swing and the ball came flying out—it was a super shot. Later, his caddie admitted that he had thrown the ball out while the golfer swung for the sound effect."

Proper Handicapping

It used to be easy to show up at a tournament and claim a higher handicap than you actually carry. But this is an old dodge, and it doesn't work often.

"We have a big two-man event every year," says Stan Shaw, a former vice president of the Florida PGA, "and we had a problem the first year. No more. When a guy comes here that I don't know, I call his club and verify his handicap. If I still feel uneasy, I tell the guy that I've rejected his entry. I'm not going to get in trouble with my members because of some ringer."

But, like all systems, this too can be beaten.

Your handicap is based on your scores. But when you play a casual match at your club, you're almost always playing hole for hole—match play—rather than stroke play. So, say you've driven into trouble on a hole and your opponent is in perfect position. Say your next shot ends up in worse trouble, and your opponent's shot is on the green. So why not run up the score? He's going to make a four, and you're going to be lucky to make a five—so make sure you get a six, the highest you can claim for handicap purposes on a par-four hole.

If every hole you lose is a double bogie on the card, that's maybe three or four shots extra per round . . . and don't think you can't use those in the next member-guest.

Or be even more blatant—say a big event is coming up, and it's one you'd love to win. For a period before the tournament, play with a group of guys who eschew gambling, and turn in some terrible scores. Miss those short putts! Skull those trap shots! Hit the wrong club! It won't hurt your game or your pocketbook, but it definitely will raise hell with your handicap.

And then you'll be ready to win the tournament.

But wait!

What is a reputable publication like this doing rattling on about cheating? And what is a reputable writer like this, one who wouldn't do anything worse than take a Mulligan, clanking on about violating all that the USGA, The Royal and Ancient and Bob Hope hold sacred?

We don't condone cheating, but it exists. And don't think that it doesn't exist on every level of golf. The lure of winning $40,000 isn't all that different from winning a $2 Nassau—it's all relative.

But . . . why does it exist?

That answer isn't always apparent. Of course, people cheat to win money. They cheat in cards, they cheat in politics, they cheat in business, they cheat on their expense accounts. Cheating is right up there with baseball as the Great American Pastime, just as it's probably right up there with the Great Russian Pastime, whatever that might be.

A trio of psychologists, all from Jacksonville, Florida, and all possessing high handicaps and self proclaimed honest dispositions, answered the "Why does it exist?" question and came up with 10 reasons:

1. Extreme stress on winning: This is particularly prevalent among those who come from extremely competitive families.

2. Peer pressure: Loss of face is worse than loss of self-esteem.

3. The loner: The guy who's left out needs a way to fit in. And what's better than being best?

4. Self-defense: Others do it, why not me?

5. Lifestyle: Some people cheat their partners, clients or the government. It carries over to the golf course.

6. Man against the elements: "That tree wouldn't be there if this were a fair course." So why not move the ball a few feet?

7. Wishful thinking: If you want a par or bogey hard enough, can't you forget that dubbed shot along the way?

8. Hostility toward others: "I'll get you, buddy."

9. Immaturity: If you can't get your own way legally, what's the alternative?

10. Insecurity: How can I reach equality?

And there's another theory.

"Some people cheat just to see how much they can get away with," says another psychologist.

Without getting into too much heavy stuff, consider the words of another mind analyst.

"The three most important things to consider are the amount of trust a person has in himself and others, the degree of self-acceptance and self-respect that a person has, and the degree of mature discipline," says the high-handicap shrink. "The best predictor is whether or not a person saw his father cheat. Parental attitudes are a big factor—if a person has seen his parents cheat, he's more likely to be a cheater himself."

* * *

But all this is getting away from the main issue—namely, how can you improve your game by cheating?

A lot, that's how.

But if you're going to go to all this trouble, why not spend your energies on something worthwhile?

"Honesty is basically functional," says psychologist Dr. Melvin Reid. "I know a lot of honest people who cheat only on their golf scores and their income tax."

Or maybe there are other places . . . did you really shell out $7.95 for this book, or did you come out of your favorite bookseller with your GOLFER'S DIGEST under a bulky overcoat?

AT AN amateur tournament luncheon in Texas when John Jacobs was 19 years old, somebody introduced a local golfer as one of the longest hitters in the world. Jacobs' California buddies jumped up and yelled, "Hey, *we* got a guy here." Before very long, the Texans were betting with both fists. Jacobs and the other fellow agreed to hit ten drives apiece, and the longest drive would be the winner. Everybody started for the door except Jacobs, who headed for the bar, telling the crowd to call him when it was his turn. When it *was* his turn, he went out into the hot sun, wobbling some, looked out at the other guy's longest drive and said, "Gimme a 3-wood. I gotta get it airborne." He took one swing and connected and as the ball sailed out, John dropped the club, grabbed his beer and headed back for the clubhouse. He won by 40 yards.

Nine years later, at the 1973 St. Louis Open, John Jacobs was on the practice tee sailing drives out over a snow fence that was 300 yards away. On a dare, he pulled out a 2-iron and hit one that rose up, went into the jetstream and landed in the top of a tree behind the fence. He gave the iron back to his caddie, and as he walked away he told the fans what they already suspected: "Folks, I don't believe anybody's ever hit an iron that far before."

The previous year, Jacobs had put together his best season as a touring golf pro. He had finished 96th on the tour in money-winnings with just under $23,000. But in 1973, and again in 1974,

BY DAN GLEASON

JOHN JACOBS IS #1 ON THE PRO GOLF TOUR... IN MONEY SPENT

he wasn't even among the top 100. He was lower than a rabbit, so obscure that if he wandered across your screen during a televised tournament, it had to be a technical error. For every golf fan who'd heard of John Jacobs, there had to be a million who'd heard of Arnold Palmer. Before I ever saw Jacobs play a round, I figured he was one of those big lugs who could just hit for show and couldn't make a 2-foot putt. But a wise old caddie said I was wrong.

"He can putt and he can chip," the caddie said. "I don't guess he's got any weaknesses except for off the course. He could probably beat most of these $100,000 players if it was for their own money. It's a whole lot different playin' for your own cash. And to J.J., money don't mean nothin'—it's just little pieces of paper."

Indeed, I soon found out that while the $100,000 players were busy planning their strategies for the Grand Slam, Jacobs was out sniffing the wind for the grand parties. He was a hard rider, a two-fisted gambler, a man who tested how fast the car could go and the life could be lived, who tumbled through The Scene and practiced wenching until he had raised it to an art. Like the fictional soldier-adventurer, the delightfully scandalous "Flashman" of George MacDonald Fraser, John Jacobs was more concerned with cutting a fine figure on parade than with the battle.

In the middle of today's recession, with a lot of big spenders holding back, it is reassuring to find a man who possesses the style of John Jacobs. Not only is he one of golf's biggest hitters and one of the world's fastest livers, but there is a third component—his attitude toward security—that makes him particularly worth viewing in these nervous days. Several months ago, I sat in his car as Jacobs scorched a Southern California four-lane at 100 miles an hour. We had been talking about the golf tour's highest echelon—the 60 men who win the most money in a year and, thus, are automatically eligible to play in the major tournaments. Jacobs leaned back in his seat and said, "*I* don't want to be in the top 60."

I know pros who've sweated and stayed awake nights thinking about being in the top 60 and not having to qualify for tournaments on Monday. I know pros who'd give their souls and 10 years of their lives to be in the top

60. But Jacobs simply shrugged. "If you're in the top 60," he said, "you just have to be a bunch of places and do a bunch of things."

The front end of the car started shaking and he let off the footfeed and eased it down under 90. His sidekick, John Nichols, was in the back trying to keep from spilling a gin-and-tonic he'd camouflaged in a Ronald McDonald glass. "This thing needs a tune-up," Nichols said.

Jacobs adjusted the rearview mirror. "Yeah, I'll take it in tomorrow and have it washed." Then he turned to me. "Look," he said, "if you run short on material and you have to make something up, it's okay. I'll understand."

It is not necessary to make up anything about John Jacobs—not even to satisfy the most avid fancier of colorful personalities. When he was 15 years old, for example, Jacobs made it to the National Junior Championship in Detroit. While the other kids were bunked in at the YMCA, sneaking puffs off cigarettes they'd smuggled in, dropping water balloons and thinking of ways to cheat the pinball machines, John Jacobs checked into a downtown Detroit hotel suite, got a fake I-D, rented a Cadillac convertible, bought a fifth of Scotch and picked up a 20-year-old girl.

When he was 19, in 1964, Jacobs went into the army and had it made, teaching golf to officers and their wives at Ft. Hood, Texas. Someone gave him a Cadillac to drive down to play in an amateur tournament in Mexico and, he says, "I figured, 'What the hell, I'm a real big man back at the base—I'll stay down here for an extra week.' " But on Jacobs' return, the general decided to teach him a lesson and told him he was going to a place called Viet Nam in southeast Asia. "I figured it was some kind of exotic island, like Hawaii, and I said, 'Great, I'll pack my swimming trunks.' And then I read where there were snakes over there that could kill you in 30 seconds, and that weekend 80 guys had been killed in Saigon—and that was just in bar fights."

Jacobs managed to survive Viet Nam, both the night life *and* the ambushes. He even survived an assignment as a forward-observer, an artillery scouting job with a life expectancy about equal to that of an ant on a Manhattan sidewalk during lunch hour.

When he got back to the U.S., he turned pro, got his tour card at 23 and headed for the Big Time. A rich friend offered him $7,000 extra to take along just to spend; Jacobs would never even have to pay it back. Jacobs said no, he had his own bankroll, but the man insisted. So Jacobs asked Nichols if he wanted to go along. They had John's bankroll, plus the $7,000, and on top of that, Jacobs immediately began averaging $1,200 a week in winnings on the tour. In less than 3 months, he and Nichols were flat broke and eating celery.

Then, as now, the problem was not Jacobs' game or swing, but his inattention to the practice and sacrifice necessary for consistency on the tour. "I'm usually sharp for a few weeks," says Jacobs, "and then my game gets sour out there. It might be different if I was married. But bachelor life on the tour gets you."

It also costs money. "I can squeeze by on the tour," says Jacobs, "for about $50,000 a year." He used to sell shares of himself to backers; "I've had more sponsors than the Johnny Carson Show." But lately he's found the international golf market and can keep up not only his bankroll, but also his spirits by playing in London one week, Tokyo the next, Paris the week after, as opposed to, say, Endicott, N.Y. one week, Bettendorf, Iowa, the next week, and Robinson, Ill., the week after that. In 1974 he earned some big checks playing in Europe, and won about $25,000 on the American tour. He picked up an additional $20,000 playing television exhibitions in England and Japan and, with his long ball as a drawing card, opening driving ranges in Japan.

"I've decided," says Jacobs, "to get a little more serious about making money."

"Yeah," says Nichols, "John's 30 going on 21. But that's a big improvement. He used to be 29 going on 18."

Jacobs is concerned about making money for his sponsors, but his sponsors—which he has cut down to two now—are sportsmen and are less concerned with profit than sport. John's "Northern California" sponsor is Syl Enea, a very rich land developer who owns the Concord Inn, a country club near San Francisco; Enea, says Jacobs, "is more like a dad than a sponsor." His "Southern California" sponsor is his close friend Ray Kawano, who owns a big produce company; Kawano is a calm, very personable man in his mid-30's who met Jacobs at Del Mar race track a few years ago.

Additionally, because Jacobs does cut such a fine parade figure, the Jantzen company sends him a steamertrunk full of clothes at a time, 90 shirts at once, and his closet is full of expensive slacks and suits. Jacobs also has more than 150 pairs of street shoes, some of which he's never worn. He is a powerful man—big in the shoulders, strong in the legs—and, with his California beach-blond hair and fashionable costuming, does not have to search hard for temptations to which to yield. Last year, on a vow, he stopped partying for 3 days and stood third in the Bing Crosby tournament when rain canceled the event after the third round. A reformed man, fresh with success, he went on to Phoenix. There, he shot a 76 in the first round, allowed two girls to escort him off the course, and several weeks went by before he was seen again on the tour.

"There isn't anybody on the tour with more talent and less motivation than John Jacobs," says Leonard Thompson, the pro from Bay Tree Golf Plantation, S.C., who himself won more than $122,000 in 1974. "John is long and straight," says Thompson, "and he has a good putting touch and all the talent anybody could hope to have."

1976 Masters champion Ray Floyd is even more lavish in his praise for Jacobs' putting and in his belief that "John has all the physical abilities it takes." And Rod Curl, who won $120,000 last year, agrees that Jacobs has talent. But, says Curl, "There's a lot of 'if' there. Mickey Mantle might have been better than Ruth and Gehrig put together if he hadn't had bad knees—and maybe J.J. could rule the world if he had different goals and attitudes. And maybe I could whip Muhammad Ali if I were 7-feet tall. But the thing is, Mickey Mantle did have bad knees and John's where he is in golf and I'm 5'-5". Maybe John already has what he wants."

What John has, in golf, is a reputation as one of the two longest hitters in the game. The other is Jim Dent, a man to whom Jacobs concedes nothing. "If Jim Dent's manager, Mark McCor-

mack, puts it in print that Jim is the longest hitter in the world, I'll sue him," says Jacobs. "What I want to do is bet Jim Dent a wheelbarrow full of cash on a one-on-one contest. I know I'm longer than Dent. And if he doesn't believe it, I'll get out the wheelbarrow."

When Jacobs was an amateur, he might very well have been the longest hitter in the world, hands down. He used to hit a low, screaming hook that would roll forever. But on the tour he cut back to get control. "A lot of times," he says, "you don't see Dent's long ball or my long ball because we're just trying to knock it down in the fairway."

Back in the Southern California amateurs, Curtis Sifford, now a touring pro, was putting out on a 400-yard hole. He heard a thump and a ball tickled up between his legs. He looked around to bawl out the guy who had hit his second shot onto the green. He looked back and saw no one. He looked back and back and back and still saw no one. He finally spotted a tiny figure 400 yards away on the tee. "Nobody had to tell me who it was," says Sifford. "I knew it had to be John Jacobs."

John Jacobs began playing golf when he was 3 years old. His father managed country clubs around Los Angeles and his older brother, Tommy Jacobs, was a golf prodigy who eventually became one of the stars of the pro tour in the 1960s. "Tommy taught me a lot about golf," says John, "but most of it I picked up by observation. I was such a wild kid that most everybody was always trying to duck me, so I had to learn a lot of it on my own."

Through Tommy, who is 10 years older, John met most of his sports contacts in Los Angeles while still a kid. Consequently, he has *always* had the best seats at all the football games and prize fights and the best tables at all of the best night clubs. "I've done everything I've ever wanted to do every day of my life since I was 17 years old," says John.

The brothers are almost complete opposites. John is 6-3 and 215 pounds; Tommy is 5-10 and 160. John is extravagantly free-spirited; Tommy is a mild-mannered man who believes in the work ethic and enjoys his current life as a club pro near San Diego. Nevertheless, the brothers are very close. Whenever the PGA has a com-

plaint about something John has done, they call Tommy.

Periodically, Tommy has long talks with John, urging him to get serious about golf and to ease back on his pace. John listens respectfully, thanks him, thinks it over, and goes back to living the way he's always lived—recklessly, honestly, happily and with high regard for the generous gesture.

A tour caddie tells a story of getting $300 from Jacobs for working his bags, even though they'd missed the cut, because Jacobs knew the caddie was broke. An assistant pro out at Tommy's club, Rancho La Costa, tells how John came home from one satellite tournament $1,200 richer. He went out on one of his buying sprees, and the assistant rode along. At a clothing store, John said, "Hey, aren't you going to buy any threads?" The assistant said no, he couldn't afford any. John peeled off a $100 bill. "Pick out some nice colors."

John Nichols enjoys recounting how Jacobs always drove his Corvette 120 miles an hour, "one-two-oh, even to the grocery store." Jacobs himself happily remembers that he used to hit the night spots before he'd leave for the tour, and eventually would get somebody to drive him to the airport in the Corvette. He'd tell the person to keep the car and drive it, he'd be back in a month or two. Sometimes he didn't even know the driver's last name. "Nobody ever stole it," he shrugs.

One evening not long ago, Jacobs, Nichols and I were headed for a night spot in La Jolla, near John's home. La Jolla is a sartorial, leisure chunk of California in the San Diego area, full of jet-setters and surf-bunnies, the new-rich, the pool lappers, and more than 10 per cent unemployment, much of which is purely by choice. There's legal nude sunbathing in La Jolla, a delicatessen that sells artichoke fritatta, another place where you can find a bottle of Chateau Lafite-Rothschild for $325 and can get fresh caviar flown in direct from Iran.

While driving, Jacobs whipped out a gold, engraved lighter and lit a cigarette. "My friend Jim Hughes from Canada told me a long time ago never to go any way but first class." He had a dark thought. "Jesus—what if you died in a plane crash and your friends found your body in the coach section?"

We arrived at one of his favorite

places, Bully's. It was crowded with people, most of whom knew Jacobs either personally or by reputation, especially the women. We took over a booth and ordered a liter of wine and started talking about the tour life. "When I'm in Florida," Jacobs said, "sometimes I get a suite at the Diplomat and do the coast up for a week or so. The Diplomat is between Miami and Lauderdale, which is strategic to the program." His favorite tour stops, he said, are Hawaii—"for pure female volume;" Ft. Worth for the Colonial—"because they party big and the girls are in a contest to see who can wear the least amount of clothing to the golf course;" and Jacksonville—"because it's the only town where the girls find out where you're staying and call *you*."

Our waitress was Sondra Buffet, a friend of John's. "Somebody asked me the other night if John plays out of a club," she said. "I told them, 'Yes, the Playboy Club.'"

John raised his glass.

Later on, when the crowd began to trickle out, the talk grew serious. "You know," Jacobs said, "I might end up broke and staggering. But this is no time to think about it, and anyway . . . it's only life."

He got up to talk to the owner. "John's not gonna starve," Nichols said. "The women won't let him starve. There's a long line of them out at La Costa, divorcees and rich widows who'd scratch each other's eyes out to make him a kept man."

By 1AM, as the music picked up and we started on our third liter of wine, we were talking about friends and how good it was to be young and in Southern California. Somewhere, people were thinking about the future and building monuments to themselves. But not Jacobs.

One of his friends was saying, "You know, whenever you have a talent, the first thing somebody says these days is, 'You can sell that.' Or, 'Hey, you can make a load of money with it.' Why don't they say, 'You can have a lot of fun with it?' Anyhow, a thousand years from now, who'll really give a damn?"

It was a good question. Billions of years from now, after we've built driving ranges and franchise hamburger stands across the rusty deserts of Mars, all our monuments will turn into dust thinner than pool chalk, and our universe will disappear. And whatever or whoever's next won't likely care that there were men on the planet Earth who were responsible, much less restrained, or made a load of money and won a lot of athletic contests. So why not try to leave heavy tracks by taking a hard ride through life, making a big dent and enjoying the music?

As we were leaving Bully's, the bartender was closing down and washing the glasses. Jacobs tossed a $50 bill out on the bar and said, "Is that gonna cover it?"

The bartender shook his head and said, "John, when are you going to start thinking about frugality?"

Jacobs' expression changed. He didn't say anything. And finally, he said, "I've been thinking about it for a long time now, more and more here lately. Frugality. But how did you know?"

I shrugged and Nichols shrugged back.

Outside in the parking lot, Jacobs had a quizzical look on his face. He shrugged and lit a cigarette and looked over at us. "*Frugality* is a three-year-old running up at Del Mar on Saturday. He's a long-shot, but if I thought the sonovabitch could get out of the gate, I'd put five grand on his nose."

"Putter."

Golf's Ball Banditos

By HARLESS WADE
(Dallas Morning News)

NEXT TIME you see some guy or gal striking a golf ball with a colored stripe around it, chances are you're looking at a petty thief.

Collectively, these thieves are anything but petty. Would you believe that golf's ball banditos, in the Dallas area alone, heist more than 100,000 golf balls a year?

Sure, it sounds wild. Outrageous and almost unbelieveable. Unfortunately, it's true.

Club pros of the area will quickly give you statistics to prove these numbers. They have just cause, since it pinches them in their pocketbooks by unhealthy margins each year.

"They pick you like a chicken," declares Buster Creagh, the head pro at Sherrill Park, Richardson, Texas. "With costs up like they are today, it's not economically sound to have a practice range. It's a break even situation at best."

Creagh cites these figures. In the first 18 months that Richardson operated its plush municipal layout, from late 1973 to early 1975, banditos plucked 400 DOZEN golf balls from the practice range.

This is not an isolated case. Nor, do the banditos confine their activities to municipal courses. The petty thieves are operating around the plushest country clubs, too.

"It's absolutely unbelievable at times," says Ron Junge, the head man at Royal Oaks CC, one of the Dallas area's rich, new spreads. "You'd think that people would be embarrassed to play with them, but they're not."

Junge says he bought 500 dozen range balls last year. Recently, he figured he had only about 50 dozen left, meaning he must now reorder some 500 dozen for consumption this year.

The Royal Oaks pro, somehow, manages to laugh about his dilemma. One thing is certain, he knows his members aren't heisting all his range balls. This he discovered one day as a train pulled to a stop on the tracks just across the fence from his range.

"I couldn't believe it," Junge chuckled. "The trainmen stopped that thing, crawled off the train and started collecting balls that had been knocked over the fence. You know, it's hard to give a lesson and chase down trains at the same time."

Every so often a professional diver goes into the lakes, ponds and creeks of all clubs to recover golf balls that have been splashed there by misspent shots. These divers work for the money in it.

"You'd be surprised at how many range balls the divers recover," Junge says. "Not just balls from our range; they find 'em from Preston Trail and Northwood and the finest places in town."

Hardy Greenwood, who has operated a driving range for 29 years, figures he loses about 4,000 balls a year. Yet, he accepts his fate and charts it off as costs, such as labor.

"It's not just kids and the guys who can't afford to buy golf balls who steal 'em," says Greenwood, who helped mold Lee Trevino into a links giant, "it's the guy who drives up in a big, black Cadillac, too. Shoot, we even caught a city judge doing it one time. I'm not kidding, we caught a city judge."

Joe Black, the former PGA tour director who heads up operations at Brookhaven CC, says he likes to keep about 1,000 dozen range balls in operation.

"I use between 500 and 700 dozen per year," Black says. "Some of these wear out and some are just naturally lost, but I venture to say I have 300 to 400 dozen stolen each year."

Black, unlike some local pros, does have some recourse. Any member caught playing one of the three Brookhaven courses with a range ball is fined $5. These banditos are forced to pay up or be suspended from the club.

"We don't have too much of this going on now," Black said, "but some strange things still happen around range balls."

Once, Black drove close to a fence at Brookhaven. When he arrived there, across the fence in his backyard, a club member was practicing with a bucket of Joe's range balls.

Did he recover them? "Sure, it'd be hard not to, since they all have my name stamped on 'em," Joe laughed.

Another time, during his annual beat-the-pro day, when he moves from group to group and plays one hole, Black walked to a new group and found a woman teeing up a range ball. He knocked the ball off her tee, put it in his pocket and she never said a thing.

"I know that some pros go through their members' bags every so often while they're stored and collect range balls," Black said. "I've never done this, but you'd be surprised how many balls those pros gather up doing it."

Jerry Andrews, the head pro at L.B. Houston, installed the first and only range at a Dallas municipal course last year. It's operating in the red.

"Conservatively, I lost 250 dozen in the first year," Andrews says. "That's a big loss. I'm operating at a loss. It's ridiculous, I know. It can only be a service, not a profit."

This sort of thing all adds up to one point: If you're ever tempted to pick up a range ball and walk off with it, don't do it.

After all, who wants to join the petty thieves who make up golf's gang of ball banditos?

Surely, not you.

THE CASE FOR LIGHTER CLUBS

By JAMES McAFEE
And the Editors of GOLFER'S DIGEST

"THE AVERAGE man could probably play better with his wife's clubs."

Frank Beard, who made the above observation, is convinced that almost every golfer should be using lighter clubs. Beard might even go so far as to swing a feather-shafted club if he could find a manufacturer with the ingenuity to produce one.

Albert Einstein was no golfer or he would have told the golfing public the same thing Beard advocates. Einstein and his fellow physicists have long known that force equals mass times velocity squared. In other words, the faster you swing a driver the farther you will hit the golf ball. You can swing a lighter club faster.

Jim Dent, the long-driving king of the tour, agrees with Einstein and the physicists. After winning the *Golf Digest*-Tournament Players Division distance contest in 1974, he told our readers to swing as light a club as possible.

Star teaching professional Bob Toski, who stresses the value of a light grip pressure, says that lighter clubs make it easier to grip the club lightly. "The average player doesn't have to work as hard to swing a lighter club," he says.

The weight of a club is the total of the head, shaft and grip. The most practical avenue to a lighter club is the shaft. It's the controlling element.

We've come a long way since the days of the hickory shaft, which weighed as much as 8½ ounces. Manufacturers steadily have trimmed the weight of shafts until today some weigh under three ounces.

The first improvement on hickory, in the 1930s, was steel, which now weighs about 4½ ounces. By the mid-1960s the weight of shafts was lowered to four ounces with the appearance of lightweight steel and aluminum. Many still feel aluminum is a useful club for the average player, but it didn't catch on. The dull appearance, the insistence of some touring pros that it felt too "soft," and its fat look worked against aluminum.

Lightweight steel gained better acceptance and accounts for about 20 per cent of the shaft market today. Although the shaft is slightly larger in diameter than regular steel, the walls aren't as thick, saving weight.

Stainless steel, which made an abortive appearance several years ago, is back on the market in limited supply. The problem with stainless has always been finding the proper alloy. It is about the same weight as lightweight steel.

Today, the golf club industry also is working with a lighter-than-lightweight steel, with titanium and with graphite. A titanium driver shaft weighs 3½ ounces, the lighter-than-lightweight steel only 3 ounces, and graphite ranges between 2.3 and 3.6 ounces.

Titanium is a metal widely used in the aerospace industry and even in pots and pans. It is plentiful and has exceptional strength, but it is expensive to extract from the earth and is difficult to shape into shafts. One of the reported assets of titanium is its resistance to torque.

The 3-ounce steel is only in the first experimental stages. The shafts have very thin walls—which is why they're lighter—and are very flexible.

Graphite, which burst onto the scene in 1973, has since captured the imagination of the golfing public—but only 2½ per cent of the club market. Graphite has been called the most dramatic single innovation in golf since hickory shafts were supplanted by steel. Stories of greater distance have been numerous. Touring pro Gay Brewer credited graphite with 30 extra yards on his drives. Jim Dent says his tee shots gained 20 yards with the new shafts.

One of graphite's most prominent advocates has been Gene Littler. After cancer surgery deprived him of some of his old strength, Littler converted to graphite. "It took me about a month to get used to it," he says. "I had to slow down my rhythm. But now I can hit the ball at least 20 yards longer off the tee than I could with steel shafts."

Many knowledgeable golf people claim graphite is a boon to women players and seniors.

Why then has graphite cornered such a small portion of the market? Several reasons, but cost remains the most conspicuous. Graphite woods run from $85 to $150 each, the irons from $70 to $125. A full set of graphite clubs can cost more than $1,500.

Top-grade graphite fibers currently sell at $50 per pound, a sixth of the original cost but still high. Only four shafts can be manufactured from a pound of graphite. Resin, mixed with the graphite fibers in manufacturing the shafts, has gone up in price recently. The production process is extensive and further contributes to the high price of the clubs.

A further development that could bring down the price of graphite shafts more sharply is the pitch process, the making of graphite fibers from natural compounds such as coal tar pitch rather than synthetic materials now used.

In the meantime, minor drops in price are being offered by some companies which cite improved production techniques. Graphite clubs that are significantly cheaper are manufactured with much less graphite or with lower-grade graphite. Unquestionably golfers are confused by all the different types of graphite clubs. Some experts feel graphite shafts only now are becoming similar. All those shafts are manufactured by more than a dozen companies, most of them having come into the golf business with the advent of graphite.

In addition to cost, another reason for the slow acceptance of graphite is con-

The Making of a Graphite Shaft

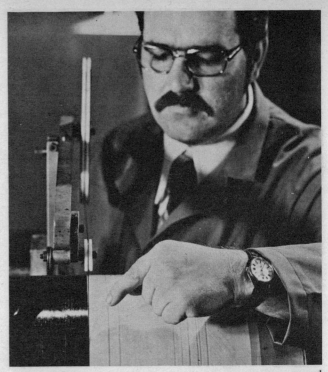

1. The basic ingredient in manufacturing graphite shafts is a supply of synthetic graphite fibers as shown on this spool. Such fibers are produced by heating rayon threads to a temperature of 5,000 degrees Fahrenheit in an oven filled with pure nitrogen. With no oxygen in the oven the rayon will not burn away, but will "carbonize" into this synthetic graphite.

2. The fibers are separated into thread and the thread is wound around a drum covered with resin-coated paper.

5. Non-stick cellophane is wrapped around the tape and the covered rods are placed for four hours in ovens heated to 250 degrees Fahrenheit. The cellophane holds in the moisture of the resin during this heating and drying process.

6. After cooling, the cellophane is removed and the steel rods pulled out, leaving the hollow graphite shafts which are smoothed by sanding.

3. When the gluey resin dries the thread has become a foot-wide layer of graphite tape about the thickness of heavy wrapping paper.

4. The tape is cut into strips 2½ inches wide and wound tightly around stainless steel rods to a thickness of several layers. (In the Shakespeare and Fansteel process the fibers as shown in photo 1 are coated with resin and wrapped around the steel rods without the intermediate step of changing the fibers into tape.)

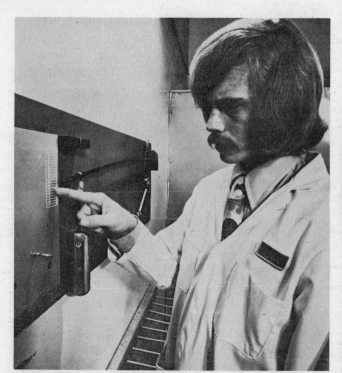

7. Each shaft is tested for flex and properly marked.

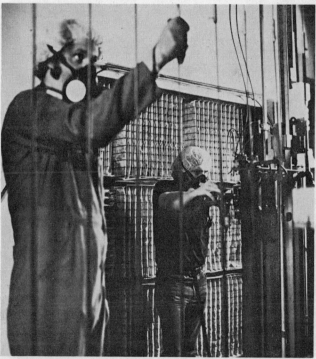

8. Finally, the shafts go to the painters, who put on the finishing touches. The shafts are now ready to be sent to the club makers.

fusion over fitting the clubs to individual players and their games. In the beginning, finding the correct shaft to match a golfer's needs was mainly a guessing game. The trial and error method is still used today, but there does seem to be a majority opinion about a starting point—going to higher swingweights and stiffer shafts.

In the beginning there were opposite viewpoints about flexes. One major company offered 15 flexes and another big firm offered only one. Today, the consensus is to offer a range of flexes comparable to those in steel.

Irv Schloss, veteran clubmaker and teacher, says, "If a guy has been using a D0 driver with a regular steel shaft, I'll recommend a D3 stiff driver. Then I'll have him hit balls with different swing-weighted clubs until he finds the one that feels best to him."

Frank Thomas, technical director of the United States Golf Ass'n and a pioneer in graphite, recommends graphite woods swingweighted D2 and graphite irons of D0 and D1 as a starting point for most golfers changing to graphite. He urges a stronger golfer who is pulling his drives to move up in swingweight, and a golfer who is leaving the ball out to the right to reduce his swingweight. Even more so than when buying other clubs, he says, golfers should try out graphite clubs enough to get a good feel for them before making a choice.

Most club golfers playing graphite have bought only drivers. Is that good or bad?

Paul Runyan warns of potential dangers. "It throws off your timing. You should use all graphite or none," he says.

On the other hand, Jimmy Wright, teaching professional from the Inwood (N.Y.) C.C., believes you can play with just a graphite driver. "I think it can help a golfer produce a smoother tempo that will carry over to his steel clubs," he says.

The USGA's Thomas takes a position in between Runyan and Wright. Thomas says, "Graphite is good if you have it in all your woods, not just your driver."

The pros and cons of graphite irons have been all but overlooked amid the hoopla about the drivers and longer belts off the tee.

Peter Kostis, professional at The Hamlet, Delray Beach, Fla., puts it this way: "With graphite I feel I'm hitting an 8-iron when I'm using a 4-iron. Who doesn't feel more comfortable hitting shorter irons?"

Touring pro Jim Wiechers says, "You can swing graphite irons with less physical effort and the ball gets in the air quicker."

Touring pro Phil Rodgers says, "I have hit more classic-looking iron shots since starting to use graphite. I'm able to stop the ball on the greens quicker since I get more spin. I feel graphite irons can be a definite advantage for the medium to high handicapper, especially older players who have lost some strength. My 70-year-old father hits the ball higher and farther with my old set of graphite irons than he has in 20 years."

Ladies PGA tournament professional Sandra Haynie says, "The ball jumps off the clubface. For irons you have to adjust your club selection or you'll be hitting the ball too far."

On the other side, some advanced players claim they cannot maneuver the ball as well with graphite shafted irons—cannot deliberately fade or draw it.

The earlier graphite shafts had less resistance to torque (or twisting) than steel. The more the shaft twists, the less chance there is of the clubface returning squarely to the ball. Although improvements have been made through the use of additives and different methods of applying the graphite fibers, many industry experts seem to feel the shafts still do not equal their steel cousins in torque-resistance.

GOLFER'S DIGEST conducted a telephone survey of 100 graphite-club purchasers across the country. Some had bought full sets and some woods, but most of them owned only graphite drivers. Fifty-nine of the 100 said they could detect little difference in their performance with graphite. Twenty-one claimed they benefited substantially from graphite, while the 20 others said they lost distance.

Jim Inman, a 9-handicapper from Greenwich, Conn., said, "I love it. I'm hitting the driver 25 yards longer when I flush it—up to 250."

Said Robert Mickler of Lexington, Ky.: "I'm hitting my driver 35 yards longer and my handicap has dropped from 14 to 12. I'm tempted to try graphite irons."

But after experimenting with seven or eight graphite drivers, Johnny South of Abilene, Tex., a low handicapper, declared, "I didn't notice enough extra distance to make it worth adding to my bag."

Del Trotter of Tulsa, Okla., a 7-handicapper, has quit using his graphite driver at least temporarily. "I lost yardage," he says, "I did hit it straighter, but just not as far as I would like."

Then there is Gov. John West of South Carolina, an 18-handicapper. He has an entire set, "I'm more confident with graphite. I can swing easier, and I get better control and a little more distance," he says.

If the survey points up nothing else, it shows the importance of experimenting with different clubs and getting the clubs properly fit to your swing.

If you're not in the market for graphite and want to try lighter clubs, what can you do?

The obvious first answer is lightweight steel.

Second, you can go to a lower swingweight. A club swingweighted C6 does not *have* to be lighter in static weight than a D2, but it normally will be. The trend on the men's tour is toward lower swingweights.

Ralph Maltby, clubmaker and designer and author of the new book, *Golf Club Design, Fitting, Alteration and Repair, The Principles and Procedures,* defines swingweight as: "The measurement of a golf club's weight distribution about a point which is established at a specified distance from the grip end of the club." Each point on the swingweight scale is figured to be 1/16th of an ounce. But there is a variance among brands, so if you go the way of lower swingweight, you should check the over-all weight of the clubs.

You can custom-order a steel-shafted club, of course, to make it lighter and still retain acceptable swing characteristics. But this can be a time-consuming and more costly process.

As a last resort, you could always take Frank Beard's advice and filch your wife's clubs. They might be shorter than yours, but that isn't all bad. Jim Flick contends that shorter clubs result in better control for the average player. Flick does warn that the more flexible shaft in women's clubs might cause increased wildness for a hard-swinging man. Besides, where would your wife go for her lighter clubs?

THE WEEK JACK FLECK SHOCKED THE GOLF WORLD

By **DWAYNE NETLAND**

EVEN THEN, two decades ago, there was about it an ethereal quality, as misty and gray as the fog that rolled in off San Francisco Bay. It was hard to believe it happened, and as the pieces are fitted back together today the picture seems as unreal as ever.

The U.S. Open this year will mark the 21st anniversary of Jack Fleck's momentous upset victory over Ben Hogan in the 1955 Open Championship at the Lake Course of the Olympic Club.

Both of them remember the incidents of that week with binocular clarity. Fleck's recall is a trifle sharper, which is not surprising, since it was the most significant event of his life.

That Open, memorable in so many ways, was the third of Fleck's career. The first two provided no hint of what was to occur at Olympic. He had missed the cut at Merion in 1950, when Hogan won, and in 1953 at Oakmont he shot rounds of 76-76-77-80 for a 309 that was 26 shots behind Hogan's winning score.

Although admittedly an obscure champion by Open standards, Fleck was not the total unknown the press made him out to be. Several accounts of that 1955 tournament referred to him as a driving-range pro. He actually was playing the tour at the time. Back home in Davenport, Iowa, he had a rather good job as head professional at the city's two municipal courses, Duck Creek and Credit Island. His wife, Lynn, ran the two courses, located eight miles apart, while her husband was on tour.

It was Lynn Fleck who prodded him into playing the tour. In the fall of 1954 Fleck, at the age of 33, was getting restless

in Davenport. He was itching to try his luck against the circuit golfers. He had played well for years in local tournaments throughout Iowa and Minnesota, and occasionally had teed it up on the tour during the winter. Time was slipping by and he couldn't afford to wait much longer.

"Try it for two years," Lynn told him. "I'll run the shops while you're gone. If you don't succeed, at least you'll have it out of your system."

Fleck then made a wise move. An old friend, Melvin Hemphill, was pro at the Forest Lake Country Club in Columbia, S.C. Fleck went to Columbia for three weeks and worked with Hemphill, who refined his setup and tempo in addition to implanting positive thoughts on the mental approach to tournament golf.

"I always regarded myself as a pretty good player," Fleck says. "Melvin turned me into a tournament player." Although Fleck earned only $2,752 in 15 tournaments preceding the 1955 Open, he made money in the last six. Jack attributed the sudden improvement to a sand wedge he had purchased that spring, by mail, from the Ben Hogan Co. in Ft. Worth.

Qualifying for the Open at Lincolnshire Country Club near Chicago, Fleck returned home for a few weeks and then drove, alone, to San Francisco in his 1954 Buick. Arriving 10 days before the start of play, he encountered Hogan on the practice tee and introduced himself. The Hogan wedges, he told Ben, were working very nicely.

Fleck was demoralized by his first look at Olympic. The fairways were narrow, the greens were small and the air was heavy. The rough, a thatchy growth of imported Italian rye,

With thousands of spectators watching from the hillside overlooking the 18th green, Jack Fleck putts toward the cup at the end of his playoff victory over Ben Hogan, who stands at the right with his caddie.

was nearly a foot high in many places. (It was after that Open that the United States Golf Ass'n began taking a more active role in course preparation. Until then the host club could pretty much control factors like the rough.)

After shooting 87 in his opening practice round, Fleck intensified his preparation by playing 36 to 45 holes a day for the week. "I discovered it was a fair course," Fleck says today. "I didn't have to worry about water hazards or a lot of tight out-of-bounds holes. The main thing was to hit it straight and stay out of the trees."

In the first round, paired with Walker Inman and Larry Tomasino, Fleck shot 76. "It was the best ball-striking round I played in that tournament," he claims, "but I couldn't putt a lick." On Friday his putting picked up and he shot 69 to move into a tie for second place at 145 with Hogan and Julius Boros, one stroke behind leader Tommy Bolt.

In those days the USGA did not arbitrarily pair the leaders together on the last day, which took in two rounds and was played in twosomes. Hogan went off on Saturday morning at 9:31 for the start of the 36 holes with Bob Harris, a Chicago pro whose score the first two rounds totaled 148. Fleck started at 10:30 with Gene Littler. There were three other twosomes behind them.

Fleck had 75 in the morning, and by the time the final round got under way in the afternoon, the battle had apparently simmered down to those old rivals, Hogan and Sam Snead. Snead frittered away his chances by missing three birdie putts of nine feet or less on 12, 13 and 14. After taking bogeys on 16 and 17, he finished at 292.

Hogan, limping on his bad knee, hit a 4-wood out of the rough to save a critical par on the long 14th and birdied the 15th before parring in for a 70 and 287. As he came off the 18th green to a thunderous ovation, Ben handed his ball to Joe Dey, then executive director of the USGA. "This is for Golf House," he said. Then he trudged slowly to the locker room to await official word that he had won his record fifth Open.

"I had been keeping track of the scoreboards all day," Hogan says now. "When I finished, I was sure I had won that tournament by at least two shots."

Hogan wasn't the only one. In the locker room, the writers pressed around him, probing for quotes. Ben quietly sipped a Scotch and water. He was packed, ready to go home after the presentation ceremonies.

The 1955 Open was the second that was telecast nationally. It was carried by NBC, with Lindsey Nelson and Gene Sarazen the announcers. Sarazen rushed down to the 18th green to congratulate Hogan and then proclaimed him the Open Champion to the television audience. It was 6 P.M. and NBC's hour of air time was over. Television viewers throughout the nation assumed Hogan had won.

Meanwhile, out on the course, Fleck was playing with an astonishing calm. On the 13th hole at the time Hogan finished, he saved par by coming out of a trap. A bogey on the 14th, however, left him needing two birdies on the last four holes to tie Hogan. "You also need a couple of pars," Littler reminded him as the gallery swelled to watch the finishing holes.

Fleck made the first birdie on 15 by hitting a 6-iron shot 9 feet away and holing the putt. Hogan got the news as he was preparing to take a shower. "Good for him." declared Ben.

Fleck parred the 603-yard 16th and then hammered two wood shots to the back of the 17th green and just missed his 40-foot putt for birdie. Lawson Little was on the course doing radio commentary for the NBC Monitor show. "Fleck could do it," Little shouted into the microphone.

As Lindsey Nelson climbed off the television tower behind the 18th green, he was approached by a concerned Tom Gallery, then NBC television sports director. "Do you think this fellow Fleck can get that last birdie?" he asked Nelson. "If he does, we aren't going to look very good."

The thought had also occurred to Lindsey Nelson. "I don't think so, Tom," he replied. "There's too much pressure on him."

The network had declined its option to carry the playoff, if one was needed. Nelson flew back to New York to accept an award the next evening on the Ed Sullivan show.

The 18th hole at Olympic measures 337 yards, with the small green tucked into the basin of a vast natural amphitheater. Fleck pulled his 3-wood tee shot just into the rough, 130 yards from the green. "I had a good lie," he recalls. "The pin was set fairly tight on the right side. I hit an easy 7-iron over the bunker, sort of punched it, and the ball wound up about 8 feet to the right of the hole. I played the putt for a slight break to the left, and looked up as the ball dropped into the cup."

When he heard the tremendous roar of the gallery, Hogan, still in the locker room, was knotting his tie. He lowered his head and cursed softly. "I was wishing he'd make either two or four," he said. "I was hoping it was all over." Hogan nodded to the locker-room attendant. "Get the clubs out," he said, "I'll be back tomorrow."

Hogan returned to the Fairmont Hotel for a quiet dinner with his wife Valerie. The last thing on earth he wanted was a playoff. His legs were aching. He had worked since March, priming himself for 72 holes, and now he had to go back out the next day and play 18 more.

On another floor of the Fairmont, where he was rooming with golf historian Fred Corcoran, Gene Sarazen was barraged with telegrams from Iowa protesting his premature declaration of Hogan as the winner. "Gene took it all in stride," Corcoran recalls. "He just said, 'Well, I was 24 hours early, that's all. Ben will still win it.' I guess all of us felt the same way."

Fleck had checked out of his motel room in suburban Daly City that morning. San Francisco hotels were jammed with conventions, and he was left homeless until some friends from Davenport, Dr. and Mrs. Paul Barton, obtained a room for him next door to theirs at the Stewart Hotel.

"I didn't sleep much that night," Fleck says. "The telegrams were pouring in, sent in care of Dr. Barton, and the phone never stopped ringing. I remember sitting there in my pajamas, talking on the phone to people from Iowa and wondering if I was ever going to get to bed."

The next morning Fleck went out for breakfast with the Bartons at Seal Rock, a tourist-type restaurant and gift shop.

"I was really edgy all morning," Fleck says. "I could hardly wait to get playing. Then, as I was standing on the first tee, someone in the pro shop leaned out the window and said there's a call for me from a Mr. Oliver. I took it, and sure enough, it was Porky. He phoned to wish me luck."

If Fleck's golf the day before had contained a chimerical quality, what of his performance in the playoff? Here he was, a municipal course pro from Davenport, Iowa, going head-to-head with the man generally considered the greatest golfer in history.

But there was an eerie assurance about Fleck. Not only did he play deliberately and without any apparent emotion, his concentration was almost trance-like. "That guy's in another world," observed Bob Roos, the tournament's general chairman. "You could stick a 6-inch needle in his back and he'd never know the difference."

Hogan, on the other hand, was a source of disquieting concern to his many rooters. Throughout the week there was a puzzling tentativeness to his play, a lack of the crisp decisiveness that had characterized his golf in the Opens of 1951 and 1953. His swing didn't look quite the same, either.

It was the deliberate result of Ben's preparations for the '55 Open. More perceptively than other contestants, he had recognized the type of golf required to win at Olympic. Distance was important, to be sure, but accuracy was paramount. Ben realized the need to control the ball, and he had altered his plan of attack to incorporate a swing that was flatter than normal; he was virtually punching the ball with his forearms. In the process he speeded up his tempo a bit, and the hills took a toll on his battered legs. Ben Hogan was 42, and he looked all of that.

Al Laney of the New York *Herald Tribune,* a Hogan-watcher since Ben's early days on the tour, discerned it better than anyone else. "The greatest golfer of his day is 2 years beyond his peak, mechanically speaking," Laney wrote. "But he is Hogan, nevertheless, and no one may still be as good as he."

The trend in the playoff was set when Hogan missed a short birdie putt on the fourth hole. He fell a stroke back with a bogey on five, and Fleck grimly held that lead with a 25-foot putt for a par on six. On the eighth, Hogan made a 50-footer for a birdie two, but Fleck threw an 8-footer right on top of that for *his* deuce. Fleck extended his margin to two strokes with a 25-foot birdie putt on nine, and to three with an 8-footer on 10.

"He was playing well and putting like crazy," Hogan said recently. "He was using those wedges we had sent him pretty effectively, too."

Hogan fought back to chop a stroke off Fleck's lead with a birdie on 14 and when Fleck bogeyed 17 Ben was one shot back with one hole left.

"We were playing from a new back tee on 18 that wasn't fully covered with grass," Hogan recalls. "They hadn't watered that tee the night before, and I noticed that as I walked up to hit. As I swung into the ball, my right foot slipped. That was the shot that killed me."

Hogan pulled his drive into the deep, heavy rough. "We had a hard time just finding the ball," he says. "I took a sand wedge and moved it about a foot. It took two more swings to get the ball back onto the fairway.''

Fleck knew he had won the Open, and he had his par all the way. Hogan, who hit his fifth shot about 25 feet above the pin, was faced with the probable humiliation of three putts and an eight. Summoning all his ineffable determination, Ben rolled the putt in for a six and a 72 to Fleck's 69.

As Hogan walked over to congratulate the new champion, he made a tremendous effort and smiled. Then he took off his cap to fan Fleck's hot putter as the photographers closed in.

Fleck was visibly moved by the gesture. ''Ben didn't say much to me on the course,'' he remembers. ''He was his usual serious self, concentrating hard, and I tried to play the same way. But there was no hostility out there, during the round or after. When we walked over to the presentation, Ben put his arm around my shoulder and said quietly, 'You did a great job'.''

Once the euphoria of his epic victory had abated, Fleck began to realize he had precipitated a certain backlash of resentment among the game's sentimentalists, who were pulling so hard for Hogan.

''I heard some comments then and for years afterward,'' Fleck says. ''But nobody could expect me to go out there and try to lose. Looking back on it now, maybe it would have been better if Ben had won. That fifth Open meant a lot to him.''

Before leaving San Francisco, Fleck was summoned to an audience with President Dwight Eisenhower, who was attending the 10-year anniversary festivities of the United Nations at the St. Francis Hotel, across the street from the Stewart. A group of secret service men spotted Fleck checking out and ushered him away.

''We've been looking all over for you,'' one of them told Fleck. ''The President wants to see you.'' Fleck spent nearly an hour with the golf-loving Ike, who also phoned his condolences to Hogan.

For Fleck, there was no returning to his municipal course job now. There was money to be made in exhibitions and personal appearances, and Fleck got his share. ''I did all right financially from the Open,'' he says, ''but I never played quite as well afterward as I would have liked. I broke my driver at the Masters the next year, and it took me a year to find another good one.'' Jack won only two tournaments on the tour after the Open, beating Bill Collins in a playoff in 1960 at Phoenix and Bob Rosburg in a playoff in 1962 at Bakersfield.

Nobody seems to remember that he almost won another Open. Hogan ironically, also was involved in 1960 at Cherry Hills in Denver. Hogan had battled winner Arnold Palmer for 36 holes the last day, hitting his first 34 greens in regulation until he caught the water with a touchy pitch shot on the 71st hole. Palmer established his charging image for all time that day with an outgoing 30 for a 65 on the final round. But Fleck, playing two groups behind Palmer, had a 31 himself on the front nine in the afternoon before missing three short putts on the closing holes to finish three strokes behind.

Fleck then drifted back into obscurity. He played the tour spasmodically the next few years while maintaining various club jobs in Illinois and California. He surfaced again briefly in 1966 when the Open returned to Olympic. Hogan was there, too. Ben had accepted a special invitation from the USGA and played superbly, despite his shaky putting, to finish 12th. Fleck, whose exemption as Open champion had expired, had to qualify. Fleck's homecoming at Olympic,

coinciding with Hogan's, provided extra flavor for the tournament but Jack played raggedly and missed the cut.

Early that week, on the putting green, Hogan spotted Fleck. The two smiled, waved and exchanged greetings. ''I saw Ben at the Open the next year at Baltusrol, too,'' Fleck says. ''Again he was very friendly.''

That was the final Open appearance for either of them. In 1973 Fleck became pro at the North Hills Country Club in suburban Milwaukee. He called Hogan that summer with an invitation for Ben to play in the Vince Lombardi Memorial Tournament at North Hills but Hogan, busily involved in the construction of two golf courses near Fort Worth, graciously declined.

Fleck is still working at North Hills. He is 53 now, and seldom plays much, except for an occasional round with his members or a Monday outing with nearby pros. Like Hogan, Fleck has mellowed over the years. For a long time he didn't like to talk about his Open victory, but he has become far more outgoing and eager to reminisce. ''I wouldn't mind playing in a few tour events,'' says Fleck, who still has a lifetime tour exemption from his Open championship. ''But I can't afford the travel expenses.''

Hogan spends his mornings these days in his office, his afternoons overseeing the completion of his 36-hole Trophy Club. He will be 64 in August.

Not long ago, Ben was asked to sum up the highlights of his career. ''The tournaments that gave me the most satisfaction,'' he replied, ''were the 1950 U.S. Open at Merion, the first one I played after the accident, and winning the British Open at Carnoustie in 1953, the only time I entered. But I remember the ones I lost a lot more than the ones I won.

''I've had many sleepless nights thinking back over the Open with Fleck in '55 and hitting the water at Cherry Hills in '60. Espceially the one in '55. Like I said, I thought I had won that one by at least two strokes.''

When contestants gather at this year's Open, someone will be sure to bring up, as someone does at every Open, the story of Fleck and Hogan at Olympic. Fleck and Hogan. An improbable pairing for sure, but because of what happened on that misty weekend in 1955, their names will be forever linked.

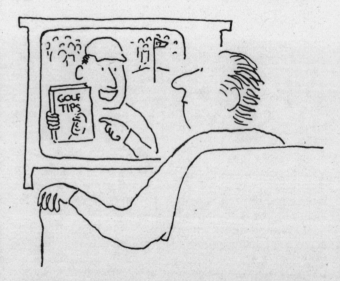

"Before I line up my putt, fans, I would like to remind all of you in the TV audience of my new book that is now available in all bookstores.

Calkins System Had Merit

By JOHN S. BRODHEAD, JR.
(The *Courier News,* Somerville, N.Y.)

EVERYBODY here who's heard of the Calkins system for handicapping golf matches stand up!

This probably won't generate much in the way of jolting golfers onto their feet but Leighton Calkins, who devised a handicap system good enough to be approved by the leaders of golf, was a real "buster."

A corporation lawyer by trade, he tackled everything from the United States Golf Association (of which he was a member) to the staid Blue Laws of New Jersey (which prohibited recreation on Sunday) to nude sun bathing (which was lawless everywhere) to politics and a few things in between and came out top cat every time—and mind you much of this was accomplished in the early 1900's.

He had studied law abroad, at Harvard and MIT and was in business by 1895, the year he established residence in Plainfield, New Jersey. It was about then he was bitten by the universal golf bug and became an immediate critic of the game, particularly when it came to balancing a method to make what appeared to be one-sided matches come out close to even around the 18th hole—enter handicapping.

Maybe he'd been stung financially by those famous "first tee" words which today still cause players with established handicaps to wrap both hands tightly around their wallets: "Well, I really don't have a real handicap but I shoot about . . ." or words to that effect.

Anyway, Calkins' mind with numbers produced a handicap system in 1904 that was designed for courses with pars from 62 to 76. It ranged from plus three for players who scored 70 or under to 27 for those who toured the course in 109 or worse. The actual handicap was determined by a player's three best scores of the year with an adjustment the next year.

The Metropolitan (NY) Golf Association and the New Jersey Golf Association, of which Calkins held excutive committee memberships (including presidencies) adopted it immediately.

It took the United States Golf Association a little longer . . . 7 years.

By then Calkins was no stranger to the USGA. He had been a member of that august body's executive committee in 1907-08 and when he left he became highly critical of its handicap system and said so . . . loudly. People must have listened.

Now no handicap system, today's included, is going to make every golfer happy immediately, or ever. But the USGA must have thought the Calkins system had merit. Let it not be said the USGA bowed to Calkins' critiques of its prior system; it was just in keeping with the trend that what Calkins wanted, Calkins got.

For instance, as member of Plainfield Country Club (which isn't and never was in Plainfield, but mainly in Edison, New Jersey) he moved the ball around in 12-handicap style but could not go with the Blue Laws that prohibited golf, baseball or any recreation on Sunday.

He started rattling the cages to bring golf to Plainfield Country Club on Sunday. Twice, just after the turn of the century, the board had put him down. But, in the fall of 1908 he was able to call a full membership meeting in a downtown casino that was destroyed by fire only a year ago.

The wearers of the cloth knew as well as the membership what was coming and denounced the plan from their pulpits. These men had been busy that year. They also had been preparing sermons against a statewide liquor law.

The membership approved Sunday golf at that meeting by the slender margin of four votes.

Calkins wins again.

But let it be noted the golfers were not boastful in their victory. They gave the men of the church one last word against golf on the Sabbath and then, when most churches had ended services, about 25 of them quietly teed off, starting at 1 PM on Sunday, October 26, 1908.

They were not vindictive in triumph. No caddies were employed; there was no prize competition (well, maybe a few Nassaus) and the women stayed off the course.

While the struggle for Sunday golf was going on, the club membership, without fanfare, had changed its name It had been known as Hillside Tennis and Golf Club. No reason was given for the change, but a nearby cemetery had (has) the same name.

Meanwhile Calkins doubtlessly was enjoying himself immensely but corporate law in New York had to be getting in the way of his golf. Although active on Plainfield's fairways, he managed to play 41 other courses in 1908 including such famous ones as Maidstone and Tuxedo in Westchester (NY) and Baltusrol and Morris County and such now defunct ones as Westfield and Cranford in New Jersey.

But now he was on the prowl for new fields to conquer. He became a bug on golf for boys and, as president of the Metropolitan Golf Association, he battled for a tournament for teens. He got it and became the father of the Metropolitan Junior Tournament when that group held its first event at Plainfield in June 1912. Stu Connolly of Rockland (NY) won the inqugural event with a rather respectable 74.

But the restless Calkins still wanted to better his track record so he took on politics, city hall and nude sun bathing . . . not necessarily in that order of importance.

He ran for mayor of Plainfield and was elected to three terms, 1915 through 1920 and quit a winner. He was backed heavily to run again but he'd had it with politics and went back to corporate law. During his term, Plainfield's city hall was under construction and the general contractor failed on the job. Calkins headed the committee to complete the edifice and there's no need to say how the job came out.

In 1934, Calkins, now semi-retired was averaging about 144 holes of golf a week but he had now adopted another avocation—following the sun—in the nude.

Now remember, this was 1934 and nude sun-bathing was not enjoying the fashion it does today—particularly in the dunes of Cape Cod. One day when Calkins was enjoying his new-found hobby on a sunny September afternoon, he was arrested and hauled into court on an exposure charge.

The good burghers of Massachusetts, not buying his explanation that sunning sans clothes was good for a nervous breakdown he said he suffered, and cuffed him with a $100 fine.

But, that's right, Calkins wins again. He took his case to the Massachusetts appellate court and the lower court's decision was overturned.

Calkins died at age 87 in 1955, maybe because he couldn't find any more mountains to tackle.

ODDEST ACES

A generations gap
Two aces were made on the 143-yard fourth hole at the Maryville Municipal Golf Course, Phoenix, on the same day, by golfers in different foursomes. Not so unusual, but the age of the acers shows that golf is a game to be enjoyed by all. Authors of the perfect tee shots were Scott Miller, 14, and Lee Bathrick, 73.

Bad timing
To be eligible for the hole-in-one "kitty" at the Sharpstown Country Club in Houston, an acer must be a member of the club's hole-in-one association and be playing with another member of that association at the time of the big event. Clayton Watkins scored an ace while playing with his wife, but unfortunately she was not a member of the hole-in-one club. After the round Mrs. Watkins decided to join the ace club. Three months later Watkins aced again. Mrs. Watkins, invited to play, had bowed out because of exhaustion from a shopping trip. No one else in Watkins' group was a member of the ace club and he lost out again.

Left arm is dominant
David Maynard, a 13-year-old from Nacogdoches, Tex., didn't let a broken right arm slow his golf. He continued to play, using his left arm only since his right arm was in a cast from fingertips to above the elbow. He one-armed an ace with a 5-iron at the 126-yard sixth hole at the Piney Woods Country Club, Nacogdoches.

Famine or feast
No holes-in-one had been made at the nine-hole, sand-green Mullen (Neb.) Golf Club since 1938. Then in July and August, 1974, the lid came off at Mullen. Four aces were made. Member Wayne Fitzgerald says a golfer from a nearby club "asked if we had replaced the cups at Mullen with horse tanks."

A straight plus one
Play was not heavy at the Cherry Hill Country Club, Andrews, S.C., so professional Wilson H. Myers didn't mind when a sixsome teed off. In fact, Myers joined the group, and on the 175-yard ninth showed some class by making a hole-in-one. The other five followed suit, in a manner of speaking. Erwin Chemons had a 2, Linwood Foster a 3, Billy Harris a 4, Dan Farrell a 5 and —aw, you guessed it—Samuel Harper a 6.

You gotta believe
Yetta Blumenthal dreamed that she made a hole-in-one at the Westwood Country Club, Vienna, Va. The dream was so vivid that the next day she joined Westwood's ace "insurance" club. Then she teed off and aced the 155-yard 17th.

Not so sudden, but sudden

George Solovich Sr. ran in a 12-foot par putt on 18 to give him and his partner, Ivan Misner, a tie for the tournament lead with Tom Sluiter and Tom Sherwood. It was a partners event at the Hidden Waters Golf Course, Arkville, N.Y. The teams started a sudden-death playoff and matched pars for seven holes. On No. 8 Solovich ran in an 18-foot putt to gain another tie. On the 145-yard 10th, the miracle-worker settled things for good with a hole-in-one.

Fame fleets

Frank (Pooch) Lombardo whopped when he aced the very first hole he played in a shotgun-start event at the Pittsburg (Calif.) Golf and Country Club. It was the 127-yard fourth. But Pooch's game quickly deteriorated. For the next 17 holes, he took 153 shots. There is a silver lining, though. Pooch won two honors—closest-to-the-hole on the No. 4 and high gross score.

Three strikes aren't out

When your tee shot strikes an overhead power line on the par-3 fourth hole at the Morehouse Country Club, Bastrop, La., you get another shot—with no charge for the first. Hugh McGeever hit the wire with his first shot, and then did the same on his second. The wire is only three eights of an inch thick. On his third shot, McGeever missed the wire—and made a hole-in-one.

Nice month

Rudy Veruto, a 10-handicapper at the Columbia Golf and Country Club, Hudson N.Y., looks with favor on the month of May, his 8-iron and the courses 141-yard seventh hole. For three consecutive years Veruto has scored a hole-in-one on No. 7 in May, each time using that trusty 8-iron.

Fore for two

Mr. and Mrs. William H. Peterson had a giddy time in 1974 between May 31 and Aug.14, when each scored two holes-in-one. All were at the Royal Poinciana Golf Club, Naples, Fla., which has two 18-hole courses. All of their aces were made on different holes.

Square-shooter

Kay Jesm knew her time to play golf was limited, so she hurried to the Valli-Vu course in Afton, Wyo. During the round, Kay scored a hole-in-one. "Quite a feat for a five-footer who is almost square," wrote her friend, Rose Wray. Kay was over eight months pregnant at the time of her ace.

Will Anyone Ever Topple Souchak's Record of 257?

By HUBERT MIZELL

EVEN GOLF'S most historically inclined chanticleers seldom mention the 257 of Mike Souchak, perhaps because it's so unreachable. Unthreatened accomplishments often become unmentioned accomplishments. Jack Nicklaus has never come close to Souchak. Neither have Palmer and Player. Johnny Miller may not know the record exists.

Twenty-seven!

That becomes the magic figure in a flashback to February 1955 when Souchak, a former Duke football tight end, authored the still-unchallenged 72-hole tour total of 257 in the Texas Open. Born in '27, Mike was then 27 years old. He had 27 birdies, and for one nine-hole round had a fantastic 27! His 257 total was 27 under par. And, as he charged through the closing 18 holes on a Sunday 21 years ago, the temperature around San Antonio plunged to—you guessed it, folks—a frigid 27 degrees.

"I would rather have won a U.S. Open in my career," says Souchak, now approaching age 49, "and God knows I came close three straight years. But since I can't look back on a great victory at Winged Foot or Cherry Hills or Oakland Hills, I'm glad I had my week at Brackenridge Park at least."

Compared to those golfing meccas, Brackenridge is a virtual poorhouse. The lowly municipal course was so grass-thin in 1955 Souchak and his tour brothers teed off from rubber mats.

Souchak's opening round began unspectacularly. He birdied the second hole, but three-putted at five, missing a 2-footer to drop back to even par. "That little 24-inch putt was to cost me a lot of golfing fame," Souchak says, "but, at the time, I sure wasn't thinking about breaking 60. I had never won on the tour. I was a rabbit, a Monday qualifier. All I wanted was to win and earn my exemption form qualifying. Nothing else mattered."

Even after eight holes, Souchak was only one under par. That's when the volcano erupted. Eagles and birdies spewed across Brackenridge like boiling lava. After the smoke cleared, Souchak had shot 33-27—60, equalling the one-round tour record that stands today.

It really began on No. 9, where Souchak crunched his drive and whistled a 5-iron to the green. He plunked in a 13-foot putt for an eagle. On No. 10, an iron shot died 18 feet from the cup and Mike holed it for a birdie. "Then came two fairly easy birdie holes, the 11th and 12th," he recalls. "I went par-par and figured the charge had ended."

It had only begun. Souchak's 3-wood on the par-five No. 13 landed 3 feet from the flagstick and he rapped home a second eagle. On the 14th, a short par-four, he nearly drove the green and then chipped to within 12 inches for an easy birdie.

On he went, dropping a 12-footer to birdie the 15th after a 7-iron approach and making a putt from 6 feet on the 16th after an 8-iron. A pitching wedge put Mike 10 feet away on the 17th and again he made the birdie putt. On the 18th, needing another birdie to tie the tour record of 60, he slapped a 5-iron to within 20 feet and sank the putt.

Tommy Bolt, Sam Snead and Ted Kroll also shot 60s on the tour. So did three lesser-knowns named Bill Nary, Wally Ulrich and Al Brosch. Although the gallery mushroomed as word spread around Brackenridge Park that some guy from Pennsylvania was blistering the back nine, the only persons to see all 60 shots were Mike's playing partners, Otto Greiner and George Buzzini.

Souchak followed the 60 with rounds of 68-64-65 for his 257, an average of 64.25 per 18 holes for the Millers, Ben Crenshaws and Hubert Greens to shoot at for years to come.

"There are many more fine young golfers today, but the tour no longer goes to courses like Brackenridge Park," Souchak says. "I would guess that the one-round record of 60 will fall sometime, maybe even the nine-hole mark of 27 will get tied or something. But that 257 will be tough to touch. If somebody beats it, my hat is off to him. It takes some great playing and some extraordinary luck—like sinking putts from all over the ballpark."

After the opening 60, Souchak shot a second-round 68 and now admits, "I felt like I was shooting 90." He led by only two shots with 60-68—128, but the weather changed for the worse and Souchak, torrid right through the bitter cold of Saturday and Sunday, pulled away from the pack.

"Under the conditions of Sunday, with the temperature hovering in the high 20s, I thought my closing 65 was as

good as my opening 60," he said. "By then, the local newspapers had let me know I was chasing the 72-hole record of 259 by two Texas immortals, Ben Hogan and Byron Nelson. I was aware I needed 67 to tie the record, 66 to beat it."

Mike wore every stitch of clothing he had on the trip for that Sunday. "I was still cold," he says. "Fortunately, after I drove on No. 1, some gentleman obviously saw I was shivering and offered me a pair of deerskin gloves. I wore them all day, removing them only when making a shot. I played super and didn't have to try anything spectacular at the end to beat the Hogan-Nelson record."

For all that he won $2,200.

"I was so psyched up that I didn't let down at Houston the next week," he says. "I won again and the first-place paycheck was $6,000, one of the tour's largest in 1955. I had gone from tour rabbit to leading money-winner in 2 weeks."

Souchak went on to win 16 tournaments in the next decade, including the St. Paul Open and the Houston event, both twice. His first victory at St. Paul was another classic Souchak birdie explosion as he closed with 63 to erase a seven-shot deficit against little Jerry Barber.

Still, he missed the big one.

"My entire career would have taken a different road if I hadn't blown three great chances in the U.S. Opens of 1959-60-61," he says. "I made some mistakes and got bugged by cameras long before Tom Weiskopf ever got mad at his photographer."

Souchak had worked as an assistant pro under Claude Harmon at Winged Foot in Mamaroneck, N.Y., before tackling the tour. When he returned to Winged Foot for the 1959 Open, Mike felt he was playing strongly and had a chance on the course he knew so well. "It came down to the final hole," he says. "I needed a birdie three to tie Billy Casper for the championship. Instead, I made bogey five. I had also bogeyed the 11th, 12th and 15th, so I felt like dying right there."

If not there, then at Cherry Hills in Denver the next year. Souchak blistered the course for 68-67 the first two rounds, an Open record of 135 for the first 36 holes. In those days the final two rounds were played on Saturday, and

Souchak came to No. 18 of the morning round needing a par four for a healthy four-stroke lead.

"Just as I started my downswing, some photographer started clicking away," he recalls. "I jumped, lurched and hit my tee shot out-of-bounds. I made a double bogey and my game fell apart for the afternoon round. On No. 1, I drove into a creek that was barely a foot wide. I was on my way to a 75. I double-bogeyed the 12th and three-putted the 18th along the way. Palmer won it, Nicklaus finished second—he was an amateur then—and I was fourth. Again, I wanted to find a hole to bury myself in."

In 1961 the Open was at Oakland Hills near Detroit, where Souchak was to become the host pro a few years later. "I was dreadfully sick, but refused to consider withdrawing," he says. "I had come so close I had to give it another try. A doctor pumped me full of penicillin and, although it was warm, I had chills and wore a sweater. Each of the first two days, I was birdie-crazy and then ran out of steam. I was three over for the last four holes in the first round, shooting 73. I was two over the final three holes the second day, shooting 70. Then, fortunately, the penicillin took hold. I was OK for the closing 36 holes."

He shot 68 Saturday morning and trailed leader Jacky Cupit by one shot. He birdied the first two holes and No. 4 to begin the afternoon round and was the sole leader—"the only SOB in red numbers." Then another cameraman came into Souchak's life to help wreck his dream of an Open title.

"I had bounced a 5-iron over the fifth green," he says. "I pulled a pitching wedge out of my bag and was about to hit my third shot, hoping to get up and down for a par four.

"A newspaper photographer, using one of those old box-type cameras they had in those days, clicked away just before I struck the ball. It sounded like a machine-gun. I jumped and hit the ball about halfway up the embankment."

Mike wound up with a double bogey and Gene Littler came on to win the tournament. Souchak was fourth, two strokes behind Littler and one back of Bob Goalby and Doug Sanders.

More than one golfing expert has speculated that if Souchak had beaten Palmer in 1960 at Denver, their careers could have been reversed. Mike had similar gallery appeal and could drive the ball a ton. He, too, was from Pennsylvania. It could have been Souchak flying around in an executive jet and earning a million a year.

But, Souchak hasn't done badly.

He had a posh club job at Oakland Hills for 5 years and then became involved in a highly profitable resort-real estate venture and golf job in Florida.

He is listed as "golf professional" at the Innisbrook resort, and is also a stockholder. Souchak lives in a hand- some waterfront home, wheels to work in a Mercedes 300SCL and owns a cache of French wine that even the Gallo brothers would admire.

The relationship with fine wine began when Souchak played in the pro-am of the Los Angeles Open with Harley Edrington, a broker for French vineyards. "He got me interested and I sure liked burgundy," Mike says. "So, when the time was right, I bought myself a nice supply." The supply is 2,400 bottles, aging in Nuit-St. George, France. Mike "visited my wine" on a recent business trip to Europe and plans to bring it over.

Last year, Souchak took on a second pro job. Golf Hosts South, the corporation which owns Innisbrook, has also become Golf Hosts West with a picturesque mountain resort at Durango, Colo. Mike has a piece of the action.

The resort, called Tamarron, is 7,800 feet above sea level. "Forget the golf and the sight is still incredible," says Souchak, with more than a taste of corporate pride. "You hit shots through the aspen and ponderosa pine, through the natural buttes, up and down the hillsides. You'll be hitting golf shots much farther, due to the 7,800 feet."

He'll be Tamarron's host professional during the summer, returning home to Innisbrook for the remainder of the year. Maybe Mike Souchak would have enjoyed a richer life if he had won a U.S. Open. Maybe, but it's hard to imagine. The fellow from Berwyck, Pa., seems to be doing quite well.

"Fore!"

"Fore!"

When Golf Is No Fun

By BEN HOGAN

Here, in a reprint of a 1942 *Esquire* article, Hogan offers consolation for the duffer who learns that form sometimes goes wrong for the best of them.

WHEN I got the man's letter I thought here is something a couple of books couldn't answer.

And he wanted me to solve his problem with an offhand reply on a sheet of paper!

What the fellow wrote was this:

"I used to play a fairly good game of golf, getting several rounds a year in the 70's and going over 85 only two or three times a year. Now my game is always around 100—a few strokes under or over. I have taken some lessons, and I practice about one evening a week on the average at a stop-and-sock place. But my game is getting no better. I certainly don't enjoy my golfing as much as I did. Is there anything I can do to get back on my game, or must I realize I am 46 years old and past the age when my golf can be improved? If I am going to be playing worse and worse all the time, then I am about ready to give up on the game entirely. It's no fun any more."

I feel sorry for that fellow. I have taken the same sort of punishment he's been giving himself. Before I really found my game I might be hot one round and cold the next for no reason I could figure out. After rounds when I wasn't scoring well I would practice for hours trying to get to hitting the ball, and finally go home disgusted.

When I found out from players like Nelson, Cooper, Armour and Smith what I was doing wrong and got ideas for correction, then I began to get some good out of practice. Now I will practice for an hour or two right after I've come in from playing a round well under par. My inquiring friend won't do that. He probably goes in, takes his shower and has a few drinks to console himself for his score. That part, at any rate, should be fun.

What I've learned is that when a fellow is hitting the golf ball well he should try to keep in that groove until it becomes a habit. If he's developed bad details in his swing and tries to get rid of them without knowing how his swing looks or without being aware of the feel he should have at different stages of the swing, then his practice only deepens his bad swing.

The chances are that the fellow who wrote me never had what could actually be called a golf swing. When he was younger, when his eyes were keener, his coordination better and his muscles more flexible, it was natural that he would be able to hack at the ball fairly well without thinking about it at all. Adjustment for error was subconscious and fairly efficient.

Then along came the day when he tried to substitute his brains for his muscles. He heard some fellow say that he should keep his right elbow close to his body on the backswing, and he got so attached to that hunch that he ended up taking a ladylike jerky hack at the ball. Or the chances are about 9 to 1 that his playing companions all kept telling him that he was taking his eye off the ball. Whereupon the victim stiffened himself so much that he almost broke his neck when he swung. Then, as he still had a miserable swing and got bad results, he gave up in profanity and dismay.

He thought he was the only one in the world who had become so stinking at golf he should give up the game. The sad part of it is that one of his type often does quit golf when some other discouragement is added to his scores. If his business slumps, then golf loses a player. Men in seed stores in the larger cities will tell you that their sales of seeds and garden tools increased to the 100-shooting members of golf clubs during the first few years of the Depression. Then golf didn't deteriorate; something else did.

There now are about 2,500,000 golfers in the United States. Authorities estimate there are about 1,500,000 men and women who once played golf but who discontinued playing for one reason or another. From what I've seen of golfers I'd say that about nine out of ten of those who gave up the game quit because there was no fun in their scores. They are like the fellow who wrote to me.

These people who get troubled about their scores to the extent that they quit the game make an expensive mistake. It's plain that if they get so disturbed about their scores when they are not in golf for prize money as a living that they worry themselves into giving up, their general morale needs attention.

The best thing golf can do for these fellows who get low-spirited when they bump into a tough problem is not to give them scores of 73, 74, and 75, but to get them to walking the 4 miles of an 18-hole round merely for the exercise and the congenial company. The first thing I'd honestly advise a fellow who is disgusted with his golf to do is to change the company he's playing in. If he changes to playing with fellows who enjoy themselves without worrying themselves and others about bad shots and high scores, he'll begin to relax at his game. He will get a better score because he won't be trying so desperately that he tightens up stiffer than a steel rail.

In tournament golf the hardest thing to do is to swing easy. I can tell you that because it took me plenty of time to learn that when I gave the ball the works I stayed on the line, but when I had to hold back I ended too often in some trouble. Consequently, I had to work hard to get a compact swing that would hold together when I didn't go to the full limit of my backswing. Even now some think I'm inclined to underclub approach shots. But they don't appreciate that I have complete confidence when hitting a shot hard—a shorter club and swinging harder give me precision.

But you take the case of this man who is discouraged with his game and you find the opposite condition. He gets disgusted with a bad shot and goes to his next shot either scared or in a mad mood. If he's scared he has an unreasoning hunch that brute force will hammer the next shot home. If he's

Ben Hogan in action during a U.S. Open tourney.

sore he wants to take out his grouch on the ball. So he doesn't stop to think about the first two things: whether his grip gives him a chance to swing the club head squarely into the ball, and whether the location of the ball with respect to placement of his feet will allow the club to do its work right.

Even if the fellow did stop to think, he probably wouldn't know what to do because he's so set in his own wrong way that the right way probably would feel awkward to him. That's why you hear men say so many times that the lesson they just took threw them off their game. It sure enough did. That is what the pro was paid for. The game the pupil had was lousy; he should have been thrown off it long ago. No effort at correction can be 100 percent successful immediately.

It would amaze the fellow who is discouraged with his golf to realize what patience and heart has been required for many of the greatest pros to discover and overcome mysterious flaws that were giving them trouble.

Denny Shute was sick of his golf in 1928. He made a change in his grip that took him about a year to master. His first big victory was in the Los Angeles Open in 1930. From that he went on to win a British Open, two P.G.A. Championships, lose a U.S. National Open title in a play-off, and keep good enough to finish second in the 1941 U.S. Open.

Ralph Guldahl went into a bad slump after finishing a stroke out of a tie for the 1933 National Open Championship. It took him three years of practicing and studying before he came back to win two U.S. Opens and three Western Opens. In the past year or so some aggravating defect has developed in Ralph's game, although 999 out of a thousand might say he's just not getting the breaks he deserves, and Ralph's again analyzing and correcting.

Hagen, Sarazen, Horton Smith, Lawson Little and other great stars have had their slumps. But they've also had the hearts that make champions. They've found out what they needed to get scoring again and they worked on it until they got it.

I wouldn't expect anyone like the man who wrote me the letter I quoted to apply himself to correcting his game with the same intensity, and as long, as the playing pros work on theirs. He'd be crazy if he did. He's primarily in the game for fun and unless he is willing to enjoy himself at supervised practice for some months, he'd better get used to the sort of golf fun that isn't dependent on the scorecard.

Thinking of the discouraged man's case and of the many pupils I've taught—or tried to teach—to score well, it occurs to me that private golf clubs and the usual procedure of the instruction are not fitted to a very large percent of club members.

The truth is that about three fourths of a golf club's membership doesn't know how to swing a golf club properly. They have just enough knowledge of the technicalities of the swing that they've read or heard to be able to mess up natural impulses toward a smooth and effective swing. They were pretty fair baseball players when they were boys so why shouldn't they be good at this game where the ball stays still? That's the notion they have.

They insist that their children take weekly piano lessons for a couple of years and practice faithfully. The children are imitative, unmarked by incorrect habits of performance, and flexible enough to have their muscles do their minds' bidding. Yet their parents don't expect the impossible development of piano maestros in a few months.

But the parents whose muscles are getting numb and whose minds rarely can be disciplined to even brief concentration on a sport come out to a golf club and expect a professional to make them good players in six lessons.

There must be genius in golf instruction or the pros wouldn't have done as well as they have in teaching in the way

that fundamentally hasn't changed for almost 100 years.

Golf has to be learned as it is being taught. If the golf clubs had night-lighted practice tees of the stop-and-sock type and the pros were paid to get the pupils set on the first principles of grip, stance and swing, then walk up and down the tee supervising the practice, you'd see the standard of golf scoring greatly improved at golf clubs. Conditions would be right for learning, as well as for teaching. And I'm sure that the pupils would get a great deal of pleasant and healthy exercise out of the change in procedure.

Consider the fellow who wrote me. This past golfing season he has probably had plenty of business problems. He made dates to take a lesson, or to play. He rushes out to the club, throws in a quick lunch, makes a telephone call he forgot to make at the office, and hurries out to the tee tired already and with his nerves dancing.

I might tell the man that if I'd go out to a golf course the way he does I'd feel lucky if I ever was able to break 90. He's a nervous basket case before he gets to the golf course—and he blames his score for making him that way! It's not the man's golf game, it's his entire physical and mental condition that has upset him about his golf. I'll bet if he'd analyze himself frankly he'd find that he was easily and severely upset about other things undoubtedly more important than his golf score.

Yet, as long as the average American has a good strong element of competition in his nature, this fellow just can't be told to forget his score and not worry. That's like somebody telling me: "Think nothing of it; all you need is three pars to win."

The situation with this man is that he hasn't got the first thing for good golf scoring, and that's a sound golf stroke. If he could combine his instruction and his practice in the evening at his club when he could apply himself in a relaxed mood to mild physical exercise,

he would get the physical part of his game in good shape. It would do him a lot of good all around. He'd probably go to bed tired enough physically to go right to sleep.

He has probably been taking his lessons in the afternoon at his club and seeing, out of a corner of his eye, pals of his in competitive play. He figures he's missing something. He can't make up his mind what he wants to do, play or practice. That doesn't contribute anything to his enjoyment of golf.

So he misses developing the second thing he needs for a good score, a disciplined temperament.

Adding it all up, I'd say that if the fellow is scoring around 100, he isn't doing bad. Considering what he's up against in factors that handicap the development of the physical and mental phases of his game the man is lucky to hit a shot well now and then.

If this man is really on the level about wanting to improve his golf, he can do what I've done for several years; take a putter and use it from 15 minutes to a couple of hours almost every night putting at a glass laid on a carpet.

If he'll see where the ball is, with respect to his feet and eyes, when he gets uniformly good results, and how his grip is, and how the path of the putter blade is when he's regularly stroking putts into the glass, then he'll begin to get fun out of really studying his golf.

If he doesn't want to do that, what he wants is a miracle worked to improve his golf. Should there be any miracle that can be worked on a golf game I want it for myself.

When you get right down to it I guess that it actually isn't a few details about golf that have been bothering the man who wrote me. Maybe it's something he ate, the war, priorities, taxes or something else far away from a golf course. Golf is a very convenient thing for him to blame as the source of his unhappiness. He should be happy he has golf handy for that alibi and relief.

GOLF WITHOUT THE BALL? WELL...

By LARRY SHEEHAN

THE FIRST and last Anglo-American summit meeting of the golfing imagination—a bizarre match played without golf balls—was held at the Old Course, St. Andrews, Scotland. No one saw the match except its organizer, Fitch, and two local caddies who by now probably have drunk themselves into oblivion to forget the whole affair.

Fitch, a former golf equipment salesman, had hoped the unusual match would become a fixture in international golf, like the Walker Cup or Ryder Cup, and set a standard of play for ordinary golfers to follow. He honestly believed that if more people played golf without a ball, many friendships and stomach linings would be restored to the pink of health.

Fitch did not get the backing he needed to *really* promote the match. Originally he had wanted to produce a film or videotape of the event and later use it to spread his message that mental golf could relieve the world's anxieties. But then this message did not come through loud and clear in the match anyway.

What follows is taken from a transcription of a cassette tape that Fitch recorded intermittently during the match. It pretty much tells the story:

Waiting to get started, sitting on bench on first tee in front of historic R & A. Old codgers from Boxer Rebellions looking out window. Aura of tradition plus misty wind off sea sends chills up spine, down. Caddies smoking hand-rolled cigarettes, faces like wineskins. No question, colorful site for major test.

Too bad film contract fell through. No use turning back, of course, already quit job, spent life savings on airline tickets, hotels, meals, phone calls, etc. Will record all, maybe get in *People* Magazine, donate tape to UNESCO if all else fails.

Chauncey Lenz-Lees makes a few practice swings. Must be 65 at least, but spry. Consummate Briton. Knickers, necktie, funny little cap, pink cheeks, lips like earthworms. Resembles Vardon on follow-through—elbows out like wings, right heel way off ground, massive chin jutting toward target.

Lenz-Lees stopped playing the game with real balls when England lost India, definitely has edge as far as experience goes. Told me as much when I flew over 2 months ago to set things up. That was when U.S. TV deal was still all systems go. Visited him at his club in Kent where his manner of play has been tolerated but unfortunately not copied. Human evolution has reached point where competitiveness and physical skill should not be paramount factors in golf—or in international relations for that matter. The two go hand in hand: both sport and politics must become more cerebral before we can have peace in our time in my opinion. Well, that's one reason I brought these two men together, after all.

Starter waves from his shed. Chauncey Lenz-Lees sticks tee in ground, addresses non-existent ball with club, swings.

Onlookers mutter. Ha! Well, they muttered at the Wright Brothers.

Al St. Louis, the man I have brought over from America to play Chauncey head on, tees up his non-ball now. Al is what you call swarthy and fat. He chews gum, has flattish swing and dogged manner of Hogan. Wearing red Bermuda shorts today, yellow socks.

Al swings, more grumbling is heard. Starter looks particularly aghast. Caddies pick up bags, we hurry off tee.

Match of Century is on.

1st Hole Went all right. Chauncey played two on, two in. I walked with Al St. Louis, who said his tee shot drifted right. Then he reported his pitch bounced short of green, dangerously near Swilken Burn, historic creek where Jones, Hagen, Palmer et al have bathed.

Al had to chip on and make 10-footer to halve. Chauncey came over and slapped him on back, said was amazed visiting American had been able to read the tricky green so well. Al graciously accepted the congrats.

Spirit of concord is gratifying, thought it would take longer to develop. They understand each other's games, must be communicating on some revolutionary new wavelength. Well, that's my theory! That's why I conceived this unique new format. Not worried that we are all alone out here. Even U.S. Open started small, unheralded, I understand.

Don't like attitude of caddies, though.

2nd Hole Halved again. Caddies are going to be a problem. Lenz-Lees criticized his for stepping on his line on the green and the old-timer said loudly, " 'owd I know wherrrr 'is bloomin' line wuz!"—or something like that. On way to 3rd tee, informed same caddie we will brook no more impertinence, guffaws, etc. Paying him three times the usual fee for extra cooperation, after all.

3rd Hole Still even. Too soon to tell, but perhaps Chauncey wants a dull, steady game today, while Al St. Louis has opted to scramble. Al nervous. Not as experienced, of course. Less than year, now, I think, since he abandoned use of sphere at his club in western Pa. Not really accepted by his fellow members out there yet; treated like pariah, actually. Remember clearly day I dropped by on sales call at pro shop and saw him on practice putting green stroking non-existent balls. Knew right away he would make great match for legendary Briton I had heard of. Thought had sold idea to network, too, began making plans, quit job, contacted Lenz-Lees, spent own money, etc.

4th Hole Al is one down. Hit tee shot

into gorse but made superb recovery. Then Lenz-Lees came over, said he was delighted to see Yankee hacker get out of alien weed so handily. Al stubbed next shot as though embarrassed to be playing well. Or maybe he is stale from waiting around in London all week while I made vain last-minute effort to find film producer over here after U.S. network let me down.

6th Hole Back to even. Al made another fine recovery from gorse to 3 feet of pin, sank putt for birdie. Accepted profuse congrats from Chauncey who declared he had never seen a foreigner in blinding red short pants master the perils of St. Andrews so quickly.

Warned caddies about guffawing again.

7th Hole Odd. Al put tee shot in pot bunker, then made what appeared to be brilliant escape. But Chauncey said too bad Al's shot had caught the lip, bounced back in. Al looked bothered, then apparently realized his imagination had played tricks on him, for he played again from bunker.

First time wavelengths have not coincided. This sort of thing probably inevitable when massive brain power is being applied to raise golf to level of art. Should not let it worry me.

10th Hole Al three putted, making him two down. Am carrying Al's bag now that his caddie quit, just walked off into gorse after Al told him to clean his non-existent ball. Good riddance, I say.

Al understandably irritable. His game plan was to remain even through the turn and then hope the pressure would get to the favorite on way in.

Weather has cleared, up ahead are gray towers of St. Andrews, cradle of golf, gleaming wet, brings lump to throat, almost like fairy tale that we are all here, this match is taking place and I am carrying heavy bag.

12th Hole Al back to one down after calling penalty stroke on Chauncey for grounding club in hazard.

13th Hole All even again! Al sank snaking 40-footer for birdie. Chauncey threw his own putter high in air in admiration, came over to shake Al's hand, declared had never seen a heavy-set, gum-chewing Yankee tourist in underdrawers read Scottish greens so well.

Warned remaining caddie to stop mumbling to himself, it might distract golfers.

15th Hole Al one down again in this exciting match of wits, seesaw battle. Tee shot landed in another one of those devilish bunkers. He thought he had escaped on his first attempt but Chauncey said he had topped it. On second try, Chauncey said he had caught lip. On third try, Chauncey said he had escaped but had hit ball twice during stroke.

Al took brutal reversal in fortune well, Chauncey did not crow, either. Amazing how their wavelengths manage to merge at critical points.

17th Hole Famed Road Hole goes past hotel where we are all staying. Wonder how much bill will come to. Not that the money, all my savings actually, matters. It was noble experiment and after all it proves how great is the potential for harmoniousness within each and every golfer, and for brotherhood.

These bags are getting heavy. Second caddie walked off course when Al accused him of kicking Chauncey's tee shot on 17 back into fairway. Nasty-tempered old man said something like, " 'ow cin I kick woot I cin't set eyes on, ya blinkin' idiot!''

Al hits approach into bunker guarding green, then overshoots, lands on dreaded road. Chauncey, on in two and 20 feet from pin, has match in grasp.

But Al makes stupendous little finesse pitch, shot hits stick, he says, and drops in for birdie.

What great TV fare! Too bad BBC didn't have budget for this sort of thing.

Chauncey nods stoically, what a man, concedes hole with odd little smile on face.

18th Hole Who could not fail to be stirred by inspiring sight from final tee? I am thinking of all the trophies and titles that have changed hands within great sporting arena formed by the gray-stoned R & A, tall brownish ex-hotel and string of quaint woolen goods stores.

Almost can picture crazed golf fans hanging out windows instead of women tending flowers, and cameramen, reporters and officials jostling each other instead of locals out walking their dogs. Can even see myself presenting the Fitch Cup up there in the shadow of the R & A.

Al St. Louis, with newly won honors, tells Chauncey Lenz-Lees to stop twitching his goddam little limey mustache so he can hit off.

Chauncey replies he can't help it, he is allergic to the sight of a man's lumpy knees.

Both drive well in spite of amusing repartee.

Al leaves his approach in Valley of Sin, that tricky hollow in the front part of finishing green, while Lenz-Lees is perhaps too strong, but safe, on far side of the pin where the green is flat, easily negotiable in two.

Al stabs nervously at first putt and leaves it well short. In fact he is still away. He summons courage from I don't know where, strokes second putt directly into the hole.

Chauncey does not question or congratulate Al. Simply stoops and studies his own 40-footer with great deliberation. Then makes a smooth-looking stroke at it. Moments later, Chauncey raises his fist in triumph.

Al St. Louis shakes his head, says no, and points to a spot 2 feet short of the hole.

Chauncey Lenz-Lees walks up, shakes head again, and points directly at the cup.

I am suddenly aware of a small crowd gathered around the home green. It worries me slightly only because I see one of our ex-caddies is in the front ranks, watching balefully. I wonder if he has perhaps spread the word that madmen are loose on the revered Old Course. Geniuses and madmen are of course practically indistinguishable, but how explain that to this curmudgeonly lot?

I ask Chauncey and Al to settle the matter quickly and avoid any difficulties. Put your wavelengths to work, I plead.

Chauncey bends over, picks out his imaginary sphere and holds it aloft.

Al St. Louis is not convinced. Understandable, perhaps, since he loses the match if in fact the putt is in. He shakes his head.

Impasse. Wait, Chauncey suddenly flings his arm outward, toward Al St. Louis. Al stumbles backward three or four paces, as though struck.

He takes his hands down from his face.

Oh no, his nose is bleeding . . .

The tape ends here, apparently because Fitch, extremely sensitive to the sight of blood, fainted. Off tape, however, he later admitted that he was disappointed in the match even though Al's bloody nose tended to prove that imaginary golf was a valid concept.

Golf and Newton's Physical Laws

By MURRAY OLDERMAN
(Newspaper Enterprise Association)

KEN ROGERS doesn't blink an eye when he reads about Jack Nicklaus soaring to a quarter of a million dollars in golf earnings. Hell, Ken made almost that in one weekend when a dollar was worth 100 cents, not 22.

In the histories of golf, you'll seldom find the name of Ken Rogers, though in his really active days he held 23 course records. One reason is he never turned pro.

But Cary Middlecoff, the trained dentist who won the U.S. Open and remains prominent as a commentator, remembers Ken Rogers.

They met in February, 1940. Ken was an Air Force officer stationed in Orlando, Florida. Rodgers had been introduced to golf exactly a decade before when, through Walter Hagen, he met the immortal Bobby Jones. "You better have the right clubs," said Bobby, "if you're going to play." He immediately presented Ken with a set of his clubs.

At 2 o'clock on Saturday morning, Rogers was awakened from his sleep by a friend calling from Memphis. "Come on up heah," said the friend. "There's a 20-year-old kid, just graduated from dental school, been beating everybody 'round heah. You got to play him. See you in the mawnin'."

Thanks to the Air Force, Ken arrived early Saturday and went out in a foursome playing $100 Nassau, with Rogers matched for $500 against the young dentist. It was Cary Middlecoff. Rogers and his partner won handily and Ken won his match. They played nine more holes for $1,500, and Cary's backers kept boosting the ante—$2,000 . . . $3,000—and Rogers kept winning. "Middlecoff," he remembers, "never won a nine."

It went the same way Sunday morning until by noon, with Nassaus, presses and straight match money, Rogers and his partner totalled their take at $190,000. "There was a real 'norther' blowing up by then," recalls Ken, "so I went inside and got a little drunk when a guy tells me that Middlecoff's mistake was having the wrong partner. He'd team with Cary and play us for $10,000. I looked outside and said, 'I wouldn't walk out there for less than $25,000.' He said, 'You're on.'

"Off we go, with me half drunk. By the 15th hole we were three down, and my partner had his ball in a shallow creek off the green. He wants to pick it up. I said, 'Go ahead and hit it.' A lefthander with a 16-handicap, he hacks at it, cuts the ball almost in two, and it goes in. Now we're two down with three to go. I say, 'Let's press 'em.' We come to the 18th and we've got to win it to collect. Middlecoff hits one less than a foot from the hole. I pull my shot off the green. My partner says, 'Let's give it to 'em.' I shake my head. I chip and the ball goes in—they measured it at 68 feet.

"Cary's putt is 11 inches. My partner wants to concede it. 'Naw,' I insist, 'let him hit it.' No one's ever putted before in the history of golf for $25,000. He stood over that ball for 10 minutes. He brought the club head back 6 inches, tapped, and the ball moved half an inch. With the press, we went away from there with $240,000 that weekend, all of it in nice green cash."

All of this is pertinent because Ken Rogers remains associated with golf, though he is 68 years old, is bent by arthritis and his handicap has increased to six. He'll still bet anyone 2-to-1 he can hole out from 100 yards in two

strokes. "Nicklaus," he says, "is the world's worst 100 yards in."

Ken's edge now is that he uses his own specially designed, revolutionary golf clubs which, he claims, will change the life and outlook of every weekend golfer.

He has an engineering degree and it struck him right from the start that golf clubs were engineered all wrong.

"How can you have a low center of gravity," he asks grumpily, "when any extra weight is added to shaft?" That has been the historical method of adding swing weight to golf clubs.

On the very first set that Bobby Jones had given him, Ken had run a flange of silver solder on the back. Four years ago, he started experimenting seriously on putting more weight directly into the club head. The inspiration hit him one day: Why not put a slot in the damn things?"

A cavity is left behind the face plate on the head of the club and the desired lead weight is dropped into it, then sealed with black epoxy and you have what is being called the first really radical change in the manufacture of irons in the last 30 years. The clubs are being produced under the Shamrock label.

The main beneficiary is the mediocre player. The tour pro doesn't have trouble getting loft with a 2-iron, and now the duffer, with that extra swing weight in the club head (via the slot) gets the ball up in the air, too.

The head man of Shamrock is Jack Kirby, who used to catch passes and run the ball for the USC Trojans—played in the Rose Bowl, too—and developed a lively interest in golf after making his million in real estate. Jack can provide instant gobbledygook about Newton's Second Law of Physics, the acceleration squared, to show why the weight should all be in the clubhead.

"We produce a lighter club," says Kirby, "with greater head feel."

And the word has even reached as far as Japan. A 6'8" Sumo wrestler named Giant Baba ordered a set of Shamrocks—his driver is 46 inches long (vs. the usual 42) and his 2-iron measures at 44 inches (vs. the regular 39).

If they can show Giant Baba how to get the club-head past his gigantic stomach, it'll be the ultimate engineering tribute.

The Feisty Genius By NICK SEITZ
Who Taught the Tour's Foreign Stars

GARY PLAYER, the winner of many major championships, was recalling the days when nobody thought he could win any minor tournaments in his lifetime. The young South African had gone to England to play, and the vaunted experts there agreed that his swing was too flat.

But Norman Von Nida, the Australian who is famous for his minority opinions, came up to Player and told him he was going to be a great champion. Shocked, Player asked why.

"Because," replied Von Nida, "you've got *IT*."

Von Nida then arranged for Player to travel to Australia, where Player stayed and studied with Von Nida and won a big tournament, a victory that gave him the financial base to get married. When Player traces the important influences on his life, he eagerly gives credit to Von Nida.

Player is probably the greatest sand

player in the world, an ability that offsets erratic streaks in his long game; if he doesn't get up and down in two shots from sand, he is mad. He learned his sophisticated sand technique from Von Nida.

Seventeen years ago Von Nida told Player he could make more money breeding horses than being the best golfer in the world. Today, Gary is heavily into horse breeding and says "There is a lot of sense in what he said."

Von Nida's guidance has been just as instrumental in the careers of other foreign stars on the American tour, including Australians Bruce Crampton, Bruce Devlin and David Graham, who still go back to him for tuneups. Together with Player they have won something like $3 million here.

Von Nida is little known in the country that has made his pupils rich, but in other parts of the golfing world he is a colorful major personality. There are countless stories of Von Nida the peerless teacher, Von Nida the artful shotmaker, Von Nida the intrepid lover, Von Nida the angriest man. Most of them sound too good to be contrived.

Von Nida is often cast in a controversial role over the question of paying appearance money to top American players. Appearance money was banned by the Australian PGA, presided over by Peter Thomson, who led the fight to put the extra money into the Australian purses. Von Nida contends that American stars won't make the long trip to Australia without the guarantee of appearance money (Lee Trevino reportedly was paid $35,000 to play in one Australian event) and that without the American stars the Australian circuit cannot grow.

For Thomson and Von Nida, the dominant forces in Australian golf, it

Bruce Devlin

Bruce Crampton

Gary Player

David Graham

is another in a long line of disagreements. Mutual friends and enemies say they will take opposite sides of an issue simply to aggravate each other. Both write pointed newspaper columns in Australia.

They once traveled together and split their prize money, but the younger Thomson eventually beat many of Von Nida's records. Von Nida believes Thomson has never acknowledged the help he gave him with his game. Von Nida won the Australian Open many times but never won the cherished British Open which Thompson took five times. That is an inevitable comparison that galls Von Nida.

"Maybe Peter became a strong individualist after Norman taught him and took him around and paid his bills," surmises Bruce Devlin.

If Thomson is reluctant to cite a Von Nida patronage, Devlin and his fellow Australians on the American tour are anything but. They say "The Von," as they call him, sharpened their games, worked on their equipment, took them into his Sydney home for months at a time, bought them what they needed if they were short of money and got them overseas. And that was after he initially had rejected two of them—Devlin and Graham.

Devlin was helping his father in the plumbing business when Von Nida appraised his golf game and suggested he stay with plumbing. Later Devlin improved and Von Nida made a public apology and worked with him for several years. "He's a hard bugger to argue with but he isn't afraid to eat his words," says Devlin. "His theories have to be adapted somewhat for the large ball and inland conditions, but thankfully he taught us to play more like the Yanks than the British, with a one-piece takeaway and a good, strong lateral move with the lower body on the downswing. Otherwise we would have been slapping at the ball with our hands, flat-footed."

Graham, himself outspoken, first observed Von Nida teaching the son of the chairman of the board of a leading Sydney newspaper at a driving range. After the lesson Graham questioned the young man. Graham said he didn't agree at all, the young man relayed that bit of intelligence to the bombastic Von Nida and Von Nida summoned Graham. "Who in hell do you think you are!" was the gist of Von Nida's message.

"I apologized for 12 months," Graham says. "Finally I got better and he said he admired me for improving on my own. From then on he couldn't do enough for me. He likes teaching—but only good players and only if you've prepared to work twice as hard as you think you need to."

Crampton was an impressionable schoolboy when his pro asked Von Nida to look at him. Von Nida drove up in the flashiest car Crampton had ever seen, a black Jaguar with red seat covers. He was dressed just as boldly. Crampton was mesmerized.

Von Nida gave him clubs and balls and taught him intensely, finding him a job with Von Nida's golf company, Slazenger, that allowed two afternoons a week off for golf. Eventually Von Nida took Crampton on a British and European golf tour and raised the money for him to come to America.

"He more or less ran my life through my teens," Crampton says. "He dressed me and I had to go to his barber and he paid. He influenced my demeanor too. He was a fiery little guy and he'd tell me to beat a club on the ground if I missed a shot . . . he said bad publicity was better than none. That led to my image as a mean man."

Von Nida's temperament on the course was Vesuvian. Once in an Australian tournament players were permitted to take a free drop away from a tree if the tree was no taller than 6 feet. Von Nida's ball rolled up against a tree and an official ruled he had to play it. Von Nida challenged the ruling, and a tape measure was brought out. The tree proved to be 6 feet and 1 inch high. Von Nida played the shot from up against the tree. Then, furiously wielding his iron like an ax, he chopped the tree to the ground.

Another time, in a British tournament, his ball landed in a contentious lie in a bunker with oppressive heather lips. Von Nida played the shot. Then, wielding his iron like a scythe, he worked his way around the bunker and chopped away the entirety of the heather lip. "Nobody will ever have to play that shot again!" he stormed.

Von Nida usually was at odds with British galleries. He abhorred them for their reserve and their war views, among other things, and frequently would halt play to lecture them at the top of his thin voice.

In America, where he played the tour

off and on before and after World War II, Von Nida became noted for his running skirmishes with journalists and photographers, especially photographers. He would sit at the edge of a green and refuse to putt until all photographers were removed.

His relationships with the American players weren't much better at first. He struck them as being excessively cocky, an attitude no doubt enhanced by his wearing a French beret set at a jaunty angle.

No one was surprised when Von Nida and Henry Ransom had a fistfight during the 1948 Rio Grande Valley Open in Texas. The two were paired on the first hole and Von Nida claimed Ransom whiffed a tiny putt before tapping it in. Von Nida later refused to sign Ransom's scorecard, reportedly proclaimed that American pros were "cheaters and chislers," and took a swipe at Ransom with a club. One taunt led to another until , the burly Ransom says, he delivered a knockdown blow to Von Nida's nose. Ransom was suspended for 2 weeks.

Ransom says Von Nida's attitude softened and a month later Von Nida agreed to babysit for the Ransoms. Ransom speculates that Von Nida was preceded to this country by a great reputation as a shotmaker and was frustrated by his inability to win with the unfamiliar big American ball. And Von Nida was under the pressure of a sensational divorce action in which he is said to have been found by a private investigator with the wife of a prominent British club member one dark evening in, of all places, a bunker.

Neither his sexual exploits nor his shotmaking ability seem to be exaggerated, although there are more witnesses to the latter than the former. With the small ball he played in Australia and Britain, Von Nida could perform feats of magic, even though it is harder to spin than the big American ball.

"He's the best maneuverer of the ball I've ever seen," says Crampton. "Bobby Locke was great but usually hit everything from right to left. The Von could turn the ball 20 yards in either direction with a wedge. He could stomp the ball into the ground and hit a magnificent shot with a 4-wood. He has a great understanding of the ballistics of shotmaking. We'd play practice rounds with several balls and he'd mix up the situations and quiz me on how the ball was going to react off the face of the club, in flight and back on the ground. He could convince you to use no more effort with a 3-iron than a 9-iron. He was a great wind player. And out of sand he was just unbelievable. He'd put five balls down in a bunker and bet he could hole one—and 99 per cent of the time he did.''

HOW TO BEAT THE WIND

Norman Von Nida was a great manipulator of the ball—but never in the wind, especially a crosswind. The key to good wind play, he says, is to use the wind.

"Adjust your aim and hit the ball straight. Let the wind work on the ball. Don't try to bend the ball in the wind.''

Bruce Devlin marvels at how Von Nida could hit a low sand shot that took two big skips and stopped dead, time after time. Devlin's favorite story is about a clinic he and Von Nida put on in the New South Wales. To end it, Von Nida picked a bunker 40 yards from the hole and tossed down 15 balls. Now, the long sand blast is probably the most difficult shot in golf, but Von Nida was telling the crowd how easy it can be. He swung at the first ball, and it bounced once and plopped into the cup! Without breaking his conversational stride he turned to the gallery and said laconically, "Now Bruce will show you how it's done.''

On Devlin's first shot, the ball bounced once—and landed in the hole on top of Von Nida's ball! Trying to appear nonchalant, Devlin picked up the rest of the balls and he and Von Nida walked off the course. "The odds against him had to be 15,000-to-one and against me a million-to-one," Devlin says. "At home, people still ask me about that.''

Von Nida's sand theories are too complicated for any but the most advanced players. For any particular sand shot he may ask you to alter your stance and the position of the ball, the depth of your feet in the sand, the length of your grip and the proportioning of your weight, to cite only a few of his variables. "He deals in sixteenths of an inch and very subtle spins," says David Graham. Generally he teaches that the good player should leave the face of the

Von Nida with Dave Hill

club open and stand closer to the ball. It is a technique that his proteges say make them particularly outstanding from buried lies.

"He thinks the club is 50 per cent of sand play," Devlin says. "He's liable to throw your sand wedge in the nearest pond. He likes more bounce in the club—a more rounded bottom so the club won't dig in." Von Nida does not see the sand wedge as a two-way club to use on grass. Gary Player carries three wedges and does not hit pitch shots with a sand iron.

"The great sand players have one thing in common," says Player. "Sam Snead, Julius Boros and Von Nida all play the shot very slowly. There has never been a better sand player than Von Nida.''

Over and above that, Player admires Von Nida's willingness to put something back into the game. "If all champions helped youngsters the way he has, the game would be better," Player says.

Why does a man, and a frequently irascible man like Von Nida at that, continue to tutor and support young prospects (he recently brought a promising young Italian player to live with him)? Partly to fill his time no doubt. Von Nida's back has all but given out "because I'm little and I hit too many practice shots" and so he no longer plays. His only strong interest other than golf is

horse racing; he rises at 5 AM to study the daily racing forms.

But more tellingly he remembers his own youth, a constant struggle to escape poverty and excel at golf, the most challenging of games. When he was 9 he caddied to make money and when he was 14 he was working full-time in a meat plant and practicing his golf after hours.

When the heroic Walter Hagen came to Australia to play, Von Nida approached him and announced that he was the finest caddie in the territory. Hagen replied that he was the finest golfer in the world, so they should get along well. They did. Von Nida asked Hagen question after question about shotmaking, went off to master Hagen's advice, and hurried back for more. "He's the keenest kid I've ever seen," Hagen said.

Von Nida, now 60, always has been grateful for the help Hagen gave him and always has been determined to follow Hagen's example. Says Graham, "It's a shame The Von isn't part of the big golfing society. He's a genius. Had he been an American, in a progressive country, he would be tremendously famous." Says Devlin, "He's given countless bloody hours and dollars to young players and never expected anything in return. Why? I guess for the satisfaction of a thank you.''

Golf: Only A Game?

By ART SPANDER
(Sports Writer,
San Francisco Chronicle)

TO THE PUBLIC, humored by the one-liners of Lee Trevino and awed by the one-putts of Jack Nicklaus, the job of playing the pro golf tour really isn't a job at all, rather a wonderful journey across the country and the calendar, full of birdies and big checks and busty blondes in places like Fort Worth and Augusta.

There's advice from Bing and repartee from Bob and enough free double-knit slacks to open a department store. The sun shines, you never have to fight traffic jams, and practically no one says a discouraging word, if you don't count those weirdos from the newspapers. It sure beats working for a living.

Sometimes. But not most. The 200 golfers who play the tour, who saw those dollar signs glittering like so many new Titleists in a pro shop window, discover quickly enough it's as bad as many occupations and worse than some. The birdies are more likely to be bogeys, the big checks are the ones you write, not receive, and the only blonde in town is throwing a hamburger at you in some all night diner. If that isn't work, neither is driving a truck.

What the people in the crowd, or in the front of the television sets, hardly comprehend, is that what they see in a pro golf tournament is not what they get. The pros will tell you. The game is played not so much on the sprawling acres of grass and sand between the gallery ropes as it is the 4 inches of gray matter between the ears.

The ultimate challenge in golf is mental instead of physical. It's easy enough to knock a 4-foot putt into the hole— unless there are headlines, a $30,000 check, and a great deal of pride involved. Then the 4 feet begins to seem more like 40.

The maxims about golf, that it's a humbling game, that a 1-inch putt counts the same number of strokes as a 250-yard drive, that confidence means more than a pretty swing, are absolutely accurate. As accurate as the putting touch Billy Casper, for years, has claimed he doesn't have.

But, if Casper indulges in a bit of fantasy, it's probably no more deplorable than Dave Hill's temper, Lee Trevino's talking, or Bruce Crampton's displeasure. Laughing or crying, shouting or silent, every man tries to find a method of coping with the pressures of reality, pressures endemic to the game, pressures the amateur golfer hasn't even considered. And some of those methods are simply more noticeable than others. If less acceptable.

These individuals, the high-strung Hill, the resolute Crampton, the devising Casper, are not unique among sportsmen. No game wrenches the mind as it does the body; no game wears down the ego before it does the muscles as does professional golf.

The pressure begins with the first shot off the first tee and doesn't end until the last putt on the last green— and sometimes, for the man who's been groping through the round as if wandering through a thick fog, it doesn't end then. There is no margin for error, no help from teammates, no escape from inadequacy.

Sam Snead, it may have been, said that in golf you have to play your foul balls. You have to play them with the wind in your face, the gallery in your line, and a thought in your mind that maybe your mother was right, you should have become a salesman.

In tennis, it doesn't matter if you lose points, if you win the game. In baseball, it does't matter if you've made a bad pitch, if the shortstop makes a good catch. In football, it doesn't matter if the quarterback was off, if the receiver was on. A man can rebound a shot in basketball, and a goalie can stop a shot in hockey. And even in the cerebral games, like chess or cards, your opponent can squander opportunities you've given him. But in golf you don't get a reprieve. Second chances only mean a second shot—and thus a second, or third, or fourth, stroke.

They'll be arguing from now to Armageddon which sport is the toughest. Fifteen rounds against George Foreman isn't exactly like an afternoon in the grill room at the club. Distance running makes you feel like you've been run over by a couple of elephants! And in pro football you probably will get run over by a couple of elephants, or gorillas, the college recruiting rules getting a trifle lax these days.

But golf tests your character as well as your stamina, and if you've ever walked 36 holes over some course that runs up-the-down-staircase, you know you've got to be in shape. Golf works on your psyche and your mettle in a manner no 260-pound tackle could work over your body.

Tension builds to a point where you imagine Jack Nicklaus is riding around on your shoulders. Or on the medulla. And there's no way of getting rid of that tension, short of hitting a few spectators, or maybe yourself, over the head with a 5-iron. "In football," explained U.S. Open champion Hale Irwin, a former all-conference defensive back at the University of Colorado, "you can take out your frustrations on someone else. But in golf you've got to keep them inside. There's no way to release them."

So those guys out there in the pastel shirts and two-tone shoes, who seem to be taking a Sunday stroll, living, to borrow a phrase from Molière, in the best of all possible worlds, are actually time bombs ready to explode. Or be defused. The pros have a word for it, "grinding." The symbolism is well taken. After 4½ hours of battling undulating greens, high rough, and a jerky putting stroke, a pro feels like he's been pressed under a millstone.

The basic problem with golf, aside from the fact it's nearly impossible to play, is that intrinsically it's a game between a man and nature, you against the world. With that match-up, you'd be better off trying to get Golda Meir elected president of Egypt.

In golf, there are no umpires to blame, no teammates to admonish, no coaches to lend reassurance. It's you alone, you and that sculptured plot of land some sadist designed to make you look like a fool—and feel like an idiot.

Practically no one is going to admit failure, not when he's an *ex officio* member of a group described as the best in the world at this particular activity. The cause for three-putts and shanked irons, and balls that just trickle into sand traps, must lie with someone else. Confidence is too valuable a commodity to relinquish easily.

That's why some men rant and others rebel. And still others ease the situation, or at least attempt to, with a few witticisms that draw attention and magazine interviews—and the ire of people around them.

Dave Hill managed to combine all three tactics during the 1970 U.S. Open at Hazeltine Country Club near Minneapolis. The end result, in a word, was amusing. Unless you happened to be a Hazeltine member, who had given up your course to Mr. Hill and comrades,

Billy Casper

or Robert Trent Jones, Sr., the course architect.

Hill is an excellent golfer—maybe one of the best—and relatively astute. But when it comes to diplomacy, Dave reminds you more of Genghis Khan than Henry Kissinger. If you wanted to settle a dispute between the factions in Northern Ireland, for example, you might want to send Dave to Hawaii.

When Hill was introduced to Hazeltine, you could tell immediately it was a meeting planned anywhere except in heaven. It was hate at first sight. In truth, many of Dave's fellow golfers didn't like the course either, but they had the acumen, or the fear of reprisal, to keep their opinions to a whisper.

It's Hill's nature to say what is going through his mind. Dave made all sorts of remarks, the majority quite critical, and the sporting journalists and radio and TV announcers kept encouraging Dave to make a few more. Not one to squander rights provided by the First Amendment—to the Constitution, not the PGA Tour bylaws—Hill kept complaining. The more he complained, the more unhappy he became. The more unhappy he became, the more he complained. It was a circle, vicious or not so, depending upon your viewpoint. His most memorable line, which now from a distance of 6 years should make even the course designer chuckle, is that all Hazeltine needed to become a good farm was 40 acres of corn and some cows.

Oh, yes. Hill did something else besides grouse. He played golf. And quite well. Hill finished second in the tournament to Tony Jacklin—the only man even to provide competition for Jacklin—who apparently failing to understand the situation, took a big lead the first day and never lost it. Why, then, did Dave Hill grumble and gripe? Put on a display of petulance that almost equalled his displays of golf? Because that is his nature, the way he reacts to the problems that work on a pro golfer's mind where he's working on those 40-plus acres—without corn and cows.

If nothing else, Dave Hill, by his presence, proves every one of the touring pros is not stamped out of the same fragment of beige material—the spectrum of personalities is as wide as the colors of their clothing, there is room for anyone who can beat his golf ball and keep from beating his head against the wall—although at times everyone has wished he could do just that.

The amazing thing about Bruce Crampton is he keeps from doing anything, except what he's supposed to do—meaning playing golf and following the rules. Well, that isn't entirely true. Bruce scowls a lot, going about his chores with all the frivolity of a surgeon. But people don't stand 3 feet from a surgeon when he's at work, kibitzing on his technique—"never cut it with that scalpel"—so no one laments over the lack of revelry in an operating room. But when an individual goes to a golf course, including the surgeon, he goes to have a good time. To enjoy himself. He doesn't understand why Crampton takes things so seriously.

Some of the other pros don't either. But then, maybe they should. Crampton undoubtedly smiles—if only secretly—each time he studies his enviable record and his bank account. The man in the gray flannel cashmere, Crampton is a no-nonsense sort who doesn't believe an $8 million-a-year business should be a training ground for the future Woody Allens of the country. "You don't see those pilots of a 747 laughing while they're trying to land," emphasized Crampton. "They're serious about doing their job well. So am I."

It is an attitude not advanced by every pro golfer. Fortunately. But if Crampton doesn't go around jingling his pocket change on other people's backswings, or stepping on their putting line, there's no reason he can't be as solemn as he desires. Someday, Crampton might get even with his critics by marching into a press tent around deadline time and ask the people behind the typewriters why they aren't in hysterics—instead of hysteria.

Sort of like Lee Trevino, who's usually in one or the other. Which is the reason he's so fascinating, not to mention appealing. A little *chile relleno* dressed in red shirt and black slacks, Trevino is the tour's answer to Muhammad Ali. And Flip Wilson. And Pancho Villa. About the only thing Trevino can't do on a golf course is an imitation of Marcel Marceau.

When Trevino isn't laughing, he's talking. Or snarling. Or knocking in a birdie putt. Life isn't one big tamale as it used to be for Trevino. There are annoyances and demands that didn't exist when Lee first came out of West Texas with the flat swing and flatter wallet. The blithe spirit has the opportunity, if not always the reason, to be a malcontent. Although the words and actions remain full of vitality, they're frequently tinged with vitriol. Still, a spiteful Lee Trevino is ultimately more interesting than most people in a good mood. And when Lee's in a fine disposition, there's no one better.

"I played like a dog today," snapped Trevino after an over-par round last year. "I'm gonna have a can of Alpo for dinner tonight." Not only did that remark crack up a room full of cynical sports writers, but it also provided considerable insight into the man who made it. Lee Trevino can put himself down as quickly as he can put down someone else. Lee Trevino didn't have to blame the greenskeeper, the humidity content, or the alignment of Jupiter and Mars for his poor play. Lee Trevino knows how dejected even a most happy fella can get after a round of golf.

The quip also tells you that two such disparate personalities as Trevino and Crampton can co-exist in a struggle against the common enemy: themselves.

That 4- to 5-hour trip is a struggle, a fight to keep your senses and self-respect, and in the process, hopefully, keep somewhere around par. A minute adjustment of the grip, a slight alteration of the stance, and the fight tends to become hopeless. You start to lose control of the ball. And your patience. And then, worst of all, your confidence.

It happens even to the best of golfers. "I've always said," insisted George Archer, "that it comes and goes faster in golf than any other sport. You never know what's going to happen. Even a guy like Nicklaus is liable to shoot 78 one day and 68 the next."

Archer became a living example of his contention. Winner of the Masters tournament and some $700,000 in purses during his career, George developed swing problems. Suddenly he was acting, and talking, like a 19-handicapper, although he wasn't playing anywhere close to one.

Steve Reid, formerly a touring pro and now working for the Tournament Player's Division, expressed a player's worst fears. "One day," said Reid, "you wake up and discover the ball may never again go where you aim it. From then on, everything is chaos.

Each golfer reacts to this chaos differently. Some have the perseverance, and the talent, to rebuild, create a new order. The confusion, the frustration, the indecision may last only hours. Or it may last months.

Jack Nicklaus, by consensus merely the world's greatest golfer, got muddled down during the 1969 U.S. Open at Houston. He began to talk like some weekend hacker. "I don't know where the ball's going," insisted Jack, bewildered. "I think I'm swinging over the ball. But one of the guys on the practice tee told me I was standing too far up on it." You were about ready to take Jack out and give him three strokes a side. But with his ability and determination, it didn't take Jack long to reconstruct his swing, and more importantly his assurance.

That assurance may be the one most important part of golf. If you lose it, or never had it, you'd better throw your clubs in the trunk and go back to sharecropping in Texas. Conversely, if it's there, you'll be in decent shape even with a swing that looks like someone trying to drive a stake in the ground. "When you come down to the final holes," Gary Player, once said after a frantic finish at the Masters, "it doesn't matter if you have a pretty swing. It only matters if you've got the proper attitude. It takes a lot of guts. You've got to believe you can do it."

So much so that many golfers won't risk losing that confidence. They find reasons—excuses might be another definition—for everything that goes wrong, and infrequently, what goes right. And maybe, when you consider the circumstances, it's a legitimate cop-out.

Arnold Palmer used, in his own words, 100 different putters last year. That's nearly one a round. How much different could one putter be from another? When Arnie was putting well in those glory days of the 1960s, he could putt with a broom. Or the big toe on his left foot. According to the other pros, Arnie willed the ball into the hole.

But willing won't seem to work any longer for Arnold Palmer. Neither will his putting stroke. Not surprisingly, Arnie can't bring himself to believe such blasphemy. It has to be the club, not the man. So, he keeps changing—his putter, not his fortune. Maybe it will help. Maybe he'll regain that confidence. But if he does, it will not be the

Arnold Palmer

Photo By CORMAN

putter that makes the difference, but the touch of the man holding it.

In 1967, Billy Casper shot a sub-par round to lead the Masters. The next day, Casper was someplace in the mid-70s and no place near the lead. The problem, Billy explained, was not in his play but in his diet. Casper had peaches and sausage for breakfast, and it made him nauseous. At least one other golfer figured the true causes of Billy's nausea was his play. "Sausage, peaches, and five bogeys," quipped Mason Rudolph, taking a skeptical look at things, "would make anyone sick."

Mason didn't intend to sound jealous. Just cute. His own philosophy is closer to Lee Trevino than Dave Hill. He has a crinkling wit and an ability to laugh at circumstances that intrude upon his tranquility. After whiffing a 1-inch backhand attempt and four-putting a green in

the 1969 U.S. Open, Mason confided, "I always did have a weak backhand."

Palmer and Casper, to be sure, are two of the finest golfers in history Each has won more than a million dollars and at least 50 tournaments. Maybe looking for a reason other than yourself, when things go wrong, is the proper method. Proper or not, it has certainly worked.

Dave Hill rants, Bruce Crampton endures, Lee Trevino jokes, and Billy Casper explains. They're different people going about the same task in different ways, trying to hold off the pressure and hold on to some peace of mind. It's like Johnny Miller said, "Serenity is knowing your worst shot is still going to be pretty good."

That serenity is not always found by serene methods. Sometimes you need to do a lot of crying or laughing.

WOMEN GOLFERS:

IRV GROSSMAN has been a publicist for a lot of sports events but a women's golf tournament at Rancho Santa Fe really tried his patience.

"What a disaster," he said.

Grossman's job was to publicize the four-day Golf Inns of America tournament and 56 members of the Ladies Professional Golf Assn. (LPGA). But few of the top-name golfers showed—they were tired or had other commitments—and Grossman acted as if he had one big white elephant on his hands.

It was one of a dozen times in the LPGA's 25-year history that it had not met a contractual agreement to provide at least 20 of the top 30 money earners. What Grossman had was 14 of the top 30, and only three of the top 10.

"Maybe it happened only 11 times before but when you're in the middle of a disaster like this, what difference does it make?" he asked.

He said he had one hell of a job getting people to come all the way to Rancho Sante Fe (near San Diego) to see a less-than-star-studded tournament.

He blamed it on the golfers—"on their attitude. I hold them culpable for this tournament," he said. "It's not smart business on their part to do this. Where's Laura Baugh? Amy Alcott? Carol Mann? Where you're successful you can blow your nose but if you're to build something up, you don't do this!"

Grossman really had to scrape to push the tournament, and he thought he had some pretty good ideas about how to market women golfers.

"Girl-watching" was the theme of his publicity campaign. He chose some of the "best lookers" and sent out a press release that described Jan Stephenson as a "dark-haired, dark-eyed beauty," Carole Jo Skala as "blonde, out-going and California-informal," Joyce Benson as "photogenic, long blonde hair, model figure," and JoAnn Washam as "pert, congenial and typical college coed."

"What's wrong with the LPGA," he said, "is that it keeps all those personalities bottled up. There's no one promoting them. These girls have personalities but they need to be less inhibited. I mean, if we have somebody out there with a sour puss when they are 36-24-36, what good is that?

". . . Look at these pictures—they got mascara all over Marlene Hagge's eyes. I refused to use these pictures. They make the girls look like they're on their way to the prom. I asked the girls how they could allow themselves to be photographed like that. But will these women listen?

"I don't care who you are. If you are a professional golfer you are in the business of entertainment. You have to understand that if you are going to succeed.

"Now what do the girls have that the men don't? Sex. There's nothing wrong with that. That's one reason men watch women golfers. These girls have a hell of an opportu-

Laura Baugh

nity. Women in action are exciting. Women are doing everything—even football. It's a turn-on for a guy.

"These women have to fact up to a reality. Arnold Palmer is an electric personality on the course. But these girls, well, it gets down to one thing—would anyone want to go to bed with them?"

Grossman's ideas, though well-intentioned, offend many people, including some golfers, who feel they are victimized by such promotion. Whether it even works is questionable. The gate at Rancho Santa Fe was not impressive. And many newspapers have become more sensitive to coverage of women, rejecting the traditional cheesecake picture in favor of serious coverage of women's sports.

Still, publicity men often go overboard to project a "feminine" image of women athletes.

"I wouldn't do it that way," said Kathy Whitworth, the all-time top money winner in women's golf. "I would promote the records of the women, how many tournaments they won. But I have gotten the impression from some people, including some golfers, that this is not the right way to do it. It doesn't matter how many tournaments you have

ATHLETES OR SEX SYMBOLS?

By CHERYL BENTSEN *(Los Angeles Times)*

won, just how many people you draw through the gate. I get the impression that I should do a strip on the 18th hole, and that irritates me.''

The LPGA has been a notoriously unaggressive organization that left promotion up to individual tournament sponsors. The sponsor, often a charity organization, would hire a local guy and let him publicize the event as he saw fit.

But that is all changing. The LPGA's goal now is to be aggressive.

"We want action now" said Carol Mann, president of the executive board.

Former LPGA commissioner Bud Erickson, described by some golfers as "lacking faith in women's sports," has been canned. Ray Volpe, a former vice president of marketing for the National Hockey League, replaced him. Bob Basche, a PR man, has been hired away from the women's tennis circuit. The stodgy oldline executive board, made up of veteran players, is being replaced by a player's council that will include rookies, so all will have a voice.

"There has been a lot of criticism about the way this tour was promoted," Volpe said. "Too many people have promoted it for the wrong reasons. It has been done without direction or continuity. We don't want to bill this as a sex tour. We don't want to say come see the girls swing, look at all the short skirts. The players are players and will be recognized accordingly. A man going to a hockey game doesn't go to see how a guy looks. But golf has been promoted to come and see the sexy girls."

Mann believes the women are taking the LPGA more seriously. "They used to laugh at it," she said. "Now we are deciding our goals and our direction. And our commissioner believes in women's sports. We still have some older, conservative women who are afraid of the style of change— to be flamboyant and more visible. Some have had to face problems for the last 20 years and that keeps them afraid. But there are only a few and I have been able to talk with all of them. I think that is changing.

"The golf industry is still a problem. That includes companies and the people or groups who support golf. In 1969 I was No. 1 and it sent me in a funk for 3 years because I got no attention. I swore that would not happen to anyone else. It was such a deflating experience. But now Sandra Palmer is No. 1 and she has not gotten many endorsements.

"I am angry at the golf industry. They have never been pro-women and still aren't. We need to make a change. Maybe we need to go outside that industry and show it can be done. Our previous commissioner (Bud Erickson) knew the golf industry wasn't supporting us but he didn't know what to do.

"We had the same problem with golf agents. They didn't believe in their women clients and helped to keep our fees low. But new, younger agents are surfacing and we are really ready to move."

Well, change is supposed to be happening but a release sent out for a recent $50,000 Colgate Triple Crown championships at Mission Hills Country Club in Palm Springs, told us, "good cooking and good golfing are not incompatible . . . Sandra Palmer's chili is a winner!"

The recipe followed, and the release continued: "I used to burn water," says the diminutive blonde pro, "but with my Fort Worth background, I learned to make a great chili, one that's a favorite one-course meal among my golfing friends." The women, it seems, are not always unwilling victims in this kind of promotion.

Colgate spent about $6 million sponsoring women's golf and using the women in soap and toothpaste ads. It gave the players more exposure than they'd ever had. In fact, some golfers say they are better known for their ads than their golf.

But a top woman tennis player recently was heard doing a parody of one ad featuring a southern player: "Oh mah. Ah got dirt all ovuh mah nahlon golf shirt. But ah know how to fix that. Ah use Tide in mah washin' machine."

At a party at the country club where the Golf Inns of America tournament was held last year, a number of club members were overheard commenting that the golfers were "masculine-looking," or more bluntly, "look like a bunch of truck drivers."

The LPGA has 115 active tournament players, and the truck driver image is unfair. Yet it sticks.

One male golfer insisted that the word "broad," when used to describe women, originated with women golfers. "They're broad in the rear," he said.

When country club members used the description "masculine-looking," there was inevitably the sly smile and the knowing look. What they were really saying is that the women golfers look like lesbians, or what they *think* lesbians look like.

Generally the sexual preferences of athletes have been considered their own business. But in women's athletics the rumors of lesbianism persist. Both straight and gay women athletes in the past refused to discuss the subject. But the question is always there. In a recent *Playboy* magazine interview, Billie Jean King was asked, "Are you a lesbian?" King refused to give a direct answer, calling it a private matter.

Recently the *Washington Star* published a fourpart series on homosexuality in sports that included strong statements about women golfers.

According to the *Star*, LPGA members told a reporter that the number of lesbians on the professional golf tour is well above "the 5 percent national average for homosexuals." The story said a feud between straight women and lesbians had split the LPGA, that the lesbian image "had cost them prize money, sponsors, endorsements and recognition."

The *Star* quoted an unidentified golfer who said the straights criticized the lesbians' dress, mannerisms and speech and said they urged them to adopt a straight lifestyle "for the sake of everybody."

Carol Mann, identified as a straight, was quoted as saying problems had arisen at private country clubs where most tournaments are held because members object to lesbianism. "It's not part of their lives and they don't have to accept it," she said. "And since it's their private club, they don't have to."

Mann, a 14-year tour veteran, said in an interview that she was upset with the *Star's* article.

"The reporter came to me with an assumption about lesbianism," she said. "I did say that about country clubs, and it is true. But I told her we had not lost endorsements because of the image. She had no right identifying me as 'straight.' I'll have to think about that, it's fantastic. I would deny that there is any split or feud. She asked leading questions which I did not buy. There may have been a split at one time but I don't want to comment on it. We may talk about it among ourselves but there is no feud."

But now image has become so important in selling professional sports that women golfers are concerned about the public impression that women golfers are masculine-looking.

"We don't want people to think that we are all real masculine-looking," Sandra Palmer says. "That is the thing that has been so hard to overcome in women's sports. We've carried it much more severely than we ever should have. We kind of got the brunt of it.

"Back when ladies golf was just starting it was really frowned on. Everybody thinks you are some kind of goon or real mannish. Well, not everyone is real attractive. Half the women in supermarkets would look mannish on a golf course. We're not all Miss Americas but we have some pleasant-looking, attractive girls.

"We can and should improve our appearance. I care and I work on it. I wash my hair every day. I try to wear clothes that are nice. I don't like to wear slacks because I have a big fanny. It is important how we look. One thing about golf, most of us are overweight. We're a little chubby. I guess I eat too much and golf doesn't really give you much exercise. But I try to run a mile every day. I think once people come out and see us, they decide we are not bad-looking girls."

Bonnie Lauer, 24, a rookie, said she was hesitant about joining the tour for several reasons, among them the image.

"You'd hear comments about truck drivers and that type of connotation about women," she said. "People might have thought they didn't want to get involved or be associated with that. I think that image is disappearing as younger women join the tour. Still, some people have stereotypical ideas about us."

Lauer noted that women athletes generally do look different from unathletic women. "I'm not sure why," she said. "When I was in college I always shied away from becoming a physical education major. I just didn't want to be involved in all that talk. So I was a PE minor. Once I got involved I saw it was not what I had heard.

"If a woman goes into sports she has to be assured of herself and her identity and have a certain amount of self-confidence. To feel that you truly are a feminine person and that it doesn't bother you to be associated with 'talk' because you know who you are and what you are trying to be, that is something that has happened in my own life. I kept saying that I didn't want to be associated with that in my life but now I have self-assurance, so why should I worry about somebody's stereotypical idea?"

Hall of Famer Betsy Rawls, the LPGA's tournament director, said the image has improved. "It is a highly acceptable image socially," she said. "Some of us are not concerned about image, but others are. I think the women would just like to go out and play, work on their game, concentrate and be accepted for what they are. It is really a waste of energy to try to prevent an image that implies something you are not.

"Maybe the women look different because they have a different kind of lifestyle. They exercise more. They are more efficient in their movements. They have a more self-sufficient air. They are not helpless in any respect, so people say this is 'masculine.' People have funny ideas about what feminity is. Feminity should be concerned with warmth, kindness, inner qualities—not the latest hairdo. It is hard for us to fit that so-called feminine image because in athletics hair can't always look nice. We have to be more muscular. We don't have the same interests as most women. We are truly concerned with physical things."

Laura Baugh has probably gotten more publicity than any woman golfer. "Beautiful, blonde, dimpled, saucy sweetheart"—all those words have been used to describe Baugh. You might think she was the best player on the tour from the amount of publicity and endorsements she gets, yet she has never won a professional tournament.

Still, Baugh is hard-working, and the other golfers admire her and consider her an asset.

"People come to our tournaments just to see Laura," Carol Mann says. "But that's OK, because she does have talent. Other players think she is a hard-working player who believes in what we are doing and holds up her end. If she couldn't play golf, I don't think you would hear about her anymore. You can't make it on good looks alone.

"I think that coldly and commercially, it is important that people who were born with pleasant physical attributes be made visible. Now I say bleep to beautiful people. Show me talent. If they have both, terrific.

"We are concerned with how we are promoted and what we are made to look like. But personally I can't stand the sexist adjectives. Many of the top players abhor sexist adjectives. We take ourselves very seriously. We want to be known as professional golfers, not ugly or beautiful women.

"I do resent that kind of promotion but I realize a sponsor has to do what he thinks will appeal to his community. We can suggest to a promoter how we want to be promoted but it can only go so far. One of my biggest pet peeves in the whole world is being called a 'pro-ette.' That is so demeaning. I would rather have sexist adjectives than 'pro-ette.'"

Still, the women expect to continue to hear comments such as this from Irv Grossman: "I look at a girl and I say, 'How can I market her?' There's nothing wrong with marketing them as women. I'll tell you, they're a lot better looking than the tennis women."

Check Points

The Grip »
Here's where a lot of trouble begins

« The 'Slot'
You can tell by the feel when you're in it

The Full Turn »
Here's a lazy fault that can become a habit

The Tempo
The golf swing is a sequence of synchronized movements

Alignment »
Are you letting yourself drift off target?

Anchor That Heel »
Because the right heel is the anchor of the swing

« Ball Position
A simple way to check your set-up

Playing poorly?
Review your swing systematically –
like PGA champions do!

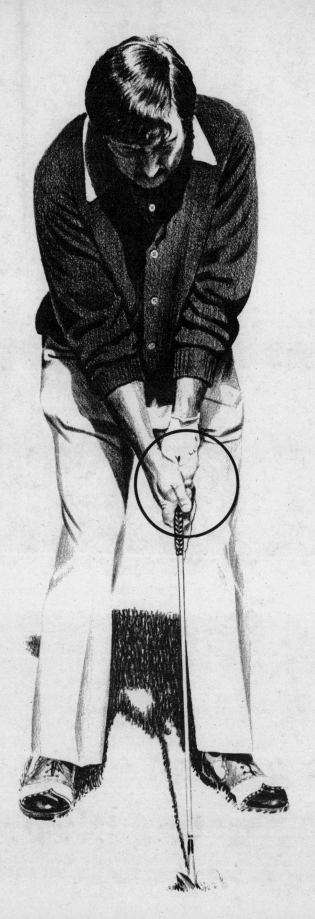

The Grip

Bill Robinson, Silver Lake Golf & Country Club, Leesburg, Fla., Florida Section Champion

When my game goes sour, first thing I do is check my grip. I sometimes fall into a careless habit of releasing the last two fingers at the top, and then regripping the club as I start down. This affects my normal tempo and tends to throw the club out of the correct plane. That's why I first check my grip at the address position, make sure I have one knuckle showing and my right palm is square to the target. Then I remind myself not to release those two last fingers at the top of the backswing.

Alignment

Denny Lyons, Niagara Falls Country Club, Lewiston, N. Y., Western New York Section Champion

I sometimes find I'm blocking out or getting over the top, and this usually comes from lining up too far left or right. So I get on the range and lay a couple of clubs down to establish the correct alignment. Then I just hit balls until I recover the "feel" of proper alignment. Eventually, it works back in. I get back on target and the ball starts flying better.

Ball Position

Clayton Cole, Dallas Country Club, Dallas, Texas, Northern Texas Section Champion

The position of the ball is one key to the swing plane. I have a tendency to move the ball a little too far forward. This tends to make me take the club back on the outside and bring it back across the ball. Conversely, if the ball is moved back too far I tend to yank the club back quickly on the inside. Then the club is committed too far right of the target at the top and there is a tendency to swing inside-out in a hooking action. To check my position at the ball, I have a little gimmick. When I set up the shot, I check the line of the shaft. This line should extend directly into my left armpit. My stance will vary as I move from woods and long irons down to the shorter clubs, but that line should always run directly through the armpit.

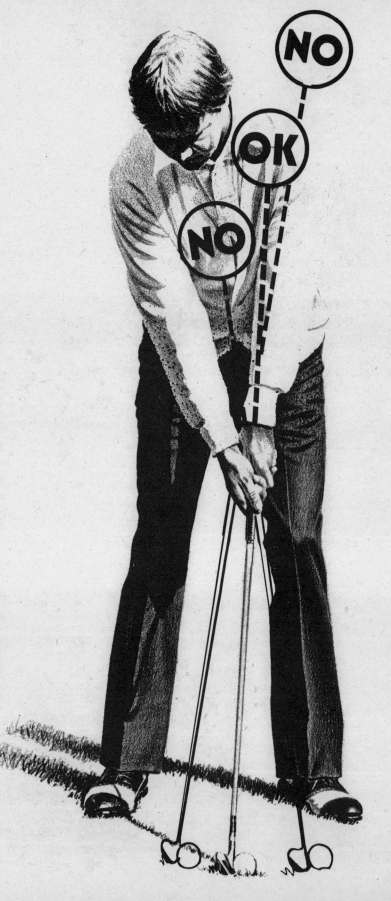

Anchor That Heel

Terry Malan, Willow Creek Country Club, Utah, Rocky Mountain Section Champion

Occasionally I find myself moving out of position and hitting from the top as I start the downswing. Result: the right shoulder moves out over the ball. The key to controlling this fault is to feel the right heel move slightly to the left as it leaves the ground. You can imagine a strong rubber band linking both heels and drawing the right heel inward. This mental image serves as a reminder that the lateral shift of the knees largely controls the timing and balance of your swing.

The Full Turn

Howell Fraser, Bay Point Yacht & Country Club, Panama City, Florida, Dixie Section Champion

I sometimes fall into a lazy habit of neglecting to make a full body turn and the result is I become something of an arm hitter. This is a very common flaw in the high handicap player's swing, and it's really a lazy fault. When I'm not playing my best game, this is the first thing I check, to make sure I'm bringing the club back on a firm inside track. The complete body turn begins right there, starting the right hip on its way.

The 'Slot'

Ron Aleks, Bloomfield Hills Country Club, Bloomfield Hills, Michigan, Michigan Section Champion

Invariably, when I'm off my game it means I've drifted out of what I call "The Slot." This is the position of the club I want at the top of the backswing. It's something you have to feel. I go to the practice tee and start hitting a bunch of 9-iron shots until I get back in The Slot, when everything is hinged together. I know when it happens by the set-up. When I place the clubhead down and all the muscles are evenly tensed, I know by the feel that I'm back in the groove. Then I can move on down to the 5-iron and begin bringing my whole game together again.

The Tempo

Terry Wilcox, The Cardinal Golf Club, Greensboro, North Carolina, Carolinas Section Champion

The first thing I do when my game goes sour is re-set my "clock." The golf swing is a sequence of movements, fixed in a pattern by timing. This timing, or tempo, is an individual thing. You may be a slow swinger or a fast swinger. In either case, the slightest unconscious variation in your normal rhythm will break the pattern. The sequence of movements becomes erratic like an automobile engine with a faulty timer, or may break down entirely and there goes the old golf swing. Now you have to set your mental clock and restore the familiar pattern of the swing. Again, we're talking about something you have to feel. When your clock starts ticking at the old pace, you know it because everything falls into place again.

I Remember Bobby Cruickshank Shot His Age More Than 200 Times

By JIM WARTERS
(Florida Golfweek)

THE DEATH of Bobby Cruickshank brought to an end one of the most phenomenal records of golfing longevity.

They talk about Sam Snead's feats as he approaches his seventh decade. But the West Virginia wizard of the fairways has a long way to go to match some of Cruickshank's octogenarian accomplishments.

Little Bobby, a pro of no mean stature during the roaring 20s, undoubtedly was the finest seniors performer in the U.S. until the final illness that felled him in Delray Beach in 1975.

Just two years before, at the age of 78, the wee Scot was bettering his age on championship layouts nearly every time he played a round. And he hardly missed a day.

"I don't shoot my age," he told me without a trace of immodesty at Naples in 1972. "I shoot under my age."

He proved he wasn't just talking through his head covers that week in the Florida PGA with four consecutive days of 75 or better.

Only 5-foot-4 and considerably under his fighting weight after a severe stroke a couple of years earlier, Bobby opened with 75, then added a trio of 73s for 294.

He didn't have to play all four days since two rounds were all that were called for in the 75-and-over division. But Bobby decided to take a chance in the overall division, winning $90, $40 more than the seniors take.

Besides the extra cash, he got priceless satisfaction in knowing his closing 73 was better than the 74s by touring pro Steve Reid and 1954 U.S. Open champion Ed Furgol or the 77 by former Florida PGA titleholder and third day leader Gordon Jones.

In fact, the last two days of the tournament over the 6,500-yard Naples Beach Club course, Cruickshank was four strokes better than both Jones and Furgol.

When Bobby was relating how "I tied the greatest golfer of them all—Bobby Jones—in the 1923 U.S. Open," Gordon Jones noted: "That was 6 years before I was born."

I wasn't really surprised at the Cruickshank magic. I had read of his age-defying antics ever since I came to Florida. In any seniors division event he entered, it was no contest. When he was 75, the 150-pounder was putting 70s and 71s on the board like he had a pencil.

So, I made a particular point of meeting him at the '72 PGA. Not only was he a fantastic shotmaker, he was a kind, courteous and gentle man.

The stroke had left him with a serious speech impediment, but he patiently talked with me, reminiscing over old times, for as long as I cared to listen.

Born in Grantown-on-the-Spey at Morayshire, Scotland, Cruickshank came to this country in 1921 as a professional golfer. Two years later he came within a stroke of winning the U.S. Open. His loss was Bobby Jones' gain.

After 72 holes at Inwood Country Club on Long Island, the two Bobbies were tied at 296. In an 18-hole playoff, the next day "Bobby Jones beat me on the last hole." Jones had 76 to Cruickshank's 78, capturing his first of 13 major championships enroute to golfing immortality.

The year before, Bobby had rounds of 69 and 70 the first 2 days of the National PGA at Oakmont, PA, gaining the semi-finals of the match play event. Gene Sarazen was his foe in the semis. "I was working on a 72 and he beat me," grinned Cruickshank, head pro at Gulfstream CC, Delray Beach, at the time of his death.

Bobby also was runnerup to Sarazen in the 1932 U.S. Open at Flushing, NY.

A veteran of World War I with the 51st Highland Infantry Regiment, Cruickshank credited his incredible tenure on the fairways to "just taking care of myself. I don't drink any more and I quit smoking 20 years ago."

Bobby would have me believe his near-par efforts at Naples came off a hot putter. "I'm just putting good," he said.

This wasn't true. As Mitch Joannes, his playing partner from Tampa pointed out: "A lot of people think he just bats it up the middle, chips up and one-putts every hole. He made some good birdie putts, but he missed a couple of 5- and 6-footers, too."

I followed him for several holes, amazed at the distance he got with a high-arching fade. And he reached enough of the greens the first 2 days to have nine birdies.

Bobby Cruickshank provided one of my most unforgettable weeks as a golf reporter. Although he won seven pro tournaments in 1927 alone, he didn't dwell on the past.

Instead, he preferred to repeat those same shots of nearly 50 years ago. He estimated he had more than 200 scores equal or better than his age in 1972. Three times that fall he posted 69s on courses in the Pittsburgh area where he lived for many years.

A couple of weeks after our visit, Bobby wrote me one of the nicest letters I ever received from a golf pro. It's one I will forever treasure along with my memories of Bobby Cruickshank and the 1972 Florida PGA.

Lament for a Vanishing Breed- The Caddie

By WAYNE THOMPSON
(Memphis Commercial Appeal)

SOMEONE, displaying a flash of genius several years ago when electric carts first started appearing on golf courses, called them "caddie-lacks."

Up to a point, that summation was entirely correct although the argument about which came first—like the old saw about the chicken or the egg—will never be completely settled.

Certainly there is plenty to be said for either thesis and the old cause and effect discussion will continue. Progress is indeed wonderful, in most cases, although someone switching from dinner at grandma's to a frozen pizza may differ.

Which leads us to this fact: At most courses, caddies are a disappearing breed. If the trend continues, in the too-near future the only place they can be seen will be on the professional tour. And, the average golfer will be worse because of it.

This discussion is about caddies, not bag-toters, which is another point. And, to find out about how the caddies themselves feel about the situation, why not go straight to the source.

Through the cooperation of Jerry Hinton, a personable Memphis pro, I was able to visit with several of them after their day's caddie chores were completed, at A. Y. Marshall's home.

Present were A. Y., his son Hines, Himmer Traylor and James A. Taylor—although the last two will be better recognized by their "calling names" of Nail and Bucket Joe.

Because of the inroads made by the carts and changes in playing habits, most hold other jobs now. But, they are caddies at heart and if the truth were known would probably prefer that vocation fulltime.

The four talked freely of the problems—and the joys—of being a caddie as well as others of their profession. Names like Early Bird, Bad Pap, Smooth, Wink, Little Larry, Jelly Roll, Beaver Hound, Bottley and Skinny punctuated the conversation.

Nail had several stories to tell about "Monkey Red," his brother and former Chickasaw caddie-master, and one of my own ambitions now is to have Nail caddie for me just one time and then watch him do his own impression, complete with facial expression and body English, of my swing.

Nail and A.Y. are two of the real oldtimers, both with more than 40 years experience, and both have worked on the course at various times.

As A.Y. said:"How many folks know that No. 17 green is built on stones or how No. 8 drains. We helped build those greens, have cut them and can tell you how they break. Can a cart do that?"

Bucket Joe broke in: "That's something else. Can a cart tell you how far it is from your ball to the pin? Can a cart notice something wrong with your swing, something not there last week when you played so good, and correct it right there on the course?"

With that, he answered his own questions with a vigorous nod of his head, looked me straight in the eye, and added:"Let me tell you something else. When you make that good shot or else get down on yourself when you make a bad one, can a cart inspire you, give you some inspiration?

"Unless something is done, pretty soon there won't be any more caddies and they can let one of the carts try to find their ball."

All pointed out how women golfers seemed to depend more on their caddies for advice than the men, not being too proud to accept help.

They talked about how the caddie fees had been raised from only 75¢ long ago to $4 a bag now, while Hines recalled the time they staged a strike, standing just outside the gate, to get their prices on a par with that paid by other clubs in the city.

They are professionals, they have a pride in their work and A.Y., despite his 67 years, still walks the course every morning so he can tell his player exactly where all the pins are located.

Many of these who try to work fulltime elsewhere still go to the club on weekends and during their vacations.

And they wonder what will happen when the oldtimers are gone. A part of golf will be missing.

Caddie! Caddie! Where Are You?

By ALLEN M. OAKLEY (Editor, *Quincy* (Ill.) *Herald-Whig*)

THE CADDIE is a dying breed. He's being carted away.

But in my 55th season I can't forget . . .

● The one who was ahead of me in high school, but took it meekly when I growled, with all the self-importance of a 16-year-old playing with his low-handicap elders, "SON, get your shadow off the hole."

● The one who said, "I told my Dad I caddied for you the other day, and my dad said he did too."

● The one who grew up to be a surgeon and a fellow-club member, who said, when I was reminiscing about an exhibition match in 1923, "You don't remember, I caddied for Chick (Evans) that day."

● The one who looked down at my shoes as we walked down the fairway and said, "Boy! THESE Foot-Joys are sure good shoes."

● The one who explained why he hadn't shown up one summer weekend: "I had to go to Forty Hours' Devotion," and was ever after known as Forty Hours.

And his little brother who came along the next year and was ever after known as Thirty-nine Hours.

● The one assigned to me for the duration at an out-of-town tournament who said, when I asked him who the stranger was following us on the third day, "That's my father. I told him what that old guy I was carrying for was doing, and he had to come see for himself."

● And, again out of town, in a four-ball tournament, the one who bubbled over with every shot, finally with a shouted "Tremendjus!" you could hear in the clubhouse when I sank a 30-footer that didn't count because my partner had already won the hole.

● And the one who needled me (in front of a girl—it stung) about my weak shots and sent me to the cross-cut saw and the woodpile all winter for a build-up program even Gary Player hasn't discovered yet.

● The three, each smaller, less able to cope and sorer of foot, that I had in one tournament round at an out-of-town club not noted for its caddie program, so that I carried the clubs up the 500-yard uphill 18th hole rather than see the survivor suffer.

● The one whose last name was Schenk, teaching me always to ask a caddie's name at the start of a round and not at some critical point later.

● There were those with Sam Snead swings to be envied, and one who kept giving my partner the wrong wood club because he didn't know the Roman numerals on the head covers. There were those who never came back for a second round, and one who grew up to fight me head-and-head in extra holes for the city championship.

● There was the one who reminded me of the 3-footer I missed to clinch the previous year's City Open when I had another 3-footer to beat an old rival for the club championship. You know what happened. I'll never forget him—and he knows it. But he knows, too, that I remember him for more than that.

Over five decades and more, they remember me and I remember them. There were those who never found a job and kept on caddying into the depression '30s. Today they discover cars and girls and hamburger jobs, and fade away as the carts rolling to the first tee go by them without a wave.

I want to *walk* down the fairway. Boy, I hope some kids show up this spring!

ALLIN'S A WINNER WITHOUT

THE NEXT TIME Buddy Allin pops up and wins a golf tournament, he'll be surprised. He prefers it that way.

"It's a surprise to me every time I win," Allin says. "I don't set goals. I don't know how good I am or how good I'll be, but I'm not going to tell myself that I've got to win or reach a certain place in life. It's not that important to me. I've already achieved more on the tour than I thought possible."

At 31, Brian Allin looks like a refugee from an old Our Gang movie. He has freckles, a shy grin and a mop of hair hanging over his forehead. He stands 5'-9" and weighs only slightly more than his golf bag at 133 pounds. There have been times when he has had trouble getting in the gate at tournaments, but in four full seasons on the professional tour he has won four times and earned $315,881.

In addition to winning at Doral in 1974, Allin also won the Byron Nelson Classic and finished second in the Tournament of Champions. He nearly doubled his previous career earnings with a cash tote of $137,950, ninth best for 1974.

None of which impresses him very much. A thoughful man, Allin is a Veitnam combat hero who underwent the additional trauma of divorce in late 1973. Winning golf tournaments just does not rank very high on his scale of values. Especially since he can't quite understand why he wins.

"My mind isn't convinced that I'm good enough to compete with the big stars," he says. "I'm going to let time tell me that. I'm tickled about winning four tournaments. That's something a lot of guys haven't done. But a lot of guys have, too, so I don't think it's any great achievement.

"Many things in life are more important. I'm not convinced the tour is the greatest life in the world. It cost me a marriage and a lot of time with my little boy, so I'm not going to tell everybody that this is great.

"It was just something that we couldn't handle, and maybe if I had done something else for a living I would have kept my family. Maybe not. I'm still trying to figure out the reasons. It's tough for two young married kids to come out here and try something this big and really come up with a lot of understanding. I don't think Cecilia and I were mature enough to cope with it. I know I wasn't. I think I forgot who my family was and put them second. It just wasn't the right way to handle it.

"But maybe it worked out for the best. I have a good relationship with Cecilia. She takes good care of my son Aaron and I get to see him any time. She's really happy now. If she were miserable, I might feel differently about the divorce.

"Those things are important in life, more than just winning," says Allin, now remarried to the former Carolyn Spring of Santa Barbara, Calif. "What's more important—to win the tournament this week or go home happy? Financially, winning is great. You have some extra bucks to spend, but I can't convince myself that this means the whole world to me.

"Not that golf isn't important to me . . . my whole life revolves around what I do out here. But if I can keep from thinking that I have to win this week or win three tournaments this year, then I can round out my life better."

Allin feels this attitude is one reason for his success, because it enables him to control emotions which in the past have tended to get out of hand.

"I've read every self-improvement book put out," he says. "I've gone on positive-thinking kicks for months at a time. But every time I try to get really positive, really try to achieve this or that, something kind of goes slack inside my head and I go the other way. If I don't put a lot of pressure on myself to do well, I play better without really thinking about it.

"All I'm really doing is trying to find peace of mind. I'm trying to curb my emotions, because I'm a very emotional person. I can watch a movie and cry. I get nervous on the course, and I think I have to have this approach to keep my nerves in check. And I've got a terrible temper. Sometimes if I have a real bad round I get sick and want to jump off a bridge or something.

"I can go the other way and be too complacent, also. Some guys have to calm themselves down and others say they've got to charge themselves up. I'm just trying to get right in the middle.

"I want to win just like anybody else, but I'm not going to take the attitude that I've got to win. I just try to keep myself on an even keel and figure that if the situations are right tomorrow and I try better, I *can* win."

In a roundabout way, Allin credits the Army for the development of his attitude. A teammate of Johnny Miller at Brigham Young University, Allin quit college after 2½ years and enlisted for three years in November, 1966.

"It was just something I felt I had to do at the time," he explains. "I had kind of a gung-ho attitude, wanted to protect our country and all that kind of stuff, and that to me was more important than college. I kind of hate to relate my experience in Vietnam to golf—that's been played up too much—but I do think it helped put me at peace with myself. I felt what I was doing was right. I didn't question the government."

Allin spend 18 months in Vietnam, volunteering for an extra 6-month

REALLY TRYING By LARRY DENNIS

hitch, and wound up an artillery first lieutenant. During that time he was awarded the Bronze Star and two commendations for valor, but he shrugs them off. "The Army just has to give so many of those decorations, really," he grins.

Allin liked the Army so well he considered making it a career, but a request for transfer to a better command slot was snafued along the way.

"One colonel didn't send it up, and when they finally found out that I had tried to transfer it was too late," he says. "I only had a month or so left and I decided to go home and play golf. But the Army almost had me."

Instead, Allin returned home in September of 1969 to Santa Barbara, where he still lives. There he agonized for 6 months over whether to return to school or try the tour. In February, 1970, he decided on the spur of the moment to try golf for pay. He worked as an assistant pro and played in some small southwestern tournaments until he could qualify for the tour in the November school.

At the time, his credentials were singularly unimpressive. A graduate of the Santa Barbara caddie ranks, Allin's only early achievement of note was finishing as low amateur in the California Open as a teen-ager, after he had hitchhiked 75 miles to get to the tournament.

"Going to Brigham Young was the thing that helped me the most, I think,"

he recalls. "I was able to play against the good schools and compare myself with better players. I won a couple of tournaments and placed high in a couple and I thought, 'Well, maybe I'm a little better than I think I am.' "

True to form, Allin set no goals for himself at the start of his pro career.

"I was scared to death," he says. "I had only seen one professional tournament in my life, the Bakersfield Open back in 1962. So I didn't know what to expect. I was just hoping to break even that year."

Operating on borrowed money, Allin made the cut in his first two post-school tournaments in late 1970. He made the cut again in the Los Angeles Open that began the 1971 tour. Suddenly, at Greensboro in the spring of his first full season, he won.

"That was kind of a fluke," he says. "The highest finish I had until then was a tie for 17th. Nobody played good that week at Greensboro."

Allin neglects to mention that he shot a second-round 64 in a rainstorm, followed with 67 and 69 and won a three-man playoff with a 32-foot birdie putt on the first extra hole. He was $38,000 richer and above the break-even mark . . . maybe too quickly.

"Instead of a help it was a setback," he says. "All of a sudden I thought I was better than I was. I thought that was fun and all I had to do was just go out and win every now and then. I thought I should probably finish in the top 10

every time. But it just doesn't work out that way. I wasn't ready. My game wasn't good enough and my concentration wasn't good enough. I didn't have enough experience, and the rest of the year was a catastrophe."

Catastrophe or not, he finished the season with $55,786 in winnings, good for 43rd on the money list and an exemption. He didn't win in 1972 but still earned $47,576. Then, early in 1973, he surfaced again to win the Florida Citrus Open with rounds of 66-65-67-67. He was 13 under par after 36 holes, 18 under after 54 and 23 under at the finish, all of which wound up as the best marks of 1973. For the year he won $77,472, good for 33rd on the money list, and was on his way into the big '74 campaign.

His improvement has been more mental than physical. "I'm a better player now than I was 2 years ago," he says. 'I think I hit the ball better, although I haven't made any changes in my swing. The big thing is that I think better on the course, and I feel I'm improving at that. The more times you finish in the top 10 and the more tournaments you win, the more your confidence is built."

An extremely straight driver, Allin says his lack of size is no handicap. "Most of them out here hit it farther than I do, but I can get within 10 or 15 yards of everybody, and that's no big hurdle."

Despite his obvious potential, Allin is not concerned about superstardom. He

would, of course, be surprised if it ever happened.

"I don't know that even if I won the Big Four it would convince me I was a superstar," he says. "I'd rather not feel I was one, even if people said I was. I'd hate to get so big that I didn't have time for my good friends. That would hurt me."

Allin plans to play the tour for the foreseeable future. But he knows it's not forever.

"I don't know how long I have," he says. "It depends on how long I can cope with the pressures, the travelling, my family situation, just a lot of things. I might break my little finger. It's conceivable I could go sour out here. I can't project myself into the future. But I think that whatever happens, I can handle it. I'll be able to make a living. Just as long as I can find something constructive . . . that's the most important thing for me. When I get down on myself out here, I don't find anything constructive about my being on the tour. It's hard for me to say if it's really right or good, or if there's something better in life.

"I'm still kind of hunting for answers. I wouldn't mind having a philosophy of life that I could live with every day for the rest of my life. I don't have that yet, but I'm working on it."

When he finds one, it no doubt will keep him on an even keel. That's what's important.

Allin's a master with the handy 5-wood

"If Jack Nicklaus pulled out a 5-wood, people would snicker," says Buddy Allin. "But they think it's OK for me to use it because they figure I need it."

The wispy Allin smiles when he says that, because he's not exactly a shrimp when it comes to hitting for distance.

"I use the 5-wood whenever I can't get there with a 2-iron," Allin says. "I figure a 5-wood is about half a club longer. I hit it about 205 yards with no wind compared to 200 for a 2-iron.

"I also think the 5-wood is easier to hit than a long iron, particularly for the average guy. It's partly psychological—with a 2-iron you don't have much loft and you feel you have to hit harder at it to get the ball up. You've got a bigger hunk of wood down there with a 5-wood and you don't feel you have to swing as hard.

"But I really feel you have more room for error with a 5-wood. It has more loft, and you have a little more flexibility with it. You can close it down and hit it a little farther, or you can take an easier swing and cut it in from 195 yards or so. If I ease off on a 2-iron, I don't get it up in the air well and don't have as much spin on the ball."

Allin uses the same swing with the 5-wood he uses for the long irons, a sweeping rather than pinching action.

He finds the 5-wood particularly valuable out of light rough, because the larger head cuts through the grass more easily and the loft gets the ball up quicker. And because of that loft, he finds he can get the ball up better off the fairway when the grass is wet.

In this sequence with the 5-wood, Allin is aiming at the tallest tree in the middle of the picture. He prefers to fade the ball and has set up with his feet open but his shoulders much more square to the target-line.

"I just can't hit it from a square position, because I can't move my bottom half out of the way on the downswing," he explains. "This is just a method for me to be able to make a good move at the ball."

From address, Allin swings the club back to a position which is virtually square to the target-line at the top (frame 4). His first downswing move with the lower body (frame 5) drops the club into a position inside the target line. He then returns the club through the ball on an ideal path from inside to along the target line- (Frames 6 through 8).

A Visit to the Cradle

Like every golfer who's heard the tales, Gordon Campbell, Golf Canada's correspondent, has made the Scottish pilgrimage to the official cradle. As he says, "St. Andrews is certainly a place every golfer should see before he dies, and, if he can find an Alex Paterson or a Bob Husband, the experience will be just that much more enjoyable."

By GORDON CAMPBELL

FOR A CITY that has hosted players of various shapes and sizes since the 1540's, St. Andrews has stood up well as the mecca where all golfers must go sometime in their lives.

Today, the common land given by a church bishop to the town 434 years ago to "play games, graze sheep, hang washing and catch rabbits" has four golf courses—the Old, the New, the Eden and the Jubilee—all open to the public plus a free nine-hole children's course.

"The Old Course was laid out 200 years ago," remarked Alex Paterson, 67-year-old native of St. Andrews. "Golf has changed but we've kept the course the same as it was when played with old hickory shafts."

Paterson probably knows more about the city, its golf and other happenings than anyone. He has been a newspaperman for 50 years and reported on the Royal and Ancient club during all that time.

An 18-handicap, once-a-week golfer now, Alex is also a playwright. He wrote a play called the "Open", based on the 1950 British Open here, and is chairman of the board of the Byre Theatre which he helped found 40 years ago.

Hence, it was to this veteran holder of the MBE (Member of the British Empire) we went to get the background on how golf came to Scotland.

"Golf was played in Holland back in the early 1500s," Paterson explained. "The Dutch traders first brought it to St. Andrews and it was played by groups to a stick in the ground.

"Research shows that the city paid two nurses to attend the injured, most of whom were hit on the head because they were standing too close to each other.

"The idea then was not strokes but the speed in getting the ball to the hole. It was a matter of hit and run. The golf hole was a Scotch innovation."

Paterson turned us over to Bob Husband, a lovable 73-year-old, who has phoned in stories for various writers from every British Open championship, except one, since 1949.

A native of nearby Dundee, Husband retired seven years ago after 20 years with the civil service following his return from a six-year sojourn with the Bell Telephone Co. in Montreal.

"I didn't realize how nice a place St. Andrews was until I came back," commented the 20-handicap, who has played three times a week for the past seven years in an attempt to catch up.

Husband, a one-time soccer star, first took us on a walking tour of the Old Course. It was during the Royal and Ancient's Autumn Medal tournament and, at the 170-yard, 11th hole, we ran into Joe Dey Jr., recently retired commissioner of the PGA Tour.

Playing with Frank J. Trumper and Capt. F. B. Lloyd, secretary of the Senior Golfers Society of Great Britain, Dey, a 15-handicap, holed a 50-footer from off the green with his putter to par the hole the late Bobby Jones called the "best par three in the world."

Trumper, a 13-handicap, used a hickory-shafted jigger to get to 10 feet of the pin on the sloping green of the 466-

Royal Ancient Golf Club at St. Andrews

yard, 17th, known as the Road Hole.

"It's rather an examination in chess, really," was the way he described the Old Course.

The next day, courtesy of Keith Mackenzie, R & A secretary, Husband and yours truly were permitted to tee off following the tourney.

Husband bogeyed the first and parred the second hole via 35 and 50-foot off the green putts indicating he knew the greens, seven of which are double on the course.

We didn't get our first par until the sixth, a 374-yarder, but then went bogey, par, par, par, bogey before reverting to our normal duffer's game.

"Secret of the course," declared Husband, "is to place the tee shot in the right position to approach the green. The five-iron—or jigger—is used to pitch and run from 60 to 100 yards out."

Needless to say, without Husband's coaching, we would have been in even more trouble. The stragetic positioning of the many small, deep bunkers, which look like shell holes, plus the heather, make local knowledge a must.

While the 5-par, 513-yard, 14th is undoubtedly the course's toughest hole, especially in the prevailing wind which was gusting over 40 miles per hour, the 18th also can be a study in frustration.

Known as the Valley of Sin, this 358-yard finishing hole has a deep depression in the left front of the green. A topped second shot can often get there better than a good shot.

Tony Lema endeared himself to the gallery when he played a pitch and run to finish off his British Open championship while Jack Nicklaus drove through the green and wound up on the bank enroute to his triumph.

We finished our fascinating round in the gathering gloom but made it in three hours and 10 minutes despite the cool, cool walk through history.

After a few cocktails in the unique and exclusive St. Andrews Golf Club, Husband revealed a few more intriguing facts about the courses, which have no professionals.

It seems that in the 19th century the town council needed some money, so it sold the course to the Cheape family. A later council decided that this was a mistake and decided to buy it back.

The Cheapes agreed but stipulated that the family may always play at any time free, which means they could appear in the middle of a British Open and have to be accommodated. They also can take shells from the courses.

Alexander Cheape, now 70, is the last remaining member of the family and, while he doesn't play golf, digs up shells every few years which he puts on the driveway of his course-bordering mansion.

Cost to play golf at St. Andrews is $4.70 for the Old Course, $2.95 for the New, $1.75 for the Eden and 85¢ for the Jubilee. The Old Course is closed on Sunday and the others have slightly higher weekend rates.

A full set of clubs may be hired from Winnie McAndrew's store for $3.05, Electric carts are not permitted except occasionally on the Eden course.

Municipal voters and wives get yearly memberships for $5.20!

A visit to St. Andrews is not complete without a chat with Laurie Auchterlonie, 70-year-old honorary pro to the Royal and Ancient club, whose family goes back to the year 1200.

Auchterlonie, whose father, Willie, was the last Scot to win the British Open (1893), was disappointed that the Hall of

Gordon Campbell and Bob Husband

Fame in Pinehurst, N.C., didn't include a Scot among its first inductees.

"Imagine that," pondered Laurie. "Not a Scot in it and this is the home of golf!"

Although he is recuperating from a heart attack, Auchterlonie was on hand for the annual ceremony that sees each new R & A captain play himself into office.

The ceremony takes place at exactly 8 AM with the new captain—six-handicap Sir John Carmichael—teeing off as a small cannon is fired. Caddies line up 200 yards down the fairway and scramble for the ball.

Bill Nicoll, a 35-year-old St. Andrews car salesman retrieved it this year as 23 competed. The 64-year-old Carmichael gave Nicoll a golden sovereign which can usually be sold for 25 pounds.

A native of St. Andrews, Nicoll said it was the first time he had ever seen the ceremony, witnessed by about 300 people, including 11 previous captains.

St. Andrews is certainly a place every golfer should see before he dies, and, if he can find an Alex Paterson or a Bob Husband, the experience will be just that much more enjoyable.

Town of St. Andrews

Bobby Jones and the British Amateur of 1930

By DAWSON TAYLOR

ALL GOLF BUFFS *know that in the year 1930 Robert Tyre Jones, Jr., won the United States and British Open and Amateur titles, a feat unique in the game's history.*

Here, in an excerpt taken from St. Andrews, Cradle of Golf *by Dawson Taylor, soon to be published by Barnes, is the story of his two matches in the British Amateur, the first of them against the defending champion, Cyril Tolley.*

Bobby Jones and Cyril Tolley were great friends and avid competitors, each one determined to beat the other if he could possibly do so. Cyril had already won the championship for a second time the year before. As defending champion he had great prestige in Great Britain and no doubt felt a great responsibility to keep the Cup on the Scottish side of the Atlantic. Tolley was a big man, a very powerful player and an especially long driver. Jones himself felt that in the entire field Tolley would be his most dangerous opponent, the one most likely to upset his chances for the first leg of the four championships. Jones and Tolley had to win two matches apiece in order to meet in the upper bracket of the draw. Jones got past Roper and won his second match, to fulfill his part in the destiny of Jones and Tolley. Tolley had a narrow squeak, however, in his first round, almost lost but did not and then came through with his second win handily. The stage was now set for the confrontation between Jones and Tolley. Jones did not particularly like eighteen-hole matches, and much preferred to battle over the thirty-six hole route, feeling that he had more room to maneuver, more of an opportunity to make a few bad shots and yet recover and win. He had beaten Tolley very badly, 12 and 11, in the thirty-six hole singles match of the Walker Cup matches of two years before over the same Old Course. Any golfer hates to be "disgraced" by being beaten in "double figures" and Tolley just might have been harboring a grudge along with an even increased desire to win this particular match and avenge his earlier trouncing by Jones.

Furthermore, on the morning of the match it was soon apparent that Tolley would have another advantage, that of familiar "St. Andrews" weather and course conditions. Jones was far less experienced than Tolley in strong wind and rain. Strong winds were blowing at half gale force, coming in off the sea. The fine seaside sand was being whipped out of the bunkers and off sandy patches of the turf and driven into the faces, sometimes the eyes of the golfers when they played into the teeth of the wind.

The match between Jones and Tolley was followed by a gallery of thousands. Tolley began like a duffer with a topped drive off the first tee, an unbelievable shot from so good a golfer. It is to his great credit that although the bad stroke cost him a 5 at the first hole to go one hole down to Jones's 4, Tolley came right back with a strong 4 at the second to an equally weak second hole on Jones' part.

Tolley one up at the 4th, Jones and Tolley even by the 7th, Jones one up at the 8th, all even at the 9th when Tolley drove the 306 yard green and got a 3 to Bobby's 5. The scores were 39 for Jones and 38 for Tolley, not very good under ordinary conditions but remarkably good for the horrible wind and rain the two golfers were forced to undergo.

Scores of other leading players in the same wind, incidentally, were much worse in comparison.

Here are the first nine scores:

Jones	Out:	4 5 4 5 5 4 4 3 5	39
Tolley	Out:	5 4 4 4 5 4 5 4 3	38	Match even

At the short eleventh hole, after both golfers had tied in 4s at No. 10, Tolley's driving iron was seen to fly as far as the putting surface in the air and then be blown backward into the fairway short of Strath bunker. Jones's shot was even stronger from the tee, caught a lull in the gusting wind and sailed over the green onto the bank of the Eden river. Cyril dubbed his next shot, did not even hit it as far as Strath bunker and then dumped the ball into Strath. Jones pitched onto the green safely, took 4 to Tolley's 5 when Tolley had a great recovery out of the bunker on his fourth shot. Jones, one up. Most incredibly, the next five holes were traded in succession, first one and then the other golfer making the superlative shot to win. Tolley eagled the 14th with two monstrous shots which reached the 5-par green, and a putt that went down to outscore Jones's equally beautifully played birdie 4.

The greens were "blown out" by the winds, dry and slick as glass. There were spike marks on them, too, which had not healed since the play of the day before and these irregularities added to the uncertainty of the players' putting. The effects of the wind itself had to be taken into consideration in calculating the line of a putt and that is most difficult when the wind is an unsteady one.

By the time the players reached the seventeenth hole, the match lead had been traded from one up to even or one down to even six separate times. Jones was one up at the end of the first and at the eighth, one down at the end of the fifth, sixth and seventh and even on the other four holes of the nine. On the back nine Jones took a one up lead at the eleventh, thirteenth and fifteenth only to see Tolley take it away each time at the twelfth, fourteenth and sixteenth holes.

Both Jones and Tolley had very long drives on the seventeenth. Jones's ball was to the left side of the fairway while Tolley's, a little bit longer, was in the center. Jones would be forced to play to the dangerous green first. The flagstick was directly behind the Road Bunker from Jones's position while the hole opened slightly for Tolley since he was more to the right.

In order for Jones to reach a position in front of the green from which he could chip to the hole it was necessary for him to land his ball very close to the road itself. If Jones hit the ball a shade too hard he would be in the road, a shade too softly and he might still be blocked from the pin by the Road Bunker. He decided to attempt to play intentionally past the Road Bunker on its left side with the idea that once past the hazard he could chip back to the hole with a better chance for a 4 than he would have if he should get into trouble in the road or by being blocked out by the bunker. Jones tried to get the massed galleries to move away from his intended target area. They moved slightly and begrudgingly. The stewards were doing their best but excitement was running so high that the people were unreasoning. They would chance being hit by a Jones shot and proudly show the bruise, no doubt, the next day.

Jones finally made the stroke, a 4-iron that caused the ball to land even with the bunker and then bound into the side of the roped gallery and there be stopped on the back edge of the green some forty or fifty feet away from the hole, but a most satisfactory shot under the circumstances, one which now threw great pressure on Tolley to equal or surpass it in order to hold the match all square.

Tolley knew he had to "go for the flag" in order to save his half on the hole. Knowing the danger in letting the ball get to the right and into the road, Tolley instinctively guarded against any kind of a "push." As a result, the shot was slightly pulled to the left, safely away from the road, it is true, but it came to rest to the left of the Road Bunker with that dreaded sandy hole between Tolley's ball and the flagstick. Moreover, the ratio of distance between Tolley's ball and the bunker, and the bunker and the flagstick was so unfavorable that it appeared probable that Tolley would not put the ball onto the putting surface and still stop it anywhere near the hole because the hole was cut extremely close to Tolley's side of the green.

O. B. Keeler, the great reporter who followed Jones's career so avidly, witnessed the shot. He said that he felt that "no man alive could execute so deft a pitch that it would clear that bunker and stop anywhere near the hole in that absurdly narrow plateau green with the road just across it." He thought Tolley would be most likely to put the ball into the road, would never be able to get it near the flag. In one minute Jones had the hole "won" and in another minute Jones was putting an eight-footer for his life because Tolley would go one up should Jones miss his putt. But Jones did not miss the putt and the history of golf was better served as a result. Without that putt in the hole at seventeen it is fairly certain there would have been no "Grand Slam" for Jones.

At this crucial moment, Tolley was able to make what he later said, some twenty-eight years afterward, "was the finest shot of my life." He was able to loft his ball off the closely cut grass of the fairway onto exactly the right spot at the green's edge where it should hit and get enough underspin on the ball to cause it to stop within inches of the hole for a certain 4. Jones, startled no doubt by the excellence of Tolley's recovery, made his run-up shot from the back edge of the green. To his horror he saw the ball sliding farther and farther away from the hole, coming to rest at least eight feet away. Now the tide had really turned. From a probable 4 for Jones and a possible 5 for Tolley at the moment before Tolley had made his approach to the green, Jones now faced the certainty of Tolley's 4 and a very possible 5 for himself if he should not sink this wicked

slippery eight foot putt.

Jones once more exhibited his silken putting stroke under pressure, holing the putt to tie Tolley. The two great golfers headed for the Home Hole with the wind now at their backs, all tied. The galleries lined both sides of the fairway and surrounded the back of the eighteenth green.

Both players drove to within ten yards of the green, helped by the powerful tail-wind. Jones was to the left and played his run-up shot first. His shot was too strong and ran up through the Valley of Sin about twenty-five feet past the hole. Tolley's shot was better than Jones's and stopped about twelve to fifteen feet away, also on the high side of the hole. Jones, of course, putted first. He missed the hole but was close enough to assure his par. Now the door was open for Tolley and Jones could do nothing about it. If Cyril downed this birdie putt he had won the match and put Jones out of the Amateur Championship.

Tolley missed, Jones, in mental agony waiting for the verdict, had another "life" in the match. They would go to extra holes.

The nineteenth hole was anti-climactic. Tolley missed the green on his second shot and chipped weakly short of the hole by seven feet.

Jones, in the meanwhile, had hit a fine drive and a superlative second shot only ten feet away from the flagstick. The stymie rule was still in effect at that time. Since both balls were on the same side of the hole it was entirely possible that if Jones did not hole his putt it might stop on Cyril's line and block his line to the cup. That is exactly what happened. Jones's ball was only a couple of inches short of the hole but Tolley had a complete stymie which he could not possibly negotiate. So, it was Jones one up in nineteen holes over Cyril Tolley. Another piece of the jig-saw puzzle, the four championships of 1930 for Jones had fallen into place, reluctantly it is true, but it had fallen.

Roger Wethered, the tall, distinguished gentleman-golfer famous as much for his own golf as for the golf swing of his famous sister, British Women's Champion, Joyce, would meet Jones in the final thirty-six hole match.

Roger had had three very easy matches to start and then had had four equally tough ones. He was hitting his irons and pitches to the green in brilliant fashion. His driving, often erratic, remained good for the first nine holes of the match with Jones and then began to get him into serious trouble from which he never would recover.

These two golfers had recently played a preview of the match at Sandwich in the Walker Cup only a few weeks before. Wethered and Jones had each shot 35s to make the turn even. Then, Roger's game went to pieces and Jones took six of the next seven holes. The same thing happened at St. Andrews. Jones won five of the first seven holes on the second nine. Although Wethered birdied the Road Hole brilliantly, Bobby, having missed a two-foot putt after recovering so close to the pin that it appeared he would make his 4 there, too, was four up at the start of the second eighteen. Roger made as good a fight as he could, battling to the turn, trying not to get any further behind, but the result was a foregone conclusion. Jones played superb golf and was two under 4s for the thirty holes of the match, for Wethered was congratulating Jones at the twelfth hole on his great victory in the championship, the first crown of the four he would gather together for his Grand Slam of 1930.

The voice of the newshawk knifed through the busy noise of Dublin.

Pars, Birdies—
and a Little Pink Colleen

By BLAIR HOLLEY
(Golf Editor, *Morristown* (N.J.) *Daily Record*)

STRIDENT AND YOUNG, the voice knifed through the busy noise of Dublin's Earl Street. It penetrated with the same intensity as the chill, Irish breeze.

The stranger first became aware of the shrill call soon after he passed the incongruous shop, Moore Ltd., which featured "Top Gear, Western Wear."

Again and again, each time a bit louder, the voice called its undecipherable message from up near the O'Connell Street corner. A mental bet was

made that it belonged to a newsboy and perhaps offered some photographic possibilities.

The visitor found his way to the newshawk, not a boy, but a girl of about 12. Slender, with close-cropped blonde hair, she wore a warm jacket against the nippy October day.

Her bike rested on the side of the simple newsstand, which was nothing more than a few boxes and planks. She lit the scene, however, with her smile of

thanks to each of her customers.

Catching her eye just after she sold a paper, the stranger asked if he might take a picture and she shyly nodded her assent. He took several shots as she went on with her work, thanked her, and slipped a coin in her small hand.

The youngster grasped his hand and the coin at the same time and held him to the spot, while she asked him to please send her a picture. Pleased, he assured her he would be glad to do so and she

12th green at Baltray golf Club

quickly scribbled her name and address on one of his business cards. Then it was his turn for that magic smile and she turned back to work.

Her name was Joan, and even that brief encounter with the child had made a lasting impression on the man. However, the charm of Dublin again caught him and he moved on to try his luck at riding the double-decker buses.

The stranger was a golf writer, in Ireland for a unique tournament labled the Irish International. The stateside competition was being provided by four New Jersey club pros.

Even though they had been in the air what seemed all night, the first day in Dublin had been spent at the famed Portmarnock Golf Club, where the four New Jersey pros and writers played a practice round.

The next day they toured Portmarnock in earnest, playing the likes of Harry Bradshaw and Patty Skerritt and taking a four to two edge in Nassau play.

A day later, they traveled some 30 miles north of Dublin to play the devilish Baltray, or County Louth, Golf Club. A rough-and-ready golf course in the oldtime tradition, it proved a wicked test of skill for the unknowing Americans.

Baltray has little which might be called plush, but you can play all year long for annual dues of under 70 dollars in United States equivalent. Its rough is

Irish caddy at Baltray with New Jersey pro Pat Schwab.

The goats on the Lahinch links.

never cut, growing a foot or more in entangled depth, and one fairway was paced off as being only 12 feet wide at one point.

When one of the visiting pros, a man of over 250 pounds with a bag to match, asked where his caddie was, the venerable Baltray caddie master indicated a boy of nine or ten complete with heavy sweater, knee wrappings and high-buttoned shoes. Fortunately, the bags were pulled on handcarts called "trolleys" and not carried.

Coming back from Baltray late that day on an Irish Tourist Board bus, the group enjoyed the magnificent views of the countryside afforded by the picture windows on the vehicle. Seated high above the stone-fenced roadsides, the golfers forgot the game as the beauty of Ireland greeted them at every turn.

As they wound through Dublin, the stranger suddenly recognized Earl Street. Nearing O'Connell, he turned to a friend and remarked that perhaps they'd see the cute, little newsgirl of whom he had spoken.

Just as the man did spot her, the child lifted her gaze and appeared to half recognize him. Raising the camera around his neck elicited a big smile and wave,

but the moment was fleeting as the light changed and the bus moved on.

The American-like Royal Dublin Golf Club was the site of the next day's play, with the tournament all tied up. Royal Dublin has a modern clubhouse and facilities, but is still a bargain at well under 200 American dollars yearly dues.

When they say "outgoing" nine at Royal Dublin they mean it, as the ninth green is the furthest point from the clubhouse. The "incoming" nine parallels the front side.

Magnetically pulled by the attraction of Dublin Town, the stranger left Royal Dublin early and again successfully rode the two-level bus to the heart of the city. After a pleasant lunch with a delightful family, whose brother in New Jersey asked him to visit, the man again walked through the city.

That family, the Morans, owned a small hotel only two blocks from Joan's corner and the impulse to see again the charming, little newsgirl was easily answered. The man was glad he stopped by that last time.

Joan's mother and smaller sister were also there, and the infectious smile was revealed as a family trait. The mother

spoke with pride about her Joan who arose every morning at six, sold morning papers until school time, then returned to the stand to sell evening papers.

The stranger was impressed with the strong family bond in Ireland, and he noticed its fine effect on the children he met. His final visit with Joan ended and he went on his way.

The golf moved over to Woodbrook Golf Club on the final day in Dublin, with the Irish pros holding a slim lead. The final matches were played in blasting wind and rain, and the Irish pros called on their bad-weather experience to score a resounding victory.

Never outclassed, the New Jersey quartet met the best Ireland had to offer. It's no shame to lose to pros such as Christy O'Connor, Christy Greene, and others of their Ryder Cup and Canada Cup stature.

Those same rains and winds had kept the stranger in Dublin that final day, with the excuse of a beginning cold and much shopping to do. One of those shopping stops took him to a men's store on O'Connell Street.

As he walked by the Earl Street corner, the man knew he might see Joan again, since the schools were closed that day. He never got to say goodbye.

A crowd surrounded the spot of the newsstand, and the stranger's breath caught with apprehension. It was not the kind of crowd which buys papers.

Finally getting through the crush of people, he saw the twisted frame of the bike and the scattered papers, wet and trampled. The stand was splintered and smashed.

"A coal truck," he was told by the red-headed Garda, "skidded on the wet pavement, the child was badly hurt and is on the way to hospital." Then the young police officer went back to his duties.

Obviously an American, many in the crowd may have wondered about his tears as the stranger stumbled away from the hurtful scene. His group was leaving Dublin within hours and he couldn't even check on Joan.

The remainder of the stay in Ireland was numbed by the Dublin experience. Even the Irish countryside on the 130-mile motorcoach trip from Dublin to Shannon was dulled.

The fantastic beauty of the Lahinch Golf Club on the Atlantic Coast, and the formidable Cliffs of Moher nearby, pushed their way into his consciousness, but never really dominated as they would with anyone else on first visit.

Looking back with some objectivity, the man would have to say that the Lahinch links offered the most exciting golf he had seen in Ireland. If he had a chance to visit only one course in that grand, green land, it would be Lahinch.

It has the most breathtaking holes and scenery you could imagine. There are also a pair of goats on the course, hobbled and tied together to prevent their roaming too far.

The goats are owned by an old man who once had a large herd, and they are welcomed on the Lahinch links as a sort of bearded, walking barometer. When the goats come in to the clubhouse shelter, it's going to storm badly and the golfers know it is time for them to also come in.

A grizzled veteran of many days on those windy links, the Lahinch pro sits in his small pro shop warming himself by the cheerful, tiny coalstove and warming visitors with his tales of the coastal golf game.

Two brief days at Shannon, with visits to Lahinch and a restored castle, punctuated by trips through the little towns of Ennistymon and Clare Castle, ended.

The trip home was both happy and sad. It had been a superb trip, but thoughts of Joan flooded the visitor's mind.

He left that handsome, green land no longer a stranger to it, and with more than a little piece of his emotional being still there.

More than a few things will some day draw him back, not the least of which will be that dear girl in the Irish hospital. He is not yet sure of her condition and is impatiently waiting answers to airmail queries.

When he returns, he will bring his family so that his wife and children may experience the joys of that land and the golf that is Ireland.

Meanwhile, Joan is on his mind, and for her he prays the old prayer:

May the road rise to meet you,
And the wind be always at your back.
May the sun shine warm upon your
face,   And, until we meet again,
May God hold you in the hollow of
His hand.

(Editor's Note: Holley later learned that Joan, altho knocked unconscious, had suffered comparatively minor injuries and was back on the corner in a few days.)

WHY GENE LITTLER HAD HIS BEST YEAR

By NICK SEITZ

PHIL RODGERS, a stubby, sometimes irascible veteran, is the resident guru of the men's professional golf tour. He is acutely knowledgeable about the game and is blessed with a photographic memory that surpasses videotape because it has a third dimension. Other players come to Rodgers for help when they're playing badly, knowing he can remember exactly how they were swinging when they were playing well—a year ago, 5 years ago, 10 years ago. In many cases Rodgers understands his fellow pros' games better than they do.

Rodgers and Gene Littler live in the San Diego area and are long-time friends, and Rodgers was the first person I wanted to talk to about Littler's unexpectedly great season. Less than three years after undergoing two grave operations for cancer—operations that laid waste much of the muscle structure of the upper left side that traditionally has been considered crucial to the golf swing—Littler in 1975 won the Crosby, Memphis and Westchester tournaments in the U.S. He finished in the top 10 in eight tournaments and earned almost $200,000. Considering how much the

competition has improved since he joined the tour, it had to be his best year yet, to the delight of the millions of people in golf who admire the quiet quality of the man.

I found Phil Rodgers after the first round of the Tournament Players Championship in Fort Worth. In a demonstration of guru wisdom, he had fled the broiling, 110-degree heat of the practice range to take up a position near the cold-drinks box in the air-conditioned locker room.

Rodgers pointed to several salient reasons for Littler's magnificent 1975 record, including changes in equipment, changes in attitude and even, to some extent, changes in Littler's classic swing. The changes reflect an incredible willingness to adapt and expand in a 46-year-old athlete, let alone one who was told by his doctors he'd never again tee it up in competition. "But the biggest difference I see is in his short game," Rodgers said. "Follow him around and you'll see what I mean. He's much more consistent at getting it up and down."

Since the temperature the following

afternoon had subsided to a mere 105 degrees, I willingly if irrationally took leave of the press lounge (temperature 70 degrees, cost of refreshments zero) to pick up Littler as he made the turn. I arrived at the ninth green to witness his short game facing a knotty test.

The ninth at Colonial is a 405-yard par-4 with a moat protecting the green. Littler's second shot had cleared the water but was deep in the rough to the left of the green. He was only about 35 feet from the cup, but it was cut immediately behind a deep bunker.

Littler flipped a wedge shot almost straight up in the air, stopped it just 10 feet beyond the hole and made the putt to save his par. Rodgers' words came back to me: "He's much more consistent at getting it up and down."

On the 416-yard 10th hole, uphill through overhanging trees, Littler missed the green short and to the left and had a chip shot of at least 100 feet. He rolled it dead a foot from the hole and tapped in for a par.

On the 11th hole, a wearing, 609-yard par-5, he was under the high lip of a greenside bunker in three. He splashed

his sand shot 15 feet from the hole and made the putt for a par.

On the 12th hole, a dogleg-left 419-yarder, he was in the deep bunker in front of the green in two and, you guessed it, lobbed out and one-putted for another par.

At this point I was conveniently close to the clubhouse and left the course, the better to keep from suffering heat prostration. I took with me a new appreciation of Gene Littler's scrambling ability. Best known for the smoothness of his full swing, which presumably would get him in trouble only once every generation or so, he had just staged a magic show that saw him wriggle out of dire predicaments on four straight holes.

"I now have a fuller repertoire of gimmicks to get the ball around the course," Littler says of his scrambling. He speaks softly and well, flavoring the words with a laconic wit. "Maybe the public doesn't realize that all the top players have to be able to save par frequently. Jack Nicklaus is powerful, but he's also one of the best up-and-downers on the tour in years and years and years. Consistently. That's why he almost never shoots a bad round. He's a great player, but there's more to the game than striking the ball purely. You can hit the ball just so well. You might go two strokes up on the field because

you hit the ball better during a round, but if you recover and putt better than the other guys you could gain a half dozen or more shots. That's why it pays to practice the short game more than the long game."

Littler's values have changed recently in this connection. Says teaching professional Paul Runyan, who has worked with him on his game, "For a long time Gene thought he had to perform perfectly to be a champion. But no one, not even the greatest champ hits every shot perfectly. Gene become more of a scrambler since he's had to."

The scrambler, of course, puts oppressive pressure on his putting stroke. It does little good to manufacture a fine recovery shot if you don't get down in one putt, and Littler's recent putting has been far and away the best of his million-dollar career. It is almost ordinary for him to knock in during the course of a day's work putts of 15, 25, 28, 18 and 35 feet, to pick a recent example.

He attributes the improvement to a new putter and a modification in his setup position. The putter, developed especially for him by Littler's "nutty inventor friend" Dave Taylor of Carmel Valley, Calif., features 11 bold, black lines running across the mallet head perpendicular to the face, giving it its name Zebra.

"Taylor is the guy who got me interested in buying and working on old Rolls-Royces," Littler says. "He told me it was easier to align this putter. I stayed at his home when I went up to play the Crosby in January, and he had a prototype of the putter. I took it to the course for a practice round on Wednesday. I putted all right with it, so I used it in the tournament. I putted super and won.

"I was able to line up those lines better than I'd been able to line up the face of the putter. I putted for more than 30 years lining up the face of the putter, and I haven't looked at the face of this one a single time. I just take those lines and line them up and drive them right straight through to where I want the ball to go. Before, I was lining up left and missing a lot of putts left. The lines straightened me out."

Partly owing to the new putter, Littler has set up to putt differently this year. "I'd been a stand-up putter, but I can see the lines on this putter better if I set up more back and under," he says. "I'm lowering my right side, more as I would for a regular shot. I noticed that Jack Nicklaus sets up this way."

Says Arnold Palmer, with no more than a touch of jealousy, "Gene seems to have everything rolling right at the hole." Palmer also has used the Zebra

The Mechanics of Gene Littler's Smooth Swing

Gene Littler's swing is an eye-opening example of the value of smooth tempo. Close examination reveals mechanical flaws that might bring a less gifted player to ruin. He is swinging a long iron here, aiming at the gap in the trees (as indicated on photos). Littler takes the club quickly inside (1), which results in a flat swing plane going back. He makes a fine shoulder turn and gets the club in excellent position at the top (4), but his first move down (5) looks to be a slight spinning of the shoulders which moves the club outside or above his backswing plane. Littler is "coming over the top" and it may be from this action that he gets a

putter, which now is in mass production. (Editor's note: See article on the Zebra putter elsewhere in this book.)

In addition to a new putter, Littler is now carrying a full set of graphite-shafted clubs. He began playing graphite woods when he came back from the cancer surgery late in 1972, then added the irons at the 1975 U.S. Open.

"I know I drive the ball farther with graphite, but it's hard to say if it's 12 yards farther or 28 yards farther, because I switched to a graphite driver when I started playing again," he says.

"I don't hit the irons any farther, but I'm really enjoying them. I think the ball flies softer and more uniformly. The trajectory is higher. I think graphite irons would help the average guy. The shaft is lighter and there's more weight in the clubhead, so it's easier to get the ball up in the air, especially with the long irons."

Littler hasn't tried to swing his woods and irons any differently than he did before his surgery, but feels that, out of necessity, he is playing more with his right side. How does he reconcile that with the gospel-like modern teaching emphasis on left-side dominance?

"I always believed that golf was played primarily with the left side—that you pulled the club down with the left-side muscles," he says. "But I am minus some big muscles in my left side now, and I have come to realize that either I never played that way or else golf is a much more right-sided game than I ever thought it was.

"Ben Hogan was so correct when he said that your left side sets up the swing so your right side can hit the heck out of the ball. That's really what happens in the best swings. You pull down with the left side to get in position to whale it with the right side at the bottom of the swing.

"I feel more right-sided even though I don't think it would show in pictures. But my left side isn't all that weak. It's a fantastic commentary on the human body the way other muscles surrounding the area where I had the surgery have strengthened. I don't miss the ones I lost that much."

Other tour players who have watched him for most of his career, like George Archer, say they can see a stronger right-side role in Littler's swing. "He's pushing the club more with the right side from the top of the swing instead of pulling down with the left side the way he used to," Archer says. "I used to look at his swing and see a car pulling a trailer. Now I see the trailer pushing the car. Gene's always been an arms swinger. He has tremendous forearms—they're thicker than Arnold Palmer's. Maybe he developed them working on his old cars."

Phil Rodgers agrees and remembers, photographically, that the medium-sized Littler was a good shot putter in high school, setting a school record. "He's not as strong with his left side since the surgery, but he can still hold a packed suitcase above his shoulder with his left hand," Rodgers says.

What message would Littler give the weekend golfer based on his intense experience with left-sidedness and right-sidedness?

"Well, I guess progbably the worst thing you can tell the average golfer is that you have to hit with your right side. But you have to hit with the right at the proper instant. This is where it gets tricky. It would be ridiculous for me to tell a guy to take the club to the top of his swing, delay his right-side action until he's almost to the bottom, and then hit it with the right side. He'd probably fall down. That move takes years of practice—you aren't going to find it on the first tee. I would never preach a delayed hit. I would tell the average golfer that the right-side hit is an involuntary move that follows from what precedes it. From the top of the swing, he should move the lower body first and leave everything else up there. But he

new feeling of right-sidedness, although his swing always has exhibited this characteristic. At this point, most players would allow the right side to overpower the left, with disasterous results. But Littler makes the change from backswing to downswing so smoothly—and keeps the left arm and side in such a firm, leading position—that he not only gets away with it, but indeed arrives at impact in a superb striking posture. Through the ball, the clubhead is traveling directly down the target line and his left arm is fully extended, still leading the right. That's a combination that produces power and accuracy.

GENE LITTLER'S TIPS ON TEMPO

• Swing all your clubs with the same tempo or pace. Swing your 2-iron as slowly as your 9-iron.

• Concentrate on smoothness and rhythm as you prepare for a shot. Take a couple of practice swings and then hit the ball with that same relaxed tempo.

• The first foot or so of your takeaway sets up good tempo. You have to be smooth there.

• The top of the swing is the most crucial area for good tempo. If you are going slowly just before you get there and just as you start down, your tempo won't be bad.

• When my tempo is good, I almost feel I'm swinging the club with my feet. Good footwork promotes good tempo. I've always liked the way Sam Snead seems to start his downswings with his feet. The top part of his body doesn't appear to move until after his feet start.

• Don't forget that a golf swing has to be greater than the sum of its parts, Sometimes we get so concerned with mechanical position we forget we have to fit them all together smoothly.

• Tempo requires practice, like everything else in this game. I'll hit dozens of practice balls thinking about nothing but smoothing out my tempo.

LITTLER'S TOUR RECORD

Year	Wins	Tour Money	Money Position
1954	1	$ 8,327	28
1955	4	28,974	5
1956	3	23,833	6
1957	1	13,427	18
1958	0	12,897	27
1959	5	38,296	2
1960	2	26,837	8
1961	1	29,245	9
1962	2	66,200	2
1963	0	32,566	12
1964	0	33,173	15
1965	1	58,898	9
1966	0	68,345	7
1967	0	38,086	32
1968	0	61,631	26
1969	2	112,737	6
1970	0	79,001	22
1971	2	98,687	14
1972	0	11,119	135
1973	1	95,308	18
1974	0	102,822	20
1975	3	182,883	5
	28	$1,223,292	

should try to keep everything coordinated. That's the meaning of good tempo."

When Littler talks about tempo, the world drops what it's doing to listen, a la those television commercials for a Wall Street firm in which someone says to someone else in the middle of a crowded scene, "My broker is H. F. Burple, and H. F. Burple says . . ." and the silence suddenly becomes deafening as everybody cranes necks to eavesdrop.

Gene Littler swings a golf club with the same elegant style Sinatra brings to a song, Nureyev to a dance, Olivier to a Shakespearean role. The pace is courtly and pervaded with poise and control, and it doesn't vary from the first shot of a tournament to the last. For all the effort he seems to expend, Littler might be pouring a glass of milk before bedtime. If his swing were a piece of music, it would be a Strauss waltz.

It is too easy to assume that he came by his rhythmic action naturally. His inherent talent is considerable, but he consciously practices tempo by the hour and has evolved definite thoughts on how to improve it (see box). Essentially, he strives to be slow in two potentially dangerous speed zones: the takeaway and at the top.

It also is too easy to assume that, because Littler's tempo is aesthetically pleasing, he has a model swing mechanically. In truth, his swing is not one of the 10 or 12 best on the tour and never has been. His tempo is so good he has time to correct positional errors; his is a forgiving swing. "Gene the Machine" in reality should be called "Gene the Metronome."

He takes the club away from the ball abruptly to the inside of the target line, until it's about horizontal. Then he lifts it almost straight up to the top, in tandem with a big hip turn. The upshot is that he tends to come over the ball with his right shoulder on the downswing. If he were to try swinging the club under Hogan's famous imaginary pane of glass that represents a prefect plane, there would be broken glass all over the place.

Through the ball, Littler turns a bit too rapidly to the left with his lower body, the left knee stiffening rather than staying fixed for maximum power. Sam Snead swings in a similar pattern, but Snead is stronger and can hang on with the left hand better through the ball.

If you aren't careful, of course, you can sound like the class dunce second-guessing a swing like Littler's. That kind of talk is best saved for late-night cocktail-lounge discussions about the ideal swing that none of us will ever see on this particular planet.

Littler is the first to admit his swing isn't what he'd like it to be—and still believes he struck the ball more purely as an amateur than he has since—but the telling point is that he gets outstanding results.

The story is told of the day perfectionist Littler was disconsolate on the practice range after a round in the Hawaiian Open, and asked another pro to give him a lesson. Littler complained that he had been outdriven by 40 yards all day, hadn't hit a shot on the face of the club and probably ought to be looking for an easier way to make a living. The other pro sympathized with him and, somewhat hesitantly, asked what Littler had shot.

Moaned Littler, "67."

Says Steve Reid, a former peer of Littler's now working for the tour office, "Gene isn't a pure striker of the ball like Hogan, but he makes up for it with great self-control. He loses his temper—I've seen him ram a club through the bottom of his bag after a bad shot—but he doesn't let himself get upset to the point it bothers his game. He's smart enough to realize that minor irritations will pass. He keeps an uncluttered mind and reasons his way through."

Since the cancer surgery, Littler's attitude is even more philosophical. "I have a little different perspective on life now," he says. "I'm not as afraid to make a mistake. I shoot at the flag a lot more than I used to. I've been very guilty in my career of thinking negatively. I was all right as long as I was playing well, but when I slumped a little I didn't think I could play at all. Now I think much more positively. My son got me interested in psychocybernetics and I took a course called PACE that helped me a great deal. I've learned that a better mental outlook is what separates the *really* good player from the good player."

For the newly positive Littler, the future is today. Speculation about his

health varies wildly on the tour. You can hear, to put it perhaps too bluntly, that he is cured of cancer, or you can hear that he does not have long to live. The most popular opinion, usually attributed to one medical source or another, is that survival is problematic for five years after the type of surgery Littler had, but after the five years you don't have to worry.

"I hear that one a lot," Littler says, "but I don't know where it comes from. My doctors have never told me anything like that, and they've been candid with me. I feel very well right now and I'm just living my life for today. I'm on sort of a health kick, not eating any white-flour or white-sugar products. Otherwise I live normally—I've always taken pretty good care of myself. As long as I feel this good, I have to be optimistic. I could learn tomorrow that I have cancer, but so could any of us.

"I feel very fortunate to be able to play golf again, and I'm paying more attention to the game. I used to come home from the tour and work with my cars and never practice. I would have to go back on the tour to get myself back in shape. Then about the time I was back in shape I'd be coming home again, because I've always wanted to be with my family. It became a vicious circle. Now I spend time at home working on my game, and my play is sharper over-all as a result.

"I used to say, 'Give me 5 more good years and I'll be off this tour so fast.' I started saying that about 15 years ago. I don't say that anymore. Maybe I'm on a little bit of a mission, trying to give some of the people who face the illness I did a little lift. I'm going to play as long as I can play well."

Everyone in golf hopes that will be a long time for Gentleman Gene Littler.

The Glorious Gambling Games—
Gamemanship and Gambitry of Golf

By CLEMENT McQUAID
(Editor of *Gambler's Digest* and
World Renowned Authority on Gambling)

YES, DUFFERS, there is a Santa! He showed up late in '75, but wrapped his golfer gifts, "Don't open 'til January 1, 1976!"

Santa, employed by the venerable USGA, gave millions of America's golfers the present of a lifetime, and, in the true Christmas spirit, magnanimously spread those presents among the stroke poor, with generous extras for them and token remembrances for those already endowed. The losers of '75 could become the winners of '76—thanks to the new USGA handicap policy issued late in '75 which became effective January 1, 1976.

You golfers already know of the change—a handicap increase from 85 percent of your scoring differentials to 96 percent. And those 11 extra percentage points become the edge—the leg up. It's what we higher handicap golfers have been waiting for. Now, finally, the 12-20 handicappers have a decent (statistically better) chance to win than ever before without charity bets! And that golfing friends is what this article and the game is all about. Winning! We duffers, who found through round after round of play that our low handicap friend(s) always (almost always) won and seemed to win by just enough to pocket the money, can truly thank Dr. Francis Scheid, GOLFER'S DIGEST, and *Gambler's Digest* and the Canadian Golf Association for the USGA's change of heart.

But it's here, it's now and Gamesmanship, Gambits and the Gambling Games of Golf need adjustment to meet the new ruling. It's a whole new betting golf game fans!

Mr. Oddsmaker, Bob Martin, of Las Vagas, in his treatise on gambling in golf in *Gambler's Digest,* was forced to concentrate his "best bets" in golf to the following:

The average golfer who bets on himself doesn't bet smartly! (His disadvantage was 23 points on the handicap system! The differential percentage established was 85, but most mathematicians including Dr. Scheid proved the truly fair handicap differential percentage should be 108!) Knowing this disadvantage, Mr. Oddsmaker told his 12-20 handicap readers to bet *only* on their strengths—putting, chipping, or driving—or "bet against your opponent's weaknesses!" Because the handicap system clearly favored the low handicapper, most 12-20 handicap golfers were destined to be born losers if they accepted the standard differentials in a Nassau game with a 3 to 8 low handicapper!

Thousands of computerized comparisons have proven that a 3 handicapper could easily spot a 15 with 12 strokes and win 70 percent of the time. What an edge!

Does the new system change all this? "Not quite," says Mr. Oddsmaker. "With the new 96 percent differential, the 12-20 handicap golfer still has less than an even chance to beat a 3 or 4 handicapper! Consistency, in golf, like any other game, pays off! I think that the USGA played a game of gradualism and gave another nod to the low handicapper by refusing to adjust to a differential of at least 100 percent!"

But our millions of duffers in the 90-100 score area now have a 50 percent better edge than they did last year. But don't double up yet. Read on to pick out the betting game that favors you and your style—one that will reward you in the payoff at the 19th hole.

Best Bet: Low handicappers put in birdies and greenies to give you an extra edge.

Best Bets:
- Know your opponent's weaknessess. Play and bet to them.
- If you don't know the course, shy away from side bets on holes.
- If you receive strokes, press when you can before stroke holes.
- Insist on Medal Play of you're more consistent than your opponent.
- Don't accept bets without full stroke concession and preferably with a ½ extra stroke per 4-stroke difference to allow for USGA vigorish!
- For best gambitry at golf, read Stephen Potter's *Gamesmanship* and *One Upmanship*. Both books will give you great psychological "edge ups!"

Golf is a great game. Over $2 billion is bet each year by the players in the perpetual quest of score reduction. Remember, every club has its hustlers, so know your game, know the bet, know your chances and, above all else, know your opponents and their playing abilities, your best bet is no bet! (Or maybe a tiny bet just to keep your interest going.)

TEMPIS FUGIT

A friend of mine went to his golf club and inquired of the threesome coming in to the 19th hole if he might join them the following day. After they agreed, he said he would meet them at 8 AM although he might be a few minutes late. The next day he is there at 8 AM and plays par golf with a left-handed set of clubs. The other three are quite impressed and agree to have him join them the following day. He said he would be there at 8 AM but again might be a few minutes late. At 8 AM the next day he is there and again plays a magnificent game but this time with a right-handed set of golf clubs. They marvel again and ask how he determines what set he should use each day. He said when he gets up in the morning, if his wife is on her right side, he plays with right-hand clubs. If she is on her left side, he plays with left-hand clubs. And what if she is on her back?—"That's when I am a few minutes late!"

HOW FAR SHOULD YOU STAND FROM THE BALL?

Jack Grout, long-time instructor of Nicklaus, found the answer by studying many of the great players

By LARRY DENNIS

Barbara Nicklaus

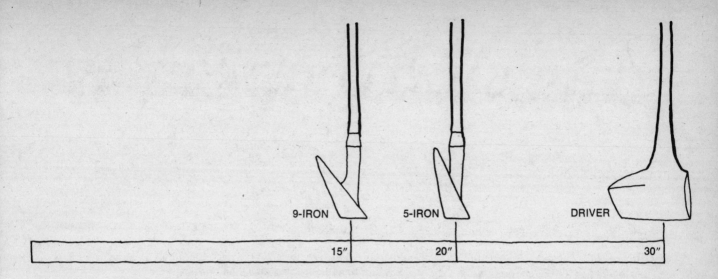

9-IRON   5-IRON   DRIVER

15″   20″   30″

MIDWAY through 1974, when Jack Nicklaus was struggling with a slight slump (his slumps are never large), Jack Grout had the answer. "Nicklaus is standing 2 inches farther from the ball than he used to," Grout declared.

He should know. As the long-time professional at Scioto C.C. in Columbus, Ohio, Grout taught Nicklaus to play. Now retired, Grout remains the man to whom golf's premier star goes for help.

Grout's diagnosis of Nicklaus' trouble was consistent with his belief that you cannot stand too close to the ball.

"In all my years of teaching, I've only seen two players stand too close to the ball," says Grout, "and I can't remember who they were."

On the other hand, Grout contends that 90 percent of the players he sees stand too far from the ball, which creates poor posture and numerous swing ailments.

Once a player on the professional tour, Grout would stand in the footprints of stars like Byron Nelson, Ben Hogan, Jimmy Demaret and others and confirm his observation that they all stood the same distance from the ball. From this experience, he developed guidelines so that any player can make sure he is standing the correct distance from the ball.

A golfer 5′-9″ or taller should stand 30 inches from the ball with a driver, 20 inches with a 5-iron and 15 inches with a 9-iron. Shorter players should stand farther away, but usually not more than an inch. Measure from the left toe to the middle of the ball.

"Those are guidelines," Grout warns. "Obviously everybody can't stand the same distance away. There has to be some adjustment for differences in height and arm length. For example, Tom Weiskopf is 6′-3″ with a 35-inch sleeve, so he'll stand half an inch closer than Nicklaus, who is 5′-11″ with a 32½-inch sleeve. But your adjustments are made simply by complying with the rules of good posture."

Grout believes good posture starts with being erect. "Hogan, Nelson and Jones all were very erect with the upper body," he says. "And Jack is perfect."

Grout wants your weight balanced between the balls and heels of the feet, your knees flexed but not too deeply, your arms extended just enough to swing clear of the body. He says this posture enables a player to turn more easily and to fully work the legs. The erect posture, combined with standing relatively close to the ball, causes the arms to swing in a more upright fashion, giving you a straighter return path through the ball.

Grout says shorter players, portly players and thick-chested players must bend over slightly more, but never too far. Bending too much, usually a result of standing too far from the ball, causes the weight to go toward the toes. The results are poor balance, a curtailed body turn, and a tendency to swing outside the target line and "come over the top" on the forward swing.

One who had this problem was touring professional Gibby Gilbert.

"Three years ago Gilbert was going to quit tournament golf," Grout recalls. "He came to me and I saw immediately he was standing 6 inches too far from the ball. This caused him to hit either duck hooks or pushes to the right. I had him assume my stance, and he immediately started hitting the ball straight. And he could fade it or draw it when he wanted to. He told me he was going to start practicing with the new stance right then. I told him to get to a phone and tell 'em he'd be at the next tournament, that he didn't need that much practice. He's been playing better ever since."

Grout feels poor posture is the main reason for George Archer's lengthly slump. "He's a marvelous putter, but he ruins himself with the probably the poorest posture on the tour. He should straighten his legs—if your knees flex past your toe line, it puts too much crouch in the hips and hinders turning. And he should stand closer to the ball. It would make him a better player because it would make his swing more upright and he'd gain both distance and accuracy."

Grout feels poor posture is the main reason for George Archer's lengthy slump. "He's a marvelous putter, but he ruins himself with probably the poorest posture on the tour. He should the shorter player who needs the longer club, he says. "Wee Bobby" Cruickshank, still an active player at the age of 81 despite a recent stroke, stands only 5′-4½″ but swings a 45½-inch driver.

"He stands fairly erect, and the longer shaft gives him better leverage, a bigger arc and more clubhead speed," Grout explains. He recommends that anybody shorter than 5′-9″ use a longer club, from 44½ to 45 inches.

"There will be no problem controlling it," Grout contends, "and the shorter player needs it for the increased distance it will give him."

Oh yes, about Nicklaus—he's back standing closer to the ball and looking for a big year. Grout is a persuasive teacher.

Ambidextrous Golfer

By TOMMY KOUZMANOFF

HARRY PEZZULLO is one golfer who would much rather switch than fight a bad score.

That's because Pezzullo, the veteran professional at Plum Tree National Golf Club in Chicago suburban Harvard, Ill., can play the game expertly—righthanded or lefthanded.

Born a righthander, Pezzullo, a pro for 40 years and known to virtually every golfer in the Chicago area because of his teaching talents and his many contributions to the game, recalls the incident that resulted in his becoming an ambidextrous player:

"That's one day in my golfing career I'll never forget because it placed me in a unique class of golfers. Here's how it happened:

"I was playing the Rhode Island Country Club course where I started as a caddie. Playing in a foursome back of us was a Catholic priest, a Rev. Peter Connoly of Providence. We lived in West Barrington, a suburb not far away. Father Connoly was impressed with the way I was hitting the ball for a 14-year-old. As we came to a long par-three hole, a water hole, Father Connoly offered a very tempting challenge:

"This next hole calls for a pretty long carry on the tee shot, sonny, 200 yards at least, maybe 225. If you can drive the ball over the pond I'll give you my set of clubs.

"Man, how I could use that set of clubs. The ones I was playing with were my brother, Jesse's, the only set among nine of us brothers. We passed them around.

"Well, I really put the screws on a spoon, known now as a 4-wood. I belted that tee shot over the drink with a few yards to spare. With that, the priest gave me his clubs.

"But, what kind do you think they were? Lefthanded! Now, I had to learn to play the game lefthanded, as well as righthanded, if I was going to use my own clubs."

Harry Pezzullo did—well enough to try the pro tour and play the game well enough to take two sets of clubs wherever he goes, one righthanded and one lefthanded. He has shot in the 60s and is the only ambidextrous golfer to have scored holes-in-one both ways.

There have been many times during his career that he wasn't sure which clubs to take to the first tee.

"If I played extra well the last time lefthanded, I'd stay lefthanded the next time out," said the 62-year-old Pezzullo who during one stage of his career was president of the Illinois PGA for 14 consecutive years and has been a vice-president of the National PGA.

"But, that didn't always work out. A person never knows when he's going to have a bad round regardless of how he feels about his game."

Like the day you were playing in a pro-am and a spectator needled you after you had played what he thought was poorly for you the first nine holes?

"Right," laughed Pezzullo, a gifted speaker who has regaled listeners with wit and quips that have trademarked him as the Bob Hope of the local

"This guy hollers to me:

"'Pezzullo, you could do better left-handed.'

"Well, he doesn't know that I'm ambidextrous, so I told him, okay, I'll try playing lefthanded the last nine holes. I told my caddie:

"'Go to my car and get my lefthanded clubs out of the trunk.'

"Okay, after shooting 39 righthanded the front side, I throw out a 32 lefthanded. That shut my heckler up for the rest of the round."

From that day on, Pezzullo's heckler became one of his best friends . . . and believers.

Another time—way back in Pezzullo's long and colorful career—a member of the Cape May Country Club, Cape May, N.J. (the club no longer exists) where Pezzullo was the pro before heading west and settling in the Chicago area, challenged Harry to an unusual match.

The member would play righthanded, the only way he could play, and Pezzullo lefthanded.

"This member said to me if he couldn't beat me playing his regular way against my lefthanded game he'd throw his clubs in the lake and buy a new set from me," recalled the straw-hatted Pezzullo who rarely takes off the hat for the same reason as Sam Snead and Byron Nelson. They're bald like Pezzullo.

"Show me the day a club pro can't use a good sale. So, I took up his challenge and did I ever throw one hot nine holes at him. I fired a 34 and whipped him. The match was only nine holes.

"The guy was so frustrated—he thought he was a pretty good player, you know—that he did go to the water hole and threw his clubs in. They were still in that lake many years later when the course gave way to a housing development. A construction crew came up with the clubs during a period of excavation."

Pezzullo was pro at Mission Hills daily fee club in Northbrook, Ill. for 25 years, then went to Plum Tree 5 years ago when Mission Hills was sold to a group that completely redesigned the course to make room for expensive condominiums.

Harry's brothers kidded him for a long time about his playing golf lefthanded and he tells why:

"I did everything righthanded. As a kid, I was a righthanded pitcher in baseball. I bowled righthanded. Jesse used to say:

"'You're all mixed up. You don't know which way to play.'"

Pezzullo's oldest brother was kidding, of course. Harry displayed poten-

tial early. In 1932, he won the highly competitive Rhode Island State Amateur. He was only 18. He became one of the youngest head professionals in the country when he took the head professionalship at Meshanticut Country Club in the Rhode Island area when he was 19.

He's made six holes-in-one—one of them lefthanded. That was the day he fired the 34 at the Cape May member.

Pezzullo doesn't claim to be a Paul Hahn, but he does have some trick shots. He tells about one:

"I carry a lefthanded 5-iron in the bag. Mostly for trouble shots. Actually, I can turn the club around and hit a ball righthanded from against a fence or a bush or a tree with the clubhead upside down."

He pulled that shot—with the head of the 5-iron upside down and swinging righthanded—a few years ago in an exhibition match commemorating the 50th year of the Chicago Park District Waveland course in Lincoln Park.

He did it on a short par 3, a 140-yarder, and he almost had a hole-in-one!

Pezzullo's lefthanded talents extend beyond golf.

"I even learned to write lefthanded," grins Pezzullo, twice winner of the Illinois PGA "Club Pro of the Year" award and once was accorded that honor by the National PGA.

While he was president of the Illinois PGA, he assisted the late Charlie Bartlett in lining up pros for the *Chicago Tribune's* outdoor golf classes which annually heralded the start of a new golf season.

Each year, he is the featured speaker at the all-sports banquet of Immaculate Conception High School in Elmhurst and highlights it by presenting the Harry Pezzullo Trophy to the school's outstanding scholar-athlete. For speaking, Harry receives no fee and the trophy he donates is paid for from his own pocket.

"You can never do too much good for kids," says Harry who can turn serious just as easily as he can turn comedian.

There are a lot of fine golfers among Italians. And Pezzullo has beaten many of them. Three times, in 1965-66, and again two years ago, he won the Italian Open in Milwaukee.

Harry feels he holds a big advantage in being able to teach the game lefty as well as righty.

"To teach lefthanded and righthanded, you should be able to demonstrate the grip, the stance, the address and the various segments of the swing. Not just talk about it. A lot of lefthanded golfers come to me for lessons because I'm the only pro around here who can play lefthanded as well as righthanded."

Quite a guy, this Harry Pezzullo. And, that's no lefthanded compliment."

Here's A Shaggy Dog Story

By HAMP ROGERS
(Sports Writer,
The Columbia (S.C.) *Record*)

MOVE OVER Rin Tin Tin and Lassie, Shag Bag Rusty has arrived.

Most Boykin spaniels aren't very good golfers. In fact, Rusty's handicap is so high he would rather not mention it. But when it comes to shagging golf balls, the 5-year-old canine is the envy of every driving range superintendent.

Nearly 5 years ago Ollie Kelly, who drifts back and forth between a scratch

and a four handicap, started teaching Rusty to retrieve golf balls while living in Savannah, Ga.

"It was by accident that Rusty learned how to pick up shag balls," said the 55-year-old Kelly. "I started hitting them to him in the yard and he would catch them in his mouth and bring them back to me."

When Kelly first started teaching his

Rusty catching a shag ball . . . .

spaniel to retrieve balls, the only problem he had was teaching Rusty to turn the shag bag upright when he put it on the ground.

"I taught Rusty to use his feet to turn the bag over so he could drop the balls in it," he added. "Once he learned that much, all I had to do was place his head in the bag and shake the balls loose. From that point on he did it like he had been shagging balls all his life."

Rusty's fielding talents don't stop on the golf course. The little canine gets his dog food dish, closes doors to the house behind him, retrieves slippers for his master and even will go on a fishing trip.

Like all good spaniels, Rusty loves the water. One day Ollie hit a ball in the lake into about 18 inches of water. Rusty walked around in the water until he felt the ball with his feet, then dipped down and picked it up.

Kelly recalls another occasion when Rusty attempted to find the newspaper in the yard during a rain storm. After an hour of searching without finding the paper anywhere, Rusty returned to the house, slamming the door behind him.

"The next time I asked him to go for the paper in the rain he looked out of the window first," Kelly said with a smile. "He's surely a smart dog."

While Kelly's partner fell upon the ancient game of golf by accident, his trainer comes from a long background of sports.

After growing up in the Atlanta, Ga., area, Kelly decided minor league baseball looked better at the time than college. So in 1940 Kelly marshalled his semi-pro experience and packed his bags for the next train to Miami.

Kelly played with a class B Miami club until he could find a spot at second base on a Salley League team in Savannah. He later was promoted to the class AA Memphis South team where he hit over .300 and was selected to play on the all-star squad in 1948.

"I loved playing baseball, but I just got tired of the traveling," recalled Kelly, who now builds houses on the Seabrook Island resort where he plays most of his golf.

With the exception of a 3½-year trek

in the Army, which Kelly served on a military baseball team where he was the only player who hadn't spent time in the major leagues, it was 10 years before the former second baseman told the White Sox organization he was ready to settle down.

The construction business keeps Kelly busy more than he would like these days, but he does find time to play a round of golf once or twice a week on one of the most beautiful courses in the nation.

The Seabrook Island course, which has known only one professional since it opened in 1973—Tom Wagner—plays to 6,850 yards from the blue tees. The par-72 layout stretches through the woods for the first nine, and then cuts back to the oceanfront clubhouse across marshes and sandy beaches.

"My four handicap here is like a scratch handicap anywhere else," Kelly explained.

"With these narrow fairways on the front side, and the wind on the back, this course is one of the most difficult I've played."

While the natural surroundings of Seabrook offers golfers a real challenge, the wilderness of the low-country island provides a perfect playground for Rusty and his poodle sidekick—Coco.

"I've never taken the dogs out on the course with me," Kelly noted. "But I don't have to worry about them on the driving range because they pick up only the white balls, not the yellow and red-striped range balls."

And who was it that said dogs are man's best friends?

and putting it back in the shag-bag.

Johnny Miller Turns Killer... On The Course

BY WELLS TWOMBLY

THE NAMES come screaming out of nowhere. They festoon the sports pages like bright lights on a honky-tonk strip. Before journalists covering the sun-kissed golf tour can turn them into living, breathing chunks of flesh and muscle, they disappear. Some of them vanish without a trace. A few end up behind the counter in the pro shop of a cheap golf club located in the middle of an expensive housing development. Most of them drop back into the great mob scene, writhing and struggling to make the cut.

They all seem to be winsome blond college graduates, who grew up watching their fathers give lessons without end to newly rich females with sagging figures. They not only talk alike—when and if they have something to say—they all seem to be punched out of the same sheet of cookies. None of them has any unusual desires, no hidden passions of any sort. At times, their names all seem interchangeable. The leader of one tournament is someone named, say, Connors Jones. The leader of the next is Ben Connors, who is followed by Gordan Grant, who is replaced by Grant Connors. They are all neat, clean and devoted to the Protestant ethic. They all went to Oklahoma State or the University of Houston or Brigham Young University.

But Johnny Miller is different. Right? Despite his tousled hair, his California beach boy good looks, his rigid conformity to the stereotype, Johnny Miller is a champion. Yes! He is the next great golfer, the imperial successor to Jack Nicklaus, Arnold Palmer, Sam Snead, Ben Hogan, Walter Hagen, Bobby Jones, a line as long as the British royal family's. Before he's through, Johnny Miller is going to be a multi-millionaire. Yes! Yes! That's because Johnny Miller is different. Yes! Yes! Yes!

Unlike the other lean, hungry, innocent-eyed blond boys, the ones who flashed and faded, Johnny Miller is bold and confident. Good grief, he's almost arrogant, although the strictness of his Mormon upbringing helps him control that dreadful sin. Johnny Miller acts as if he ought to be shooting in the high 50s, as if God came to him in a dream and told him that it was possible. A round of 71, acceptable to anybody else, can send him into a mumbling, muttering spasm of public apology. If Palmer was a reckless adventurer with a puzzled look and a hacker's follow-through, if Nicklaus was a flawless piece of fine machinery with so much money in the family that he didn't really need to turn professional, then Johnny Miller is the most intense perfectionist the game has ever known, a white-hot piece of metal who enjoys taking the lead and then reducing the golf course to a pile of burned grass and blistered sand.

And what marketing potential the man has! That is, after all, the real name of the game these days. Toss that name around on your tongue for awhile . . . Johnny Miller . . . Johnnnnnnnnny

Miller . . . Johnnnnnnnnnny Miller. Good, solid, substantial name, Johnny Miller. He is the ultimate end product of the white man's culture, playing what is still largely a white man's sport. Small wonder that by the start of spring, his agent, Ed Barner of Los Angeles, had turned down more than $500,000 in endorsement offers, evil stuff like booze and tobacco and pizza parlors. The horizons are unlimited. Somebody wants him to do five challenge matches for television—Johnny Miller Against The World. The winner would get $150,000 and the loser $50,000. Johnnnnnnnnny Miller! Beautiful!

"The man behaves as if he has discovered the secret of the game," says Tony Jacklin, who shakes his head in bemusement, as most of the other professionals do when they discuss this devastating wunderkind. "If he continues to improve, the rest of us might as well stay home and watch on television to see how close Johnny Miller can come to shooting a 55."

That is what Johnny Miller feels he is capable of. He thinks he can dominate the game of golf for the next decade as no man ever has before him. Certainly, no man has ever had such amazing streaks. It was Miller who won the first three tournaments of 1974, won eight tournaments in all and set a record with $353,021 in prize money. ("Only one-third of what he made," says his agent.) It was Miller who opened the tour in 1975 by sweeping the first two events, in Phoenix and Tucson, by an incredible 23 strokes, firing eight of the best consecutive rounds anybody could remember.

It was Miller who floundered embarrassingly in the Bing Crosby National Pro-Am at Pebble Beach, after predicting that a 64 over one of America's most treacherous courses was not an impossibility for him. "I've created a monster," he conceded. But it was also Miller who took a week off, actually went fishing and then devastated the Bob Hope Desert Classic, his third victory in four tournaments.

Johnny Miller is a ruthless competitor. Forget those talks he makes to Mormon youth groups. Ignore the fact that he does not smoke, drink, swear or consume such mild stimulants as coffee or cola drinks. Overlook, too, the fact that his idea of dissipation is taking his wife and three small children out for double hamburgers and milk shakes. On the course, with sticks in his hands, this noble young human being is a blue-eyed assassin. When he missed the green on the 16th hole at Cypress Point, he entertained the customers at the Crosby by flinging his iron in the best tradition of Tommy Bolt.

"He doesn't need booze or pills to get high," says prosaic old Gene Littler, the recovered cancer patient who defeated Miller at Crosby's little lawn party. "When he starts rolling in those birdies and eagles, he's flying. That's what the kids call a 'natural high.' That's what he's on. He gets high on golf. It'll tell you what the test of young Johnny Miller is going to be. Pretty soon the public is going to get tired of watching him run off these streaks of tournament victories. They'll ask him to prove how great he is by winning the major tournaments. He won't be allowed to forget that Nicklaus has won 14 majors and he's had only one (the U.S. Open in 1973). You fellows in the press will hound him

Johnny Miller does not smoke, drink or swear, but on the golf course, he is transformed into a blue-eyed assassin.

about that."

Fade quickly to a magazine headline, designed to stun hell out of the casual reader: "Why Can't Johnny Miller Win The Big Ones?" It will neglect to mention anywhere in the text that in his own unusual way Johnny Miller does not give a good gosh-darn whether he wins the U.S. Open, the PGA, the Masters or the British Open every year for the next decade. What he wants to do is exactly what he's been doing, string tournament victories together like jewels on a dowager's clavicle.

"All the tournaments on the tour are important," says Miller. "A lot of hard work, a lot of money and a lot of love goes into each one. They're going to say that I psyche out when one of the majors comes up. Let them. They mean a lot to me, but I'm not going to tear myself up worrying about them. I bear down regardless of whether I'm playing at the Masters in Augusta or in the Gomer Pyle-Peanut Butter Open in Possum Trot. I'm proud to win any tournaments."

There are two distinct Johnny Millers, inseparable, but different in texture and context.

The religious, highly domesticated Miller smiles relentlessly, signs autographs behind the 18th green for interminable periods and speaks with plausible humility. Golf is something he could give up tomorrow. It is far less important to him than his family or his church, both of which bring deep personal comfort. Just watching the children throw bits of hamburger bun back and forth across the table is better than shooting a 64.

Then there is the bumptious, aggressive young warrior who cannot stop talking about his own ability and his relative place in the history of the game. This is a Johnny Miller of materialism, even though ten percent of his earnings are tithed to the Church of Jesus Christ of Latter Day Saints. His closets contain so many clothes that he was named one of the world's 12 best dressed men and Sears, Roebuck Inc. offers a "Johnny Miller Collection." He has a condominium at Hilton Head, S.C. He is building a $300,000 villa with six bedrooms near the tenth green at Silverado Golf Club, an oasis in the vineyards of Napa County. He owns a number of elegant automobiles and admits to driving them beyond the limits sanctioned by the California

Highway Patrol. He drives his Porsche Carrera at speeds up to 140 mph—he does not say where—and envisions himself at LeMans.

Already he is receiving $15,000 for a one-day exhibition. Nicklaus gets $12,000, Plamer gets $10,000 and Lee Trevino gets $8,000. He will make approximately $1.25 million this year endorsing tomato juice in Japan, men's slacks in Switzerland and golf camps in the United Kingdom. When the gallery insists on taking his picture, he is capable of saying, with muted sarcasm, "There were so many cameras out there, I thought I was playing in the Tokyo Open."

When a newsman laughs at the remark, he replies that he is a private sort of person and doesn't really need to tell jokes the way Lee Trevino does, a surprisingly catty observation. Asked about his own skills, he has no difficulty saying, "I think golf historians will probably say that I was the greatest front-runner of my time. When I get the lead, I'm nearly impossible to catch." He does not consider himself cocky, merely honest.

Ever since he shot that astonishing 63 on the final round and won the U.S. Open at Oakmont, Johnny Miller has been laboring mightily to establish the illusion of a great cheek-to-jowl confrontation between Nicklaus and himself. It is possible that the 35-year-old Nicklaus has become an obsession with Miller. Friends have suggested to him privately that he cool it. But he won't.

More then likely, it is part of the strong vein of romanticism in his soul. When he strides out to meet Nicklaus, he is, at age 28, the classic young upstart of Western mythology challenging the quickest gun in the territory.

Miller says he is always aware of Nicklaus' presence on the course; he listens for the gallery shouting on some distant meadow. Nicklaus, on the other hand, says he is not preoccupied with Miller; still, he is careful to lather his young opponent with soothing praise.

"Whenever Johnny is out on the course, he is a danger to everyone, not just to me," says Nicklaus. "Miller has the soundest swing on the tour. What's

more, he knows exactly how to use it. I've never seen such confident putting. If I were a teaching pro, I'd start by showing students films of Johnny Miller swinging his clubs. He's just reaching his physical peak. He has great powers of concentration. Miller can close out the rest of the world when he plays. I admire that."

Yet Nicklaus is not above a little gamesmanship: There is Miller sitting in the press room listening while somebody asks Nicklaus if he is always conscious of what Miller is up to. With a moderate smirk, Nicklaus says: "No, not really. By the way, Johnny, what *did* you shoot out there today?"

Miller's psyche escapes intact. He admits that the best player in the world is still Jack Nicklaus. "I have to admit that he's No. 1," he says. "Anything else would be foolish on my part. I'd also have to put Gary Player and Lee Trevino ahead of me, because they have more experience. However, I think I'm the best young player on the tour. Jerry Heard has potential. So have John Mahaffey, Hubert Green and Tom Watson. Ben Crenshaw has talent, but he needs to learn his swing. Tom Weiskopf has as much talent as anyone, but who knows what makes him tick. I'm not the best on the tour, but I'm not far from it."

Offering opinions does not trouble Johnny Miller at all. He is even willing to show Jack Nicklaus how he can grow in grace. "I disagree with Jack on one crucial point," he says. "He says that if he can stay with the pack until the final day, he can break out and win. I can't imagine how many tournaments he's lost with an attitude like that. I like being a front-runner because that puts the pressure on the other fellow. I tell Jack that right to his face."

There is no need for Nicklaus to be offended, because Miller is willing to criticize his own attitudes, too. One question can send him prowling through a series of odd, but connected mental themes. At times he speaks in sentences that seem to be searching for a period.

"A few years ago, I thought my nerves weren't good enough to let me win a lot of tournaments," he says. "My choke level was much lower . . . there I was looking to make the cut, you know—looking for the $3,000 that would get me to the next tournament. The mind is a powerful force. I don't

Jack Nicklaus is the man Miller must beat for the title of world's best golfer—and Nicklaus has the trophies to prove it.

think we know all we can ever hope to know about it. That one round in the 1973 Open convinced me that I could play under pressure.

"Most of my game is excellent, but I'm a terrible chipper and I used to let that get me down. When I'm playing well, it takes a heck of a lot to disturb me now. I've grown since I was 22, you know. I'm six-two now and 180 pounds. That's a gain of 30 pounds and an inch and a half. That's given me strengh . . . my swing is 99 percent address position . . . stance, grip and body position. It produces a good shot.

"If I had to depend on my chipping for a living, I'd be selling hot dogs . . . do you know that somebody wanted to know if I thought golfers were athletes or not. What was I supposed to say? I exercise every day and do a lot of running. I can't play well unless I'm physically rested and mentally alert. Lots of guys on the tour don't take care of themselves. Watch and see how long they last."

The older of the two Miller boys—as pale blond as his younger brother, John—had been perched on the high slimy rocks near the entrance to San Francisco's Golden Gate all morning without catching a thing. Cautiously, he moved down past a couple of slumbering sea lions and took a position nearer the water. He was watching a freighter steam toward the Farallon Islands, some 30 miles out into the Pacific, when a large wave caught him broadside and swept him away into the greenish-white foam. Some other children who had been fishing with him ran for help, but it was useless.

Weeks passed before Johnny Miller could force himself to believe what had happened. Finally his parents convinced him that he should leave the darkness of his bedroom and go to church. It was there that he was introduced to John Geertsen, the former teaching pro at the San Francisco Golf Club. For want of anything truly appropriate to say, Geertsen asked the 7-year-old Johnny how he'd like to take some golf lessons.

"It was just an effort to get his mind off what had happened," says Geertsen. "Johnny was the smallest 7-year-old I'd ever seen. He was so frail and unathletic that it was almost

pitiful. But I felt I could do something for him. He wanted to learn so badly that it was fun teaching him. It was almost as if he knew he was supposed to play golf for a living. Inside a couple of months, he had a canvas net in his basement and he'd spend hours slamming away with his driver."

By the time he was in the seventh grade, he was hanging around a municipal course, winning dimes and quarters from other children and putting better than he ever has since. His skills matured more quickly than his self-control. In the clubhouse at the State Amateur tournament at Pebble Beach in 1963, after he was penalized for carrying one club too many, he sat and wept uncontrollably. He was, according to Geertsen, one of the worst caddies in the city of San Francisco. "Johnny was too busy practicing his swing to worry about whether the guy who had hired him had the proper club," he says. "In tournament play, he kept blowing up. There's more emotion inside him than the public ever sees."

In 1966, he was a 19-year-old sophomore at Brigham Young University, carrying both a B-plus average and a

rating as a scratch golfer, when sports writer Nelson Cullenward of The *San Francisco Examiner* arranged for him to play in a foursome with Nicklaus. It was a practice round the week before the Open was to be played on San Francisco's stately Olympic Club course. Miller had qualified for the tournament, but he had little hope of being in contention until he matched Nicklaus stroke for stroke over 18 holes. Both men shot an even-par 72 and Miller came away convinced of his potential as a legitimate contender.

"Jack was just reaching his true greatness and I had this unusual feeling that I would play against him again and again," Miller said. "I think we became friends that day. I knew that I wanted to play as well as Jack Nicklaus. He was only 26 at the time. I don't want to embarrass him by saying that he was my boyhood idol, but he came close. By shooting the same thing he did, I knew that I belonged with the best. Jack is so great that when some of the younger players are paired with him, they have trouble drawing the club back."

Unbelievably, Johnny Miller tied for eighth in the 1966 Open. He was beaten

Between eagles and endorsements, Johnny Miller still manages to find time for his wife, Linda, and their three children.

by Arnold Palmer, Billy Casper, Jack Nicklaus, Dave Marr, Tony Lema, Phil Rodgers and Bobby Nichols. His score of 290 for 72 holes was better than anything Ben Hogan, Gary Player, Ken Venturi, Julius Boros, Gene Littler and Ed Furgol did and they were all former Open champions. They gave him a trophy for being the best amateur in the field. Just three years later, he turned professional, got married and started playing like an amateur. His first year on the tour, he won only $8,364. It was 1971 before the nation seriously considered Johnny Miller again. He almost won the Masters, tying for second.

"I choked," he said, with utmost honesty. "I blew a lead on the last few holes because of the pressure. I simply have to learn to play under pressure. I'll do it, though. I'm sure I can."

The desert sun, filtering through the low-hanging branch of a pepper tree, casts odd geometric patterns on Johnny Miller's white turtle neck shirt and his sky-blue slacks as he addresses his approach shot, which lies about 18 inches from the trunk. Behind him stands Andy Martinez, his executive assistant and one of the highest-paid caddies on the tour. They make an attractive couple, this handsome blond capitalist and his dark, moustachioed adjutant. They confer constantly.

Miller has Andy on a weekly salary, plus seven percent of his tournament earnings, plus some of his expenses. It is said that Martinez made $45,000 last year.

Miller and Martinez took a chance on each other about 4 years ago. At the time, Martinez was working for Grier Jones, who was supposed to be ready for a run at Nicklaus' sovereignty himself. The caddie had only one year's experience, but when Miller asked him to work for him, Martinez acted strictly on impulse and accepted. They grew up together on the tour. Their working relationship is generally acknowledged to be one of the best in the history of the game.

Miller's shot is nearly perfect, bouncing just past the pin. The gallery applauds. Miller and Martinez march forward together. The putt rolls in for a birdie. The caddie nods and semi-grins. On the next tee, Miller gets off a poor drive. "Crummy," he says. "Absolutely crummy. Geez!"

"Not anywhere near as crummy as the one you hit here last year. That one went halfway up the mountain," says Martinez, breaking the tension. "Stop complaining. You're getting better every year."

"Now there's type of encouragement I need," says Miller, laughing. "Some partner, you are. Why don't you go work for somebody else?"

"You're too good a meal ticket and I need the money," says Martinez. So Miller birdies the par-five hole.

There is no question that Andy Martinez is the celebrity caddie of the year. He has even taken to using a euphemism for his work. He is, he says, Johnny Miller's Weapons Carrier. He is also Miller's defensive platoon. There is something in Miller's nervous system that reacts violently to movement behind him when he's on the green. So Martinez drops down into a catcher's stance and blocks the distraction.

"It's comforting to have Andy back there," says Miller. "A strange noise could take my eye off the ball. He helps me line up putts. I think I can read a line better than most golfers, but Andy isn't far behind me. I make the decision but I value his judgment. It's like having another pro golfer out there."

Regardless of his blatant self-confidence, Miller does not really enjoy going into battle without Martinez. He does not like the U.S. Open system of assigning caddies to golfers by a drawing. Miller wants to fight that system, to the point of threatening not to appear unless he can bring Martinez with him.

"My caddie isn't a crutch," says Miller. "Andy is very helpful to me, but I can win or lose without him. Since he is part of my team, why can't he win

Behind every great golfer stands a caddie, but very few of them are as knowledgeable as Miller's—Andy Martinez.

the big one right along with me if it happens to be our week? I may just insist that he be included and see what happens. There's no law that he can't be with me. If they stop Andy, we might get a lawyer."

As Johnny Miller walks from green to tee during the Bob Hope Desert Classic, a woman in dark glasses with a hat made out of beer-can halves comes running up with a program in her hand.

"Would you mind signing an autograph?" she asks.

Miller signs and then asks: "Would you mind if I asked you if you were in the middle of making dinner?"

Later on, he stands around the press room trying to explain the customers to the working press.

"The fans are strange," he says. "Autographs are the cheapest kind of good publicity. It's also the cheapest way to get a bad name. You have to do it. You just stand there and sign and sign and sign. All the time you want to go someplace else. If you sign for a hundred people and don't sign for the next, he'll tell his friends what a rat Johnny Miller is and what a waste of time going to a golf tournament is. You

have nothing to gain from signing autographs and everything to lose if you don't. They never stop to think you might have a family waiting for you."

The third round of the Crosby is slipping away into darkness. On the expensive walkways of Del Monte Lodge, expensive people are walking toward their expensive cars. Linda Miller has one child by the hand. Back at the house where they are staying with friends during the tournament, a young Irish nurse is watching the other two little Millers in a confusion of toys, picture books and disposable diapers.

"It's really strange," says Linda Miller, dark and attractive in a homey, earth-mother sort of way, "they make such a big deal out of us being Mormons. I never see a story that refers to the fact that 'Roman Catholic Lee Trevino' won a tournament. They also think we don't have fun because we don't drink. That's not so. We aren't prudes at all. It's fine if our friends drink. Nobody feels uncomfortable because our religion forbids us to drink. Our family life is very important . . . that's one of the reasons Johnny likes and admires Andy Martinez so much. Andy goes out and inspects the

course and measures the yardage. Johnny says that gives him a chance to spend an extra day with us. How you raise your family is important, at least to us."

Through a tangle of humanity moves the new golden hero of golf, stopping to sign autographs and say something pleasant to people who buy tickets to watch him play.

"Johnny's the one!" yell a couple of lacquered ladies, waving champagne glasses as they squeal their way forward. Miller beats them to his car and slips in beside his wife and son. The ladies rap on the window and offer him a sip. He smiles so fiercely that it is almost a frown. They insist.

"Please," he says, "I don't drink and this is my wife with me. Please be pleasant, so I can be pleasant, too."

They continue to insist. So Johnny Miller rolls the window up, still somewhat reluctant to offend anyone. Isolated from the wickedness of the professional golf tour, he heads up the road to the manor house where he is staying. The lacquered ladies stand around wishing he were an agnostic. Walter Hagen would never have deserted their grandmothers like that.

"If there's something about me you don't like, Mr. Davis, I wish you'd tell me."

Pioneer Woman Golfer Tells How It Was

By FRANK LITTLER

CHAMPION golfers are as willing to abandon competitive play as a cardinal is prone to abandon his religion. And in the 1970s they are less likely than ever to limit themselves to friendly games. There are more senior events, pro and amateur, male and female, than there are balls on the practice tee. With card and pencil in their pockets, half the septuagenarians in the nation are obsessed with beating their age. Many of them do it.

But history does record a few notable withdrawals from the arena. The best-remembered occurred in 1930, when Bobby Jones quit the scene after winning the Opens and Amateurs of Britain and the United States. Then, when Walter Hagen formally bowed out a few years later, the two dominant golfers of their day had ceased to pursue anything but peace and quiet.

After World War II the situation changed. Players not yet decrepit were dropping out of contention for reasons of *force majeure*. There wasn't much percentage in continuing, when trophies or money were getting harder to win, defeat was becoming too predictable, and nobody was sponsoring tournaments for gramps and grannies.

One of the very few indisputable champions who quit when they were ahead—and, as Jones and Hagen did,

abstained from second thoughts on the subject—was Virginia Van Wie. When she captured the U.S. Women's Amateur in 1932-33-34 she had become the last golfer to hold the title in three consecutive years. (It had been done before, but it was never done again.) And that, she decided, was enough.

In a sport that has never been shy of amazonian contenders, of unfeminine strength and femoral bulk, Miss Van Wie teed off with a slim build and a sweet swing. Now, more than 40 years later, her figure is still shapely, her eyes still alert. She looks at first sight to be the kind of golfer, casually but stylishly dressed, who, on any sunny Tuesday morning, might step out of a Ford Torino in the parking lot of a typical suburban country club and head for the ladies' locker room. But on closer acquaintance you can detect a latent athleticism that not all the years of retirement have sapped. You can distinguish too that look of poise and far-sightedness, hard to define in any terms, that never seems to leave a celebrity. And especially a celebrity who has heard prolonged applause in the open air.

A lifelong Chicagoan, and one of the tiny clutch of Midwesterners who achieved golfing fame, she lives on the 18th floor of a South Side high-rise. Her integrated neighborhood is well within

the city limits, and from the windows of her apartment she can see segments of two golf courses—Jackson Park, a municipal layout, and farther south the now-defunct South Shore Country Club. Beverly, her own club, is several miles to the west.

The names she recalls include some that are better remembered than her own, and others that few historians would cite in the age of an LPGA's Sandras, Sharons, and Kathy's. Give or take a few years, she was a contemporary of Glenna Collett (later Mrs. Vare), Maureen Orcutt, hard-hitting Helen Hicks, Opal Hill, Betty Jameson, and Marion Hollins. On the international scene she knew Enid Wilson, Joyce Wethered, Molly Gourlay, and Pam Barton.

She won her three straight titles at match play. And if a feat like that is tough to accomplish over 72 holes of stroke, it is harder still when an unlucky bounce of the ball can wreck your prospects in one single moment of an 18-hole tussle. To judge from the records, she must have survived that danger twice. She played 16 matches in the three championships. One of them she won on the last green, and one at the 19th. But there were no cliffhangers in the other 14 duels, and several of them she coasted through.

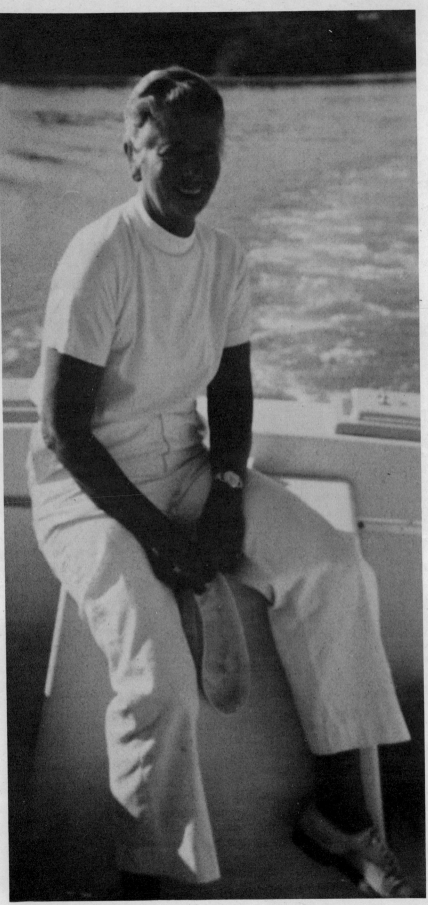

Today she has no particular handicap, but generally shoots in the low 80s—when she does play. Much of her vacations in Florida she spends with a fishing rod, and golf receded further from her mind during the 11 years she worked on market research with a prominent food company.

"Now," she said, "tell me what this interview is all about."

"The men's National Amateur has gone back to match play, and many of the contestants aren't happy about it. What's your own preference?"
"We had qualifying scores for the Amateur, but in my day there weren't many stroke play events as such. I do remember competing in what was called a 'derby.' It was about the time Patty Berg was coming up. I'd say the real reason for less match play nowadays is that the promoters and the networks feel public interest will drop if the stars are eliminated early in the contest. A bad spell won't necessarily eliminate you from stroke play. You can recover and come from behind."

"Did you enjoy match play because it's possible to take chances without spoiling a scorecard?"
"No. I didn't see match play in terms of risky and spectacular shots. Even in a friendly game I never did anything reckless. Once you start doing that you get into bad habits."

"What are the principal differences in women's golf between then and now?"
"I'm not the best person to ask. There's so much that happened that I haven't been involved in—and you know, we do change. We change our interests and our attitudes, and it would be hard for *me* to relate the present to the past."

"Did you foresee the effects of professionalism?"
"I think that what I noticed more were the beginnings of commercialism. Now you may think this is trivial, but I can remember the first time I saw peanuts being sold on the course. That was in the 1930s, and in an amateur contest it just hadn't happened before. As for tournament pros, I doubt we ever thought the day would come. You have to remember that the best of the men pros didn't make a fortune in those days, and there certainly wasn't a Palmer or a

Nicklaus for us to envy. But Helen Hicks—and I was closer to her than anyone—did turn pro. That was in 1934, and she was the very first to do it. There was no women's circuit, as I've said, so Helen undertook exhibition matches, and she represented the Wilson company. She was touring the world with Gene Sarazen and his wife when World War II broke out—they were in Australia about that time—and I remember her telling me that she had played 21 exhibitions in 21 days, under all kinds of conditions. She wanted me to turn pro, and so did a number of others who took the same step. But I determined I wouldn't. I became a non-playing pro eventually, when I started giving lessons."

"Where did you teach?"
"I had two schools—one on 75th Street and one out in Hinsdale. The one in Hinsdale was in the garden of a friend of mine—I used to drive out there with the practice net and then set it up."

"Did you have to inform anyone of your business? The USGA, for example?"
"No. If you're no longer playing competitively you do what you like. But I do regret commercialism, as I've said. Nowadays everything seems to be money."

"Ladies never play in mixed events beyond the club level, and I think the girl pros were sorry when the Haig Mixed Foursomes came to an end. What was your experience of playing with the men?"
"It didn't occur to me that it would help my game, and I never recall actually seeking the opportunity. But I played with Leo Diegel once, in an event in California, and after he died I was in touch with his brother George for a long time."

"Who was the best player you knew?"
"Glenna. She was particularly good coming out of a trap, but actually she had all the shots. When I beat her in the Amateur, I really felt I'd earned the title."

"Would you say that the women pros of today are more intense—that they're playing under greater pressure?"

"No. Because we played in the Curtis Cup matches, and it wasn't only our individual reputations that were at stake. We were playing for our country too."

"When were you selected?"
"The first match in the series was played in 1932, and I was on the team. You know Link Werden, the golf writer? Well, I was with him shortly before we sailed, and all of a sudden I realized I didn't have my golf shoes with me. The last thing I wanted to do was buy another pair and to break them in before the match. So we drove out to where I'd left them. He brought me to the dockside just in time. Helen was frantic—she wanted the captain to hold the ship. I started telling him about the people I should write to, and he said 'For heaven's sake—I'll write to them. Just get on board.' They pulled the gangway up the moment I stepped off it. The match was played at Wentworth, and Helen and I beat Enid Wilson and Mrs. Watson. And it was a good thing we did. We didn't have any experience of alternate-shot partnerships, so before the match began we played our combined ball against the substitute player on the team. And she taught us a lesson. She beat us. Anyway, the U.S. won and in 1936 we kept the trophy at Chevy Chase, Maryland. I was chosen that year too."

"Had you played overseas before?"
"Yes. I was with a party of about 24 women who toured England, Scotland, and France. There was a man named Kennedy in charge of the trip, and it couldn't have been easy for him. I'm sure we didn't give him any trouble, but when we disembarked in New York and he knew it was all over, I don't think I'd ever seen such an expression of relief on anyone's face."

"To go back to Miss Hicks. Was she really hard-hitting? Or was it a journalistic gimmick?"
"She hit a longer ball than most of us. But she wasn't really exceptional."

"Did you hit hard?"
"I'll tell you something. Until I went to Ernest Jones, I'd never got beyond a 36-hole final. I just couldn't win. I first met him through Marion Hollins, and he gave me lessons on the Pacific Coast

and later in New York. He taught all his pupils to *swing*. It was the creed of his whole life. And I can't help noticing that his theories are coming back. There hasn't been as much emphasis lately on hitting. He used to say 'You can hit harder when you swing than you can any other way.' And he was right."

"About the time you were making your name there were changes in equipment. Did you go along with them?"
"Ernest Jones made steel-shafted woods, and I used them. But for my irons I stuck to hickory. It was a question of torsion. Put your fingers on a steel shaft and try to do a little twisting. You can't feel what you can feel with hickory."

"The year you won the Amateur for the first time Sarazen invented the wedge. Did you use it?"
"I bought my first sand wedge just 2 years ago. It *does* help—there's no doubt about that. But all the time I was playing I stayed with the 9-iron."

"Which is your favorite course?"
"Cypress Point."

"And your favorite shot?"
"I always enjoyed playing the woods. But I think the shot I liked best was the pitch."

"What distance? Eighty to 100 yards?"
"Well, there again you're talking about a different era. We didn't think mathematically. We looked at the flagstick, we sized up the situation, and we took the club we thought we needed."

Whatever the spectators thought, and however much the USGA might have deplored it, it is for Miss Van Wie to decide whether she retired too soon. Obviously she hasn't regretted her choice, and championship play on the highest level—given a fresh impetus by Babe Didrikson—did continue for several years after her departure. By dropping out in 1934 she didn't bring women's amateurism to a full stop. But it's hard to deny that her decision at least put a significant semicolon into the text.

14-YEAR-OLD WITH THE GOLDEN SWING

By CLARK CARPENTER
(Member, GWAA)

YOUNGSTERS, duffers, scratch players and even pros sometimes wonder if the myriad of articles seen on how to improve your game in many different golf publications are really beneficial.

But not the people in Monroe, La. They are convinced.

Johnny Myers, head pro at the municipal golf course and president ot the Gulf States Section of the PGA, has had two such articles in *Pro Shop Operations,* a national publication.

The first was on the psychological approach to teaching juniors and the second was concerned with detailed planning being the key to the success of a junior clinic.

All the members of Neville High's Louisiana state championship team of 1975, including individual winner Bob Cooper, were graduates of Myers' junior programs.

But perhaps the most outstanding alumnus to come out of these clinics lives right under Myers' roof!

Scott Myers, 14, has rolled up a list of accomplishments that would tend to make the casual reader believe he is closer to 24 than 14.

His name has been listed in *Golf World* and his picture appeared when he was only 12 in the "Faces in a Crowd" section of *Sports Illustrated.*

But his greatest golfing feats came at 14, under the hot Southern sun in 1975.

Scott ran away with the Twin City Juniors title by scoring a fantastic 64 on the final day, including an incredible 29 on the back nine of Monroe's municipal course.

This tied the back nine record held by his older brother Steven and it came on an incoming nine that measured 3,055. Steven was also 14 when he shot 29.

To illustrate what kind of shotmaker young Scott is, the Monroe course has been played by Byron Nelson, Tommy Bolt, Dutch Harrison and Gil Morgan, 1975s 60th-place money winner on the tour.

Nelson and Bolt are former U.S. Open champions and Nelson's best was 65. Morgan's lowest effort netted him a 66.

Like a razor that was honed to a fine edge, Myers set out in quest of a title that had always eluded him, entering the Future

Masters in Dothan, Ala.

Scott won his age group and finished ninth in a field of 670. And he wasn't through yet!

Next stop was Pensacola, Fla., and the Southern Juniors Tournament. It was here that young Myers had his greatest hour and most heartbreaking defeat, although winning his fourth straight divisional Southern title.

He toured the Perdido Bay Country Club course in a neat 67 strokes, giving him a 13-shot advantage on his nearest rival in his age bracket.

Perdido Bay, incidentally, was the course used by the PGA for its Tour Qualifying School the year Ben Crenshaw and Morgan received cards to compete.

Such a course is the type the Tournament Players Division usually chooses for its qualifying school, one that demands all the shots. This lends more credibility to Myers' score.

His 67 was a tournament record, and it let him set his sights on winning the overall title as he had a five-shot lead on the field.

But on the final day he ballooned to a 79 and lost the overall title by one shot. But, out of the ashes of defeat came a valuable lesson.

"You've got to keep your concentration," Myers said. "I didn't and I lost it all. But I'm going back."

Concentration and motivation. Whether young Myers will be able to blend these two, to incorporate them in his daily playing habits may well determine if he has a future on the tour.

It was a mental lapse that cost Myers a double bogey and the overall title of the Southern Juniors. Having used a 4-wood or 1-iron before with great success on No. 12, Myers took out his driver on the final round and hooked into a water hazard.

Ironically, there was an article by Ben Hogan in a golfing publication at his dad's pro shop in which Hogan said, "Good swings don't win tournaments, good management does."

Scott recalled the incident well, saying, "I never realized how important the mental side of golf was until this tournament.

"Now I know I can shoot good golf in a tournament. But I need to do a lot of work on my concentration."

But the motivation factor is something that must come from within. They can teach you how to swing, how to putt and, in time, you can learn course management.

No person, however, can *make* you swing.

Different things seem to motivate different people. For instance, since Lee Trevino comes from a poor family, it may have been the vast amount of money for the winner that had its effect on him.

But for Jack Nicklaus, the motivation in his game could be to build up a total of major championships that no one ever will be able to surpass.

Scott already has had his bout with a bad round due to hasty club selection, so he is not liable to forget when it comes to the concentration department.

But as for motivation, not even his dad, who has been his teacher through the years, knows the answer. This is one that Scott will have to handle by himself.

David Steel, host pro at Pine Hills Golf Club, felt these two factors would determine Myers' future.

"He has a super future if he keeps his interest. He is so good now, I hope he doesn't lose his interest. I've seen this happen.

"He has a great swing and more potential than anyone I have ever seen."

A story on Scott in *Golf* Magazine in October, 1974, is headlined "Another Nicklaus? Why Not?"

This comparison was made before his triumphant trips to the Future Masters and the Southern Juniors.

"Such an early comparison must be out of proportion" would be perhaps the first reaction. But when you realize the capabilities of this young man, you run out of adjectives to describe his game.

An early portent came when, at the age of 12 and playing from the back tees, he shot 72 and finished one shot in back of three pros who tied for first at an Alexandria, La., Pro-Am—one of whom was Johnny Myers, his dad.

Also at the age of 12, Scott played Morehouse Country Club in nearby Bastrop with the top player at Northeast Louisiana University, his dad and two other pros.

Playing from the championship tees on a course that measures 6,467 yards long, Scott carded a nifty 69!

And Morehouse C.C. is no pushover. It was selected as the site of the 1976 Louisiana State Amateur Golf Tournament.

Although only 14, Scott has all the tools it takes. He is greatly poised for his age and has a build like "Gentle Ben" Crenshaw, who dominated the college golf scene for 3 years at Texas University.

Much of this poise, on and off the course, is the result of fine training. Scott always uses the men's tees and has been exposed to adult golf from the beginning.

He has been urged to squeeze a rubber ball to strengthen his golfing muscles and to enter competition at every opportunity.

Golf writers are hesitant to label even the most promising youngster with a "can't miss" tag. For those who have been around the game know the pitfalls that can trap any golfer between tee and green.

There can be bunkers, bad lies, water hazards and out-of-bounds markers all waiting to catch errant shots.

But right now Scott Myers looks like a 250-yard drive right down the center of the fairway.

With all his local and national titles, Scott is off the tee in good shape.

It will be interesting to see whether he's a morning glory or another Golden Bear as the years go by.

JIM DENT'S DISTANCE TIPS

"Creep" club back for smoother tempo

"I 'creep' the club away from the ball," says Jim Dent, the long-drive champion. "It's my only thought at address. Just creep the club back. The start of the swing pretty much sets your pace, and if you start too fast, you're dead. Sometimes I'll get on the practice tee and just work on bringing the club back properly."

Dent, like most golfers, had to learn his tempo. "Mine wasn't good at first," he says. "It was way too fast. It's better now. It's slow and easy. I'm not jumping out of my shoes."

Drag right foot to stay behind shot

Dent gets a big part of his power with leg action and a strong lower-body move on the downswing. Dragging his right foot is his main objective here.

Observant and eager to learn during his early days on tour, Dent admired the way Billy Casper swung with complete control. Dent noticed that Casper dragged his right foot toward the target on the downswing. "Watch him some time," Dent says. "He does it better than anybody."

Dent discovered that this foot action encourages him to keep his upper body behind the ball and make a proper rotation of the shoulders instead of turning the shoulders out and around his axis. It keeps his head steady by reducing the tendency to sway. "If the head goes," Dent says, "the shot goes."

Use a lightweight driver for more clubhead speed

Blessed with size, strength and quick hands, Dent maximizes those attributes by using lightweight clubs for greater clubhead speed. "The average golfer tries to swing much too heavy a club," Dent says. "He's just cutting down his own clubhead speed through the ball."

Dent's regular graphite-shafted driver has a D2 weight, comparable to the D0 he uses in a steel-shafted driver.

"I heard where Ben Hogan swung a C9, a lady's weight," Dent adds. "Most sets I see in pro shops are D3 or D4. That's too heavy. Don't just buy what the man has to sell. Get a club you can swing."

KEY THOUGHTS OF OTHER LONG HITTERS

TOM WATSON: "I try to make sure I stay behind the ball, and then swing as hard as I can. I like to catch the ball on the upswing to use the full impact of the clubhead."

JOHN SCHROEDER: "I was so pumped up for the driving contest that I may have been swinging faster than normal. I know I hit three balls right on the nose. But my key thought is to keep the swing as smooth as possible."

CURTIS SIFFORD: "I tee the ball a little higher and try to sweep it off. Bob Wynn teed his ball on a scoring pencil to get it even higher."

CHI CHI RODRIGUEZ: "The best way to get extra distance is to draw the ball. To do that, I swing on a flatter plane. A flat swing produces a hook and that's where you get the added yardage."

LARRY ZIEGLER: "You've got to get the legs into the swing. I try to get them working through the ball as much as possible."

FORREST FEZLER: "I think about waiting on the club coming down. I avoid rushing the swing. I use a 100-compression ball."

PHIL RODGERS: "Pick your landing area. Use the terrain. If the fairway slopes a little to the left, hit on the right side with a slight draw and watch it roll."

BEN CRENSHAW: "The temptation in a driving contest is to try to reach back and let everything out. What you're doing then is putting on a new swing. I prefer to take my normal pass at the ball and hope I catch it just right."

WHAT'S NEW IN GOLF BOOKS

By ROBERT CROMIE

THERE ARE rainswept days, and snow-deep days, and days when illness or bad luck or a nagging conscience keep you from the golf course. As a consolation, when evening comes at one of those wasted times, you might try sitting down with a good book on the subject. Here are some recent ones:

THE STORY OF AMERICAN GOLF, by Herbert Warren Wind (revised and enlarged; Knopf, $20)

This is the third edition of an excellent volume which first appeared in 1948 and is now regarded as a classic. Herbert Warren Wind, a member of the *New Yorker* staff, has been known for several decades as one of the world's finest golf writers. The book traces the history of the game in the United States from the Apple Tree Gang (which founded the first "permanent" U.S. golf club in 1888) up to the present.

There probably is almost nothing you want to know about the development of the sport in the United States that you won't find here: winners of the major tournaments down the years; Gene Sarazen's incredible double-eagle to steal the 1935 Masters' crown; Ben Hogan's near-fatal accident; and names such as Patty Berg, Babe Zaharias, Nicklaus, Arnie Palmer, Johnny Miller, Mickey Wright, Louise Suggs, Chick Evans; Bob Jones and his Grand Slam; the Open, Masters, Western, U.S. Amateur; Champagne Tony Lema, Porky Oliver, Samuel Jackson Snead, Byron Nelson, Ben Crenshaw, Gary Player, etc., etc., etc. . .

The book, as those who know Wind's work do not have to be told, is superbly done. Whether you're reading about Lee Trevino's childhood background (Texas poverty); Jerry Barber and the series of unbelievable birdie putts that kept him alive in the 1961 P.G.A., or other dramatic accounts of dozens of major moments, you can rely on this superb stylist to breathe life into them.

Wind himself has golfed and loved the game since he was a youngster. He has played on courses around the world, too, although he admits—ruefully I suspect—that he's never teed it up on two of the seven continents: Africa and the Antarctic.

It seems only fair to give you a brief look of the Wind at work, and because of the overall quality making a choice would be an aggravating chore. So this—a picture of the early Nicklaus—is a selection made by opening this well-illustrated volume at random:

"Since the America in which Jack Nicklaus was growing up was peopled with dozens of hotshot young golfers, anyone who did as well as he did had to be imbued with a formidable competitive spirit. He had one other tremendous asset. This was not his staggering power, though he was longer off the tee than anyone else in his age group, but the soundness of his swing. In Jack Grout he had one of the finest teachers in the country. Grout had been an assistant to

Henry Picard, who in turn had studied with Alex Morrison, far and away the game's most *avant garde* scholar in the period between the two world wars. From his many hours of listening, reading, thought, and experiment, Grout had concluded that a correct golf swing rested mainly on the execution of three fundamentals. 1. The head had to be kept still throughout the swing, since it was the balance center of the swing. 2. In order for a golfer to move swiftly and correctly through the ball on the downswing, he had to have excellent balance. Balance depended on proper foot action. And proper foot action meant the correct rolling of the ankles—the left ankle rolled in on the backswing and the right ankle braced, with the reverse taking place on the downswing. (When Morrison first propounded this theory, he was ridiculed—he was that far ahead of his time.) 3. A golfer should try to develop the fullest possible arc by making the fullest possible shoulder turn. Like Deacon Palmer, Grout believed that golfers should be encouraged to hit the ball as hard as they could when they were young and their muscles were flexible and stretchable. They could work on control afterwards. This went headlong against the traditional advice given for eons to young players. Learn to control the ball first; distance will come later. How long, you ask, did Jack, when he had grown up, hit the ball? Try this one for size: In a warmup round for the 1960 Open at Cherry Hills when he was 20, on the 550-yard seventeenth, aided by a mild following wind, he was home in two on the island green with a drive and 7-iron."

Now that's when Wind is only *coasting*. Get the book and see what he does when he slides into high.

THE PGA, by Herb Graffis (Crowell, $16.95)

Another of the great golfing historians, Herb Graffis, a former Chicago sports columnist, has done a job many of his confreres would have found too formidable to attempt: He has managed to make the story of the Professional Golfers' Association both tidily complete and far livelier than any such potentially pedestrian account has any right to be. It is a book no golf library can afford to be without.

Graffis, who with his equally delightful brother, Joe, used to own and run *Golfing* and *Golfdom* magazines, uses his own tremendous personal knowledge and an unrivaled store of anecdotes to spice the history of the organization and keep the reader reading. Graffis, now retired to Florida, where he still retains his keen interest in the game, is known—literally—to hundreds of persons in the golf world both here and abroad. He has other books in the field to his credit, most notably a couple done in collaboration with Tommy Armour that have gone into multiple printings.

This is far more than just the history of the P.G.A. from 1916 to the present. It also is a history of the game from its birth at some unkown time and place, and of the people who govern it, and of the people who play it. Graffis proves once more that professionals can perform miracles with even the most unpromising material. *The PGA* is at least a literary birdie and possibly an eagle.

A taste from the book:

"The story of the Masters Tournament is relevant to PGA history because the Masters came along at the right time to prove that class outranked money in the public eye where golf tournaments were concerned. The Masters has been top class from the start. There have been no robbery prices at the concessions, no parking in remote spots at fancy prices, and no program advertising waste. Sheets on pairing and starting times and information booklets on contestants are provided free to the public.

"So the Masters became world famous as the tournament most intelligently conducted by men whose dream was to share a wonderful show with others who also loved golf. And the dates of the Masters are right. (Bobby) Jones had retired as master of all he surveyed and sat at the top of the mountain as the Perfect Gentleman Sportsman. (Clifford) Roberts, a country boy who'd tamed the wolves of Wall Street and had a passion for anonymity and the quiet, friendly pleasures of golf, turned his attention to Augusta National. Of course, there were problems during its infancy, but Roberts and Jones triumphed by maintaining the high quality that was part of their character.

"The Augusta National membership list was and continues to be a high-bracket golf Who's Who. Before Dwight Eisenhower knew whether he was a Republican or a Democrat, his presidential destiny may well have been born at Augusta National with Roberts and Jones as mid-wives. Both of them were just too old-fashioned honorable to think of Ike in any way other than the best man for the country, and away from work, a perfect golfing companion."

Plenty of photos.

THE METHODS OF GOLF'S MASTERS, by Dick Aultman and Ken Bowden (Coward, McCann, Geoghegan, $12.95)

This excellent work deals with the ways in which the following universally-recognized masters of the game hit the ball: Vardon, Hagen, Sarazen, Jones, Cotton, Nelson, Snead, Hogan, Locke, Middlecoff, Thomson, Palmer, Casper, Player, Trevino and Nicklaus. And now we cheat a bit. For this is a quotation from the foreword, written by none other than the remarkable Herbert Warren Wind, which describes the book to perfection:

"My guess is that *The Methods of Golf's Masters* will become one of those uncommon sports books to which golfers will return time and time again—intellectual golfers, weekend golfers, and serious tournament-level golfers. After all, it never hurts to refresh one's understanding of, say, why Walter Hagen might have fared even better with metal-shafted clubs, how Gene Sarazen went about assembling the swing that would complement the dominant left hand in his interlocking grip, why it was that Bobby Jones placed so much value on the extension through the ball, how it was Henry Cotton came to emphasize hand action primarily, why it was important for Byron Nelson to have his legs lead on the downswing, what facets of Sam Snead's style account for his amazing longevity, and how Lee Trevino was able to compound a remarkably dependable hitting action out of five unorthodox moves. It is all here in a book that both informs and entertains and that possesses the real flavor of the game."

Now an example of the Aultman-Bowden touch:

"It was impossible in his day not to admire Sarazen as a golfer and not to be entertained and intrigued by him as a man . . . He was one of the fastest golfers in history—once shooting 70 in the final round of the Masters in 1 hour, 57 minutes—and a vociferous critic of tardy play. He habitually wore what the British call plus fours and Americans knickers on and off the golf course (and, suggested some of his rivals, also in bed) . . . He was the smallest great golfer pre-Gary Player—5 feet, 5 inches and 145 pounds in his spikes . . . He fought a sometimes bitter, sometimes good-natured battle with Walter Hagen for titles, money, recognition, and the *bon mot*—a battle often enlivened by the fact that in many personal tastes and habits he was Hagen's opposite: openly ambitious, industrious, intense, mercurial, health-conscious, temperate, and usually early to bed. And he was a self-admitted loner; a man who never tried to hide the fact that he was out for himself; who said many times in his career: 'Your game counts for you and mine for me. In other words, look out for number one, because in doing that you'll find you have plenty to care for.' "

Wind is right, as usual. It's a lovely book.

A NATURAL WAY TO GOLF POWER, by Judy Rankin with Michael Aronstein; foreword by Bob Toski (Harper & Row, $8.95)

For less than the price of a dozen of the best golf balls, you *may* acquire pointers (whether you're male or female) that will improve your game to the point where you will retrieve your outlay many times over in winnings from rivals to whom you have—wisely—neglected to mention Ms. Rankin's book.

There are several reasons to read what she sets down (with the aid of Aronstein, a staffer for *Golf* magazine). Among them are that despite her diminutive size, she is one of the best players on the women's tour, and led the LPGA in scoring in 33 events in 1973 and was second in money winnings. Also, because this is what Bob Toski wrote:

"I'll never forget meeting Judy when she arrived at the Miami airport (for an analysis of her game by Toski, a great teacher). This tiny, freckle-faced girl walked toward me and I immediately said 'Oh God!'—she is so small she might get lost in an unreplaced divot. Little did I realize that an ounce of touch is worth a ton of brawn . . .

"Now Judy Rankin is without question, pound for pound, the finest player I have ever seen. She combines great arm and hand speed with a superb lower body action to produce an unbelievable golf swing. Her lower action through the ball is amazing. She utilizes it to the maximum, playing as well beneath herself as any player I have ever seen, with the exception of the great Mickey Wright. Every part of her body is playing an important role to produce the full effect of the clubhead against the ball. For a person her size to do this consistently and effectively, as she has, over a long period of time is tribute to her dedication to the art of mastering the golf swing . . .

"She is an example of the maxim that if you're good enough you're big enough to succeed."

If only a little of her style and skill rub off, you'll be on your way up. Happy reading.

ALL THAT'S NEW IN GOLF CLUBS
ACUSHNET

Model: AC 108

WOODS (1-3-4-5)
Head: Laminated—mahogany finish
Shaft: Acushnet steel L-A-R-S flexes
Length: 43" #1
Grip: Composition
Also stocked in ladies models.

IRONS (2 through 9 P.W. & S.W.)
Head: Investment cast stainless steel—shaft in
hosel design
Shaft: Acushnet steel L-A-R-S
Length: 38¾" #2 iron
Grip: Composition

Model: PRO 100

WOODS (1-3-4-5)
Head: Laminated—black finish
Shaft: Acushnet steel R & S flex
Length: 43" #1
Grip: Composition

IRONS (1 through 9 P.W. & S.W.)
Head: Forged carbon steel—shaft in hosel design
Shaft: Acushnet steel R & S flex
Length: 39" #2 iron
Grip: Composition

Acushnet Sales Co.
Slocum Street
Acushnet, Massachusetts 02743
(617) 997-2811

AMERICAN PRECISION GOLF

WOODS
Head: Laminated
Shaft: Unilite steel in R, MS, S flexes. Dynamic
steel and graphite in R, MS, X flex.
Length: 43" in stock
Grip: Composition. Cord or leather on special
order.

IRONS
Head: Investment cast stainless steel
Shaft: Unilite steel in R, MS, S flexes. Dynamic
steel and graphite in R, MS, S and XS
flexes.
Length: 38¾" in stock
Grip: Composition. Cord or leather on special
order.

American Precision Golf Corp.
1566 Rowe Avenue
Worthington, Minnesota 56187
(507) 376-4183

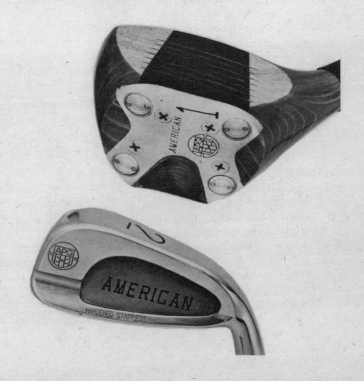

CON-SOLE

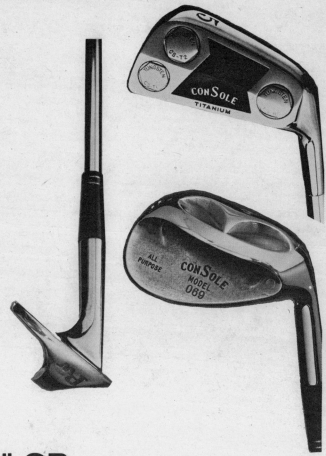

IRONS
Head: Investment cast titanium
Shaft: Dynamic steel in L-A-R-S-X flexes
Length: Mens 39″ #2, Ladies 38″ #2
Grip: Leather or composition
Available in mens and ladies right hand models 2
through 9 and P.W.

WEDGES
Head: Investment cast stainless steel
Shaft: Dynamic steel
Length: Mens 35″, Ladies 33¾″
Grip: Composition
All purpose—pitching—sand
All 3 wedges feature concave sole design.

Con-Sole
P.O. Box 679
Kennet Square, Pa. 19348
(215) 444-1120

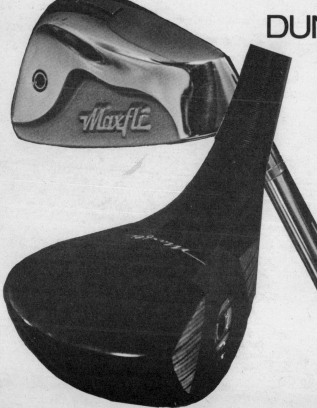

DUNLOP

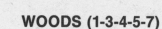

WOODS (1-3-4-5-7)
Head: Laminated—black finish
Shaft: Dynamic steel R & S flex, A & X special
order
Length: 43⅜″ #1
Grip: Composition

IRONS (2 through 9 P.W. & S.W.)
Head: Investment cast stainless steel—shaft over
hosel & in hosel designs
Shaft: Dynamic steel R & S flex
Length: 39″ #2 iron
Grip: Composition

Dunlop
Box 1109
Buffalo, New York 14240
(716) 877-2200

FIRST FLIGHT

Model: THE PHANTOM

WOODS
Head: Persimmon—black finish
Shaft: Dynamic—R & S flex—Driver available in graphite R & S flex
Length: 43" #1
Grip: Composition

IRONS
Head: Investment cast-stainless steel shaft over hosel design
Shaft: Dynamic—R & S flex
Length: 38½" #2 iron
Grip: Composition

Model: FTD

WOODS (1-3-4-5)
Head: Persimmon—walnut finish
Shaft: Dynamic R & S flex driver available in graphite R & S flex
Length: 43" #1
Grip: Composition

IRONS (2 through 9 P.W. & S.W.)
Head: Forged steel—shaft over hosel design
Shaft: Dynamic R & S
Length: 38½" #2 iron
Grip: Composition

Pro-Group Inc.
99 Tremont
Chattanooga, Tenn. 37405
(615) 267-5631

WALTER HAGEN GOLF EQUIPMENT

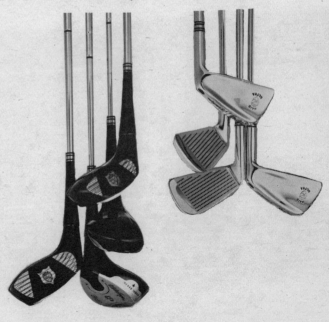

Model: HAIG ULTRA 66

WOODS
Head: Laminated head
Shaft: R & S flex in stock, A & X flex on special order
Length: 43" & 43½"
Grip: Composition & leather
Mens left hand available in 43" & 43½" R flex in stock. A-S-X special order.

IRONS
Head: Forged steel
Shaft: R & S flex in stock, A & X flex special order
Length: 38" & 39½"
Grip: Composition & leather
Mens left hand available in 38½" length only, R & S flex in stock. A & X special order.

WALTER HAGEN GOLF EQUIPMENT

Model: ULTRA DYNE II

WOODS
Head: Laminated
Shaft: Countertorque. R & S flex in stock, A & X flex special order
Length: 43″ & 43½″
Grip: Composition—half cord grip
Mens left hand model available in 43″ R & S flex in stock.

IRONS
Head: Investment cast stainless steel
Shaft: Countertorque R & S flex in stock—A & X special order
Length: 38½″ & 39″
Grip: Composition—half cord grip
Mens left hand model available in 38½″ R & S flex in stock.

Walter Hagen Golf Equipment
2233 West Street
River Grove, Illinois 60171
(312) 456-6100

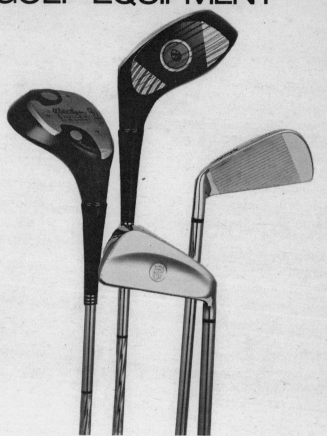

HILLERICH & BRADSBY

Model: POWER-BILT CITATION

WOODS
Head: Laminated #519 and Persimmon #319—black finish
Shaft: Dynamic steel—A-R and S in stock
Length: 43″ & 44″
Grip: Composition & leather

IRONS
Head: Forged—over hosel shaft design
Shaft: Dynamic steel—A-R & S flexes
Length: 38½″ & 39″
Grip: Composition & leather

Hillerich & Bradsby
P.O. Box 506
Louisville, Kentucky 40201
(502) 585-5226

HILLERICH & BRADSBY

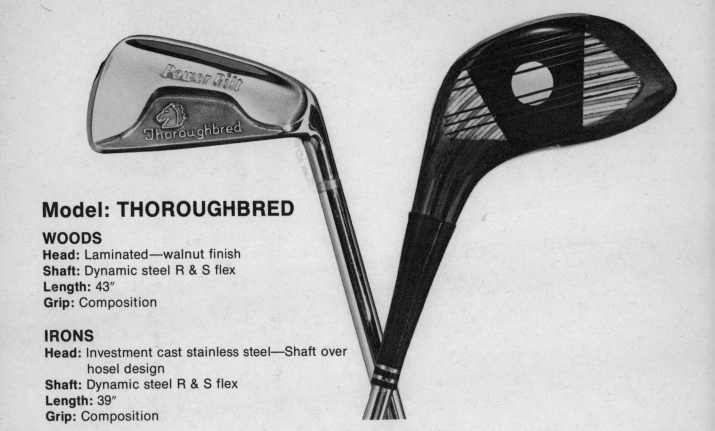

Model: THOROUGHBRED

WOODS
Head: Laminated—walnut finish
Shaft: Dynamic steel R & S flex
Length: 43″
Grip: Composition

IRONS
Head: Investment cast stainless steel—Shaft over
　　　hosel design
Shaft: Dynamic steel R & S flex
Length: 39″
Grip: Composition

BEN HOGAN

Model: PRODUCER

WOODS
Head: Laminated—black finish
Shaft: Apex lightweight steel. Available in #2
　　　(flexible), #3 (medium), #4 (stiff).
Length: 43″ #1
Grip: Composition

IRONS (2 through 9 plus equalizer (P.W.)
Head: Investment cast stainless steel. Shaft in
　　　hosel design.
Shaft: Apex #2, #3 & #4 flexes
Length: 38½″ #2 iron
Grip: Composition
Woods and Irons available in left hand model with
#3 & #4 flex shafts only.

BEN HOGAN

Model: DIRECTOR

WOODS (1-3-4-5)
Head: Laminated—black finish
Shaft: Apex lightweight steel available in #2, #3, #4 flex
Length: 43″ #1
Grip: Composition

IRONS (2 through 9 and equalizer [P.W.]. 1 iron available on special order)
Head: Forged shaft in hosel design
Shaft: Apex #2, #3, #4 flexes
Length: 38½″ #2 iron
Grip: Composition
Director irons available in womens model also

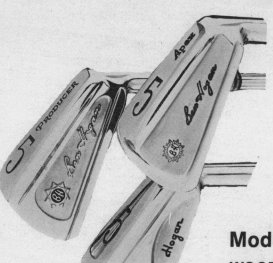

Ben Hogan Irons: From top to bottom the Apex, Producer and Director.

Model: APEX

WOODS (1-3-4-5-7)
Head: Laminated—black finish
Shaft: Apex #2 & #3 flexes only
Length: 43″ #1
Grip: Composition

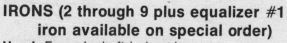

IRONS (2 through 9 plus equalizer #1 iron available on special order)
Head: Forged, shaft in hosel
Shaft: Apex #3, #4, #5 flexes
Length: 38½″ #1
Grip: Composition
Apex irons available in women's model also.

Ben Hogan
2912 West Pafford Street
Ft. Worth, Texas 76110
(817) 921-2661

OSCAR JONES COMPANY INC.

Model: CUSTOM CREST

WOODS (1-3-4-5)
Head: Laminated with dark walnut finish
Shaft: Dynamic steel
Length: To individual specification
Grip: Leather or composition

IRONS (1 through 9—P.W. & S.W.)
Head: Investment cast stainless steel shaft in hosel design
Shaft: Dynamic steel—R flex in stock, others on request
Length: To individual specification
Grip: Leather or composition

Oscar Jones Company, Inc.
P.O. Box 11203
2080 South Grand Avenue
Santa Ana, California 92705
(714) 549-8494

KELLER GOLF CLUBS INC.

WOODS (1-3-4-5)
Head: Persimmon—black finish
Shaft: Dynamic steel L-A-R-S flexes
Length: 43″ #1
Grip: Composition

IRONS (2 through 9 P.W. & S.W.)
Head: Investment cast stainless steel shaft over hosel design
Shaft: Dynamic steel L-A-R-S flexes
Length: 38½″ #2 iron
Grip: Composition

Keller Golf Clubs, Inc.
2140 Westwood Blvd.
Los Angeles, California 90025
(213) 879-5992

LYNX PRECISION GOLF EQUIPMENT

Model: U.S.A.

WOODS (Mens and womens models available)
Head: Persimmon—ebony finish
Shaft: Dynamic L-A-R-S flexes. Also available in titanium.
Length: To individual specification
Grip: Composition

IRONS (U.S.A.—available in mens and womens models)

Head: Investment cast stainless steel
Shaft: Dynamic L-A-R-S
Length: To individual specification
Grip: Composition

Lynx Precision Golf Equipment
7302 Adams Street
Paramount, California 90723
(213) 531-2333

Model: LIBERTY "76" LIMITED EDITION IRONS

Head: Investment cast stainless steel—shaft in hosel design
Shaft, Length, Grip: Shaft, length, grip swing weight and lie manufactured to individual specification

MacGREGOR

Model: VIP

WOODS (1-3-4-5)
Head: Laminated with soft applewood finish
Shaft: Available in medium and stiff flexes only
Length: 43" #1
Grip: Composition

IRONS (2 through 9 P.W. & S.W.)

Head: Investment cast stainless steel shaft in hosel design
Shaft: Medium and stiff flexes only
Length: 38½" #2 iron
Grip: Composition

MacGregor
P.O. Box 1005
Skokie, Illinois 60076
(312) 982-6000

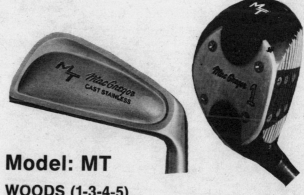

Model: MT

WOODS (1-3-4-5)
Head: Laminated—black finish
Shaft: Available in ladies—mens medium and stiff flexes
Length: 43" #1
Grip: Composition

IRONS

Head: Investment cast stainless steel—shaft in hosel design
Shaft: Available in ladies—mens medium and stiff flexes
Length: 38½" #2
Grip: Composition

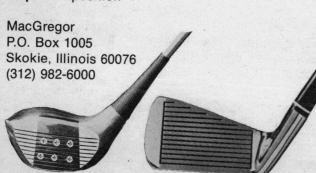

ARNOLD PALMER COMPANY

Model: PERSONAL

WOODS
Head: Laminated—two tone walnut finish
Shaft: Dynamic steel R & S flexes
Length: 43" #1
Grip: Composition

IRONS
Head: Investment cast stainless steel shaft over hosel design
Shaft: Dynamic R & S flexes
Length: 38½" #2 iron
Grip: Composition

Arnold Palmer Company
99 Tremont Street
Chattanooga, Tenn. 37405
(615) 267-5631

PEDERSEN

Model: 100

WOODS
Head: Persimmon with antique pecan finish
Shaft: Available in dynamic steel, titanium & graphite L-A-R-S flexes
Length: 43" #1
Grip: Composition

IRONS (2 through 9 P.W. & S.W.)
Head: Investment cast stainless steel shaft in hosel design
Shaft: Available in dynamic steel, titanium & graphite L-A-R-S flexes
Length: 38½" #2 iron
Grip: Composition

Model: SPOILER

WOODS (1-3-4-5-7)
Head: Laminated—walnut finish
Shaft: Dynamic steel available in L-A-R-S flexes. Also available in titanium and graphite shafts in L-R-S flexes.
Length: 43" #1
Grip: Composition

IRONS
Head: Investment cast shaft in hosel design
Shaft: Dynamic steel—titanium and graphite in L-A-R-S flexes
Length: 38½" #2 iron
Grip: Composition

Pedersen
101 Powdered Metal Drive
North Haven, Connecticut 06473
(203) 288-5611

PING

WOODS (1-2-3-4-5-6)
Head: Laminated—black finish
Shaft: Ping special steel—available in L-R-S flex
Length: 43″ #1
Grip: Composition

IRONS (1 through 9 P.W. & S.W.)
Head: Investment cast stainless steel shaft in hosel design
Shaft: Ping special steel—available in L-R-S flex
Length: 38½″ #2 iron
Grip: Composition

Karsten Mfg. Corp.
2201 West Desert Cove
Phoenix, Arizona 85029
(602) 943-7243

P.G.A.-VICTOR GOLF

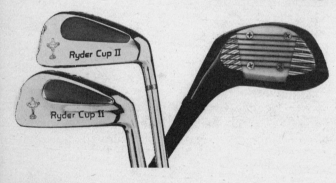

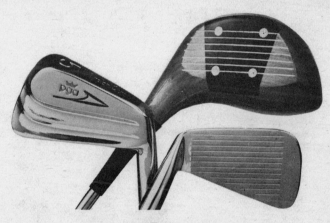

Model: RYDER CUP II

WOODS (1-3-4-5)
Head: Laminated—maroon glaze finish
Shaft: Dynamic steel R & S flex. Graphite shaft available on special order.
Length: 43″ #1
Grip: Composition
Left hand model also available in stock.

IRONS (1 through 9 P.W. & S.W.)
Head: Investment cast stainless steel. Both shaft in hosel and shaft over hosel available.
Shaft: Dynamic steel R & S flex. Graphite shaft available in the hosel model on special order.
Length: 39″ #2 iron
Grip: Composition

Model: VARDON CUP

WOODS (1-3-4-5)
Head: Laminated—soft honey finish
Shaft: Dynamic R & S flex. Graphite available on special order.
Length: 43″ #1
Grip: Composition

IRONS (2 through 9 P.W. & S.W.)
Head: Forged shaft in hosel design
Shaft: Dynamic R & S flex. Graphite available on special order.
Length: 39″ #2 iron
Grip: Composition

P.G.A.-VICTOR GOLF

Model: PAR-EX
WOODS (1-3-4-5-7)
Head: Laminated—black finish
Shaft: Par-Ex steel—flexible, regular & stiff flexes
Length: 43½″ #1
Grip: Composition

IRONS (1 through 9 P.W. & S.W.)
Head: Investment cast stainless steel shaft over
  hosel design
Shaft: Par-Ex steel—flexible, regular & stiff flexes
Length: 39″ #2 iron
Grip: Composition

P.G.A.-Victor Golf
8350 North Lehigh Avenue
Morton Grove, Illinois 60053
(312) 966-6300

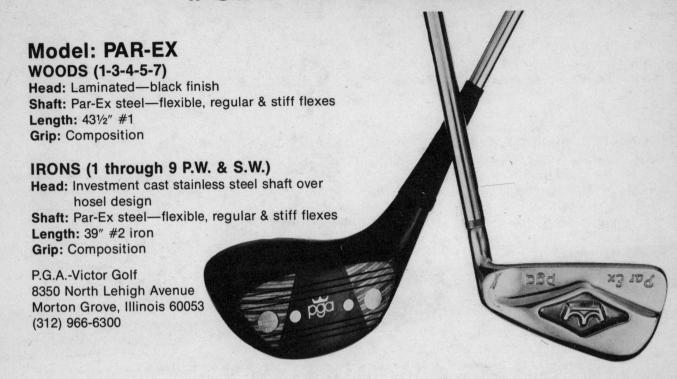

SHAMROCK GOLF COMPANY

WOODS (Men #301   Ladies #301-L)
Head: Laminated—forest green/black walnut
  finish
Shaft: Dynamic steel L-A-R-S-X flexes
Length: 43″ #1   Ladies 42″ #1
Grip: Composition

IRONS (Men #201   Ladies #201-L)
Head: Investment cast stainless
Shaft: Dynamic L-A-R-S-X flexes
Length: Men 39″ #2 iron   Ladies 38″ #2 iron
Grip: Composition. Leather and cord special
  order.

Shamrock Golf Company
1745 - 21st Street
Santa Monica, California 90404
(213) 828-7431

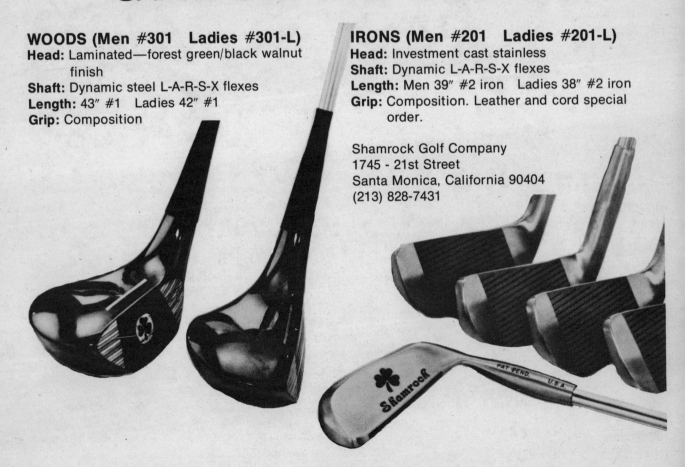

SIMMONS INTERNATIONAL

Model: MERLIN

WOODS (1-3-4-5)
Head: Laminated—walnut finish
Shaft: True temper steel
Length: 43″ #1
Grip: Composition

IRONS (2 through 9 P.W. & S.W.)
Head: Investment cast stainless steel. Shaft over
      hosel design.
Shaft: True temper steel
Length: 38½″ #2 iron
Grip: Composition

Model: STINGER WOODS

Head: Laminated—walnut finish
Shaft: Dynamic
Length: 43″ #1
Grip: Composition

Model: HONEYCOMB IRONS

Head: Investment cast stainless steel
Shaft: Dynamic
Length: 38½″ #2 iron
Grip: Composition

Simmons International
1048 E. Burgrove Street
Carson, California 90746
(213) 537-6690

KENNETH SMITH

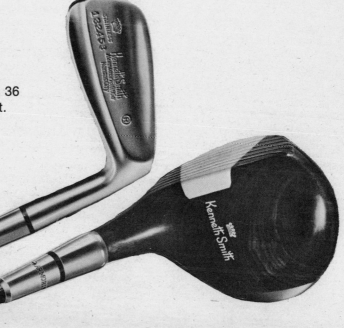

Model: HANDMADE CLUBS TO FIT YOU

WOODS
Head: Persimmon or laminated
Shaft: Rex alloy steel or graphite. Available in 36
      flexes from the whippiest to the stiffest.
Length: To fit the individual specification
Grip: Leather or composition

IRONS (1 through 9 P.W. & S.W.)
Head: Forged stainless steel
Shaft: Rex steel or graphite
Length: To fit individual specification
Grip: Leather or composition

Kenneth Smith
Box 41
Kansas City, Missouri 64141
(913) 631-5100

SPALDING

Model: ELITE CENTURION

WOODS (1-3-4-5)
Head: Laminated—black finish
Shaft: Lightweight or dynamic steel
Length: 43″ #1
Grip: Composition or leather

IRONS (2 through 9 P.W. & S.W.)
Head: Investment cast stainless steel
Shaft: Lightweight or dynamic steel
Length: 38½″ #2 iron
Grip: Composition or leather

Model: TOP FLITE LEGACY

WOODS (1-3-4-5)
Head: Laminated—black finish
Shaft: Dynamic steel R & S flex
Length: 43″ #1
Grip: Composition

IRONS (2 through 10)
Head: Investment cast stainless steel chrome
plated
Shaft: Dynamic steel R & S flex
Length: 38½″ #2 iron
Grip: Composition

Spalding
Meadow Street
Chicopee, Mass. 01014
(413) 536-1200

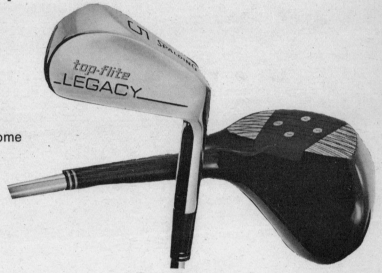

SQUARE TWO GOLF CORPORATION

Model: SQUARE TWO

WOODS (1-2-3-4)
Head: Laminated—black finish
Shaft: Dynamic steel L-A-R-S-X flex. Graphite in
R-S-X flex.
Length: 43″ #1
Grip: Composition

IRONS (2 through 9 P.W. & S.W.)
Head: Investment cast stainless steel
Shaft: Dynamic steel, L-A-R-S-X flex
Length: 39″ #2 iron
Grip: Composition

Square Two Golf Corp.
6 Franklin Avenue
Oakland, New Jersey 07436
(201) 337-3037

STAG

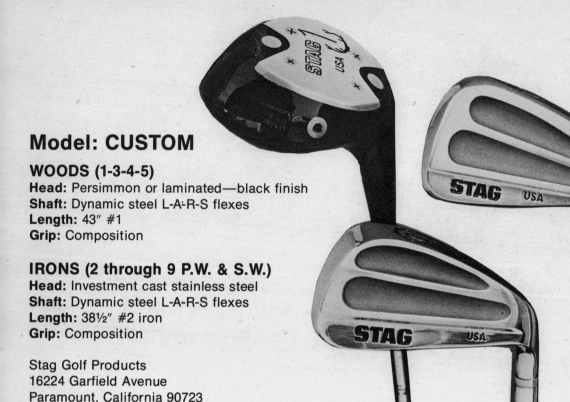

Model: CUSTOM

WOODS (1-3-4-5)
Head: Persimmon or laminated—black finish
Shaft: Dynamic steel L-A-R-S flexes
Length: 43" #1
Grip: Composition

IRONS (2 through 9 P.W. & S.W.)
Head: Investment cast stainless steel
Shaft: Dynamic steel L-A-R-S flexes
Length: 38½" #2 iron
Grip: Composition

Stag Golf Products
16224 Garfield Avenue
Paramount, California 90723
(213) 633-7080

WILSON SPORTING GOODS COMPANY

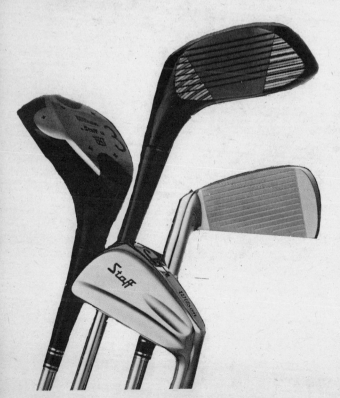

Model: STAFF

WOODS (1-3-4-5)
Head: Laminated head—black finish
Shaft: Dynamic steel R & S flex in stock, A & X on
special order
Length: 43" & 43½" #1
Grip: Panel leather or composition
Left hand model available 43" length only. R & S
flex in stock, others on special order.

IRONS
Head: Forged—shaft in hosel design
Shaft: Dynamic steel, R & S flex in stock, A & X
on special order
Length: 38½" & 39" #2 iron
Grip: Panel leather or composition

WILSON SPORTING GOODS COMPANY

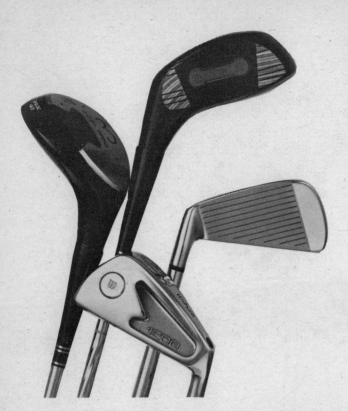

Model: 1200

WOODS (1-3-4-5)
Head: Laminated—black finish
Shaft: Counter torque lightweight steel. R & S
flex in stock, A & X flex on special order.
Length: 43" & 43½" #1
Grip: Leather or composition
Mens left hand available in 43" length R & S flex
only.

IRONS (2 through 9 P.W. & S.W.)
Head: Investment cast stainless steel shaft over
hosel design
Shaft: Counter torque lightweight steel R & S flex
in stock. A & X flex on special order.
Length: 38½" & 39" #2 iron
Grip: Leather or composition
Mens left hand available in 38½" length. R & S
flex only.

Model: WILSON X-31

WOODS
Head: Strata block—laminated
Shaft: Pro Fit steel
Length: 43" & 43½" R & S flex only
Grip: Composition
6 & 7 wood also available.

IRONS
Head: Forged
Shaft: Pro Fit steel
Length: 38" & 39½" R & S flex only
Grip: Composition

Wilson Sporting Goods Company
2233 West Street
River Grove, Illinois 60171
(312) 456-6100

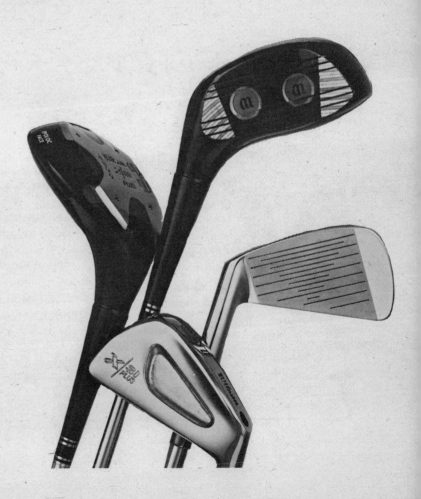

THE RECORD BOOK

Snead Wright

Zaharias Jones

USGA MEN'S OPEN

Year	Site	Winner	Score
1895	Newport (R.I.) G.C.	Horace Rawlins	173
1896	Shinnecock Hills	James Foulis	152
1897	Chicago G.C.	Joe Lloyd	162
1898	Myopia Hunt C.	Fred Herd	328
1899	Baltimore C.C.	Willie Smith	315
1900	Chicago G.C.	Harry Vardon	313
1901	Myopia Hunt C.	Willie Anderson	331-85
1902	Garden City C.C.	L. Auchterlonie	307
1903	Baltusrol G.C.	Willie Anderson	307-82
1904	Glen View (Ill.) C.	Willie Anderson	303
1905	Myopia Hunt C.	Willie Anderson	314
1906	Onwentsia C.	Alex Smith	295
1907	Philadelphia C.C.	Alex Ross	302
1908	Myopia Hunt C.	Fred McLeod	322-77
1909	Englewood (N.J.) G.C.	George Sargent	290
1910	Philadelphia C.C.	Alex Smith	298-71
1911	Chicago G.C.	John McDermott	307-80
1912	C.C. of Buffalo	John McDermott	294
1913	The Country Club	*Francis Ouimet	304-72
1914	Midlothian	Walter Hagen	290
1915	Baltusrol G.C.	*J. D. Travers	297
1916	Minikahda C.	*Charles Evans, Jr.	286
1917-18	No championship		
1919	Brae Burn C.C.	Walter Hagen	301-77
1920	Inverness C.	Edward Ray	295
1921	Columbia C.C.	James M. Barnes	289
1922	Skokie (Ill.) C.C.	Gene Sarazen	288
1923	Inwood (N.Y.) C.C.	*R. T. Jones, Jr.	296-76
1924	Oakland Hills	Cyril Walker	297
1925	Worcester (Mass.) C.C.	Wm. MacFarlane	291-75-72
		*R. T. Jones, Jr.	291-75-73
1926	Scioto C.C.	*R. T. Jones, Jr.	293
1927	Oakmont (Pa.)	Tommy Armour	301-76
		Harry Cooper	301-79
1928	Olympia Fields (Ill.) C.C.	Johnny Farrell	294-143
		*R. T. Jones, Jr.	294-144
1929	Winged Foot G.C.	*R. T. Jones, Jr.	294-141
		Al Espinosa	294-164
1930	Interlachen C.C.	*R. T. Jones, Jr.	287
1931	Inverness C.	Billy Burke	292-149-148
		Geo. Von Elm	292-149-149
1932	Fresh Meadow	Gene Sarazen	286
1933	North Shore G.C.	*Johnny Goodman	287
1934	Merion Cricket C.	Olin Dutra	293
1935	Oakmont (Pa.)	Sam Parks, Jr.	299
1936	Baltusrol G.C.	Tony Manero	282
1937	Oakland Hills C.C.	Ralph Guldahl	281
1938	Cherry Hills C.C.	Ralph Guldahl	284
1939	Phila. C.C. W. Consho-hocken, Pa.	Byron Nelson	284-68-70
		Craig Wood	284-68-73
		Denny Shute	284-76
1940	Canterbury G.C. Cleveland	Lawson Little	287-70
		Gene Sarazen	287-73
1941	Colonial C.C. Ft. Worth, Tex.	Craig Wood	284
1942-45	No championship held		
1946	Canterbury G.C. Cleveland	Lloyd Mangrum	284-72-72
		Byron Nelson	284-72-73
		Vic Ghezzi	284-72-73
1947	St. Louis C.C. Clayton, Mo.	Lew Worsham	282-69
		Sam Snead	282-70
1948	Riviera C.C.	Ben Hogan	276
1949	Medinah C.C.	Cary Middlecoff	286
1950	Merion Cricket C. Ardmore, Pa.	Ben Hogan	287-69
		Lloyd Mangrum	287-73
		George Fazio	287-75
1951	Oakland Hills C.C.	Ben Hogan	287
1952	Dallas Northwood	Julius Boros	281
1953	Oakmont C.C.	Ben Hogan	283
1954	Baltusrol G.C.	Ed Furgol	284
1955	Olympic C.C. San Francisco	Jack Fleck	287-69
		Ben Hogan	287-72
1956	Oak Hill C.C.	Cary Middlecoff	281
1957	Inverness C.	Dick Mayer	282-72
		Cary Middlecoff	282-79
1958	Southern Hills	Tommy Bolt	283
1959	Winged Foot G.C.	Bill Casper	282
1960	Cherry Hills C.C.	Arnold Palmer	280
1961	Oakland Hills	Gene Littler	281
1962	Oakmont (Pa.)	Jack Nicklaus	283-71
		Arnold Palmer	283-74
1963	The Country Club	Julius Boros	293-70
		Jacky Cupit	293-73
		Arnold Palmer	293-76
1964	Congressional C.C.	Ken Venturi	278
1965	Bellerive, C.C., Creve Coeur, Mo.	Gary Player	282-71
		Kel Nagle	282-74
1966	Olympic C.C., San Francisco	Billy Casper	278-69
		Arnold Palmer	278-73
1967	Baltusrol G.C.	Jack Nicklaus	275**
1968	Oak Hill C.C.	Lee Trevino	275**
1969	Champions G.C.	Orville Moody	281
1970	Hazeltine Ntl.	Tony Jacklin	281
1971	Merion G.C., Ardmore, Pa.	Lee Trevino	280-68
		Jack Nicklaus	280-71
1972	Pebble Beach	Jack Nicklaus	290
1973	Oakmont (Pa.) C.C.	Johnny Miller	279
1974	Winged Foot G.C.	Hale Irwin	287
1975	Medinah C.C., Medinah, Ill.	Lou Graham	287-71
		John Mahaffey	287-73

PGA CHAMPIONSHIP

Year	Site	Result	Margin
1916	Siwanoy C.C., Bronxville, N.Y.	James Barnes d. J. Hutchison	1 up
1917-18	No tournament		
1919	Engineers C.C., Roslyn, L.I., N.Y.	James Barnes d. Fred McLeod	5 and 4
1920	Flossmoor (Ill.) C.C.	Jock Hutchison d. J. D. Edgar	1 up
1921	Inwood C.C., Far Rockaway, N.Y.	Walter Hagen d. J. Barnes	3 and 2
1922	Oakmont (Pa.) C.C.	Gene Sarazen d. E. French	4 and 3
1923	Pelham (N.Y.) C.C.	Gene Sarazen d. W. Hagen	1 up (38)
1924	French Lick (Ind.) C.C.	Walter Hagen d. J. Barnes	2 up
1925	Olympia Fields (Ill.) C.C.	Walter Hagen d. B. Mehlhorn	6 and 5
1926	Salisbury G.C., Westbury, N.Y.	Walter Hagen d. L. Diegel	5 and 3
1927	Cedar Crest C.C., Dallas, Tex.	Walter Hagen d. J. Turnesa	1 up
1928	Five Farms C.C. Baltimore, Md.	Leo Diegel d. Al Espinosa	6 and 5
1929	Hillcrest C.C., Los Angeles, Calif.	Leo Diegel d. J. Farrell	6 and 4
1930	Fresh Meadows C.C., Flushing, N.Y.	Tommy Armour d. G. Sarazen	1 up
1931	Wannamoisett C.C., Rumford, R.I.	Tom Creavy d. D. Shute	2 and 1
1932	Keller G.C., St. Paul, Minn.	Olin Dutra d. F. Walsh	4 and 3
1933	Blue Mound C.C., Milwaukee, Wis.	Gene Sarazen d. W. Goggin	5 and 4
1934	Park C.C., W'msville, N.Y.	Paul Runyan d. C. Wood	1 up (38)
1935	Twin Hills C.C., Oklahoma City	Johnny Revolta d. T. Armour	5 and 4
1936	Pinehurst (N.C.) C.C.	Denny Shute d. J. Thomson	3 and 2
1937	Pittsburgh, F.C.	Denny Shute d. H. McSpaden	1 up (37)
1938	Shawnee (Pa.) C.C.	Paul Runyan d. S. Snead	8 and 7
1939	Pomonok C.C., Flushing, N.Y.	Henry Picard d. B. Nelson	1 up (37)
1940	Hershey (Pa.) C.C.	Byron Nelson d. S. Snead	1 up
1941	Cherry Hills C.C., Denver, Colo.	Vic Ghezzi d. B. Nelson	1 up (38)
1942	Seaview C.C., Atlantic City, N.J.	Sam Snead d. J. Turnesa	2 and 1
1943	No tournament		
1944	Manito G. & C.C., Spokane, Wash.	Bob Hamilton d. B. Nelson	1 up
1945	Moraine C.C., Dayton, O.	Byron Nelson d. S. Byrd	4 and 3
1946	Portland (Ore.) C.C.	Ben Hogan d. E. Oliver	6 and 4
1947	Plum Hollow C.C., Detroit	Jim Ferrier d. C. Harbert	2 and 1
1948	Norwood Hills C.C., St. Louis	Ben Hogan d. M. Turnesa	7 and 6
1949	Hermitage C.C., Richmond, Va.	Sam Snead d. J. Palmer	3 and 2
1950	Scioto C.C., Columbus, O.	Chandler Harper d. H. Williams, Jr.	4 and 3
1951	Oakmont (Pa.) C.C.	Sam Snead d. W. Burkemo	7 and 6
1952	Big Spring C.C., Louisville, Ky.	Jim Turnesa d. C. Harbert	1 up
1953	Birmingham (Mich.) C.C.	Walter Burkemo d. F. Torza	2 and 1
1954	Keller G.C., St. Paul, Minn.	Chick Harbert d. W. Burkemo	4 and 3
1955	Meadowbrook, Detroit, Mich.	Doug Ford d. C. Middlecoff	4 and 3
1956	Blue Hill C.C., Canton, Mass.	Jack Burke d. T. Kroll	3 and 2
1957	Miami Valley, Dayton, O.	Lionel Hebert d. D. Finsterwald	2 and 1
1958	Llanerch C.C.	Dow Finsterwald	276
1959	Minneapolis	Bob Rosburg	277
1960	Firestone C.C.	Jay Hebert	281
1961	Olympia Fields (Ill.) C.C.	Jerry Barber	277-67
		Don January	277-68
1962	Aronimink G.C.	Gary Player	278
1963	Dallas (Tex.) A.C.	Jack Nicklaus	279
1964	Columbus C.C.	Bobby Nichols	271**
1965	Laurel Valley G.C.	Dave Marr	280
1966	Firestone C.C.	Al Geiberger	280
1967	Columbine C.C., Denver, Colo.	Don January	281-69
		Don Massengale	281-71
1968	Pecan Valley C.C.	Julius Boros	281
1969	NCR, Dayton	Ray Floyd	276
1970	Southern Hills	Dave Stockton	279
1971	PGA National G.C.	Jack Nicklaus	281
1972	Oakland Hills C.C.	Gary Player	281
1973	Canterbury G.C.	Jack Nicklaus	277
1974	Tanglewood G.C.	Lee Trevino	276
1975	Firestone C.C.	Jack Nicklaus	276

MASTERS

Site: Augusta National G.C., Augusta, Ga.

Year	Winner	Score
1934	Horton Smith	284
1935	Gene Sarazen	282-144
	Craig Wood	282-149
1936	Horton Smith	285
1937	Byron Nelson	283
1938	Henry Picard	285
1939	Ralph Guldahl	279
1940	Jimmy Demaret	280
1941	Craig Wood	280
1942	Byron Nelson	280-69
	Ben Hogan	280-70
1943-45	No championships	
1946	Herman Keiser	282
1947	Jimmy Demaret	281
1948	Claude Harmon	279
1949	Sam Snead	282
1950	Jimmy Demaret	283
1951	Ben Hogan	280
1952	Sam Snead	286
1953	Ben Hogan	274
1954	Sam Snead	289-70
	Ben Hogan	289-71
1955	Cary Middlecoff	279
1956	Jack Burke	289
1957	Doug Ford	283
1958	Arnold Palmer	284
1959	Art Wall	284
1960	Arnold Palmer	282
1961	Gary Player	280
1962	Arnold Palmer	280-68
	Gary Player	280-71
	Dow Finsterwald	280-77
1963	Jack Nicklaus	286
1964	Arnold Palmer	276
1965	Jack Nicklaus	271**
1966	Jack Nicklaus	288-70
	Tommy Jacobs	288-72
	Gay Brewer	288-78
1967	Gay Brewer	280
1968	Bob Goalby	277
1969	George Archer	281
1970	Billy Casper	279-69
	Gene Littler	279-74
1971	Charles Coody	279
1972	Jack Nicklaus	286
1973	Tommy Aaron	283
1974	Gary Player	278
1975	Jack Nicklaus	276

*Denotes amateur. **Record.

LEADER BOARD OF MAJOR-CHAMPIONSHIP WINNERS

	U.S. Open	British Open	PGA	Masters	U.S. Amateur	British Amateur	Total Titles
Jack Nicklaus	3	2	4	5	2	0	16
Bobby Jones	4	3	0	0	5	1	13
Walter Hagen	2	4	5	0	0	0	11
Ben Hogan	4	1	2	2	0	0	9
Arnold Palmer	1	2	0	4	1	0	8
Gary Player	1	3	2	2	0	0	8
Gene Sarazen	2	1	3	1	0	0	7
Sam Snead	0	1	3	3	0	0	7
Harry Vardon	1	6	0	0	0	0	7
Byron Nelson	1	0	2	2	0	0	5
Lee Trevino	2	2	1	0	0	0	5
Peter Thomson	0	5	0	0	0	0	5

MEN'S PROFESSIONAL RECORDS

Past Leading Money Winners

1963
	Player	Money
1.	Arnold Palmer	$128,230
2.	Jack Nicklaus	100,040
3.	Julius Boros	77,356
4.	Tony Lema	67,112
5.	Gary Player	55,455
6.	Dow Finsterwald	49,862
7.	Mason Rudolph	39,120
8.	Al Geiberger	34,126
9.	Don January	33,754
10.	Bobby Nichols	33,604

1964
	Player	Money
1.	Jack Nicklaus	$113,284
2.	Arnold Palmer	113,203
3.	Bill Casper	90,653
4.	Tony Lema	74,130
5.	Bobby Nichols	74,012
6.	Ken Venturi	62,465
7.	Gary Player	61,449
8.	Mason Rudolph	52,568
9.	Juan Rodriguez	48,338
10.	Mike Souchak	39,559

1965
	Player	Money
1.	Jack Nicklaus	$140,752
2.	Tony Lema	101,816
3.	Bill Casper	99,931
4.	Doug Sanders	72,182
5.	Gary Player	69,964
6.	Bruce Devlin	67,657
7.	Dave Marr	63,375
8.	Al Geiberger	59,699
9.	Gene Littler	58,898
10.	Arnold Palmer	57,770

1966
	Player	Money
1.	Bill Casper	$121,944
2.	Jack Nicklaus	111,419
3.	Arnold Palmer	110,467
4.	Doug Sanders	80,096
5.	Gay Brewer	75,687
6.	Phil Rodgers	68,360
7.	Gene Littler	68,345
8.	R. H. Sikes	67,348
9.	Frank Beard	66,041
10.	Al Geiberger	63,220

1967
	Player	Money
1.	Jack Nicklaus	$188,988
2.	Arnold Palmer	184,065
3.	Bill Casper	129,423
4.	Julius Boros	126,785
5.	Dan Sikes	111,508
6.	Doug Sanders	109,455
7.	Frank Beard	105,778
8.	George Archer	84,344
9.	Gay Brewer	78,548
10.	Bob Goalby	77,106

1968
	Player	Money
1.	Bill Casper	$205,168
2.	Jack Nicklaus	155,285
3.	Tom Weiskopf	152,946
4.	George Archer	150,972
5.	Julius Boros	148,310
6.	Lee Trevino	132,127
7.	Arnold Palmer	114,602
8.	Dan Sikes	108,330
9.	Miller Barber	105,845
10.	Bob Murphy	105,595

1969
	Player	Money
1.	Frank Beard	$175,223
2.	Dave Hill	156,423
3.	Jack Nicklaus	140,167
4.	Gary Player	123,897
5.	Bruce Crampton	118,955
6.	Gene Littler	112,737
7.	Lee Trevino	112,417
8.	Ray Floyd	109,956
9.	Arnold Palmer	105,128
10.	Bill Casper	104,689

1970
	Player	Money
1.	Lee Trevino	$157,037
2.	Bill Casper	147,372
3.	Bruce Crampton	142,609
4.	Jack Nicklaus	142,148
5.	Arnold Palmer	128,853
6.	Frank Beard	124,690
7.	Dick Lotz	124,539
8.	Larry Hinson	120,897
9.	Bob Murphy	120,639
10.	Dave Hill	118,415

1971
	Player	Money
1.	Jack Nicklaus	$244,490
2.	Lee Trevino	231,202
3.	Arnold Palmer	209,603
4.	George Archer	147,769
5.	Gary Player	120,916
6.	Miller Barber	117,359
7.	Jerry Heard	112,389
8.	Frank Beard	112,337
9.	Dave Eichelberger	108,312
10.	Bill Casper	107,276

1972
	Player	Money
1.	Jack Nicklaus	$320,542
2.	Lee Trevino	214,805
3.	George Archer	145,027
4.	Grier Jones	140,177
5.	Jerry Heard	137,198
6.	Tom Weiskopf	129,422
7.	Gary Player	120,719
8.	Bruce Devlin	119,768
9.	Tommy Aaron	118,924
10.	Lanny Wadkins	116,616

1973
	Player	Money
1.	Jack Nicklaus	$308,362
2.	Bruce Crampton	274,266
3.	Tom Weiskopf	245,463
4.	Lee Trevino	210,017
5.	Lanny Wadkins	200,455
6.	Miller Barber	184,014
7.	Hale Irwin	130,388
8.	Billy Casper	129,474
9.	Johnny Miller	127,833
10.	John Schlee	118,017

1974
	Player	Money
1.	Johnny Miller	$353,021
2.	Jack Nicklaus	238,178
3.	Hubert Green	211,709
4.	Lee Trevino	203,422
5.	J. C. Snead	164,486
6.	Dave Stockton	155,105
7.	Hale Irwin	152,520
8.	Jerry Heard	145,788
9.	Brian Allin	137,950
10.	Tom Watson	135,474

LEADERS FROM 1941 TO 1962
Year	Player	Money
1941	Ben Hogan	$18,358
1942	Ben Hogan	13,143
1943	War bond prizes.	
1944	Byron Nelson	37,967
1945	Byron Nelson	63,335
1946	Ben Hogan	42,556
1947	Jimmy Demaret	27,936
1948	Ben Hogan	32,112
1949	Sam Snead	31,593
1950	Sam Snead	35,758
1951	Lloyd Mangrum	26,088
1952	Julius Boros	37,032
1953	Lew Worsham	34,002
1954	Bob Toski	65,819
1955	Julius Boros	63,121
1956	Ted Kroll	72,835
1957	Dick Mayer	65,835
1958	Arnold Palmer	42,607
1959	Art Wall	53,167
1960	Arnold Palmer	75,262
1961	Gary Player	64,450
1962	Arnold Palmer	81,448

Byron Nelson . . . $63,335 was a record haul in 1945.

ALL-TIME MONEY LEADERS
(In tour events, through 1975)
	Player	Since	Total
1.	Jack Nicklaus	1962	$2,541,772
2.	Arnold Palmer	1955	1,723,113
3.	Billy Casper	1955	1,581,605
4.	Lee Trevino	1966	1,398,651
5.	Bruce Crampton	1957	1,323,399
6.	Tom Weiskopf	1964	1,224,854
7.	Gene Littler	1954	1,203,541
8.	Gary Player	1957	1,163,153
9.	Miller Barber	1959	994,868
10.	Julius Boros	1950	993,756
11.	Frank Beard	1962	951,596
12.	Johnny Miller	1969	947,152
13.	Dave Hill	1959	922,233
14.	Bobby Nichols	1960	906,276
15.	Dave Stockton	1964	814,483
16.	George Archer	1964	810,020
17.	Al Geiberger	1960	794,505
18.	Dan Sikes	1961	773,508
19.	Doug Sanders	1957	767,434
20.	Hale Irwin	1968	760,054
21.	Tommy Aaron	1961	745,707
22.	Gay Brewer	1956	712,087
23.	Bob Murphy	1968	708,392
24.	Ray Floyd	1963	697,587
25.	Bert Yancey	1964	688,124
26.	Charles Coody	1963	663,253
27.	Bruce Devlin	1962	660,454
28.	Don January	1956	655,189
29.	Juan Rodriguez	1960	650,969
30.	Bob Goalby	1957	629,457
31.	Jerry Heard	1969	618,320
32.	Lou Graham	1964	617,842
33.	Sam Snead	1937	611,886
34.	Homero Blancas	1965	593,586
35.	Art Wall	1950	585,837
36.	Mason Rudolph	1959	535,942
37.	Gardner Dickinson	1952	533,795
38.	J. C. Snead	1968	530,692
39.	Hubert Green	1970	527,408
40.	Bob Charles	1962	524,301
41.	George Knudson	1959	490,243
42.	Jim Colbert	1966	464,490
43.	Kermit Zarley	1963	463,926
44.	Dale Douglass	1963	457,714
45.	Rod Funseth	1961	453,694
46.	Ken Still	1961	453,140
47.	Phil Rodgers	1961	452,005
48.	Bob Rosburg	1953	435,498
49.	Bob Lunn	1967	426,643
50.	John Mahaffey	1971	423,153

ALL-TIME TOURNAMENT WINNERS
(In tour events, through 1975)
	Player	Since	Total
1.	Sam Snead	1937	84
2.	Ben Hogan*	1938	62
3.	Arnold Palmer	1955	61
4.	Jack Nicklaus	1962	58
5.	Byron Nelson*	1935	54
6.	Billy Casper	1955	51
7.	Lloyd Mangrum**	1939	34
8.	Cary Middlecoff*	1947	33
9.	Jimmy Demaret*	1935	31
10.	Gene Littler	1954	28
11.	Jim Ferrier	1944	21
12.	Doug Sanders*	1957	20
13.	Doug Ford*	1950	19
14.	Julius Boros	1950	18
	Gary Player	1957	18
	Lee Trevino	1966	18
17.	Harold McSpaden*	1932	17
18.	Mike Souchak*	1953	16
19.	Dutch Harrison*	1930	15
	Paul Runyan*	1929	15
	Tommy Bolt*	1946	15
	Jack Burke Jr.*	1947	15
	Bruce Crampton	1957	15
	Johnny Miller	1969	15
25.	Art Wall	1950	14
26.	Dow Finsterwald*	1952	12
	Bobby Nichols	1960	12
	Dave Hill	1959	12
29.	Bob Goalby*	1957	11
	Don January	1955	11
	Frank Beard	1962	11
	George Archer	1964	11
	Gay Brewer	1956	11
	Tom Weiskopf	1964	11

*Not active on tour.
**Deceased 11/17/73.

TOURNAMENT PRIZE MONEY
(In tour events only)
Year	Events	Total Purses	Average Purse
1945	36	$435,380	$12,094
1946	37	411,533	11,123
1947	31	352,500	11,371
1948	34	427,000	12,559
1949	25	338,200	13,528
1950	33	459,950	13,938
1951	30	460,200	15,340
1952	32	498,016	15,563
1953	32	562,704	17,585
1954	26	600,819	23,108
1955	36	782,010	21,723
1956	36	847,070	23,530
1957	32	820,360	25,636
1958	39	1,005,800	25,789
1959	43	1,102,474	25,639
1960	41	1,187,340	28,959
1961	45	1,461,830	32,485
1962	49	1,790,320	36,537
1963	43	2,044,900	47,497
1964	41	2,301,063	56,123
1965	36	2,848,515	79,403
1966	36	3,074,445	85,401
1967	37	3,979,162	108,356
1968	45	5,077,600	112,835
1969	47	5,465,875	116,295
1970	47	6,259,501	133,181
1971	52	6,587,976	126,689
1972	47	6,954,649	151,188
1973	47	8,657,225	184,196
1974	43	7,764,449	180,568
1975	41	7,402,750	180,555

VARDON TROPHY WINNERS
Year	Player	Average
1947	Jimmy Demaret	69.90
1948	Ben Hogan	69.30
1949	Sam Snead	69.37
1950	Sam Snead	69.23
1951	Lloyd Mangrum	70.05
1952	Jack Burke	70.54
1953	Lloyd Mangrum	70.22
1954	E. J. Harrison	70.41
1955	Sam Snead	69.86
1956	Cary Middlecoff	70.35
1957	Dow Finsterwald	70.29
1958	Bob Rosburg	70.11
1959	Art Wall	70.35
1960	Bill Casper	69.95
1961	Arnold Palmer	69.82
1962	Arnold Palmer	70.27
1963	Bill Casper	70.58
1964	Arnold Palmer	70.01
1965	Bill Casper	70.59
1966	Bill Casper	70.16
1967	Arnold Palmer	70.18
1968	Bill Casper	69.98
1969	Dave Hill	70.34
1970	Lee Trevino	70.64
1971	Lee Trevino	70.41
1972	Lee Trevino	70.91
1973	Bruce Crampton	70.69
1974	Lee Trevino	70.53
1975	Bruce Crampton	70.50

PHOENIX OPEN ($150,000), Phoenix C.C. (71-6,709), Jan. 9-12.

J. Miller	**67-61-68-64—260**	**$30,000**
Heard	74-68-67-65—274	17,100
Aaron	68-72-69-67—276	10,650
M. Hill	71-63-69-74—277	7,050
Pace	68-69-69-72—278	6,150
J. Snead	68-72-67-72—279	5,400
Lotz	69-68-72-71—280	4,095
Mahaffey	67-71-72-70—280	4,095
Littler	71-67-70-72—280	4,095
Watson	73-71-68-68—280	4,095
Baird	71-74-67-68—280	4,095

DEAN MARTIN TUCSON OPEN ($200,000), Tucson Ntl. G.C. (72-7,305), Jan. 16-19.

J. Miller	**66-69-67-61—263**	**$40,000**
Mahaff'y	67-69-69-67—272	22,800
Watson	72-67-67-67—273	14,200
M. Hill	68-72-67-69—276	8,800
Iverson	67-74-66-69—276	8,800
Geib'ger	71-69-69-69—278	7,200
Crampt'n	71-72-70-66—279	5,900
Aaron	71-66-70-72—279	5,900
Th'pson	68-70-69-72—279	5,900
Palmer	72-71-67-70—280	5,000

BING CROSBY NTL. PRO-AM ($185,000), Pebble Beach G. L. (72-6,815), Spyglass Hill G.C. (72-6,810), Cypress Point C. (72-6,464), Pebble Beach, Calif., Jan. 23-26.

Littler	**68-71-68-73—280**	**$37,000**
Green	66-75-74-69—284	21,090
Kite	70-76-69-70—285	13,135
L.Grah'm	72-70-70-75—287	8,695
Fezler	71-73-72-72—288	7,585
D. Hill	76-72-69-72—289	5,319
Nicklaus	71-74-72-72—289	5,319
Devlin	73-71-69-76—289	5,319
J. Miller	71-74-70-74—289	5,319
Th'pson	74-71-71-73—289	5,319
R. Massengale	72-71-74-72—289	5,319

HAWAIIAN OPEN ($220,000), Waialae C.C. (72-7,154), Honolulu, Hawaii, Jan. 30-Feb. 2.

Groh	**68-68-70-68—274**	**$44,000**
Geib'ger	66-69-71-69—275	25,080
Palmer	69-67-69-71—276	15,620
Crampt'n	69-70-70-68—277	9,680
L.Grah'm	69-71-65-72—277	9,680
Fezler	69-67-68-74—278	7,920
Crawf'rd	72-70-66-71—279	6,765
Rogers	69-71-71-68—279	6,675

BOB HOPE DESERT CLASSIC ($160,000), Bermuda Dunes C.C. (72-7,010); also at La-Quinta, Tamarisk & Indian Wells C.C.s, all in Palm Springs, Calif., area, Feb. 5-9.

J. Miller	**205-66-68—339**	**$32,000**
Murphy	208-68-66—342	18,240
Heard	206-68-69—343	11,360
T. Shaw	205-71-69—345	7,520
Mahaffey	206-69-71—346	6,160
Fitzsimons	213-67-66—346	6,160
Casper	209-68-70—347	4,920
McLendon	207-74-66—347	4,920
M. Barber	206-70-72—348	4,160
Bies	204-72-72—348	4,160

ANDY WILLIAMS SAN DIEGO OPEN ($170,000), Torrey Pines G.C. (No., 72-6,667; So., 72-7,047), San Diego, Feb. 13-16.

J.Snead*	**69-71-71-68—279**	**$34,000**
Nichols	71-69-68-71—279	15,725
Floyd	68-71-68-72—279	15,725
Funseth	70-67-69-74—280	7,990
Kite	72-68-70-71—281	6,970
Mahaff'y	69-71-71-71—282	5,525
Irwin	70-71-73-68—282	5,525
Casper	69-68-72-73—282	5,525
Douglass	71-71-72-70—284	4,250
L.Th'pson	72-69-68-75—284	4,250
F'simons	71-74-71-68—284	4,250

*Won sudden-death playoff.

GLEN CAMPBELL LOS ANGELES OPEN ($150,000), Riviera Country Club (6,847-71), Pacific Palisades, Calif., Feb. 20-23.

Fitzsmns	**70-71-64-70—275**	**$30,000**
Kite	71-69-71-68—279	17,100
Nicklaus	69-75-71-65—280	10,650
Irwin	72-72-71-67—282	6,600
Weiskopf	67-75-72-68—282	6,600
Watson	67-73-72-71—283	4,668
McGee	70-73-70-70—283	4,668
Casper	69-74-71-69—283	4,668
Dent	69-73-71-70—283	4,668
Stockton	68-75-69-72—284	3,600
Douglass	68-69-74-73—284	3,600

JACKIE GLEASON INVERRARY CLASSIC ($260,000), Inverrary C.C. (7,128-72), Lauderhill, Fla., Feb. 27-March 2.

Murphy	**68-71-66-68—273**	**$52,000**
Pearce	67-64-72-71—274	29,640
Nicklaus	67-69-66-73—275	18,460
M.Barb'r	67-70-71-68—276	12,220
Trevino	70-70-71-66—277	10,010
Irwin	68-66-72-70—277	10,010
Palmer	68-66-71-74—279	7,995
Weiskopf	72-68-66-73—279	7,995
Littler	70-66-72-72—280	6,240
Coody	68-69-71-72—280	6,240
R. Massengale	68-74-65-73—280	6,240
Kite	68-67-70-75—280	6,240

FLORIDA CITRUS OPEN ($200,000), Rio Pinar C.C. (72-6,929), Orlando, Fla., March 6-9.

Trevino	**69-66-70-71—276**	**$40,000**
Irwin	68-67-74-68—277	22,800
Crensh'w	72-68-67-71—278	14,200
Coody	71-66-71-71—279	9,400
Devlin	72-71-66-72—281	7,267
R. Massengale	68-71-72-70—281	7,267
Fezler	71-74-69-67—281	7,267
Watson	70-69-73-70—282	5,225
Ziegler	71-70-72-69—282	5,225
Hinson	68-68-74-72—282	5,225
Schlee	72-72-69-69—282	5,225

DORAL-EASTERN OPEN ($150,000), Doral C.C. (Blue cse., 72-7,065), Miami, March 13-16.

Nicklaus	**69-70-69-68—276**	**$30,000**
Fezler	71-70-67-71—279	13,875
Yancey	71-72-69-67—279	13,875
J. Miller	72-69-72-67—280	7,050
Crampt'n	73-69-68-71—281	5,775
Allin	70-72-70-69—281	5,775
M. Hill	69-71-72-70—282	4,612
Melnyk	72-71-70-69—282	4,612

*Won sudden-death playoff.

GR. JACKSONVILLE OPEN ($150,000), Deerwood C.C. (72-7,143), Jacksonville, Fla., March 20-23.

Ziegler	**73-69-69-65—276**	**$30,000**
McL'don	67-72-71-68—278	13,875
Morley	72-71-65-70—278	13,875
L.Gra'hm	74-69-71-65—279	7,050
North	71-71-70-68—280	5,450
Armstr'g	71-73-66-70—280	5,450
Shaw	70-67-72-71—280	5,450
Cole	69-69-74-69—281	3,765
Inman	70-68-73-70—281	3,765
Dickson	68-71-71-71—281	3,765
Crensh'w	68-73-69-71—281	3,765
McGee	70-68-71-72—281	3,765
Hinson	71-70-69-72—282	2,850

HERITAGE CLASSIC ($200,000), Harbour Town G. Links (71-6,655), Hilton Head Island, S.C., March 27-30.

Nicklaus	**66-63-74-68—271**	**$40,000**
Weiskopf	70-65-68-71—274	22,800
Coody	71-69-74-65—279	14,200
Mahaff'y	70-70-70-70—280	9,400
Crampt'n	69-70-71-71—281	7,700
Kite	69-68-69-75—281	7,700
McL'don	73-68-72-69—282	6,400
Schlee	73-70-68-72—283	5,900
Archer	71-68-76-69—284	4,800
M.Barber	72-66-74-72—284	4,800
January	69-70-69-76—284	4,800
Irwin	69-68-72-75—284	4,800

Jerry McGee's Pensacola win was his first.

GR. GREENSBORO OPEN ($225,000), Sedgefield C.C. (71-6,643), Greensboro, N.C., April 3-6.

Weiskopf	**64-71-72-68—275**	**$45,000**
G'berger	71-75-66-66—278	25,650
McGee	77-67-68-68—280	15,975
Trevino	71-70-72-68—281	10,575
D. Hill	67-73-72-70—282	9,225
Still	74-68-69-72—283	7,650
J. Miller	72-70-70-71—283	7,650
Bembridge	72-73-70-69—284	6,650
Marsh	73-70-72-70—285	5,625
Rudolph	73-72-70-70—285	5,625
Melnyk	77-70-70-68—285	5,625

MASTERS ($250,000), Augusta (Ga.) Nt'l G.C. (72-6,980), April 10-13.

Nicklaus	**68-67-73-68—276**	**$40,000**
Weiskopf	69-72-66-70—277	21,250
J. Miller	75-71-65-66—277	21,250
Irwin	73-74-71-64—282	12,500
Nichols	67-74-72-69—282	12,500
Casper	70-70-73-70—283	7,500
D. Hill	75-71-70-68—284	6,000
Watson	70-70-72-73—285	4,500
Green	74-71-70-70—285	4,500
Trevino	71-70-74-71—286	3,600
J. Snead	69-72-75-70—286	3,600
Kite	72-74-71-69—286	3,600
Palmer	69-71-75-72—287	3,250
Ziegler	71-73-74-69—287	3,250
A. Miller	68-75-72-73—288	2,900
Cole	73-71-73-71—288	2,900
Devlin	72-70-76-70—288	2,900
Curl	72-70-76-70—288	2,900
Wall	72-74-72-70—288	2,900
Allin	73-69-73-74—289	2,550
Johnston	74-73-69-73—289	2,550

PENSACOLA OPEN ($125,000), Pensacola C.C. (71-6,679), Pensacola, Fla., April 17-20.

McGee	**69-66-66-70—271**	**$25,000**
Armstr'g	70-66-66-71—273	14,250
Nevil	71-69-69-65—274	6,625
Crampt'n	65-72-68-69—274	6,625
M.Barber	67-69-70-68—274	6,625
Pate*	69-71-69-66—275	
Mitchell	73-70-67-66—276	4,062
Murphy	69-73-67-67—276	4,062
Sikes	72-69-66-69—276	4,062
Coody	65-71-73-68—277	2,770
Sanders	73-64-71-69—277	2,770
L.Grah'm	68-70-70-69—277	2,770
North	64-73-70-70—277	2,770
Elder	70-68-69-70—277	2,770
Maltbie	69-67-69-72—277	2,770

TOURNAMENT OF CHAMPIONS ($200,000), La Costa C.C. (72-6,855), Rancho La Costa, Calif., April 24-27.

Geib'ger*	**67-67-70-73—277**	**$40,000**
Player	72-70-68-67—277	23,700
Trevino	72-65-70-71—278	14,812
Colbert	65-73-70-71—279	9,503
Allin	73-69-70-72—284	7,792
Irwin	70-73-71-70—284	7,792
Littler	69-72-74-70—285	6,667
Watson	69-75-71-70—285	6,667
Nicklaus	70-72-71-74—287	5,944
Stockton	72-71-71-73—287	5,944
F'simons	74-72-74-68—288	5,104
Weiskopf	71-76-70-71—288	5,104
Murphy	74-73-69-72—288	5,104

*Won sudden-death playoff.

TALLAHASSEE OPEN ($90,000), Killearn G. & C.C. (72-7,124), Tallahassee, Fla., April 24-27.

R.Massengale	**67-67-68-72—274**	**$12,000**
Kelley	69-70-69-68—276	5,550
Yancey	69-70-68-69—276	5,550
Johnston	67-70-69-72—278	2,820
Charles	71-69-70-69—279	2,460
Adams	73-70-70-67—280	2,040
Toepel	67-69-75-69—280	2,040
Panasiuk	73-69-69-70—281	1,567
Dill	70-71-69-71—281	1,567
Mitchell	67-70-72-72—281	1,567
Brown	71-69-69-72—281	1,567
Floyd	74-71-70-67—282	1,125
Hayes	74-70-69-69—282	1,125
Melnyk	67-70-74-71—282	1,125
Schr'der	72-68-69-73—282	1,125

HOUSTON OPEN, ($150,000), The Woodlands C.C. (72-6,929), Woodlands, Tex., May 1-4.

Crampt'n	**68-70-66-69—273**	**$30,000**
Morgan	70-68-67-70—275	17,100
J. Inman	68-70-71-67—276	10,650
Schr'der	68-72-67-71—278	7,050
L. Hebert	69-71-70-69—279	5,194
Kite	70-71-70-68—279	5,194
Nelson	68-71-70-70—279	5,194
Pearce	67-70-71-71—279	5,194
Maltbie	69-70-70-71—280	3,900
Tapie	67-71-73-69—280	3,900
Trevino	66-69-73-74—282	3,450

Gary Groh was 14 under in winning Hawaiian.

BYRON NELSON CLASSIC ($175,000), Preston Trail G.C. (71-6,983), Dallas, May 8-12.

Watson	**72-63-69-65—269**	**$35,000**
Smith	67-68-69-67—271	19,950
Ewing	74-63-68-67—272	12,425
L. Nelson	69-65-71-68—273	7,700
Funseth	69-68-66-70—273	7,700
Nevil	68-68-71-67—274	5,950
Crampt'n	66-70-67-71—274	5,950
Hinkle	69-71-68-67—275	4,392
Morley	71-71-65-68—275	4,392
Knudson	68-69-68-70—275	4,392
M.Barber	68-69-67-71—275	4,392
Eastw'd	73-65-65-72—275	4,392

NEW ORLEANS OPEN ($150,000), Lakewood C.C. (72-7,080), New Orleans, May 12-18.

Casper	**67-68-66-70—271**	**$30,000**
Oosterh's	68-68-69-68—273	17,100
Wadkins	69-68-70-69—276	10,650
Wynn	71-66-70-70—277	7,050
January	69-72-71-66—278	5,450
Hinson	73-70-67-68—278	5,450
Melnyk	69-69-68-72—278	5,450
D.Grah'm	70-69-73-67—279	4,075
Porter	74-66-71-68—279	4,075
Shaw	69-67-73-70—279	4,075
Douglass	73-67-69-71—280	3,300
Knudson	70-70-69-71—280	3,300
Funseth	70-67-72-72—281	2,850

DANNY THOMAS MEMPHIS CLASSIC ($175,000), Colonial C.C. (72-7,173), Memphis, May 22-25.

Littler	**67-68-69-66—270**	**$35,000**
Mahaff'y	65-68-71-71—275	19,950
Weiskopf	65-71-73-68—277	10,325
Nicklaus	66-70-73-68—277	10,325
Simons	69-70-72-70—281	6,737
Kite	67-73-70-71—281	6,737
Watson	69-72-73-68—282	5,600
Dent	72-70-74-67—283	5,163
Trevino	74-67-73-70—284	3,750
Gilbert	72-71-71-70—284	3,750
Inman	71-72-71-70—284	3,750
Pace	74-70-69-71—284	3,750
January	73-71-69-71—284	3,750
Lister	68-71-73-72—284	3,750
Floyd	69-74-69-72—284	3,750

ATLANTA CLASSIC ($225,000), Atlanta (Ga.) C.C. (72-6,883), May 29-June 1.

Irwin	**66-69-68-68—271**	**$45,000**
Watson	71-71-65-68—275	25,650
Coody	71-68-67-70—276	15,975
M.Barber	71-64-73-69—277	9,300
Nicklaus	68-63-67-69—277	9,300
J. Miller	68-71-68-70—277	9,300
Colbert	70-74-68-67—279	6,925
Dent	70-68-69-72—279	6,925
Schlee	71-74-67-68—280	5,625
Casper	66-73-70-71—280	5,625
Gilbert	75-65-70-70—280	5,625
McGee	72-73-70-67—282	4,219
Trevino	69-76-69-68—282	4,219
Zarley	73-71-67-71—282	4,219
L.Th'pson	68-75-67-72—282	4,219

AT A GLANCE

KEMPER OPEN ($250,000), Quail Hollow C.C. (72-7,160), Charlotte, N.C., June 5-8.

Floyd	**65-71-73-69—278**	**$50,000**
Player	69-70-69-73—281	23,125
Mahaff'y	71-69-71-70—281	23,125
Heard	71-70-69-72—282	11,750
Masserio	71-70-69-73—283	9,083
Oosterh's	70-73-69-71—283	9,083
Murphy	68-72-72-71—283	9,083
Stanton	70-75-69-70—284	6,531
D.Grah'm	73-68-71-72—284	6,531
Nichols	71-69-69-75—284	6,531
Melnyk	71-68-74-71—284	6,531
Coody	72-72-74-67—285	4,687
Bies	70-71-73-71—285	4,687
Maltbie	67-77-70-71—285	4,687
Hayes	70-70-72-73—285	4,687

IVB PHILADELPHIA CLASSIC ($150,000), Whitemarsh Valley C.C. (71-6,687), Chestnut Hill, Pa., June 12-15.

Jenkins	**69-65-69-72—275**	**$30,000**
J. Miller	71-69-68-68—276	17,100
Wynn	73-70-65-69—277	10,650
Simons	69-71-68-71—279	7,050
Allin	71-70-69-70—280	6,150
Groh	73-71-71-66—281	4,485
McGee	69-72-68-72—281	4,485
Bies	71-71-71-68—281	4,485
Shaw	70-71-70-70—281	4,485
J. Snead	69-72-69-71—281	4,485
A. Miller	71-71-66-74—282	3,450
D. Hill	74-69-70-70—283	2,900
Erskine	74-68-73-68—283	2,900
Hayes	70-72-68-73—283	2,900

U.S. OPEN ($240,000), Medinah (Ill.) C.C., (71-7,032), June 19-22.

L. Graham*	**74-72-68-73—287**	**$40,000**
Mahaff'y	73-71-72-71—287	20,000
Murphy	74-73-72-69—288	10,875
Irwin	74-71-73-70—288	10,875
Crensh'w	70-68-76-74—288	10,875
Beard	74-69-67-78—288	10,875
Nicklaus	72-70-75-72—289	7,500
Oosterh's	69-73-72-75—289	7,500
Palmer	69-75-73-73—290	5,000
Watson	67-68-78-77—290	5,000
Fitzsimons	67-73-73-77—290	5,000
North	75-72-72-72—291	2,800
Floyd	76-71-72-72—291	2,800
Wiech'rs	68-73-76-75—292	2,025
Massengale	71-74-71-76—292	2,025
Inman	72-72-71-77—292	2,025
Pearce	75-71-70-76—292	2,025
Jones	69-73-79-72—293	1,675
Groh	73-74-73-73—293	1,675
Dill	72-69-77-75—293	1,675

*Won 18 hole playoff, 71-73.

WESTERN OPEN ($200,000), Butler Ntl. G.C. (71-7,002), Oak Brook, Ill., June 26-30.

Irwin	**71-68-71-73—283**	**$40,000**
Cole	74-71-70-69—284	22,800
Sneed	71-74-69-73—287	14,200
Lister	76-75-65-72—288	8,266
Heard	69-74-72-73—288	8,266
Gilbert	71-71-73-73—288	8,266
Brewer	75-70-69-75—289	5,460
Molina	70-73-71-75—289	5,460
Geib'ger	71-73-76-69—289	5,460
Simons	71-73-70-75—289	5,460
G.Johns'n	72-66-72-79—289	5,460

Don Bies takes first win, at Hartford.

GR. MILWAUKEE OPEN ($130,000), Tuckaway C.C. (72-7,010), Franklin, Wis., July 2-5.

Wall	**67-67-67-70—271**	**$26,080**
McCord	69-71-65-67—272	14,820
Curl	69-70-66-68—273	9,230
D. Hill	68-68-69-69—274	5,720
Gilbert	69-66-69-70—274	5,720
Stockton	68-71-68-68—275	4,680
Still	68-67-70-71—276	4,160
Elder	69-69-70-69—277	3,673
Hayes	71-68-66-72—277	3,673
L. Hebert	69-71-68-70—278	3,120
Maltbie	72-67-68-71—278	3,120

QUAD CITIES OPEN ($75,000), Oakwood C.C. (71-6,305), Moline, Ill., July 10-13.

Maltbie	**74-65-72-64—275**	**$15,000**
Eichelberger	67-75-72-72—276	8,550
Hayes	70-68-70-69—277	5,325
McCord	72-66-70-70—278	3,525
Blancas	70-67-73-69—279	2,725
Dill	67-71-69-72—279	2,725
Twitty	66-73-68-72—279	2,725
Cerda	73-73-68-66—280	2,213

PLEASANT VALLEY CLASSIC ($200,000), Pleasant Valley C.C. (71-7,179), Sutton, Mass., July 17-20.

Maltbie	**72-71-67-66—276**	**$40,000**
McLend'n	70-68-70-69—277	22,800
Simons	69-70-74-65—278	9,750
Allin	70-67-72-69—278	9,750
M.Barb'r	67-74-69-68—278	9,750
Crensh'w	69-68-71-70—278	9,750
Trevino	70-66-74-70—280	6,150
Knudson	69-69-72-70—280	6,150
Geib'ger	70-71-70-70—281	4,600
Irwin	70-68-73-70—281	4,600
G.Johns'n	69-68-72-72—281	4,600
Elder	68-67-73-73—281	4,600
Curl	66-71-71-73—281	4,600

CANADIAN OPEN ($200,000), Royal Montreal G.C. (70-6,628), Ile Bizard, Quebec, July 24-27.

W'skopf*	**65-74-68-67—274**	**$40,000**
Nicklaus	65-71-70-68—274	22,800
Brewer	68-68-70-69—275	14,200
Palmer	68-73-69-67—277	9,400
Crampt'n	74-68-67-69—278	8,200
S. Snead	73-68-72-66—279	7,200
Player	67-73-73-67—280	5,675
B. Wynn	69-74-69-68—280	5,675
Trevino	71-72-68-69—280	5,675
Still	70-67-74-69—280	5,675
Coody	70-70-75-66—281	3,920
Floyd	70-73-72-66—281	3,920
Knudson	68-74-71-68—281	3,920
Maltbie	72-72-69-68—281	3,920
Watson	72-71-68-70—281	3,920

*Won sudden-death playoff.

WESTCHESTER CLASSIC ($250,000), Westchester C.C. (72-6,614), Harrison, N.Y., July 31-Aug. 3.

Littler*	**68-68-69-66—271**	**$50,000**
Boros	70-66-70-65—271	28,500
Weisk'pf	66-63-72-71—272	17,750
Lietzke	70-71-66-67—274	11,750
Fitzsimons	67-70-66-73—276	10,250
Shaw	72-71-67-67—277	8,125
Heard	73-70-67-67—277	8,125
Irwin	72-65-71-69—277	8,125
D. Sikes	72-71-69-66—278	6,000
R. Massengale	65-74-72-67—278	6,000
Cadle	71-69-69-69—278	6,000
Wall	72-68-69-69—278	6,000

*Won sudden-death playoff.

PGA CHAMPIONSHIP ($225,000), Firestone C.C. South (70-7,180), Akron, Ohio, Aug. 7-10.

Nicklaus	**70-68-67-71—276**	**$45,000**
Crampt'n	71-63-75-69—278	25,700
Weisk'pf	70-71-70-68—279	16,000
North	72-74-70-65—281	10,500
Irwin	72-65-73-73—283	8,662
Casper	69-72-72-70—283	8,662
D. Hill	71-71-74-68—284	6,917
Littler	76-71-66-71—284	6,917
Watson	70-71-71-73—285	6,075
January	72-70-71-73—286	4,468
D.Grah'm	72-70-70-74—286	4,468
Allin	73-72-70-71—286	4,468
Schlee	71-68-75-72—286	4,468
Floyd	70-73-72-71—286	4,468
Th'pson	74-69-72-71—286	4,468
Crensh'w	73-72-71-70—286	4,468
M. Hill	72-71-70-74—287	2,923
Morgan	73-71-71-72—287	2,923
Melnyk	71-72-74-70—287	2,923
Gilbert	73-70-77-67—287	2,923
Douglass	74-72-74-67—287	2,923

SAMMY DAVIS JR.-GR. HARTFORD OPEN ($200,000), Wethersfield (Conn.) C.C. (71-6,598), Aug. 14-17.

Bies*	**65-66-67-69—267**	**$40,000**
Green	66-65-68-68—267	22,800
J. Snead	66-68-67-67—268	14,200
Nelson	68-66-67-68—269	8,800
Regalado	69-68-65-67—269	8,800
Blancas	67-69-68-66—270	7,200
Miller	69-67-68-67—271	6,150
North	66-69-67-69—271	6,150
Player	69-68-69-66—272	5,200
Floyd	67-69-71-65—272	5,200
Simons	71-69-70-63—273	4,400
M. Hill	66-71-68-68—273	4,400

*Won sudden-death playoff.

TOURN. PLAYERS CH. ($250,000), Colonial C.C. (70-7,160), Fort Worth, Tex., Aug. 21-24.

Geiberg'r	**66-68-67-69—270**	**$50,000**
Stockton	72-64-68-69—273	28,500
Green	71-65-70-69—275	17,750
Murphy	73-69-71-68—281	10,333
Dickson	67-69-72-73—281	10,333
Rudolph	69-70-72-70—281	10,333
Irwin	67-72-72-72—283	8,000
Watson	73-69-75-67—284	6,791
Porter	72-72-68-72—284	6,791
B. Wadkins	76-69-68-71—284	6,791
Rogers	69-70-76-70—285	5,062
Littler	73-71-70-71—285	5,062
Allin	68-73-71-73—285	5,062
Mahaff'y	69-75-69-72—285	5,062

B.C. OPEN ($175,000), En-Joie G.C. (71-6,815), Endicott, N.Y., Aug. 29-Sept. 1.

Iverson	**66-69-71-68—274**	**$35,000**
Colbert	69-69-69-68—275	16,187
D.Grah'm	68-68-71-68—275	16,187
Diehl	69-70-71-66—276	8,225
Green	70-69-71-67—277	6,358
McGee	69-72-70-66—277	6,358
Wiech'rs	72-67-71-67—277	6,358
Baird	66-67-71-74—278	4,944
S.Snead	69-73-69-67—278	4,944
Hayes	71-69-68-71—279	4,025
Jaeckel	72-68-68-71—279	4,025
McCord	70-70-71-68—279	4,025

SOUTHERN OPEN ($100,000), Green Island C.C. (72-6,791), Columbus, Ga., Sept. 4-7.

Green	**68-66-66-64—264**	**$20,000**
Schr'der	65-66-68-68—267	11,400
Dill	66-69-69-68—272	7,100
Rogers	70-69-63-71—273	4,700
Gilbert	69-68-69-68—274	4,100
Crensh'w	68-69-70-68—275	3,600
Burns	70-65-71-70—276	2,950
J. Snead	68-68-72-68—276	2,950
Nelson	70-71-70-65—276	2,950

WORLD SERIES OF GOLF, Firestone C.C. South (70-7,180), Akron, Ohio, Sept. 6-7.

Watson	**69-71—140**	**$50,000**
Nicklaus	72-70—142	15,000
Weiskopf	75-70—145	7,500
L. Graham	76-71—147	5,000

WORLD OPEN ($200,000), Pinehurst (N.C.) C.C. (No. 2 cse., 71-7,007), Sept. 11-14.

Nicklaus*	**70-71-70-69—280**	**$40,000**
Casper	70-72-68-70—280	22,800
Weiskopf	67-71-68-75—281	14,200
Fitzsimons	67-69-71-75—282	9,400
Sneed	68-70-70-75—283	8,200
Nelson	70-71-69-74—284	6,255
Funseth	67-70-74-73—284	6,255
Mahaff'y	70-71-70-73—284	6,255
Schlee	68-72-73-71—284	6,255
Zender	72-71-71-71—285	4,240
Zarley	71-69-74-71—285	4,240
Armstr'g	69-72-71-73—285	4,240
Twitty	69-68-73-75—285	4,240
Lietzke	72-72-71-70—285	4,240

*Won sudden-death playoff.

DEL WEBB SAHARA INV. ($135,000), Sahara-Nevada C.C. (71-6,800), Las Vegas, Nev., Sept. 25-28.

D. Hill*	**68-66-67-69—270**	**$27,000**
Mas'gale	70-64-67-69—270	15,390
Mitchell	70-64-67-70—271	7,965
Inman	67-70-67-67—271	7,965
Cadle	69-66-67-70—272	4,674
Crampt'n	72-65-65-70—272	4,674
Coody	70-69-65-68—272	4,674
January	70-66-70-66—272	4,674

*Won sudden-death playoff.

KAISER INT'L OPEN ($175,000), Silverado C.C. (No., 72-6,828, So., 72-6,619), Napa, Calif., Oct. 2-5.

Miller	**68-67-68-69—272**	**$35,000**
Curl	73-67-64-71—275	19,950
Fleckm'n	68-67-71-70—276	9,275
Littler	65-70-71-70—276	9,275
Trevino	70-65-72-69—276	9,275
Nicklaus	72-67-69-69—277	6,300
Lietzke	70-70-68-70—278	5,382
Cerda	69-70-73-66—278	5,382

SAN ANTONIO-TEXAS OPEN ($125,000), Woodlake G.C. (72-7,038), San Antonio, Oct. 16-19.

January*	**71-67-71-66—275**	**$25,000**
Hinson	70-73-64-68—275	14,250
Morgan	66-68-75-68—277	8,875
Lietzke	70-71-70-67—278	5,166
Johnston	67-68-73-70—278	5,166
Barber	66-71-70-71—278	5,166
McCullough	73-67-70-69—279	4,000
B. Shaw	71-72-68-69—280	3,137
Cole	74-66-71-69—280	3,137
Crawf'rd	68-69-70-73—280	3,137
Coody	68-69-70-73—280	3,137
Funseth	73-69-66-72—280	3,137
Hinkle	71-66-73-71—281	2,375

*Won sudden-death playoff.

WALT DISNEY WORLD NTL. TEAM CH. ($200,000), Palm (72-6,951) & Magnolia (72-7,162) G. Cses., Lake Buena Vista, Fla., Oct. 23-26.

Refram-Colbert	63-63-62-64—252	$20,000
Cu. Sifford-Regalado	66-65-62-62—255	10,504
Cole-Schlee	67-64-62-62—255	10,504
Mitchell-Gilbert	62-66-66-63—257	5,336
Rudolph-Sikes	64-66-61-67—258	4,372
J. Miller-Jones	63-65-67-63—258	4,372
L. & B. Wadkins	65-66-63-65—259	3,492
J. & S. Snead	65-65-66-63—259	3,492
Wittenberg-Abbott	62-64-65-69—260	2,837
Allin-Geiberger	68-61-65-66—260	2,837
Dent-Johnson	66-66-65-63—260	2,837

SECOND TOUR WINNERS

SUN CITY OPEN—Bob Risch, 139, $2,000.

YUMA OPEN — Dave Shuster, 138, $2,000.

LITTLE CROSBY PRO-AM — Billy Ziobro, 138, $1,700.

HOPE OF TOMORROW — Rik Massengale, 206, $2,400.

PINE TREE OPEN—Florentino Molino, 134, $2,000.

MAGNOLIA CLASSIC — Bob Wynn, 270, $7,000.

MINI-KEMPER OPEN — Perry Leslie, 67, $3,000.

BUICK OPEN — Spike Kelley, 208, $4,200.

JR. SAMMY DAVIS OPEN — Randy Erskine, 66, $1,000.

EVENT BY EVENT WITH THE TOP 25 PROS

(Players listed from left in money-winning rank. Tournaments listed from top in chronological order.)

T means tied for that position. WD means withdrew, DQ means disqualified. FQ means failed to qualify for final 36. Winners of tour events not among top 25 money-winners: Groh (Hawaiian), Ziegler (Jacksonville), Jenkins (Philadelphia), Wall (Milwaukee), Bies (Hartford), Iverson (B.C.), January (Texas), Colbert-Refram (Natl. Team). Second-tour events are not listed.

	JACK NICKLAUS ($298,149)	JOHNNY MILLER ($226,118)	TOM WEISKOPF ($219,140)	HALE IRWIN ($205,380)	GENE LITTLER ($182,883)	AL GEIBERGER ($175,404)	TOM WATSON ($153,795)	JOHN MAHAFFEY ($141,471)	LEE TREVINO ($134,206)	BRUCE CRAMPTON ($132,532)	BOB MURPHY ($127,471)	HUBERT GREEN ($113,569)	RAY FLOYD ($103,627)	BILLY CASPER ($102,275)	LOU GRAHAM ($96,425)	JERRY McGEE ($93,569)	J. C. SNEAD ($91,822)	TOM KITE ($87,045)	CHARLES COODY ($86,812)	PAT FITZSIMONS ($86,181)	MILLER BARBER ($81,993)	JERRY HEARD ($81,687)	ROGER MALTBIE ($81,035)	DAVE HILL ($80,533)	RIK MASSENGALE ($77,079)
PHOENIX OPEN	—	1	FQ	T13	T7	—	T7	T7	T34	T42	—	FQ	—	FQ	—	T53	6	T57	FQ	—	68	2	T69	T34	T66
MARTIN TUCSON OPEN	—	1	FQ	FQ	T11	6	3	2	T20	T7	—	—	—	T25	T31	T20	T20	—	FQ	—	T52	T52	T41	T25	T11
CROSBY NTL. PRO-AM	T6	T6	T14	T16	1	T52	T16	FQ	—	FQ	FQ	2	T12	T30	4	T16	—	3	—	—	FQ	T24	T6	T6	—
HAWAIIAN OPEN	T14	—	T14	T14	T26	2	T14	T9	FQ	T4	T69	FQ	T26	T26	4	T26	T42	T9	T21	FQ	FQ	—	T71	—	—
HOPE DESERT CLASSIC	—	1	—	—	—	—	T5	—	T11	2	T32	T25	7	—	T25	T25	—	—	FQ	T5	T9	3	T43	T11	—
WILLIAMS SAN DIEGO OPEN	—	T16	FQ	T6	T21	T21	FQ	T6	—	T30	T12	—	T2	T6	T16	T27	1	5	—	T9	T21	—	T43	—	T21
CAMPBELL LOS ANGELES OPEN	3	T15	T4	T4	T12	FQ	T6	T12	T34	—	—	T49	T6	T38	T6	T23	2	—	—	1	FQ	T61	—	WD	T23
GLEASON INVERRARY CLASSIC	3	—	T7	T5	T9	—	T13	—	T5	T13	1	70	T46	—	T33	T22	T53	T9	T9	T65	4	—	T39	T9	—
FLORIDA CITRUS OPEN	—	—	2	T49	T42	T8	—	1	T12	T33	T42	—	—	—	—	—	—	—	4	T12	T30	72	FQ	T33	T5
DORAL EASTERN OPEN	1	4	T63	—	—	T18	FQ	—	T9	T5	—	T50	—	—	FQ	T29	FQ	T29	—	T50	T29	T42	—	—	—
JACKSONVILLE OPEN	—	—	T31	T63	—	—	WD	—	T24	—	T58	T14	—	4	T8	FQ	—	FQ	—	T70	T31	T54	—	—	—
HERITAGE CLASSIC	1	FQ	2	T9	—	T28	T13	4	T13	T5	T38	T28	T48	—	T38	16	FQ	T5	3	T17	T9	T42	—	—	DQ
GREENSBORO OPEN	—	T6	1	—	T44	2	T20	WD	4	—	—	—	WD	T32	T12	3	FQ	T54	—	FQ	T27	T20	FQ	5	T16
MASTERS	1	T2	T2	T4	T22	FQ	T8	FQ	T10	FQ	42	T8	T30	6	T40	—	T10	T10	T40	T22	T26	T26	—	7	T24
PENSACOLA OPEN	—	—	—	—	T15	—	T3	T6	T30	—	T15	T9	1	—	—	—	—	T36	T3	—	—	T9	—	—	T24
TOURNAMENT OF CHAMPIONS	T9	T15	T11	T5	T7	1	T7	—	3	—	T11	19	—	—	14	T17	—	—	T11	T25	—	—	T17	—	—
TALLAHASSEE OPEN	—	—	—	—	—	—	—	—	—	—	—	T12	—	—	—	—	—	—	—	—	—	—	—	FQ	1
HOUSTON OPEN	—	—	—	T12	T41	—	T66	11	1	—	—	FQ	—	T41	T25	T32	T5	T12	—	—	—	T9	FQ	—	T12
BYRON NELSON CLASSIC	—	T35	—	T49	T21	—	1	—	FQ	T6	—	T28	—	—	—	T21	—	FQ	T21	—	T8	64	FQ	—	FQ
NEW ORLEANS OPEN	—	—	—	—	—	—	T52	—	T14	—	T32	—	—	1	T72	—	—	—	—	T26	T52	—	T40	T26	—
THOMAS MEMPHIS CLASSIC	T3	—	T3	—	1	T30	7	2	T9	—	T41	T9	T30	T21	—	T30	T5	—	T30	FQ	—	T60	T21	—	—
ATLANTA GOLF CLASSIC	T4	T4	T26	1	T33	FQ	2	T48	T12	T33	T16	FQ	T26	T9	T23	T12	T39	T23	3	FQ	T4	T16	FQ	T60	T66
KEMPER OPEN	—	—	T41	T21	FQ	—	T2	FQ	WD	T5	T21	1	FQ	T51	T41	FQ	—	T12	FQ	T21	4	T12	FQ	—	T41
IVB PHILADELPHIA CLASSIC	—	2	WD	—	—	—	—	—	T37	T25	FQ	T53	T34	T6	T6	T61	—	—	—	T55	WD	T12	T61	—	—
U.S. OPEN	T7	T38	T29	T3	T49	T38	T9	2	T29	—	T3	T18	T12	—	1	FQ	T49	FQ	FQ	T9	T24	T29	—	—	T14
WESTERN OPEN	—	FQ	1	—	T7	T12	—	WD	—	WD	T34	WD	FQ	—	WD	T50	T12	T43	—	T12	T4	—	FQ	T19	—
MILWAUKEE OPEN	—	—	—	—	—	—	—	—	—	—	—	—	—	—	FQ	—	—	—	—	—	T12	—	T10	4	T21
QUAD CITIES OPEN	—	—	—	—	—	—	—	—	—	—	—	—	—	—	—	—	—	—	—	—	—	—	1	T15	—
PLEASANT VALLEY CLASSIC	—	T9	—	T9	—	—	—	T7	T17	T30	—	—	—	—	—	FQ	FQ	FQ	—	—	T3	T40	1	T40	FQ
CANADIAN OPEN	2	T16	1	—	T52	—	T11	FQ	T7	5	FQ	T23	T11	—	T41	FQ	6	T23	T11	T28	T28	T41	T11	—	T28
WESTCHESTER CLASSIC	—	T49	3	T6	1	FQ	13	T21	—	T28	T36	FQ	FQ	—	FQ	FQ	FQ	T21	T14	5	FQ	T6	—	FQ	T9
PGA CHAMPIONSHIP	1	FQ	3	T5	T7	T33	9	T28	T60	2	T25	—	T10	T5	T54	T40	T28	T33	FQ	FQ	—	T25	FQ	T7	FQ
DAVIS-HARTFORD OPEN	—	T7	—	—	—	T13	—	—	T13	—	T27	—	2	T9	—	T34	T27	3	—	—	—	T13	FQ	—	—
TOURNAMENT PLAYERS CHAMP.	T18	—	T29	7	T11	1	T8	T11	T50	T34	T4	3	T21	T15	T29	T40	T34	T40	T29	T60	T29	T21	T21	WD	FQ
B.C. OPEN	—	—	—	—	—	—	—	—	—	T5	—	—	—	—	—	T5	—	—	—	—	—	—	FQ	—	—
SOUTHERN OPEN	—	—	—	—	—	—	—	—	—	—	—	1	—	—	—	—	T7	T32	—	—	—	—	—	WD	—
WORLD OPEN	1	T32	3	T64	—	T39	—	T6	T17	T32	T39	T39	FQ	—	2	T17	T39	T17	T25	T17	4	T25	T58	FQ	T17
SAHARA INVITATIONAL	—	—	—	—	—	T12	T18	T32	—	T5	—	T12	—	—	—	T45	—	T32	T5	T18	T39	T39	FQ	1	2
KAISER INTERNATIONAL	6	1	3	—	T3	T24	FQ	T13	T3	—	—	—	—	—	—	T9	T18	—	T13	T18	T27	T9	FQ	FQ	FQ
SAN ANTONIO-TEXAS OPEN	—	—	—	—	—	—	—	T24	T14	—	—	—	—	—	—	—	—	—	—	FQ	T8	—	T4	—	FQ
NATIONAL TEAM CHAMP.	—	4	—	—	—	—	T9	T21	T21	—	—	—	43	24	—	—	T18	7	T30	T30	—	T12	T12	—	—

1975 PGA TOUR CHART

Player	Tour Events[1]	Finishes 1st	2nd	3rd	Scoring Average	Perf. Average	Official Money for 1975	Average Money Per Tour Event	Career Earnings
1. Jack Nicklaus (2)	16	5	1	3	69.88	.909	$298,149	$18,634	$2,541,172
2. Johnny Miller (1)	21	4	2	0	70.24	.663	226,118	10,767	947,152
3. Tom Weiskopf (13)	23	2	2	4	71.11	.580	219,140	9,527	1,224,854
4. Hale Irwin (7)	22	2	1	1	70.90	.678	205,380	9,335	760,054
5. Gene Littler (20)	22	3	0	1	70.93	.611	182,883	8,312	1,203,541
6. Al Geiberger (23)	25	2	2	0	71.38	.453	175,693	7,027	794,505
7. Tom Watson (10)	25	1	1	1	70.88	.672	153,795	6,151	390,105
8. John Mahaffey (16)	25	0	4	0	71.00	.556	141,471	5,658	423,153
9. Lee Trevino (4)	27	1	0	2	71.11	.569	134,206	4,970	1,398,651
10. Bruce Crampton (12)	24	1	1	1	70.60	.601	132,532	5,522	1,323,399
11. Bob Murphy (44)	23	1	1	1	71.68	.465	127,471	5,542	708,392
12. Hubert Green (3)	26	1	2	1	71.37	.441	113,569	4,368	527,408
13. Ray Floyd (18)	25	1	1	0	71.78	.417	103,627	4,145	697,587
14. Billy Casper (35)	19	1	1	0	71.19	.553	102,275	5,383	1,581,605
15. Lou Graham (29)	26	1	0	0	71.70	.426	96,425	3,708	617,842
16. Jerry McGee (51)	30	1	0	1	71.26	.450	93,569	3,118	334,707
17. J. C. Snead (5)	28	1	0	1	71.83	.398	91,822	3,279	530,692
18. Tom Kite (26)	26	0	1	1	71.43	.457	87,045	3,347	221,923
19. Charles Coody (42)	27	0	0	2	71.21	.493	86,812	3,215	663,253
20. Pat Fitzsimons (143)	23	1	0	0	71.59	.447	86,181	3,747	112,875
21. Miller Barber (22)	31	0	0	2	71.56	.447	81,993	2,645	994,868
22. Jerry Heard (8)	26	0	1	1	71.71	.391	81,687	3,141	618,320
23. Roger Maltbie	29	2	0	0	72.19	.267	81,035	2,794	81,035
24. Dave Hill (11)	27	1	0	0	71.61	.403	80,533	2,982	922,233
25. Rik Massengale (127)	28	1	1	0	71.64	.433	77,079	2,752	164,306
26. B. R. McLendon (76)	30	0	2	0	75.27	.374	76,971	2,566	260,892
27. Gary Player (19)	15	0	2	0	71.45	.490	73,943	4,930	1,163,153
28. Dave Stockton (6)	28	0	1	0	71.56	.384	72,885	2,513	814,483
29. Don Bies (32)	23	1	0	0	71.90	.340	69,968	3,042	350,140
30. Don January	24	1	0	0	71.48	.427	69,034	2,876	655,189
31. Gary Groh (103)	30	1	0	0	72.79	.204	68,296	2,277	117,959
32. Ben Crenshaw (31)	27	0	0	3	71.66	.360	63,528	2,353	206,727
33. Brian Allin (9)	28	0	0	1	71.91	.390	60,326	2,155	370,206
34. Peter Oosterhuis	31	0	1	0	71.97	.291	59,935	1,933	81,848
35. Rod Curl (17)	31	0	1	1	72.04	.283	59,599	1,923	270,056
36. Arnold Palmer (72)	19	0	0	1	71.77	.469	59,017	3,106	1,723,113
37. Don Iverson (99)	31	1	0	0	72.59	.190	56,560	1,825	152,632
38. Gibby Gilbert (33)	32	0	0	0	71.81	.347	56,279	1,759	345,647
39. Eddie Pearce (47)	25	0	1	0	72.59	.254	54,595	2,184	111,467
40. Larry Ziegler (27)	31	1	0	0	72.23	.198	54,265	1,750	363,400
41. Joe Inman Jr. (61)	30	0	0	2	71.84	.334	53,225	1,774	100,820
42. Bob Wynn (67)	28	0	0	1	71.57	.279	52,414	1,872	134,192
43. Forrest Fezler (24)	28	0	1	0	72.47	.247	52,157	1,863	272,809
44. David Graham (41)	30	0	1	0	72.02	.298	51,642	1,721	209,923
45. Jim Colbert (21)	31	1	1	0	72.34	.255	50,111	1,616	464,490
46. Bobby Nichols (14)	23	0	1	0	72.40	.261	49,835	2,167	906,276
47. Mark Hayes (68)	32	0	0	1	71.83	.390	49,297	1,541	89,917
48. Leonard Thompson (15)	31	0	0	0	71.90	.327	48,748	1,573	296,365
49. Rod Funseth (89)	26	0	0	0	71.70	.351	48,453	1,864	453,694
50. Jim Simons (87)	30	0	0	1	71.89	.264	47,724	1,591	106,957
51. Ed Sneed (34)	29	0	0	1	72.30	.270	46,635	1,608	191,113
52. Tom Jenkins (86)	30	1	0	0	72.66	.174	45,267	1,509	115,651
53. Andy North (46)	32	0	0	0	72.08	.272	44,729	1,398	148,320
54. Bob E. Smith (104)	29	0	1	0	72.12	.217	44,720	1,542	267,909
55. Steve Melnyk (52)	34	0	0	0	72.19	.280	44,707	1,315	165,091
56. John Schlee (37)	24	0	0	0	71.95	.335	44,337	1,847	404,425
57. Wally Armstrong (74)	32	0	1	0	72.36	.239	44,078	1,377	80,235
58. Art Wall (109)	22	1	0	0	72.28	.189	43,589	1,981	585,837
59. Gary McCord (78)	31	0	1	0	72.17	.263	43,028	1,388	76,668
60. Gil Morgan (94)	27	0	1	1	72.01	.237	42,772	1,584	70,452

Other money-winners

61. Bobby Cole	$42,441	91. Mason Rudolph	$23,084	121. Mike Reasor	$11,229
62. Larry Hinson	41,843	92. Butch Baird	23,033	122. Fred Marti	11,024
63. Mike Hill	41,696	93. Chuck Courtney	22,840	123. Tony Jacklin	10,824
64. Mike Morley	41,102	94. Alan Tapie	22,547	124. Lionel Hebert	10,647
65. Tom Shaw	39,948	95. John Lister	22,447	125. Bob Menne	10,423
66. Larry Nelson	39,810	96. Frank Beard	22,433	126. Graham Marsh	9,837
67. Julius Boros	36,311	97. Homero Blancas	22,419	127. George Archer	9,777
68. Dale Douglass	34,583	98. Jim Masserio	22,188	128. Nate Starks	9,058
69. Jim Dent	33,649	99. Jim Wiechers	22,138	129. Ed Dougherty	9,373
70. George Knudson	32,554	100. Dan Sikes	22,127	130. Ron Cerrudo	9,363
71. Allen Miller	31,640	101. Dick Crawford	21,630	131. Bobby Walzel	9,362
72. Ken Still	31,413	102. Ralph Johnston	20,846	132. Bob Goalby	9,039
73. Bert Yancey	31,290	103. Jack Ewing	20,726	133. Barry Jaeckel	8,883
74. Bruce Lietzke	30,780	104. Dwight Nevil	20,043	134. Florentino Molina	8,669
75. Terry Diehl	30,691	105. Joe Porter	19,819	135. Sammy Rachels	8,534
76. Bob Stanton	29,737	106. Lyn Lott	18,522	136. Lon Hinkle	8,420
77. Tommy Aaron	29,612	107. George Cadle	18,481	137. Rick Rhyan	8,302
78. Bill Rogers	29,302	108. Roy Pace	17,846	138. Sam Snead	8,285
79. Bobby Mitchell	28,862	109. Mike McCullough	17,706	139. Howard Twitty	8,211
80. Danny Edwards	27,301	110. Bob Eastwood	16,683	140. Barney Thompson	7,991
81. Lee Elder	26,809	111. George Johnson	16,236	141. Bruce Fleisher	7,773
82. Bruce Devlin	26,627	112. Grier Jones	15,719	142. Tony Cerda	7,594
83. Terry Dill	26,065	113. Randy Erskine	15,297	143. Spike Kelley	7,563
84. Kermit Zarley	25,897	114. Bob Zender	15,114	144. Doug Sanders	7,431
85. Victor Regalado	25,833	115. Juan Rodriguez	13,955	145. Dick Lotz	7,360
86. John Schroeder	25,520	116. Marty Fleckman	13,399	146. Fuzzy Zoeller	7,318
87. Bob Dickson	24,408	117. Dave Eichelberger	12,780	147. Bob Charles	7,225
88. Lanny Wadkins	23,582	118. David Glenz	12,186	148. Curtis Sifford	7,001
89. Gay Brewer	23,498	119. Mike Wynn	12,122	149. Bob Payne	6,874
90. Bobby Wadkins	23,330	120. Maurice Bembridge	11,436	150. John Jacobs	6,725

Event Winners: J. Miller (Phoenix, Tucson, Hope, Kaiser), G. Littler (Crosby, Memphis, Westchester), Groh (Hawaiian), J. C. Snead (San Diego), Fitzsimons (Los Angeles), Murphy (Inverrary), Trevino (Fla. Citrus), Nicklaus (Doral, Heritage, Masters, PGA, World), Ziegler (Jacksonville), Weiskopf (Greensboro, Canadian), McGee (Pensacola), Geiberger (T of C, TPC), R. Massengale (Tallahassee), Crampton (Houston), Watson (Nelson), Casper (New Orleans), Irwin (Atlanta, Western), Floyd (Kemper), Jenkins (Philadelphia), L. Graham (U.S. Open), Wall (Milwaukee), Maltbie (Quad Cities, Pleasant Valley), Bies (Hartford), Iverson (B.C.), H. Green (Southern), D. Hill (Sahara), January (Texas), Colbert and Dean Refram (National Team Championship).

[1]Includes only regular tour events.

Notes: Figures in parentheses after players' names indicate 1974 money-winning rank. Results of National Team Championship (won by Colbert and Refram) are reflected only in finishes. Top 60-ranked players are exempt from qualifying for 1976 PGA co-sponsored events.

HIGHLIGHTS

Lowest scores

9 holes: 27 (7 under par, ties all-time record), Andy North, B.C.; 28 (7 under), Bruce Crampton, Sahara; 29 (7 under), Hale Irwin, Phoenix, and Tom Weiskopf, Westchester; 29 (6 under), Jim Simons, Hartford.

18 holes: 61 (11 under), Johnny Miller, Tucson; 61 (10 under), J. Miller, Phoenix.

36 holes: 128 (14 under), Johnny Miller, Phoenix; 129 (15 under), Tom Weiskopf, Westchester; 129 (13 under), Jack Nicklaus, Heritage.

54 holes: 196 (17 under), Johnny Miller, Phoenix.

72 holes: 260 (24 under), Johnny Miller, Phoenix; 263 (25 under), J. Miller, Tucson.

Largest winning margin

14 strokes, by Johnny Miller, Phoenix.

Highest winning score

287 (3 over), Lou Graham and John Mahaffey (tied), U.S. Open.

Best winning comeback

7 strokes, made up in the last round in the Quad Cities by Roger Maltbie.

Largest 36-hole lead

7 strokes, by Tom Weiskopf, Westchester (he did not win).

Largest 54-hole lead

7 strokes, by Johnny Miller, Phoenix (he won).

Best start by winner

64, by Johnny Miller, Hope.

Worst start by winner

74, by Lou Graham, U.S. Open.

Best finish by winner

61, by Johnny Miller, Tucson.

Worst finish by winner

73, by Lou Graham, U.S. Open, and Hale Irwin, Western.

Lowest 36-hole cut

142 (even par), at Hartford, Sahara. 144 (even par), at Gleason-Inverrary, Houston, Westchester, Kaiser, San Antonio.

Highest 36-hole cut

151 (9 over), at Western.

Holes-in-one

17 were made, by Bobby Mitchell and Homero Blancas, Jacksonville; Nate Starks and Jim Jamieson, Tallahassee; Pete Brown, Forrest Fezler and Joe Inman, Nelson; Gary Wintz, New Orleans; Hubert Green, Memphis; Pat Fitzsimons, U.S. Open; Carl Lohren and Gene Littler, Westchester; Hale Irwin, PGA; Ras Allen, Hartford; Bob Menne, B.C.; Larry Nelson, World, and Johnny Stevens, Disney Team. In 1974, 17 were also made; 1973, 26; 1972, 24; 1971, 8; 1970, 16; 1969, 20; 1968, 20; 1967, 15; 1966, 18; 1965, 7; 1964, 19; 1963, 19; 1962, 16; 1961, 14; 1960, 17; 1959, 30 (record).

Double eagles

Lee Elder, Greensboro (driver, 5-iron, 477 yards), and Miller Barber, Canadian (driver, 3-wood, 525 yards).

Most consecutive birdies

6, by Johnny Miller, third round of Masters. 5 in succession, by Tom Weiskopf and Bert Yancey, Doral; Babe Hiskey, Nelson; Jerry Heard, U.S. Open, and Roger Maltbie, Quad Cities.

Most successive holes without 3-putt

319, by Jerry McGee (9th green, first round, at Doral through 4th green, fourth round, Tournament of Champions).

Consecutive rounds at par or under

13 in succession, by John Mahaffey (Hawaiian 4, Hope 5, San Diego 4) and Tom Weiskopf (Heritage 4, Greensboro 4, Masters 4, Tournament of Champions 1).

Consecutive rounds under 70

8 in succession, by Johnny Miller at Phoenix and Tucson.

First-time winners

Gary Groh, Hawaiian; Pat Fitzsimons, Los Angeles; Jerry McGee, Pensacola; Rik Massengale, Tallahassee; Tom Jenkins, Philadelphia; Roger Maltbie, Quad Cities; Don Bies, Hartford, and Don Iverson, B.C.

Youngest winner

Roger Maltbie was 24 when he won the Quad Cities and Pleasant Valley titles.

Oldest winner

Art Wall was 51 when he won at Milwaukee.

1975 PERFORMANCE AVERAGE LEADERS

MEN

Player	Possible Points	Points Earned[2]	Perf. Ave.[3]
1. Jack Nicklaus (16)	800	727.00	.909
2. Hale Irwin (22)	1,100	746.00	.678
3. Tom Watson (25)	1,250	840.50	.672
4. John Miller (21)	1,050	696.56	.663
5. Gene Littler (22)	1,100	672.53	.611
6. Bruce Crampton (24)	1,200	721.00	.601
7. Tom Weiskopf (23)	1,150	667.00	.580
8. Lee Trevino (27)	1,350	767.70	.569
9. John Mahaffey (25)	1,250	695.00	.556
10. Billy Casper (19)	950	525.50	.553
11. Charles Coody (27)	1,350	654.00	.493
12. Gary Player (15)	750	368.00	.490
13. Arnold Palmer (19)	950	446.00	.469
14. Bob Murphy (23)	1,150	535.00	.465
15. Tom Kite (26)	1,300	593.50	.457
16. Al Geiberger (25)	1,250	566.00	.453
17. Jerry McGee (30)	1,500	674.50	.450
18. Miller Barber (31)	1,550	693.50	.447
Pat Fitzsimons (23)	1,150	514.00	.447
20. Hubert Green (26)	1,300	523.00	.441
21. Rik Massengale (28)	1,450	606.00	.433
22. Don January (24)	1,200	512.63	.427
23. Lou Graham (26)	1,300	554.00	.426
24. Ray Floyd (25)	1,250	520.69	.417
25. Dave Hill (27)	1,350	544.00	.403
26. J. C. Snead (28)	1,400	556.76	.398
27. Jerry Heard (26)	1,300	508.14	.391
28. Brian Allin (28)	1,400	547.10	.390
Mark Hayes (32)	1,600	625.00	.390
30. Dave Stockton (28)	1,450	557.50	.384
31. B. R. McLendon (30)	1,500	561.00	.374
32. Ben Crenshaw (27)	1,350	486.20	.360
33. Rod Funseth (26)	1,300	457.50	.351
34. Gibby Gilbert (32)	1,600	556.17	.347
35. Don Bies (23)	1,150	391.70	.340
36. John Schlee (24)	1,200	402.75	.335
37. Joe Inman Jr. (30)	1,500	501.46	.334
38. Len Thompson (31)	1,550	508.00	.327
39. David Graham (30)	1,550	448.30	.298
40. Peter Oosterhuis (31)	1,550	452.33	.291
41. Rod Curl (31)	1,550	439.50	.283
42. Steve Melnyk (34)	1,700	477.00	.280
43. Bob Wynn (28)	1,400	391.10	.279
44. Andy North (32)	1,600	436.00	.272
45. Ed Sneed (29)	1,450	391.70	.270
46. Roger Maltbie (29)	1,450	387.43	.267
47. Jim Simons (30)	1,500	397.00	.264
48. Gary McCord (31)	1,550	408.00	.263
49. Bobby Nichols (23)	1,150	300.70	.261
50. Jim Colbert (31)	1,550	396.00	.255

[1] On basis of 50 points per tournament entered.
[2] On basis of 50 points for win, 49 for second, and so on down to one point for 50th place.
[3] Possible Points divided into Points Earned.
Figures in parentheses indicate number of events entered. Only those eligible — having played in at least 15 regular tour events — are listed. This is the minimum number of events in which a player must compete to retain his playing card, according to PGA rules. National Team Championship does not count.

WOMEN

Player	Possible Points[1]	Points Earned[2]	Perf. Ave.[3]
1. Sandra Haynie (19)	475	356.50	.751
2. Judy Rankin (22)	550	360.00	.655
3. JoAnne Carner (23)	575	374.00	.650
4. Carol Mann (21)	525	333.50	.635
5. Sandra Palmer (25)	625	374.50	.599
6. Jane Blalock (22)	550	325.00	.591
7. Donna Young (21)	525	302.50	.576
8. Sandra Post (22)	550	286.50	.521
Kathy Whitworth (21)	525	273.50	.521
10. Amy Alcott (21)	525	229.00	.436
11. Pat Bradley (24)	600	259.25	.432
12. Carole Jo Skala (22)	425	181.50	.427
13. JoAnn Washam (20)	500	192.75	.386
14. Suzie McAllister (27)	675	241.75	.358
15. Jocelyne Bourassa (25)	625	216.00	.346
16. Kathy McMullen (25)	625	196.25	.314
17. Betsy Cullen (22)	550	170.50	.310
18. Murle Breer (20)	500	150.50	.301
19. Debbie Austin (24)	600	173.50	.289
20. Betty Burfeindt (24)	600	160.50	.267
21. Joyce Kazmierski (25)	625	163.42	.261
22. Jan Stephenson (25)	625	159.50	.255
23. Gerda Boykin (14)	350	84.50	.241
24. Laura Baugh (24)	600	142.17	.237
25. JoAnn Prentice (26)	650	153.00	.235

[1] On basis of 25 points per official tournament entered.
[2] On basis of 25 points for win, 24 for second and so on down to one point for 25th place.
[3] Possible Points divided into Points Earned.
Figures in parentheses indicate number of official events entered. Only those having competed in at least half (14) of the 27 official events are eligible.

PAST PERFORMANCE AVERAGE LEADERS

	MEN	Performance Average
1955	Cary Middlecoff (20)	.659
1956	Ed Furgol (22)	.550
1957	Dow Finsterwald (27)	.643
1958	Bill Casper (26)	.611
1959	Gene Littler (29)	.603
1960	Arnold Palmer (26)	.706
1961	Arnold Palmer (25)	.725
1962	Jack Nicklaus (26)	.601
1963	Gary Player (22)	.864
1964	Jack Nicklaus (24)	.875
1965	Jack Nicklaus (20)	.828
1966	Bill Casper (22)	.791
1967	Arnold Palmer (23)	.739
1968	Bill Casper (23)	.803
1969	Dave Hill (25)	.643
1970	Dave Hill (25)	.673
1971	Arnold Palmer (22)	.737
1972	Jack Nicklaus (18)	.801
1973	Jack Nicklaus (17)	.894
1974	Jack Nicklaus (17)	.841

	WOMEN	Performance Average
1955	Patty Berg (20)	.894
1956	Patty Berg (22)	.882
1957	Patty Berg (20)	.830
1958	Mickey Wright (17)	.819
1959	Louise Suggs (21)	.905
1960	Mickey Wright (21)	.883
1961	Mickey Wright (24)	.891
1962	Ruth Jessen (24)	.798
1963	Mickey Wright (28)	.907
1964	Mickey Wright (27)	.838
1965	Kathy Whitworth (30)	.862
1966	Mickey Wright (22)	.900
1967	Sandra Haynie (27)	.826
1968	Kathy Whitworth (30)	.883
1969	Kathy Whitworth (28)	.855
1970	Kathy Whitworth (21)	.831
1971	Kathy Whitworth (20)	.740
1972	Kathy Whitworth (27)	.782
1973	Judy Rankin (33)	.668
1974	Jane Blalock (29)	.707

SENIOR PROFESSIONALS

PGA SENIORS' CHAMPIONSHIP

Year	Winner	Score
1945	Eddie Williams	148
1946	Eddie Williams*	146
1947	Jock Hutchison	145
1948	Charles McKenna	141
1949	Marshall Crichton	145
1950	Al Watrous	142
1951	Al Watrous*	142
1952	Ernest Newham	146
1953	Harry Schwab	142
1954	Gene Sarazen	214
1955	Mortie Dutra	213
1956	Pete Burke	215
1957	Al Watrous	210
1958	Gene Sarazen	288
1959	Willie Goggin	284
1960	Dick Metz	284
1961	Paul Runyan	278
1962	Paul Runyan	278
1963	Herman Barron	272
1964	Sam Snead	279
1965	Sam Snead	278
1966	Fred Haas	286
1967	Sam Snead	279
1968	Chandler Harper	279
1969	Tommy Bolt	278
1970	Sam Snead	290
1971	Julius Boros	285
1972	Sam Snead	286
1973	Sam Snead	268
1974	Roberto de Vicenzo	273
1975	Charlie Sifford*	280

*Won playoff.

NATIONAL SENIOR OPEN

Year	Winner	Location	Score
1957	Fred Wood*	Vancouver, B.C.	270
1958	Willie Goggin	San Jose, Calif.	270
1959	Willie Goggin*	San Jose, Calif.	289
1960	Chas. Congdon	Tacoma, Wash.	281
1961	Dutch Harrison	San Francisco	273
1962	Dutch Harrison	St. Louis	278
1963	Dutch Harrison	St. Louis	270
1964	Dutch Harrison	St. Louis	276
1965	Chandler Harper	Chesapeake, Va.	280
1966	Dutch Harrison	St. Louis, Mo.	277
1967	Pete Fleming	Las Vegas, Nev.	271
1968	Tommy Bolt	Sarasota, Fla.	265
1969	Tommy Bolt	Sarasota, Fla.	277
1970	Tommy Bolt	Sarasota, Fla.	267
1971	Tommy Bolt	Sarasota, Fla.	279
1972	Tommy Bolt	Sarasota, Fla.	274
1973	Manuel de la Torre	Milwaukee	278
1974	Willie Barber	Costa Mesa, Calif.	278
1975	Willie Barber	Costa Mesa, Calif.	281

*Won playoff.

WORLD PROFESSIONAL SENIOR CHAMPIONSHIP

Year	Winner	Runner-up
1961	Paul Runyan (U.S.)	Sam King (G.B.)
1962	Paul Runyan (U.S.)	Sam King (G.B.)
1963	Herman Barron (U.S.)	George Evans (G.B.)
1964	Sam Snead (U.S.)	Sydney Scott (G.B.)
1965	Sam Snead (U.S.)	Charles Ward (G.B.)
1966	Fred Haas (U.S.)	Dai Rees (G.B.)
1967	John Panton (G.B.)	Sam Snead (U.S.)
1968	Chandler Harper (U.S.)	Max Faulkner (G.B.)
1969	Tommy Bolt (U.S.)	John Panton (G.B.)
1970	Sam Snead (U.S.)	Max Faulkner (G.B.)
1971	Kel Nagle (Aust.)	Julius Boros (U.S.)
1972	Sam Snead (U.S.)	Ken Bousfield (G.B.)
1973	Sam Snead (U.S.)	Kel Nagle (Aust.)
1974	R. de Vicenzo (Arg.)	Eric Lester (G.B.)
1975	Kel Nagle (Aust.)	Charlie Sifford (U.S.)

Charlie Sifford won PGA Seniors in first try.

1975 PGA SECTION CHAMPIONS

Aloha: John Kalinka, Honolulu, Hawaii.
Carolinas: Roger Watson, Cary, N.C.
Central New York: Jerry Steelsmith, Syracuse, N.Y.
Colorado: Rich Bland, Denver, Colo.
Connecticut: Dennis Coscina, Simsbury, Conn.
Dixie: Hubert Green, Bay Point, Fla.
Eastern Missouri: Al Chandler, Columbia, Mo.
Florida: Julius Boros, Fort Lauderdale, Fla.
Georgia: Paul Moran, Newnan, Ga.
Gulf States: David Smith, Ocean Springs, Miss.
Illinois: Shelby Futch, Long Grove, Ill.
Indiana: Don Padgett II, Carmel, Ind.
Iowa: Hank Stukart, Galesburg, Ill.
Kentucky: Gordon Waldespuhl, Florence, Ky.
Metropolitan: Bill Collins, Purchase, N.Y.
Michigan: Gene Bone, West Bloomfield, Mich.
Middle Atlantic: Robert Post, Locust Grove, Va.
Mid-West: Bob Stone, Lee's Summit, Mo.
Minnesota: Jack Baldwin, Lafayette, Minn.
Nebraska: John Frillman, Omaha.

New England: Joe Carr, Spencer, Mass.
New Jersey: Gary Head, West Caldwell, N.J.
Northeast New York: Ron Phile, Scotia, N.Y.
Northern California: Ken Towns, Tracy, Calif.
Northern Ohio: Charlie Sifford Sr., Brecksville, Ohio.
Northern Texas: Don January, Dallas.
Pacific Northwest: Rick Acton, Kirkland, Wash.
Philadelphia: Ed Dougherty, Edgemont, Pa.
Rocky Mountain: Bill Farkas, Las Vegas, Nev.
South Central: Labron Harris Jr., Stillwater, Okla.
Southern California: Jimmy Powell, San Dimas, Calif.
Southern Ohio: Jeffrey Mays, Cincinnati, Ohio.
Southern Texas: Don Massengale, Conroe, Tex.
Southwest: Jim Marshall, Scottsdale, Ariz.
Sun Country: Darrell Hickok, El Paso, Tex.
Tennessee: Bert Weaver, Cordova, Tenn.
Tri-State: Chuck Scally, Coraopoalis, Pa.
Western New York: Denny Lyons, Lewiston, N.Y.
Wisconsin: Rolf Deming, Appleton, Wis.

WOMEN'S PROFESSIONAL RECORDS

Past Leading Money Winners

1965
Player	Money
1. Kathy Whitworth	$28,658
2. Marlene Hagge	21,532
3. Carol Mann	20,875
4. Clifford Ann Creed	20,795
5. Sandra Haynie	17,722
6. Marilynn Smith	16,692
7. Mary Mills	13,007
8. Susie Maxwell	12,982
9. Judy Torluemke	12,237
10. Betsy Rawls	10,898

1966
Player	Money
1. Kathy Whitworth	$33,517
2. Sandra Haynie	30,157
3. Mickey Wright	26,672
4. Carol Mann	23,246
5. Clifford Ann Creed	21,089
6. Marilynn Smith	16,412
7. Judy Torluemke	15,180
8. Judy Kimball	13,571
9. Shirley Englehorn	13,405
10. Mary Mills	12,823

1967
Player	Money
1. Kathy Whitworth	$32,937
2. Sandra Haynie	26,543
3. Carol Mann	24,666
4. Mickey Wright	20,613
5. Susie Maxwell	19,537
6. Clifford Ann Creed	17,940
7. Judy Kimball	14,722
8. Marilynn Smith	13,045
9. Shirley Englehorn	11,786
10. Margee Masters	11,725

1968
Player	Money
1. Kathy Whitworth	$48,379
2. Carol Mann	45,921
3. Sandra Haynie	25,992
4. Marilynn Smith	20,945
5. Sandra Spuzich	19,325
6. Clifford Ann Gordon	17,619
7. Mickey Wright	17,147
8. Sandra Palmer	16,906
9. Shirley Englehorn	15,579
10. Donna Caponi	14,563

1969
Player	Money
1. Carol Mann	$49,152
2. Kathy Whitworth	48,171
3. Donna Caponi	30,067
4. Shirley Englehorn	24,486
5. Sandra Haynie	24,276
6. Sandra Spuzich	20,339
7. Susie Berning	19,966
8. Murle Lindstrom	19,630
9. Sandra Palmer	18,319
10. Mickey Wright	17,851

1970
Player	Money
1. Kathy Whitworth	$30,235
2. Sandra Haynie	26,626
3. Shirley Englehorn	22,727
4. Marilynn Smith	22,391
5. Judy Rankin	22,195
6. Carol Mann	20,907
7. Donna Caponi	19,369
8. Sandra Palmer	18,424
9. Betsy Rawls	17,897
10. Mary Mills	15,055

1971
Player	Money
1. Kathy Whitworth	$41,181
2. Sandra Haynie	36,219
3. Jane Blalock	34,492
4. Sandra Palmer	34,035
5. Donna Caponi	23,069
6. JoAnne Carner	21,604
7. Jo Ann Prentice	20,138
8. Pam Barnett	18,801
9. Judy Rankin	17,294
10. Marlene Hagge	16,514

1972
Player	Money
1. Kathy Whitworth	$65,063
2. Jane Blalock	57,323
3. Judy Rankin	49,183
4. Betty Burfeindt	47,548
5. Sandra Haynie	39,701
6. Kathy Ahern	38,072
7. Sandra Palmer	36,715
8. Carol Mann	36,452
9. Marilynn Smith	29,910
10. Jo Ann Prentice	27,583

1973
Player	Money
1. Kathy Whitworth	$82,864
2. Judy Rankin	72,989
3. Sandra Palmer	55,439
4. Betty Burfeindt	51,030
5. Carol Mann	47,734
6. Mary Mills	47,638
7. Sandra Haynie	47,353
8. Kathy Cornelius	44,246
9. Jane Blalock	40,710
10. Joyce Kazmierski	38,973

1974
Player	Money
1. JoAnne Carner	$87,570
2. Jane Blalock	87,266
3. Sandra Haynie	76,480
4. Jo Ann Prentice	69,451
5. Sandra Palmer	55,113
6. Kathy Whitworth	52,596
7. Carol Mann	48,688
8. Carole Jo Skala	47,939
9. Judy Rankin	48,151
10. Donna Young	38,950

PAST MONEY LEADERS
Year	Player	Money
1948	Babe Zaharias	$ 3,400
1949	Babe Zaharias	4,650
1950	Babe Zaharias	14,800
1951	Babe Zaharias	15,087
1952	Betsy Rawls	14,505
1953	Louise Suggs	19,816
1954	Patty Berg	16,011
1955	Patty Berg	16,497
1956	Marlene Hagge	20,235
1957	Patty Berg	16,272
1958	Beverly Hanson	12,639
1959	Betsy Rawls	26,774
1960	Louise Suggs	16,892
1961	Mickey Wright	22,236
1962	Mickey Wright	21,641
1963	Mickey Wright	31,269
1964	Mickey Wright	29,800

1975 LPGA TOUR STATISTICS

Player	Tour Events	1st	2nd	3rd	Scoring Average	Perf. Average[1]	Official Money for 1975[2]	Average Money Per Tour Event	Career Earnings
1. Sandra Palmer (5)	25	2	2	3	72.72	.599	$76,374	$3,055	$331,293
2. JoAnne Carner (1)	23	3	4	2	72.40	.650	64,842	2,819	226,681
3. Carol Mann (7)	21	4	1	3	72.48	.635	64,727	3,082	413,301
4. Sandra Haynie (3)	19	4	3	2	72.00	.751	61,614	3,243	449,003
5. Judy Rankin (9)	22	1	5	1	72.36	.655	50,174	2,281	327,165
6. Jane Blalock (2)	22	1	2	1	73.06	.591	45,478	2,067	276,936
7. Donna Young (10)	21	2	2	1	72.87	.576	43,291	2,061	225,963
8. Kathy McMullen (24)	25	0	1	1	73.92	.314	39,555	1,582	65,087
9. Kathy Whitworth (6)	21	2	0	2	73.15	.521	36,422	1,734	576,766
10. Sandra Post (15)	22	0	3	1	76.30	.521	34,853	1,584	121,447
11. Suzie McAllister (55)	27	1	1	2	73.98	.358	31,437	1,164	58,326
12. JoAnn Washam (32)	20	2	0	1	73.33	.386	30,950	1,548	50,721
13. Carole Jo Skala (8)	17	0	0	2	73.85	.427	29,493	1,735	109,221
14. Pat Bradley (39)	24	0	1	1	73.43	.432	28,293	1,179	39,133
15. Amy Alcott	21	1	1	0	73.21	.436	26,798	1,276	26,798
16. Jocelyne Bourassa (48)	25	0	1	0	74.26	.346	26,518	1,061	65,504
17. Betsy Cullen (17)	22	1	0	0	74.04	.310	22,933	1,042	149,479
18. Sue Roberts (19)	22	1	0	1	74.55	.220	21,154	962	70,377
19. Debbie Austin (20)	24	0	0	2	74.11	.289	20,513	855	110,396
20. Joyce Kazmierski (23)	25	0	0	0	74.08	.261	20,098	804	92,459
21. Jan Stephenson (28)	25	0	0	2	74.43	.255	20,066	802	36,337
22. Jan Ferraris (41)	23	0	2	0	74.96	.189	19,316	840	91,918
23. Sandra Spuzich (14)	25	0	1	0	74.29	.219	18,372	735	171,388
24. Maria Astrologes (21)	23	1	0	0	74.34	.205	17,537	762	42,192
25. Laura Baugh (12)	24	0	0	0	74.42	.237	16,902	704	68,124

Player	Money		Player	Money		Player	Money
26. Betty Burfeindt	$16,029		35. Kathy Postlewait	12,468		44. Beth Stone	8,613
27. Shelley Hamlin	15,980		36. Louise Bruce	11,936		45. S. Bertolaccini	8,408
28. Chako Higuchi	15,678		37. Mary Bea Porter	11,665		46. Karolyn Kertzman	7,818
29. JoAnn Prentice	15,660		38. Mary Mills	11,653		47. Diane Patterson	7,511
30. Murle Breer	15,231		39. Judy Kimball	11,086		48. Kathy Cornelius	7,423
31. Kathy Ahern	14,721		40. Marlene Hagge	11,020		49. Pam Barnett	7,401
32. Gloria Ehret	14,683		41. Janet LePera	9,508		50. Sally Little	7,107
33. Hollis Stacy	14,409		42. Bonnie Bryant	9,139			
34. Gerda Boykin	13,113		43. Pam Higgins	8,994			

Event Winners: Young (Burdines, Lady Tara), Haynie (Naples, Charity, Jacksonville, Ft. Myers), Alcott (Orange Blossom), Roberts (Crosby Int'l), Blalock (Ping), Palmer (Colgate, U.S. Open), Astrologes (Birmingham), Carner (Amer. Defender, Girl Talk, Jackson), Whitworth (LPGA Championship, Southgate), Mann (Lawson's, Borden, Washington, Dallas), Cullen (Hoosier), McAllister (Wheeling), Washam (Patty Berg, Portland), Rankin (Nat'l Jewish), Porter (Golf Inns of America). **Unofficial:** Whitworth (Colgate Triple Crown), Blalock (Japan Classic), Berning (Lady Keystone), Young (Colgate-European).

[1]Performance Average is an exclusive Golf Digest method of measuring performance relative to the performance of other players in official events. It is calculated by dividing the number of possible points (25 points per tournament entered) into points earned (25 points awarded for first place, 24 for second and so on down to one point for 25th place).

[2]Includes money won in regular tour events, but no pro-am competition. Players are ranked according to this official money figure.

Note: Figures in parentheses after players' names indicate 1974 money-winning rank.

Kathy Whitworth is the LPGA's all-time money-winner.

ALL-TIME MONEY LEADERS
Player	Since	Money
1. Kathy Whitworth (1)	1958	$576,766
2. Sandra Haynie (2)	1960	449,003
3. Carol Mann (3)	1960	413,301
4. Sandra Palmer (10)	1964	331,293
5. Mickey Wright (4)*	1954	330,413
6. Judy Rankin (8)	1962	327,165
7. Betsy Rawls (5)*	1951	302,665
8. Marlene Hagge (6)	1950	300,617
9. Marilynn Smith (7)	1949	284,868
10. Jo Ann Prentice (9)	1956	279,630
11. Jane Blalock (11)	1969	276,936
12. JoAnne Carner (18)	1970	226,681
13. Mary Mills (12)	1962	226,566
14. Donna Young (16)	1965	225,963
15. Clifford Ann Creed (15)	1962	192,564

Figures in parentheses indicate 1974 rank.
*Not active on tour.

ALL-TIME TOURNAMENT LEADERS
Player	Since	Total
1. Mickey Wright (1)	1954	82
2. Kathy Whitworth (2)	1958	74
3. Betsy Rawls (3)	1951	53
4. Louise Suggs (4)	1948	50
5. Patty Berg (5)	1948	41
6. Sandra Haynie (6)	1960	39
7. Carol Mann (7)	1960	38
8. Babe Zaharias* (8)	1948	31
9. Marlene Hagge (9)	1950	25
10. Marilynn Smith (10)	1949	21

Figures in parentheses indicate 1974 rank.
*Deceased.

COLGATE TRIPLE CROWN ($50,000), Doral C.C. (Blue Cse., 72-6,239), Miami, Jan. 18-19.

Whitworth	71-73—144	$15,000
Rankin	73-73—146	10,000
Post	72-75—147	7,500
Breer	76-73—149	4,250
Mills	74-75—149	4,250
Cullen	74-77—151	2,000
Matsui	76-75—151	2,000
Prentice	77-74—151	2,000
Masters	80-80—160	1,000

BURDINE'S INV. ($40,000), Kendale Lakes C.C. (72-6,300), Miami, Jan. 31-Feb. 2.

Young	70-71-67—208	$5,700
Cornelius	71-70-70—211	4,170
LePera	69-71-72—212	2,900
McAllister	72-71-69—212	2,900
Baugh	68-75-70—213	1,478
Blalock	70-70-73—213	1,478
Carner	71-72-70—213	1,478
Mann	71-71-71—213	1,478
Patterson	74-70-69—213	1,478
Rankin	70-75-68—213	1,478
Skala	71-71-71—213	1,478

NAPLES-LELY CLASSIC, Lely G.C. (72-6,200), Naples, Fla., Feb. 7-9.

Haynie	71-72-68—211	$5,700
Smith	70-70-72—212	3,685
Young	69-71-72—212	3,685
Austin	69-71-73—213	2,600
Post	71-75-68—214	1,900
Hamlin	70-72-72—214	1,900

ORANGE BLOSSOM CLASSIC ($35,000), Pasadena G.C. (72-6,311), St. Petersburg, Fla., Feb. 28-March 2.

Alcott	68-68-71—207	$5,000
Post	73-66-69—208	3,750
Kimball	71-71-71—213	2,850
Bradley	73-70-71—214	2,350
Little	69-71-75—215	1,737
McAllister	72-69-74—215	1,737

BING CROSBY INV. ($40,000), San Isidro Cse. (72-6,300), Guadalajara, Mexico, March 21-23.

Roberts	68-74-72—214	$6,400
Blalock	74-72-71—217	4,750
Palmer	74-74-72—220	3,100
Rankin	71-75-74—220	3,100
Post	72-74-76—222	2,150
Barnett	75-72-76—223	1,575
Bradley	78-70-75—223	1,575
Bruce	75-75-73—223	1,575
Young	79-74-70—223	1,575

KARSTEN-PING CLASSIC ($70,000), Camelback C.C. (72-6,002), Scottsdale, Ariz., March 27-29.

Blalock	70-71-68—209	$10,000
Carner	67-72-71—210	7,000
Haynie	73-69-69—211	5,500
Boykin	73-69-70—212	3,770
Ahern	70-72-70—212	3,770

COLGATE-DINAH SHORE WINNERS CIRCLE ($180,000), Mission Hills C.C. (72-6,347), Palm Springs, Calif., April 17-20.

Palmer	70-70-70-73—283	$32,000
McMull'n	71-76-66-71—284	21,000
Mann	73-72-71-71—287	10,500
Skala	74-70-75-68—287	10,500
Higuchi	74-72-74-67—287	10,500
Bourassa	71-70-73-75—289	4,825
Blalock	72-73-70-74—289	4,825
Bryant	75-71-70-73—289	4,825
Cullen	73-70-74-72—289	4,825
Roberts	73-72-66-74—290	3,875
Kazm'ski	74-70-73-73—290	3,875

CHARITY CLASSIC ($45,000), Woodhaven C.C. (71-6,009), Fort Worth, Tex., April 25-27.

Haynie*	69-73-70—212	$6,400
Alcott	69-73-70—212	4,100
Rankin	71-72-69—212	4,100
Young	76-67-70—214	2,450
Bradley	71-71-72—214	2,450
Carner	74-72-69—215	1,458
Mann	72-72-71—215	1,458
Palmer	68-73-74—215	1,458
Denenberg	67-72-76—215	1,458
Post	72-70-73—215	1,458
McMullen	72-67-76—215	1,458

*Won playoff.

Maria Astrologes won first at Birmingham.

BIRMINGHAM CLASSIC ($40,000), Green Valley C.C. (72-5,741), Birmingham, Ala., May 1-4.

Astrologes*	66-74-70—210	$5,700
Rankin	71-66-73—210	3,685
Carner	72-65-73—210	3,685
Young	69-71-71—211	2,325
Blalock	67-72-72—211	2,325
Denenberg	75-70-68—213	1,567
Palmer	71-72-70—213	1,567
Mills	70-71-72—213	1,567
Kazmierski	70-73-71—214	1,250
Bradley	70-72-72—214	1,250

*Won playoff.

LADY TARA CLASSIC ($40,000), Indian Hills C.C. (73-6,335), Marietta, Ga., May 9-11.

Young	72-70-72—214	$5,700
Palmer	75-71-69—215	3,685
Ehret	73-71-71—215	3,685
Whitworth	72-73-71—216	2,600
McAllister	72-72-73—217	2,050
Crocker	71-78-69—218	1,500
Astrologes	72-76-70—218	1,500
Higuchi	70-76-72—218	1,500
Carner	73-73-72—218	1,500
Cullen	70-78-72—220	1,100

AMERICAN DEFENDER CLASSIC ($40,000), North Ridge C.C. (72-6,100), Raleigh, N.C., May 23-25.

Carner*	69-68-69—206	$5,700
Rankin	66-69-71—206	4,170
Stephenson	69-70-68—207	3,200
Skala	71-70-68—209	2,600
Bourassa	72-70-68—210	1,900
Mann	73-68-69—210	1,900
Palmer	71-72-68—211	1,416
Whitworth	73-68-70—211	1,416
Haynie	72-68-71—211	1,416
McMullen	72-73-68—213	1,050

*Won playoff.

LPGA CHAMPIONSHIP ($50,000), Pine Ridge G.C. (73-6,449), Baltimore, May 29-June 1.

Whitw'th	70-70-75-73—288	$8,000
Haynie	72-74-72-71-74—289	5,650
Washam	71-76-72-71—290	4,300
Young	72-73-73-73—291	3,300
Mann	71-77-72-72—292	2,550
Spuzich	68-78-75-72—293	1,875
Bourassa	74-74-72-73—293	1,875
Palmer	74-71-73-75—293	1,875
Carner	73-77-74-70—294	1,475
Higuchi	75-74-74-71—294	1,475

GIRL TALK CLASSIC ($50,000), Sports City G. Cse. (73-6,001), Pine Plains, N.Y., June 6-8.

Carner	68-72-73—213	$7,000
Spuzich	71-73-75—219	5,200
Mann	77-73-72—222	3,230
Roberts	72-73-77—222	3,230

LAWSON'S LPGA CLASSIC ($50,000), Weymouth Valley C.C. (72-6,142), Medina, Ohio, June 13-15.

Mann	71-72-74—217	$7,000
Rankin	70-75-74—219	5,200
Palmer	74-74-72—220	3,600
Whitworth	73-74-74—221	2,555
Breer	71-75-75—221	2,555
Baugh	73-71-78—222	1,800
Washam	72-70-80—222	1,800

HOOSIER CLASSIC ($40,000), Plymouth C.C. (72-6,134), Plymouth, Ind., June 20-22.

Cullen	71-70-70—211	$5,700
Rankin	71-71-70—212	4,170
Post	74-71-68—213	2,230
Carner	72-71-70—213	2,230
Palmer	71-71-71—213	2,230
Postlewait	70-70-73—213	2,230
Austin	69-72-72—213	2,230

PETER JACKSON CLASSIC ($60,000), St. George's C.C. (73-6,265), Toronto, June 27-29.

Carner*	73-69-72—214	$12,000
Mann	69-76-69—214	6,500
Englehorn	71-74-70—215	3,800
Haynie	71-70-74—215	3,800

*Won playoff.

WHEELING CLASSIC ($40,000), Oglebay Park (72-6,050), Wheeling, W.Va., July 4-6.

McAllister	72-70-70—212	$5,700
Ferraris	67-74-72—213	4,170
Kertzman	66-73-75—214	3,200
Ehret	70-73-72—215	2,325
Stacy	73-71-71—215	2,325

BORDEN CLASSIC ($65,000), Riviera C.C. (72-6,200), Columbus, Ohio, July 10-13.

Mann	66-70-73—209	$9,200
Ferraris	73-68-69—210	6,750
Skala	70-71-70—211	5,275
Pulz	69-73-70—212	3,025
Carner	71-71-70—212	3,025
Baugh	72-69-71—212	3,025
Haynie	68-72-72—212	3,025

U.S. WOMEN'S OPEN ($55,000), Atlantic City (N.J.) C.C. (72-6,165), July 17-20.

Palmer	78-74-71-72—295	$8,045
Lopez†	73-74-77-75—299	
Carner	73-77-74-75—299	4,045
Post	74-73-76-76—299	4,045
McAllister	79-75-74-72—300	2,445
Haynie	74-74-76-77—301	2,245
Whitworth	76-76-75-75—302	2,045
Austin	76-76-72-79—303	1,945
Rankin	72-77-79-76—304	1,745
Little	80-70-73-81—304	1,745
Bourassa	77-76-75-76—304	1,745

†Amateur.

GEORGE WASHINGTON CLASSIC ($40,000), Hidden Springs Golf & C.C. (73-6,150), Horsham, Pa., July 25-27.

Mann	68-66-72—206	$5,700
McAllister	72-68-70—210	4,170
Whitworth	72-67-74—213	2,900
Prentice	74-68-71—213	2,900
Washam	70-72-72—214	2,050

COLGATE EUROPEAN LADIES OPEN ($75,000), Sunningdale C.C. (74-6,174), Berkshire, England, Aug. 6-9.

Young	68-71-74-70—283	$11,000
Palmer	70-69-72-74—285	7,700
Higuchi	77-69-72-71—289	5,500
Carner	71-72-73-74—290	3,630
Mann	74-74-74-68—290	3,630
McAllister		
	72-72-69-78—291	2,750
Washam	73-74-76-69—292	2,310
Boykin	75-73-77-67—292	2,310

PATTY BERG CLASSIC ($45,000), Keller G.C. (73-6,000), St. Paul, Minn., Aug. 15-17.

Washam	69-69-68—206	$6,400
Bourassa	73-68-69—210	4,100
Carner	68-72-70—210	4,100
Kazmierski	72-69-70—211	2,750
Palmer	71-69-72—212	1,866
Mann	69-71-72—212	1,866
Rankin	69-71-72—212	1,866

NAT. JEWISH HOSPITAL OPEN ($40,000), Pinehurst C.C. (72-6,229), Denver, Aug. 22-24.

Rankin	68-68-71—207	$5,700
Blalock	69-72-68—209	3,685
Haynie	68-69-72—209	3,685
Stephenson	73-69-68—210	2,600

DALLAS CIVITAN OPEN ($40,000), Brookhaven C.C. (72-6,121), Dallas, Sept. 5-7.

Mann	67-70-71—208	$6,200
Palmer	71-69-73—213	4,500
Austin	73-75-67—215	3,075
Young	71-69-75—215	3,075
Rankin	70-71-75—216	2,200

SOUTHGATE OPEN ($40,000), Leawood South C.C. (71-6,085), Prairie Village, Kan., Sept. 12-14.

Whitworth	72-72-69—213	$5,700
Boykin	78-69-70—217	4,170
Bertolaccini	71-72-75—218	3,200
Blalock	72-73-74—219	2,600
Stephenson	76-70-74—220	2,050
Postlewait	75-74-72—221	1,650
Bradley	72-73-76—221	1,650

PORTLAND CLASSIC ($40,000), Portland (Ore.) G.C. (73-6,207), Sept. 19-21.

Washam	71-75-69—215	$5,700
Haynie	71-73-72—216	4,170
Hamlin	72-71-74—217	3,200
Young	70-77-72—219	2,600
Baugh	72-76-72—220	2,050
Hagge	77-73-71—221	1,500
McMullen	75-75-71—221	1,500
Palmer	71-76-74—221	1,500
Stone	72-75-75—222	1,200

GOLF INNS OF AMERICA CL., Whispering Palms C.C. (73-6,105), Rancho Santa Fe, Calif., Oct. 23-26.

Porter	68-72-71-76—287	$5,700
Young	75-71-70-74—290	4,170
Stephenson		
	71-76-73-71—291	3,200
Bruce	76-74-70-72—292	2,133
Bradley	74-69-76-73—292	2,133
Bourassa	74-74-71-77—292	2,133

LADY JACKSONVILLE OPEN ($50,000), Selva Marina C.C. (72-6,239), Jacksonville, Fla., Nov. 14-16.

Haynie	75-71-77—223	$7,000
Post	77-74-73—224	5,200
Carner	78-74-74—226	2,187
Burfeindt	76-74-74—226	2,187
Bradley	79-74-73—226	2,187
Blalock	78-76-72—226	2,187
Whitworth	76-76-74—226	2,187
McMullen	75-77-74—226	2,187
Hamlin	76-79-71—226	2,187

GR. FORT MYERS CLASSIC ($40,000), Lockmoor C.C. (72-6,150), Ft. Myers, Fla., Nov. 21-23.

Haynie*	66-71-73—210	$5,700
Bradley	68-69-73—210	4,107
Mann	71-72-70—213	2,900
McAllister	71-70-72—213	2,900
Blalock	68-74-73—215	1,900
Kazmierski	73-73-69—215	1,900

*Won playoff.

OTHER WINNERS

AUSTRALIAN CLASSIC, JoAnne Carner, 228, $10,000.

KEYSTONE TOURN., Sue Berning, 142, $4,000.

SUNSTAR JAPAN-U.S. MATCH (Japan), Sandra Haynie, 212, $1,333.

JAPAN CLASSIC, Shelley Hamlin, 218, $15,000.

COLGATE FAR EAST CH., Pat Bradley, U.S., 216, $12,560.

Mary Bea Porter took Golf Inns for first title.

LPGA'S TOP 25—EVENT BY EVENT

(Players listed from left in money-winning rank. Tournaments listed from top in chronological order.)

T means tied for that position. WD means withdrew. FQ means failed to qualify.
Event winner not among top 25 money-winners: Mary Bea Porter (Golf Inns of America).

	SANDRA PALMER ($76,374)	JOANNE CARNER ($64,842)	CAROL MANN ($54,727)	SANDRA HAYNIE ($61,614)	JUDY RANKIN ($50,174)	JANE BLALOCK ($45,478)	DONNA YOUNG ($43,291)	KATHY McMULLEN ($39,555)	KATHY WHITWORTH ($36,422)	SANDRA POST ($34,852)	SUSIE McALLISTER ($31,437)	JOANN WASHAM ($30,950)	CAROLE JO SKALA ($29,493)	PAT BRADLEY ($28,293)	AMY ALCOTT ($26,798)	JOCELYNE BOURASSA ($26,518)	BETSY CULLEN ($22,933)	SUE ROBERTS ($21,154)	DEBBIE AUSTIN ($20,513)	JOYCE KAZMIERSKI ($20,098)	JAN STEPHENSON ($20,066)	JAN FERRARIS ($19,316)	SANDRA SPUZICH ($18,372)	MARIA ASTROLOGES ($17,537)	LAURA BAUGH ($16,902)
BURDINE'S	T19	T5	T5	T13	T5	T5	1	T27	T13	12	T3	T23	T5	T27	T31	T51	T58	T35	FQ	T13	T23	FQ	T48	T13	T5
NAPLES LELY	T7	T15	T7	1	T31	T15	T2	T22	T15	T5	T13	T27	T15	T11	T22	T15	T36	T46	4	T31	FQ	T42	FQ	T7	T44
ORANGE BLOSSOM	—	T35	—	—	T8	7	—	T8	T31	2	T5	T43	—	4	1	T43	—	T13	T16	T25	T61	T40	T56	T25	T25
CROSBY INTERNATIONAL	T3	—	—	T3	2	T6	T25	—	5	T10	—	T16	T6	—	T41	—	1	T18	T16	T21	T44	T25	—		
KARSTEN-PING	T22	2	T38	3	T8	1	T26	T33	T8	T17	T6	—	T6	T17	FQ	FQ	T11	WD	T11	10	T38	FQ	T26	T44	T56
COLGATE-DINAH SHORE	1	T19	T3	22	T14	T6	T31	2	T38	T14	T41	T12	T3	—	T12	T6	T6	T10	T19	T10	—	T38	T23	T27	T31
CHARITY GOLF CLASSIC	T6	T6	T6	1	T2	12	T4	T6	T36	T6	T47	T24	—	T4	T2	T47	T20	—	13	T14	T59	T31	T31	T28	
BIRMINGHAM CLASSIC	T6	T2	T30	T14	T2	T4	T4	T30	—	T14	T24	T16	—	T9	T19	T35	—	—	T24	T9	T11	T22	T16	1	FQ
LADY TARA CLASSIC	T2	T6	—	—	T17	T10	1	T35	4	T44	5	—	T26	T17	T22	T10	WD	T46	T15	T13	T26	25	T6	FQ	
AMERICAN DEFENDER	T7	1	T5	T7	2	—	—	T10	T7	T10	T49	T10	—	T15	—	T5	T15	T33	T33	T23	—	T15	T15	T23	T38
LPGA CHAMPIONSHIP	T6	T9	5	2	T20	T38	4	T29	1	T11	T49	3	T11	T26	FQ	T6	T35	45	T20	T20	T29	T14	T6	FQ	FQ
GIRL TALK CLASSIC	T9	4	T3	—	T9	T5	—	T16	—	T25	WD	—	T16	T13	T5	T5	—	T3	T16	T27	T27	55	2	T41	T44
LAWSON'S LPGA CLASSIC	3	T29	1	T14	2	T14	—	T32	4	T32	T41	T6	—	T11	T20	T14	T18	T52	—	T14	T37	T24	T52	T24	T6
HOOSIER CLASSIC	T3	T3	—	2	—	8	T9	T3	T13	—	T33	T9	—	1	T9	T3	T38	T18	—	T21	T27	T27			
PETER JACKSON CLASSIC	T22	1	2	T3	T10	T17	T43	T8	T17	T14	T50	T50	T10	T17	T14	T5	T39	T5	FQ	T33	T33	T5	T17	T39	T22
WHEELING CLASSIC	—	—	T44	—	WD	—	T15	T11	—	—	1	—	T11	—	—	T15	—	10	T32	—	2	T6	T15		
BORDEN CLASSIC	T8	T4	1	T4	T8	T8	T32	T22	—	T22	T38	T57	3	T16	T14	T8	T38	T43	T16	T51	T51	2	T32	T43	T4
U.S. OPEN	1	T2	FQ	6	T9	T14	T16	T19	7	T2	5	FQ	T39	T16	T19	9	T33	T25	8	T45	T36	FQ	FQ	T12	T14
GEO. WASHINGTON CLASSIC	T17	T11	1	T7	—	WD	10	—	T3	T21	2	5	T15	T43	T17	T15	—	T25	T40	—	T21	T32	—	T25	20
PATTY BERG CLASSIC	T5	T2	T5	T11	T5	—	T8	T31	T11	T15	T24	1	—	T8	—	T2	T20	T15	T20	4	T35	—	T15	—	T35
NATIONAL JEWISH OPEN	T26	T5	T14	T2	1	T2	T10	T5	T5	T10	T19	T14	—	T34	T5	T40	10	32	T48	T30	4	T52	T19	—	9
DALLAS CIVITAN OPEN	2	T6	1	T12	5	T31	T3	T29	16	—	T9	T16	T42	T25	T12	T55	T9	T25	3	T20	T31	T25	T6	T31	T16
SOUTHGATE OPEN	T6	—	—	—	T6	4	—	T6	1	—	T24	—	T43	—	20	T43	T11	T45	T28	T24	5	T32	T32	—	T32
PORTLAND CLASSIC	T17	T35	8	2	—	14	4	T26	T15	—	T23	1	T30	T6	T9	T30	T17	—	—	T17	T35	T26	T17	51	5
GOLF INNS	T7	—	—	—	—	2	—	T30	—	T11	—	DQ	T4	—	T4	7	—	—	—	3	T7	—	T13	—	
LADY JACKSONVILLE	27	T3	T39	1	—	T3	T14	T3	T5	2	T34	T23	—	T3	10	T14	27	27	T34	T20	27	—	T34	T14	T39
FORT MYERS CLASSIC	T17	T17	T3	1	—	T5	T22	T48	T17	T12	T3	T34	—	2	—	WD	T41	WD	T22	T5	7	—	T17	T26	T8

WOMEN'S MAJOR CHAMPIONSHIPS

U.S. OPEN

1946	Spokane C.C., Spokane, Wash.	Patty Berg d. Betty Jameson 5 and 4	
1947	Star. Forest C.C., Greensboro, N.C.	Betty Jameson *Sally Sessions	295 301
1948	Atlantic City C.C., Northfield, N.J.	Babe Zaharias Betty Hicks	300 308
1949	Prince George's, Landover, Md.	Louise Suggs Babe Zaharias	291 305
1950	Rolling Hills C.C., Wichita, Kan.	Babe Zaharias *Betsy Rawls	291 300
1951	Druid Hills G.C., Atlanta, Ga.	Betsy Rawls Louise Suggs	293 298
1952	Bala G.C., Philadelphia, Pa.	Louise Suggs M. Bauer, Jameson	284 291
1953	C.C. of Rochester, Rochester, N.Y.	Betsy Rawls Jackie Pung	302-71 302-77
1954	Salem C.C., Peabody, Mass.	Babe Zaharias Betty Hicks	291 303
1955	Wichita C.C., Wichita, Kan.	Fay Crocker Faulk, Suggs	299 303
1956	Northland C.C. Duluth, Minn.	Kathy Cornelius *B. McIntire	302-75 302-82
1957	Winged Foot C.C., Mamaroneck, N.Y.	Betsy Rawls Patty Berg	299 305
1958	Forest Lake C.C., Detroit, Mich.	Mickey Wright Louise Suggs	290 295
1959	Churchill Valley C.C., Pittsburgh	Mickey Wright Louise Suggs	287 289
1960	Worcester C.C., Worcester, Mass.	Betsy Rawls Joyce Ziske	292 293
1961	Baltusrol G.C., Springfield, N.J.	Mickey Wright Betsy Rawls	293 299
1962	Dunes G.&B.C. Myrtle Beach, S.C.	Murle Lindstrom Prentice, Jessen	301 303
1963	Kenwood C.C., Cincinnati, O.	Mary Mills Suggs. Haynie	289 292
1964	San Diego C.C., Chula Vista, Calif.	Mickey Wright Ruth Jessen	290-70 290-72
1965	Atl. City C.C., Northfield, N.J.	Carol Mann Kathy Cornelius	290 292
1966	Hazeltine Ntl. G.C., Chaska, Minn.	Sandra Spuzich Carol Mann	297 298
1967	Cascades G.C. Hot Springs, Va.	*Catherine Lacoste Stone, Maxwell	294 296
1968	Moselem Springs (Pa.) C.C.	Susie Berning Mickey Wright	289 292
1969	Scenic Hills C.C., Pensacola, Fla.	Donna Caponi Peggy Wilson	294 295
1970	Muskogee C.C., Muskogee, Okla.	Donna Caponi Haynie, Spuzich	287 288
1971	Kahkwa C.C., Erie, Pa.	JoAnne Carner Kathy Whitworth	288 295
1972	Winged Foot G.C., Mamaroneck, N.Y.	Susie Berning Rankin, Barnett, Ahern	299 300
1973	C.C. of Rochester, Rochester, N.Y.	Susie Berning Ehret, Hamlin	290 295
1974	LaGrange C.C., LaGrange, Ill.	Sandra Haynie Stone, Mann	295 296
1975	Atlantic City C.C., Atlantic City, N.J.	Sandra Palmer *Lopez, Carner, Post	295 299

*Amateur

Sandra Palmer won the U.S. Women's Open and Colgate-Dinah Shore Winners Circle titles on way to money-earning championship.

JoAnne Carner won three events, placed second in earnings in 1975 and was winner of the Vare Trophy.

LPGA CHAMPIONSHIP

1955	Orchard Ridge C.C., Ft. Wayne	Beverly Hanson d. L. Suggs 4 and 3	
1956	Forest Lake C.C., Detroit, Mich.	†Marlene Hagge Patty Berg	291 291
1957	Churchill Valley C.C., Pittsburgh	Louise Suggs Wiffi Smith	285 288
1958	Churchill Valley C.C., Pittsburgh	Mickey Wright Fay Crocker	288 294
1959	Sheraton Hotel C.C., French Lick, Ind.	Betsy Rawls Patty Berg	288 289
1960	Sheraton Hotel C.C., French Lick, Ind.	Mickey Wright Louise Suggs	292 295
1961	Stardust C.C., Las Vegas, Nev.	Mickey Wright Louise Suggs	287 296
1962	Stardust C.C., Las Vegas, Nev.	Judy Kimball Shirley Spork	282 286
1963	Stardust C.C., Las Vegas, Nev.	Mickey Wright Mills, Faulk, Suggs	294 296
1964	Stardust C.C., Las Vegas, Nev.	Mary Mills Mickey Wright	278 280
1965	Stardust C.C., Las Vegas, Nev.	Sandra Haynie Clifford A. Creed	279 280
1966	Stardust C.C., Las Vegas, Nev.	Gloria Ehret Mickey Wright	282 285
1967	Pleasant Valley C.C., Sutton, Mass.	Kathy Whitworth Shirley Englehorn	284 285
1968	Pleasant Valley C.C., Sutton, Mass.	Sandra Post Kathy Whitworth	294-68 294-75
1969	Concord G.C., Kiamesha Lake, N.Y.	Betsy Rawls Mann, Berning	293 297
1970	Pleasant Valley C.C., Sutton, Mass.	Shirley Englehorn Kathy Whitworth	285-74 285-78
1971	Pleasant Valley C.C., Sutton, Mass.	Kathy Whitworth Kathy Ahern	288 292
1972	Pleasant Valley C.C., Sutton, Mass.	Kathy Ahern Jane Blalock	293 299
1973	Pleasant Valley C.C., Sutton, Mass.	Mary Mills Betty Burfeindt	288 289
1974	Pleasant Valley C.C., Sutton, Mass.	Sandra Haynie JoAnne Carner	288 290
1975	Pine Ridge G.C., Baltimore	Kathy Whitworth Sandra Haynie	288 289

†Won sudden-death playoff.

Vare Trophy Winners

Year	Player	Ave.	Year	Player	Ave.
1953	P. Berg	75.00	1965	K. Whitworth	72.61
1954	B. Zaharias	75.48	1966	K. Whitworth	72.60
1955	P. Berg	74.47	1967	K. Whitworth	72.74
1956	P. Berg	74.57	1968	Carol Mann	72.04
1957	L. Suggs	74.64	1969	K. Whitworth	72.38
1958	B. Hanson	74.92	1970	K. Whitworth	72.26
1959	B. Rawls	74.03	1971	K. Whitworth	72.88
1960	M. Wright	73.25	1972	K. Whitworth	72.50
1961	M. Wright	73.55	1973	Judy Rankin	73.08
1962	M. Wright	73.67	1974	J. Carner	72.87
1963	M. Wright	72.81	1975	J. Carner	72.40
1964	M. Wright	72.46			

HIGHLIGHTS OF THE 1975 LPGA TOUR

Lowest scores

9 holes: 29 (7 under par), by Carol Mann on the first nine in the second round at Columbus, Ohio.

18 holes: 65 (7 under par), JoAnne Carner, Birmingham; 66 (7 under), Carol Mann, Horsham, Pa.

36 holes (in 54-hole events): First two—134 (12 under), Carol Mann, Horsham; Second two—137 (7 under), JoAnne Carner, Raleigh; 138 (8 under), Susie McAllister and Carol Mann, Horsham, Pa.

54 holes (in 54-hole events): 206 (10 under), Carol Mann, Horsham, Pa.; 206 (10 under), JoAnne Carner and Judy Rankin, Raleigh.

36 holes (in 72-hole events): 140 (6 under), Kathy Whitworth, LPGA at Baltimore, and Sandra Palmer (4 under), Colgate-Shore.

72 holes: 283 (5 under), Sandra Palmer, Colgate-Shore.

Best start by winner

65 (6 under), Maria Astrologes, Birmingham.

Worst start by winner

75 (3 over), Sandra Haynie, Jacksonville.

Best finish by winner

67 (5 under), Donna Young, Burdine's.

Worst finish by winner

77 (5 over), Sandra Haynie, Jacksonville.

First-time winners

Amy Alcott, St. Petersburg; Maria Astrologes, Birmingham; Susie McAllister, Wheeling; JoAnn Washam, St. Paul (also Portland); Mary Bea Porter, Golf Inns. Shelley Hamlin won unofficial Japan Classic, Pat Bradley the unofficial Colgate-Far East.

Largest winning margin

6 strokes, JoAnne Carner, Girl Talk.

Best amateur finish

Tied for second, Nancy Lopez, U.S. Open.

Successive wins

Sandra Haynie was the only winner in consecutive weeks, at Jacksonville, Fla., and Ft. Myers, Fla., the last two events.

Most dramatic winning putt

Amy Alcott made a 20-foot birdie putt on the last hole at St. Petersburg to win by one shot over Sandra Post.

Best comeback

Sandra Haynie came from three strokes off the pace going into the last round to win at Naples, Fla., and Maria Astrologes did the same at Birmingham.

Worst run of luck

Judy Rankin lost in two consecutive playoffs, at Fort Worth and Birmingham; then two weeks later lost in another playoff, at Raleigh. She was second five times during the year, the most runner-up spots of any tour competitor.

Most disappointing year

After appearing ready to make it big in 1974 with $36,563 in money won, Laura Baugh could take home only $16,902 in 1975.

Most times in top 10

Judy Rankin led with 18 of these finishes. Sandra Palmer and JoAnne Carner had 17 each, and Carol Mann 15.

Most rounds in 60s

Carol Mann and JoAnne Carner each had 12 rounds in the 60s, while Judy Rankin had 11.

Consecutive birdies

Carol Mann set an LPGA record of seven for consecutive birdies during the second round of the Borden's at Columbus, Ohio. She birdied the first seven holes of the first nine and scored 29.

MEN'S AMATEUR RECORDS

USGA MEN'S NATIONAL AMATEUR

Year	Site	Winner, Runner-up	Score
1895	Newport G.C. Newport, R.I.	Charles B. Macdonald d. C. E. Sands	12 and 11
1896	Shinnecock Southampton, N.Y.	H. J. Whigham d. J. G. Throp	8 and 7
1897	Chicago G.C. Wheaton, Ill.	H. J. Whigham d. W. R. Betts	8 and 6
1898	Morris County G.C. Morristown, N.J.	Findley S. Douglas d. W. B. Smith	5 and 3
1899	Onwentsia Club Lake Forest, Ill.	H. M. Harriman d. F. S. Douglas	3 and 2
1900	Garden City (N.Y.) G.C.	Walter J. Travis d. F. S. Douglas	2 up
1901	C.C. of Atlantic City, N.J.	Walter J. Travis d.W. E. Egan	5 and 4
1902	Glen View Golf, Ill.	Louis N. James d. E. M. Byers	4 and 2
1903	Nassau C.C. Glen Cove, N.Y.	Walter J. Travis d. E. M. Byers	5 and 4
1904	Baltusrol G.C. Springfield, N.J.	H. Chandler Egan d. F. Herreshoff	8 and 6
1905	Chicago G.C. Wheaton, Ill.	H. Chandler Egan d. D. E. Sawyer	6 and 5
1906	Englewood (N.J.) G.C.	Eben M. Byers d. G. S. Lyon	2 up
1907	Euclid Club Cleveland, O.	Jerome D. Travers d. A. Graham	6 and 5
1908	Garden City (N.Y.) G.C.	Jerome D. Travers d. Max H. Behr	8 and 7
1909	Chicago G.C. Wheaton, Ill.	Robert A. Gardner d. H. C. Egan	4 and 3
1910	The Country Club Brookline, Mass.	William C. Fownes, Jr. d. W. K. Wood	4 and 3
1911	The Apawamis C., Rye, N.Y.	Harold H. Hilton d. F. Herreshoff	1 up, 37
1912	Chicago G.C. Wheaton, Ill.	Jerome D. Travers d. C. Evans, Jr.	7 and 6
1913	Garden City (N.Y.) G.C.	Jerome D. Travers d. J. G. Anderson	5 and 4
1914	Ekwanok C.C. Manchester, Vt.	Francis Ouimet d. J. D. Travers	6 and 5
1915	C.C. of Detroit Grosse Pointe Farms, Mich.	Robert A. Gardner d. J. G. Anderson	5 and 4
1916	Merion Cricket C. Ardmore, Pa.	Charles Evans, Jr. d. R. A. Gardner	4 and 3
1917-1918 No championships			
1919	Oakmont (Pa.) C.C.	Davidson Herron d. R. T. Jones, Jr.	5 and 4
1920	Engineers' C.C. Roslyn, N.Y.	Charles Evans, Jr. d. F. Ouimet	7 and 6
1921	St. Louis C.C. Clayton, Mo.	Jesse P. Guilford d. R. A. Gardner	7 and 6
1922	The Country Club Brookline, Mass.	Jess W. Sweetser d. C. Evans, Jr.	3 and 2
1923	Flossmoor (Ill.) C.C.	Max R. Marston J. W. Sweetser	1 up, 38
1924	Merion Cricket C. Ardmore, Pa.	Robert T. Jones, Jr. d. G. Von Elm	9 and 8
1925	Oakmont (Pa.) C.C.	Robert T. Jones, Jr. d. Watts Gunn	8 and 7
1926	Baltusrol G.C. Springfield, N.J.	George Von Elm d. R. T. Jones, Jr.	2 and 1
1927	Minikahda C.C. Minneapolis, Minn.	Robert T. Jones, Jr. d. C. Evans, Jr.	8 and 7
1928	Brae Burn C.C. West Newton, Mass.	Robert T. Jones, Jr. d. T. P. Perkins	10 and 9
1929	Del Monte G. & C.C., Pebble Beach	Harrison R. Johnston d. Dr. O. F. Willing	4 and 3
1930	Merion Cricket C. Ardmore, Pa.	Robert T. Jones, Jr. d. E. V. Homans	8 and 7
1931	Beverly C.C. Chicago, Ill.	Francis Ouimet d. J. Westland	6 and 5
1932	Baltimore (Md.) C.C.	C. Ross Somerville d. J. Goodman	2 and 1
1933	Kenwood C.C. Cincinnati, O.	George T. Dunlap, Jr. d. M. Marston	6 and 5
1934	The Country Club Brookline, Mass.	W. Lawson Little, Jr. d. D. Goldman	8 and 7
1935	The Country Club Cleveland, O.	W. Lawson Little, Jr. d. W. Emery	4 and 2
1936	Garden City (N.Y.) G.C.	John W. Fischer d. J. McLean	1 up, 37 hls.
1937	Alderwood C.C. Portland, Ore.	John G. Goodman d. R. E. Billows	2 up
1938	Oakmont (Pa.) C.C.	William P. Turnesa d. B. P. Abbott	8 and 7
1939	North Shore C.C. Glenview, Ill.	Marvin H. Ward d. R. E. Billows	7 and 5
1940	Winged Foot G.C. Mamaroneck, N.Y.	Richard D. Chapman d. W. B. McCullough, Jr.	11 and 9
1941	Omaha Field C. Omaha, Neb.	Marvin H. Ward d. B. P. Abbott	4 and 3
1942-45 No championships			
1946	Baltusrol G.C. Springfield, N.J.	Stanley E. Bishop d. S. L. Quick	1 up, 37 hls.
1947	Del Monte G. & C.C., Pebble Beach	Robert H. Riegel d. J. W. Dawson	2 and 1
1948	Memphis C.C. Memphis, Tenn.	William P. Turnesa d. R. E. Billows	2 and 1
1949	Oak Hill C.C. Rochester, N.Y.	Charles R. Coe d. R. King	11 and 10
1950	Minneapolis G.C. Minneapolis, Minn.	Sam Urzetta d. F. Stranahan	1 up, 39
1951	Saucon Valley C.C. Bethlehem, Pa.	Billy Maxwell d. J. F. Gagliardi	4 and 3
1952	Seattle G.C. Seattle, Wash.	Jack Westland d. Al Mengert	3 and 2
1953	Oklahoma City G. & C.C.	Gene A. Littler d. Dale Morey	1 up
1954	C.C. of Detroit Grosse Pointe	Arnold D. Palmer d. R. Sweeney	1 up
1955	C.C. of Virginia Richmond, Va.	E. Harvie Ward d. W. Hyndman, III	9 and 8
1956	Knollwood C.C. Lake Forest, Ill.	E. Harvie Ward d. C. Kocsis	5 and 4
1957	The Country Club Brookline, Mass.	Hillman Robbins d. Dr. F. Taylor	5 and 4
1958	Olympia C.C. San Francisco	Charles Coe d. T. Aaron	5 and 4
1959	Broadmoor G.C., Colorado Springs	Jack Nicklaus d. Charles Coe	1 up
1960	St. Louis C.C. Clayton, Mo.	Deane Beman d. B. Gardner	6 and 4
1961	Pebble Beach (Calif.) C.C.	Jack Nicklaus d. D. D. Wysong, Jr.	8 and 6
1962	Pinehurst (N.C.) C.C.	Labron Harris, Jr. d. Downing Gray	1 up
1963	Wakonda C.C. Des Moines, Ia.	Deane Beman d. R. H. Sikes	2 and 1
1964	Canterbury G.C. Cleveland, O.	Bill Campbell d. Ed Tutwiler	1 up
1965	Southern Hills C.C., Tulsa, Okla.	Bob Murphy Bob Dickson	291
1966	Merion G.C., Ardmore, Penn.	Gary Cowan Deane Beman	285-75 285-76
1967	Broadmoor C.C., Colorado Springs	Bob Dickson Vinny Giles	285 286
1968	Scioto C.C., Columbus, O.	Bruce Fleisher Vinny Giles	284 285
1969	Oakmont C.C., Oakmont, Pa.	Steve Melnyk Vinny Giles	286 291
1970	Waverley C.C., Portland, Ore.	Lanny Wadkins Tom Kite	279 280
1971	Wilmington, C.C., Wilmington, Del.	Gary Cowan Eddie Pearce	280 283
1972	Charlotte C.C. Charlotte, N.C.	Vinny Giles Ben Crenshaw	285 288
1973	Inverness C., Toledo, O.	Craig Stadler d. David Strawn	6 and 5
1974	Ridgewood (N.J.) C.C.	Jerry Pate d. John Grace	2 and 1
1975	C.C. of Virginia, Richmond	Fred Ridley d. Keith Fergus	2 up

Fred Ridley holds U.S. Amateur trophy he won at Richmond, Va.

AMATEUR PUBLIC LINKS CHAMPIONSHIPS

Year	Team Champ.	Ind. Champ.
1950	Los Angeles, Calif.	Stan Bielat
1951	Dayton, Ohio	Dave Stanley
1952	Chicago, Ill.	Omer Bogan
1953	Jacksonville, Fla.	Ted Richards
1954	Dallas, Tex.	Gene Andrews
1955	Miami, Fla.	Sam Kocsis
1956	Memphis, Tenn.	James Buxbaum
1957	Honolulu, Hawaii	Don Essig, III
1958	St. Paul, Minn.	Dan Sikes, Jr.
1959	Dallas, Tex.	Bill Wright
1960	Pasadena, Calif.	Verne Callison
1961	Honolulu, Hawaii	R. H. Sikes
1962	Seattle, Wash.	R. H. Sikes
1963	Toledo, Ohio	Bobby Lunn
1964	Los Angeles, Calif.	Bill McDonald
1965	Phoenix, Ariz.	Arne Dokka
1966	Pittsburgh, Pa.	Monty Kaser
1967	Dayton, Ohio	Verne Callison
1968	Dallas, Tex.	Gene Towry
1969	Pasadena, Calif.	John Jackson
1970	Chicago, Ill.	Robert Risch
1971	Portland, Ore.	Fred Haney
1972	Portland, Ore.	Bob Allard
1973	Flanders, N.J.	Stan Stopa
1974	San Francisco	C. Barenaba Jr.
1975	Honolulu	Randy Barenaba

WESTERN AMATEUR

Year	Site	Winner, Runner-up	Score
1950	Dallas (Tex.) C.C.	Charles Coe R. Goldwater	7 and 6
1951	South Bend (Ind.) C.C.	Frank Stranahan d. J. T. Blair	7 and 6
1952	Exmoor C.C., Highland Pk., Ill.	Frank Stranahan d. Harvie Ward	4 and 2
1953	Blythefield C.C., Grand Rapids, Mich.	Dale Morey d. R. Norton	8 and 6
1954	Broadmoor G.C., Colorado Springs, Colo.	Bruce Cudd d. P. Getchell	1 up (37)
1955	Rockford (Ill.) C.C.	Edward Merrins d. H. Robbins	1 up (37)
1956	Belle Meade C.C., Nashville, Tenn.	Mason Rudolph d. J. Parnell	6 and 4
1957	Old Warson C.C., St. Louis, Mo.	Dr. Ed. Updegraff d. J. Campbell	9 and 8
1958	The C.C. of Florida, Delray Beach, Fla.	James Key d. M. Rudolph	3 and 2
1959	Waverley C.C., Portland, Ore.	Dr. Ed. Updegraff d. C. Hunter	7 and 6
1960	Northland C.C., Duluth, Mich.	Tommy Aaron d. Bob Cochran	Default
1961	New Orleans (La.) C.C.	Jack Nicklaus d. James Key	4 and 3
1962	Orchard Lake C.C., Detroit, Mich.	Art Hudnutt d. Bud Stevens	1 up
1963	Point O'Woods G. & C.C.	Tom Weiskopf d. Labron-Harris, Jr.	5 and 4
1964	Tucson C.C. Tucson, Ariz.	Steve Oppermann d. Dr. Ed Updegraff	3 and 2
1965	Point O'Woods G. & C.C.	Bob Smith d. George Boutell	1 up (37)
1966	Pinehurst C.C., Pinehurst, N.C.	Jim Wiechers d. Ron Cerrudo	1 up
1967	Milburn C.C., Kansas City, Mo.	Bob Smith d. Marty Fleckman	3 and 1
1968	Grosse Ile (Mich.) G. & C.C.	Rik Massengale d. Kemp Richardson	3 and 1
1969	Rockford C.C., Rockford, Ill.	Steve Melnyk d. Howard Twitty	3 and 1
1970	Wichita C.C., Wichita, Kan.	Lanny Wadkins d. Charlie Borner	4 and 2
1971	Point O'Woods G. & C.C.	Andy North d. Barney Thompson	1 up
1972	Point O'Woods G. & C.C.	Gary Sanders d. Gil Morgan	19 holes
1973	Point O'Woods G. & C.C.	Ben Crenshaw d. Jimmy Ellis	4 and 3
1974	Point O'Woods G. & C.C.	Curtis Strange d. Jay Haas	20 holes
1975	Point O'Woods G. & C.C.	Andy Bean d. Randy Simmons	1 up

PORTER CUP TOURNAMENT
Site: Niagara Falls C.C., Lewiston, N.Y.

Year	Winner	Score
1959	John Konsek (54 holes)	215
1960	Ward Wettlaufer	282
1961	John Konsek	285
1962	Ed Tutwiler	281
1963	Bill Harvey	274
1964	Deane Beman	277
1965	Ward Wettlaufer	268
1966	Bob Smith	276
1967	Bob Smith	276
1968	Randy Wolff	282
1969	Gary Cowan	281
1970	Howard Twitty	276
1971	Cameron Quinn	279
1972	Ben Crenshaw	276
1973	Vinny Giles	274
1974	George Burns	276
1975	Jay Sigel	274

SUNNEHANNA AMATEUR
Site: Sunnehanna C.C., Johnstown, Pa.

Year	Winner	Score
1954	Don Cherry	280
1955	Hillman Robbins	280
1956	Gene Dahlbender	276
1957	Joe Campbell	283
1958	Bill Hyndman	280
1959	Tommy Aaron	277
1960	Gene Dahlbender	273
1961	Dick Siderowf	281
1962	Dr. Ed. Updegraff	278
1963	Roger McManus	282
1964	Gary Cowan	278
1965	Bobby Greenwood	269
1966	Jack Lewis	273
1967	Bill Hyndman*	275
1968	Bobby Greenwood	280
1969	Len Thompson	273
1970	Howard Twitty	276
1971	Bob Zender	278
1972	Mark Hayes	277
1973	Ben Crenshaw	275
1974	David Strawn	274
1975	Jaime Gonzalez (54 holes)	209

*Won playoff.

TRANS-MISSISSIPPI AMATEUR

Year	Winner, Runner-up
1950	James English d. Jack Vickers
1951	L. M. Crannell d. Don Addington, 7 and 6
1952	Charles Coe d. Buster Reed, 3 and 2
1953	Joe Conrad d. Jim Vickers, 1 up
1954	Jimmy Jackson d. Rex Baxter, 4 and 3
1955	Jimmy Jackson d. Rex Baxter, 2 and 1
1956	Charles Coe d. Ron Wenzler, 11 and 9
1957	Rex Baxter d. John Zibnack, 8 and 6
1958	Jack Nicklaus d. Dick Norville, 9 and 8
1959	Jack Nicklaus d. Deane Beman, 3 and 2
1960	Deane Beman d. Jack Cupit, 1 up
1961	Herb Durham d. Matt Taber, 1 up (38)
1962	Frank Ryan d. Harry Toscano, Jr., 1 up
1963	George Archer d. Steve Marad, 6 and 5
1964	Wright Garrett d. Dave Eichelberger, 3 and 2
1965	George Boutell d. Jim Hardy, 1 up
1966	Jim Wiechers d. Bob Smith, 3 and 2
1967	Hal Underwood d. Larry Hinson, 3 and 2
1968	Bill Hyndman d. Ed Hopkins, 2 and 1
1969	Allen Miller d. Dean Overturf, 4 and 3
1970	Allen Miller d. Joe Inman Jr., 4 and 3
1971	Allen Miller d. Alan Tapie, 3 and 1
1972	Ben Crenshaw d. John Cain, 4 and 3
1973	Gary Koch d. Guy Cullins, 1 up
1974	Tom Jones d. Mike Brannan, 3 and 2
1975	Tim Wilson d. Warren Aune, 1 up

NORTH AND SOUTH CHAMPIONSHIP

Site: Pinehurst (N.C.) C.C.

Year	Winner, Runner-up
1950	Bill Campbell d. W. Spencer, 1 up (37)
1951	Hobart Manley d. Billy Joe Patton, 1 up
1952	Frank Stranahan d. Frank Strafaci, 8 and 7
1953	Bill Campbell d. Mal Galletta, 2 and 1
1954	Billy Joe Patton d. Alex Welsh, 1 up (37)
1955	Don Bisplinghoff d. Bill Campbell, 5 and 4
1956	Hillman Robbins d. Bill Hyndman, 1 up
1957	Bill Campbell d. Hillman Robbins, 3 and 2
1958	Dick Chapman d. Herb. Durham, 11 and 10
1959	Jack Nicklaus d. Gene Andrews, 1 up
1960	Charlie Smith d. Peter Green, 5 and 3
1961	Bill Hyndman d. Dick Chapman, 4 and 3
1962	Billy Joe Patton d. Hobart Manley, 7 and 6
1963	Billy Joe Patton d. Bob Allen, 7 and 6
1964	Dale Morey d. Billy Joe Patton, 3 and 2
1965	Tom Draper d. Don Allen, 4 and 3
1966	Ward Wettlaufer d. Marion Heck, 4 and 2
1967	Bill Campbell d. Bill Hyndman, 10 and 9
1968	Jack Lewis df. Bill Hyndman, 7 and 6
1969	Joe Inman, Jr., df. Lanny Wadkins, 2 and 1
1970	Gary Cowan d. Dale Morey, 5 and 4
1971	Eddie Pearce d. Vinny Giles, 5 and 4
1972	Danny Edwards d. Eddie Pearce, 3 and 1
1973	Mike Ford d. Bill Harvey, 1 up
1974	George Burns III d. Danny Yates, 4 and 2
1975	Curtis Strange d. George Burns III, 2 up

SOUTHERN AMATEUR

Year	Site	Winner
1950	New Orleans, La.	Dale Morey
1951	Columbus, Ga.	Arnold Blum
1952	Knoxville, Tenn.	Gay Brewer
1953	Dallas, Tex.	Joe Conrad
1954	Memphis, Tenn.	Joe Conrad
1955	Linville, N.C.	Charles Harrison
1956	Atlanta, Ga.	Arnold Blum
1957	Miami Beach, Fla.	Ed Brantley
1958	Birmingham, Ala.	Hugh Royer, Jr.
1959	Jackson, Miss.	Richard Crawford
1960	Myrtle Beach, S.C.	Charles Smith
1961	Knoxville, Tenn.	Billy Joe Patton
1962	Ormond Beach, Fla.	Bunky Henry
1963	Rome, Ga.	Mike Malarkey
1964	Shreveport, La.	Dale Morey
1965	Pinehurst, N.C.	Billy Joe Patton
1966	Birmingham Ala.	Herbert Green
1967	Richmond, Va.	Vinny Giles
1968	N. Palm Beach, Fla.	Lanny Wadkins
1969	Nashville, Tenn.	Hubert Green
1970	New Orleans, La.	Lanny Wadkins
1971	Pinehurst, N.C.	Ben Crenshaw
1972	Green Island C.C.	Bill Rogers
1973	Champions G.C.	Ben Crenshaw
1974	Bay Hill C.	Danny Yates
1975	Pinehurst C.C.	Vinny Giles

NATIONAL LEFT-HANDERS' CHAMPIONSHIP

Year	Site	Winner
1960	Tacoma, Wash.	Jack Walters
1961	Greensboro, N.C.	Ed Sweetman
1962	Houston, Tex.	Alvin Odom
1963	Pebble Beach, Calif.	Bob Wilson
1964	Baton Rouge, La.	Stuart Chancellor
1965	Las Vegas, Nev.	Fred Blackmar
1966	Victoria, B.C.	Tim Reisert
1967	Orland Park, Ill.	Dr. G. N. Noss
1968	Gaithersburg, Md.	Bill Whitaker
1969	Oklahoma City, Okla.	Gary Terry
1970	Montgomery, Ala.	Richard Tinsley
1971	Myrtle Beach, S.C.	Bob Dargan
1972	Galesburg, Ill.	Richard Tinsley
1973	Tacoma, Wash.	Jack Ruhs
1974	Dallas	Bob Michael
1975	Myrtle Beach, S.C.	Bobby Malone

MISCELLANEOUS CHAMPIONS

MEN

National

American Airlines Classic: Sal Bando and Marv Hubbard
American Open: Bruce Ashworth
Championship of Golf Titleholders: Todd Crandall, Ashtabula, Ohio
Florida International Fourball: Robert Ault, New Mexico State and Mark Lye, San Jose State
Golf Writers Ass'n Championship: Jim McAfee, Golf Digest
Life Begins at 40: Billy Bob Coffey, Fort Worth
National Ass'n of Left-Handed Golfers Lefty-Righty: Dick Bily, Tampa, and Wayne Rudzewucz, Tampa
National Ass'n of Left-Handed Golfers: Bobby Malone, Fort Worth
National Father and Son: Robert and John Harris, Roseau, Minn.

East

Amateur Championship of the Metropolitan (N.Y.) GA: Bill Britton, Staten Island
Anderson Memorial Fourball: J. P. O'Hara and Neil Christie, Winged Foot
Belle Haven Fourball Invitational: Mike Ball, Rockville, Md., and Brooks Bolte, Baltimore
Cottonwood Invitational: Ed Flori, Wharton Jr. College
Dope Open: Skip Tellefson
Hochster Memorial: Charles Fatum
Hornblower Memorial: Bill Buttner
Ike Golf Tournament: (Team) Chet and Dave Sanok; (Ind) Chet Sanok
Long Island Amateur: Bob Murphy
Long Island GA Mixed Foursomes: Mag Cullen and Lou Body
New England Publinx: Mike Colandro, Goodwin, Conn.
New Jersey Fourball: Howard Pierson and Steve Dropkin
New York City Publinks: Leonard Dahl, Staten Island
Ouimet Memorial: Paul Murphy, Newton Centre, Mass.
Philadelphia Amateur: Art Jacoby, Philadelphia
Philadelphia Open: Jay Sigel, Philadelphia
Pittsburgh City Publinks: Frank Harbist
Walter J. Travis Memorial: Gary Koch
West Penn Open: Ron Milanovich
Westchester Amateur: Jack Dalrymple
Woodstock Open: Bill Van Aken

South

Atlanta Men's: Tim Simpson
Azalea Invitational: Skip Dunaway, Charlotte, N.C.
Bel-Aire Left-Handed Invitational: Mike Thurston, Asheboro, N.C.
Carolina GA Championship: Jim Holmes
Carolinas GA Father-Son: Harold and Chris Newman, Fayetteville
Carolinas GA Fourball: Mike Holland, Bishopville, S.C. and Marion Fowler, Lake City, S.C.
Carolinas Husband and Wife: Jim and Clara Jane Pou
Chattanooga Open: Clay Holloway
Coastal Empire: Jimmy White
Gator Pro-Am Better Ball: (Team) Bunky Henry, Jack Oliver, Joe Kunes, Valdosta, Ga., and Lanny Roy, Gainesville, Fla., (Ind) Andy Bean, Lakeland, Fla.
Golden Horseshoe Better-Ball: Larry Wheeler and Moss Beecroft
Jacksonville Area GA Father-Son: Joe and Jerry LaBarbera
Left-Handed Carolinas Championship: Richard Hoffman, Hilton Head Island, S.C.
Memphis Tournament of Champions: Kirk Bailey, Memphis
Metro Amateur (Fla.): Charles Musick
Mid-South Four-Ball Invitational: Sam Hall and Barry Gore
New Year's Invitational: Bill Harvey, Greensboro, N.C.
North Florida Invitational: Gary Holmes, Jacksonville
Olympia Spa Invitational: Sam Maddox, Dothan, Ala.
Payton Memorial: Ricardo Britt, Virginia Beach, Va.
Regional Explorer Scout Golf Tournament: Terry Anton, Doraville, Ga.
Shriners Classic: Buddy Brooks Chester, S.C.
South Carolina GA Championship: Parker Moore, Laurens
Southeastern Amateur: Ed Davis III, Shawmut, Ala.
Tennessee GA Fourball: Lew Conner and Ed Brantly

Midwest

Amana VIP Pro-Am: (Team) Julius Boros (pro), Jack Miller, Ed Robinette, Charles Smith and Bill MacDonald, (Ind) Bobby Mitchell (pro)
Billy Sixty Wisconsin Better-Ball: Mark Bemowski and Randy Warobick
Chicago District GA Championship: Jim Joseph
Chick Evans Amateur: Tom Benjamin
Cleveland District GA's Invitational: Bill Spiccia and Paul Minnich
Frank Syron Memorial Tournament: Brian Mills, Northville, Mich.
GA of Michigan Championship: Mark Henrickson, Grand Blanc
Horton Smith-Michigan Medal Play Tournament: Pete Green, Franklin, Mich.
Iowa Tournament of Champions: Lon Nielson
KOLN-KGIN Midwest Golf Classic: Dan Bahensky, St. Paul, Minn.
Radix Cup Match: Jim Joseph and Lance TenBroeck
Toledo Open: Pat Lindsey
Wisconsin State GA Best Ball: Harry Simonson and Brent Beer, Madison, Wis.

West

Appleknockers Tournament: Bruce Richards, Bellevue, Wash.
Broadmoor GC Championship: John Paul Cain, Houston
Goldwater Cup Matches: Bill Garrett (pro), Scottsdale, Ariz.
Greater Denver Golf Classic: Bill Clark, Denver
Illahe Hills Match Play Championship: Mike Fitch
Lilac City Open: Gary Floan, Spokane
Los Angeles City: Brian Lindley
Manito Pow Wow Invitational: Gary Floan, Spokane
Memorial Day Tournament: Harold Pasechnik, Calgary
North Idaho Invitational: Dick Harmon, Twin Lakes Village, Idaho
Northern California GA Amateur: Scott Hoyt, San Jose
Northwest Invitational: Peter Jacobsen
Pacific Coast Amateur: John Fought, Portland, Ore
Pacific Northwest GA Championship: Bob Mitchell, Vancouver, B.C.
Pacific Northwest Left-Handers: Simon Fraser, Pitt Meadows, B.C.
Seattle City Tournament: Bill Sander
Southern Arizona Partnership: Brian Shanks and Charlie Lamb
Southern California Amateur: Lee Davis, Los Angeles
Tacoma City Title: Gary House, Tacoma

WOMEN

International Fourball: Dale Shaw and Lancy Smith, Canada
Ada Mackenzie Challenge Trophy: Nancy Rutter and Janet McLeod, Ontario
New Jersey Shore Stroke-Play Championship: Mrs. Walter Cooperstein, Long Island
Long Island Women's GA Match-Play: Mrs. Walter Cooperstein, Long Island
New York City Publinks: Susan Morrison, Queens
West Penn Women's: Laura Beeken, Pittsburgh
Women's Metropolitan GA 54-Hole Medal Championship: Judy Cooperstein, Glen Oaks
Women's Metropolitan GA: Barbara Israel, Century C.C.
Atlanta Women's Championship: Eleanor Walker, Atlanta
Jacksonville Women's GA Championship: Mrs. Jim Pringle, Jacksonville
Louisville City: Mrs. Gaines Wilson
Virginia vs. Carolinas Team Match: Virginia
Greater Cleveland GA Title: Sheila Scott
Indianapolis Championship: Nancy Fitzgerald, Indianapolis
Michigan Closed Championship: Suzanne Conlin, Ann Arbor, Mich.
Southern Oregon Amateur: Ann Swanson, Seattle
Southwestern Amateur: Donna Cunning, Phoenix
Pacific Northwest Women's Amateur: Flo McFall, Vancouver, B.C.

SENIORS

Men

Breakers Hotel: William Horvath, Roslyn, N.Y.
Carolinas GA: Des Sullivan, Myrtle Beach, S.C.
Carolinas PGA Seniors: Joe Cheves, Morgantown, N.C.
Francis H. I. Brown International Team Matches: Australia
Great Lakes Senior: Ed Preisler, Cleveland
Great Lakes Winter Championship: William Spiccia, Lehigh Acres, Fla.
Greater Cincinnati Senior: Bill Deupree
Indiana PGA Senior: Jim Guinnup, Lafayette
Jacksonville Area GA Seniors: Bobby Walker, Ponte Vedra Beach, Fla.
Kentucky Senior Team: Tom Dickinson, Owensboro, and Roy Settle, Owensboro
Long Island Senior GA: John Humm, Baldwin, N.Y.
Metairie C.C. Seniors Invitational: Andy Pilney, New Orleans
Metropolitan GA Senior: John Humm, Baldwin, N.Y.
Michigan PGA Senior: Gaylon (Tex) Simon, Benton Harbor, Mich.
New England Seniors: Dr. J. Paul Sheeran, Winchester, Mass.
New York City Publinks: Will Ireland
North Carolina GA Seniors Pairs Event: Bud Davis and Carl Holstrom
Northern California GA Fourball: Tom Culligan III and Dan James, Foster City, Calif.
Northwest GA Seniors: Carl Jonson, Seattle
Southern Seniors' GA's Invitational Fourball: Bob Loufek and Norton Harris
Southern Seniors' GA Men's Team Medal Championship: Dr. John C. Meroer, Sarasota, Fla., and Dexter H. Daniels, Winter Haven, Fla.
Southern Seniors GA Sandhill Country Tournament: Dewey P. Bowen, Atlanta, Ga.
Southern Seniors GA Spring Tournament: Evan Schlitz
Spring Tournament of the Free State GA of Maryland: Trevor Lewis, Hillendale C.C., and Travis Barham, C.C. of Maryland
Suncoast Seniors: Billy Watts, St. Petersburg, Fla.
West Penn Senior Title: Arnold Horelick

Women

Carolina's Women's GA Amateur: Carolyn Cudone, Myrtle Beach, S.C.
Great Lakes Sr. Golfing Wives Ass'n: Mrs. August Ganzenmuller, Sea Cliff, N.Y.
New York City Publinks: Rita Hellman
West Penn Senior: Mrs. H. S. Semple, Sewickley, Pa.

JUNIORS

Boys

Arthur Jeffors: Griff Moody, Athens, Ga.
Carolinas: James McNair Jr., Aiken, S.C.
Crutchfield Junior Citrus: Steve Guttman, Pensacola, Fla.
Dixie Section: Steven Hudson, Jasper, Ala.
Donald Ross: Chris Tucker, Midland, N.C.
Greater Cincinnati: Alex Whaling
Indianapolis: Chuck Wenning
Insurance Agents Youth Classic: Bob Clampett, Carmel, Calif.
International Pee Wee: (3-5) Chuckie Wamsley, Orlando, Fla.; (6-7) John Secunda, Pompano Beach, Fla.; (8-9) Bobby Hunt, Deland, Fla.; (10-11) Jerry Haas, Belleview, Ill.; (12-13) Matthew Woods, Columbia, Mo.; (14-15) Lock Kyle. Jacksonville, Fla.
Jacksonville Area GA: Bill Hardaker
Junior America's Cup Matches: (Team) Oregon, (Ind) Scott Krieger, Oregon, and Chip Larsen, Arizona (tie)
Junior World: (10 and under) Joey Plenaflor; (11-12) Robert Meyer and Tim Robinson (tie); (13-14) Albert Flores, (15-17) John Cook
Little People's Championship: Ed Walsworth, Marceline, Mo.
Metropolitan (N.Y.) GA: Bill Newman, Scotch Plains, N.J.
Metropolitan Washington (D.C.) Schoolboy Championship: Wayne DeFrancesco, Langley High
New York City Publinks: Kevin Joyce, Tottenville
Orange Bowl: David Abell, Ft. Pierce, Fla.
Philadelphia GA: John Peterson, Riverton, N.J.
Press Thornton Future Masters: (10 and under) Billy Bulmer, Tifton, Ga.; (11-12) Brad Weaver, Memphis; (13-14) Scott Myers, Monroe, La.; (15-16) Joey Sadowski, Hickory, N.C.; (17-18) Griff Moody, Athens, Ga.
Southern GA: Allen Ritchie, Birmingham, Ala.
Southern Junior Invitational: Stuart Rumph, Montezuma, Ga.
U.S. Junior Championship: Brett Mullin, Riverside, Calif.
Westchester: Bob Cloughen Jr.
Western Junior Championship: Britt Harrison, Beaumont, Tex.

Girls

Dixie Section: Vicki Coker, Montgomery, Ala.
Greater Cincinnati: Linda Grayson
International Pee Wee: (3-5) Michelle Samulak, Lakeland, Fla.; (6-7) Pam Hardcastle, Houston; (8-9) Aubrey Bendick, Windsor, Ontario; (10-11) Brenda Corrie, Dominican Republic; (12-13) Tracey Gaster, Winter Springs, Fla.; (14-15) Jenny Davis, Valencia, Calif.
Junior World: (10 and under) Karen Nicoletti; (11-12) Jo Anne Pacillo; (13-14) Lori Castillo and Michelle Jordan (tie); (15-17) Debbie Spencer
Pacific Northwest: Sydney Thomson, Victoria, B.C.
St. Louis Women's District GA: Gail Kiplinger
USGA Girls Championship: Dayna Benson, Anaheim, Calif.
Women's Western GA Junior: Connie Chillemi, Naples, Fla.

Against the backdrop of New York's Rockefeller Center, the 1975 college All-American golf team, left to right: Curtis Strange, Wake Forest; Jay Haas, Wake Forest; Jerry Pate, Alabama; Andy Bean, Florida; Jaime Gonzalez, Oklahoma State; Kelly Roberts, Indiana; Mike Reid, Brigham Young; Mark Lye, San Jose State; Phil Hancock, Florida; Keith Fergus, Houston.

NATIONAL COLLEGIATE GOLF CHAMPIONSHIP (NCAA)

Year	Team Champ.	Ind. Champ.
1950	San Jose	Fred Wampler
1951	N. Texas State	Tom Neiporte
1952	N. Texas State	Jim Vickers
1953	Stanford	Earl Moeller
1954	S. Methodist	Hillman Robbins
1955	Louisiana State U.	Joe Campbell
1956	Houston	Rick Jones
1957	Houston	Rex Baxter, Jr.
1958	Houston	Phil Rodgers
1959	Houston	Dick Crawford
1960	Houston	Dick Crawford
1961	Purdue	Jack Nicklaus
1962	Houston	Kermit Zarley
1963	Oklahoma State	R. H. Sikes
1964	Houston	Terry Small
1965	Houston	Marty Fleckman
1966	Houston	Bob Murphy
1967	Houston	Hale Irwin
1968	Florida	Grier Jones
1969	Houston	Bob Clark
1970	Houston	John Mahaffey
1971	Texas	Ben Crenshaw
1972	Texas	Tom Kite
		Ben Crenshaw
1973	Florida	Ben Crenshaw
1974	Wake Forest	Curtis Strange
1975	Wake Forest	Jay Haas

ALL-AMERICAN COLLEGIATE TEAMS
Selected by
All-American Collegiate Foundation

1968: Hal Underwood, Houston; Grier Jones, Okla. St.; Ben Kern, New Mexico; Jack Lewis, Wake Forest; Steve Melnyk, Florida; Mike Morley, Arizona St.; Kemp Richardson, U. of So. Cal.; Bill Brask, Minnesota.

1969: Bob Clark, Calif. State at L.A.; Joe Inman, Jr., Wake Forest; Drue Johnson, Arizona; Wayne McDonald, Indiana; Steve Melnyk, Florida; John Mahaffey, Houston; Jack Lewis, Jr., Wake Forest; Gary Sanders, U. of S. Calif.

1970: John Mahaffey, Houston; Bob Clark, Calif. State at L.A.; Wayne McDonald, Indiana; Howard Twitty, Arizona State; Tom Valentine, Georgia; Mark Hayes, Oklahoma State; Bruce Ashworth, Houston; Lanny Wadkins, Wake Forest.

1971: Jim Simons and Lanny Wadkins, Wake Forest; Ben Crenshaw, Texas; Gary Sanders, So. Calif.; Mark Hayes, Okla. St.; Bill Hoffer, Purdue; Ray Leach, Brig. Young; John Mills, Houston; Andy North, Fla.

1972: Ben Crenshaw and Tom Kite, Texas; Jim Simons, Wake Forest; Danny Edwards, Okla. St.; Craig Griswold, Oregon; Steve Groves, Ohio St.; Gary Koch, Florida; Howard Twitty, Arizona St.

1973: Ben Crenshaw, Texas; Danny Edwards, Okla. St.; Jimmy Ellis, Ga. Southern; Steve Groves, Ohio St.; Gary Koch, Florida; Craig Stadler, So. Calif.; Lance Suzuki, Brigham Young; Bill Rogers, Houston.

1974: Keith Fergus, Houston; John Harris, Minnesota; Tom Jones, Oklahoma State; Gary Koch, Florida; Bill Kratzert, Georgia; Mike Reid, Brigham Young; Craig Stadler, Southern California; Curtis Strange, Wake Forest.

1975 COLLEGE RESULTS

ACC Big Four: Wake Forest; ind., Jay Haas, Wake Forest
Alabama Junior College Conference Championship: Alexander City State Jr. College; ind., Al Hayes, Marion Institute
Alabama Women's Intercollegiate: Alabama; ind., Denis Snellman, Alabama
All-American Intercollegiate: Florida; ind., Andy Bean, Florida.
Arizona Intercollegiate: Arizona State; ind., Charlie Gibson, Arizona State
Arkansas Women's Invitation: Texas; ind., Nancy Hager, Texas
Ass'n of Intercollegiate Athletics for Women: Arizona State; ind., Barbara Barrow, San Diego State
Atascosita Intercollegiate: Houston; ind., Keith Fergus, Houston.
Atlantic Coast Conference: Wake Forest; ind., Curtis Strange, Wake Forest
Big Eight Conference: Oklahoma State; ind., Tom Jones, Oklahoma State
Big Ten Conference: Indiana; ind., Bob Ackerman, Indiana, and Gary Biddinger, Indiana
Big Ten Women's: Michigan State; ind., June Oldman, Michigan State
Border Olympics: Houston; ind., Keith Fergus, Houston
Bowling Green Invitational (Women's): Michigan State; ind., Nancy Bunton, Marshall
Buckeye Invitational: Kentucky; ind., Myra Van Hoose, Kentucky
California (Irvine) Anteater Invitational: U.S. International; ind., Craig Stadler, Southern California.
California Women's Intercollegiate: Arizona State; ind., Robin Walton, Arizona State
Carolinas Women's Collegiate: Furman; ind., Betsy King, Furman
Chris Schenkel Invitational: Florida; ind., Andy Bean, Florida
Connecticut Collegiate: Univ. of Connecticut; ind., Kevin McGarry, Connecticut
Cowboy Invitational: Oklahoma State; ind., Jim Sargent, Oral Roberts
East Coast Conference: Temple; ind., Shaun Prendergast, Delaware
Eastern Intercollegiate: Temple; ind., Walter Brown, Temple
Florida Women's Collegiate: Miami-Dade North; ind., Donna Horton, Florida
Four-States Invitational: Oklahoma State; ind., Tom Jones and Lindy Miller, Oklahoma State (tie)
Fresno State Classic: Brigham Young; ind., Mike Brannan, Brigham Young
Furman Invitational: East Tennessee State; ind., Skeeter Heath, East Tennessee State
Galveston Island Tourney: Texas Tech; ind., Jeff Mitchell, Texas Tech
Great Plains Invitational: Oklahoma State; ind., Mike Clayton, Oklahoma State
Gulf South Conference: Troy State; ind., Ronny Mobley, Troy State
Iron Duke Classic: Wake Forest; ind., Bob Byman, Wake Forest

North Carolina Women's Collegiate: Univ. of North Carolina; ind., Betsy Waynick, Univ. of N.C.-Greensboro
Northern Intercollegiate: Indiana; ind., Kelly Roberts, Indiana
Northwest Conference: Pacific Lutheran; ind., Mark Clinton, Pacific Lutheran
Northwest Small College: Pacific Lutheran; ind., Mark Clinton, Pacific Lutheran
Ohio Valley Conference: Eastern Kentucky; ind., Skeeter Heath, East Tennessee
Oklahoma Intercollegiate: Oklahoma State; ind., Jaime Gonzales, Oklahoma State
Opryland Collegiate Classic: Tennessee; ind., Bowers, Western Kentucky
Oregon State Invitational: Oregon; ind., Peter Jacobson, Oregon
Pacific Coast Athletic Ass'n: San Jose State; ind., Jim Knoll, San Jose State
Pacific Coast Intercollegiate: Southern California; ind., Jim Ruziecki, Southern California
Pacific Coast Invitational: Southern California; ind., Charlie Gibson, Arizona State
Pacific Eight Conference: Southern California; ind., Scott Simpson, Southern California
Palmetto Invitational: Wake Forest; ind., Tim Simpson, Georgia
Pan American Intercollegiate: Texas; ind., Charlie Gibson, Arizona State
Pan American Invitational: Pan American; ind., Jerry Smith, Pan American
Ivy League: Harvard; ind., Alex Vik, Harvard
Jim Corbett Classic: Louisiana State; ind., Stan Lee, LSU
Kansas Relays: Missouri; ind., Denny Decker, Missouri
Kepler Invitational: Ohio State Scarlet; ind., Wayne Bartolacci, Ohio State
Lone Star Conference: Howard Payne; ind., Tim Little, Howard Payne
Long Island Intercollegiate: St. John's; ind., David Kaplow, C. W. Post
Metropolitan GA Intercollegiate: St. John's; ind., Bill Haughton, New York Tech
Miami Invitational: Florida; ind., Andy Bean, Florida
Mid-American Conference: Ball State; ind., Mick Soli, Northern Illinois
Mid-American Invitational: Bowling Green; ind., Paul Kaproski, Notre Dame
Mid-South Classic: Southern Illinois; ind., Leon Hawk, Austin Peay
Mike McKenzie Invitational: (Princeville) Oklahoma State; ind., Robert Hoyt, Houston. (Hawaii Kai G.C.)
Oklahoma State; ind., Jaime Gonzales, Oklahoma State
Missouri Valley Conference: North Texas State; ind., Ron Streck, Tulsa
National Junior College Championship: Miami-Dade North; ind., Bill Britton, Miami-Dade North
Nittany Lion Invitational: Penn State Blue; ind., Sherm Hostetter, Penn State Blue
North Carolina Collegiate: North Carolina; ind., Tom Barnes, Atlantic Christian

Pinehurst Invitational: Georgia Southern; ind., Curtis Strange, Wake Forest
Red Fox (C.C.) Invitational: East Tennessee State; ind., Skeeter Heath, East Tennessee State
Rollins Women's Invitational: Miami-Dade Community College North; ind., Donna Horton, Florida
Sam Houston Invitational: Rice; ind., Barton Goodwin, Rice
South Carolina State Intercollegiate: Clemson; ind., Jimmy White, Clemson
Southeastern Invitational: Florida; ind., Phil Hancock, Florida
Southern Conference: Furman; ind., Ken Ezell, Furman
Southern Independent Conference: Georgia Southern; ind., Mike Fox, Jacksonville
Southern Intercollegiate: Indiana; ind., Kelly Roberts; Indiana
Southern Junior-Senior Intercollegiate: (Senior Division) Troy State; ind., Johnny Lang, Mississippi. (Junior Division) Dekalb; ind., Mike Maynard, Brevard
Southland Conference: Southwestern Louisiana; ind., John Davis, Southwestern Louisiana
Southwest Conference: Houston and Texas (tie); ind., Lance Ten Broeck, Texas
Southwestern Athletic Conference: Jackson State; ind., Alfred Harris, Jackson State
Spartan Invitational: Illinois State; ind., Mark Western, Michigan State
Spartanette Invitational: Michigan State; ind., June Oldman, Michigan State
Sun Devil Thunderbird National Collegiate: Brigham Young; ind., Scott Simpson, Southern California
Sun Devil Women's Intercollegiate: Arizona State (Four-women), Stanford (Two-women)
Tennessee Intercollegiate: East Tennessee State; ind., Bill Rislove, East Tennessee State. (College Division) Tennessee-Martin; ind., Chip Rockholt, Tennessee-Martin
Texas Ass'n of Intercollegiate Athletics for Women: Texas; ind., Nancy Hager, Texas
Trojan Invitational: Southern California; ind., Ron Hinds, California State-Northridge
U.S. Collegiate Invitational: Stanford; ind., Mark Lye, San Jose State
Virginia College Athletic Ass'n Tournament: Madison; ind., Fordy Gardner, Washington and Lee
West Coast Athletic Conference: Seattle; ind., Ed Jonson and Rob Watson (tie)
West Coast Invitational: San Francisco State; ind., Dan Dwyer, San Francisco State
West Texas Intercollegiate: Eastern New Mexico; ind., Gary Hammer, Hardin-Simmons
Western Athletic Conference: Brigham Young; ind., Mike Reid, Brigham Young
Western Intercollegiate: Brigham Young; ind., Mark Lye, San Jose State

SENIOR AMATEUR RECORDS

USGA SENIORS' CHAMPIONSHIP

Year	Winner, Runner-up	Score
1955	J. Wood Platt, Philadelphia d. Geo. Studinger, S.F.	5 and 4
1956	Fred Wright, Watertown, Mass. d. J. C. Espie, Indianapolis	4 and 3
1957	J. C. Espie, Indianapolis d. Fred Wright, Watertown, Mass.	2 and 1
1958	Thomas G. Robbins, Pinehurst, N.C. d. J. Dawson, Palm Springs, Cal.	2 and 1
1959	J. C. Espie, Indianapolis, Ind. d. J. W. Brown, Sea Girt, N.J.	3 and 1
1960	Michael Cestone, Jamesburg, N.J. d. David Rose, Cleveland	1 up (20)
1961	Dexter Daniels, Winter Haven, Fla. d. Col. Wm. K. Lanman, Golf, Ill.	2 and 1
1962	Merrill Carlsmith, Hilo, Hawaii d. Willis Blakely, Portland, Ore.	4 and 2
1963	Merrill Carlsmith, Hilo, Hawaii d. Bill Higgins, San Francisco	3 and 2
1964	Bill Higgins, San Francisco d. Eddie Murphy, Portland, Ore.	2 and 1
1965	Robert Kiersky, Oakmont, Pa. d. Geo. Beechler, Pineville, Ore.	19 holes
1966	Dexter Daniels, Winter Haven, Fla. d. George Beechler, Prineville, Ore.	1 up
1967	Ray Palmer, Lincoln Park, Mich., d. Walter Bronson, Oak Brook, Ill.	3 and 2
1968	Curtis Person, Memphis, Tenn., d. Ben Goodes, Reidsville, N.C.	2 and 1
1969	Curtis Person, Memphis, Tenn., d. David Goldman, Dallas, Tex.	1 up
1970	Gene Andrews, Whittier, Calif. d. Jim Ferrie, Indian Wells, Calif.	1 up
1971	Tom Draper, Troy, Mich. d. Ernie Pieper, S. J. Batista, Cal.	3 and 1
1972	Lew Oehmig, Lookout Mtn., Tenn. d. Ernie Pieper, San Jose, Calif.	1 up, 20
1973	Bill Hyndman, Huntingdon Valley, Pa. d. Harry Welch, Salisbury, N.C.	3 and 2
1974	Dale Morey, High Point, N.C. d. Lew Oehmig, Lookout Mtn., Tenn.	3 and 2
1975	Bill Colm, Pebble Beach, Calif. d. Steve Stimac, Walnut Creek, Calif.	4 and 3

U.S. SENIORS CHAMPIONSHIP

Site: Apawamis Country Club, Rye, N.Y.

Year	Winner, club
1950	Alfred C. Ulmer, Timuquana (N.Y.) C.C.
1951	Thomas C. Robbins, Winged Foot C.C., Mamaroneck, N.Y.
1952	Thomas C. Robbins, Winged Foot C.C., Mamaroneck, N.Y.
1953	Frank D. Ross, Wampanoag C.C.
1954	J. Ellis Knowles, Apawamis C.
1955	John W. Roberts, Scioto C.C., Columbus, O.
1956	Franklin G. Clement, Fort Sheridan, Ill.
1957	Franklin G. Clement, Fort Sheridan, Ill.
1958	John Dawson, Palm Desert, Calif.
1959	John Dawson, Palm Desert, Calif.
1960	John Dawson, Palm Desert, Calif.
1961	Joseph Morrill, Jr., Great Barrington, Mass.
1962	George Dawson, Glen Ellyn, Ill.
1963	Jack Westland, Seattle, Wash.
1964	J. Wolcott Brown, Sea Girt, N.J.
1965	Fred Brand, Pittsburgh, Pa.
1966	George Haggarty, Detroit, Mich.
1967	Robert Kiersky, Winnetka, Ill.
1968	Curtis Person, Memphis, Tenn.
1969	William Scott, San Francisco, Calif.
1970	David Goldman, Dallas, Tex.
1971	Jim Knowles, Greenwich, Conn.
1972	David Goldman, Dallas, Tex.
1973	Bob Kiersky, Delray Beach, Fla.
1974	James Knowles, So. Londonderry, Vt.
1975	Dale Morey, High Point, N.C.

WORLD SENIOR AMATEUR

Year	Winner, Runner-up	Score
1960	Harry Strasburger, Coffeyville, Kan. d. John Roberts, Chicago	2 and 1
1961	Howard Creel, Colo. Springs, Colo. d. Adrian McManus, Pasadena, Cal.	19 holes
1962	Howard Creel, Colo. Springs, Colo. d. Adrian McManus, Pasadena, Calif.,	7 and 5
1963	George Haggarty, Detroit, Mich. d. Fred Siegel, Scottsdale, Ariz.	3 and 2
1964	Dorsey Nevergall, Pompano Bch., Fla. d. Jack Barkel, Australia	5 and 4
1965	Jack Barkel, Australia, d. Adrian French, Los Angeles	1 up
1966	Cecil Dees, Glendale, Calif., d. Walter Dowell, Walnut Ridge, Ark.	4 and 3
1967	Cecil Dees Glendale, Calif., d. James Quinn, Kansas City, Mo.	3 and 1
1968	David Goldman, Dallas, Tex. d. Walter Dowell, Walnut Ridge, Ark.	2 up
1969	David Goldman, Dallas, Tex. d. Curtis Person, Memphis, Tenn.	2 and 1
1970	Merrill Carlsmith, Hilo, Hawaii, d. Jack Walters, Tacoma, Wash.	2 and 1
1971	Jude Poynter, Beverly Hills, Calif., d. Merrill Carlsmith, Hilo, Hawaii 1 up d. Curtis Person, Memphis, Tenn.	6 and 4
1972	Howard Everitt, Jupiter, Fla.	
1973	W. F. Colm, Bakersfield, Calif. d. Truman Connell, Boynton Bch., Fla.	3 and 2
1974	Larry Pendleton, Glendale, Calif. d. O. W. Nelson, Wheat Ridge, Colo.	4 and 3
1975	Truman Connell, Pompano Beach, Fla. d. Merrill Carlsmith, Hilo, Hawaii	5 and 3

AMERICAN SENIORS' CHAMPIONSHIP

Year	Winner, Runner-up	
1955	Edward H. Randall, Rochester, N.Y. d. Judd Brumley, Greeneville, Tenn.	
1956	Judd Brumley, Greeneville, Tenn. d. Peter Snekser, Rochester, N.Y.	
1957	Leon R. Sikes, W. Palm Beach, Fla. d. Frank D. Ross, Hartford, Ky.	
1958	Edward Randall, Rochester, N.Y. d. John Roberts, Columbus, O.	
1959	Leon R. Sikes, W. Palm Beach, Fla. d. Bruce Coffin, Marblehead, Mass.	
1960	Egon Quittner, Rydal, Pa. d. J. W. Brown, Sea Girt, N.J.	
1961	Jack Russell, Clearwater, Fla. d. George Haggarty, Detroit, Mich.	
1962	John Roberts, Chicago, Ill. d. Clyde Haynie, Largo, Fla.	
1963	Bruce Coffin, Marblehead, Mass. d. Jack Russell, Clearwater, Fla.	
1964	Robert Kiersky, W. Palm Beach, Fla. d. Adrian McManus, Windmere, Fla.	
1965	Dr. John Mercer, Sarasota, Fla. d. Jack Russell, Clearwater, Fla.	1 up
1966	Walter A. Dowell, Walnut Ridge, Ark. d. Adrian McManus, Windermere, Fla.	4 and 3
1967	Joel Shepherd, Kalamazoo, Mich., d. J. W. Brown, Sea Girt, N.J.	2 and 1
1968	Walter Dowell, Walnut Ridge, Ark., d. J. W. Brown, Sea Girt, N.J.	4 and 2
1969	Curtis Person, Memphis, Tenn., d. J. W. Brown, Sea Girt, N.J.	1 up
1970	J. Wolcott Brown, Sea Girt, N.J., d. Robert Loufek, Moline, Ill.	2 and 1
1971	Truman Connell, Boynton Beach, Fla. d. J.B. Davis, Melvin Village, N.H.	5 and 4
1972	Howard Everitt, Tequesta, Fla. d. Truman Connell, Boynton Beach, Fla.	4 and 2
1973	Bill Hyndman, Huntingdon Valley, Pa. d. John K. McCue, Winter Park, Fla.	2 and 1
1974	Ray Palmer, Largo, Fla. d. Dick Giddings, Fresno, Calif.	1 up
1975	Edward Ervasti, Canada d. John Pottle, Linville, N.C.	2 and 1

NORTH & SOUTH SENIORS

Site: Pinehurst (N.C.) Country Club

Year	Winner, Runner-up	Score
1955	Benjamin K. Kraffert, Titusville, Pa. d. John Roberts, Columbus, O.	1 up
1956	Tom Robbins, Larchmont, N.Y. d. J. W. Platt, Philadelphia	1 up
1957	J. W. Platt, Philadelphia d. J. Ackerman, Princeton, N.J.	4 and 2
1958	J.W. Brown, Sea Girt, N.J. d. Jack Brittain, Hempstead, N.Y.	7 and 6
1959	Walter Pease, Plainfield, N.J. d. Paul Dunkel, Hackensack, N.J.	4 and 3
1960	Tom Robbins, Pinehurst, N.C. d. J. W. Brown, Sea Girt, N.J.	2 and 1
1961	Robert Bell, Worthington, O. d. Dr. J. Mercer, Fitchburg, Mass.	1 up
1962	William K. Lanman, Glenview, Ill. d. Frank Ross, W. Hartford, Conn.	2 and 1
1963	James McAlvin, Lake Forest, Ill. d. Merrill Carlsmith, Hilo, Hawaii	2 and 1
1964	James McAlvin, Lake Forest, Ill. d. J. W. Brown, Sea Girt, N.J.	2 and 1
1965	David Goldman, Dallas, Tex. d. Curtis Person, Memphis, Tenn.	1 up
1966	Curtis Person, Memphis, Tenn. d. David Goldman, Dallas, Tex.	2 and 1
1967	Bob Cochran, St. Louis, Mo., d. Dr. John Mercer, Sarasota, Fla.	1 up (20)
1968	Curtis Person, Memphis, Tenn., d. Mickey Bellande, Biloxi, Miss.	1 up
1969	Curtis Person, Memphis, Tenn., d. David Goldman, Dallas, Tex.	2 and 1
1970	Bob Cochran, St. Louis, Mo., d. John Pottle, Linville, N.C.	1 up
1971	Dave Goldman, Dallas, Tex. d. Byron Jilek, Worthington, O.	4 and 2
1972	Bill Hyndman, Huntington Valley, Pa. d. Curtis Person, Memphis, Tenn.	3 and 2
1973	Ray Palmer, Grosse Ile, Mich. d. Tom Draper, Troy, Mich.	1 up
1974	David Goldman, Dallas d. Harry Welch, Salisbury, N.C.	2 and 1
1975	Harry Welch, Salisbury N.C. d. Neil Croonquist, Edina, Minn.	3 and 2

John Cook and Debrah Spencer won World Junior titles.

JUNIORS

USGA JUNIOR BOYS

Year	Site	Winner
1950	Denver C.C.	Mason Rudolph
1951	U. of Illinois G.C.	Tommy Jacobs, Jr.
1952	Yale G.C.	Don Bisplingoff
1953	Southern Hills C.C.	Rex Baxter, Jr.
1954	Los Angeles C.C.	Foster Bradley, Jr.
1955	Purdue G.C.	William Dunn
1956	Taconic C.C.	Harlan Stevenson
1957	Manor C.C.	Larry Beck
1958	U. of Minn.	Buddy Baker
1959	Stanford U.	Larry Lee
1960	Milburn G. & C.C.	Bill Tindall
1961	Cornell U.	Charles McDowell
1962	Lochmoor C.	Jim Wiechers
1963	Florence C.C.	Gregg McHatton
1964	Eugene C.C.	John Miller
1965	Wilmington C.C.	James Masserio
1966	California C.C.	Gary Sanders
1967	Twin Hills G. & C.C.	John Crooks
1968	The C.C., Brookline, Mass.	Eddie Pearce
1969	Spokane C.C.	Aly Trompas
1970	Athens C.C.	Gary Koch
1971	Manor C.C.	Mike Brannan
1972	Brookhaven C.C.	Bob Byman
1973	Singing Hills C.C.	Jack Renner
1974	Brooklawn C.C.	David Nevatt
1975	Richland C.C.	Brett Mullin

WORLD JUNIOR GOLF CHAMPIONSHIP

Site: Torrey Pines G.C., San Diego, Calif.

1968	Bob Martin, San Diego, Calif., and Susan Rapp, San Diego, Calif.
1969	Dale Hayes, South Africa, and Jane Renner, San Diego, Calif.
1970	Craig Stadler, La Jolla, Calif., and Louise Bruce, La Mesa, Calif.
1971	Charles Barenaba, Hanuki, Hawaii, and Denise Bebernes, Santa Maria, Calif.
1972	Jack Renner, San Diego, Calif., and Anne-Marie Palli, La Ferriere, France.
1973	Randy Barenaba, Honolulu, Hawaii, and Suzanne Cadden, Scotland.
1974	Nicky Price, Rhodesia, and Lori Nelson, West Chester, Pa.
1975	John Cook, Rolling Hills, Calif., and Debrah Spencer, Honolulu.

USGA JUNIOR GIRLS

Year	Site	Winner
1949	Philadelphia C.C.	Marlene Bauer
1950	Wanakah C.C.	Patricia Lesser
1951	Onwentsia C.C.	Arlene Brooks
1952	Monterey Pen. C.C.	Mickey Wright
1953	Brookline C.C.	Millie Meyerson
1954	Gulph Mills C.C.	Margaret Smith
1955	Florence C.C.	Carole Jo Kabler
1956	Heather Downs C.C.	JoAnne Gunderson
1957	Lakewood C.C.	Judy Eller
1958	Greenwich C.C.	Judy Eller
1959	Manor C.C.	Judy Rand
1960	Oaks C.C.	Carol Sorenson
1961	Broadmoor C.C.	Mary Lowell
1962	C.C. of Buffalo	Mary Lou Daniel
1963	Woolfert's Roost C.C.	Janis Ferraris
1964	Leavenworth C.C.	Peggy Conley
1965	Hiwan G.C.	Gail Sykes
1966	Longue Vue C.	Claudia Mayhew
1967	Hacienda G.C.	Elizabeth Story
1968	Flint G.C.	Peggy Harmon
1969	Brookhaven C.C.	Hollis Stacy
1970	Apawamis C.	Hollis Stacy
1971	Augusta C.C.	Hollis Stacy
1972	Jefferson City C.C.	Nancy Lopez
1973	Somerset Hills C.C.	Amy Alcott
1974	Columbia Edgewater	Nancy Lopez
1975	Dedham C.	Dayna Benson

WOMEN'S AMATEUR RECORDS

USGA WOMEN'S AMATEUR CHAMPIONSHIP

Year	Site	Winner, runner-up	Score
1895	Meadow Brook C., Hempstead, N.Y.	C. S. Brown / N. C. Sargent	132 / 134
1896	Morris County G.C., N.J.	Beatrix Hoyt d. Mrs. Turnure	2 and 1
1897	Essex C.C., Manchester, Mass.	Beatrix Hoyt d. N. C. Sargent	5 and 4
1898	Ardsley C., N.Y.	Beatrix Hoyt d. M. Wetmore	5 and 3
1899	Philadelphia (Pa.) C.C.	Ruth Underhill d. C. F. Box	2 and 1
1900	Shinnecock Hills (N.Y.) G.C.	Frances Griscom d. M. Curtis	6 and 5
1901	Baltusrol G.C., Springfield, N.J.	Genevieve Hecker d. Lucy Herron	5 and 3
1902	The Country Club, Brookline, Mass.	Genevieve Hecker d. Louisa Wells	4 and 3
1903	Chicago, G.C., Wheaton, Ill.	Bessie Anthony d. J. A. Carpenter	7 and 6
1904	Merion Cricket C., Haverford, Pa.	Georgianna Bishop d. E. F. Sanford	5 and 3
1905	Morris County G.C., N.J.	Pauline Mackay d. M. Curtis	1 up
1906	Brae Burn C.C., Newton, Mass.	Harriot Curtis d. M. B. Adams	2 and 1
1907	Midlothian C.C., Blue Island, Ill.	Margaret Curtis d. H. Curtis	2 and 1
1908	Chevy Chase (Md.) C.	Katherine Harley d. T. H. Polhemus	6 and 5
1909	Merion Cricket C., Haverford, Pa.	Dorothy Campbell d. R. H. Barlow	3 and 2
1910	Homewood C.C., Flossmoor, Ill.	Dorothy Campbell d. G. M. Martin	2 and 1
1911	Baltusrol G.C., Springfield, N.J.	Margaret Curtis d. L. Hyde	5 and 3
1912	Essex C.C., Manchester, Mass.	Margaret Curtis d. R. H. Barlow	3 and 2
1913	Wilmington (Del.) C.C.	Gladys Ravenscroft d. M. Hollins	2 up
1914	Nassau C.C., Glen Cove, N.Y.	H. A. Jackson d. E. Rosenthal	1 up
1915	Onwentsia C., Lake Forest, Ill.	C. H. Vanderbeck d. W. A. Gavin	3 and 2
1916	Belmont Springs C.C., Mass.	Alexa Stirling d. M. Caverly	2 and 1
1917-18	No tournament.		
1919	Shawnee C.C., Pa.	Alexa Stirling d. W. A. Gavin	6 and 5
1920	Mayfield C.C., Cleveland, O.	Alexa Stirling d. J. V. Hurd	5 and 4
1921	Hollywood G.C., Deal, N.J.	Marion Hollins d. A. Stirling	5 and 4
1922	Greenbrier G.C., W.Va.	Glenna Collett d. W. A. Gavin	5 and 4
1923	Westchester-Biltmore C.C., N.Y.	Edith Cummings d. A. Stirling	5 and 4
1924	Rhode Island C.C., Nyatt, R.I.	Dorothy Hurd d. M. K. Browne	7 and 6
1925	St. Louis C.C., Clayton, Mo.	Glenna Collett d. W. G. Fraser	9 and 8
1926	Merion Cricket C., Haverford, Pa.	G. H. Stetson d. W. D. Goss	3 and 1
1927	Cherry Valley C., Garden City, N.Y.	M. B. Horn d. M. Orcutt	5 and 4
1928	Hot Springs (W. Va.) G.C.	Glenna Collett d. V. Van Wie	13 and 12
1929	Oakland Hills C.C., Mich.	Glenna Collett d. L. Pressler	4 and 3
1930	Los Angeles C.C., Beverly Hills, Cal.	Glenna Collett d. V. Van Wie	6 and 5
1931	C.C. of Buffalo, Williamsville, N.Y.	Helen Hicks d. Glenna Vare	2 and 1
1932	Salem C.C., Peabody, Mass.	Virginia Van Wie d. Glenna Vare	10 and 8
1933	Exmoor C.C., Highland Park, Ill.	Virginia Van Wie d. H. Hicks	4 and 3
1934	Whitemarsh Valley C.C., Pa.	Virginia Van Wie d. D. Traung	2 and 1
1935	Interlachen C.C., Hopkins, Minn.	Glenna Vare d. P. Berg	3 and 2
1936	Canoe Brook C.C., Summit, N.J.	Pamela Barton d. J. D. Crews	4 and 3
1937	Memphis (Tenn.) C.C.	J. A. Page, Jr. d. P. Berg	7 and 6
1938	Westmoreland Wilmette, Ill.	Patty Berg d. J. A. Page, Jr.	6 and 5
1939	Wee Burn C.C., Darien, Conn.	Betty Jameson d. D. Kirby	3 and 2
1940	Del Monte G. & C.C.	Betty Jameson d. J. Cochran	6 and 5
1941	The Country Club, Brookline, Mass.	Mrs. Frank Newell d. H. Sigel	5 and 3
1942-45	No tournament.		
1946	Southern Hills C.C., Tulsa, Okla.	Mrs. George Zaharias d. C. C. Sherman	11 and 9
1947	Franklin Hills, Franklin, Mich.	Louise Suggs d. D. Kirby	2 up
1948	Del Monte G. & C.C.	Grace Lenczyk d. H. Sigel	4 and 3
1949	Merion G.C., Ardmore, Pa.	Mrs. Mark Porter d. D. Kielty	3 and 2
1950	Atlanta A.C. Atlanta, Ga.	Beverly Hanson d. Mae Murray	6 and 4
1951	Town & C.C., St. Paul, Minn.	Dorothy Kirby d. C. Doran	2 and 1
1952	Waverley C.C., Portland, Ore.	Mrs. Jackie Pung d. S. McFedters	2 and 1
1953	Rhode Island C.C.	Mary Lena Faulk d. Polly Riley	3 and 2
1954	Allegheny C.C., Sewickley, Pa.	Barbara Romack d. M. Wright	4 and 2
1955	Myers Park C.C., Charlotte, N.C.	Pat Lesser d. J. Nelson	7 and 6
1956	Meridian Hills, Indianapolis	Marlene Stewart d. J. Gunderson	2 and 1
1957	Del Paso C.C., Sacramento	JoAnne Gunderson d. A. Johnstone	8 and 6
1958	Wee Burn C.C., Darien, Conn.	Anne Quast d. B. Romack	3 and 2
1959	Congressional, Washington, D.C.	Barbara McIntire d. J. Goodwin	4 and 3
1960	Tulsa (Okla.) C.C.	JoAnne Gunderson d. Jean Ashley	6 and 5
1961	Tacoma (Wash.) C.C.	Anne Quast Decker d. Phyllis Preuss	14 and 13
1962	C.C. of Rochester, N.Y.	JoAnne Gunderson d. Ann Baker	9 and 8
1963	Taconic G.C., Williamstown, Mass.	Anne Quast Welts d. Peggy Conley	2 and 1
1964	Prairie Dunes, Hutchinson, Kan.	Barbara McIntire d. J. Gunderson	3 and 2
1965	Lakewood C.C., Denver, Colo.	Jean Ashley d. Anne Q. Welts	5 and 4
1966	Sewickley Hts. G.C. (Pa.)	JoAnne Gunderson Carner d. Marlene Streit	41 holes
1967	Annandale G.C., Pasadena, Calif.	Lou Dill d. Jean Ashley	5 and 4
1968	Birmingham (Mich) C.C.	JoAnne Gunderson Carner d. Anne Q. Welts	5 and 4
1969	Las Colinas C.C., Irving, Tex.	Catherine Lacoste d. Shelley Hamlin	3 and 2
1970	Wee Burn C.C., Darien, Conn.	Martha Wilkinson d. Cynthia Hill	3 and 2
1971	Atlanta C.C., Atlanta, Ga.	Laura Baugh d. Beth Barry	1 up
1972	St. Louis C.C., St. Louis, Mo.	Mary Budke d. Cynthia Hill	5 and 4
1973	Montclair G.C., N.J.	Carol Semple d. Mrs. Anne Sander	1 up
1974	Broadmoor G.C., Seattle	Cynthia Hill d. Carol Semple	5 and 4
1975	Brae Burn C.C., W. Newton, Mass.	Beth Daniel d. Donna Horton	3 and 2

NORTH and SOUTH AMATEUR
Site: Pinehurst (N.C.) C.C.

Year	Winner, runner-up	Score
1950	Pat O'Sullivan d. Mae Murray	1 up
1951	Pat O'Sullivan d. Mrs. E. L. Page	3 and 2
1952	Barbara Romack d. Pat O'Sullivan	2 and 1
1953	Pat O'Sullivan d. Mary L. Faulk	2 and 1
1954	Joyce Ziske d. Mary L. Faulk	1 up
1955	Wiffi Smith d. Pat Lesser	3 and 2
1956	Marlene Stewart d. Wanda Sanches	1 up
1957	Barbara McIntire d. Ann Casey Johnstone	3 and 2
1958	Mrs. Phillip Cudone d. Barbara McIntire	1 up
1959	Ann Casey Johnstone d. Joanne Goodwin	19 hls.
1960	Barbara McIntire d. Joanne Goodwin	5 and 4
1961	Barbara McIntire d. Judy Bell	3 and 1
1962	Clifford Ann Creed d. Mrs. Charles Wilson	6 and 4
1963	Nancy Roth d. Phyllis Preuss	2 and 1
1964	Phyllis Preuss d. Mrs. George Trainor	7 and 6
1965	Barbara McIntire d. Nancy Roth	1 up
1966	Nancy Roth Syms d. Phyllis Preuss	1 up
1967	Phyllis Preuss d. Connie Day	1 up
1968	Mrs. Pete Dye d. Connie Day	1 up
1969	Barbara McIntire d. Jane Blalock	4 and 3
1970	Hollis Stacy d. Mrs. Paul Dye	6 and 4
1971	Barbara McIntire d. Hollis Stacy	6 and 5
1972	Jane Booth d. Beth Barry	2 and 1
1973	Beth Barry d. Mrs. Jane Booth	6 and 5
1974	Mrs. Marlene Streit d. Mrs. Nancy Syms	5 and 4
1975	Cynthia Hill d. Judy Oliver	8 and 7

Barbara Barrow added 1975 Collegiate title to fine record.

WOMEN'S TRANS-NATIONAL AMATEUR

Year	Site	Winner
1950	Lakewood C.C.	Marjorie Lindsay
1951	Quincy C.C.	Mary Ann Downey
1952	Arizona C.C.	Mrs. Lyle Bowman
1953	Arizona C.C.	Mrs. Edean Ihlanfeldt
1954	Glen Arven C.C.	Vonnie Colby
1955	Twin Hills C.C.	Polly Riley
1956	Monterey C.C.	Wiffi Smith
1957	Desert Inn C.C.	Mrs. James Ferrie
1958	Hickory Hills C.C.	Marjorie Lindsay
1959	Hot Springs C.C.	Mrs. A. C. Johnstone
1960	Kenwood C.C.	Sandra Haynie
1961	Eugene C.C.	JoAnne Gunderson
1962	Wichita C.C.	Jeannie Thompson
1963	Pinehurst C.C.	Judy Bell
1964	Arizona C.C.	Carol Sorenson
1965	Dubuque C.C.	Sharon Miller
1966	Hardscrabble C.C.	Roberta Albers
1967	Rochester G. & C.C.	Jane Bastanchury
1968	Battle Creek C.C.	Mrs. Michael Skala
1969	Midland C.C.	Jane Bastanchury
1970	Manor C.C.	Martha Wilkinson
1971	San Diego C.C.	Jane Bastanchury
1972	Omaha C.C.	Mickey Walker
1973	Mt. Snow C.C.	Liana Zambresky
1974	Eugene C.C.	Barbara Barrow
1975	Oaks C.C.	Beverley Davis

WOMEN'S WESTERN AMATEUR

Year	Site	Winner
1950	Exmoor C.C.	Polly Riley
1951	Plum Hollow G.C.	Marjorie Lindsay
1952	Los Angeles C.C.	Polly Riley
1953	Camargo C.	Claire Doran
1954	Broadmoor C.C.	Claire Doran
1955	Olympia Fields C.C.	Pat Lesser
1956	Guyan C.C.	Anne Quast
1957	Omaha C.C.	Meriam Bailey
1958	Oak Park C.C.	Barbara McIntire
1959	Exmoor C.C.	JoAnne Gunderson
1960	Mission Hills C.C.	Ann C. Johnstone
1961	Annandale C.C.	Anne Q. Decker
1962	South Bend C.C.	Carol Sorenson
1963	Broadmoor G.C.	Barbara McIntire
1964	Oak Park C.C.	Barbara Fay White
1965	Wayzata G.C.	Barbara Fay White
1966	Barrington Hills C.C.	Peggy Conley
1967	Bellefonte C.C.	Mrs. Mark Porter
1968	Broadmoor C.C.	Catherine Lacoste
1969	Oak Park C.C.	Jane Bastanchury
1970	Rockford C.C.	Jane Bastanchury
1971	Flossmoor C.C.	Beth Barry
1972	Blue Hills C.C.	Debbie Massey
1973	Maple Bluff C.C.	Kathy Falk
1974	C.C. Indianapolis	Lancy Smith
1975	Tanglewood G.C.	Debbie Massey

WOMEN'S NATIONAL COLLEGIATE

Year	Site	Winner
1950	Ohio State	Betty Rowland
1951	Ohio State	Barbara Bruning
1952	Ohio State	Mary Ann Villegas
1953	N.C. Women's Col.	Pat Lesser
1954	N.C. Women's Col.	Nancy Reed
1955	Lake Forest Col.	Jackie Yates
1956	Purdue	Marlene Stewart
1957	Illinois	Meriam Bailey
1958	Iowa	Carole Pushing
1959	North Carolina	Judy Eller
1960	Stanford	JoAnne Gunderson
1961	Michigan	Judy Hoetmer
1962	New Mexico	Carol Sorenson
1963	Penn State	Claudia Lindor
1964	Michigan State	Patti Shook
1965	Florida	Roberta Albers
1966	Ohio State	Joyce Kazmierski
1967	Sand Point C.C.	Martha Wilkinson
1968	Duke	Gail Sykes
1969	Penn State	Jane Bastanchury
1970	San Diego State	Cathy Gaughan
1971	Georgia	Shelley Hamlin
1972	New Mexico	Ann Laughlin
1973	Mount Holyoke	Bonnie Lauer
1974	Singing Hills C.C.	Mary Budke
1975	U. of Arizona	Barbara Barrow

SENIORS

USGA NTL. WOMEN'S SENIOR

Year	Site	Winner
1962	Manufacturer's C.C.	Maureen Orcutt
1963	C.C. of Florida	Mrs. Allison Choate
1964	Del Paso C.C.	Mrs. Hulet P. Smith
1965	Exmoor C.C.	Mrs. Hulet P. Smith
1966	Lakewood C.C.	Maureen Orcutt
1967	Atlantic City C.C.	Mrs. Marge Mason
1968	Westchester C.C.	Mrs. Philip Cudone
1969	Ridglea C.C.	Mrs. Philip Cudone
1970	Coral Ridge C.C.	Mrs. Philip Cudone
1971	Sea Island, G.C.	Mrs. Philip Cudone
1972	Manufacturer's G.&C.C.	Mrs. Philip Cudone
1973	San Marcos C.C.	Mrs. David Hibbs
1974	Lakewood C.C.	Mrs. Justine Cushing
1975	Rhode Island G.C.	Mrs. Albert Bower

MAJOR INTERNATIONAL RESULTS

BRITISH OPEN

Year	Site	Winner	Score
1860	Prestwick	Willie Park, Sr.	174
1861	Prestwick	Tom Morris, Sr.	163
1862	Prestwick	Tom Morris, Sr.	163
1863	Prestwick	Willie Park, Sr.	168
1864	Prestwick	Tom Morris, Sr.	167
1865	Prestwick	Andrew Strath	162
1866	Prestwick	Willie Park, Sr.	169
1867	Prestwick	Tom Morris, Sr.	170
1868	Prestwick	Tom Morris, Jr.	170
1869	Prestwick	Tom Morris, Jr.	157
1870	Prestwick	Tom Morris, Jr.	149
1871	Not played		
1872	Prestwick	Tom Morris, Jr.	166
1873	St. Andrews	Tom Kidd	179
1874	Musselburgh	Mungo Park	159
1875	Prestwick	Willie Park, Sr.	166
1876	St. Andrews	Robert Martin	176
1877	Musselburgh	Jamie Anderson	160
1878	Prestwick	Jamie Anderson	157
1879	St. Andrews	Jamie Anderson	170
1880	Musselburgh	Robert Ferguson	162
1881	Prestwick	Robert Ferguson	170
1882	St. Andrews	Robert Ferguson	171
1883	Musselburgh	*Willie Fernie	159
1884	Prestwick	Jack Simpson	160
1885	St. Andrews	Robert Martin	171
1886	Musselburgh	David Brown	157
1887	Prestwick	Willie Park Jr.	161
1888	St. Andrews	Jack Burns	171
1889	Musselburgh	Willie Park Jr.	155
1890	Prestwick	*John Ball	164
1891	St. Andrews	Hugh Kirkaldy	166
1892	Muirfield	*Harold H. Hilton	305
1893	Prestwick	William Auchterionie	322
1894	Sandwich	John H. Taylor	326
1895	St. Andrews	John H. Taylor	322
1896	Muirfield	*Harry Vardon	316
1897	Hoylake	*Harold H. Hilton	314
1898	Prestwick	Harry Vardon	307
1899	Sandwich	Harry Vardon	310
1900	St. Andrews	John H. Taylor	309
1901	Muirfield	James Braid	309
1902	Hoylake	Alexander Herd	307
1903	Prestwick	Harry Vardon	300
1904	Sandwich	Jack White	296
1905	St. Andrews	James Braid	318
1906	Muirfield	James Braid	300
1907	Hoylake	Arnaud Massy	312
1908	Prestwick	James Braid	291
1909	Deal	John H. Taylor	295
1910	St. Andrews	James Braid	299
1911	Sandwich	Harry Vardon	303
1912	Muirfield	Edward Ray	295
1913	Hoylake	John H. Taylor	304
1914	Prestwick	Harry Vardon	306
1915-1919	Not played		
1920	Deal	George Duncan	303
1921	St. Andrews	Jock Hutchison	296
1922	Sandwich	Walter Hagen	300
1923	Troon	Arthur Havers	295
1924	Hoylake	Walter Hagen	301
1925	Prestwick	James Barnes	300
1926	Royal Lytham and St. Annes	*Robert T. Jones Jr.	291
1927	St. Andrews	*Robert T. Jones Jr.	285
1928	Sandwich	Walter Hagen	292
1929	Muirfield	Walter Hagen	292
1930	Hoylake	*Robert T. Jones Jr.	291
1931	Carnoustie	Tommy Armour	296
1932	Princes	Gene Sarazen	283
1933	St. Andrews	Denny Shute	292
1934	Sandwich	T. Henry Cotton	283
1935	Muirfield	Alfred Perry	283
1936	Hoylake	Alfred Padgham	287
1937	Carnoustie	T. Henry Cotton	290
1938	Sandwich	R. A. Whitcombe	295
1939	St. Andrews	Richard Burton	290
1940-45	Not played		
1946	St. Andrews	Sam Snead	290
1947	Hoylake	Fred Daly	293
1948	Muirfield	Henry Cotton	284
1949	Sandwich	Bobby Locke	283
1950	Troon	Bobby Locke	279
1951	Portrush	Max Faulkner	285
1952	Royal Lytham and St. Annes	Bobby Locke	287
1953	Carnoustie	Ben Hogan	282
1954	Royal Birkdale	Peter Thomson	283
1955	St. Andrews	Peter Thomson	281
1956	Royal Liverpool	Peter Thomson	286
1957	St. Andrews	Bobby Locke	279
1958	Royal Lytham and St. Annes	Peter Thomson David Thomas	278-139 278-143
1959	Muirfield	Gary Player	284
1960	St. Andrews	Kel Nagle	278
1961	Royal Birkdale	Arnold Palmer	284
1962	Troon	Arnold Palmer	276
1963	Royal Lytham and St. Annes	Bob Charles Phil Rodgers	277-140 277-148
1964	St. Andrews	Tony Lema	279
1965	Royal Birkdale	Peter Thomson	285
1966	Muirfield	Jack Nicklaus	282
1967	Royal Liverpool	Roberto de Vicenzo	278
1968	Carnoustie	Gary Player	289
1969	Royal Lytham and St. Anne's	Tony Jacklin	280
1970	St. Andrews	Jack Nicklaus Doug Sanders	283-72 283-73
1971	Royal Birkdale	Lee Trevino	278
1972	Muirfield	Lee Trevino	278
1973	Troon	Tom Weiskopf	276
1974	Royal Lytham and St. Annes	Gary Player	282
1975	Carnoustie	Tom Watson	279

*Amateur.

1975 BRITISH OPEN LEADERS

Tom Watson*	**71-67-69-72—279**	**$16,500**
Jack Newton	69-71-65-74—279	13,200
Johnny Miller	71-69-66-74—280	8,507
Bobby Cole	72-66-66-76—280	8,507
Jack Nicklaus	69-71-68-72—280	8,507
Graham Marsh	72-67-71-71—281	6,600
Peter Oosterhuis	68-70-71-73—283	5,940
Neil Coles	72-69-67-74—282	5,940

*Won 18-hole playoff, 71-72.

RYDER CUP

Year	Site	Team	Points
1951	Pinehurst C.C., Pinehurst, N.C.	United States Great Britain	9½ 2½
1953	Wentworth, England	United States Great Britain	6½ 5½
1955	Thunderbird R.&G.C., Palm Springs, Calif.	United States Great Britain	8 4
1957	Lindrick C., Workshop, Eng.	Great Britain United States	7 4
1959	Eldorado C.C., Palm Desert, Calif.	United States Great Britain	8½ 3½
1961	Lytham-St. Anne's G.C., Lancashire, Eng.	United States Great Britain	14½ 9½
1963	East Lake C.C., Atlanta, Ga.	United States Great Britain	23 9
1965	Royal Birkdale C., Southport, England	United States Great Britain	19½ 12½
1967	Champions G.C., Houston, Tex.	United States Great Britain	23½ 8½
1969	Royal Birkdale G.C., Southport, England	United States Great Britain	16 16
1971	Old Warson C.C., St. Louis, Mo.	United States Great Britain	18½ 13½
1973	Muirfield G.L., Gullane, Scotland	United States Great Britain	19 13
1975	Laurel Valley G.C., Ligonier, Pa.	United States Great Britain	21 11

Event inaugurated in 1927.

WORLD CUP

Year	Site	Winner, runner-up	Score
1953	Beaconsfield G.C., Montreal, Can.	Argentina Canada	287 297
1954	Laval-sur-lac, Montreal, Can.	Australia Argentina	556 560
1955	Columbia C.C., Washington, D.C.	United States Australia	560 569
1956	Wentworth C., England	United States South Africa	567 581
1957	Kasumigaseki C.C., Tokyo, Japan	Japan United States	557 566
1958	Club de Golf, Mexico City, Mex.	Ireland Spain	579 582
1959	Royal Melbourne C., Melbourne, Aust.	Australia United States	563 573
1960	Portmarnock G.C., Ireland	United States England	565 573
1961	Dorado Beach G.C., Dorado, Puerto Rico	United States Australia	560 572
	Winning team: Snead, Demaret. Individual champion: Snead, 272.		
1962	Jockey C., Buenos Aires, Argentina	United States Argentina	557 559
	Winning team: Arnold Palmer, Sam Snead. Individual: Roberto de Vicenzo, Argentina, 276.		
1963	Saint Nom la Breteche C., Versailles, France	United States Spain	482 485
	Winning team: Nicklaus, Palmer. Individual champion: Nicklaus 237 (63 holes).		
1964	Royal Kaanapali G. Cse., Maui, Hawaii	United States Argentina	554 564
	Winning team: Nicklaus, Palmer. Individual champion: Nicklaus, 276.		
1965	C. de Campo, Madrid Spain	South Africa Spain	571 579
	Winning team: Gary Player, Harold Henning. Individual champion: Player, 281.		
1966	Yomiuri C.C., Tokyo, Japan	United States South Africa	548 553
	Winning team: Palmer, Nicklaus. Individual champion: George Knudson, Canada, 272 (won playoff from Hideyo Sugimoto, Japan)		
1967	C. de Golf Mexico, Mexico City, Mex.	United States New Zealand	557 570
	Winning team: Arnold Palmer, Jack Nicklaus. Individual champion: Palmer, 276.		
1968	Olgiata G.C., Rome, Italy	Canada United States	569 571
	Winning team: Knudson, Balding. Individual champion: Al Balding, 274.		
1969	Singapore Island C.C., Singapore	United States Japan	552 560
	Winning team: Lee Trevino, Orville Moody, Individual champion: Trevino, 275		
1970	Jockey Club, Buenos Aires, Arg.	Australia Argentina	545 555
	Winning team: David Graham, Bruce Devlin. Individual champion: Roberto de Vicenzo, Argentina, 269.		
1971	PGA Ntl. G.C., Palm Beach, Fla.	United States South Africa	555 567
	Winning team: Jack Nicklaus, Lee Trevino. Individual champion: Nicklaus, 271.		
1972	Royal Melbourne C.C., Melbourne, Australia	Taiwan Japan	438 440
	Winning team: Hsieh Min-nan, Lu Liang-Huan Individual champion: Hsieh Min-nan, 217.		
1973	Nueva Andalucia Cse., Marbella, Spain	United States South Africa	558 564
	Winning team: Johnny Miller, Jack Nicklaus. Individual champion: Miller, 277.		
1974	Lagunita C.C., Caracas, Venezuela	South Africa Japan	554 559
	Winning team: Bobby Cole, Dale Hayes. Individual champion: Cole, 271.		
1975	Navatanee G.Cse., Bangkok, Thailand	United States Taiwan	554 564
	Winning team: Johnny Miller, Lou Graham. Individual champion: Miller, 275.		

BRITISH AMATEUR CHAMPIONSHIP

Year	Site	Winner, runner-up	Score
1950	St. Andrews	Frank Stranahan d. Richard Chapman	8 and 6
1951	Porthcawl	Richard Chapman d. Charles Coe	5 and 4
1952	Prestwick	Harvie Ward d. Frank Stranahan	6 and 5
1953	Hoylake	Joe Carr d. Harvie Ward	2 up
1954	Muirfield	Doug Bachli d. Wm. C. Campbell	2 and 1
1955	Royal Lytham and St. Annes	Joe Conrad d. Alan Slater	3 and 2
1956	Troon	John Beharrell d. Leslie Taylor	5 and 4
1957	Formby	Reid Jack d. Harold Ridgley	2 and 1
1958	St. Andrews	Joe Carr d. Alan Thirlwell	3 and 2
1959	Royal St. George's	Deane Beman d. Bill Hyndman	3 and 2
1960	Royal Portrush	Joe Carr d. Bob Cochran	7 and 6
1961	Turnberry	Mike Bonallack d. Jimmy Walker	6 and 4
1962	Hoylake	Richard Davies d. John Povall	1 up
1963	St. Andrews	Michael Lunt d. John Blackwell	2 and 1
1964	Ganton	Gordon Clarke d. Michael Lunt	1 up, 39 hls.
1965	Royal Porthcawl	Mike Bonallack d. Clive Clark	2 and 1
1966	Carnoustie	Bobby Cole d. Ron Shade	3 and 2
1967	Formby	Bob Dickson d. Ron Cerrudo	2 and 1
1968	Troon	Mike Bonallack d. Joe Carr	7 and 6
1969	Royal Liverpool	Mike Bonallack d. Bill Hyndman	3 and 2
1970	Royal County Down	Mike Bonallack d. Bill Hyndman	7 and 6
1971	Carnoustie	Steve Melnyk d. Jim Simons	3 and 2
1972	Royal St. George's	Trevor Homer d. Alan Thirlwell	4 and 3
1973	Royal Porthcawl	Dick Siderowf d. Peter Moody	5 and 3
1974	Muirfield	Trevor Homer d. Jim Gabrielsen	2 up
1975	Royal Liverpool	Vinny Giles d. Mark James	8 and 7

Event inaugurated in 1885.

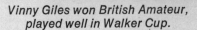

Vinny Giles won British Amateur, played well in Walker Cup.

WALKER CUP MATCHES

Year	Site	Team	Points
1955	St. Andrews,	United States	10
	Scotland	Great Britain	2
1957	Minikahda C.,	United States	8
	Minneapolis	Great Britain	3
	One match halved.		
1959	Muirfield,	United States	9
	Scotland.	Great Britain	3
1961	Seattle C.C.,	United States	11
	Seattle, Wash.	Great Britain	1
1963	Turnberry G.C.,	United States	12
	Alisa, Scotland.	Great Britain	8
1965	Baltimore (Md.)	United States	11
	C.C.	Great Britain	11
1967	R. St. George's,	United States	13
	Sandwich, England	Great Britain	7
1969	Milwaukee C.C.,	United States	10
	Milwaukee, Wis.	Great Britain	8
1971	St. Andrews,	Great Britain	13
	Scotland	United States	11
1973	The Country Club,	United States	14
	Brookline, Mass.	Great Britain	10
1975	St. Andrews,	United States	15½
	Scotland	Great Britain	8½

Event inaugurated in 1922.

WORLD AMATEUR TEAM (MEN)

Year	Site	Winner, runner-up	Score
1960	Merion G.C.,	United States	834
	Ardmore, Pa.	Australia	876
	Winning team: Jack Nicklaus, Deane Beman, Bill Hyndman, Bob Gardner.		
1962	Kawana Fuji G. Cse.	United States	854
	Ito, Japan	Canada	862
	Winning team: Deane Beman, Labron Harris, Dick Sikes, Billy Joe Patton.		
1964	Olgiata C.C.,	G. Britain	895
	Rome, Italy	Canada	899
	Winning team: Ronnie Shade, Rodney Foster, Michael Bonallack, Michael Lunt.		
1966	C. de Golf Mexico,	Australia	877
	Mexico City, Mex.	United States	879
	Winning team: Kevin Donahue, Kevin Hartley, Harry Berwick, Phil Billings.		
1968	Royal Melbourne	United States	868
	G.C., Australia	Great Britain	869
	Winning team: Bruce Fleisher, Jack Lewis, Jr., Marvin Giles III, Dick Siderowf.		
1970	Real C.,	United States	857
	Madrid, Spain	New Zealand	869
	Winning team: Lanny Wadkins, Vinny Giles, Allen Miller, Tom Kite.		
1972	Olivos C.,	United States	865
	Buenos Aires, Argentina	Australia	870
	Winning team: Ben Crenshaw, Vinny Giles, Mark Hayes, Marty West.		
1974	Cajuiles Cse., La Romana	United States	888
	Dominican Republic	Japan	898
	Winning team: Jerry Pate, Gary Koch, George Burns, Curtis Strange.		

WOMEN

Year	Site	Winner, runner-up	Score
1964	St. Germain G.C.,	France	588
	Paris, France	United States	589
	Winning team: Claudine Cros, Catherine Lacoste, Brigitte Varangot.		
1966	Mexico City C.C.,	United States	580
	Mexico City, Mex.	Canada	589
	Winning team: Mrs. Teddy Boddie, Shelley Hamlin, Mrs. David Welts.		
1968	Royal Melbourne	United States	616
	G.C., Australia	Australia	621
	Winning team: Jane Bastanchury, Shelley Hamlin, Mrs. David Welts.		
1970	C. de Campo,	United States	598
	Madrid, Spain	France	599
	Winning team: Martha Wilkinson, Jane Bastanchury, Cynthia Hill.		
1972	Hindu Club,	United States	583
	Buenos Aires, Argentina	France	587
	Winning team: Laura Baugh, Jane Booth, Mary Budke.		
1974	Cajuiles Cse., La Romana	United States	620
	Dominican Republic	Gr. Brit.-Ireland	636
	Winning team: Cynthia Hill, Debbie Massey, Carole Semple.		

CURTIS CUP MATCHES

Year	Site	Team	Points
1954	Merion G.C.,	United States	6
	Admore, Pa.	Great Britain	3
1956	Prince's Course,	Great Britain	5
	Sandwich, Eng.	United States	4
1958	Brae Burn, C.C.	Great Britain	4½
	W. Newton, Mass.	United States	4½
1960	Lindrick C.,	United States	6½
	Workshop, Eng.	Great Britain	2½
1962	Broadmoor G.C.,	United States	8
	Colorado Spgs., Colo.	Great Britain	1
1964	Royal Porthcawl G.C.,	United States	10½
	Wales, G. Britain	Great Britain	7½
1966	Cascades Cse.,	United States	13
	Hot Springs, Va.	Great Britain	5
1968	Royal County Down	United States	10½
	G.C., N. Ireland	Great Britain	7½
1970	Brae Burn, C.C.,	United States	11½
	W. Newton, Mass.	Great Britain	6½
1972	Western Gailes G.C.,	United States	10
	Scotland	Great Britain	8
1974	San Francisco G.C.	United States	10
		Great Britain	4

Event inaugurated in 1932.

FOREIGN CHAMPIONS OF 1975

MEN PROFESSIONALS

AUSTRALIA: Australian Open, Jack Nicklaus, USA; Blue Lake Classic, Mark Tapper; Chrysler Classic, Billy Dunk; Murray Bridge Open, Wayne Simpson, Riverside; New South Wales Open, A. Y. Gresham (am); South Australia Medal, Dean Wiles; South Australian Professional, Vaugan Somers; Tasmanian Open, Stewart Ginn; Victorian Open, Stewart Ginn

BERMUDA: Bermuda Goodwill Pro-Am, (Team) Richelieu Valley G.C., Canada; (Ind) Glenn Stuart, USA; (Sr) Dai Rees, England; Bermuda Open, Brendan Ingham (am)

BRAZIL: Brazil Open, P. Gonzalez

CANADA: Alberta Open, Bob Panasiuk; British Columbia Open, Dave Barr; Canadian Open, Tom Weiskopf, USA; Candian PGA, Bill Tape; Manitoba Open, Ed Byman. USA; Peter Jackson Atlantic Open, Bob Panasiuk; Peter Jackson Ontario Open, Michel Boyer; Peter Jackson Quebec Open, John Kindred, USA; Peter Jackson Saskatchewan Open, Greg Piklaski

COLOMBIA: Caribbean Open, Gene Borek, USA; Colombian Open, Peter Butler, Great Britain

EGYPT: Egyptian Open, Mohammed Said Moussa

ENGLAND: British Left-Handers, Ian Stephenson; British PGA, Arnold Palmer, USA; Commonwealth Tournament, (Team) Great Britain; Devon Open, John Green; PGA Championship, Arnold Palmer, USA; Piccadilly Medal, Bob Shearer, Australia; Royston G.C. Pro-Am Competition, Jimmy Hamilton; Southern Uniroyal Pro Championship, Dai Rees; Sumrie Fourball Better-Ball Tournament, Jack Newton, Australia and John O'Leary, Ireland; Surrey Match-Play Championship, Neil Coles; Surrey Open, K. Bousfield; Uniroyal Midland Professionals Championship, Hugh Boyle

FRANCE: American Express Pro-Am, Manuel Montes, Spain; Championship of French Professionals, Jean Garaialde; France-South Africa Team International, (Team) France, (Ind) Jean Garaialde; French Open, Brian Barnes, Scotland; International Open of the Riviera, J. P. Charpenel; Lancôme Trophy, Gary Player, South Africa; Philip Morris International Championship, Bernard Pascassio and Jean Garaialde

GERMANY: German National Closed Open Championship, Bernhard Langer.

IRELAND: Guinness Championship, Christy O'Connor; Hilary Outing Tournament, Paddy Skerritt; Irish Dunlop Tournament, Eddie Polland; Irish Open, Christy O'Connor Jr.; Kerrygold Classic, George Burns, USA; Links Pro at Royal Dublin, Bobby Browne; Ryan Pro-Am, John McGuirk and Jimmy Kinsella (tie); Connacht Alliance, Don Wallace

JAMAICA: Jamaica International Pro-Am, (Team) Del Snyder and Greenbrier; (Pro Ind) Art Silvestrone, USA; (Am) Maxie Lyn & Diane Aris; Jamaican Open, Mike Higuera, USA

JAPAN: All-Nippon Airways Tournament, Hsieh Young-yo, Taiwan; Australia-Japan Team Match, (Team) Australia, (Ind) Stewart Ginn, Australia; Chunichi Crowns International, Isao Aoki; Dunlop Phoenix International, Johnny Miller, USA; Dunlop Tournament, Norio Suzuki; Fuji Sankei Classic, Lu Liang-huan, Taiwan; Japan Open, Takashi Murakami; Japanese PGA Match-Play Championship, Takashi Murakami; Japan Pro Golfers' East-West Tournament, Teruo Sugihara; Japan-United Kingdom Match, (Team) Japan, (Ind) Kosaku Shimada; Sapporo Tokyo Open, Graham Marsh, Australia; Sobu International Open, Teruo Sugihara; Sony Classic International Open, Masaji Kusakabe; Sports Shinko Open, Yasuhiro Miyamoto; Suntory Open, Yoshitaka Yamamoto; Tohoku Classic, Masashi Ozaki; Wizard Tournament, Graham Marsh. Australia

KENYA: Kenya Open, Gary Smith, Britain

MEXICO: Atlas International Golf Tournament, Ernesto Perez Acosta; Lil' David Pro-Am, Kurt Cox, USA; Mexican Masters, Ernesto Perez Acosta; "Taxco 75" Pro-Am, Angel Lizarraga; Valle Alto Pro-Am, Wallace Marker, USA

MOROCCO: Dar-Es-Salam Pro-Am, Brian Waites, England

NEW ZEALAND: Air New Zealand Fiji Open, Frank Phillips; Auckland Anniversary Championship, P. M. Burney; Hutt Pro-Am, John Carter; Marlborough Pro-Am, Frank Malloy; Nelson Pro-Am, Wayne McIntosh and Alan Snape (tie); New Zealand Open, Bill Dunk, Australia

NIGERIA: Nigerian Open, David Jagger, Britain; Nigerian Open Pro-Am, Guy Hunt and Tony Jackson (am), Britain

PORTUGAL: Norwest Holst Pro-Am, J. Garner, J. Hume, R. Cameron, Britain; Portuguese Open, Hal Underwood, USA; Vale do Lobo Pro-Am, Stuart Brown, England

SCOTLAND: Scottish Midland Alliance Ch., Jim Farmer; Scottish Northern Open, Willie Milne; Scottish Uniroyal Tournament, Sam Torrance; Usher Scottish Championship, David Huish; Whyte and Mackay Tournament, J. Panton; Scottish Professional Championship; David Huish

SOUTH AFRICA: Dunlop Masters, John Fourie; Holiday Inn Tournament, John O'Leary, Ireland; ICL International, Vince Baker; Lion International Pro-Am, Andries Costhuizen; PGA, Graham Henning and John Fourie (tie); Rand Classic, Allan Henning, Rhodesia; Rondebosch Stroke-Play Open, Gerald Williams; South African Masters, John Fourie; South African Open, Gary Player

SOUTH KOREA: South Korean Open, Kuo Chie-hsiung, Taiwan

SPAIN: Foot-Joy International Pro-Am, (Team) Texas, USA, (Am) Bob Cowin, USA, (Pro) Jaimie Roqueni; Golf-Masters,Severiano Ballesteros; La Manga International Pro-Am, Angel Gallardo; Madrid Open, Bob Shearer, Australia; Sherry Cup, Veit Pagel; Spanish Open, Arnold Palmer, USA

SWAZILAND: Holiday Inns Tournament, John O'Leary, Ireland

SWITZERLAND: Blumisberg Open, F. Schiroli; Lucerne Open, Sooky Maharaj; Swiss Open, Dale Hayes, South Africa

THAILAND: Thailand Open Championship, Howard Twitty, USA; World Cup: (Team) USA, (Ind) Johnny Miller, USA

TOBAGO: Mount Irvin Bay 36-Hole Professional Tournament, Tommy Horton, Britain

VENEZUELA: Simon Bolivar Tournament, (Team) Venezuela, (Ind) Horacio Carbonetti

ZAMBIA: Lusaka Open, Carl Mason, Britain; Mufulira Open, Ronnie Shade, Scotland; Zambia Open, Sam Torrance, Scotland

MEN AMATEURS

AUSTRALIA: Blackwood Open, David Threlfall; South Australian Amateur, John Muller; 1975 Victorian Amateur, Ricky Wines

AUSTRIA: Austrian International Amateur, Gery Wattine, France

BERMUDA: Bermuda Invitation, Louis Moniz; Bermuda Junior, Blake Marshall

BELGIUM: Belgium International Amateur, Craig Francis

CANADA: British Columbia Amateur, Jim Nelford; British Columbia Junior, Jim Goddard; British Columbia GA Seniors, Bill Thompson; British Columbia Seniors' Championship, Jack Ellis; Canadian Amateur, Jim Nelford; Canadian Left-Handers, Jim King; Canadian Seniors, John Poyen; Dave McDonald Memorial Trophy, Harry Critchley; Manitoba Amateur, Jimmy Doyle; Manitoba Junior, Darrell McDonald; Northwest GA Seniors, Harold Weston, USA; Ontario Amateur, Gary Cowan; Ontario Junior, Gary Stickl; Ontario Public Course, Bill Laughlin, England.

COLOMBIA: Colombian Open Amateur, (Team) Rhodesia, (Ind) Dennis Watson, Rhodesia

CZECHOSLOVAKIA: Czechoslovakian National Amateur, Andreas Cobler, Germany

EGYPT: Egyptian Amateur, Amr Mahfouz

ENGLAND: British Amateur, Vinny Giles, USA; British Youths Ch., Nick Faldo; Carris Trophy, Sandy Lyle; Devon Amateur, A. P. Vicary; Duncan Putter, J. Germine; East and West Yorkshire Alliances Annual Combined Fourball, Mike Kelley and Clive Duck; East Riding and District Alliance's Fourball, Derek Rigby and David Hunter; Eastern Counties Cup, J. Marks; English Amateur, Nick Faldo; English Amateur Stroke-Play, Sandy Lyle; Lytham Trophy, George Macgregor, Scotland; Midlands Amateur, Martin Poxon; National Public Courses Championship, Tony Sullivan; Northumberland County Amateur, Peter Deeble

FRANCE: Coupe International Universitaire, Philippe Ploujoux; Coupe Murat, T. Planchin; French Amateur Championship, Georgy Leven; French International Amateur. Thierry Planchin; French Men's Fourball, Jean-Baptiste Corre and Sven Boinet; French Seniors, G. Huet; International Junior, G. Brand, England; Kas Trophy, (Team) Spain, (Ind) R. LaGarde

GERMANY: Junior Championship, Ulrich Born; German Open Amateur, Robert Stewart, South Africa

ICELAND: Uniroyal Championship, Magnus Haldorsson

IRELAND: Cork Scratch Cup, Jerry Mehigan; European Amateur Team Championship, Scotland; Irish Amateur, M. D. O'Brien; Leinster Alliance, Paul Henry; Leinster Alliance McGrath Cups, Paddy Caul; New Ross Scratch Cup, Liam McNamara; North of Ireland Open Amateur, J. Heggarty; Northwesterern Alliance, Brian Hoey; Ryan Pro-Am, John McGuirk; South of Ireland Amateur, B. P. Malone; West of Ireland Amateur Ian Elliott

JAPAN: American-Japan Society Summer Championship, Siro Omata, Asia Amateur Team Championship, Japan, (Ind) Masahiro Kuramoto

LEBANON: Pan Arab Amateur, (Team) Egypt, (Ind) Mohammed El-Sayed

MEXICO: Mexican National Interclub Tournament, (Team) Guadalajara C.C., (Ind) Rafael Alarcon

MOROCCO: Moroccan International Amateur, (Men Team) Switzerland, (Men Ind) Hamid Gartite, (Women Team) Italy, (Women Ind) Marina Ragher

NEW ZEALAND: Auckland Veteran's Tournament, D. Munro; Champion-of-Champions Tournament, Owen Kendall; Chisholm Park 36-Hole Festival Tournament, Murray Newall; Dunedin Senior Stroke-Play, Ron Johnston

PORTUGAL: Portuguese International Amateur, Pedro Caupers

SAUDI ARABIA: Arabian American Oil Co. Invitational. Saif Sa'ad

SCOTLAND: British Boys Championship, Brian Marchbank; Championship of the Edinburgh and East of Scotland Alliance, Morris S. J. McEwan; East of Scotland Amateur Stroke Play, Sandy Pirie; Edward Trophy, Charles Green; European Amateur, (Team) Scotland; Scottish Amateur, David Greig; Scottish Boys, Alistair Webster; Scottish Open Amateur Stroke, Charles W. Green

SOUTH AFRICA: Clovelly Stroke-Play Open, John Pickering; King David Open, Peter Todt; National Championship, David Stratton (won playoff); Slazenger Trophy, Nicky Price, Rhodesia; South African Amateur, Peter Vorster; South African Junior Championship, David Stratton; South African Seniors, Ken Bain; Vaal Amateur, David Stratton; West Province Amateur, Bobby Gould

SPAIN: El Cid Trophy, Carlos Miguel; International Amateur of Spain, S. Boinet, France

SWEDEN: Swedish Open Amateur Stroke, Hans Hedjerson

SWITZERLAND: Swiss Seniors' National Championship, F. Kunkler

WALES: Lanland Bay Golf Club Winter Foursomes, John Radcliffe and Peter Radcliffe; Welsh Amateur, Jeff Toye; Welsh Stroke, David McLean

WOMEN PROFESSIONALS

AUSTRALIA: Australian Women's Open, JoAnne Carner, USA; Rene Erichsen Even, J. Crafter

ENGLAND: Colgate-European Women's Open, Donna Young, USA

FRANCE: Women's European Championship, (Team) France

GERMANY: German Women's Native Open Championship, Irene Koehler

JAPAN: Hiroshima Ladies Open, Tu A-Yu, Taiwan; Japanese Women's PGA, Sayoko Yamazaki; World Ladies, Jane Blalock, USA

SOUTH AFRICA: South African Women's Championship, Jenny Bruce

WALES: Welsh Women's 54-Hole Tournament, Tegwen Perkins

WOMEN AMATEURS

AUSTRIA: Austrian International Women's Amateur, Marie-Christine Hueber

BERMUDA: Bermuda Invitation Ladies Amateur, Debbie Massey, USA

BELGIUM: Belgium International Ladies Amateur, L. van den Berghe

CANADA: British Columbia Junior Girls', Paula Phillips; Canadian Junior Girls, Pamela Johns; Canadian Women's Amateur, Debbie Massey, USA; Manitoba Ladies' Amateur, Pam Falk; Ontario Women's Amateur, Sue Wickware

COLOMBIA: International Women's Amateur, Tsai Li-hsian and Wu Ming-yeh, Taiwan

ENGLAND: Avia Ladies' International Foursomes, Mrs. S. P. Sander, USA, and A. Irvin, Mrs. A. Bonallack and Mrs. S. Barber; Berkshire Championship, Stephanie Jolly; British Girls Championship, Suzanne Cadden, Scotland; Durham Title, Anne Biggs; English Rose Spoons, (Div. 1) Mrs. P. E. Benge, (Div. 2) Mrs. J. Myring, (Div. 3) Mrs. P. Sword; English Women's Amateur Championship, Beverly Huke, Scotland; Gloucester Championship, Ruth Porter.

FRANCE: Esperance Dames, Mme. Mahe; European Women's Team Amateur Championship, France; French International Women's Amateur, Mme. I. Goldschmid; French Women's Amateur Championship, Martine Giraud.

GERMANY: German Girls Junior Championship, Sybille Bartels; German Women's Open Amateur Championship, Marietta Gutermann, Ladies International Amateur Stroke Championship, Marietta Buertermann

HOLLAND: Dutch Ladies International Stroke, Anne Marie Palli

INDIA: Ladies Open Amateur Championship of India, Tiru Fernando, Sri Lanka, Colombo

IRELAND: Inter-Women's Alliance, (Team) Leinster, (Ind) Mary McKenna; Irish Women's Close Championship, Mary Gorry Leinster Women's Alliance Foursomes Cup, Rhona Fanagan and Ann O'Reilly; Woodbrook Scratch Cup, Clare Nesbitt

JAPAN: Mizuno Shinjin Tournament, Saburo Kubo

MEXICO: Mexico Women's Amateur, Nancy Lopez, USA

PHILIPPINES: Philippine Women's Open Amateur, Wu Ming-yueh, Taiwan

PORTUGAL: Portuguese Ladies International Amateurs Championship, Christine Marcusson, Sweden

SCOTLAND: Aberdeenshire Championship, Mrs. R. J. Milne; Angus Championship, Joan Smith; Ayshire Title, Sharon Lambie; British Women's Amateur, Nancy Syms, USA; Cambs. & Hunts, Marion Maddocks; Dunbartonshire and Argyll Championship, Vicki McAlister; East Lothian Championship, Mrs. J. G. Brown; Scottish Girls' Championship, Wilma Aitken; Scottish Universities Women's Golf Championships, (Team) Edinburgh, (Ind) Maureen Walker; Scottish Women's Championship, Leslie Hope.

SPAIN: International Women's Amateur, N. Jeanson, France

SWEDEN: Swedish Open Ladies Stroke-Play Championship, Marie Wennersten

WALES: Glamorgan Championship, Tegwen Perkins; Welsh Girls, Lisa Isherwood; Welsh Women's Amateur Championship, Ann Johnson

ALL-TIME RECORDS

PGA TOUR RECORDS

72 holes: 257 (60-68-64-65) by Mike Souchak at Brackenridge Park Golf Course, San Antonio, Tex., in 1955 Texas Open.

54 holes: 189 (63-63-63), by Chandler Harper at Brackenridge Park Golf Course, San Antonio, Tex., in 1954 Texas Open.

36 holes: 126, shared by Johnny Palmer, Tucson, 1948; Sam Snead, San Antonio (Tex.), 1950 and Dallas, 1957; Chandler Harper, Texas (twice) 1954; Tommy Bolt, Virginia Beach, 1954; Jack Rule, St. Paul, 1963.

18 holes: 60, shared by Al Brosch, San Antonio (Tex.), 1951; Bill Nary, El Paso, 1952; Ted Kroll, San Antonio (Tex.), 1954; Wally Ulrich, Virginia Beach, 1954; Tommy Bolt, Hartford, 1954; Mike Souchak, San Antonio (Tex.), 1955; Sam Snead, Dallas, 1957.

9 holes: 27, by Mike Souchak during his round of 60 (27-33) in the 1955 Texas Open.

Consecutive birdies: 8, by Bob Goalby in the fourth round of the 1961 St. Petersburg Open.

Fewest Putts: 19, by Randy Glover in 1965 St. Paul Open, by Bill Nary in 1952 Texas Open, by Bob Rosburg in 1959 Pensacola Open, by Deane Beman in 1968 Haig Ntl. Open, and by Dave Stockton in 1971 Monsanto Open.

Fewest putts (72 holes): Bert Yancey, 102, at Columbia-Edgewater C.C. in 1966 Portland Open.

Consecutive wins: 11, by Byron Nelson in 1945.

Consecutive times in money: 113, by Byron Nelson in the 1940s. Dow Finsterwald had a 72-event money skein going from 1955 through 1958.

Most wins in single season: 18, by Byron Nelson, 1945.

Consecutive major championships: Walter Hagen's 4 PGA Championships (1924-1927).

Youngest tournament winner: Gene Sarazen, 20, when he won the 1922 U.S. Open, is the youngest pro winner of an official tournament since the PGA was formed in 1917.

Oldest tournament winner: Sam Snead was 52 years, 10 months and 7 days old when he won the 1965 Greensboro (N.C.) Open.

Million-dollar career money-winners: Jack Nicklaus, $2,541,772; Arnold Palmer, $1,723,113; Billy Casper, $1,581,605; Lee Trevino, $1,398,651; Bruce Crampton, $1,323,399; Tom Weiskopf, $1,224,854; Gene Littler, $1,203,541; Gary Player, $1,163,153.

Most money for a single season: $353,021, by Johnny Miller, 1974.

LONGEST SUDDEN-DEATH PLAYOFF

Lloyd Mangrum and Cary Middlecoff played 11 extra holes after they had tied for the 72-hole lead in the 1949 Motor City Open in Detroit without deciding the title. Darkness intervened and the players were declared co-champions. There have been longer playoffs, but all started with an 18-hole stroke round which was tied, then went on more holes.

LPGA TOUR RECORDS

(Scores under "preferred lie" rule not admitted)

72 holes: 273 (68-71-69-65), by Kathy Whitworth in the 1966 Milwaukee Jaycee Open.

54 holes (in 72-hole tournament): 206 (68-68-70) by Mickey Wright in 1962 Spokane Open; also by Jo Ann Prentice (67-71-68) in 1967 Dallas Civitan Open.

54 holes (in 54-hole tournament): 200, by Carol Mann in 1968 Lady Carling Open, Palmetto, Ga. Ruth Jessen also shot 200, in the 1964 Omaha Jaycee Open, but record invalidated by "preferred lie" local rule in effect at time.

36 holes (in 72-hole tournament): 136, by Jackie Pung in 1958 St. Petersburg Open and Mickey Wright in 1962 Spokane Open (first 2 rounds). Wright had 135 (67-68) in 2nd and 3rd rounds of 1964 LPGA Championship.

36 holes (in 54-hole tournament): 132 (66-66), by Carol Mann in 1968 Lady Carling Open, Palmetto, Ga.

18 holes: 62, by Mickey Wright in 1964 Tall City Open, Midland, Tex. Other 62s, by Miss Wright in 1967 Bluegrass Inv., Louisville, Ky., and by Kathy Whitworth in 1968 Holiday Inn Classic, St. Louis, Mo., invalidated by "preferred lie" local rule in effect at time.

9 holes: 29, by Marlene Hagge, on 1st 9 in 1st round of 1971 Immke Open, Columbus, O.

Most wins in single season: 13, by Mickey Wright in 1963.

Most official money in single season: $87,094, by JoAnne Carner, 1974.

Most total money in single season: $87,750, by JoAnne Carner, 1974 (inc. tour purses, pro-ams).

Most consecutive victories: 4, by Mickey Wright; twice, in 1962 and 1963; Kathy Whitworth, 1969; Shirley Englehorn, 1970.

Most birdies in round: Nine, by Mickey Wright in 1964 Tall City Open; 3rd (final) round; also by JoAnne Carner in 1971 Lady Pepsi Open, Atlanta, Ga.; 3rd (final) round.

Fewest putts: 20, by Judy Kimball in 4th round of 1961 Am. Women's Open. Also by Cynthia Sullivan in 3rd round of 1967 Amarillo (Tex.) Open.

Youngest winner: Marlene Hagge, 18 when she won 1952 Sarasota Open.

Oldest winner: Patty Berg, 44 when she won 1962 Muskogee Open.

MISCELLANEOUS

MARATHON RECORD

Dick Kimbrough of North Platte, Neb., holds the all-time record for the number of holes played on a regulation course within a 24-hour period. On June 18-19, 1972, Kimbrough played 364 holes at the 6,068, par-70 North Platte Country Club course.

The best record in this department by a woman is 156 holes, played by Katherine Murphy, a nurse from Los Angeles, Calif., on June 19, 1967, at the 6,130-yard (women's yardage) San Luis Rey resort course in Bonsall, Calif.

The only rules in this department are that the golfer must walk (or run) all the way, and that the courses over which the records are set must be 6,000 or more yards long.

LONGEST "PUTT"

Playing in a friendly match in which each player was limited to one club, R. W. Bridges chose a putter. He made a hole-in-one measuring 196 yards at the Woodlawn C.C., Kirkwood, Mo., in 1931, surely the longest "putt" in history!

MOST UNDER-PAR HOLES IN SUCCESSION

Professional Roberto de Vicenzo scored six birdies, an eagle, then three more birdies on holes one through 10, on April 6, 1974, at the Villa Allende Golf Club, Province of Cordoba, Argentina. He eventually scored 61 for the round.

The amateur record is nine, by Jimmy Smith, Nashville, Tenn., with birdies on holes four through 12 at McCabe G.C., Nashville, on Aug. 15, 1969.

FASTEST ROUND

Dick Kimbrough, North Platte, Neb., holds the all-time speed record in playing a course of at least 6,000 yards afoot, holing out on every green. On Aug. 8, 1972, Kimbrough ran the 6,068-yard par-70, North Platte Country Club course in 30 minutes, 10 seconds. Three timers with stop-watches accompanied Kimbrough.

LOWEST ROUNDS

Lowest known round on a regulation course was a 55 made by E. F. Staugaard on the 6,419-yard Montebello Park (Calif.) G.C. Staugaard had 13 birdies, two eagles and three pars, according to a Ripley "Believe It or Not" cartoon of 1936.

Staugaard's score was tied by Homero Blancas, U. of Houston golfer, in 1962. Blancas shot his 55 at the Premier Golf Course in Longview, Tex. However, the course measured only 5,002 yards.

Lowest 9-hole score is a 26 (10 under par) by professional Tom Doty on the first nine (3,300 yards) of Brookwood C.C., Woodale, Ill., on Nov. 10, 1971. He scored 33 coming back for a 59, 13 under par.

FEWEST PUTTS

Four amateurs, Bob Rogers, Moorestown, N.J., M. D. (Chick) Chatten, Elkhart, Ind., Henry H. Zeckser, Seattle, Wash., and George Lockwood, Los Angeles, and a professional, Tom Doty, Woodale, Ill., had rounds in which each used only 16 putts. Women's putting record is 19, by Beverly Whitaker, Pasadena, Calif.

LONGEST DRIVE

Longest known drive in major competition was made by American pro Craig Wood in the 1933 British Open at St. Andrews, Scotland. Wood cranked out a 430-yarder on the fifth hole. The course was dry and there was a strong following wind. U.S. Pro George Bayer recorded a drive of 426 yards in the 1955 Tucson Open.

GOLF DIGEST DOUBLE EAGLE RECORDS

Longest: 609 yards, by John W. Eakin, San Jose, Calif., on the 15th hole at the Makaha Inn West course, Hawaii, Nov. 12, 1972.

Oldest: Luke Sewell, 74, Akron, Ohio, on the 510-yard second hole of the Cardinal Course at the Country Club of North Carolina, Pinehurst, May 24, 1975.

Youngest: George Foster, 14, Cameron, Tex., in 1964, on the 471-yard 4th at the Cameron C.C.; Dan Ashdown, Marshall, Mich., in 1968, on the 485-yard 18th at Alwyn Downs G.C., Marshall, and Steve Blumkin, Omaha, Neb., in 1968, on the 479-yard 15th at Highland C.C., Omaha. This is only for double eagles made on par-5 holes. Other 14-year-olds have made technical double eagles by holing out tee shots on par-4 holes.

GOLF DIGEST AGE SHOOTING RECORDS

(Matching or shooting better than one's age on a course of at least 6,000 yards.)

Oldest

Arthur Thompson, Victoria, B.C., Canada, was 100 when he shot 97 at the 6,215-yard Uplands G.C., Victoria, in 1969.

Youngest

Bob Hamilton, professional, matched his age of 59 on the 6,233-yard, par-71 Blue course at Hamilton's Golf Club, Evansville, Ind., on June 4, 1975. The amateur record is 62, scored by A. C. Brown, 62, Chattanooga, Tenn., on June 8, 1968, at the 6,529-yard, par-72 Rivermont G. & C.C., Chattanooga.

Most strokes under age

12, by William Diddel, 86, who shot 74 at the 6,289-yard Country Club of Naples (Fla.) on Nov. 19, 1970.

Most times in career

1,954 by Frank Bailey, now 86, most of them at the 6,440-yard Maxwell Municipal course in Abilene, Tex. Bailey first began matching his age at 71.

HOLE-IN-ONE RECORDS

(As established by the Golf Digest Hole-In-One Clearing House)

Longest

444 yards, by Robert Mitera, Omaha, Neb., on the 10th hole at Miracle Hills Golf Course, Omaha, on Oct. 7, 1965.

Longest by woman

393 yards, by Marie Robie, Wollaston, Mass., on the first hole at Furnace Brook Golf Club, Wollaston, on Sept. 4, 1949.

Longest by left-hander

400 yards, by Tom Cheatwood, Oklahoma City, Okla., on the 6th hole at Lake Hefner G.C., Oklahoma City, on July 23, 1964.

Oldest man

George Henry Miller, 93, Anaheim, Calif., on 116-yard 11th at Anaheim Mun. G.Cse., Dec. 4, 1970.

Oldest woman

Edna Hussey, 81, Cincinnati, O., on the 135-yard fifth hole at the California Municipal Golf Course, Cincinnati, on June 26, 1969.

Youngest boy

Tommy Moore, 6 (plus one month, 7 days), Hagerstown, Md., on the 145-yard fourth hole at Woodbrier Golf Course, Martinsville, W. Va., on Mar. 8, 1968. Tommy also made another hole-in-one on this hole before he turned seven.

Youngest girl

Mary Venker, 9, Bloomington, Ill., on the 128-yard 12th hole at the Bloomington C.C., on Aug. 13, 1971; also, Susan Thompson, 9, Garden Grove, Calif., on the 115-yard ninth hole at the Riverview Golf Club, Santa Ana, Calif., on July 19, 1973.

Successive aces

Norman Manley, Saugus, Calif., holed out successive tee shots on the 330-yard, par-4 7th and the 290-yard, par-4 8th at the Del Valley C.C., Saugus, on Aug. 4, 1964, the only time par-4 holes have been consecutively aced. Only four other instances of successive holes-in-one by a single player have been recorded. All these were on par-3 holes.

Most in career

40, by Art Wall, a professional tournament golfer from Honesdale, Penn. His most recent came in 1973 on the 196-yard 16th hole at the Inverrary G. & C.C., Lauderhill, Fla.

Most in one calendar year

11, by Dr. Joseph O. Boydstone, Bakersfield, Calif., in 1962.

AWARGS

AWARDS

PGA PLAYER OF THE YEAR

1948	Ben Hogan	1962	Arnold Palmer
1949	Sam Snead	1963	Julius Boros
1950	Ben Hogan	1964	Ken Venturi
1951	Ben Hogan	1965	Dave Marr
1952	Julius Boros	1966	Billy Casper
1953	Ben Hogan	1967	Jack Nicklaus
1954	Ed Furgol	1968	No Award
1955	Doug Ford	1969	Orville Moody
1956	Jack Burke	1970	Billy Casper
1957	Dick Mayer	1971	Lee Trevino
1958	Dow Finsterwald	1972	Jack Nicklaus
1959	Art Wall	1973	Jack Nicklaus
1960	Arnold Palmer	1974	Johnny Miller
1961	Jerry Barber	1975	Jack Nicklaus

PLAYER OF THE YEAR

(Awarded by the Golf Writers Association of America.)

1968	Billy Casper	1973	Tom Weiskopf & Kathy Whitworth
1969	Orville Moody		
1970	Billy Casper	1974	Johnny Miller & JoAnne Carner
1971	Lee Trevino		
1972	Jack Nicklaus & Kathy Whitworth	1975	Jack Nicklaus & Sandra Palmer

BOBBY JONES AWARD

(Given annually by the United States Golf Association for distinguished sportsmanship in golf.)

1955	Francis D. Ouimet	1966	Gary Player
1956	Bill Campbell	1967	Richard S. Tufts
1957	Babe Zaharias	1968	Robert Dickson
1958	Margaret Curtis	1969	Gerald Micklem
1959	Findlay S. Douglas	1970	Roberto de Vicenzo
1960	Charles Evans, Jr.	1971	Arnold Palmer
1961	Joe Carr	1972	Michael Bonallack
1962	Horton Smith	1973	Gene Littler
1963	Patty Berg	1974	Byron Nelson
1964	Charles Coe	1975	Jack Nicklaus
1965	Mrs. Edwin Vare Jr.		

BEN HOGAN AWARD

(Given annually by Golf Writers Association of America to individual who has continued to be active in golf despite a physical handicap.)

1954	Babe Zaharias	1965	Ernest Jones
1955	Ed Furgol	1966	Ken Venturi
1956	Dwight Eisenhower	1967	Warren Pease
1957	Clint Russell	1968	Shirley Englehorn
1958	Dale Bourisseau	1969	Curtis Person
1959	Charlie Boswell	1970	Joe Lazaro
1960	Skip Alexander	1971	Larry Hinson
1961	Horton Smith	1972	Ruth Jessen
1962	Jimmy Nichols	1973	Gene Littler
1963	Bobby Nichols	1974	Gay Brewer
1964	Bob Morgan	1975	Patty Berg

CHARLIE BARTLETT AWARD

(Given annually by Golf Writers Association of America to a playing professional for unselfish contribution to the betterment of society.)

1971	Billy Casper	1974	Chi Chi Rodriguez
1972	Lee Trevino	1975	Gene Littler
1973	Gary Player		

JOE GRAFFIS AWARD

(Given by National Golf Foundation to individual who has contributed to golf education, juniors.)

1970	Ellen Griffin	1973	No award
1971	Barbara Rotuig	1974	Opal Hill
1972	Les Bolstad	1975	Patty Berg

Patty Berg is winner of the Joe Graffis Award.

PGA CLUB PROFESSIONALS OF YEAR

1955	Bill Gordon, Niles, Ill.
1956	Harry Shepherd, Elmira, N.Y.
1957	Dugan Aycock, Lexington, N.C.
1958	Harry Pezzullo, Northbrook, Ill.
1959	Edde Duino, San Jose, Calif.
1960	Warren Orlick, Orchard Lake, Mch.
1961	Don Padgett, Selma, Ind.
1962	Tom LoPresti, Sacramento, Calif.
1963	Bruce Herd, Flossmoor, Ill.
1964	Lyle Wehrman, Merced, Calif.
1965	Hubby Habjan, Lake Forest, Ill.
1966	Bill Strausbaugh, Jr., Ellicott City, Md.
1967	Ernie Vossler, Oklahoma City, Okla.
1968	Hardy Loudermilk, San Antonio, Tex.
1969	Wally Mund, St. Paul, Minn., and A. Hubert Smith, Tullahoma, Tenn.
1970	Grady Shumate, Clemmons, S.C.
1971	Ross T. Collins, Dallas, Tex.
1972	Howard Morrette, Kent, Ohio
1973	Warren Smith, Denver
1974	Paul Harney, Hatchville, Mass.
1975	Walker Inman, Columbus, Ohio

HORTON SMITH TROPHY WINNERS

(Awarded by PGA to golf professionals who have made outstanding contributions to golf professional education.)

1965	Emil Beck, Port Huron, Mich.
1966	Gene C. Mason, Portland, Ore.
1967	Donald E. Fischesser, Evansville, Ind.
1968	R. William Clarke, Phoenix, Md.
1969	Paul Hahn, Miami, Fla.
1970	Joe Walser, Oklahoma City, Okla.
1971	Irv Schloss, Dunelin, Fla.
1972	John Budd, New Port Richey, Fla.
1973	George Aulbach, San Antonio, Tex.
1974	Bill Hardy, Chevy Chase, Md.
1975	John Henrich, Clarence, N.Y.

LPGA TEACHERS OF THE YEAR

Awarded by Ladies' PGA

1958	Helen Dettweiler	1967	Jackie Pung
1959	Shirley Spork	1968	Gloria Fecht
1960	Barbara Rotvig	1969	Joanne Winter
1961	Peggy Kirk Bell	1970	Gloria Armstrong
1962	Ellen Griffin	1971	Jeanette Rector
1963	Vonnie Colby	1972	Lee Spencer
1964	Sally Doyle	1973	Penny Zachivas
1965	Goldie Bateson	1974	Mary Dagraedt
1966	Ann C. Johnstone		

VARDON CUP AWARD

(Given by PGA Victor Golf for best overall play in PGA, PGA Club Ch., PGA section.)

1974	Sam Snead	1975	Jimmy Powell

RICHARDSON AWARD

(Given annually by Golf Writers Association of America to individual who has made consistently outstanding contributions to golf.)

1948	Robert A. Hudson	1962	Walter Hagen
1949	Scotty Fessenden	1963	Joe & Herb Graffis
1950	Bing Crosby	1964	Cliff Roberts
1951	Richard Tufts	1965	Gene Sarazen
1952	Chick Evans	1966	Robert E. Harlow
1953	Bob Hope	1967	Max Elbin
1954	Babe Zaharias	1968	Charles Bartlett
1955	Dwight Eisenhower	1969	Arnold Palmer
1956	George S. May	1970	Roberto de Vicenzo
1957	Francis Ouimet	1971	Lincoln Werden
1958	Bob Jones	1972	Leo Fraser
1959	Patty Berg	1973	Ben Hogan
1960	Fred Corcoran	1974	Byron Nelson
1961	Joseph C. Dey, Jr.	1975	Gary Player

MOST IMPROVED GOLFERS—MEN PROS

Awarded by Golf Digest

1953	Doug Ford	1965	Randy Glover
1954	Bob Toski	1966	Gay Brewer
1955	Mike Souchak	1967	Dave Stockton
1956	Dow Finsterwald	1968	Bob Lunn
1957	Paul Harney	1969	Dave Hill
1958	Ernie Vossler	1970	Dick Lotz
1959	Don Whitt	1971	Jerry Heard
1960	Don January	1972	Jim Jamieson
1961	Gary Player	1973	Tom Weiskopf
1962	Bobby Nichols	1974	Tom Watson
1963	Tony Lema	1975	Pat Fitzsimons
1964	Ken Venturi		

MOST IMPROVED GOLFERS—WOMEN PROS

Awarded by Golf Digest

1954	Beverly Hanson	1965	Carol Mann
1955	Fay Crocker	1966	Gloria Ehret
1956	Marlene Hagge	1967	Susie Maxwell
1957	Mickey Wright	1968	Gerda Whalen
1958	Bonnie Randolph	1969	Donna Caponi
1959	Murle MacKenzie	1970	Jane Blalock
1960	Kathy Whitworth	1971	Jane Blalock
1961	Mary Lena Faulk	1972	Betty Burfeindt
1962	Kathy Whitworth	1973	Mary Mills
1963	Marilynn Smith	1974	JoAnne Carner
1964	Judy Torluemke	1975	JoAnn Washam

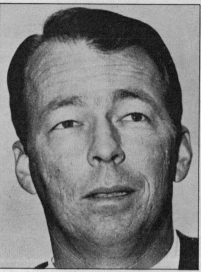

Walker Inman was named 1975 Professional of Year by PGA.

GOLF WRITING AWARDS

(Awarded by Brunswick-MacGregor. Entries are collected by the Golf Writers Association of America.)

1965	News: Bruce Phillips, Raleigh (N.C.) Times. Feature: Jerry Izenberg, Newark (N.J.) Star-Ledger.
1966	News: Sam Blair, Dallas Morning News. Feature: Phil Taylor, Seattle Post Intelligencer. Magazine: Gwilym S. Brown, Sports Illustrated.
1967	News: Art Spander, San Francisco Chronicle; Feature: Joe Schwendeman, Philadelphia Eve. Bulletin. Magazine: Herbert Warren Wind, Golf Digest.
1968	News: Jim Trinkle, Forth Worth Star-Telegram. Feature: Jack Patterson, Akron (O.) Beacon-Journal. Magazine: Cal Brown, Golf Digest.
1969	News, Gene Roswell, N.Y. Post (afternoon); Jim Trinkle, Ft. Worth Star-Telegram (morning); Feature: Doug Mintline, Flint (Mich.) Journal; Magazine, Dan Jenkins, Sports Illustrated.
1970	News, Blackie Sherrod, Dallas Times-Herald (afternoon); Art Spander, San Francisco Chronicle (morning); Feature, Sam Blair, Dallas Morning News; Magazine, Dan Jenkins, Sports Illustrated.
1971	News, Jack Patterson, Seattle Post (afternoon); Phil Taylor, Akron Beacon Journal (morning); Feature, Maury White, Des Moines Register; Magazine, Dan Jenkins, Sports Illustrated.
1972	News, Fred Russell, Nashville Banner (afternoon); D. L. Stewart, Dayton Herald-Journal (morning); Feature, Bill Beck, St. Louis Post-Dispatch; Magazine, Lee Mueller, Golf.
1973	News, Blackie Sherrod, Dallas Times-Herald (afternoon); D. L. Stewart, Dayton (Ohio) Journal Herald (morning); Feature, Dave Nightingale, Chicago Daily News; Magazine, Jim Trinkle, Golf.
1974	News, Bill Beck, St. Louis Post-Dispatch (afternoon); Marv Moss, Montreal Gazette (morning); Feature, Blackie Sherrod, Dallas Times-Herald; Magazine, Ross Goodner, Golf.

"MOST BEAUTIFUL GOLFER" WINNERS

Named by Golf Digest

1954	Dimmie Thompson, Greenville, S.C.
1955	Betty Jane Martinez, San Antonio, Tex., and Paula Ann West, Sacramento, Calif.
1956	Barbara Williams, Richmond, Calif.
1957	Judy Easterbrook, Peoria, Ill.
1958	Sally Bergman Robb, Cleveland, O.
1959	Elaine Woodman, Wichita, Kan.
1960	Florence Zupnik, Washington, D.C.
1961	Sue Dobson, Macomb, Ill.
1962	Carol Sorenson, Janesville, Wis.
1963	Nancy Albert, Trenton, N.J.
1964	Marlene Floyd, Fayetteville, N.C.
1965	Laura Anne MacIvor, Fort Walton Beach, Fla.
1966	Sharron Moran, Carlsbad, Calif.
1967	Margo Fletcher Brinkley, Raleigh, N.C.
1968	Carolyn Finley, Huntington Beach, Calif.
1969	Priscilla Sauter Grosch, Switzerland
1970	Jane Fassinger, New Wilmington, Pa.
1971	Laura Baugh, Long Beach, Calif.
1972	Jonya Stapp, Miami, Okla.
1973	Debbie De Agostine, Walkill, N.Y.
1974	Mary Cushing, San Antonio, Tex.
1975	Beth Boozer, Lawrence, Kan.

1975 STATE CHAMPIONS

LEGEND: O—Open; MA—Men's Amateur; WA—Women's Amateur; Pub—Publinks; LH—Left-handed; Sr—Senior; Jr—Junior; HS—High School.

ALABAMA: O-Rick Sirmon, Birmingham (am); MA-Frank (Buddy) Gardner, Montgomery; WA-Jane Reynolds, Huntsville; LH-Rickie Stukes, Decatur; Sr-Ossie Botwell, Mobile; Mrs. Conway Ellers, Enterprise; Jr-Allen Ritchie, Birmingham; Leah Oldacre, Prattville; HS (boys team)-Mountain Brook; (ind)- Allen Ritchie, Mountain Brook.

ARIZONA: O-Bill Garrett (pro); MA-Bill Meyers, Phoenix; WA-Diane Wolta, Phoenix (match); Mrs. Frank Bostock, Scottsdale (stroke); Pub-Mark Sollenberger, Tempe; LH-Andy Toth, Scottsdale; Sr-Ken Storey, Phoenix; Merle Windatt, Phoenix; Jr-Rip Vaugh, Lake Montezuma; Ann Feist, Phoenix; HS (boys team)-Coronado; (ind)-Mike Linsdey, Tempe; (girls team)-Maryvale; (ind)-Kelly Fuiks, Phoenix.

ARKANSAS: O-George McKeown (pro);MA-Louis Lee, Herber Springs (stroke); Ed Harris, N. Little Rock (match); WA-Rosemarye Bartlett, Little Rock; Pub-Ronald Richard, Ft. Smith; Sr-Willis Watkins, Conway; Jr-Doug Ward, Little Rock (match); Steve McElhonon, Fort Smith (stroke); HS (boys 4A-3A, 4-man team)-Northeast of North Little Rock; (ind)-John Juvenal, North Little Rock; (2A, 4-man team)-Camden; (ind)-Mark Bradshaw, Fordyce; (2A, 2-man team)-Van Buren; (ind)-Randy Buford, Fordyce; (A-B, 2-man team)-Gravette; (ind)-Charles Nuckles, Manila; (girls ind)-Leigh Bilger, El Dorado.

CALIFORNIA: O-Jimmy Powell, Los Angeles (pro); MA-John Cook, Rolling Hills Estates; No. Calif. MA-Scott Hoyt, Menlo Park; So. Calif. MA-Lee Davis, Los Angeles; WA-Jane Booth, Whittier; So. Calif. WA-Mrs. Paul E. Travis, Wilshire C.C.; No. Calif. Pub-Kim Flint, Sacramento; So. Calif. Pub-Roger Fagan, Western GC; Sr-Jude Poynter, Beverly Hills; No. Calif. Sr-Mat Palacio, San Rafael; So. Calif. Sr-John L. Connelly, Virginian C.C.; Jr-John Cook, Rolling Hills Estates; Debbie Stewart, Long Beach; No. Calif. Jr-Joe Rassett, Turlock; So. Calif. Jr-John Cook, Rolling Hills and Brett Mullin, Canyon Crest C.C.; Dayna Bensen, California C.C.; So. Calif. HS (boys team)-San Marcos of Santa Barbara; (ind)-Lennie Clements, Poway.

COLORADO: O-Pat Rea, Pueblo (pro) (stroke); Tim Branch, Boulder (match); MA-Larry Maurer, Boulder (stroke); Mark Crabtree, Ft. Collins (match); WA-Lynn Zmistowski, Boulder; Pub-Pat Eggling; Sr-Claude Wright, Denver (stroke); Les Fowler, Boulder (match); Vivian Dorsey, Denver; Jr-Kevin Spencer, Longmont (stroke); Terry Kahl, Aurora (match); Lauren Howe, Colorado Springs; HS (boys team)-Pueblo Centennial; (ind)-Jeff Armstrong, Pueblo.

CONNECTICUT: O-Jim Becker, Windsor (am); MA-Rev. William Lee, New Haven; WA-Marcia Dolan, Ridgewood CC; Sr-Sam Petrone, Bruce CC; Jr-Jerry Courville Jr.; Laura Vautrain, Wallingford; HS (boys team)-Westport, Staples; (ind) (div. 1)-Bob Wells, Westport; (div. 2)-Jeff Torrance, Manchester.

DELAWARE: O-Rick Osberg, Dover (pro), MA-Dave Corzillius, Smyrna; WA-Judy Robinson, Dover; Sr-Joe Sylvester; Jr-Larry Jones, Milford; HS (team)-Mt. Pleasant of Wilmington; (ind)-Larry Jones, Milford.

DISTRICT OF COLUMBIA: MA-Dave Allen, Mt. Vernon; WA-Sue Keeney, Arlington; Sr-Robert Morris, Argyl CC; Mrs. Amuel, Indian Spring CC; Jr-Mike Hopke, Belle Haven CC; Sally Voss, Congressional CC.

FLORIDA: O-Lee Wykle, Ormond Beach (pro); MA-Jack Veghte, Clearwater; WA-Evie Kirkland, Pensacola; LH-Keith Foster, Miami Springs; Sr-Norton Harris; Jr-Kevin Janiga; Connie Chillemi, Naples; HS (boys team)-John Carrol, Ft. Pierce; (ind)-Eric Slovenkay, Winter Park; (girls team) Lake Worth; (ind)-Constance Chillemi, Naples.

GEORGIA: O-Tommy Aaron (pro); MA-Mark Mike, LaGrange; WA-Ceil MacLaurin; LH-Farrell Hayes, Ringgold; Sr-Bill Zimmerman; Mrs. James Patton, Atlanta; Jr-Mike Cook, Cartersville; Teri Moody, Athens; HS (boys 3A team)-Columbus Hardaway; (ind)-Tom Brannen, Marietta; (2A team)-Forsyth County, Cumming; (ind)-James Black, College Park; (A team)-Riverwood; (ind)-Jay Lumpkin, Atlanta; (B team)-Athens Academy; (ind)- Griff Moody, Athens.

HAWAII: O-Allan Yamomoto (am) Hilo: O-Walter Kawakami, Honolulu; Kauai O-Randy Barenaba, Honolulu; Maui O-Clyde Kahalehau, Maui; MA-Keith Kollmeyer, Honolulu (stroke); Ken Miyaoka (match); WA-Debra Spencer, Honolulu; Pub-Allan Yamomoto; Sr-Walter Takiguchi, Honolulu; Jr-Clyde Rego (match); Kalua Makalena (stroke); Debra Spencer (match) Althea Tome (stroke).

IDAHO: O-Tom Storey, Las Vegas (pro); MA-Dave Molitor, Boise; WA-Kalli Voyce, Boise; Jr-Jo Lodge, Caldwell; Brenda Leese, Pocatello; HS (coed A team)-Caldwell; (ind)-Dee Swartz, Pocatello, and Jo Hubbard, Boise (tie); (B team)-Buhl; (ind)-Sam Hopkins, Middleton.

ILLINOIS: O-Bill Erfurth, Glencoe; MA-Mick Soli, DeKalb; WA-Desiree Alley, Waukegan; Sr-John Vogler, Downers Grove; Mrs. Edward Cooley, Winnetka; Jr-Lance Ten-Broeck, Chicago (stroke); Scot Brewster, Lake Forest (match); HS (boys 2A team)-Rockford Guilford; (ind)-Dave Ogrin, Waukegan; (A team)-Carmi HS; (ind)-Pat Venker, Normal; (girls team)-Waukegan East; (ind)-Ann Atwood, Bloomington.

INDIANA: O-Don Padgett II, Carmel (pro); MA-Scott Steger, Anderson; MA-Mrs. Cookie English, Indianapolis; Pub-Mike Komalanc, Indianapolis; Sr-Charles Harrell, Bloomington; Jr-Scott Bidimos, Gary; Kyle O'Brien, Indianapolis; HS (boys team) Yorktown; (ind)-Don LaPierre, Yorktown; (girls team)-North Central of Indianapolis; (ind)-Kyle O'Brien, North Central.

IOWA: O-John Frillman, Omaha; MA-Lon Neilsen, Belle Plaine; WA-Anita Harsch, Burlington; Jr-Mike McCutchen, Des Moines; Barbara Jo Miller, Lake Mills; HS (boys 2A team)-Oskaloosa; (ind)-Charley Porter, Oskaloosa; (A team)-Algona; (ind)-Dave Rummells, West Branch; (girls team)-Cedar Falls; (ind)-Deb Moler.

KANSAS: MA-Frank Rose, Topeka; WA-Karen McGee, Overland Park; Sr-Ralph Bevan, Wichita; Jean Metz; Jr-Steve Brown, Salina; Jennie Huvendick, Leavenworth; HS (boys 4-man team)-Shawnee Mission NW; (2-man team)-Wichita East; (ind)-Jeb Jenkins, Shawnee Mission; (girls 4-woman team)-Great Bend; (2-woman team)-Wichita North; (ind)-Nancy Horns, Leavenworth.

KENTUCKY: O-Larry Gilbert, Brandenbury (pro); MA-Kevin Proctor, Bowling Green; WA-Myra Van Hoose, Bowling Green; Pub-Mike Perpich, Louisville; Sr-Howard Jones, London; Mrs. E. Carter; Jr-Ralph Landrum, Elsmere; HS (boys team)- Doss; (ind)-Russ Cochoran, Paducah; (girls team)-Ballard; (ind)-Charlotte Allen.

LOUISIANA: O-Larry Griffen, New Orleans (pro); MA-Randy Simmons, Shreveport; WA-Ann Hollier, Opelousas; Sr-Andy Pilney, Metairie; Jr-Tim Graham, Baton Rouge; Deannie Wood, Shreveport; HS (boys team)-Nevil, Monroe; (ind)-Bob Cooper, Monroe.

MAINE: O-Bob Menne, Fla. (pro); MA-Ron Brown Jr., Riverside; WA-Mrs. Gordon White; Sr-Steve Polackwich; Mrs. Winslow Grant; Jr-Mike Nimi; HS (boys team)-Edward Little, Auburn; (ind)-Brian Hurley, Portland; Terry Holden, Bridgeton; Gary Varney, Milo (three-way tie); (girls ind)-Vicki Marceau.

MARYLAND: O-Marty West, Columbia (am); MA-Gary Mankulish, Crofton; WA-Joan Winchester, Baltimore; Sr-Robert Morris, Prince Georges; Mrs. Joseph Smyth, Congressional CC; Jr-Wayne DeFrancisco, Lakewood CC; Nancy Maunder, Baltimore; HS (coed team) Walt Whitman, Montgomery County; (ind)-David Hughes, Walt Whitman.

MASSACHUSETTS: O-Dick Hanscom, Newton; MA-Bruce Douglass, Brockton; WA-Jeanne-Marie Boylan, Milton; Pub-James Sullivan, Wellesley; Sr-Warren Tibbetts, Manchester, N.H.; Mrs. Paul G. Black, Marshfield; Jr-Paul Littlejohn, Braintree; Leslie Greis, Holden; HS (boys team)-Dennis-Yarmouth; (ind)-Flint Lincoln, E. Longmeadow; (girls ind)-Judy Farrell, Scituate.

MICHIGAN: O-Bob Ackerman, Bridgman (am); MA-Dan Pohl, Mt. Pleasant (match); Peter Green (stroke); WA-Suzanne Conklin, Ann Arbor; Pub-Bill MacDonald, Pontiac (match); Tom Proben (stroke); LH-Ron Kardynski, Livonia; Sr-Frank E. Richart Jr., Ann Arbor; Mrs. W. R. Dixon, Ann Arbor; Jr-Don Beardon and Jo Morris (tie); HS (boys A team)- Loy Norrix of Kalamazoo; (ind)-Dale Rob, Eisenhower; (B team)-Parma Western; (ind)-John Gibson, Tecumseh; (C team)-Detroit Country Day; (ind)-Glen Alexander, Detroit Country Day; (D team)-Catholic Central Manistee; (ind)-Neil Cichy, Catholic Central; (girls team)-Clarkston; (ind)-Martha Panfil, Hastings.

MINNESOTA: O-Mike Morley, Minot, N.D.; MA-Steve Johnson, North Branch; WA-Joan Garwin, Minneapolis (match); Julie Gumlia, Bemidji (stroke); Pub-Jeff Krummel, Duluth; Kay McMahon, Minneapolis; LH-Giles Koblika, St. Paul; Sr-Roy Widstrom, Minneapolis; Mrs. Edward J. Monahan Jr., Minneapolis; Jr-Bill Israelson, Bemidji; Julie Gumlia, Bemidji; HS (team)-Bemidji; (ind)-Dan Croonquist, St. Paul.

MISSISSIPPI: O-Mike Taylor, Meridian (am); MA-Mike Taylor, Meridian; WA-Wanda Hendrix, Jackson; Sr-Walter Johnson, Jackson; Jr-Robert Fulton, Pascagoula; Dale Bounds, Meridian.

MISSOURI: O-Bob Stone, Independence (pro); MA-Bruce Hollowell; WA-Barbara Berkmeyer, Glendale; Sr-Jack House; Jr-Bill Landis, Jefferson City; HS (boys team)-Springfield Glendale; (ind)-John Gentry, Glendale; (girls team)-Marceline; (ind)-Mary Smith, Marceline.

MONTANA: MA-Mike Barnett, Missoula; WA-Helen Tremper, Missoula; Sr-Maury Colberg, Billings; Jr-Rick Kloepfer, Billings; HS (boys team)-Missoula Sentinel; (ind)-Dave Kenyon, Sentinel; (girls team)-Roundup; (nd)-Shanda Imlay, Sentinel.

NEBRASKA: MA-Mike Klein, Scottsbluff (stroke); Dan Bahensky, Lincoln (match); WA-Theresa Wanek, Omaha; Sr-Gordon Saffer, Omaha; Jr (A)-Steve Buel, Omaha; (B)-John Donachie, Grand Island; Cathy Curry, Columbus; HS (boys A team)-Grand Island; (ind)-Greg Howell, Beatrice; Jay Huston, Grand Island; Bill Henderson, Scottsbluff (3-way tie); (B team)-Sidney; (ind)-Jeff Erwin, O'Neill; (C team)-Woodriver; (ind)-Sam Moyer, Woodriver; (girls team)-Omaha Marion; (ind)-Cathy Curry, Columbus.

NEVADA: O-Tom Storey, Las Vegas (pro); MA-Butch Sheehan, Reno; WA-Patty Sheehan, Reno; Pub-Phil Dickinson, Las Vegas; HS (boys team)-Wooster, Reno; (ind)-Alah Mahterian, Reno; (girls team)-Wooster, Reno; (ind)-Sally Sire, Reno.

NEW HAMPSHIRE: O-Byron Abbott, Keene (pro); MA-Paul Moriarty Jr., Nassua; WA-Sue Jordan, Franklin; LH-Glenn Dick, Charingfare; Sr-Henry Robbins; Kate Guest, Hanover; Jr-John Gimas, Derryfield; HS (boys team)-Keene; (ind)-Rick Palmer, Lebanon.

NEW JERSEY: O-Jack Keifer, Emerson (pro); MA-Chet Sanok, Montclair; WA-Cindy Ferro, Lawrenceville (match); Mrs. David Johnstone, Montclair (stroke); Pub-Norman Becker, Carteret; Sr-Chet Sanok, Montclair; Mrs. Pat Fisher; Jr-Bill Snouffer, Belleville.

NEW MEXICO: O-Jim Marshall, Phoenix (pro); MA-Ray Cragun, Albuquerque; WA-Nancy Romero, Soccoro; Jr-Steve Haskins, El Paso; Sherry Chandler, Las Cruces; HS (boys team)-Sandia; (ind)-Mark Pelletier, Sandia.

NEW YORK: MA-Alan Foster, Bellevue; WA-Sara Jane Stuhler, Ft. Johnson; Sr-Burt Kling, Rochester; Mrs. Philip Allen, Syracuse; Jr-James Gridley, Syracuse; Cindy Pietrusik, Lackawanna; HS (boys team)-Southwestern, Lakewood; (ind)-Rick Bell, Southwestern.

NORTH CAROLINA: O-Sam Adams (pro); MA-Lee Keesler, Charlotte; WA-Jan Disque, Greensboro; Sr-R. L. Rigsbee; Mary Emma Manley; Jr-Chris Newman; HS (boys team)-South Mecklenburg of Pineville; (ind)-Frank Acker, Fayetteville; (girls team)-Sanford Central; (ind)-Susan Cary, Raleigh.

NORTH DAKOTA: MA-Bob Dahm, Fargo; Sr-Loyd Orser, Bismark; Jr-Jeff Jessen, Dickinson; HS (boys team)-Red River of Grand Forks; (ind)-Dave Brown, Fargo South; (girls team)-Fargo South; (ind)-Wendy Wenz, Fargo South.

OHIO: O-Todd Crandall, Ashtabula (pro); MA-Rick Jones, Youngstown; WA-Gail Clayton, Portsmouth; Pub-Ken Hyland, Hartville; Sr-Dudley Humphrey, Cleveland; Jr-Mort Bertram, Portsmouth, and Ted Moore, Findley (tie); HS (boys 3A team)-Youngstown Ursuline; (A team)-Tuscarawas Central Catholic; (ind)-Mitch Camp, Orrville.

OKLAHOMA: O-Danny Edwards (pro); MA-Bill de Tournillon, Lubbock, Tex.; WA-Dale McNamara, Tulsa; Sr-Stormy Williams, Oklahoma City; Jr-Jeff McMillan; Margret Ward; HS (boys 4A team)-Putnam City; (ind)-Jim Woodard, Oklahoma City; (3A team)-Stillwater Donart; (ind)-Terry Collier, Ada; (2A team)-Comanche; (ind)-Dennis Lewis, Anadarko.

OREGON: O-Craig Griswold (pro); MA-Mitch Mooney, Seaside (match); John Pennington (stroke); WA-Judy Hoetmer, San Leandro, Calif.; Jr-Mitch Mooney, Seaside; Mary Lou Mulflur, Portland; HS (boys 3A team)-Portland Madison; (ind)-Glen Luikart, Grants Pass, and Jack Schneider, Clackamas (tie); (2A-A team)-Seaside; (ind)-Mitch Mooney, Seaside; (girls team)-Portland Parkrose; (ind)-Mary Mulflur, Portland.

PENNSYLVANIA: O-Steve Brewton, Valley Brook (am); MA-Jay Sigel, Philadelphia; WA-Carol Semple, Sewickley; Pub-Ed Malehorn, York; Sr-Russ Maitland, Gettysburg; Mrs. Harton Semple, Sewickley; Jr-Mike Forgash, Philadelphia; Mary Beth Lange, Philadelphia; HS (boys ind)-Russ Elken, Pennsbury; (girls ind)-Joan Hubbert, Upper Dublin.

RHODE ISLAND: O-Norm Lutz, Pawtucket (am); MA-Stan Abrams, E. Providence; WA-Mrs. Robert Kirouak, Barrington; Pub-Leo Marcotte Jr., N. Providence; Sr-Charles Pound; Barbara Groves; Jr-Matt Zito, Lincoln; Susan Santucci, Woonsocket; HS (boys team)-North Kingston; (ind)-Scott Teller, North Kingston.

SOUTH CAROLINA: O-Dick Horne, Mt. Pleasant (am); MA-Ken Wiland, Aiken (match); Parker Moore (stroke); WA-Carolyn Cudone, Myrtle Beach; LH-James W. Ford, Sumter; Sr-Jack Gordan, Clover; Jr-Bret Bauer, Summerville; HS (boys 4A team)-Aiken; (ind)-Mike King, Anderson; (3A team)-Greenville Bera; (ind)-Bruce Ericson, Myrtle Beach; (2A team)-Barnwell; (ind)-Randy Kinard, Georgetown; (A team)-Holly Hill; (ind)-Steven Bear, Holly Hill.

SOUTH DAKOTA: MA-Dave Hanten, Rapid City (stroke); Tom Hendricks, Yankton (match); WA-Peggy Schock, Sioux Falls; Pub-Jim Sorensen, Sioux Falls; Sr-Bob Walrath, Watertown; Jr-Pat McNeill, Sioux Falls; Coleen Darrah, Brookings; HS (boys A team)-Sioux Falls Washington; (B team)-Sully Buttes; (ind)-Scott Hofer.

TENNESSEE: O-Greg Powers, Nashville; MA-Frank Gusmus, Memphis; WA-Nancy Homes, Nashville; Sr-Jim Edwards; Jr-Lee Cheairs, Memphis; Charlotte Grant, Chattanooga; HS (boys team)-Memphis Christian Brothers; (ind)-Putter Robbins.

TEXAS: O-Ben Crenshaw, Austin; MA-Robert Hoyt, Houston; WA-Debbie Skelly, San Antonio; Pub-Judy Casey, Abilene; LH-Fred Blackmar, Corpus Christi; Sr-Frank Guernsey, Houston; Janet Blair, Dallas; Jr-Steven Bowman, Tyler; Sandy Young, Plano; HS (boys 4A team)-San Angelo Central; (ind)-Britt Harrison, Beaumont Forest Park; (3A team)-Eisenhower HS, Houston; (ind)-Craig Barton; (2A team)-McCamey HS; (ind)-Doug Adams, McCamey; (A team)-Rankin HS; (ind)-Donnie O'Bannon; (girls 4A team)-Midland; (ind)-Liz Norton, Midland Lee; (3A team)-San Antonio East Central; (ind)-Peggy Guestavson, Brenham; (2A team)-Spearman; (ind)-Linda Hunt, Olney; (A team)-Farwell; (ind)-Sheri Haynes, McLean.

UTAH: O-Mike Brannan, San Jose, Calif. (am); MA-Don Branca, Salt Lake City; WA-Bev Nelson, Salt Lake City; Sr-Walt Gresham, Salt Lake City; Jr-Mike Bouich, Salt Lake City; Jody Reuss, Salt Lake City; HS (boys 4A team)-Brighton HS; (ind)-Scott Brandt, Brighton; (3A team)-Jordan HS; (ind)-Jay Don Blake, Dixie; (2A-A team)-Richfield; (ind)-John Hummel, Richfield.

VERMONT: O-Jim Browning; MA-John Donnelly, Kwiniaska C.C.; WA-Cindy Paquet, Kwiniaska C.C.; Sr-Bob Clifford, Burlington; Jr-Steve Salerno, Montpelier; HS boys team)-Champlain Valley Union; (ind)-Gary Shover, Kwiniaska; (girls ind)-Marsha Hier.

VIRGINIA: O-Chip Heyl, Reston (am); MA-Curtis Strange, Suffolk; WA-Nancy Hollenbeck, Arlington; Sr-Landon Buchanan, Roanoke; Mrs. Donald O'Brien, Virginia Beach; Jr-Bill Woolard, Virginia Beach; Barbara Moran, Richmond; HS (boys team)-Charlottesville Albermarle; (ind)-Richard Tucker, Virginia Beach.

WASHINGTON: O-Fred Haney, Portland; A-Bob Burton, Everett; WA-Edean Ihlanfeldt, Seattle; Pub-Shirley Fopp, Tacoma; Sr-Manley McDowell, Seattle; Jr-Mike Hammermeister, Yakima; HS (boys 3A team)-Burlington Edison; (ind)-Jeff McMillen; (2A team)-Eastmont; (ind)-Ron Jones.

WEST VIRGINIA: O-Barney Thompson, Barboursville; MA-Bill Campbell, Huntington; WA-Caroline Hornor, Clarksburg; Sr-Henry McCoy, Sistersville; Maxine Gilmore; HS (boys team)-S. Charleston; (ind)-Bryan Beymer, Huntington.

WISCONSIN: O-Rick Rasmussen, Madison (am); MA-John Pallin, Fond du Lac; WA-Jackie Hayes, Madison; Pub-Mike Plantz, O'Dana Hills Club; LH-Dave Wernicker, Whitnall Park Club; Sr-Sam Ruskin, Brynwood Club; Jr-Steve Krause, Muskego; Andrea Welch, Black Hawk Club; HS (boys team)-Fond du Lac; (ind)-Dan Nimtz; (girls team)-Madison West; (ind)-Larl Huxhold, Fond du Lac.

WYOMING: O-Mel Curci, Indian Wells, Calif.; MA-Brad Butler, Casper; WA-Kandy Holmes, Cheyenne; Pub-Laura Bencriscutto, Racine; Jr-Larry Uroszek, Sheridan; HS (boys 2A team)-Gillette; (ind)-Bob Bennett, Casper; (A team)-Green River; (ind)-Brant Williams, Newcastle.

1975 CLUB CHAMPIONS

ALABAMA
Andalusia: M. Mathews; C. Kyzar
Anniston: J. Phillips
Birmingham: A. Yeilding; J. Miller
Bonnie Crest: E. Vaughan; C. Wilder
Burningtree: A. Jones; E. Tannehill
Clay County: C. Chapman
Demopolis: M. Bell
Dothan: J. Brennan; C. Harris
Fayette: D. Bell; J. Martin
Florence: D. White; K. Atkins
Green Valley: C. Stanford; M. Bartz
Huntsville: F. Campbell Sr.;
    F. Edmondson
Indian Hills: B. Mullins; N. McCall
Maxwell AFB: B. Carroll;
    R. Meyer, J. Johnson
Musgrove: S. Hudson; D. Gold
Saugahatchee: B. Dumas; W. Boyd
Turtlepoint: J. Stockard; B. Price

ARIZONA
Ahwatukee: R. Worsley; F. Bourdette
Alpine: B. Collins; M. Parizek
Antelope Hills: A. Edwards; M. Albee
Arizona: A. Thum; M. Hornbake
Cobre Valley: A. Ambros; B. Grice
Desert Hills: J. Russell; B. Cooper
Desert Sands: B. Bentley; B. Bentley
Encanto: B. Meyer; K. Mancuso

Golden Hills: M. Whitelawn; P. Spelta
Lake Havasu: J. Meyers; T. Stone
Maryvale: M. Shepard; K. Mancuso
Oakcreek: D. Watson; E. Mahannah
Phoenix: P. Brignall; J. Thomas
Pima: J. Mitchell; B. Gantz
Prescott: H. Alexander; J. Clark
Rolling Hills: C. Sosa; S. Sisk
Show Low: J. Coppedge; K. Chapman
Sierra Estrella: T. Hasbrouck
Sun City: H. Sapakie; G. Strecker
Thunderbird: J. Bodell; D. Smid
Tubac: H. Wheless; H. Hansman
Villa Monterey: L. Amato; D. Egan
Yuma: D. Brown; R. Brasher

ARKANSAS
Blytheville: C. Campbell Jr.; M. Hale
Camden: B. Cook; P. Kyser
Dawn Hill: D. Crockett, J. Hayes,
    R. Syler
El Dorado: S. Saulsbury; Mrs. N. Price
Fayetteville: J. Shreve; Mrs. C. Elwell
Jaycee: O. Taylor; M. Bryant
Jonesboro: S. Puryear; L. Kirkley
Little Rock AFB: J. Adkins; J. Tarver
Little Rock: W. Daniels Jr.;
    Mrs. T. Shea
North Hills: T. Williams; S. Bost
Pleasant Valley: D. Thornally;
    Mrs. J. Fryer
Prairie Creek: B. Whitaker; M. Warden

Riverlawn: D. Donaldson; D. Anderson
South Haven: G. Long; M. Miers
Western Hills: G. Carter

CALIFORNIA
Alisal: M. Muraoka; J. Pedersen
Almaden: D. Allen; L. Hodge
Altadena: M. Estes; A. Frost
Anaheim: G. Ledford
Ancil Hoffman Park: J. Cronick;
    S. Dauber
Annandale: B. Gaddy; V. Smith
Antelope Valley: R. Munoy; C. Anthony
Auburn Valley: D. Bingham;
    J. Fitzgerald
Bakersfield: R. Hestley; A. Bury
Bel-Air: J. Miles; P. MacCullum
Bishop: T. Murphy; L. Hudec
Blackberry Farm: R. Harmon; P. Ogden
Bonita: N. Therkien; A. Osborn
Brookside: C. Wilson; M. Newcomb
Calabasas Park: D. Barth; J. Paul
Calero Hills: B. Bennert; D. Pugh
California: D. Rasley; Mrs. R. Schulz
Cameron Park: D. Johnson;
    K. Woodward
Carlton Oaks: T. Kuhn
Chevy Chase: R. Detman; A. Hays
Chimney Park: J. Smock; D. Hunter
Chula Vista: B. Johnson; P. Majors
Center: W. Price; S. Sanchez
Cold Springs: R. Grove; C. Edwards

Costa Mesa: E. Cabrera; B. Leonard
Cottonwood: T. Prince; C. Hadl
Crystal Aire: J. Gibbons; L. Howard
Cypress Hills: Mrs. H. Canavan
Davis Municipal: L. Caster;
    W. Whitson
Debell: G. Pelow; M. Scozzola
Deep Cliff: T. Bertken
Del Norte: W. Speer III; B. Spencer
Del Safari: J. Thompson; M. Grimelli
Diamond Oaks: J. Liskum; S. Dauber
El Caballero: S. Gealer; H. Knight
Elkins Ranch: C. Smith
Fairway Glen: Mrs. T. Winters
Fig Garden: P. Carosso; A. Costales
Fort Ord: R. Hammel; Mrs. R. Robbins
Fort Washington: G. Moran;
    E. Merzoian
Haggin Oaks: B. McInroe; K. Derby
Hasley Canyon: B. Smith;
    S. O'Callaghan
Healdsburg: B. Simon; B. McCaffrey
Indian Creek: R. Germona; C. Jordan
Jurupa Hills: G. Hoxie; I. Lusk
King City: A. Kinney; E. Clark
La Costa: G. Hodde; M. Gray
LaCumbre: D. Baskous; Mrs. G. Orr
Laguna Hills: R. Gregg; V. Royer
La Jolla: T. Brown; A. Schroeder
Lake Chabot: T. McElhatton;
    N. Stevenson
Lake Charles: G. Quarles; J. Smith
Lake Don Padro: B. Reeves

Lake of the Pines: G. Topper;
    H. Rothschild
Lake Shastina: E. Irwin; M. Zvehlke
Las Positas: V. Wolfe, J. Griffin;
    L. Prince, P. Rodermund
Lincoln Park: H. Canavan
Little Knoll: L. Banchero; D. Swenson
Little River: T. McBroom; E. Chernoff
Los Robles Greens: S. Swain;
    C. Mansbridge
Los Serranos: Mrs. B. Hallum
Los Verdes: C. Hunt; R. Bills
Madera: T. Ortiz; A. Leming
Marina: F. Green
Marine Memorial: C. Scaran;
    J. Abrahams
Mather: J. Turnbull Jr.; P. Ross
Meadow Lake: J. Marshall; A. Johnston
Meadowood: Mrs. R. Boucke
Montebello: D. Brown; T. Blyth
Napa Valley: N. Kincaid; B. Sands
Naval Postgraduate School:
    E. Johnson; T. Brown
Navy: L. Merrick; S. Bennett
North Ridge: B. Chatham; K. Dushane
Norwalk: D. Ashcraft; B. Gilliland
Oakmont: G. Goodman; M. Hansen
Old Ranch: T. Gorelli; B. Straub
Olympic: J. Luceti; E. Guggenhime
Osbrinks: A. Hetherington; E. Carlin
Pala Mesa: T. Beck
Palos Verdes: S. Croft; A. McAllister
Pauma Valley: S. Erickson; R. Hume

That championship spirit

When a man wins his club championship for the ninth time it shouldn't come as much of a surprise, but the members of Twin Orchard Country Club near Chicago regard the triumph of Bernie Katz last fall as little short of a miracle.

Katz, 58, had come back from a herniated disc on the spinal cord, an ailment which required surgery and 17 weeks of hospitalization and left him paralyzed.

"If it weren't for golf," Katz says, "I wouldn't be walking. It gave me an incentive, something to keep working for."

Katz, co-owner of a sportswear store in Chicago, formerly played to a scratch handicap. He set his course record of 65, which still stands. He qualified for the U.S. Amateur in 1956, beat Bob Willits of Kansas City in his first match and took Walker Cupper Ward Wettlaufer to the 19th hole before losing in the second round.

In 1970, while playing golf in Florida, Katz bent down to tee the ball, stepped back to glance down the fairway—and couldn't move his legs. He underwent surgery and for the next six weeks was carried from

treatment room to treatment room on a table. Later he got around in a wheelchair, then graduated to crutches and special braces.

Two years after his surgery, Katz returned to the golf course with a brace on his right leg and a crutch in his left hand. He swung the club with his right hand.

Among those who wrote letters of encouragement were Ben Hogan, Chi Chi Rodriguez and Bob Toski.

Katz continued to improve his golf and entered the 1975 club championship, a 72-hole, stroke-play event held over two weekends in September, with a 6-handicap.

Gone were the brace and the crutch, but Katz's legs were still so weak he could walk only a few steps at a time, so he rode a car. He shot rounds of 81-77-78-77 and won the championship by two strokes.

Following him down the 18th fairway the final day were 150 club members who joined in a tumultuous cheer after Katz putted out.

"I've had many happy days in golf," Katz said, "but nothing compared to this."

Point Mugu: M. Brown; W. Tibbs
Porter Valley: B. Ritzinger; R. Dwyer
Rancho Calif.: B. Cavic
Redlands: J. Foley; M. Farquhar
Riverside: B. Williams
River View: J. Wood; N. Brown
San Jose: N. Woodruff; S. Woodruff
Santa Ana: B. Selman; C. Kinzie
San Gabriel: R. Hatfield;
Mrs. R. Fogwell
San Geronimo Nat'l: Mrs. N. Gapinski
San Marcos: W. Shipley
Santa Teresa: Mrs. P. Hamilton
Saticoy: R. Honeycutt; A. Green
Sebastopol: T. Birnie; D. Cate
Sepulveda: J. Short; D. Romain
Sharp Park: H. Canavan
Singing Hills: Mrs. D. Peters
Skylinks: J. Newell; E. Wigton
Sonoma Nat'l: J. Knego; R. Stone
Spring Valley: J. Barr; A. Amundsen
Spyglass Hill: D. Silva; P. Patch
Stardust: D. Keith; M. Kiner
Stone Ridge: L. Kubiak; S. Brownbeck
Sun City: G. Lance; J. Thorpe
Sunnyside: D. Makasian;
Mrs. C. Hamlin
Sunol Valley: R. Keller; J. Warwick
Table Mountain: C. Martens; N. Grieb
Tahoe City: R. Doyle; P. Cross
Torrey Pines: B. Imlay; D. Skinner
Tracy: J. Landis; L. Ruis
Tucker Oaks (Anderson):
D. Dallagiacomo; B. Bennett
Turlock: J. Rassett; L. Maruer
Twain Harte: J. Turner; H. Recek
US Army Hawaii G.A.: R. Gomard;
J. Kamisugi
University Village: W. Dyer;
I. Hollarman
Valley Hi: R. Levin; Mrs. L. Browning
Van Buskirk Park: D. Codog
Vandenberg AFB: M. Kazak; J. Peyrot
Victoria: A. Wilson; V. Halbrooks
Warmen's: E. Kelly
Western Hills: D. Good; B. Miller
West Winds: E. Gillberg
Wikiup: B. Scuri; M. Helmy
Wilshire: J. Williams; Mrs. P. Travis
Yolo Fliers: P. Perugino;
Mrs. G. Yeager

CANADA
Aurora Highlands: A. Albright;
M. Chapman
Beloeil: A. Jette; M. Klassen
Burlington: T. Zaw; J. Rosart
Calgary: R. Alexander; T. McCaffery
Canyon Meadows: L. Parks;
D. Kortgaard
Cataraqui: M. Amson; C. Cartwright
Chedoke: B. LeMaire, W. Wilton;
J. Ricker
Chinguacousy: G. Anderson;
D. Anderson
Cutten: P. McGregor; D. Morgan
Glendale: W. Abbot; C. Abel
Glen Eagle: B. Street; H. Johnson
Hamilton: G. Gibson; Mrs. D. Parks
Highland: R. Rhoades; B. Cole
Islington: P. Gilbert; B. Gilbert
Ki-8-eb: R. Sicard; Y. Picotte
Lambton: L. Biddie; J. Kirkpatrick
LaTuque: D. Merril; D. Savoy
Laval Sur Le Lac: P. Archambault;
S. Labrie
Lookout Point: S. Billyard; A. Sharpe
Lorraine: A. Dutriszc; M. Garneau
Maple Downs: M. Firestone; E. Waxer
Norfolk: H. McGhie; D. McDowell
Point Grey: J. Russell;
Mrs. L. McCulloch
Port Colborne: R. Noyes; S. Sherk
Richmond: T. Nemetz; J. Kless
St. Catherine's: R. Laugher;
H. Chyplick
St. Georges Beauce: Y. Pelletier;
F. Veilleux
Southwood: G. Speirs; S. Thomson
Thunderbay: T. Stokaluk
Wainwright: J. McDonald; R. Percival
Westfield: J. Golding; C. Deakin

COLORADO
Adams County: A. Stinnett; J. Hetzler
Applewood: D. Einspahr; J. Lambert
Aurora: D. Johnson; R. Bartlett
Boulder: R. Pierson; J. Bailey
Chatfield: P. Pollard; M. Dorr
Cherry Hills: R. Moore; Mrs. G. Wright
Collindale: R. Vanderslice; C. Ward
Colorado City: K. Kepley; L. White
Colorado Springs: B. Veigele Jr.;
L. Brunkhorst
Columbine: T. Grant III;
Mrs. F. Richards
Cortez: C. Herndon; E. Skinner
Eaton: M. Spencer; G. Childers
Eisenhower: W. Simmons; M. Miller
Flatirons: N. Renfro; Mrs. B. Ross
Foothills: Mrs. J. Laraby
Fort Collins: R. Baker; V. Shaner
Greeley: L. Eaton; T. King
Green Gables: S. Miller;
Mrs. E. Hyman
Heather Ridge: J. Loechel;
P. Anderson
Highland Hills: B. Heiny
Hillcrest: J. Young; G. Thompson
Inverness: H. Parker
Lakewood: V. Sachs; A. Grady
Loveland: H. Squier; M. Giaque
Lowry: G. Brown; M. Shockley
Meadow Hills: G. Baxstrom;
P. Chambers
Perry Park: L. Tolley; S. Henderson
Pueblo City Park: P. Ivan; E. Morgan
Ranch: B. Drake; R. Young
Rolling Hills: J. Woodard; T. Fleming
Shadow Hills: B. Lynn; D. Payne
Sterling: M. Bodkin; R. Bruce
Sunset: D. Schoy; M. Wolfe
Tiara Rado: R. Olson; B. Hickman
Vail: P. Etters; P. Wolfe
Valley: L. Scott; J. Settle
Walsenburg: B. Hyde
Willis Case: J. Rozmiarek;
K. Fiorella
Woodmoor: D. DeGeare; B. Bartlett

Home run
Baseball fans will remember southpaw Jack Harshman's effective pitching for the Chicago White Sox a few years ago. Now 46, Harshman has found a new love—golf. A 2-handicapper, Harshman in 1975 won his seventh men's title at the Cedar Knob Golf Club, Somers, Conn. Yes, he's a left-handed golfer.

CONNECTICUT
Aspetuck Valley: K. Bowden;
N. Putnam
Avon: J. Brunoli; G. Appell, P. Mandly
Banksville: J. Kennedy; D. Collins
Bel Compo: P. Marquis
Black Hall: D. Soccoli;
Mrs. S. Comstock
Brooklawn: R. Bodine Jr.; G. Felis
Brownson: D. Hotchkiss; J. Bondos
Bruce: A. Beatini; Mrs. A. Evans
Burning Tree: M. Sullivan;
A. Chambless
Candlewood Lake: D. Baines;
D. Luckenbill
Cedar Knob: J. Harshman; M. Masley
Cedar Ridge: G. Smith; S. Bond
Century Hills: J. Crosby;
E. Donaldson
Chippanee: G. McQuillan; M. Funk
Cliffside: S. Liebman; E. Zieky
Clinton: B. Coman; J. Kinsley
Darien: B. Whaley; P. Everson
East Hartford: T. Gorman;
G. Toussaint
Ellington Ridge: S. Goodman;
W. Ehrlich
Fairchild/Wheeler: N. Mastroni
Farmington: D. Britschgi;
Mrs. W. MacLachlan
Farmington Woods: D. Garczewski;
L. D'Addabbo
Farms: M. Buck III; Mrs. N. Johnson
Glastonbury Hills: J. Nikander;
Mrs. E. Daly
Glen Hollow: M. Block;
Mrs. H. Gutwillig
Grassy Hill: G. Leahy; L. Perl
Greenwich: B. Shea; Mrs. L. Dennis
Green Woods: J. Staszowski;
M. Staszowski
Harrisville: W. Cooke
Hartford: J. Suisman; J. Kohn
Hillandale: M. Tishler; K. Fahy
Hop Brook: M. Baronowski
Hop Meadow: D. Haley;
Mrs. J. Kurek Jr.
Hubbard Heights: B. Fitzpatrick;
Mrs. A. Clepea
Indian Hill: D. Zimonis; I. Scauillo
Innis Arden: E. Cleaves; L. Munro
Lake Waramaug: B. Baxter; S. Angell
Laurel View: W. Miller; D. Barnes
Litchfield: D. Goss; Mrs. L. Cornell
Lyman Meadow: R. Shaw
Madison: S. Hadfield; A. Welsh
Milbrook: D. Smith; Mrs. W. Goelkel
Mill River: J. Pinto; H. Rossi
New Haven: B. Clinton;
Mrs. C. Anderson
New London: T. Daniels; D. Turisco
Newtown: S. Tilly; D. Cubelli
Norwich: R. Tangari
Oak Hills: J. Russo; A. Whitman
Oak Lane: L. Liebman;
Mrs. M. Scholsohn
Old Lyme: R. Ebbets;
Mrs. S. Comstock
Orange Hills: J. Buraceski;
L. Petitte
Oronoque Valley: B. Ruby;
Mrs. J. MacDonald
Patterson: B. Hajas; Mrs. B. Peck
Patton Brook: J. Dulac; P. Fancher
Pautipaug: C. Peichowski;
N. Ruszyk
Pequot: P. Stefanski; L. Jacobik
Pine Orchard: S. Martin; S. Ford
Pine Valley: R. Defosses
Ridgewood: A. Butera; M. Dolan
Rockledge: J. Pinto; T. Schuman
Rock Rimmon: R. Epstein; D. Epstein
Round Hill: C. McAdam;
Mrs. C. Chadsey
Sharon: F. Noyes Jr.; P. Robinson
Shennecossett: L. Demers; L. D'Atri
Shorehaven: E. Berndt; Mrs. R. Graf
Shuttle Meadow: W. Watson Jr.;
M. Crothers
Silvermine: S. Caulkin; M. Squires
Simsbury Farms: K. Foster; V. Huckel
Stanwich: S. Green; Mrs. R. Bendheim
Sterling Farms: B. Thieme;
J. Van Munching
Suffield: B. Magnuson; A. Hanzalek
Tamarack: P. Fiorita; Mrs. P. Dinter
Torrington: R. Weigold; A. Merchand
Wallingford: B. McCaw Jr.;
Mrs. C. Earley
Wampanoag: R. Long; D. McKown
Waterbury: T. Gleeton; Mrs. K. Keggi
Watertown: Ms. J. Zailckas
Wee Burn: T. Robbins; B. Montgelas
Western Hills: B. Loman; B. Danaher
Woodbridge: S. Kroop; Mrs. H. Levine
Woodway: J. Kelly; N. Wolcott

DELAWARE
Cavaliers: P. Freccia; T. Locke
Dover: W. Dembrock
Garrison's Lake: J. Bernard
Hercules: J. Osberg; C. Dawson
Maple Dale: R. Faries; T. Wood
Newark: J. Tutthe; Mrs. M. McDowell
Rehoboth Beach: D. Grayes; J. McNatt
Seaford: D. Eisenhauer; D. Bremner

DISTRICT OF COLUMBIA
Andrews AFB: R. Spiers; A. Gentle
Rock Creek: P. Fogarty; H. Liana

FLORIDA
Airport Inn: S. Doolin; I. Larson
T. Bolt's: P. Moody; E. Anderson
Bradentown; P. Catalano; A. Sanford
Broken Woods: C. Hess; E. Pierce
Brooksville: R. Anderson;
C. Wainwright
Calusa: J. Haverty; J. Brezin
Capri Isles: L. Huston; B. Overby
Cocoa/Rockledge: M. Smyth
Continental: J. Otto; E. Ryan
Coral Ridge: H. MacCallum; C. Lowell
Delray Dunes: P. Demick; E. Heath
East Bay: B. Curtis; M. Howell
Eglin: G. Nelson; B. Mickael
Errol Estate: H. Marchman;
H. Gregoire
Fort Lauderdale: P. Dixon;
J. Brumbaugh
Gainesville: B. Mims; N. Coons
Indian Rocks: J. Bielat; E. Morrow
Inverness: E. Libert; E. Hick
Jacarande: R. Griffiths;
P. Lindbloom
John's Island: B. Young; L. Cassady
Kings Bay: J. Feinberg; D. Macht
Lago Mar: T. Templin; C. Templin
Lake City: J. Rountree; F. Bowling
Lake Lorraine: Mrs. J. Hart
Longboat Key: J. Tanner; J. Corley
Lost Tree: W. Bronson;
Mrs. J. Whitaker
Mount Dora: C. Bowman; R. Norton
Naples: L. Cunningham; S. Fyke
Naval Training Center: D. Brague;
J. Hichew
Oak Hill: J. Grice
Palma Ceia: J. Hodge; O. Byars
Palm Beach Lakes: A. Menne
Pelican: D. Ahern; J. Eckstein
Point o' Woods: L. Fraser;
E. Donovan
Port Malabar: M. Arbogast; E. Gera
Punta Gorda: J. Walker; L. McFee
Redland: B. Fitzpatrick Jr.; T. Munz
Riomar: R. Dodge; B. Wilson
Rio Pinar: J. Byington; S. Carter
Rolling Hills: B. Shoemaker Jr.;
P. Lucas
Sara Bay: S. LeBlanc; K. Mann
Sebring: F. Voxbrich; T. Akin
Sombrero: C. Bayles; Mrs. B. Thomas
Timuquana: G. Conner;
Mrs. T. Madison
University: P. Smith;
Mrs. J. Landversicht
University Park: R. McCahan;
C. Bryant
Westview: J. Langer; R. Leoni
Willow Brook: Mrs. H. Kesterson
Winewood: T. Brown Jr.; L. Duke
Winter Park: D. Bailey; L. McElroy
Yacht: M. Hamilton; E. Destefano

Try, try again
Seven times Whitey Richey, 62, had been runner-up in the men's championship at the Indian Lake Country Club, Indianapolis. But in 1975 he ruined his image—he won.

GEORGIA
Atlanta: J. Olsen; Mrs. J. LeCraw
Arrowhead: K. Blevins
Brookfield West: C. Uhl; M. Van Horn
Brunswick: S. Torbett; M. Melnyk
Callier Springs: M. Ball; L. Horton
Canongate-on-Lanier: B. Johnson;
J. Acker
Canton: K. Page
Cartersville: M. Cook
Chattahoochee: S. Towson;
T. Maginnis
Cherokee: J. Brennan III; N. Agry
Columbus: J. Holman; S. Fabian
East Lake: R. McClearen; L. Ford
Elks (Calhoun): R. Davis
Fairington: J. Stevenson; E. Thorton
Flat Creek: S. Powers; P. Hubbard
Ft. McPherson: B. Reimers; S. Johnson
Georgia Warm Springs: S. Waller;
M. McKenzie
Green Island: A. Dudley
Griffin: T. Smith Jr.; M. Burdeshaw
Houston Lake: B. McDonald; C. Gann
Hunter: R. Nonnenberg
Lakeside: R. Samples; M. Wise
Marshwood at the Landings: B. Jones;
Mrs. H. Bouchillon
Newnan: J. Mottola; P. Keiser
Northwood: B. Dahlgren; E. Hannan
Peachtree: J. Cleveland
Pinetree: J. Mitchell; F. Cox
Riverside: W. Robertson; A. Prickett
Sandy Run: K. Onsted
Snapfinger Woods: L. Kelly
Spring Hill: V. Marcoullier; J. Milam
Standard Club: A. Kaminsky; R. Edlin
Swainsboro: L. Parrish
West Lake: M. Steed; Mrs. L. Pogue

HAWAII
Mid-Pacific: C. Kong; T. Nagatoshi
Waialae: P. Spengler Jr.; P. Anderson

IDAHO
Aspen Acres: W. Robertson; N. Algood
Broadmore: W. Peterson; C. Lindsey
Burley: K. Huizinga; S. Sorenson
Crane Creek: J. Bunker; C. Ayres
Hillcrest: F. Bento; J. Teters
Jefferson Hills: J. George; M. Williams
Lewiston: V. Thomas; B. Bond
Plantation: T. West; R. Stone
Rexburg: K. Vernon; L. Womack
Soda Springs: D. Allred;
R. Transtrum
Warm Springs: R. Spaeth; L. Blade

ILLINOIS
American Legion (Edwardsville):
T. Martin; B. Bates
Aurora: J. Haried; S. Arendt
Barrington Hills: J. Wagner; J. Kinne
Bartlett Hills: G. Roloff; J. Pitchitino
Benton: J. Hill; V. Wyskiver
Big Run: J. Heimann; K. Newman
Biltmore: B. Heyn; S. Douglas
Bloomington: M. Milligan; M. Vaughn
Bob O'Link: P. Day Jr.
Briarwood: R. Cole; S. Mandel
Brookwood: D. Nudelman; D. Shaffer
Bryn Mawr: L. Rosenberg; B. Cohen
Buffalo Grove: D. Vandersande;
J. Laurie
Bureau Valley: M. Morel; Mrs. T. Cook
Burnham Woods: R. Brown;
S. Lashbrook
Butler National: B. Shean Jr.
Butterfield: J. Flanagan;
Mrs. E. Somerville
Calumet: J. Aurelio; Mrs. L. Boewe
Cary: R. Carroll; C. Grelle
Cherry Hills: R. Pavlowski; J. Grobner
Chicago: T. Cisar
Chicago Heights: A. Paci; A. Costello
Cog Hill: V. Salmans
Crab Orchard: J. Tucker; S. McCree
Crawford County: K. Correll;
B. Cunningham
Cress Creek: L. Gibson; Mrs. D. Scott
Crystal Woods: D. Rosing; C. Craig
Danville: M. Hoffman; J. Miller
Decatur: K. Wilson, V. Barnes
Dixon: W. Clevenger; M. Krahenbuhl
Edgewood: H. Gahr; G. Macchio
Edgewood Valley: G. Warner; M. Olson
Effingham: S. Hancock; D. Pillers
Elgin: T. Boyer; S. Reagan
Elks (Danville): J. Springer;
G. Rausch
Elks (Lincoln): P. Werkman;
B. Peacock
Evanston: M. McDermott; N. Meinken
Florrmoor: F. Meekins; H. Parrad
Fox Bend: K. Arnold; M. McKenzie
Freeport: T. Seely; L. Steenrod
Fresh Meadow: G. Straka
Geneva: R. Bricher; G. Barse
Gillespie: P. Brown
Glen Flora: D. Hiner; C. Reedy
Glen Oak: D. Huske; J. Kuoni
Glen View: M. Louis; Mrs. H. Becker
Glenview Park: D. Rowlands;
B. Sterner
Green Acres: R. Welch; G. Luckman
Hickory Point: R. Goodman; E. Pope
Highland: W. Tuffli; D. Basler
Highland Park: B. Barnett; J. Baltimore
Highland Park (Bloomington):
L. Berner III; N. McMeekan
Hillcrest (Long Grove):
G. Bartelstein; L. Matlin
Hillcrest (Washington): J.Theine;
S. Boyle
Hinsdale: B. Creed; M. Haarlow
HISA: D. Haney; F. Phipps
Idlewild: S. Cole; M. Rosenthal
Illini: R. Leistner; J. Foran
Indian Bluff: M. Madden; D. Schuber
Indian Creek: D. Vaughan;
J. Stephens
Indian Hill: R. Porter Jr.;
Mrs. E. Cooley
Inverness: P. John; H. Clitherow
Ithasca: P. Busch; J. Schwarz
Jacksonville: R. Neff; L. Cox
Jasper County: D. Hout; V. Spencer
Joliet: J. Oberwortmann; M. Silk
Kankakee: R. Ferrias; E. Wertz
Kaufman Park: L. Zibert; W. Sauder
LaGrange: S. Vidmer; Mrs. D. Metzg
Lake Bluff: J. Ryskiewicz; M. Miller
Lake Bracken: J. Foutch; C. Graham
Lake Shore: H. Foreman Jr.;
Mrs. F. Mayer
Lakeview: T. Schofield; E. Schimans
Lawrence County: D. Greenlee;
T. Scott
Lena: G. Taylor; R. Ziegler
Lincolnshire: T. Elmblad; D. Pilotto
Lincolnshire Fields: B. Rice;
D. Higgins
Longwood: B. Scardine
MAC Scott: J. Hall; G. Freas
Marengo Ridge: R. Ellett;
C. Hellemann
Mattoon: D. Stapleton; M. Hoots
Meadow Woods: C. Pitee; K. Saul
Medinah: J. Green Jr.; Mrs. B. Carls
McHenry: A. Jackson; M. Bishoff
Midlothian: T. Cramsie; M. McDoug
NAS (Glenview): G. Manning; J. Ill
Nelson Park: R. Anderson
North Shore: A. Ellis; Mrs. J. Thoma
Oak Park: J. Wheatland;
Mrs. P. Goodwillie
Oakwood: D. Willard; B. Johnson
Old Elm: H. Gardner
Olympia Fields: B. Gunn; U. Walton
Onwentsia: G. Bennett;
Mrs. D. Cottrell
Pana: J. Fribley; C. McClaren
Park Hills: B. Brinkopf; M. Dust
Park Ridge: F. Hianik; M. Rolston
Peoria: M. McCord; A. Watson
Plum Tree: A. Oldenburger;
D. Dimoff
Quincy: D. Weibring Jr.; Mrs. J. Dav
Ravinia Green: B. Zino; J. Eisen
Ravisloe: J. Joseph; F. Heiss
Renwood: J. Pichla; D. Johnson
Ridge: P. Johnson; P. Ahern
Ridgemoor: S. Kubiatowski;
M. Grimelli
River Forest: R. Allen; L. Conkel
Riverside: D. McLanchlan; B. Kubik
Rockford: P. North; P. Huston
Rock River: J. Allen; G. Hungate
Rock Spring: J. Hand Jr.; P. Pitt
Rolling Green: L. Westol; L. Strobe
Ruth Lake: J. Voyda; J. Jones
Scripps Park: C. Settles; S. Heflin
Shady Lawn: G. Gilroy; M. Grubach
Shambolee: S. Sinclair; D. Helm
Shoreacres: C. Brown III; N. Victor
Skokie: B. Schmid; N. Guthrie
Spring Creek: V. Pyszka; T. Blanco
Sunset Ridge: D. Kennedy; M. Gag
Thorngate: J. Keane; E. Maiorano
Timber Trails: J. Marsh
Urban Hills: B. Bryson; A. Gardner
Valley-Lo: J. Anton; H. Reed
Village Links: T. Johnston;
G. Wermine
Waveland: J. Catomer; A. Schonfie
E. Dunn
Westgate Valley: W. Linn; A. Walsh
Westlake: W. Calvey
Westmoreland: P. Holm; S. Hustea
White Pines: T. Jacobsen; M. Fred
Willow Run: N. Kent; B. Clegg
Wilmette: J. Versino; T. Robey
Winnetka: S. McElroy; N. Hellstron
Yorktown: T. Berger; P. Pitt

INDIANA
American Legion (New Castle):
E. Smith
Augusta Hills: S. Norris; M. Berkes
Bass Lake: R. Pettinato; M. Peters
Broadmoor: J. Kroot; Mrs. M. Bern
Brook Hill: M. Douglass; J. Nau
Brookshire: C. Weinkauf;
L. Farrington
Cedar Lake: A. Miller; H. Persons
Christmas Lake: H. Bennett Jr.;
F. Witte
Colonial Oaks: M. Egley; B. Banet
Connersville: D. Fischesser;
L. Werking
Corydon: J. Miles; M. Moss
Crawfordsville: E. Selby;
L. Branstetter
Crestview: M. Cravens; L. Andersc
Crooked Stick: B. Hovde; P. Wyck
Dearborn: J. Williamson; M. Leeds
Decatur: F. James; T. Baker
Delaware: G. Ryan; Mrs. P. Pipper
Edgewood: S. Douglass; J. Martin
Edwood Glen: J. Vaughn;
H. Patterson
Elbel Park: T. Bujeker; G. Kroll
Elcona: I. Kloska; B. Schricker
Elks (Blue River): B. Moore;
P. Dovidas
Elks (Elkhart): K. Everett; B. Thom
Elks (Ft. Wayne): J. Morris; M. Be
Elks (Kendallville): L. Patton;
B. Zawadzke
Elks (Lafayette): R. Fairman;
D. Schuette
Elks (LaPorte): K. Young; M. You
Elks (Plainfield): D. Pagach; L. M
Elks (Richmond): J. Brzuzy;
Mrs. V. Bartlemay
Elks (Rushville): W. Hartzler;
J. Benson
Elks (Seymour): F. Wilson;
S. Lonowski
Elks (Sullivan): B. Pierce; D. Boc
Erskine: S. Gebo; B. Henry
Etna Acres: T. Manley; C. Gosset
Forest Hills: S. Porter;
Mrs. V. Bartlemay
Forest Park: D. Butterfield; C. Sa
Foxcliff: S. Hardin
Frankfort: T. Conard; M. Snyder
Gary: J. Rasmusen; L. Magnetti
Grandview: J. Steenerson; B. Kol
Green Acres: J. Farrington; J. Ha
Greenfield: A. Griffin; S. Kirby
Green Hill: P. Hodson; A. Dixon
Greenburg: L. Hoffman; M. Linvil
Harrison Lake: R. Dice; Mrs. H. J
Hart: B. Brunner; M. Henchon
Heather Hills: M. Clifton; Mrs. G.

Highland: L. Bola; Mrs. W. Siegrist
Highland Lake: R. Melling; D. MacIntosh
Hillcrest: R. Walsman; M. Kelley
Hoosier Heights: T. Koressel; R. Koressel
Hoosier Links: T. Bush; Mrs. E. Prange
Indian Lake: W. Richey
Jasper: S. Schneider; E. Moore
Killbuck: J. Dixon; B. Kolins
Kokomo: J. Jackson; Mrs. S. Kubesch
LaFontaine: M. Houtz; M. Jeffrey
LaGrange: J. Ulery; J. Ulery
Lakeside: R. Pence
Liberty: M. Mullin
Limberlost: G. Davis; J. Williams
Maplecrest: G. Morehead; Mrs. M. Hollinger
Martinsville: J. Blickenstaff
Meshingomesia: G. Coryea; M. Herrick
Michigan City: L. Cheek
Morris Park: B. Whitmer; G. Krizman
New Albany: W. Richard; L. Richard
Norwood: M. John; C. Schumaker
Oak Meadow: W. Henry; C. King, B. Elmendorf
Old Oakland: D. Burton
Orchard Ridge: K. Rodewald; D. Hoffman
Otter Creek: C. Gossman; M. Fox
Parmore: Mrs. M. Price
Pheasant Valley: R. McDonald; N. Clarkson
Pine Valley: H. Athanson; E. Zumbrun
Plymouth: L. Roahrig; E. Ritzenthaler
Pottawattomie: M. Winski; R. Spencer
Prestwick: B. Ludlow; B. Money
Robin Hood: W. Ostrowski; A. Irish, F. Janssen
Rolling Hills (Loganport): B. Winters; A. Snapp
Rolling Hills (Newburg): G. Mankowski; K. Mankowski
Rozella Ford: J. Nelson; Mrs. J. Bess
Shady Hills: L. Morris; J. Druck
Sarah Shank: J. Hook Jr.; E. Preston
South Bend: B. Roberts; Mrs. D. Burnside
South Shore: J. Abrams; L. Harper
Sprig-O-Mint: N. Yeager; K. Stine
Terre Haute: R. Holmes; Mrs. E. Dede
Tippecanoe: A. Schledmilch; I. Hubbard
Tippecanoe Lake: J. Nelson; B. Clarke
Ulen: D. Heath; V. Walker
Union City: S. Mote; M. Jones
Valparaiso: G. Grieger; F. Dunleavy
Wabash: B. Herrell; J. Harris
Walnut Creek: T. Schaumleffel
Wawasee: J. Hartsough; J. Rice
Western Hills: J. Atkins; J. Moll
Westwood: J. Fischer; J. Becker
Woodmar: T. Schock; Mrs. C. Loane
Youche: J. Hershman; L. Wiles
Zollner: L. Davis; C. Clark

IOWA

Algona: E. Repschlaeger; D. Erickson
American Legion (Ft. Dodge): T. Miller; I. Adams
Ames: M. Miller; L. Barnett
Ankeny: M. Alexander; E. Burt
Atlantic: C. Waugh; K. Friday
Boone: C. Updegraff
Byrnes Park: J. Scheppele; S. McCunniff
Carroll: S. Crane; J. Blohm
Charles City: D. Fisher; D. Jacobson
Clinton: G. Moore; H. Volckmann
Crow Valley: J. Lujack; A. Clark
Des Moines: M. Schuchat; E. Van Horn
Dubuque: W. Hodge Jr.; A. M. Aschenbrener
Elmhurst: C. Porter; R. Stanley
Emerald Hills: A. Barriage Jr.; A. Kelloway
Floyd Park: Mrs. M. Bard
Friendly Fairways: C. Drake
Gates Park: E. Scheppelle; B. Meewes
Green Valley: G. Hagen; J. Prescott
Grinnell: J. Switzer; A. Wack
Hawarden: C. McManaman; J. Bradley
Highland Park: A. Cates; D. Flores
Hillside: B. LaBarre; S. Raney
Hyperion Field: J. Mitchell; Mrs. C. Erickson
Lake MacBride: J. Devine
Logan-Missouri Valley: H. Erickson; D. Erickson
Maple Hills: K. Kehe; J. Poock
Mason City: H. Anderson; C. Torgerson
Newell: M. Smith; J. Galbraith
New Hampton: D. Gates; P. Carney
Newton: H. Skow; J. Ferguson
Oneonta: A. Lynnes; P. Dahly
Ottumwa: G. Engle; J. Yetley
Prairie Knolls: A. Stewart
Raintree: J. Perkins; K. Balzer
Sheaffer: J. Druppel
Sioux City: D. Mogren; D. Marsh
Spencer: R. Sopeland; L. Johnson
Spring Lake: J. Slykhuis; J. McCarty
Sunny Brae: J. Lessard; L. Christiansen
Sunnyside: J. Schall; K. Tyler
Valley Oaks: D. Cavanaugh; D. Andersen
Wakonda: R. Bliss III; S. Scarlett, J. Miller
Washington: J. Carr; R. Nemmers
West Liberty: M. Nortman
Westwood: I. Altman; W. Jess
Willow Creek: C. Campbell; V. Trent
Woodward: T. Ledvina; J. Ledvina

KANSAS

Alvamar Hills: B. Scarborough; J. Woolard
Cedar Crest: D. Calderwood; P. Hulteen
Elks (Salina): R. Bennett; J. Hagen
Fort Hays: J. Drake
Fort Leavenworth: J. Nelson
Garnett: R. Powers; J. Cooper
Hiawatha: N. Parrigo; J. Bavans
Lake Quivira: J. Johnson; L. Devers
Lake Shawnee: E. Weber, D. Pressler; M. Waddell, L. Caleb
Leawood South: J. Clark; M. Ronsick
Liberty: T. Graber; B. Sturdy
Meadowbrook: D. Kay; M. Krigel
Ness: P. Richolson
Osawatomie: P. Reyburn; S. Cortner
Ottawa: R. Moline; J. Foulks
Overland Park: D. Cox; C. Yarr
Stagg Hill: G. Furney Jr.; G. Ewing
Town & Country: T. Sherman
Victory Hills: D. Brewer; N. Allen
Wamego: J. Clark; K. Kinderknecht
Wichita State: J. Denver; A. Stevens

KENTUCKY

Arlington: V. Stubblefield; K. Wylie
Bellefonte: G. Rupert; E. Nelson
Benton: P. Howard; J. Bradley
Big Elm: D. Standafer; T. Mayes
Big Spring: M. Thorp; Mrs. J. Hutson
Bon Harbor: W. Rightmyer Jr.
Boone Aire: W. Farrell; L. Peck
Bowling Green: H. Hinton; V. Perkins
Chenoweth: T. Crowley; M. Kammerdiener
Cherokee: B. Miller; M. Roll
Danville: H. McGuire; P. Caldwell
Fulton: J. Vowell; V. Rogers
Glenwood Hall: G. Boyles; J. Zembrodt
Harmony Landing: D. Kohler; Mrs. A. Peer
Henry County: C. Wetenkamp; M. Vaughn
Highland: G. Herfel; R. Zint
Hillcrest: P. Wilson; M. Alexander
Hunting Creek: L. Horn; Mrs. R. Hawkins, Mrs. R. Kalembes
Hurstbourne: R. Siegelin; F. Baldridge
Idle Hour: J. Owens; Mrs. E. Freeman
Lakeshore: L. Ruth; G. Omer
Lakeside: J. Newton
Lebanon: B. Leake; J. Isaacs
Louisville: H. Kemp; Mrs. T. Wall III
Madisonville: C. Riddle; M. Riddle
Mt. Sterling: J. Brock; B. Evans
Murray: N. Hood; J. Sullivan
Oldham: W. Morgan; C. Stavenow
Owl Creek: O. Spears; Mrs. O. Spears
Paintsville: C. Adkins; Mrs. R. Hall
Ponderosa: C. Armstrong; M. White
Ryland Lakes: P. VanCuren; J. Gentner
Shelbyville: D. Logan; Mrs. R. Logan
Stearns: E. Upchurch; A. Hile
Tates Creek: P. Schultte
Windridge: B. Foster; S. Ham
Woodhaven: D. Smith; J. Denham
Woodson Bend: Mrs. B. Burgess

One more time!

Bill Gressard won his first club championship at the Twin Lakes Country Club, Kent, Ohio, 38 years ago. In 1975, at age 60, he won his 15th title at Twin Lakes. In the finals, scheduled for 36 holes, he defeated a local high school golf coach, 9 and 8. Gressard played the final 10 holes in three under par. He says it was the last time he'd go after the Twin Lakes title. But his friends are taking that with a grain of salt.

LOUISIANA

Advance: M. Baragona; J. Castello
Audubon: W. Barcelo; J. Rosen
Avoyelles: S. Juneau
Baton Rouge: R. Didier Jr.; Mrs. F. Henry
Bayou De Biard: R. Shelton; F. Holt
Beauregard: M. Weigand; Mrs. R. Scalfi
Belleview: W. Clayton
Bogalusa:T. Tullos
Briarwood: L. Irvin; D. Vaughn
City Park: S. Picard; L. Short
Colonial: Mrs. L. Miczli
Covington: T. Danos; S. Hatfield
Eastwood Fairways: M. Buchanan; N. Floyd
Franklinton: A. Stafford; K. Bell
Monterey: B. Clements; H. Williamson
Springhill: M. Whitlow; M. Kottenbrook
Tri-Parish: P. Darcey; S. Eastin
Webb Memorial: S. Reeves; B. Michael

MAINE

Apple Valley: A. Durisko; A. Rylander
Augusta: M. Plummer; P. Widdoes
Bangor: B. Hobert; A. Mooney
Bethel Inn: D. Dolven; M. Dolven
Brunswick: M. Alford; S. Coombs
Fairlawn: D. Bartasius; A. Heldman
Fort Kent: E. Pelletier; Mrs. G. Ouellette
Gorham: J. Hadlock; Mrs. R. Labrecque
Grand View: M. Davis; P. Willey
Kebo Valley: P. Schuller; H. Linnehan
Kenduskeag Valley: R. Girvan II
Lakeview: B. Jones
Lucerno: B. Shapero; L. Koritzky
Meadowhill: B. Nason; B. Davis
Oakdale: D. Brown; P. Cloutier
Old Orchard Beach: B. Dodge
Portland: R. Lebel; Mrs. C. Milliken
Presque Isle: B. Madore; B. Giberson
Prospect Hill: R. Shea
Purpoodock: T. Palanza Jr.; Mrs. F. Beecher
Riverside: A. Bouchard; Mrs. M. Young
Summit: D. Johnson
Sunrise Acres: R. Miller
Waterville: O. Shiro; D. Graffman
Webhannet: B. Bonney; S. Brown
Western View: D. Katon; A. Stanley
White Birches: K. Jordan
Willowdale: B. Wood; J. Farley

MARYLAND

Bay Hills: G. Picard; A. Hopper
Beaver Creek: R. Roulette; L. Slocum
Belair: J. Deck; Mrs. H. Benson
Bonnie View: H. Leavy; J. Greenberg
Brandywine: E. Myer; B. Van Dyke
Bretton Woods: M. Martin; J. Gerstein
Chartwell: T. Flory; S. Hull
Chesapeake: R. Fischer Jr.; M. Sieder
Chestnut Ridge: J. Kaye; T. Abrams
Clifton Park: O. Wilcox; L. Martinak
Columbia: G. Nye Jr.; Mrs. D. Carpenter
Congressional: B. Johnston; P. Smyth
Crofton: J. Finneran III; M. King
Diamond Ridge: C. Fisher
Elks (Salisbury): B. Bradway; M. Lloyd
Greencastle: D. Stewart; B. Kaufman
Green Hill: B. Bradway; P. Hendrikson
Hobbit's Glen: B. Gillham; J. Takesian
Laytonsville: B. Mort
Manor: E. Ball; M. Booth
Maplehurst: T. Graff; B. Hanna
Martingham: S. Blades; B. Rodgers
Maryland: J. Kleman; Mrs. C. McComas Jr.
Nassawango: B. Groton; D. Stotts
Norbeck: D. Cohn; H. Feldman
Ocean City: A. Whaley; P. Parker
Piney Branch: J. Jones; J. Stull
Potomac Valley: W. Wheeler; K. Smith
Rocky Point: D. Corbin Jr.
Rolling Road: R. Slaght; Mrs. J. Rogers
Rossmoor Leisure World: D. Sartwell; D. Roane
Suburban Club: C. Hurst; S. Abeshouse
Swan Creek: C. Mitchell; L. Painter
Tantallon: T. Smialek; D. Coulther
University of Maryland: W. Moore; J. Nisonger
USNA: T. Herbin; A. Hopper
VFW: G. Graefe; L. Demchak
Washingtonian: M. Han; E. Baker
Worthington Valley: H. Wallett; C. Taylor

MASSACHUSETTS

Amesbury: S. Frank
Amherst: O. Brassard; J. McConnell
Bass River: R. Hewins; B. Mayo
Bass Rocks: J. Frithsen; N. Tarr
Bellevue: W. Brown Jr.; J. Field
Belmont: D. Brilliant; H. Sobin
Brae Burn: S. Dewire; Mrs. G. Gibson
Braintree: R. Lyons; P. Mansbach
Cherry Hill: D. Farrar
Chestnut Hill: B. Kolikof; D. Suvalle
Chicopee: K. Wajda
Cohasset: R. Towle Jr.; Mrs. C. Hitchcock
Cranwell: W. Salinetti
Crestview: J. Isenberg; L. Fodiman
Dedham: S. Smith; S. Foehl
Dennis Pines: T. Chase; T. Anderson
Duxbury: J. Alexander IV; S. White
Eastward Ho: M. Cotton; D. Bohman
Eden: D. Boyer; L. Corsetti
Edgartown: F. Garron; Mrs. F. Dickinson Jr.
Edgewood: R. Levesque
Elmcrest: J. Hunt; M. Ruggiero
Ferncroft; S. Tomasello; M. Dinerman
D. W. Field: W. Donahue
Forest Park: C. Mendel; M. Dolan
Fresh Pond: R. Quimby
Grand View: F. Lucier; B. Spencer
Greenfield: R. Ducharme; J. McConnell
Groton: J. Dwyer
Halifax: J. Crowley; A. Jacobs
Hampden: E. Polchlopek; I. Gendron
Hawthorne: D. Turner
Hickory Ridge: F. Godek; P. Mullins
Hillcrest: D. Larsen; P. Paulauskas
Juniper Hill: W. Porkula; D. Rosenberg
Kernwood: P. Oppenheim; B. Beckwith
Kittansett: D. Cassell; M. Marlio
Ledgemont: D. Loebenberg; P. Granoff
Little Harbor: R. Hunter; M. Nicholson
Long Meadow: F. Lincoln; A. Southworth
Lynnfield Centre: D. Burnham
Marlboro: D. Kelleher; F. Deruvo
Marshfield: G. Gearhart; L. Mariani
Leo J. Martin: J. Harris
Meadow Brook: S. Campbell; B. Keane
Middlebrook: P. Annarummo; B. Spooner
Middleton: R. Delorey
Milford: J. Senkarik
Monoosmock: R. Cross; Mrs. E. Bigelow
Nabnasset Lake: P. Walsh; P. Eastman
Needham: R. Hasenfus; S. Bergin
New Seabury: R. King; B. Fitzpatrick
Norfolk: P. Seddon; P. Ainsworth
North Andover: V. Morton Jr.; Mrs. J. McClintock
Northfield Inn: D. Lanphear
Northampton: E. Skroski; P. Wentworth
North Hill: M. Garrity
Norton: A. Love; A. Turgeon
Oakley: J. Wolf; Mrs. L. Olmsted
Oak Ridge: J. Helbig Jr.
Ould Newburg: J. O'Keefe; D. Cullen
Petersham: L. Smith; R. Kemmey
Pine Brook: P. Drooker; Mrs. P. Dine
Pinecrest: C. Fasick
Pine Grove: D. Jesanis; L. Cowell
Pine Valley: A. Barros; D. McAvoy
Pleasant Valley: R. Ciociolo; V. Rowe
Plymouth: B. Bottner; K. Withington
Pocasset: P. Stephen; D. McCullough
Ponkapoag: J. Sullivan; J. Depckelo
Pontoosuc Lake: G. Kubica
Powder Horn: B. Watts; C. Monahan
Quaboag: J. Hinchey; E. Wysmutek
Reservation: A. Mezlo; M. Ahlander
Salem: A. Kiernan; M. Marquis
Sandy Burr: C. Orkeny
Scituate: E. Stewart; E. Shone
Shaker Farms: T. Mack; J. Pratte
Skyline: S. Albano; J. Guftufson
Springfield: J. Cibrowski; C. Dalton
Spring Valley: S. Borr; Mrs. A. Klein
Strawberry Valley: L. Larson; B. Keene
Taconic: W. Pringle; Mrs. R. Deuber
Tatnuck: P. Bennett; Mrs. W. Brown
Tedesco: D. Duffy; B. Thorner
Thomson: P. Twomey; A. Locke
Thorny Lea: B. Chalas; B. Wind
Twin Hills: C. Dempsey; B. Orenstein
Veteran's Memorial: M. Gibson
Wahconah: R. Dinofrio; E. Carver
Walpole: J. Calf; K. O'Leary
Westboro: E. Porter; V. Williamson
Westminster: D. LeBlanc; J. LeBlanc
Winchester: L. Grace; J. Welch
Winnesuket: D. Adamonis
Woburn: J. Keddle; G. Worth
Worcester: R. Duprey; Mrs. P. Callahan
Worthington: B. Smith; S. Whitcomb

MICHIGAN

American Legion (Holland): B. McKnight; M. Cobb
Ann Arbor: D. Navarre; B. McCallum
Arbor Hills: D. Kelosky; J. Johnston
Barton Hills: B. Gustine; S. Conlin
Battle Creek: J. Taylor; D. Hunaker
Bay Pointe: T. Olk
Bay Valley: C. Sturm; L. Bush
Birmingham: R. Weyand; Mrs. C. Byrne Jr.
Black River: J. Robb; M. Luber
Bonnie Brook: N. Lasky; D. LePla
Boondocks: M. Randall; L. Gallas
Briar Hill: J. McKinley J. Hagerman
Burning Tree: D. VanErd; J. Large
Cadillac: J. Hand D. McCormick
Carleton Glen: R. Post
Caro Golf: D. Sherman; D. McNeil
Cascade Hills: R. Brown; D. Scripsema
Chardill: D. Vandenberg; J. Bollman
Clearbrook: T. Vantongeren; M. Colenbrander
Coldwater: B. Reynolds; T. Young
Corunna Hills: J. Vogl; L. Worthington
Detroit: R. Tolleson; Mrs. J. Hartzell
Edgewood: M. Seremjian; D. Button
El Dorado: R. Flading
Elks (Kalamazoo): R. Steffen; P. Anderson
Elks (Muskegon): D. DeWitt; D. Meier
Flint: S. Braun; A. Hagan
Flushing Valley: C. Lucia; D. Wilson
Forest Lake: K. Daiek; H. O'Connell
Four Lakes: L. Evans; Mrs. L. Evans
Frankenmuth: D. Zehnder
Frankfort: R. Clement
Franklin Hills: J. Straus; Mrs. L. Sherman
Genesee Hills: J. Ortiz; V. Reid
Germania of Saginaw: T. Russell; S. Schrock
Gogebic: J. Milakovich; D. Ahonen
Gowanie: J. Marshall; A. Ramge
Grand Haven: D. Singleton Jr.; S. Nietering
Gratiot: P. Mahoney; L. McKinney
Grayling: G. Schwarz; C. Smith
Great Oaks: T. Watrous; R. Aucott
Green Ridge: J. O'Donovan; M. O'Donovan
Greenville: D. Cushman; G. Gowans
Grosse Ile: T. Bolthouse; L. Mahanti
Gull Lake: S. Malaney; Mrs. T. Harding
Hampshire: E. Meyer; L. Heiden
Hunt Valley: T. Hofmann; J. Noel
Huron Shores: F. Gerhardt; B. Gross
Indianwood: R. Vershure; E. Vershure
Inverness: A. Clemes; B. Farrell
Ionia: B. Bowne; S. Ertl
Kalamazoo: B. Western; K. Kukolich
Kent: J. Glerum; L. Miller
Kincheloe: J. Hagan; R. Krig
Knollwood: M. Bleznak; B. Levitt
Lake Doster: D. Llewellyn; S. Boylan
Lake Isabella: P. Mack; E. Harkins
Lansing: F. Benymer Jr.; P. Bearden
Lapeer: G. Vaughn; R. MacFarlane
Lost Lake Woods: D. MacLeod; E. Freitas
Ludington Hills: J. Quinn; M. Semrad
Manistee: D. Flarity; L. Sandborg
Marshall: G. Zollner; K. O'Connor
McGuires: E. Tanner; B. McGrew
Meceola: C. Christensen
Midland: J. Tucker; Mrs. M. Nelson
Milham Park: D. Parker; S. Den-Otter
Mill Race: S. Miller; C. Spencer
Monroe: R. McAuliffe III; D. Stougaard
Mt. Pleasant: K. Mohr; Mrs. J. Murray
Muskegon: C. Munson; G. Stevens
Northwood: D. Outwin; I. Breuker
Oakland Hills: R. McDonald; A. Wright
Oceana: B. Peets; J. Bullough
Old Channel Trail: J. Bendelow; G. Richlen
Orchard Hills: G. Clemens; J. Beistle
Oxford Hills: B. Hubbard
Pine Lake: J. Grace Jr.; J. Kelchner
Plum Hollow: T. Rex Jr.; C. Vollmer
Point o' Woods: R. Mack; D. Ryan
Port Huron: R. Schultheiss; A. Yull
Portage Lake: E. Hughes; A. Hauge

Good hands

Dr. Tom Brown, a dentist, has now won five consecutive club championships at the La Jolla (Calif.) Country Club although his work limits him to about three rounds a month. "I think dentists make good golfers," he says, "because we work with our hands."

A 2-handicapper, Dr. Brown prefers La Jolla's match-play format because "I don't play enough to put four good rounds together." The year before he began his run of five straight titles he went to the finals and lost to Craig Stadler, who went on to win the 1973 U.S. Amateur championship.

Radrick Farms: G. Forrest; C. Dixon
Raisin Valley: J. Kennedy;
M. Rosancrans
Riverside (Battle Creek): K. Aubuchon;
D. Shay
Riverside (Menominee): W. Thomsen;
M. Stillman
Rolling Hills: B. Flowers, P. Skinner;
T. Weaver
Saginaw: D. Franz; P. Theuer
St. Ignace: M. MacDonald; S. Pierson
Saskatoon: D. Olinger; D. Campbell
Schuss Mountain Royal: K. Wells;
E. Manville
Scott Lake: M. VanDyke; J. Faber
Shenandoah: D. Burnstein; S. Garzia
Signal Point: B. Kasler; T. Childs
Spring Lake: C. Taylor; D. Johnson
Spring Meadows: J. Lind; J. Cramer
Sunnybrook: J. Bishop; M. Nordyke
Tam O'Shanter: B. Kamin;
Mrs. F. Schwartz
Tecumseh: B. Holmes; M. Hannibal
Tomac Woods: B. Murphy
Traverse City: R. Newman; J. Norcross
Twin Beach: R. Herpich;
Mrs. R. Heincelman
Verona Hills: S. MacGregor; V. Hilla
Walnut Hills: S. Eckert; J. LaBelle
Warwick Hills: D. Marr; L. Hilkene
West Branch: H. Minor; M. Smith
Western: G. Petosky; Mrs. D. Martin
West Shore: T. Campau; J. Vida
Whispering Willows: D. Wall;
L. Waldecker
White Ford Valley: B. Kreuz;
R. Garrison
Wilderness: R. Hart; S. Wrona
Willow Brook: P. Brooks;
Mrs. I. Muchler
Ye Nyne Olde Holles: D. Peak Jr.
Ye Olde: D. Myer; B. Stough

MINNESOTA

Albany: D. Schiffler; M. Luethmers
Albert Lea: J. Rasmussen; N. Haney
Austin: D. Seltz; Mrs. R. Moen
Balmoral: D. Stickel; J. Anderson
Benson: B. Force; J. Peterson
Brainerd: J. Boileau; L. Willis
Burl: D. Reimer; B. Morton
Castle Highlands: M. Port; D. Harmon
Cimarron Public: J. Wolff
Coffee Mill: L. Ekstrand; M. Gosse
Coon Rapids: A. Kauppi Jr.;
R. Glassman
Crow River: D. Prochnow; C. Swanson
Dellwood Hills: N. Anderson;
P. Erickson
Dodge: L. Blow; E. Slukich
Dwan: J. DuPont; J. McWilliams
Faribault: D. Deem; A. Olson
Forest Hills: C. Kelsey; Mrs. R. Pepin
Golden Valley: J. Gruidl; B. Markham
Gross: J. Jaros; Y. Walters
Hazeltine Nat'l: J. Beck; Mrs. P. Olson
Ironman: T. Welle; M. Santwire
Island View: D. Wilson; D. Moonen
Jackson: B. Chozen; C. Muir
Lafayette: G. Garner; Mrs. M. Bolin
Lake Miltona: R. Shields;
J. Freudenberg
Lakeway: R. Risbrudt; E. Ness
Little Crow: J. Golla; N. Jacobson
Lost Spur: G. Wilson; A. Nelson
Meadowbrook: J. Belfry; M. Jodell
Midland Hills: J. Fehling; E. Sullivan
Minikahda: J. Seidel; Mrs. J. Turner
Minneopa: R. Anderson; E. Yeomans
Minneapolis: L. Chapman; N. Harris
Minnetonka: M. Korte; E. Lee
Minnesota Valley: R. Render;
J. Lindsey
Moorhead: J. Dorsey; P. Phillipp
Normandale: J. Lassley; S. Grosklags
Northfield: R. Witheron; S. Nelson
Northland: D. Kohlbry; G. Carlson
North Oaks: P. Turner; N. Hay
Oak Ridge: B. Wernick; V. Werner
Olympic Hills: L. Evans
Osakis: A. Kluver; J. Randahl
Pebble Lake: B. Riviere; J. Gustufson
Pipestone: W. Bailey; M. Lange
Ridgeview: G. Kaskala; H. Randall
Rochester: B. Reichart; N. Schnabel
Scottdale: B. Carlson
Somerset: T. Garrett III; R. Cole
Springfield: R. Loomis; V. Johnston
Stillwater: B. Miller; P. Giebler
Terrace: G. Hasselberg; J. Palmer
Thief River: M. McGrath; L. Kotlke
Tianna: E. Sauer; B. Iverson
Town & Country: J. Knutson; J. Calin
Veterans: R. Erickson; P. Fredlund
Virginia: B. Loushine; C. Peterson
Westfield: D. Cleveland; Y. Carpenter
White Bear: C. Vollhabek;
Mrs. W. Motter
Willmar: H. Caldwell; K. Skinner
Willow Creek: B. Hagen; D. Bergeson
Worthington: G. O'Brien;
T. Schimbeno
Zumbrota: K. Kish; P. Anderson

MISSISSIPPI

Aberdeen: B. Miley; Mrs. B. Rhea
Brookwood: B. Harper; H. Stodghill
Canton: J. Iupe Jr.; C. Hailey
Clarksdale: V. Hughes; H. Cauthen
Colonial: W. Mowat; Mrs. D. Little
Dixie G. A.: J. Smith; Mrs. D. Garick
Greenville: J. McGough; M. Lingle
Grenada: R. Ross; J. Carroll
Hickory Hill: L. Justice; B. Bocklett
Hattiesburg: J. Pittman; A. Johnson
Indianola: C. Webb; J. Miller
Jackson: M. Tullos; M. White
Keesler AFB: D. Detiege; S. Barbaree
Millbrook: S. Boudreau Jr.;
M. Tucker
Olive Branch: R. Black; K. Zeip
Pascagoula: J. Logan; T. Gianatsis
Prentiss: W. Cook
Tupelo: Z. Hodges
University: J. Lang
Univ. of Southern Miss.: E. Thames

MISSOURI

Ambo River Valley: T. Mohan;

Hat tricks

At least two golfers won championships at three different clubs in 1975. Helene Canavan, 61, San Francisco, won at the Lincoln Park Golf Course, a San Francisco municipal layout; Cypress Hills Golf Club in Daly City, and at Sharp Park Municipal in Pacifica. She won by 27 strokes at Lincoln Park, by eight in the other two.

Another three-timer is Jerry R. Clark, 26, Pleasant Hill, Mo. He won at the Pleasant Hill Golf and Country Club and also at the Shamrock Hills Golf Club and Leawood South Golf and Country Club in Leawood, Kan.

E. Mohan
Blue Hills: J. Krause; K. Cooper
Bogey Hills: G. Hall; P. Hall
Bolivar: J. Henrikson; Mrs. L. Roberts
Briarbrook: G. Phillips; C. McKenzie
Brookfield: B. Mendenhall; C. Miller
Cameron Memorial: R. Skidmore
Caruthersville: W. Pate
Cassville: R. Haynes; R. Barnes
Chillicothe: B. Welch; S. Welch
Columbia: R. Jones; M. Diehl
Daviess County: I. Bridgman;
E. Morrissey
Excelsior Springs: S. Zimmerman;
A. Tinsman
Fayette: M. Cochran; M. Diehl
Forest Hill: H. Miller; L. Miller
Forest Hills: C. Abel; J. Klaus
Ft. Leonard Wood: C. Chishulm;
B. Fellows
Fulton: R. Niedergerke; C. Kurtz
Glen Echo: M. Prendergast; L. Chrenka
Hickory Hills: B. Hollowell; J. Mahoney
Hillcrest: B. Bannon; A. Lawrence
HOK Valley: J. Hames; V. Kerr
Indian Foothills: J. Simmons;
D. Potter
Joachim: L. Johnston; L. Harmon
Kirksville: B. Daniels; D. Link
Lake Valley: A. Phillips; B. Hagadorn
Liberty Hills: J. Houston; E. Schmidt
Marceline: E. Walsworth; M. Tillotson
Meadowbrook: S. Stone; Mrs. R. Korn
Meadow Lake: C. Patterson III;
S. Wetzel
Meadow Lake Acres: R. Boyce;
D. Hempe
Moila: W. Riepen; B. Meredith
Norwood Hills: D. Brookreson;
B. Beuckman
Oak Meadow: S. Hill; B. Moore
Oakwood: A. Garfinkel
Paradise Valley: D. Medlock; B. Gaus
Pike County: F. Branstetter; M. Martin
Pleasant Hill: J. Clark; A. Clark
Pro-Am: C. Hutton; T. Springli
River Valley: S. Owsley; B. Smith
Rockwood: D. Clark; G. Scott
Rolla: L. Stites; E. Parker
Ruth Park: J. Pozzo; M. Bell
St. Joseph: R. Finch; Mrs. T. Potter
Sedalia: G. Thompson; H. Brown
Shirkey: W. McAllister; J. Robinson
Southview: J. Hillstrom
Stayton Meadows: R. Brewer
Sunset: C. Morgan; Mrs. J. Spitzfaden
Triple A: J. Hillwick; B. Lehr
Twin Oaks: T. Glass; G. Johnson
Westborough: J. Holtgrieve;
Mrs. W. Parshall
Westwood: B. Schulein; M. Dalton

MONTANA

Butte: E. Zemljak; R. Canty
Elks (Lewistown): M. Field; D. Horning
Green Meadow: M. Majors; E. Hagler
Hamilton: J. Moss; S. Philip
Hilands: G. Schuyler; L. Prill
Kalispell: M. Hanson; V. Gustin
Laurel: M. Oliver; J. Bailey
Missoula: G. Koprivica; H. Tremper
Polson: J. McKethan;
D. Christofferson
Bill Robert's: D. Sidor; J. Jones
Signal Point: G. Erickson;
O. Erickson
Robert Speck: G. Yowell; V. Dunn
Yellowstone: B. Meek; M. Clark

NEBRASKA

Alliance: P. Kunzman; E. Smith
Aurora: D. Morgan; S. Core
Blair: M. Wallin; D. Harrison
Chappell: T. Kastler; W. Clark
Elks (McCook): M. Broderson;
N. Mullen
Falls City: E. Comfort; I. Brecht
Fontenelle Hills: R. Gaylord;
M. Huck
Four Winds: C. Christensen; B. Brown
Fremont: J. Liechty; J. Gillen
Happy Hollow: P. Peartree; N. Circo
Highland: G. Gratton; M. L. Walker
Hillcrest: M. Hughett;
D. Schwartzkopf
Lincoln: D. Spangler; S. Roper,
L. Sundberg
Lochland: S. Stewart; B. Hopp
Miller Park: M. Fitzgerald; E. Hult
Norfolk: K. French; J. Hall
North Platte: D. Cander; S. Roberts
Oakland: G. Peterson; B. Peterson
Omaha Field Club: A. Ludwig;
D. Sandstedt
Riverside: S. Beltzer; P. Shull
Rolling Hills: D. Christensen;
M. Adkins
Schuyler: D. Vest
Scotts Bluff: K. Powell; A. Finke
Southern Hills: L. Phillips; N. Thiel
Sunset Valley: B. Wright; J. Helgesen
Wayne: B. Reeg; A. Barclay
Woodland: B. Ditter; M. Weiland

NEVADA

Black Mountain: Mrs. B. Anderson
Desert Inn: H. Fletcher; M. Smith
Edgewood Tahoe: B. Young
Hidden Valley: H. Larsen; P. Sheehan
Incline Village: J. Johnson; R. Hume
Las Vegas: W. Pearson; L. Nelson
Sahara Nevada: B. Hinkley; E. Moelter
Sierra Sage: D. Finley; M. Johnson
Wahoe: F. Menante; P. Sheehan
White Pine: H. Ford; C. Boyce
Winnemucca: D. Verner; G. Duvivier

NEW HAMPSHIRE

Abenaqui: J. Tinios; P. Patton
Amherst: F. Britton; Y. Kelly
Ammonoosuc: K. Hartwell; T. Burlock
Beaver Meadow: L. Dupuis;
A. Clemons
Bethlehem: F. Page; B. Enderson
Bretwood: D. Costello; L. Thoin
John H. Cain: W. Fennessy;
B. Murgatroy
Charming Fare Links: G. Dick;
A. Green
Claremont: K. Paton; E. Thoresen
Cochecho: D. Goldstein;
E. Lauterborn
Den Brae: B. Batchelder; I. Smith
Derryfield: J. Cullify; B. Sante
Exeter: D. Kukesh; A. Abbott
Goffstown: R. Lamy; H. Martel
Green Meadow: J. Harrington;
R. Thornton
Hanover: T. Staples; K. Slattery
Hoodkroft: A. McNeilly; B. Misiaszak
Keene: E. Niemela; M. Snow
Manchester: L. Hillsgrove; R. Plante
Nashua: H. Beaulieu; D. Gardler
North Conway: G. Chandler; J. Harvey
Oak Hill: H. Staubitz; E. Estes
Pease AFB: J. Warren; J. Conry
Plausawa Valley: D. Carroll; L. Morey
Portsmouth: M. Healy; B. Baird
Rockingham: R. Shelton
Waukewan: J. Schenk; M. Moore
Waumbek Inn.: J. Kovalik
Wentworth Fairways: J. Weldon;
D. Gaulin

NEW JERSEY

Alpine: B. Goldberg; J. Baris
Apple Ridge: T. Lynch; E. Madden
Atlantic City: D. Delcher; B. Knorr
Atlantis: F. Curtis Jr.; S. Doenges
Bamm Hollow: D. Mazza; P. Rohrey
Beaver Brook: C. Peck; J. Frazee
Bedens Brook: A. Schwartz; S. Blair
Bowling Green: J. Van Vooran;
A. Johnston
Burlington County: J. Helhowski;
B. Moyerman
Cedar Hill: M. Goldman; S. Abramson
Clearbrook: F. Quinn; M. Hadley
Cranbury: D. Provow
Cream Ridge: J. Aaronson; T. Miscoski
Crestmont: I. Samuels; R. Sabin
Deal: J. Wilcoxen; Mrs. D. Corwin
Essex County: R. Saugstad;
Mrs. H. Barrett
Essex Fells: B. Connell
Great Gorge: J. Connoly; B. Hansen
Goldon Pheasant: J. Adams
Green Acres: G. Schafer;
Mrs. K. Zeltmacher
Greenbrook: H. Schinman;
B. Glucksman
Hackensack: J. Flanagan; E. Weiss
Hanover: E. Biehl; R. Roberts
High Mountain: C. Najziejka; P. Busch
Holly Hills: R. Boss; J. Watkins
Hollywood: P. Schottland;
Mrs. K. Weinstein
Hopewell Valley: F. Oshel; S. Rosser
Knickerbocker: R. Riseley;
Mrs. F. VonHessert
Linwood: A. Shuster; J. Gottlieb
Manasquan River: G. Barnett III;
Mrs. L. Dwulet
Maplewood: F. Brown; Mrs. R. Fisher
Mendham: D. Lamp; C. Dahlenburg
Merchantville: A. Andreola;
S. Hutchinson
Metuchen: P. Maglione Jr.; C. Jarema
Montclair: K. Gordon;
Mrs. P. Johnstone
Moorestown Field: P. Allen;
B. Kichline
Morris County: J. Wight Jr.;
M. Harris
Mt. Tabor: F. Sullivan; G. Mercer
Newton: B. Dolan; S. Swayze
North Jersey: P. Samanchik;
Mrs. G. Guard
Oak Hill: A. Biggs; M. Campbell
Oak Ridge: D. PiPala
Old Orchard: R. Colaguori;
A. Calabrese
Pitman: L. Glutting; D. Smith
Plainfield: B. Milligan; Mrs. N. Lyman
Preakness Hills: P. Mucci Jr.;
A. Brawer
Ramsey: D. Hovermale; J. Baucom
Raritan Valley: R. Hunt Jr.;
Mrs. R. Hunt Sr.
Rock Spring: L. Willhelm;
Mrs. T. Paluck
Roselle: D. Pitman; P. Hatfield
Rutgers: N. Jacobs; K. Boyer
Shackamaxon: D. Kopelman; L. Gale
Sharon: W. Sawka Jr.; D. Young
Short Hills: S. Gray; M. Monaghan
Somerset Hills: R. Johnson;
Mrs. E. Burke
Spring Brook: A. Melillo; C. O'Connor
Stony Brook: C. Boone; J. Jones
Suburban: J. Paskowitz; Mrs. J. Faraci
Summit Municipal: B. Parkins;
D. DeRosa
Tamarack: J. Spangler; H. Creighton
Tamcrest: N. DeFazio
Trenton: T. Sawyer; Mrs. O. Brown
Twin Brooks: M. Wichansky; T. Prince
Upper Montclair: T. Potter; C. Gaston
Wildwood: J. Byrne; M. Samson
Woodbury: T. Simpson; N. Blemker
Woodcrest: M. Cohen; Mrs. E. Corwin
Woodlake: C. Siciliano; P. Brooke

NEW MEXICO

Albuquerque: R. Marron; J. Greiner
Arroyo Del Oso: M. Pelletier;
N. Knickerbocker
Cahoon Park: G. Martinez; D. Meyer
Colonial Park: P. Tankersley;
G. Kinyon
Eunice: J. Bentle; A. Cypert
Hidden Valley: B. Whipple; V. Morris
Hobbs: O. Seilheimer; B. Clarke
Los Alamos: B. Black; E. Griggs
Paradise Hills: L. Greene; E. Morales
Riverside: D. Skarda; M. Culpepper
San Juan: D. McLaughlin; B. Salmon
University of New Mexico: D. Hood

NEW YORK

Afton: C. Putrino; M. Nesbit
Albany: C. Murphy Jr.; M. Battaglia
Apawamis: S. Karlen; S. Paus
Arrowhead: P. Hagen; A. Sloan
Attica: J. Beitz; H. Godfrey
Ballston: R. Pegg; M. Mottau
Bartlett: J. Brady; K. Freitas
Bath: B. Perkins; J. LeRay
Battenkill: E. Donnelly; V. Stants
Bay Meadows: E. Cavazos;
E. Marzola
Beaver Meadows: W. Knych;
P. Morabito
Bedford: D. Ewing; Mrs. R. Welch
Beekman: R. Metz
Belden Hill: J. Gresham; B. Gresham
Bellport: N. Raimondo; E. Czaja
Bethlehem Management; E. Pasnik;
M. Hacic
Binghamton: R. Baldwin; S. Sullivan
Bolivar: R. Dwaileebe; C. Hannon
Bonavista: G. Lucas
Bonnie Briar: M. Carpiniello;
C. Algiero
Brae Burn: M. Doppelt;
Mrs. M. Doppelt
Brentwood: L. Austin
Briar Hall: M. Sugarman;
R. Saterberg
Bristol Harbour: D. BeVier;
Mrs. H. BeVier
Brookville: R. Hoshino; B. Cotter
Caledonia: S. Weitzel; M. Hartford
Camillus: D. Campbell; G. Kush
Canasawacta: B. Branham; J. Eaton
Catatonk: S. Manning; P. Wade
Cedar Brook: B. Albert; C. Bologna
Cedar Lake: F. Smith; R. Kelleher
Central Valley: F. O'Connor; W. Wolf
Charter Oaks: R. Stanley;
Mrs. M. Wiltsek
Chenango Valley: B. McCarthy
Cherry Valley: R. Gregerson;
Mrs. E. Walsh
Chili: D. Hahn; B. Walsh
Cold Spring: J. Tomasello;
R. Goldzier
College: R. Ide; J. Sholes
College Hill: E. Allen
Colonie: N. Spitalny; D. Rome
Commack Hills: P. Conte
Cordial Greens: H. Carroll;
A. Szembrot
Corning: J. Kempf; Mrs. J. Carver
Crag Burn: M. Balen; Mrs. P. Vogt
Craig Hill: B. Sluman; G. Freese
Creek Club: S. Titus; Mrs. C. Cullen
Dogwood Knolls: G. Carter; R. Devins
Dunwoodie: M. Pylypshyn; I. Gaito
Dutch Hollow: K. King; N. Murphy
Dutchess: R. DeStefano; J. Mertz
Edison: G. Freeman; J. Sayles
Elma Meadows: D. Morris; C. Steiner
Elmira: G. Girmindl; M. Clute
Elms: M. Patell; E. Taggert
Elm Tree: L. Gokey; B. Contento
Elmwood: W. Birnbaum; Mrs. H. Libert
Engineers: B. Gold; G. Katz
Ford Hill: W. Hogan
Frear Park: W. Kalbaugh;
Mrs. R. Krause
Fresh Meadow: A. Greene;
B. Finkelstein
Garden City: B. Murphy; H. Lawkins
Gardiners Bay: G. Dickerson;
A. Woodcock
Genegantslet: C. Babcock;
N. Dietrich
Geneva: D. Purbeck; J. Dwyer
Glen Cove: L. Curcio; S. Vuillet
Glen Head: M. Winkelman; D. Lovell
Glen Oaks: R. Spring
Glens Falls: B. Folley; G. Brophy
Green Hills: J. Infantino; A. Collins
Grossinger's: P. Zintel; S. Needel
Hampton: D. Tanner; G. Richmond
Hauppauge: M. Friedman
Heatherwood: R. Lynch; E. Munzer
Heritage Hills: V. Turchick;
M. Lawrenz
Hidden Waters: J. Martin
Highland Park: B. Chalanick; I. Tarby
Hill 'n Dale: P. Austin;
W. Vandewalker
Homowack Lodge: M. Robbins;
H. Stoller
Honey Hill: S. Crane; M. Hensel
Hornell: T. Giedlin; Mrs. D. Blades
Hudson Hills: B. Sarroff; Mrs. H. Pear
Huntington: G. Gilbert; E. Walker
Huntington Crescent: P. Caricola;
J. Cornacchia
IBM: L. Coble; G. Bradicich
Indian Hills: J. Broere; T. Odenwald
Irondequoit: K. Weiner; F. Sand
Island's End: B. White; M. Strasser
Island Valley: H. McLaughlin;
L. Johnson
Ithaca: R. Shulman; D. Kostrinsky
Inlet: L. Baerman
Ives Hill: K. Leon; M. Gerken
Kanandaque: B. Attardo; M. Munger
Knollwood: E. Tompkins;
Mrs. E. Hayes
Lake Shore: B. McLaughlin;
V. Carbone
Lake Shore Yacht: J. Bialek;
L. Barzee
Lakeview: M. Hutton
Lancaster: J. Lindner; P. Ploysa
Lawrence: B. Yacker; B. Krass
Leewood: F. Gorda; M. Walsh
LeRoy: P. McGrath; M. Antinore
Livingston: J. Fitzgerald; J. Adams
Lochmor: S. Solomon; M. Crawford
Mahopac: A. Variano; C. Puchir
Malone: G. Gokey; M. Tulloch
Marvin's: D. Peshek; M. Hoffer
McConnellsville: J. Prozny;
Mrs. R. Archibee
Metropolis: R. Hurvitz; Mrs. A. Schu
Middle Bay: N. Goland; J. Schiff
Midvale: T. Carlisi; C. Mass
Mill River: A. Goore; J. Pearlman
Monroe: B. Bettin; M. Kircher
Montauk: L. Ialacci; B. DiPalma
Moon Brook: D. Young; E. O'Neill
Mt. Kisco: C. Bohmert; L. Ebert
Muttontown: J. Braun; N. Platzer
Nassau: J. Stalarow; Mrs. V. Larkin
Newark: H. Van Demortal; J. Graybi
Newman: J. Atsedes
Niagara Falls: F. Silver; M. Stefik
North County: W. Valenze;
H. Archibald
North Hills: M. Galletta; Mrs. M. Re
Northern Pines: R. Russo; A. Misen
North Fork: J. Ehlers; A. Suter
North Shore: T. Ryan; R. Bitz
Northway Heights: R. Graham;
C. Carter
Noyac: P. Hickey; C. Desch
Oak Hill: C. Lillich; L. Willard
Old Westbury: R. Kaplowitz;
Mrs. B. Franklin
Oneonta: S. Torrey; P. Seybolt
1000 Acres: Al Wittekind
Orange County: R. Mulqueen;
G. Dunning
Oriskany Hills: R. Misiasrek;
K. Jacobson
Osiris: J. Richards; L. Kastelic
Oswego: F. Plata Jr.; M. Walcott
Owasco: G. Lesch; M. MacKay
Pelham: B. Haggerty; Mrs. A. Bowe
Pine Crest: W. Richard; A. Fusaro
Piping Rock: R. Millen;
Mrs. G. McGrath
Pleasant View: W. Vaughn; D. Vaug
Pompey Hills: M. Novak; A. Roy
Potsdam Town & Country:
A. Papayanakos; C. Baker
Powelton: J. Smith Jr.; Mrs. R. Och
Quaker Hill: S. Busby; C. Laporte
Quoguefield: T. Mullen; G. Lanyon
Rainbow: R. Merchant
Richmond: S. Tellefsen; N. Avis
Ridgeway: S. Frankel; M. Springer
Rochester: D. Allen; Mrs. G. Train
Rock Hill: J. French; A. Simson
Rye: T. Pike; O. Slegar
Sacandaga: M. Sturm; D. Venner
St. Andrew's: R. Darmstadt;
Mrs. C. Schneider
St. George's: R. Jones Jr.;
Mrs. W. Miller
St. Lawrence: W. Christy;
M. Lawrence
Saratoga: P. Baruzzi; B. Curtis
Schuyler Meadows: H. Wood; L. E
Sedgewood: G. Dickinson;
Mrs. G. Dickinson
Seneca: W. Grygiel III; R. Kassel
Seven Oaks: F. Potter; M. Burke
Shaker Ridge: L. Apple; J. Ripps
Shawangunk: F. Muller; R. Murray
Shelridge: J. Castle; H. Graham
Shinnecock Hills: S. Sherrill;
A. Enstine
Six—X: E. Roeske; G. Knapp
Skenandoa: B. Curtis; M. Carville
Smithtown Landing: F. White;

M. Stauder
Soaring Eagles: E. Hughes
Sodus Bay Heights: J. Brado; J. White
Southampton: R. Marcincuk;
M. Hedges
Spring Lake: R. Davis
Springville: W. Lowe; E. Berst
Stamford: G. Lewis; M. Govern
Tall Timber: J. Wilde; A. Baker
Tam O'Shanter: K. Jampolis;
L. Alberts
Tan-Tara: F. McCarthy; J. Jerauld
Thendara: R. Christy; P. McCormack
Ticonderoga: J. Dreimiller; M. Gijanto
Transit Valley: B. Boles; V. Diebold
Tupper Lake: J. Smith; S. Young
Turin Highlands: E. Johnson; M. Reed
Twaalfskill: D. Gaffney;
Mrs. J. Edwards
Twin Hickory: K. Cregan; R. Coleman
Vails Grove: R. Dlugo; G. Guglielmo
Van Schaick Island: J. Owens; M. Dow
Vestal Hills: S. Drazen; B. Slutzker
Waccabuc: W. Fenton; L. Brockelman
Walden: F. Scott; P. Merrill
Wanakah: D. Koch; L. Ward
Watkins Glen: T. Franzese; L. Smythe
Wayne Hills: N. Forgiome; K. Bowler
Westchester: D. Scanlon; K. Scanlon
Westchester Hills: C. Hansen;
C. Brown
Whispering Pines: E. Febbie;
L. Marchione
Willowbrook: W. Cravener;
A. Bergeron
Willow Ridge: M. Sheib; M. Edelman
Willow Run: J. Pickard; S. Mulkin
Wiltwyck: W. Van Aken; M. Motzkin
Windham: R. Ahern; K. Krug
Winding Brook: C. O'Rourke;
H. Marshall
Winged Foot: J. O'Hara; M. Christie
Wolferts Roost: J. Murphy;
Mrs. R. Sauers
Woodcrest: T. Schaeffer;
Mrs. R. Barna
Woodmen: A. Finkelstein; R. Bender
Wykagyl: D. Ragaini; P. Fisher

NORTH CAROLINA

Arrowhead: C. Sharpe; P. Bulter
Asheville: B. Van Arsdale;
A. Brandis
Beechwood: J. Edwards;
Mrs. A. McLean
Bermuda Run: D. Anderson;
C. Sandefur
Boone: E. Taylor; C. Hodges
Brookwood: M. Guthrie
Brushy Mountain: J. Queen
Buccaneer: R. Ferrell; C. Brown
Cape Fear: D. Sloan; D. Oxenfeld
Cashie: S. Rogerson; C. Jordan
Catawba: J. Sadowski; L. Lofland
Charlotte: R. Shull III; E. McKee
Chatuge Shores: K. Kilpatrick
Deep Springs: B. Pearce,
M. Claybrook; E. Martin
Emerywood: L. Higgins; P. Webster
Gaston: J. Gray III; K. Yarbrough
Gates Four: R. Barbee; M. Snowden
Grandfather: W. Bissette;
Mrs. P. Rendleman
Grassy Creek: C. Greene; J. Long
Greenville: V. Taylor; H. White
Hendersonville: T. Hadley; B. Haile
Highland: M. Waren; E. McNeill
Hound Ears: M. Bean; K. Mann
Kern Lake: R. Godwin; E. Faulkner
Lakeside: B. Harrell; J. Seavers
Lakewood: J. Warren; V. Strickland

Family affairs

Larry and Robin Chilson (above) of Williamsport, Pa., were one of several husband-wife tandems to win club championships in 1975. The Chilsons took the men's and women's titles at the Coudersport (Pa.) Golf Club. Robin, seven months pregnant when she won, said, "I was playing the best golf of my life."

Harley and Donna Erickson have a great record at the Logan-Missouri Valley Country Club in Missouri Valley, Iowa. Harley has been the club champion for the past seven years, and his wife has won the women's title the past two years. It isn't surprising that they've won the club's husband-wife title every year since 1972.

Tim and Carol Templin have won championships at the Lago Mar Country Club in Fort Lauderdale, Fla., the past two years. They're a tough team—Tim's a scratch and Carol's a 2-handicapper. Not far behind are Neil (scratch) and Sandy (4) Woodruff, who overcame big fields to win titles at the San Jose Country Club.

MacGregor Downs: D. Rizzo;
F. Henderson
Meadowbrook: C. Keever
Mimosa Hills: Z. Zimmerman;
L. Byrnes
Monroeton: C. Williams
Morehead City: S. McConkey;
N. Crumley
Mountain Glen: E. Berry; G. Tatum
Myers Park: T. Smith; C. Pou
New Bern: G. Collins; N. Sullivan
North Ridge: H. Powell III; E. Rein
Occoneechee: J. Durham
Old Town: J. Eller Jr.;
Mrs. G. Mountcastle
Paschal: M. Marshall; F. Wilkinson
Pennrose Park: P. Brady; F. Hooper
Piedmont Crescent: E. Hughes;
M. Thaxton
Pine Island: L. Tucker; A. Friday
Quaker Meadows: W. Burkert
Red Fox: B. Black; D. Griffith
River Bend: B. Sherman; Mrs. B. Switt
Rutherfordton: R. Robertson
Scotfield: T. Malinowski; L. Hale
Shamrock: S. Isley; A. Finch
Tryon: K. Casey; M. Hannon
Waynesville: B. Deweese; H. Griffith
Willow Creek: M. Stephens; K. Spaugh
Wilson: T. Barner; S. Helmes
Wolf Creek: M. Thore Jr.
Wolf Laurel: W. Jeffries;
Mrs. G. Maiden
Zebulon: R. James; B. Roberson

NORTH DAKOTA

Apple Creek: R. Ledebuhr;
Y. Ellingson
Fargo: J. Mayer
Grand Forks: G. Pearson; S. Ryan
Hettinger: S. Dannenfelzer; S. Long
Hillcrest: C. Hall; B. Galloway
Jamestown: L. Niemeyer;
J. Lidstrand
Langdon: R. Haaven; J. Smith
Leonard: K. Richards
Mandan: R. Stecher; G. Heinsohn
Mayville: D. Ralston; Mrs. M. Carter
Minot: J. Haider; B. Rocle
Oxbow: D. Schnell
Rugby: W. Paterson
Westhope: R. Floberg

OHIO

Alliance: A. Rotar; Z. Bradshaw
Apple Valley: N. Woodward;
H. Workman
Ashland: J. Nordstrum; B. Curran
Athens: A. Smith; T. Kendall
Bath: J. Estep; A. Alameda
Beechmont: S. Neye; S. Reitman
Bellefontaine; R. Weeks;
Mrs. D. Hilliker
Belleview: T. Kurty; H. Galownia
Belmont Hills: E. G. Mehallis;
M. Burnett
Bel-Wood: S. Busam; S. Schilling
Berkshire Hills: T. Spena Jr.; V. Toth
Blackhawk: H. Norman
Bluffton: B. Garrison; P. Nigh
Bowling Green: B. Gwin; S. Muir
Briar Hill: D. Brown Jr.
Bridgeview: R. Eversole; M. Grube
Brookside (Canton): E. Schlitz;
Mrs. D. Peppard
Brookside (Worthington): L. Turkelson;
J. Moran
Brown's Run: R. Martin; G. Shull
California: R. Wilson; P. Hilb
Camargo: Mrs. W. Lillard Jr.
Candywood: R. Lindsey
Canterbury: R. Fairchild;
Mrs. M. Hattenbach
Chagrin Valley: J. Nordine; P. Santor
Chapel Hills: J. Ball; J. Jacobs
Chillicothe: N. Holmes Jr.;
J. Climer
Cincinnati: S. Strauchen; E. Mosher
Clearview: W. Cost; M. Pellegrene
Clinton Height: R. Bibcock; L. Pharges
Clover Nook: T. Baker; R. Shepard
Coldstream: E. Heimann; J. Diem
Columbia Hills: J. Donasky; M. Dipple
Columbus: G. Woodworth Jr.;
Mrs. W. Williams
Community: D. Dickman; D. Hamilton
Congress Lake: W. Hackett Jr.;
K. Oldham
Countryide: D. Hetrick
Crest Hills: S. Silverman; M. Elkus
Dayton: J. Deuser; Mrs. R. Donnelly,
Mrs. C. Wilson
Echo Hills: R. Ramer; M. Leeper
Edgecreek: S. Boley
Elks (Hamilton): D. Thomas;
Mrs. R. Gard
Elks (Norwalk): E. Barker; C. Spaar
Elyria: R. Sanker; L. Field
Fairlawn: T. Edwards; H. Bonner
Fairview: R. Moor; S. Yerkes
Firestone: R. Ambrose; R. Cooper
Fonderlac: E. Connor; M. Landis
Forest Hills: S. Taulbee;
M. Dickerson
Forest Hills Public: R. Maltby;
E. Coverdale
Fox Den Fairways: S. Weld;
P. Parmelee
Glengarry: J. Silverman; C. Paris
Hartwell: T. Proud; K. Langenbahn
Hickory Grove: D. Ruby; J. Bower
Hickory Hills: C. Slattery; L. Jones
Hidden Valley: D. Farahay; E. Davis
Hilltop: T. Boden; E. Mahaffey
Hocking Hills: C. York; G. Eymon
Homestead: E. Rose; C. Paxton
Hubbard: B. Getz; S. Hill
Hyde Park: S. Gonzalez; Mrs. R. Hall
Inverness: G. Mouen; Mrs. C. Betz
Irish Hills: R. Mayhew; P. Stull
Ironwood (Cincinnati): L. Fluharty;
M. Ferdon
Ironwood (Wauseon): Mrs. M. Fichter
Kenwood: B. Cowgill; J. Stoffregen
Ketteníng: R. Anderson; M. Mallott
Kildaire: G. Tallman Jr.;
L. Mershman
Kirtland: E. Meister Jr.;
Mrs. W. Stewart
Lake Forest: T. Biskind;
Mrs. M. Meltzer
Lakewood: S. Hughes; Mrs. D. Given
Larch Tree: J. Shroyer; P. Behlav
L. C. Boles: B. Schubert; N. Newman
Legend Lake: T. Richards; F. Rauh
Lincoln Hills: R. Donelson; C. Bastel
Llanerch: G. Marucci Jr.;
Mrs. D. Comly
Losantiville: J. Schloss; C. Ratzkin
Locust Hills: J. Miller
Madison: S. Francis; J. Dunning
Maketewah: M. Snodgrass;
B. Gallagher
Maple Ridge: J. Locke; A. Niemela
Marion: J. Conkle; L. Phillips
Mar-O-Del: H. Newell; L. Wells
Marysville: R. Martin;
K. Strausbaugh
Mayfield: R. Bingham;
Mrs. W. Bierman
Meadowood: C. Fitzwilliam;
Mrs. L. Green
Memorial Park: D. Deliz; P. Nicely
Miami Valley: J. Herbig;
Mrs. C. Beardsley
Miami View: B. Krueger; J. Fessel
Miami Whitewater: J. Day
Moraine: J. Fisher Jr.;
Mrs. R. Eshelman
Moundbuilders: R. Hannum;
S. Litwiller
Mount Vernon: W. Curry; B. Barry
Muirfield Village: F. Schmidt
NCR: L. Harper, J. Neff; R. Smith
Northwood Hills: H. Quinn;
B. Sowards
Oak Harbor: E. Hamlin; Mrs. A. Dohy
Oakhurst: I. Smith; J. Smith
Oak Knolls: M. Follin; M. Ambler
Orchard Hills: J. Jereb; K. Parshall
Pine Hills: G. Kaltenbach; D. Reeve
Pleasant Run: D. Cochan; S. Reichert
Pleasant Valley: T. Rosswurm Jr.;
Mrs. E. Harp
Pleasant View: W. Blanc; J. Chlebeck
Portage: D. Voth; M. Foster
Potters Park; J. Urso
Ridgewood: H. Murphy; O. Zwiener
Rolling Acres: S. Clark
Rolling Green: Mrs. R. Smith
Salem: R. Pasko; Mrs. E. Pukalski
Scioto: J. Hesler; Mrs. C. Brewer
Shady Hollow: J. Laubacher;
Mrs. W. Seese
Shaker Heights: S. Findlay;
G. Hendricks
Sharon: R. Beallo
Silver Lake: G. Lyle; B. Allen
Skyland Pines: J. Spitale; H. Bush
Sleepy Hollow (Brecksville):
Ms. K. Clarke
Sleepy Hollow (Clyde): B. Houle;
A. Scagnetti
Springvale: J. Scheel; C. Schenk
Spring Valley: J. Kuhl; G. McGreevey
Henry Stambaugh: B. Santor
Steubenville: C. Klasic; J. Dyer
Sugar Valley: F. Henley; H. Johnson
Sunbury: L. Luthi; J. Shumway
Switzerland of Ohio: J. Heidelbach;
J. Kurtz
Sycamore Creek: G. Frankenfeld;
K. Jordan
Sycamore Hills: J. Swint; K. Stein
Sylvania: T. Moore; Mrs. S. LaBohn
Tanager Woods: D. Gruber;
A. Davidson
Tanglewood: J. Skinner Jr.; M. Althans
Toledo: B. Williams; Mrs. G. Urschel
Troy: B. Gregg; J. Adkins
Trumbull: G. Kline Jr.; N. Lewis
TRW: D. Minick; E. Croninger
Turkeyfoot Lake: B. Dudra;
M. Mozingo
Twin Lakes: W. Gressard; B. Byrne
Twin Run: C. Chadwell
Urbana: C. Mullen; Mrs. R. Bohl
Valley: R. Jackson; M. Allison
Valley View: R. Gardner; H. Poling
Valleywood: G. Hallett;
G. Greiffendorf
Villages of Wildwood: B. Tague;
J. Gentner
Walnut Grove: J. Kronauge;
K. Kronauge
Washington: R. Herron; Mrs. C. Mason
Wayside Manor: K. Jenkins; M. Cam
Wedgewood: R. Widener;
E. Winstanley
Westbrook: Mrs. R. Flockenzier
Western Hills: J. Esselman; M. Bernet
Westfield: O. Bosshard; S. Glass
Wildwood: R. Connor; M. Mack
Willard: D. Hartenstein; M. Miller
Willoughby: W. Cooks; B. Jacobs
Willow Bend: F. Purmort Jr.;
L. Purmort
Winding Hollow: S. Friedman;
Mrs. D. Roth
Windton Woods: D. Friedhoff
Woodland: J. Wilkins
Worthington Hills: T. Reardon;
B. DeYoung
Xenia: S. Bogenschutz
Yankee Run: T. Torma; C. Marion
York Temple: T. Truitt; M. Etzel

OKLAHOMA

Adams: D. Wilber; J. Brown
Cedar Ridge: M. McKenzie; J. Barnes
Golden Green: A. Deaver
The Greens: S. Williams; P. Stinson
Hillcrest: G. Witzel; Mrs. L. Gadner
Indian Springs: B. Henry; G. Sherman
Kicking Bird: J. Matheson; J. Cole
Lake Hefner: D. Brown
Lakeside: T. Craft; M. Reynolds
Lindsay: B. Cook
McAlester: J. Baumert; C. Pyle
Muskogee: D. Grover; R. Deckert
Oaks: G. Burton; Mrs. C. Pelton
Oakwood: N. Oxford; C. Collins
Oklahoma City: D. Stuart Jr.;
L. Stuart
Okmulgee Town & Country: G. York;
G. Grant
Perry: K. Kasper
Quail Creek: M. Hendrickson; J. Brett
Trosper Park: J. Jodlowski
Tulsa: J. Harris; B. Brown

OREGON

Agate Beach: C. Taylor; D. Hans n
Alderbrook: P. Nelson; P. Wirth
Astoria: J. Leinassar; C. Leinassa
Bowman's: H. Richardson;
L. Lythgoe
Cedar Bend: A. Burgess; L. Bice
Cedar Links: B. Phillips; J. Rodman
Charbonneau: J. Niederkorn; J. Bristol
Columbia-Edgewater: D. Kreiger;
J. Berkis
Coos: D. Hanen; P. Aleksa
Corvallis: L. Soule; Mrs. D. Ash
Dalles: G. Giese; R. Koch
Elks (Coquille Valley): J. Metcalf;
J. Bridgham
Emerald Valley: G. Daulsson;
J. Swadener
Eugene: K. Gubrad; S. Teatsch
Forest Hills: C. Hikes; I. Rupprecht
Green Acres: Mrs. B. Hix
Gresham: J. Whitehead; D. Achison
Hidden Valley: L. Emery
Illahe Hills: K. Forster; A. Cross
Juniper: E. Reynolds; M. Wood
King City: J. Abbott; J. Lattanzi
Marysville: D. Sluick
Mountain View: P. Sutton; J. Miller
Oak Knoll: G. Fueston; M. Patterson
Orenco Woods: B. Dreyer;
G. Wheelock
Pendleton: N. Nelson; Mrs. J. Clubb
Pleasant Valley: B. Prentiss;
K. Brumbaugh
Portland: J. Cundari;
Mrs. E. Bowers Jr.
Seaside: L. Johnson
Senior Estates: R. Ernstrom;
A. Eikenberry
Shadow Hills: J. Shupe; S. Fullerton
Summerfield: S. Fischer;
L. Blumenfeld
Sutherlin Knolls: G. Walker; N. Pine
Willamette Valley: A. Forrest;
W. Renoud
Wilson's Willow Run: J. Harper;
S. Green

PENNSYLVANIA

Allegheny: G. McQuone;
Mrs. R. Semple Jr.
Aliquippa: V. Daniels; N. Figley
Ambridge: J. Montagna;
K. Steekewsky
American Legion (Mt. Union):
M. Uelovich Jr.; E. Wible
Bala: D. Adam; Mrs. J. Galen
Beaver Lakes: V. Daniels; N. Figley
Berkleigh: A. Shapiro; Mrs. L. Dunitz
Berkshire: R. Palmer; Mrs. A. Jay
Bethlehem: M. Palos; D. Ellsworth
Blairmont Club: R. Bishop, K. Brua;
Mrs. C. Wilson
Brackenridge Heights: R. Young;
Mrs. M. DiGirolamo
Briarwood: B. Brenner
Brockway Glass: J. Binney
Brookside (Macungie): D. Holman;
Mrs. S. Oatman
Brookside (Pottstown): E. Ermisch;
Mrs. R. Gross
Bucknell University: J. Maier;
J. Millward
Burn Brae: J. Lemmel, W. Hubicki,
V. Milks
Butler's: R. Davis; P. Sarmento
Carlisle: R. Hrip; B. Rankin
Cedar Brook: C. Goldate; J. Greco
Centre Hills: R. Rutherford III;
K. Christoffers
Chartiers: W. Glikes; Mrs. F. Herold
Chester Valley: C. Terebesi; I. Albano
Churchill Valley: F. Malay; D. Rizta
Clearfield Curwensville: S. Butler;
C. Gosch
Coatesville: F. Root; E. Keyes
Colonial: P. McLaughlin; S. Shuey
Concord: S. Pahls; Mrs. B. Johnson
Conewango Valley: T. Kottraba;
R. Grimaldi
Conocodell: R. Fitzgerald
Cool Creek: R. Heller
Corey Creek: R. Cole; Mrs. M. Strange
Cornwells: G. Wolff; J. Platt
Crucible Management: R. Kelker Jr.;
J. Slater
Cumberland: H. Bly
Del-Mar: G. Friello; P. Franus
DuBois: D. Erickson III; H. Harriger
Duquesne: K. Mayher; Mrs. H. Turnbull
Eagles Mere: J. Moyer; Mrs. C. Brogan
Edgewood: J. Salonik;
Mrs. G. Evashavik
Elks (Johnstown): R. Burk;
Mrs. Y. Shubick
Elks (State College): B. Houtz
Gilbertsville: R. Bateman; G. Morris
Glen Oak: W. Chomicz; L. Ellowitz
Green Acres: J. Armatas; M. Dingle
Green Oaks: R. Brourman;
Mrs. J. Alexander
Greensburg: R. Allshouse; L. Conley
Greenville: E. Kenyon; N. Oliver
Gulph Mills: W. Dixon;
Ms. E. Slaymaker
Hanover: S. Fitzgibbons; C. Sneddon
Harrisburg: E. Rhodes;
Mrs. G. Nielsen
Hidden Valley: A. Ferrara; F. Davis
Highland: R. Reilly; Mrs. G. Shore
Hi-Point: D. Powell
Hollenback: F. Brzycki
Honey Run: D. Lankford
Huntingdon: R. Cirignano; G. Dore
Immergrun: M. Springer
Indian Mountain: R. Neff
Irem Temple: T. Gauntlett Jr.;
Mrs. E. McKeage
Iron Masters: W. Lingenfelter;
P. Dodson
Jackson Valley: W. Johnson; N. Hillard
Johnstown: R. McLaughlin;
S. Antonikas
Kahkwa: J. Spath; Mrs. D. Fessler
Kennett Square: J. Tigani Jr.;
Mrs. T. Mitchell
Kimberton: B. Faust; D. Seitz
Lancaster: B. Davidson Jr.;
Mrs. C. Heath
Lebanon: B. Weik; J. Meyer

Pabulum and par

One of the youngest 1975 club champions is Peter Reyburn, 14, who won the Osawatomie (Kan.) Golf Club title. Peter, a 6-handicapper, overcame a 50-man field.

Through 1974, Mari McDougall, 15, had broken 100 only once, but in 1975 Mari scored 86-82-83 to become the youngest women's champion in the history of the Midlothian (Ill.) Country Club, which dates to 1898. Another 15-year-old girl, Amy Resetar of Camp Hill, Pa., was the youngest entry in the women's championship of the Silver Spring Golf Course, Mechanicsburg, Pa., and she won. The men's winner there was Stanley Willis, who at 65 was the oldest entry in the men's field.

LeHigh: S. Demchyk; A. Devaney
Lewistown: K. Hidlay; N. Bryant
Ligonier: R. Johnson;
 Mrs. M. Goehring
Limekiln: A. Camasso
Locust Valley: B. Smith; R. Smolow
Longue Vue: R. Merchant Jr.;
 S. Royston
Lords Valley: E. Jansak;
 Mrs. A. Jackson
Lost Creek: R. Roush; D. Zeiders
Lulu Temple: E. Patten Jr.; N. Tither
Manada: J. Hileman
J. C. Martin: D. Salvatore
Meadia Heights: J. Burkholder;
 Mrs. R. Rummel
Meadowlands: A. Jacoby; I. Seiver
Melrose: J. Katziner; G. Katz
Middlecreel: M. Jones; L. Pritts
Montour Heights: J. Vernocy;
 L. Wilken
Moselem Springs: S. Codi;
 Mrs. H. Flippin
Nemacolin: F. Shuler; S. Misenko
Northampton: G. Riddagh;
 Mrs. A. Nolan
Northampton Valley: R. White;
 S. Harrigan
North Hills: R. Lazar; Mrs. D. Lowe
Oakmont: J. Malone; C. Seely
Oak Terrace: A. Malloy; S. Miller
Old York Road: D. Burton;
 Mrs. E. Wagner
Overlook: G. Weyhausen; J. Kuhrman
Park Hills: S. Stultz; J. DelGrosso
Pennhills: B. Bowler; H. Digel
Penn National: D. Richards
Penn Oaks: W. Casto; G. Brown
Penn State University: T. Sulkowski
Philadelphia Cricket: M. Fetterolf III;
 Mrs. H. Cross Jr.
Phoenixville: J. Nattie; L. Martin
Picasso: M. Kudlick; K. Watkinson
Pine Acres: D. Reiley; B. Sankner
Pinecrest: D. McLaughlin; V. Smith
Pine Meadow: R. Page
Pittsburgh Field Club: F. Fuhrer III;
 L. Clark
Pleasant Valley (Connellsville):
 G. Stone; M. Forys
Pleasant Valley (Stewartstown):
 J. Hoover
Pleasant Valley (Vintondale): C. Fox;
 R. Strenko
Plymouth: E. Stevenson; J. Coe
Pocono Manor: B. Nixon; J. Taylor
Punxstawney: J. Benson; H. Johnson
Radnor Valley: S. Robinson; B. Kay
Reading: M. Heller; J. Matz
Red Lion: P. Rank; F. Sutton
River Forest: G. Applegarth
River's Bend: R. Grubb;
 J. Showalter
Rolling Acres: P. Vukson
Rolling Green: F. DiPrima;
 Mrs. J. Matsinger
St. Clair: P. Perry; Mrs. J. Brodhurst
Sandy Run: M. Lombardo;
 C. Gallagher
Saucon Valley: R. Hunsicker;
 S. Ramonat
Schenley Park: D. Steranchak;
 G. Votilla
Seven Springs: T. Timko; S. Dupre
Sewickley Heights: T. Lenz; B. Sweet
Shadow Brook: W. Gaylord;
 M. Claypoole
Shamokin Valley: D. Kohler;
 Mrs. G. Cox
Shannopin: R. Hofmann II;
 N. Hollstein
Shawnee: D. MacDonough; B. Deihl
Silver Spring: S. Willis; A. Resetar
Sinking Valley: R. DelGrosso;
 J. Stiffler
Skytop: W. Wolak Jr.
Somerset: R. Cober; Mrs. D. Schenck
South Hills: D. Helwig
Springdale: G. Franko
Spring-Ford: H. Nettles;
 J. Cardamone

Springhaven: M. Howanski;
 Mrs. R. Bigelow
Standing Stone: L. Bock Jr.
Sunnehanna: B. Crooks; P. Stull
Sunnybrook: R. Campbell;
 Mrs. H. Nalle
Sunset: R. Gumpper
Titusville: J. Steinbuhler; R. Martin
Towanda: G. Smith; S. Ohart
Toresol Frankford: S. Haman;
 Mrs. G. Penrose
Tower Vue: M. Supira; I. Supira
Treasure Lake: J. Filsinger;
 L. Ulerich
Twin Woods: B. Cramer; P. Cangiano
Tyoga: B. Hotchkiss; C. Mertes
Valley Brook: J. Wales;
 Mrs. J. Faulkner
Valley: F. Olander; L. Gieking
Valley Green: B. Hippensteel Sr.;
 J. Short
Wanango: T. McGuire
Waynesborough: M. Forgash;
 M. Markle
Westmoreland: C. Whitehill; F. Caplan
Westover: R. DeFranco
West Shore: E. Tabor; Mrs. E. Miller
Whitford: C. Curtis; Mrs. P. Emory
Willow Brook: J. Fromhartz
Windber: R. Kendig; P. Stull
Wyoming Valley: E. Kaminski;
 C. Lippincott
Yardley: T. Bartolacci Jr.; B. Nini
Youghioghenv: C. Walters; S. Kostelac

RHODE ISLAND
Alpine: J. Bordieri; G. Compagnone
Coventry Pines: R. Fusco
East Greenwich: T. McDermott;
 M. Gray
Green Valley: B. Victor; L. Keene
Kirk Brae: M. St. Martin; M. Symons
Laurel Lane: J. Neronha
Louisquisset: B. Carline

SOUTH CAROLINA
Anderson: M. King; A. Chapman
Berkeley: B. Jones; J. Wenningham
Clavendon: G. Laing;
 Mrs. T. McKenzie
Conway: C. Wade
Cooper's Creek: S. Carter; V. Tyler
Cheraw: J. Isgett
Crestwood: J. Edwards
Lan Yair: L. Edwards
Mid-Carolina: F. Caldwell; E. Taylor
Pine Lakes: B. Ericson; Mrs. E. Hall
Pineland: R. Smith
Sedgewood: J. Plyler; E. Jeffrey
Shaw: B. Mitchell; F. Kuhn
Spartanburg: B. Price; P. Wardlaw
Star Fort National: E. Bolton;
 A. Barnes
Tifton: C. Register
Twin Lakes: M. Baucom; A. Baucom

SOUTH DAKOTA
Cactus Heights: S. Kolsrud; L. Geraci
Elks (Rapid City): J. Magstadt;
 A. Colgan
Huron: C. Rink; B. Brinkman
Lenkota: W. Brigger; L. Hofer
Madison: D. Fawbush; V. Das
Minnehaha: M. Getten; G. Idema
Par-Mar: D. Richards; D. Lehman
Parkston: J. Jones; G. Murphy
Rocky Knolls: D. Williamson
Westward Ho: W. Rausch; N. Stevens
Winner: T. King; K. Ochsner

TENNESSEE
Beaver Brook: G. McCloud; H. Bowers
Carroll Lake: S. Welch; M. Brush
Cherokee: S. Mayo; Mrs. L. Wright
Chicasaw: W. Carrier III;
 Mrs. M. Eckman
Cookeville: K. Hounihan
Gatlinburg: P. Maples: B. Maples

Graymere: T. Thompson; N. Thompson
Green River: L. Clemmons;
 M. Beckham
Hickory Valley: D. Roberson
Hillwood: J. Rose; Mrs. W. Bosworth
Hohenwald: D. Barber; B. Hinson
Holly Hills: M. Pettit;
 Mrs. M. Jackson
Jackson: C. Bennett; B. Pearce
Johnson City: O. Haws;
 Mrs. W. Anderson
Link Hills: R. May; Mrs. S. Gass
Meadow View: J. Lane; L. Negrotto
N.A.S. Memphis: J. Schneider;
 F. Griffin
Old Hickory: M. Graham Jr.;
 Mrs. L. Potter
Pine Oaks: G. Carrier; L. Hyder
Richland: C. Whittemore; P. Wallace
Sequatchie Valley: R. Rankin
Skyview: B. Maddox; N. Harney
Springbrook: R. Penley; E. Cute
Stonebridge: L. Shaffer; Mrs. J. Brode
Stones River: C. Holloway;
 J. Alexander
Valleybrook: G. Liner III; R. Avery
Windyke: K. Walsh; B. Foster

TEXAS
Abilene: S. Fox; J. Casey
Amarillo: J. Herring; Mrs. T. Jones
April Sound: R. Boyt; H. Bradley
Austin: L. Lundell; M. Rader
Bear Creek: J. Jones III; J. Raymond
Bent Tree: L. Blanks
Big Spring: J. Thomas;
 Mrs. A. Marshall
Bryan Municipal: T. Bryan Jr.;
 K. Sippel
Canyon Creek: R. Anderson; D. Meyers
Colonial: P. Darwin; D. Thomason
Comanche Trail: B. Rains;
 Mrs. J. Buchanan
Coronado: R. Hibler; M. Hoover
Dac: B. Mitchella; C. Albers
Dallas: C. Adams; J. Munger
Devine: E. Jungman; J. Parker
Diamond Oaks: J. Olsen;
 B. Christensen
Dumas: P. Boyd; A. Morrison
Elkins Lake: J. Register;
 M. Hornbuckle
Graham: J. Wells; P. Bussey
Great Southwest: R. Fels; Mrs. B. Klug
Greggton County: B. Brewer
Hill Crest: E. Gauldin; I. Sheridan
H & H: B. Gilliam; R. A. Ward
Lake Waco: D. Carlisle; Mrs. L. Ford
Las Colinas: R. Rawlins;
 Mrs. C. Holland
Marshall Lakeside: D. Taylor; L. Arnold
Meadowbrook: F. Duphorne;
 A. Hammer
Morris Williams: N. Puett; N. Frasher
Newport Yacht: C. Ahrens;
 L. Branscome
Northern Hills: H. Buntyn; R. Bogan
Oak Cliff: R. Meeks; Mrs. W. Gregory
Oak Grove: D. Gilbert; K. Moore
Oak Hills: J. Thornton; H. Keene
Odessa: R. Folk; Mrs. J. Tidwell
Onion Creek: E. Kohl
Packsaddle: R. Bevill; L. Delz
Padre Isles: B. Lewis
Pharaoh's: Mrs. J. Pagan
Pinewood: T. Philips; B. Hand
Preston Trail: D. Gray
Prestonwood: J. Perry; E. Finigan
River Hills: G. Muckleroy;
 S. Christopher
Sotogrande: J. Browne; A. Duncan
Spring Creek: H. Edmiston; S. Walker
Stratford: E. Oquin; R. Pittman
Sugar Creek: H. Price; K. Spencer
Tanglewood on Texoma: H. Summer;
 D. Johnson
Tascosa: T. Dement; R. Thompson
Tawakoni: F. Torres
Temple: J. Harlan; B. Janeway
Waxahachie: M. Hastings; E. Foster
Willow Brook: A. Wall;
 Mrs. D. Cameron
Winkler: R. Peden; B. Worrell
Woodlands: D. Custer; Mrs. J. Bishop

UTAH
Canyon Breeze: H. Gray; I. Harris
Country Club: L. Moench
Dinaland: E. Gudac; B. Hart
Dixie Red Hills: J. Blake; E. Shell
El Monte: P. Christiansen;
 J. Christiansen
Forest Dale: J. Ferney; J. Showell
Ben Lomond: T. Hulmston; K. Jensen
Mountain View: G. Ryther;
 B. Betteridge
Oakridge: K. Olsen; L. Randall
Ogden: A. Lieshman; V. Ferguson
Oquirrh Hills: T. Leonelli; N. Pitt
Painted Hills: I. Isom
Provo City Timpanogos: C. Barton;
 M. Norman
Rose Park: D. Pronk; J. Malin
Schneiter's Riverside: S. Woodland;
 J. Porter, M. Steeke
Sherwood Hills: B. Blackburn;
 E. Ballif
Spanish Fork: S. Bingham; M. G. Amos
Valley View: T. Leslie; M. Lund
Willow Creek: R. Magario; B. Jenson

VERMONT
Barre: J. Wood; M. Hamilton
Burlington: L. Rozzi; M. LaCroix
Champlain: R. Coleman; M. Coleman
Copley: R. Reynolds
Lake Morey Inn: O. Miller; D. Butler
Manchester: J. Gallagher Jr.;
 A. Waters
Montague: L. Thurston; B. Allen
Quechee: B. Purcell; R. Katz
Rocky Ridge: G. Rotelli; N. Riggs
Stowe: S. Dresser; A. Savela
Stratton Mountain: H. Miller;
 Mrs. W. LeGrow
Stowe: S. Dresser; A. Savela
Williston: J. Murray; G. Church
Woodstock: R. Tracy; B. Nilson

VIRGINIA
Amelia: M. Flippen
Arrow Wood: C. Powers; P. Stallins
Bedford: W. Proffitt;
 Mrs. B. Overstreet
Bide-A-Wee: B. Hartsell; M. Rawls
Brunswick: S. Smith
Carper's Valley: D. Oates;
 G. Boettner
Cypress Cove: D. Morgan; D. Hubbard
Elizabeth Manor: S. Liebler;
 M. Belcher
Evergreen: J. Woodard Jr.;
 Mrs. W. Kite
Fairfax: N. McClary; A. Geithner
Falling River: J. Conner; J. Lyon
Farmington: J. Hoy; Mrs. J. Stillwell
Ft. Belvoir: W. Haraway; M. Freimark
Fredericksburg: M. Corter; J. Perrin
Galax: G. Adams; S. Morris
Giles: R. James; Mrs. J. Mullins
Goose Creek: G. Bobby; P. Smyth
Gypsy Hill: B. Hanson
Hunting Hills: C. Sellers;
 Mrs. M. Cline
International: H. Bowers Jr.;
 D. Grappone
James River: T. Savas;
 Mrs. J. Peake III
Jefferson Lakeside: J. Flax; L. Milkin
Kempsville Meadows: T. Miller;
 M. Skinner
Leesburg: V. DeMott
Lake Bonaventure: W. Ferguson;
 S. Elliott
Lakeview: B. Lam
Lake of the Woods: J. Parker; D. Post
Lake Wright: H. Baskette; K. Roman
Laurel: C. Loehr; J. Nagle
Princess Ann: C. Ball Jr.; M. Smith
Red Wing: J. Hughes; A. Heinbockel
Retreat: D. Holdren; E. Howard
Richwood: H. Cutlip Jr.
Round Meadow: S. Gilley; P. Crockett
Salisbury: D. Sobrito; Mrs. R. Duma
Sewells Point: J. Saunders; J. Gallant
Shenandoah Valley: L. Sealock;
 E. Jones
Spotswood: P. Estep; N. Bronson
Thorn Spring: C. Tickle; V. DeVilbiss
Tuscarora: E. F. Jones III; J. Jones
Warrenton: J. Zaleski; V. Rosser
West Point: R. Betts
Westwood: P. Healy; A. Templeton
Willow Creek: R. Robinson;
 R. Chitwood
Willow Oaks: L. Isaacs;
 Mrs. J. Smith Jr.
Wytheville: K. Baumgardner;
 Mrs. S. Tarter

WASHINGTON
Bellingham: O. Arford; Mrs. H. Powers
Elks (Allenmore): C. Hunter;
 E. Kirkes
Everett: L. Wilson; H. Odegard
Fairwood: B. Morganstern; R. Tudeth
Fircrest: J. Baty; H. Johnson
Ft. Steilacoom: A. Anderson;
 S. Kaempfer
Foster: D. Schoner; G. Davis
Glendale: J. Blechman; T. Pharr
Grays Harbor: J. Paul; D. McGuire
Interbay: L. Daniels
Juanita: T. Leavitt; M. Fisher
Moses Lake: K. Anderson; P. Larson
McChord AFB: J. Kahaniak; D. Smith
Nile: F. Wolgamott; M. Allison
North Shore: T. Bearman; D. Young
Oakbrook: C. Johnson; P. Strait
Okanogan Valley: J. Knight;
 N. Baines
Olympia: B. Dobbins; M. Zech
Olympic Hills: E. Pearsall
Orcas Island: W. Giswold;
 M. Petterson
Othello: D. Buck; R. Livczey
Overlake: D. Hay; B. Thorlakson
Rainier: J. Colello; G. Colello
San Juan: A. Scribner; E. Johnson
Shamnapum: B. McElroy; S. Zahler
Similk Beach: R. Freier; Mrs. W. Wade
Skagit Valley: T. Perry; K. King
Sundance: K. Schroeder; H. Mackey
Tumwater Valley: F. Nelson; J. Uhlman
Tyee Valley: B. Tessandore; K. Puetz
Useless Bay: B. Eyman; A. Cocklin
Wandermere: J. Leahy;
 Mrs. D. Van Hook
Wayne: D. Wynia; B. Bryan
Willapa Harbor: L. Runge
Wing Point: C. Leimback; B. Green
Yakima: R. Twiss; T. Powell

WEST VIRGINIA
Bluefield: D. Modena; R. Meem
Cherry Hill: M. Blake
Elks (Princeton): R. Sink; E. Legg
Grandview: D. Vass; R. Scott
Greenbrier Valley: W. Burns
Kanawha: D. Dickerson; J. Tondreau
Lakeview: S. Misgalla; C. Costaines
Opequon: L. Staples; M. Speer
Parkersburg: B. Hissam; M. Gilmore
Par-Mar Pines: F. Rake; B. Abels
Pocahontas: J. Hooke
Preston: R. Witt; S. Beneke
Sisterville: A. Licchillo; Mrs. H. Barth
Sleepy Hollow: M. Brown; N. Roth

Spring Valley: J. Feaganes;
 Joan Davidson
Valley View: H. Fitswater; E. Kindle
Waterford Park: J. Finley; G. Jackson
Wheeling: J. Guthrie; S. Carroll
Williams: H. Peterson Jr.; J. Garvey
Woodbrier: G. Roach
Worthington: J. Dotson; S. Beckwith

WISCONSIN
Alaskan Motor Inn: R. Ray;
 S. Bournoville
Antigo Bass Lake: B. Martine;
 K. Curran
Beloit: C. Ramsden; C. Tensfeldt
Blackhawk: M. Murphy; D. Lindsay
Blue Mound: D. Hanley;
 Mrs. P. Stieber
Bridgewood: T. Stinski
Brown County: J. Zeise; F. Denessen
Brynwood: J. Wagner; J. Shlimovitz
Butte Des Morts: P. Malloy;
 S. Gustman
Camelot: C. Eichstedt; L. Wiegert
Chenequa: J. Wheeler III; M. Nunz
Cherokee: M. McFarland; B. Erickson
Clifton Highlands: T. Magee;
 M. Mercord
Crystal Springs: M. Mullen; D. Reed
Darlington: M. Howery; R. Parkinson
Dell View: F. Anderson; K. Butler
Dodge Point: R. Jacobson;
 L. Van Epps
Eagle River: L. Vandervest; K. Pohni
Eau Claire: S. Jensen;
 Mrs. R. Schwartz
Edelweiss Chalet: M. Duerst; E. Genin
Edgewater: B. Gullickson; D. Kelly
Fox Valley: R. Vanderwyst;
 J. Schomisch
Golden Sands: P. Wallrich
Hallie: B. Rolland; N. Friede
Hill Crest: D. Hanson; D. Witzig
Hilly Haven: C. Diny; Mrs. A. Davis
Hudson: R. Lohman; S. Anderson
Janesville: J. Brennan; Mrs. F. Russo
Kenosha: D. Adamson; N. Donnell
LaCrosse: B. Johns Jr.; R. Johns
Lac La Belle: L. Jones;
 Mrs. F. Voreck
Little River: P. Krause; G. Korbury
Maple Grove: Mrs. L. Harris
Mayville: R. Bachhuber; D. Steinbach
Meadowbrook: B. Hansen; R. Dill
Merrill: D. Preboske; S. Hacker
Merrill Hills: K. Gavre; S. Murray
Mid-Vallee: D. Alft; G. Arndt
Milwaukee: R. Quinlevan III;
 Mrs. E. Von Estorff
Monroe: J. Lovelace; J. Smith
Nakoma: M. Goode; K. Julson
Nippersink Manor: R. Seagren;
 C. Seagren
Norsk Bowl: M. Tvedt
Northbrook: J. Haack; S. Gehrke
North Shore (Menasha): J. Konsek;
 C. Mosher
North Shore (Mequon):
 E. Meisenheimer; S. O'Connor
Osseo: H. Johnson; M. Oftedahl
Ozaukee: B. Boegel; Mrs. B. Reid
Pine Acres: R. Lindner; J. Alsteen
Pine Crest: J. Sevals; C. Thompson
Pine Hills: S. Sousek; M. Magnuson
Port Washington: M. Metera;
 L. Molynex
Quit-Qui-Oc: T. Weedman; S. Kahl
Racine: G. Goodsell; M. Farley
Reedsburg: J. Hasler; M. Gschwind
Reid: D. Babb
Rhinelander: A. Loomans; B. Marko
Rice Lake: B. Day; B. Rydell
Ridges: D. Ebacher; B. Lowell
Ridgeway: M. Benner; S. Verstegen
Riverdale: H. Fischer; H. Liebl
River View: D. Swenson
Sheboygan: J. Radder;
 M. Hollingsworth
Shoop Park: Mrs. I. Vold
South Hills: J. Gilles; M. McGallowa
Spread Eagle: T. Wittkopf
Stevens Point: R. Lundquist;
 M. Lundquist
Sun Prairie: B. Langer; P. Rardin
Sunset View: A. Cernohous;
 J. Follien
Tee-A-Way: D. Lemke; Y. Root
Tee-Hi: L. Connor; K. Connor
Tripoli: D. Higgins; Mrs. A. Wakefor
Tuckaway: B. Wisniewski; L. Rice
Tumblebrook: B. Witt; C. Chmela
Tuscumbia City: J. Diedrich; A. Car
Village Green: A. Carlotto
Viroqua: G. Faherty; M. Burkhardt
Watertown: J. Wade; S. Wilkes
Wausau: L. Kordus; L. Post
Waushara: W. Tess
West Bend: B. Meler; M. Hateman
Westmoor: T. Stouthamer; D. Baker
Yahara Hills: M. Plautz; J. Walker

WYOMING
Airport: B. Ortega; M. Longpre
Buffalo: A. McBridge; S. Polrot
Gillette: S. Paulsen; P. Paulsen
Olive Glenn: T. Cole; D. Kousoulos
Rolling Green: P. Bunning; R. Gues
Sheridan: C. Stewart; M. Stout

A lock, wouldn't you say?

Sergene Sorenson, 43, has won 18 consecutive women's championships at the Burley (Idaho) Municipal Golf Club, including 1975. Sergene is a 9-handicapper.